RETURN TO

A STUDY OF

Rural Society

J. H. Kolb

COLLEGE OF AGRICULTURE, UNIVERSITY OF WISCONSIN

Edmund de S. Brunner

TEACHERS COLLEGE, COLUMBIA UNIVERSITY

EDITED BY

William F. Ogburn

THE UNIVERSITY OF CHICAGO

Third Edition

HOUGHTON MIFFLIN COMPANY · BOSTON

New York · Chicago · Dallas · Atlanta · San Francisco

The Riverside Press Cambridge

The Riverside Press

CAMBRIDGE · MASSACHUSETTS

PRINTED IN THE U.S.A.

We Dedicate This Book
to the Youth of
Rural America
Whose Intellectual and
Spiritual Powers and Desires
Will Determine Her Future

Editor's Introduction

THE STUDY OF RURAL SOCIETY had a distinguished origin. It grew out of a research monograph done by Professors Kolb and Brunner for the President's Research Committee on Social Trends appointed by President Herbert Hoover in 1929. In the Committee's final report, *Recent Social Trends*, the authors also had a chapter on rural society. On the basis of these researches, the authors, with a lifetime of research and service in this field, were persuaded to present a systematic study of rural society and make it available to the many thousands of students of social science and of social problems.

The book became at once a standard treatise on the subject and was commonly accepted as such by the colleges and universities of America. As a further testimonial to its high place in the literature was its choice as the one text in rural sociology for our service men in the United States Armed Forces Institute. The selection was made by a committee of experts after an extensive canvass of other specialists.

That so important and useful a text should be kept up to date was obvious. It was revised in 1940, but before the new material of the Census of 1940 was available. Then too, the war, that great precipitator of vast and revolutionary changes throughout society, made necessary a thorough rewriting. The airplane has made all the nations of the world our neighbors. Accordingly the authors have added extensive analyses of rural society in other countries. Other changes which mark this new treatise are reported in the authors' preface. The permanence of the book is due however to its consistent treatment of fundamentals.

WILLIAM F. OGBURN

Preface to the Third Edition

IT HAS BEEN SIX YEARS since the second edition of *A Study of Rural Society* appeared. Since that time the full results of the 1940 Census have become available and World War II has produced many changes in rural society. Throughout the period the generous reception accorded the earlier editions has continued. This has included the selection of the book as the text in rural sociology used by the United States Armed Forces Institute. These facts, together with the considerable volume of new research findings which have appeared, seem to make it desirable to present a fundamental revision of the volume.

This revision employs a new outline. Rural people receive first consideration after the Prologue. The next part considers making a living in the agrarian culture. Group relationships, beginning with the family, through neighborhoods, villages, and communities to rural-urban relationships, are then discussed. Finally the institutional arrangements of rural society are studied.

This outline appears to conform to the preferences of many users of the text, but for classroom purposes the chapters can be interchanged without difficulty.

Within this revised outline certain other changes have been made. Material on rural merchandising has been included in the village chapter. Since the interests of rural youth are as broad as rural society, material concerning this very important group will be found throughout the text instead of largely in one chapter. The section on farm labor has been considerably expanded. Background economic data have been brought up to date, and the chapters on rural education include some very significant new data. Completely reorganized chapters with new material on rural health, rural welfare, and local government have been included. Every effort has been made to bring the bibliography on rural life in foreign lands up to date.

The prefaces of the two previous editions give the point of view of the authors with respect to the study of rural society. These should be examined by the reader. However, three of these may be briefly summarized.

1. Rural society is considered as a unit made up of both farmers

and villagers, and the modern rural community as a town-country community. The rural and urban elements in general society are regarded throughout as interdependent parts of the larger whole.

2. Economic factors are not considered as separate from social life. Rather, the myriad activities and institutions associated with making a living are regarded as an essential part of rural society and of the social behavior of its people. In other words, the social sciences are social. The economic behavior of men is social behavior. There are no economic problems or policies which do not have real social consequences and implications, nor can social problems and policies be divorced from their economic bases.

3. While there is no chapter or section devoted exclusively to social theory as such, there is a definite frame of reference within which the materials are organized and there is a conscious plan and theory implicit in the discussion throughout. In short, theory is viewed as a tool for study and as a means for understanding.

The authors express their renewed obligations to readers who have made helpful suggestions. In addition to others specifically mentioned in earlier prefaces, they are under obligation to Doctor Ellwood Hsin-Pao Yang for extensive bibliographic research, to Doctor William Wiser for assistance on the India section of the bibliography of rural life in foreign lands, to Mr. Joao de Souza on the South American section, and finally to the Misses Josephine Kronenberg and Ruth O'Donnell, who prepared this edition for the press.

J. H. KOLB
EDMUND DE S. BRUNNER

Preface to the Second Edition

THE GENEROUS RECEPTION accorded the first edition of A *Study of Rural Society*, together with the rapid pace of social change, accounts for the appearance of this second edition at this time.

The chief changes are these: the inclusion of a new chapter dealing with rural youth, and a new section on the agricultural laborer; rewriting and bringing up-to-date the chapters and sections dealing with rural relief, public health and welfare, and agricultural legislation and policy, including an expansion of the discussion on farm tenancy; and a bringing up-to-date of the rest of the volume on the basis of the new knowledge rural social research has made available since 1935. This last type of change is to be found particularly in the chapters on the rural community, standards of living, education, religion, merchandising, and recreation. The new data have been drawn especially from the studies of the rural research unit of the Work Projects Administration, from the Division of Farm Population and Rural Welfare of the United States Department of Agriculture, and from the third study of village-centered farming communities, *Rural Trends in Depression Years*. Thanks are due to the publishers of this lastnamed work, the Columbia University Press, for permission to quote therefrom.

One comment about the use of the book, in addition to those in the opening paragraphs of the Preface to the first edition, may be made. This is done in response to suggestions received. While there is no chapter or section devoted exclusively to social theory as such, there is a definite frame of reference within which the materials are organized and there is a conscious plan and theory implicit in the discussion throughout. In short, theory is viewed as a tool for study and as a means for understanding. Much concrete material is purposely presented because the authors believe that this is the best way to study society. It is recognized, of course, that it is not possible for one study of the rural life in America to describe in detail every area or every kind of situation or institution. Hence, selection is necessary. For example, much use is made of the studies of the 140 village-centered communities because they make possible comparisons over time and indicate changes under way. Similarly, many of the materials on neighborhoods, communities, and the various social institutions are drawn from studies made in particular localities. They are oriented to reveal certain types of situations or problems or trends. The reader is expected to regard them, not as representing universals, but as types with which to compare or to contrast those conditions with which he is familiar, either by his own direct experience or by his own study and observation. In fact, we believe that in this way the science of rural society will advance. Readers can thus make their contributions whether they live in New England, the Deep South, the Far West, or elsewhere. It is the hope of the authors that this book will stimulate many to re-examine their own experiences in rural society and to carry forward the study of rural life in their own immediate areas. To these ends, many of the topics for discussion found at the close of the chapters were formulated. References in footnotes and at the conclusions of chapters will be helpful for exploring in greater detail the case materials which have been included.

It is the authors' hope that the new edition may serve its purpose even better than did the last. Many of the changes made were suggested by readers, and to them real gratitude is hereby expressed. It is the expectation that when the data of the 1940 Census become fully available, those portions of the volume dealing with census facts will be brought up-to-date.

In addition to the indebtedness to the first two of the authors' secretaries mentioned in the Preface to the first edition, acknowledgment is made to Miss Jeanne Weiss who prepared nearly half of this edition for the press.

Preface to the First Edition

THIS BOOK IS OFFERED because of a sincere desire to stimulate greater interest in and to promote more study of Rural Society. It is, in fact, a study of rural society, its organization and changes, from the point of view of important backgrounds, recent developments, and significant trends. It stresses the forces and the tendencies which have developed in the rapidly shifting rural scene since the advent of modern inventions like the automobile and the radio, and since the disturbing consequences of the World War and the long-continued agricultural depression have become all too apparent. Therefore, it gives considerable space to such movements as the Agricultural Adjustment Act, the Federal Relief Administration, and the rise of Adult Education.

Rural society is considered as a unit made up of both farmers and villagers and the modern rural community as a town-country community. The rural and urban elements in general society are regarded throughout as interdependent parts of the larger whole. At the same time, a number of neglected aspects of rural life are discussed, such as the social influences of school curricula, the institutions of rural retail trade, local government, and national policies affecting agricultural life. While problems are not treated as such, many troublesome problems of rural life do emerge from these pages; nor are economic factors considered as separate from rural social life. Rather, the myriad activities and institutions associated with making a living are regarded as an essential part of rural society and of the social behavior of its people.

Opening with a brief discussion of the nature of rural society, which constitutes the first chapter, the book is organized into five parts. Part I considers the group life of rural people, the family, the neighborhood, the village, the community, and the interrelations of town and country as well as rural and urban. Part II directs attention to rural people themselves, their origins and characteristics, the composition of the rural population and its mobility. Part III reviews the social economics of agriculture and the institutions associated with farming as a means of earning a livelihood, with special reference to the events of the last few years and the New Deal. Part IV describes the organization, recent changes, and trends of rural institutions such as the home, school, church, and agencies for recreation, health and social welfare, and then, in national terms, the apparent trends and possible future policies for rural America are considered in Part V.

In classroom use these five parts may be interchanged, provided their relationships are made clear. Individual chapters may also be given detailed or limited study depending upon the degree of specialization of courses within the institution.

Two main sources of data are utilized: the 1930 Censuses of Population, Agriculture, and Retail Distribution, together with numerous other official reports published since then; and numerous field surveys conducted by the authors since 1919, many of them nation-wide in scope, and culminating in the survey, *Rural Social Trends*, the rural section of President Hoover's Research Committee on Recent Social Trends.

The authors desire to acknowledge their indebtedness to the McGraw-Hill Book Company of New York City for permission to quote frequently from their previous book, already alluded to, *Rural Social Trends*, and to Harper and Brothers of New York City for similar permission to reproduce a few paragraphs from their publication, *The Protestant Church as a Social Institution*.

Thanks are also due to a number of their colleagues who have read and helpfully criticized various chapters, including Professor W. F. Ogburn of the University of Chicago, Professors Kimball Young, E. L. Kirkpatrick, and A. F. Wileden of the University of Wisconsin, and Professors Frank W. Cyr, Fannie Dunn, Mabel Carney, Harold F. Clark, and Lyman Bryson and Dr. Irving Lorge of Columbia University.

Special thanks are due to Mr. Anthony Netboy who read and edited the entire work, and to the authors' secretaries who typed and prepared the manuscript for the printer, the Misses Josephine Kronenberg, Aileen Karppinen, and Katherine McGrattan.

CONTENTS

THE STUDY OF RURAL SOCIETY

1

What Is Rural Society — Why Study It?

AMERICA, despite her recently acquired huge cities, is a nation of rural backgrounds and traditions. Few are the families of native stock that do not trace back to the soil within two generations. The imagery of the national anthem is rural. The democracy so widely cherished is soil-born. Many social attitudes have their root in the experiences of frontier and farm.

Notwithstanding the great industrial zones, agriculture is still a very important part of the nation's total economic life. More capital is invested in it than in any other type of enterprise. It gives employment to more persons than any other single industry; indeed, it is exceeded by only two major occupation groups in its share of the nation's gainfully employed. Its purchases keep the wheels of industry turning one third or more of the time. Its products load the majority of the freight cars outside of the East. Its surpluses make up an important fraction of our export trade even in peace times. And, of course, its soils bear and sustain the crops, and livestock that answer the daily prayer for bread.

The human side of agriculture. Soils, crops, and livestock are the concern of the physical sciences related to agriculture, but there is also a human side to agriculture. The tiller of the soil and his family, and those who care for his immediate physical, social, and economic needs are at least as important as the soil and its products. In short, successful agriculture has three concerns: farming as such, the efficient, profitable marketing of the products of the farm, and living the good life. To overlook any one of these three is dangerous for the individual farmer and for society. The aim of better farming is to secure better returns. The objective of better business is to support or achieve security, justice, culture, education, and all those personal and social satisfactions that enter into winning the final objective of human effort, better living. Neither efficient farming nor plentiful profits, however, are guarantees in themselves of better living. There is still the question of the human material and its capacity to measure up to the standards that better living

1

demands. Consequently, the study of rural society and of the human element in agriculture is one of vast importance.

In the expansion period of national development this fact, axiomatic as it seems, was given little attention. It did not achieve official recognition until 1908 when President Theodore Roosevelt appointed his now famous Country Life Commission. The classic report of this commission marks the real beginning of the country life movement in the United States. It dealt with the conditions, needs, and aspirations of rural people. It pointed out both deficiencies and assets in rural life, and showed how rural social institutions, such as the school and church, could be improved. These and other institutions gradually began to respond to the challenge of this report. The movement that resulted is today carried on by the American Country Life Association, an agency through which the various specific agencies of rural service are co-ordinated and in which they participate.

It is the purpose of this book to examine the whole complex of social arrangements, group characteristics, traits, and institutions that are concerned with rural living and go to make up rural society.

RURAL SOCIETY

Its people. In any consideration, then, of rural society, the people composing it are a basic consideration. America was once, of course, entirely rural. Up to our entry into World War I it was half rural, and even today the percentage is well over two fifths. Twenty-eight of our forty-eight states in 1940 were more rural than urban, all but a few more rural than the nation as a whole. Moreover, from these rural people has come a crop more important than any other: perhaps half the boys and girls born into rural homes, at least in the half-century period prior to 1930, migrated to the city and thus replenished the less fertile urban population. These matters are given detailed attention in Part I.

Its institutions. So, too, a study of rural society is concerned with a study of social institutions and social relationships and their changes, with the reasons for such changes. The school is a social as well as an educational institution; the church is social as well as religious, and so with others. This is to say that basic interests such as education, religion, health, government, and the like, institutionalize themselves in organizations through which persons co-operate in achieving their expressed ends. These organizations influence and are influenced by the community. Much of the life of rural society flows through them.

Its groups. There have been those who argued that the citizens of rural society were individualists, living alone and caring little for friend or foe. Evidence for this conclusion is hard to find. Even the hardy pioneers took their families with them or they soon acquired them. "Neighbor" became a trenchant term, setting off in sharp relief those who were entitled to friendly confidence from those who were regarded as strangers or "foreigners." Neighborhood groups and family groups have played and continue to play very important rôles in the more personal drama of rural life. Modern facilities for travel and communication give the community of town and country its opportunity and permit rural people to seek companionship on the basis of special interests. In fact, so specialized have some of these special interest groups become that concern is expressed in some quarters lest families, communities, and even personalities be pulled apart. For this reason, questions of community organization and integration are most timely.

Its wealth. The consumption of wealth becomes an important consideration, fully as significant as its production and even its distribution. This has for some time been clear to rural leaders, and in these days when the federal government is so largely devoting its efforts to balancing the production of goods and their consumption, it is probably self-evident. The consumption of wealth in any community may be an aid in analyzing its standards of living. The distribution of expenses within the total income available indicates the values that are held by the family or community. For example, many a family or community prefers to do without electricity and modern heating equipment in order to have automobiles.

But the matter goes deeper. American economic society is organized on the basis of the profit motive, however variously that term is defined, and this has resulted in a certain mode of life. It accounts, for instance, for the protection society affords the institution of private property, which in rural society is so closely associated with land possession, and for the insistence of business upon "free enterprise." One has only to consider the contrasting attitude in present-day Russia to realize how completely different attitudes toward wealth and its consumption, profits and their making, possession and use, change drastically the social arrangements, laws, and institutions of a people, so far as they relate to these things. Thus, the whole consumption of wealth, not only of food, clothing, and shelter within the home, but of those social utilities including education, religion, recreation, and welfare within the community, must be considered in any study of rural society.

Its policies. Although the phrase "social planning" has only recently become a shibboleth, planning and policy-making have always been functions of any society and they must probably become even more important functions. In planning for rural America, a study of rural society is essential, for policy-making requires knowledge of the situations and agencies involved in the plans. People require study in planning as well as land in zoning, or crops and livestock in farming. The naïve assumption that any group of persons will fall in with any plan about which they have not been consulted and which has not taken the social situation into account has been proved false so often in history that its survival is one of the world's mysteries.

Tradition plays its part here. Despite the lowest cotton price in years, the head of a large plantation in the South, scion of a family of distinction in his state, remarked in 1932, "The Lord meant this country to grow cotton. It's done so for two and a half centuries. Why should I change?" Religion and nationality play their parts also. The Japanese have never competed with the wheat-growers of the Pacific Coast. Their excursions into agriculture were confined to those specialties requiring intensive hand cultivation, the stoop-and-squat labor that was so largely required in their rice paddies at home.

Sentiment, too, plays its part. It may be a common-sense matter for a few isolated families in the Ozarks or on the too sterile soil of some dry-farming area to avail themselves of a plan to move elsewhere. But perhaps they share the pioneer's love of solitude, perhaps they have a deep attachment to the familiar scenes of their home, perhaps life gains in zest because of their constant battle to outwit Nature and wrest a living from soil never intended to support human life. Perhaps the little community is one bound by religious ties and settled in such a place to keep itself "unspotted from the world." Such social and socio-psychological considerations will, if not taken into account, upset the best-laid plans.

SOCIAL CHANGE

All society is caught in the grip of social changes of considerable moment and velocity, and rural society is no exception. No one, of course, can predict how long this period will continue. In such times of adjustment, much of the surface interest is naturally captured by political changes, nor are these unimportant. But political arrangements are but a device for expressing social judgments. Public opinion often changes before shifts in the political scenery occur. More fundamental are economic changes, and more important are changes in attitudes and philosophies, registering profound shifts in convictions. With these latter come changes in the social processes themselves.

The discussion to follow does not explain how to organize and manage an agricultural marketing co-operative, how to draw up contracts, deal with the railroads and the terminal markets, and so on. That is outside its province. It is, however, concerned with the growth of the co-operative movement in rural America as a social movement; with the fact that in many respects organizations for economic co-operation are affected by the same factors and in somewhat similar ways as are rural organizations for non-economic co-operation; and with the all-social implications of economic co-operation. It is important to grasp this distinction. Social science is the poorer because of the assumption on the part of some of its scientists that anything somewhat economic is wholly economic. Sociology has much to contribute through adequate analysis of the social aspects of economic events, movements, and organizations. It can, if it will, breathe the breath of life into the "average man" and the "economic man" of the older schools of economists. These convictions are the reasons for including Part II on the social economics of agriculture and the changes in thought and action which are taking place in this sphere of agricultural life.

The challenge of the future arising out of these and other changes is sounded by Charles Beard and it lays a responsibility upon citizen and physical and social scientist alike. Doctor Beard, in a recent article in which he considers "The Promise of American Life," points out three fundamental ideas which he says have taken form in the United States in recent years and are finding ever deeper lodgment in the American mind. Putting the case in simple terms he says: "Americans are now asking themselves three questions: What do we need in the way of food, clothes, shelter, comforts, and conveniences for a decent, universal standard of life? What natural resources, technical arts, and managerial skills do we have for supplying these needs? Shall we not call our civilization a failure if it cannot bring the economy of abundance into realization?" [1]

[1] Cf. *The New Republic*, February 6, 1935, p. 352.

CHARACTERISTICS OF RURAL AS COMPARED WITH GENERAL SOCIETY

Thus far in this introductory discussion no definition or characterization of rural society has been attempted. It is important before going further, both to define and to note some of the distinctive characteristics of rural society, in order to recognize why it should be studied apart from society in general and, in a sense, contrasted with it.

The United States Census counts as rural the farm population and all the non-farm population living in places of less than 2500 population. For the most part, this is the definition of this book, although here and there the rural affiliations of places up to 10,000 population are considered.

In the midst of a natural environment. Most obvious in a comparison of rural and urban society is the immediate environment. Rural people have space, especially the farm people. Once this meant isolation, but that has been greatly reduced by modern invention. They are close to Nature. The "fruited plains" stretch away from the door of the farm home over which trees cast their protecting shade in summer and from which, perhaps in the distance, tower "the purple mountain majesties." Even in the villages and towns there are trees, gardens, lawns, detached houses. Nowhere are there the narrow streets, sky-reaching buildings, the elbowing crowds, the snarling traffic, and the congestion, noise, and turmoil of the city.

The rural scene shifts, of course, according to soil and topography. Here it is level, there rolling, yonder hilly. Here there is black loam, there sandy soil, or again the firmer texture of shale or lime; there waving grain, yonder the regimented rows of fruit trees, elsewhere the fluffy cotton or the myriad vegetable plants, never venturing far from the earth from which they forced their way into the light. Save along trunk highways, none of the earth is hidden by solid concrete with which man protects the earth's surface from the scarring pressure of mechanized transportation.

Climate, too, plays its part. The graceful date palm never courts the breezes where they bear any touch of the North. The sun of the plains is just enough for the grain, but its greater generosity to the South and Southeast produces cotton or perhaps citrus fruit. Alfalfa yields to man five or six times a year in the frostless areas, once or twice in the regions mantled by snow and ice, through one third of the year. The machinist, the typist, the clerk, the banker, carried to and from work, perhaps beneath the ground in roaring subways, pursue their accustomed tasks without regard to wind or weather. The farmer and even the villager fit their task to Nature's mood and the rhythm of the seasons and by the same token shift to a certain extent their attitudes and organizational programs. In short, rural Americans are close to Nature. Urban Americans have built an artificial structure to escape Nature so far as possible. Even where the cities have saved oases of trees and open spaces whither their inhabitants may crowd to remind themselves of what the country is like, Nature is, so to speak, artificially on exhibit.

The family, a unit. In rural society people live in close proximity to their work. They can see the fields and orchards where their toil lies. They can hear the animals and chickens that are theirs to tend. They are never out of sight of their enterprise. For this reason the family has an absorbing common interest. Father, mother, and children are associated with living things, plants and animals, in the task of feeding the world. Every meal has the possibility of being a staff conference. Commutation is a word unused in the daily vocabulary of the rural family. Its members do not scatter to widely diversified tasks in different parts of the community by means of various sorts of transportation. In the rural world the individual adapts himself to the family situation. In the urban, the family adapts itself to the individuals that comprise it.

The family is, therefore, a supremely important rural social unit. In the economic life of the city family means little. In the country it means much. Especially in older communities the actions, achievements, and mistakes are judged in the light of the community's knowledge of the family unto the third and fourth generation. Measurably, though to a less extent, this is true in social relationships as well.

Rural organization simple. The physical spaciousness of rural life makes for a far lower density of population and restricts the number and possibly the power of human contacts, although not their depth. Conversely, within the community local group organization is simpler and not so highly specialized as in the city. Invariably the larger the community, even in rural terms, the larger the number of organized interests and agencies there are. But local rural communities do not possess medical and bar associations, councils of churches, and specialized trade groups, as do cities. If these and others exist at all, they are on a county basis.

Country and village, separate but united. The chapter thus far

has several times differentiated between farm and village and yet
has included both as belonging to rural society, as indeed the
United States Census does by its definition. What are the relations
between these two great elements in rural society?

In many parts of the world, notably in the Orient, this distinction cannot be drawn. There the agricultural village is the
home of the farmer. From it each day he trudges to his fields. To
it each night he returns, to mingle with his neighbors or join the
village elders as they discuss the affairs of the community. Indeed
in many parts of Europe this age-old pattern still persists and may
never change. It is to be found chiefly where farms are small and
easily reached. It is appearing again in certain restricted areas of
specialized farming in this country where farms are small as farms
go in the United States, and where they can be reached quickly by
automobile. This is especially noticeable in a few citrus-fruit centers on the Pacific Coast.

This, too, was the pattern in early colonial days, but soon the
huge tracts of land to be had for the taking and the clearing
spurred men to venture to live upon the broad acres they could not
well reach daily from the village. It was in the Americas that agriculture first meant isolation for the farmer and his family. For a
time it seemed as if the agricultural village was thereby doomed.
The self-sufficing plantations of the South seemed to show the trend.
They needed but one center to a county and the county seat came
to be something of what the market town is to much of the Orient
today, a place whither the farmer went periodically for the relatively rare goods and services he could not supply for himself.

Self-sufficing agriculture did not continue in the United States,
however. Specialization set in as will be seen later. More and
more, the farmer needed a near-by center where he could secure
supplies, clothing, medicine, and other professional services. As
time went on, spurred by the automobile which reduced the time
required to cover the distance from farm to town, the farmer, as
Part III shows, tended to use his village more and more. It became
increasingly a social as well as an economic center and rural America has shifted its capital from the crossroads hamlet to the village
or town. There the farmer trades and banks. Thither he goes more
and more for the education of his children, for his organized religion, for social life and recreation. The use he makes of it varies
with the region, the crop, and the distance from the center, but the
trend is clear throughout the nation. This dualism in the structure
of the rural community, accompanied by a high degree of integra-

tion and division of labor, is another of the distinctive characteristics of rural society.

ELEMENTS OF RURAL POPULATION

The whole matter of rural population is discussed in Part I, but in this preview of rural society it is necessary to point out that it is made up of various elements, more or less akin, more or less different.

Farm population. There is first of all the great group numbering over 30,000,000 people in 1940 in the open country, who live on the land, on farms, and whose major or sole task is to raise food or fiber from the soil. They are the primary producers, the followers of man's oldest occupation and most ancient art.

Non-farm population. Over 27,000,000 more persons live in close proximity to the farm group, under varying but essentially rural conditions. They are of several types. First of all are the 10,000,000 or more who reside in villages and hamlets which are within agricultural communities and which exist, as the previous section showed, to serve the farm group and themselves as well, in ways essential for rural and especially agricultural society as it has been organized in this nation during the last century.

Secondly, there are some 4,000,000 who live in industrial villages, given over to a single economic pursuit, such as mining, forestry, or the manufacturing of textiles. These people, as will be explained later, are in rural America but not completely of it. Their approximation of urban industrial conditions in units of population as small as these centers are creates situations and problems, not only unique in rural society and social organization, but also largely neglected. All these groups vary significantly in the composition and characteristics of their population and in their occupational distribution.

Finally, there are those who from choice, though city toilers, wish to approximate as closely as possible at least the physical setting that differentiates the setting of rural society: space, trees, gardens, sunlight, quiet. Numerically and socially, in terms of total interest, this is by far the least important group. Nevertheless, observing the growing numbers of this group, the increasing social integration of farm and village, and the influence of the automobile, the radio, and motion pictures in reducing isolation and spreading understanding, there are those who follow Doctor Galpin in characterizing not only rural population but rural society as "rurban."

WHY STUDY RURAL SOCIETY?

The study of rural society is a practical as well as a scientific pursuit. It supplies at least a knowledge of the importance of rural America in the national life, of the rural heritage of that life, and of rural-urban relationships. It shows the importance of social forces, groups, and organizations and the parts they play in national and community life. It furnishes, if not techniques, at least clues for the understanding of places where one works and lives, and indeed of the backgrounds of associates and friends.

These values grow out of such a study only if the attitude toward this subject of rural society is that of the student, of the scientist seeking facts and understanding, laying aside, so far as possible, preconceptions and adopting instead an objective approach. Such values may accrue to members of both rural and urban society. A study of rural society should give to rural residents a better understanding of the life about them which they are all too likely to take completely for granted. Rural leadership to be effective today needs the attitude of the student. City dwellers should benefit from a study of rural society if they come to recognize more fully the real interplay and interdependence of the great rural and urban forces and fortunes which, working together, may realize the dream of America, but which, pulling apart, may tear her asunder.

DISCUSSION TOPICS

1. List and describe very briefly five distinctive characteristics of rural society.
2. Make a list of what you consider the six chief deficiencies or problems in rural society today. How does your list compare with that of the Roosevelt Country Life Commission of 1908?
3. Rural society is said by some writers to be "individualistic." What do they mean by this? What do you think of this explanation?
4. What are the chief reasons for a study of the social and consumption relations of agriculture as compared, for example, with its production or distribution problems?
5. What social forces have been released by science and invention during the past ten years which are producing social changes and posing social problems in rural society?

REFERENCE READINGS

Adams, James Truslow, *The Epic of America*. Revised edition. Boston: Little, Brown & Co., 1933. An excellent statement regarding the influence of the frontier upon American life.

Galpin, C. J., *Rural Life*, chap. 3. New York: Century Company, 1918. Statement of rural social problem.

Macklin, Grimes, and Kolb, *Making the Most of Agriculture*, chaps. 1 and 26. Boston: Ginn & Co., 1926. A social point of view for agriculture.

Plunkett, Sir Horace, *Rural Life Problem of the United States*. New York: The Macmillan Company, 1911. A very interesting statement of American rural problems by a famous Irish observer.

Roosevelt Country Life Commission, *Report of Commission on Country Life*. New York: Sturgis & Walton, 1911. Read especially first fifty pages. An important and historical document giving rural social problems their setting in the national life.

Williams, J. M., *Our Rural Heritage*. New York: Alfred Knopf, 1925. An interpretation of the backgrounds of rural life, especially from the viewpoints of New England.

Wilson, Warren H., *The Evolution of the Country Community*. Boston: Pilgrim Press, 1923. A very clear explanation and analysis of the growth and development of group relations in rural society.

PART ONE

RURAL PEOPLE · THEIR DISTINGUISHING CHARACTERISTICS

2

Cultural Origins and Regional Distribution

PEOPLE constitute the element that gives the breath of life to the social structure. The structure itself evolves from the complexity of cultural heritages and experiences, of mores and acquired social habits which any given unit of population possesses. In an aggregate population as large as that of rural America there is great cultural diversity. Interaction takes place, modifications in social behavior occur. The culture is an on-going process, never quite the same, but never wholly losing the heritages of the past. This is true also in single communities. The larger the number of cultural influences that have gone into the make-up of a given community, the broader its experience and the more fluid its local culture is likely to be. The converse is also true. This explains some of the differences between communities on the West Coast of the United States and other communities in the Mid-West or the East, where the bulk of the population has sprung perhaps from a single racial group.

But any such group is influenced, not only by the physical environment, but also by the national climate of opinion. Thus, viewed from the air the physical structure of communities founded by German migrants to eastern Pennsylvania or central Wisconsin is closely similar, even to the architecture of churches and barns, to communities of similar origin in southern Australia or Queensland. The policy and creed of churches in such communities are closely akin. Cultural practices in agriculture are similar, but show differences forced by variations in climate and soils. Attitudes show far greater diversity.

It is necessary, therefore, before considering the social arrangements, institutions, and behaviors of any society to understand something about the people themselves. The origins, characteristics, distribution, and attitudes of the population and their interaction with the environment are of importance, because without people there would be no society.

This is especially true in rural America. Many countries, such as

Australia, New Zealand, the islands of the Pacific, and to a lesser extent, such areas as Holland, Scotland, Egypt, and others, are relatively homogeneous. Thus, well over ninety per cent of the population of the firstnamed of these lands is of English origin. On the other hand, the population of rural America is composed of many diverse strains. Each of these originally had its own culture. Some groups attempted to set up cultural islands and preserve their accustomed ways of life, but slowly the changed environment and the unique place of the United States in the world undermined the cultural foundations of such groups and commanded adaptations. It was not until the late nineteen-tens and early twenties that religious services in the mother tongue were largely abandoned in areas settled by some German groups.

Over a period of years the population of rural communities often became quite heterogeneous, with two or more racial stocks represented. The various cultures interacted, but some traits of each almost always remained and are clearly discernible. Such cultural impedimenta have to be taken into account in all local planning. This interaction and the influence of the total environment — physical, social, and economic — resulted in the evolution of a societal structure describable by no other term than American. For instance, the Portuguese in Barnstable County, Massachusetts, retain their Catholic religion and marry largely within their own group, but they join the same co-operatives, trade at the same stores, send their children to the same public schools as do the descendants of the first settlers, the English. Almost every nation in the world has had a part in the development of our present rural society, some, of course, more than others. The contribution of a few of those races whose influence is still traceable and vital will be briefly examined.

The English. Two predominating English strains founded our first agricultural colonies, the country gentleman and the yeoman. The former settled in the South, the latter left his impress chiefly in New England. From the beginning, the South concentrated on export crops, first on tobacco, later on cotton. The history of the section is closely linked with the story of cotton and tobacco; in fact its very agricultural geography is determined by them. The South was not tilled so much by small holders as it was divided into large estates or plantations, which were mostly self-subsisting. The plantation form of agriculture was a direct descendant of the old English manor. Since cotton and tobacco required cheap labor, a slave economy arose, accompanied by an enormous influx of

Negroes for two hundred and fifty years after the country was first settled. Except for the political necessity of a county seat, the self-contained plantation had little if any need for the services of towns and villages, and this accounts for the fact that the number of Southern villages per one hundred square miles is today only half that in the Northern Colonial States.

The rise of isolation. The yeomen settled for the most part in New England, and to some extent in the Middle Atlantic States. They were freeholders, and participated in the great westward migration toward the cheap virgin land so different from that which their European forbears had tilled and exploited for centuries. The lure of these large holdings, the prospect of possessing land in such quantities as dwarfed their European experiences, seduced the imagination of these men, and in effect did away with the im-memorial agricultural village in which their ancestors had resided, the village (still predominant in much of Europe and the Orient) from which they went forth to their fields in the morning, and to which they returned at night. In America, agriculture and isola-tion first united, and the result was the solitary homestead set in the midst of the farmer's acres, miles from the nearest town. Such was the pattern which came to characterize American agriculture.

It is hard now to realize how revolutionary the change was his-torically, and to appraise its influence in the development in the pioneer of such qualities as self-reliance, and rugged independence, qualities which contributed immensely, in the North and South alike, toward the drive for national liberty, and which account in part for the intense individualism that for decades characterized the economic, social, and religious life of the United States. Never-theless, as will be shown in Part III, the village could not be en-tirely dispensed with, and today it has become the service station for the farming population.

In time the yeoman stream divided. Some, as we have seen, migrated to the west, and traces of their influence can be found now in many Middle and even Far-Western States, for example, in such colleges as Grinnell, Earlham, and Whitman. Some, turn-ing southwest in search of a kindlier climate than New England's, were marooned in the Appalachian Highlands and the Ozarks, along with many Southern *émigrés*. Even today, in the more iso-lated sections of these areas, one finds many household arts of pioneer days and hears English words which have passed out of currency everywhere else. Other New Englanders forsook agri-culture for the sea and in their famous clipper ships carried the

American flag and American trade over the seven seas, contributing, in this way, to the economic development of the young republic.

The Scotch and Irish. Another racial stream came from Ireland, driven out in the middle of the last century by successive crop failures and other economic maladjustment. The Irish settled from Maryland northward, for the most part in non-rural areas. The North-Irish and Scotch-Irish, who came earlier, established a considerable number of farming communities in Pennsylvania and northern Maryland, and their descendants are still living in scores of communities in those states, each settlement possessing its two-century-old Presbyterian church, and other relics of Irish and Scotch pioneering.

The Dutch. The Dutch, two of whose progeny have occupied the White House in this century, were rather more important in urban than in rural American development.

The Germans. The Germans, whose cultural contributions are very significant, came in two waves, the smaller from southern Germany in the eighteenth century, and the larger, from central and northern Germany in the century following.

The first are the so-called Pennsylvania Germans, sociologically a highly interesting race. Originally extremely poor and tenacious of their Germanic traditions, they remained for nearly two centuries an almost alien group, not only in southeastern Pennsylvania where they first settled, but wherever they chanced to migrate. They took their form of religion with them when they migrated, and in their churches and parochial schools their dialect has been preserved in many places until this day. Moreover, they invariably cling to the limestone soil to which their ancestors were accustomed in the German Palatinate.[1] These people fled to America partly because of untoward economic conditions, and partly to safeguard their religious liberty and avoid joining the German State Church.

The bulk of the North-German immigration, greatly stimulated by the German Revolution of 1848 and the conditions that produced and followed it, took place between 1836 and 1886. These people were agrarians, and settled for the most part in the West North Central States, as did a considerable stream which arrived

[1] Cf. Brunner, *Co-operation in Coopersburg* (New York, 1915), chapter II, for a more extensive discussion of this subject. See also the *Proceedings* of the Pennsylvania German Society. It would be quite possible and sociologically valuable to follow all population groups in greater detail, unfolding the influences which brought them to America, which molded them, and the contributions they have made to American rural life.

about the same time from the Scandinavian peninsula. For a time the East regarded the rapid settlement of the frontier by people of alien tongues as highly dangerous, but this opposition began to fade when these immigrants responded wholeheartedly to the Northern spirit during the Civil War. They did, however, change the local scene. Places whose English names still betray their New England origin are engulfed by Germans and Scandinavians and their postoffice rosters now reveal no English stock. The Congregational Church was replaced by the Reformed or Lutheran. The parochial school was introduced. The *Verein* became the leading social organization. Only the American forms of government and the physical structure of the community persisted.

The flood of immigrants, especially from southern and southeastern Europe, increased enormously with the turn of the century, but for the most part these people settled in cities. The Czechs, who came earlier, did settle on the land, as did some of the Italians and Poles, especially in the East. These people, and the French Canadians who poured into Vermont and New Hampshire, and the Portuguese, who dominate some types of agriculture in eastern New England, introduced their diverse social elements. So, too, the Mexican has invaded the Southwest, though far more as an agricultural laborer than as a farmer.

The blending of these various racial streams with American rural life has been widespread and far-reaching in effect. In many communities, now apparently typically American, close study discloses influences, attitudes, and cultural deposits which reflect diverse racial local origins, without an understanding of which the community itself cannot be fully understood.

Obviously, all the members of these racial groups did not remain where they first settled. Most of them spread far and wide, mingling with new people, contributing and assimilating cultural and ethnological heritages. Today the actual number of foreign-born on farms and in villages of the United States is relatively small, and because of our present immigration laws, this number is declining, but the record of the achievements of immigrant farmers, as gathered from the United States Census tabulations and field studies, is highly significant.[2]

[2] Cf. Brunner, *Immigrant Farmers and Their Children*. New York: Institute of Social and Religious Research, 1929. In areas where there are considerable numbers of foreign-born or sons of foreign-born the report of this nation-wide field and census study may well be used for further exploration as to the present status of the foreign-born on the land. The 1940 Census figures should, however, be secured and substituted for those of 1920 in chapters I and II.

THE SIZE AND LOCATION OF THE PRESENT RURAL POPULATION

But while rural America cannot be fully understood without a knowledge of the racial streams that contributed to it, it is more pertinent for our present purposes to consider the size, distribution, and importance of the rural population in the nation.

Rural proportion declines. At the time of the federal census of 1820 the country was almost entirely rural, 93 per cent to be exact, but with each succeeding census the urban proportion increased, although the total number of rural people has never failed to gain.

By 1890, the United States had grown from the less than four million pioneers clinging to the Eastern seaboard in 1790 to a nation of over fifty millions, more than 70 per cent rural.[3] By the turn of the century, our more than seventy-five millions were exactly 60 per cent rural and 40 per cent urban. Somewhere between 1910 and 1920 the urban population became the majority group, for the 1920 Census showed 51.4 per cent of the population living in urban territory. By 1940 this proportion had increased to 56.5 per cent. Table 1 tells the story of the gain in rural and urban population and of the changing proportion of these two groups in the national total since 1880.[4]

TABLE 1. RURAL AND URBAN POPULATION IN THE UNITED
STATES, 1880–1940 *

(Population in millions)

Year	Total	Rural	Urban	Rural Per cent	Urban Per cent
1880	50.16	35.80	14.36	71.4	28.6
1890	62.95	40.65	22.30	64.6	35.4
1900	75.99	45.61	30.38	60.0	40.0
1910	91.97	49.81	42.16	54.2	45.8
1920	105.71	51.41	54.30	48.6	51.4
1940	131.67	57.24	74.42	43.5	56.5

* *Sixteenth Census of the United States*, 1940, vol. I, *Population.*

[3] The definition of *rural* of the present United States Census of Population is used here. It includes the farm population, those living in incorporated centers of less than 2500 population and others living in rural territory but not engaged in farming.

[4] These census figures are based on an arbitrary dividing line between rural and urban. Some such line must, of course, be drawn. Because an agricultural village grows from 2450 to 2550 population in ten years, however, it does not cease to be a farmers' service station. At one time the United States Census used 8000 as the dividing line between rural and urban. If it had continued to do so 49.1 per cent of the population would have been classed as rural in 1930. The United States Census of Retail Distribution classes together rural and small town communities, including all centers of less than 10,000 inhabitants, or 52.4 per cent of the total population of the nation.

It will be observed that during the first decade of the century the rate of urban gain, 38.8 per cent, was four times the rural increase of 9.2 per cent. Between 1910 and 1920 urban population grew nine times as fast as rural, 28.8 per cent as against 3.2 per cent. Between 1920 and 1930 the rates of gain were respectively about 28 and 5 per cent, but between 1930 and 1940 they were about equal. The rural population is an appreciable part of the nation. It includes for one thing a disproportionate number, over 48 per cent of those under nineteen years of age, in the total population. Twenty-eight of the states, one more than in 1930, were more rural than urban. Eight others were more rural than the nation as a whole. Seventeen of the states and four of the nine census divisions, including the more urbanized, were more rural in 1940 than in 1930. The details are given in Table 2. The urban population is obviously concentrated in a minority of the states, so that in the majority, educators, clergymen, social workers, and governmental officers will have to deal with predominately rural groups. Even so highly an industrialized state as Pennsylvania has nearly 1,000,000 farm population and a total rural population of over 3,300,000.

It is obvious that World War II has further changed this distribution, as will be shown later in this section. Several millions of the rural population, both farm and non-farm, entered war industries. A few rural villages were transformed into industrial cities by the location of large war plants in their midst. The degree to which this happened exceeded that of similar developments during World War I. Some industries were designedly located in rural areas to tap surplus population, changing certain open-country areas and villages to metropolitan industrial centers. Postwar economic developments will have great influence on this situation. The end of the war has produced a movement back to rural areas on the part of workers. Indeed, such a tendency was noted by personnel managers in a number of war industrial centers both after the invasion of North Africa and the invasion of France.

But even with these war and postwar dislocations, it is clear that, with the factor of natural increase taken into account, there are more than twenty-five million people on the farms and at least twice that number in rural America. The 1945 agricultural census, when available, will give an answer to the effect of the war on the size of the farm population. There is one other indication. On November 1, 1943, the United States Bureau of the Census estimated that the civilian population of the United States had declined by just over four million, or 3.1 per cent since April 1, 1940. Thirty-

TABLE 2. PROPORTION OF RURAL AND URBAN POPULATION BY STATES, 1920, 1930 AND 1940

State	1920 Rural	1920 Urban	1930 Rural	1930 Urban	1940 Rural	1940 Urban
North Dakota	86.4	13.6	83.4	16.6	79.4	20.6
Mississippi	86.6	13.4	83.1	16.9	80.2	19.8
South Dakota	84.0	16.0	81.1	18.9	75.4	24.6
Arkansas	83.4	16.6	79.4	20.6	77.8	22.2
South Carolina	82.5	17.5	78.7	21.3	75.5	24.5
New Mexico	82.0	18.0	74.8	25.2	66.8	33.2
North Carolina	80.8	19.2	74.5	25.5	72.7	27.3
Alabama	78.3	21.7	71.9	28.1	69.8	30.2
West Virginia	74.8	25.2	71.6	28.4	71.9	28.1
Idaho	72.4	27.6	70.9	29.1	66.3	33.7
Kentucky	73.8	26.2	69.4	30.6	70.2	29.8
Georgia	74.9	25.1	69.2	30.8	65.6	34.4
Wyoming	70.5	29.5	68.9	31.1	62.7	37.3
Virginia	70.8	29.2	67.6	32.4	64.7	35.3
Vermont	68.8	31.2	67.0	33.0	65.7	34.3
Montana	68.7	31.3	66.3	33.7	62.2	37.8
Tennessee	73.9	26.1	65.7	34.3	64.8	35.2
Oklahoma	73.4	26.6	65.7	34.3	62.4	37.6
Arizona	64.8	35.2	65.6	34.4	65.2	34.8
Nebraska	68.7	31.3	64.7	35.3	60.9	39.1
Nevada	80.3	19.7	62.2	37.8	60.7	39.3
Kansas	65.1	34.9	61.2	38.8	58.1	41.9
Iowa	63.6	36.4	60.4	39.6	57.3	42.7
Louisiana	65.1	34.9	60.3	39.7	58.5	41.5
Maine	61.0	39.0	59.7	40.3	59.5	40.5
Texas	67.6	32.4	59.0	41.0	54.6	45.4
Minnesota	55.9	44.1	51.0	49.0	50.2	49.8
Colorado	51.8	48.2	49.8	50.2	47.7	52.3
Missouri	53.4	46.6	48.8	51.2	48.2	51.8
Oregon	50.1	49.9	48.7	51.3	51.2	48.8
Delaware	45.8	54.2	48.3	51.7	47.7	52.3
Florida	63.3	36.7	48.3	51.7	44.9	55.4
Utah	52.0	48.0	47.6	52.4	44.5	55.5
Wisconsin	52.7	47.3	47.1	52.9	46.5	53.5
Indiana	49.4	50.6	44.5	55.5	44.9	55.1
Washington	44.8	55.2	43.4	56.6	46.9	53.1
New Hampshire	36.9	63.1	41.3	58.7	42.4	57.6
Maryland	40.0	60.0	40.2	59.8	40.7	59.3
Pennsylvania	35.7	64.3	32.2	67.8	33.5	66.5
Ohio	36.2	63.8	32.2	67.8	33.2	66.8
Michigan	38.9	61.1	31.8	68.2	34.3	65.7
Connecticut	32.2	67.8	29.6	70.4	32.2	67.8
California	32.0	68.0	26.7	73.3	29.0	71.0
Illinois	32.1	67.9	26.1	73.9	26.4	73.6
New Jersey	21.6	78.4	17.4	82.6	18.4	81.6
New York	17.3	82.7	16.4	83.6	17.2	82.8
Massachusetts	5.2	94.8	9.8	90.2	10.6	89.4
Rhode Island	2.5	97.5	7.6	92.4	8.4	91.6

Source: *Sixteenth Census of the United States*, 1940, vol. I, Population.

six states showed a loss, twelve a gain. Of the twenty-seven states which are more rural than urban, twenty-three showed declines, totaling about four fifths of the national total. Only two of these states lost at a rate lower than the nation's, four more exceeded it by only one point or less, nine lost between 4.1 and 9.9 per cent. The other eight lost up to 16.4 per cent. Obviously, however, if the men and women in the armed services had been counted as well as civilians, these twenty-three states would have shown little or no loss.

The causes which transformed the United States from an almost completely rural nation to one which is more than half urban will be discussed more fully in the next chapter. Briefly, the explanation lies in the rapid growth of industrialism. Of course this phenomenon operated also elsewhere in the world. For example, the farming population of England declined from about one third the total in 1810 to about one tenth in 1860, the period which embraces the first industrial revolution.

Japan more recently repeated the experience. From 1898 to 1925, the urban population of this most industrialized of the Oriental nations went from 15,000,000 to 32,300,000 and from 32.6 to 55.8 per cent of the total population. Conversely the rural population dropped from 30,500,000 to 26,400,000, and its share of the total from 67.4 to 44.2 per cent. According to a special tabulation made in 1927 by Professor S. Nasu, using the American definition of rural, taking all places of 10,000 residents or less as rural,[5] the Japanese census shows that the total population in such districts declined from 67.7 per cent to 54.1 between 1920 and 1935. This decline has continued.

Similarly, in countries as young as New Zealand and Australia the urbanization has gone on rapidly. In 1901, the former country was 64.6 per cent rural; in 1911, 58.2 per cent; in 1936, 47.2 per cent. Australia, with a land area almost identical to that of the United States, and settled only a century and a half ago, had 47 per cent of its population in its six largest cities in 1936. Only 36 per cent of its people were rural: one half of them on farms.

The density of rural population. One highly important characteristic of rural area is, of course, a relatively low population density. For the nation as a whole 44.2 persons live on the average square mile, but in New York City the figure is 24,937.7 and in Chicago 16,824.2. Even the density of rural population varies widely, a variation which may be ascribed to many factors, such as crops, topog-

[5] That is, United States Census of Distribution.

raphy, climate, proximity to large cities, and length of settlement in the area. For example, in Salem County, New Jersey, a fruit and trucking region, population density is 120.8 persons per square mile, but in Hunterdon County in the same state, which is devoted to dairying and general farming, the figure is 84.5. Walworth County, Wisconsin, a dairying district, registered a density of 59.1 persons in 1940. A representative section in the corn belt, Pocahontas County, Iowa, had a density of 28. Wheat, a crop more highly mechanized than corn, brings a lower population density, since individual farms are larger. For example, Stutsman County, North Dakota, in 1940 had a density of 10.3. In areas of sparse rainfall where dry-farming is practiced, farms become larger, thus reducing the density, as in McKenzie County in western North Dakota, where the figure is 3. Mountainous areas are not generally favorable for farming, and are likely to be devoted to stock-raising or forestry, which accounts for the low point in population density in Beaverhead County, Montana, where there are only 1.2 persons to the square mile. A relatively new state like Wyoming, which is both mountainous and deficient in rainfall, has only two cities of over 10,000, and is an important stock-raising area, showed a population density of only 2.3 in 1930; 2.6 in 1940.

Importance of density. The low density of population in rural areas as compared with urban and suburban centers is one of the major difficulties that must be overcome in the social organization of rural America. Des Moines, Iowa, has a population of nearly 160,000 persons living in an area of 54 square miles, a density of over 2900 persons per square mile. This city possesses several dozen schoolhouses, a paid fire department with fire stations strategically located over the city, a fine library with several branches, a paid police force, and an efficient health department as well as other social utilities, such as hospitals, clinics, street lighting, and water mains.

A township of similar area in a near-by rural county with a population density of twenty-five to thirty persons on each of its thirty-six square miles, has no fire or police protection, probably no library, or at best only a small one, and a part-time health officer whose duties are confined to tacking up quarantine signs and making routine reports. Street lighting and water mains are absent. Such a township has a few one- or two-room schools, or if it has a consolidated school, an appreciable part of its budget is spent in transporting the pupils to and from their homes.

Obviously no such rural township needs social utilities in the same amount and degree as a city like Des Moines, but just as obviously it has need for educational facilities, fire and police protection, and health and social services. The absence of these used to be taken as one of the handicaps of rural living, but more and more ruralites are seeking and even demanding service along these lines. It is often difficult for the township or even the county to supply these, and for this reason rural people are beginning to demand state support for certain minimum institutional services.

REGIONAL CHARACTERISTICS IN RURAL AMERICA

Comparisons in this chapter and elsewhere in this book contrast various sections of the United States. These distinctions are very important for our discussion. As will be shown again and again, conditions in many regions vary sharply from national averages and from one another. It is necessary, therefore, to study the social influences of regional peculiarities, and this study in turn involves an understanding of the regions themselves.

Census divisions. The best-known national classification is that of the United States Census which divides the country into nine sections, as follows:

New England — Maine, New Hampshire, Vermont, Massachusetts, Rhode Island, and Connecticut.

Middle Atlantic — New York, Pennsylvania, New Jersey.

East North Central — Ohio, Indiana, Illinois, Michigan, Wisconsin.

West North Central — Minnesota, Iowa, Missouri, North Dakota, South Dakota, Nebraska, Kansas.

South Atlantic — Delaware, Maryland, Virginia, West Virginia, North Carolina, South Carolina, Georgia. Florida.

East South Central — Kentucky, Tennessee, Alabama, Mississippi.

West South Central — Arkansas, Louisiana, Oklahoma, Texas.

Mountain — Montana, Idaho, Wyoming. Colorado, New Mexico, Arizona, Utah, Nevada.

Pacific — California, Oregon, Washington.

Crop areas. Another official division is that of the United States Department of Agriculture, made on the basis of crop areas.[6] The

[6] This plan of classification divided the country into two parts: the eastern half with a sufficient amount of rainfall for agricultural production by ordinary methods, and the western half with less adequate rainfall except in certain districts. Each of these halves is subdivided into six areas. Those in the East are classified according to temperature and crops grown: (1) hay and pasture, (2) corn, (3) corn and winter wheat, (4) cotton, (5) sub-tropical gulf coast region, (6) spring wheat. In the West, where rainfall and topography deter-

effect of these crop areas on social conditions may be illustrated by reference to two factors, the community area, and the open-country population of the community, both discussed in Chapter 13. Small groups of villages, where the factors of topography and proximity to cities did not appear, were selected from the corn, wheat, and fruit belts, encompassing Iowa, North Dakota, and California respectively. The average extent of the community area in square miles was computed for each of these three groups and compared with open-country population and density, with the results shown in Table 3.

TABLE 3. AVERAGE AREA OF COMMUNITIES AND AVERAGE COUNTRY POPULATION

Crop Area	Number of Villages *	Average Area of Community (Square Miles)	Average Country Population	Persons Per Square Mile
Corn..............	10	80.0	1640	20.5
Wheat..............	9	294.4	1908	6.5
Citrus..............	6	40.0	1443	31.1

* The communities selected for this table were as nearly as possible one-crop communities.

It will be observed that the area of a community in the wheat belt is seven times greater than in a fruit-growing district, but that the density of population in the latter is five times that of the former. As far as the factors of transportation or topography are concerned, there is no reason why the California communities should not be larger. The average number of farmers served does not vary greatly, regardless of the size of the village. This is largely because other centers spring up, each serving its own closely integrated group of farmers.[7]

mine the nature and amount of agricultural production, the areas derive their names from their physical features: (1) Great Plains, (2) Rocky Mountain, (3) Arid Intermountain Plateaus, (4) North Pacific, (5) South Pacific, (6) California-Arizona desert region.

For a detailed analysis of the agricultural production of each area in 1920, see "A Geographic Summary of American Agriculture," by O. E. Baker, in the *Yearbook* of the United States Department of Agriculture, 1921, pp. 407-507.

[7] Still another classification, adopted by the Institute of Social and Religious Research, sought to reveal certain differences which the other two classifications seemed to obscure. Its classification differs from that of the census chiefly because it sets aside the Southern mountains as a separate region totally unlike the rest of the South. This dividing line is drawn to allow also for certain situations where characteristics of one state or census division dominate bordering counties of another.

The National Resources Planning Board worked in six regions, namely, Northeast, Southeast, Middle States, Northwest, Southwest, Far West. One of the most careful delineations of regions and sub-regions is that developed by A. R. Mangus.[8] Using such indices as proportion of urban population to total, plane of living, ratio of children under five years of age to one thousand women twenty to forty-four years inclusive, percentage of tenant-operated farms and several others, he divided the United States into thirty-two rural farm and thirty-four rural non-farm regions with over two hundred sub-regions in each group.

The type of regional classification used depends upon the purposes of a given discussion. In this work we are concerned with population regionalism and with certain sociological data varying significantly with population. For this reason the federal census divisions are frequently used, or, as in many studies of the above-mentioned Institute of Social and Religious Research, regions or census divisions have been combined into the following units: New England, Middle Atlantic, South, Middle West, and Far West. In this classification the South includes the three Southern census divisions or regions; the Middle West, the two Central Western regions, and the Far West and Mountain and Pacific.[9] Some of the chief regional characteristics and their significance will now be described.

New England and Middle Atlantic regions. The New England and Middle Atlantic regions, rurally, bear unmistakable marks of their peculiar situation. More than any other regions, they carry on the colonial tradition. This is manifested even in their domestic and ecclesiastical architecture. Their agriculture is conditioned by proximity to urban markets, but urban opportunity has drained off more of their youth than elsewhere, so that their farmers are on the average older. But although the number of their farms may continue to decrease in any predictable future, agriculture, and therefore rural life in these regions, have achieved during the last decade or two, a relative balance with industry and the city, or at least more of a balance than other regions.

The Middle West. The Middle West, on the other hand, was invaded by various migratory streams, and therefore, by various cultures. As already described, its relative lack of cities and large farms forced it into cereal farming, and thus made it more de-

---

[8] Cf. *Rural Regions of the United States.* Washington, D.C., 1940.

[9] For a detailed discussion of these regions and their economic and social characteristics in 1920, with maps, see Morse and Brunner, *The Town and Country Church in the United States,* pp. 17-36. New York, 1923.

pendent upon world economic conditions than any other region except the South. Fluctuations in these conditions have been responsible for prosperity, a land boom, and finally, depression with foreclosures, tax sales, and increasing tenancy, all of which have brought a cessation of social progress, as will be shown later.

The Far West. The Far West was settled last. It profited by the accumulated experience of the territories whence its population came. Its pioneering stage was brief. Aided by splendid mineral and agricultural resources, and a well-advertised climate, it eagerly appropriated the best experience of the nation.   Co-operation flourished. Public schools were excellent. The level of rural social life remained high between 1920 and 1930, but progressed little, if at all, after that.

The South. The South, with its high proportion of Negroes, its absence of foreign-born, and its cotton and tobacco culture conducted by an increasing number of tenants, evolved an economy peculiar to itself: large plantations, comparatively few villages, and the socially and economically important county seat. All these things have also produced a relatively lower standard of community life, especially among the Negroes and in the Southern Highlands. But in the decades from 1920 to 1940, the South has made much progress, in some respects more than other regions. It has, for instance, created county health units, in which it leads the nation.

Yet in one village in the Far South, where climate and irrigation made possible the growth of such Southern California crops as citrus fruit, melons, and early spring vegetables, for winter sale in the North, cotton-growing had disappeared by 1924. The population was drawn from many regions, farms were small, churches variegated, and even architecture and speech were affected by the new industry. Field workers described it as a California village set down in the Far South. Southern mores were on the defensive. Southern traditions were not binding on the community. The Mexican, rather than the Negro, furnished the farm labor. In population growth, school construction, farm ownership, and per capita retail sales, this community in the decade prior to the last survey ranked first or second among thirty agricultural villages studied in the South. Even regional influences, powerful as they are, exercise no unimpregnable control, as this illustration shows. Regional boundaries themselves may not be fixed for all time.

There has been a great increase in the use of regional classifications in the last decade. Various departments and agencies of the federal government use no less than 110 different regional classifications, many of which vary but slightly. The regions of the Federal Reserve banks and of the Farm Credit Administration are illustrations. Many corporations also have regional divisions. Social agencies like the American Red Cross have regional offices. The excellent studies of the National Resources Committee make much of regional planning and have stimulated the interest in regional matters. These studies indicate that many conditions and problems overlap state lines, that they affect and are the concern of regional groupings of states, and that necessary action therefore must also transcend state lines. Some political scientists have even proposed that the numbers of states be reduced from forty-eight to six or twelve. Unquestionably the trend is for an increasing use to be made of regional divisions for planning and administration and by the same token the subject of regionalism will become increasingly important.

This chapter has described briefly some of the racial streams, now largely assimilated, which have contributed to American rural life. It has shown that despite the fact that rural people were becoming up to 1940 more and more a minority in the nation, they are still, nevertheless, a very important element in the population, and do indeed dominate, numerically, a majority of the states. The importance of low density of population, a characteristic of ruralism, has been pointed out, as well as the relation of geographic and economic factors to population and to social institutions. But two important questions have not been answered: What has brought about the present distribution of our rural population? Why has urban population forged ahead of rural? A third topic injects itself here also: What of the future trend regarding population? These questions will be answered in the next chapter.

DISCUSSION TOPICS

1. Trace the early settlements in your county. Where did the first settlers come from? What racial groups did they include?
2. Trace the changing proportions of rural and urban population for your state given in Table 2 on page 22 and explain changes. Refer to the *United States Census of Population: 1940* and explain similarly changes in your county.
3. Is the decline in the proportion of rural people in the total population good or bad from the point of view of national welfare? Defend your point of view.

4. What, if any, are the evidences that the interests of the rural population as a minority group may be overlooked in national policy-making?

5. Should matters of regional concern be handled by regional organizations or by co-operation among the states? Defend your point of view in terms of your own general region.

6. What have been the effects of the war on the population of your community or county?

REFERENCE READINGS

Brunner, E. de S., *Immigrant Farmers and Their Children*. New York: Harper & Bros., 1929.

Brunner, E. de S., and J. H. Kolb, *Rural Social Trends*, chap. I. New York: McGraw-Hill, 1933.

Brunner, E. de S., and I. Lorge, *Rural Trends in Depression Years*. New York: Columbia University Press, 1937.

Mangus, A. R., *Rural Regions of the United States*. Washington, D.C.: Government Printing Office, 1940.

Odum, H., *Southern Regions*. Chapel Hill: University of North Carolina Press, 1936.

Odum, H., and H. E. Moore, *American Regionalism*. Chapel Hill: University of North Carolina Press, 1938.

Population Statistics: I, National Data; II, State Data. Washington, D.C.: National Resources Committee, October, 1937.

Problems of a Changing Population. Washington, D.C.: National Resources Committee, May, 1938, chaps. II and IX.

Thompson, Warren, and P. K. Whelpton, *Population Trends in the United States*, chap. III. New York: McGraw-Hill, 1933.

Vance, Rupert B. *All These People: The Nation's Human Resources in the South*. Chapel Hill: University of North Carolina Press, 1945.

3

The Mobility of Rural Population

MIGRATION FROM EUROPE to the rural areas of America, which began almost as soon as the first colonies were permanently established, and which continued to the close of the last century, is by no means the only migrational influence in rural America. Once the nation was firmly established, the ceaseless movement of people hither and thither across the continent was of even greater importance.

AMERICA'S GREAT MIGRATIONS

Before 1930, this movement was characterized by two drifts, one westward, the other toward the cities. The former came first, and was the more important for many decades. The latter movement began slowly, at the beginning of the nineteenth century, but in the fifty or sixty years prior to 1930 it gradually became more significant than the westward trek.

Westward ho! Westward expansion began in colonial times. The English who settled Plymouth, Cape Cod, and Boston, penetrated to the Berkshires in a few decades, to central New York by 1800, and thence continued to move westward. So with other groups. The indentured servants of the early Virginia planters, after serving their time, pushed up the Virginia rivers toward the west. In Washington's day, the site of Pittsburgh was the western outpost of the European *émigré*. Expansion accelerated with time, led by frontiersmen of the Daniel Boone type, in whose wake followed hardy pioneer farmers like the parents of Abraham Lincoln. So it continued until the comparatively recent days of homesteading, the frontier and the center of population moving farther west every year.

The frontier. The frontier left a tremendous mark on American life, rural and urban. Pioneering involved ceaseless, unaided struggle. Land had to be cleared and cultivated; civilization with its well-established and comfortable institutions was left behind.

31

Neighbors were few and far between. Only the strong, the fittest, survived. Migration meant a definite break with Europe, the parent continent, and a repudiation of the eastern United States, whence the pioneers had come.[1]

In the main, the frontier drive was economic. Cheap Western land, the chance to become monarchs of vast acres, lured the masses. Land was wealth in those days, as in all agrarian civilizations, and these migrants were Europeans, or the descendants of Europeans, and accustomed to the meager holdings of Continental peasantry. They were willing to make any sacrifice to obtain and hold these vast acres of the West.[2] A movement similar to ours was that from China proper and Korea into Manchuria, which, between 1900 and 1930, brought a fifteen-fold increase in the population of this fertile empire which then totaled thirty million people.

Westward expansion carried 3,500,000 people into the eastern Middle West, including Iowa and Minnesota, between 1850 and 1860. The importance of this enormous mass migration, as indeed of all interstate migrations, is recognized by the United States Census, which, for the last eight enumerations, has attempted a rough measure of the migrational force by noting how many people are living in states where they were not born. For example, by 1870, one twelfth of all persons born east of the Mississippi were residing west of it; that is, two fifths of the West's six million population. Horace Greeley's slogan, "Go West, young man!" described a national movement.

The period ends. In 1890, one tenth of those born east of the Mississippi, about four and a half million, had crossed it, and almost another million was added by 1910. Thereafter the pace slackened, both because free land was getting scarce, and because of the rise of the "industrial frontier" in the East. The 5,200,000 Easterners reported living in the West in the 1930 Census constituted but a sixth of all Western population, and less than one thirteenth of all living Easterners. By 1940, the number of Easterners living west of the Mississippi River had actually declined

---

[1] The influence of the frontier has been well discussed by the historian Turner. See also Eggleston's *Hoosier Schoolmaster* and James T. Adams's *Epic of America*, chaps. IV, V, VI. Boston: Little, Brown & Co., 1932.

[2] See Herbert Quick, *Vandermark's Folly* (Indianapolis: Bobbs-Merrill, 1923), for an excellent description in fictional form of the American migration and its motives. See also sections of Phillips's *Life and Labor in the Old South* (Boston: Little, Brown & Co., 1931) for family case histories based on old records and materials relating to the causes of migration and the experience of migrants from the Old South.

by half a million and was but 5.5 per cent of the total number of Easterners. Indeed, the movement had reversed itself, and the flow was toward the east; by 1940, 1,920,000 Westerners were living east of the Mississippi, about 272,000 more than in 1930, nearly a million more than in 1920. Interestingly enough, the proportion of all native Westerners living in the East was also 5.5 per cent.

Similarly, the movement from the South to the North was two to three times as strong as the movement from North to South. This included Negro migration from the South. (The North constitutes New England, Middle Atlantic, East North Central, and West North Central Census divisions. The South embraces South Atlantic, East South Central, and West South Central divisions.) Each census since 1910 has found just over 3 per cent of all those Northern-born residing in the South — double the figure of 1870. On the other hand, Southerners in the North equaled 5.3 per cent of all Southern-born in 1900, and 8.6 per cent in 1930, but 8.2 per cent in 1940.

Migrations are more than movements of people. Along with the baggage stowed in the prairie schooner were transplanted distinctive social and cultural ideas: ideas of local government, of community organization, education, architecture, even modes of speech and superstitions. The farther west the pioneers traveled and the more they mingled with natives of other regions and countries, the more their traditional personal and social mores were modified by environmental and social contacts.[3]

Pioneer influences. It is not difficult, now, when westward expansion has largely ceased and the nation has become comparatively stabilized, to detect some of the more abiding results of migration. Most important of all, the pioneer engrafted on American culture the idea of "rugged individualism" by which alone the pioneer survived and which has only recently, and perhaps temporarily, been more or less abandoned. Furthermore, the pioneer had his share in our continuing "splendid isolation" from the rest of the world, in the face of rather intricate economic and cultural ties with all lands. The westward movement gave us our great dramatic era of railroad-building, the by-product of which was the creation and growth of towns and villages. The rapidity of agricultural and transportation development increased the value of land and helped create a speculative attitude toward it. The necessity of

[3] Cf. Brunner and Kolb, *Rural Social Trends* (New York: McGraw-Hill, 1933), for further discussion of this topic. The above paragraph is quoted from chapter I of that work.

having governmental units of manageable areas resulted in our three thousand local counties, our tens of thousands of townships, and our hundreds of thousands of school districts. These divisions are less necessary now than in the last century, since today the fast-moving automobile has replaced the horse and a plane can span the continent in eight hours. Frequently, therefore, throughout this volume, problems and conditions will be discussed which have their roots in an age that is past, outmoded by the rush of inventions, but persisting as part of a tradition or because social inventiveness lags behind mechanical discovery.

It is obvious from Table 4 that the proportion of the native pop-

TABLE 4.   NATIVE POPULATION BORN IN OTHER CENSUS DIVISIONS, LIVING IN SPECIFIED DIVISION

Residence in Census Division	Born in Other Divisions							
	1870 per cent	1880 per cent	1890 per cent	1900 per cent	1910 per cent	1920 per cent	1930 per cent	1940 per cent
New England............	4.0	5.0	5.9	7.5	7.7	8.2	7.8	7.7
Middle Atlantic.........	5.0	4.9	4.9	6.0	6.6	7.3	9.5	9.4
East North Central......	23.8	17.9	13.7	12.2	11.3	13.0	15.8	14.7
West North Central.....	48.9	42.9	35.8	27.7	23.6	19.9	16.6	13.8
South Atlantic..........	3.1	3.4	3.5	4.1	4.9	6.7	7.6	9.2
East South Central......	14.9	11.2	9.0	8.1	7.4	7.0	7.5	6.7
West South Central.....	37.1	31.9	27.7	25.9	24.4	21.1	17.1	13.7
Mountain...............	34.5	45.6	50.9	44.8	49.0	46.4	40.6	37.8
Pacific.................	50.6	44.0	48.7	44.6	53.0	51.1	52.5	52.0

Source: *State of Birth of the Native Population, Sixteenth Census of the United States*, 1940, p. 5.

ulation living in divisions other than that of birth, began to decline in most regions after 1930. The war may have changed this situation, but how much or how permanently cannot be determined until the 1950 Census results become available.

INTERSTATE MOVEMENT OF FARM AND RURAL NON-FARM POPULATION

The 1940 Census gives more detailed information on the subject of migration than had been previously available.[4] Between 1930 and 1940, twenty states gained in farm population through inter-

[4] Cf. *State of Birth of the Native Population: 1940* (Washington, D.C., 1944), and *Internal Migration 1935 to 1940* (Washington, D.C., 1943).

state migration. Almost half of these states were in the Mountain and Pacific census divisions, in which all gained except Utah. All four West South Central states gained. Two thirds of the New England states also scored net increases, although the division lost, as a whole. The other states of these twenty were scattered, but only the East South Central division failed to have at least one state which received more farmers than it lost through interstate migration.

The rural non-farm story was much the same. Nineteen states made a net gain; again, all but Utah in the two western divisions were included in this group. No state in the West North and South Central divisions added to its rural non-farm population through migration from other states.

These voluminous data which must be studied by those who desire to understand the population composition of their own states, raise vital questions for the social scientist. It is not unexpected to find that more farmers migrated to California than to any other state, but perhaps few would have guessed, remembering the droughts of 1934 and 1936, that Oklahoma would rank second in new farm population. Illinois lost more of its native farmers to other states than any other state in the union, although Missouri, Iowa, and Arkansas, in that order, are close behind. More native sons among the farm population of California left that state to farm elsewhere than was the case in any other Far-Western state save Colorado. Her rural non-farm loss to other states was also high, third among the ten Far-Western states. The largest losers in this class were, in order, Pennsylvania, Illinois, Missouri, although the lastnamed led in net loss of rural non-farm population by interstate migration. California, of course, gained more than it lost in both categories. It is often the case, not only in the United States but also in other countries, that where there is a considerable in-movement of population there is also an above normal, although smaller, out-movement.

URBAN-RURAL DIFFERENCES

The behavior of rural and urban people in interstate migration differs in degree. When first measured in 1920, 28 per cent of all city dwellers were born in states other than those in which they resided at the time of that census. The comparable rural figure was 18.5 per cent. In 1940 the same fact was revealed. Of the urban population, 18 per cent were found living in a census division other than that in which they had been born, and 26.6 per cent were living in a different state. For the rural non-farm population the respective proportions were 14.6 and 22.5 per cent. Only 8.4 per cent of the rural farm population were living in other divisions than that of birth, and only 13.4 per cent in other states. Summing up, 29.7 per cent of the total population in 1940 were residing in a state other than that of birth. Considering only those who were born in the United States, the proportion is 22.4 per cent.

The explanations of these and other facts in the census sources alluded to lie beyond the scope of this text, and in some instances would require research. The total picture, however, is one of a mobility probably greater than that in almost all other countries, except perhaps a few of the most recently settled. It is this ceaseless movement across the face of the continent which, through the interaction of people from varying regions and sub-cultures, helps to make America what it is, to make similar attitudes of its citizens, to smooth the sharp corners of peculiar local cultural traits, and so build more unified permanent culture.

MIGRATION: 1935-40

A more recent picture of the mobility of our population is given by the census study of the half-decade prior to 1940. In the latter half of the nineteen-thirties, one person in every eight in the United States moved to a location outside the governmental area in which he resided in 1935. Of these migrants three fifths stayed in the same state, one fifth moved only to a contiguous state, and one fifth went farther away. Proportionately there was slightly less mobility among non-whites than among whites. The migratory pattern naturally varied by states and regions, but it followed closely the trends indicated, regarding persons born in one state but living in another. Thus, the North Central and Southern states were close to the national average. The Northeastern states showed a mobility slightly above one half; the Far-Western states about twice that level.

Rural migrants also varied. One tenth of the farm population and one sixth of the rural non-farm were enumerated in 1940 at a place other than that in which they resided in 1935. Thus, in the half-decade under consideration these groups also followed the pattern already indicated from the analysis of state of birth compared to state of residence for the total population.

Table 5 presents the census data on the proportion of migrants

TABLE 5. MIGRATION STATUS OF THE RURAL FARM AND RURAL NON-FARM POPULATION BY DIVISIONS: 1940

| Census Division | Per cent Migrants in Total Population | | Per cent All Migrants by Type of Migration | | | | | |
| | | | Within a State | | Between Contiguous States | | Between Non-Contiguous States | |
	R.F.	R.N.-F.	R.F.	R.N.-F.	R.F.	R.N.-F.	R.F.	R.N.-F.
New England............	8.8	12.0	56.0	55.3	27.7	26.5	16.3	18.2
Middle Atlantic......	8.6	11.3	75.0	74.0	17.2	16.6	7.8	9.4
East North Central..	10.7	16.1	74.7	74.7	15.8	12.1	9.5	13.2
West North Central .	10.2	15.8	69.2	71.2	23.4	19.7	7.4	9.1
South Atlantic......	7.6	15.3	73.5	56.4	21.2	25.7	5.3	17.9
East South Central..	7.5	13.2	80.0	69.3	15.5	20.7	4.5	10.0
West South Central..	11.5	19.2	77.2	74.3	17.4	17.0	5.4	8.7
Mountain...........	15.5	23.4	42.4	42.0	28.9	27.3	28.7	30.7
Pacific.............	21.7	31.6	46.1	52.5	10.2	8.3	43.7	39.2

Source: Washington, D.C.: *Sixteenth Census of the United States*, 1940, *Internal Migration 1935 to 1940*, pp. 10 and 11.

in these two rural groups by census divisions, and also lists the proportion of migrants who remained within the state of residence in 1935, who migrated to a contiguous state, or who went farther away.

It will be observed that for most divisions the greatest proportion of movement was within the state, and that in over half the divisions this accounted for two thirds to three fourths of the mobility. This, of course, was to be expected. People prefer to remain in a comparatively familiar locale. This was even more true for farmers than for the rural non-farm population in the half-decade reported upon. The greater mobility of the latter is in part related to the more varied economic life of villages, and especially to the rural industrial centers. The proportion of migrants from non-contiguous states in New England is interesting, and is one evidence of the improved opportunity for agriculture in this region, owing to the proximity of urban markets for fruit, vegetables, and dairy products. Except for the Far West it was the only region having over ten per cent of the migrants from non-contiguous states. It must be remembered, however, that these figures are percentages. The total number of people involved in New England in all types of migration was smaller than the number moving within a given state in all other census divisions. The data are given in terms of percentages, both for comparative purposes and because the proportions give a better measure of the problem of assimilating persons with different backgrounds into the social structure.

It is clear from the data that this is a greater problem for villages than for farming neighborhoods, and that this is least important in the South. This latter fact is doubtless because of the large proportion of sharecroppers and other tenants in this region. Although they move frequently, they rarely move far. The Far West, on the other hand, attracts large proportions of persons from outside state boundaries.

Effect of the war. It is obvious that the war has disturbed many patterns of life and social behavior. There has been no measure of gross migration such as that just discussed. But in June, 1945, it was estimated by the Census and the Bureau of Agricultural Economics that between April, 1940, and April, 1944, there had been a net movement from the farms to villages, towns and cities and into the armed services of 5,160,000 persons fourteen years of age and over, or an annual average of almost 1,300,000. This is twice the average of the nineteen-twenties and over three times that of the thirties. About one half the net loss occurred among males of military age. Though some of these went into essential industry, a large portion of this group was taken by the armed services. The demobilization of the services and of war industry will doubtless produce another considerable population movement. The final results of this are problematical. It is important that they be measured carefully by the Census of 1950.

These data raise the fundamental questions as to migration and its social consequences, especially as to migration from the rural sections to cities.

RURAL-URBAN MIGRATION

Data already discussed in this chapter mentioned the second great population current, that from country to city. Until 1940 the Census never published figures showing the number of city residents born in rural areas, farm or non-farm. But up to 1930 rural-urban migration was too well recognized to need proof. Though never measured scientifically in all its aspects, it had been described again and again in fiction and in such works of art as the picture, "The Breaking of Home Ties." The study of migration, 1935 to 1940, supplies this lack of information for those years.

Leaving the farm. Moreover, the Bureau of Agricultural Economics of the United States Department of Agriculture attempted to estimate the drift of people from farm to city and from city to farm. These estimates give only the statistical story since 1920, but the movement began in the eighteen-seventies, particularly in New England, and became a national phenomenon by 1910.[5] In the main report on *Recent Social Trends*, Mr. O. E. Baker calculates that the net migration from country to city between 1920 and 1930 was 5,898,000; 60 per cent of these wanderers came from the South, and one third were Negroes.[6]

The county story. As a result of migration, 1086 of our 3065 counties lost population between 1910 and 1920; 1265 of our 3079 counties between 1920 and 1930 lost population from the same cause. Roughly speaking, the proportion these counties had of the total land area of the nation was twice their proportionate share of the population. Between 1930 and 1940 the number of counties losing population dropped well below 900, generally those most affected by the Great Drought.

Table 6 shows that the movement from the farms reached its first peak in the latter half of the nineteen-twenties. Although the net movement from the farms began to recede in 1926, the Great Depression reduced the movement from the farms, and in its earlier years increased the counter-swing from the urban areas to the land. Indeed, in 1931 the net gain to the cities as estimated by the Bureau of Agricultural Economics was only 20,000 persons. In 1932 the farms gained 262,000 from the cities. In addition, the Bureau of Agricultural Economics estimates that in the first four years of the present decade there has been a net movement of over 1,500,000 persons from the farms into the armed services. This movment from the farms in the first half of the nineteen-forties reduced the population on farms to under 30,000,000 for the first time since 1910, when the annual estimates were begun. On January 1, 1944, it was estimated that the population on farms was 25,521,000.

Migration, 1935 to 1940. The special migration study of the census, already alluded to, clearly shows that the people who leave

[5] Cf. O. E. Baker, "Utilization of Natural Wealth," *Recent Social Trends in the United States*, chap. II, Part I, pp. 110-11. New York: McGraw-Hill, 1933.

[6] O. E. Baker, *op. cit.* The migration is estimated by comparing the number of persons in each five-year age group of the rural non-farm population in 1930, with the number in each age group ten years younger in 1920, who would naturally be expected to survive in 1930, using expectation of life figures evolved by comparing the 1920 and 1930 figures for native whites in such age groups in the country as a whole and Negroes as a whole with the Negro population of the Southern states. Migration of children born on farms during the decade is not included.

TABLE 6. ESTIMATED POPULATION MOVEMENT
TO AND FROM FARMS

(In thousands)

During Year	To Cities * from Farms	To Farms from Cities *	Net Movement to	
			Cities	Farms
1920–24.................	8,701	5,370	3,331	
1925–29.................	10,735	7,770	2,965	
1930–34.................	7,176	6,578	598	
1935–39.................	6,816	4,044	2,772	
1940...................	1,296	690	606	
1941...................	1,960	814	1,146	
1942...................	2,739	819	1,920	
1943...................	1,982	994	988	
1944...................	1,293	817	476	

* "Cities" here includes towns and villages. The net loss by migration from farms is therefore greater than the loss to the total rural population as it includes migrants from the farm joining both the urban and rural non-farm groups.

Source: *Farm Population Estimates*. Washington, D.C.: Bureau of Agricultural Economics, United States Department of Agriculture.

one location for another tend to go first to a comparable environment. Thus, more than half (53 per cent) of the farm population
which moved in this period, moved to another farm location. More
rural non-farm residents moved to other such areas (38.3 per cent)
than went elsewhere.[7] In addition, 12.3 per cent of the migrants
from rural non-farm residences moved to the farm.

The areas of greatest mobility of the farm population correlate
highly with a high percentage of tenancy and sharecropping and
somewhat in recent years with untoward climatic conditions. Tenants move from two to six times as frequently as farm-owners. Presumably migration of this sort, counting those who move within
the same community, affects more than a million farm families in
some years. It is often an effort to improve the economic conditions
of the family. But such constant shifting calls for constant readjustment on the part of the family as well as on the part of social
institutions and communities. There are clearly social losses too
subtle to measure with precision and the change is frequently an

[7] Actually the proportions may be higher, since about 11 per cent of the
rural migrants failed to indicate to the census enumerator whether theirs had
been a farm or rural non-farm residence in 1935. Of these, over 650,000 persons, 34.5 per cent, were on farms in 1940 and 31.6 per cent were in rural
non-farm territory. Thus, 66.1 per cent of these unclassified 1935 rural residents stayed in rural territory as against 62.7 per cent of those whose 1935
residence was classified as either farm or rural non-farm.

economic gamble as well. In the long run it might be better in an average situation for the community or county to seek to so improve conditions that some of the incentive to migrate would disappear.

In view of the migration estimates of the Bureau of Agricultural Economics, given above, which perforce count all migration from farms as migration to towns and cities, it is interesting to observe that between 1935 and 1940, 645,776 farm persons moved only to rural non-farm locations. This represented more than a fifth, 21.4 per cent, of all migration from farms. Presumably, a number of these persons were simply retiring to the service-station village or town of their own community. Barely one quarter of the farm population moved to urban territory, and well over half of this move was to towns of less than 100,000 population. Many such places, especially those of 2500 to 10,000 population, are also the centers of rural communities. Migration to these was partly, therefore, normal retirement.

The proportions of urban people moving to rural non-farm territory in the years 1935 to 1940 are fairly high. This movement involved more than one quarter of the city migrants. This is probably a reflection of the suburban trend. It is more than possible that a considerable proportion of the city to farm migration is also part of this movement. In recent years, especially near large metropolitan areas, there has been a considerable movement to suburban acres. Such holdings often meet the census definition of farm. This may help to account for the increase in small farms noted in a later chapter. The migration facts discussed above are summarized in Table 7.

TABLE 7. PROPORTION OF MIGRANTS, 1935–1940, MOVING TO SPECIFIED TYPES OF LOCALITIES

Number Migrants, 1935–1940, in Thousands from	Per cent Going to Specified Locations			
	Cities over 100,000	Other Urban	Rural Non-Farm	Rural Farm
Cities over 100,000......4341	23.8	38.4	29.5	8.3
Other urban...........4554	26.6	39.3	24.9	10.1
Rural non-farm........2988	17.8	31.6	38.3	12.3
Rural farm............3015	9.8	15.6	21.4	53.2

Source: Washington, D.C.: *Sixteenth Census of the United States*, 1940, *Internal Migration, 1935–1940*, Table 16, p. 27.

Types of migrants. Numerous studies indicate that rural-urban migrants included young adults, older but still vigorous people searching for greater economic opportunity, the upper middle-aged, frequently retired, desiring an easier life, and finally, people who could no longer endure agricultural toil. In short, the country contributed to the city a steady supply of youth, and many who took with them the savings of years of farming; this loss of money as well as of people proved, of course, a serious economic loss to some communities.

In the city trek, the ages between eighteen and thirty predominated. Females, the children of tenants, and younger sons of landlords, were most likely to leave home. Four fifths or more of all migrants settled within a hundred miles of home, a majority of these within fifty miles. Those who went to the city were more likely than not either to enter the professions or to remain at the bottom of the scale as unskilled or semi-skilled laborers. In short, the best and the poorest of farm youth apparently wandered to the city.[8]

These generalizations vary, of course, by regions and even states. The South appears to lose more of its superior youth, measured by school achievement and similar indices, than other regions. Such variations arise because of differences in economic opportunity, size of family, education, and other socio-economic factors.

Reasons for migration. Why did these people leave the country? Their own answers show that high taxes and small profits drove many away, while others craved richer educational, social, and cultural opportunities. But the social scientist probes beneath these replies. His answers are that, first of all, land lost its importance as a means of livelihood, that more alluring and profitable means of subsistence were found in the cities. In 1820, agriculture, the leading American occupation, absorbed two thirds of those gainfully employed; in 1940 less than one fourth. In the interval of one hundred and ten years manufacturing and trade surpassed agriculture in national importance; but of this more elsewhere.

Moreover, mechanization decreased the need of manpower on the farm, and helped to increase the efficiency of those who remained. Indeed, many tasks, such as butter and soap making, and butchering, were transferred from farmhouse to commercial institutions, often located in town or city. Many such impersonal factors influenced migration. Depletion of soil fertility through ero-

[8] These statements are based on studies by colleges of agriculture, representing every region and covering over six thousand farm families.

sion and in other ways, discussed in another chapter, played its part also. As opportunity on the land waned, it waxed in the city.

Underlying all these phenomena, however, was the natural increase of farm population; as the next chapter will show, ruralites are more fertile than urbanites. The country supplied not only the surplus food for national consumption, but the excess population for the replenishment of cities. Overpopulation in the country made a cityward trek imperative, and for this reason rural America was called "the seed-bed of the nation."

Youth as migrants. The importance of youth in the rural urban migration has already been noted, but it is of such significance that it should be studied further. Between 1920 and 1930 about 2,000,-000 persons fifteen to twenty-four years of age migrated to the cities from farms. This represents one third of the total net migration, though in 1930 this age group made up slightly less than one fifth of the total rural farm population. No data exist on the urban movement of the village youth, but probably at least another million persons were involved. With urban birth rates as they are, the present levels of population in almost all of the cities of America cannot be sustained without this renewal of their human resources from the farms and villages.

The extent of this migration, its destination, and the proportions coming from farm and non-farm localities vary with the region. So, too, does the number and proportion of rural farm and non-farm youth. In the main these variations follow the patterns of the general population. In the more industrialized areas, such as the Northeast and Pacific, non-farm youth form a majority of rural youth and their problems show greater divergencies from those of farm youth than elsewhere. In other regions similarities are far closer.

One important element in the situation is the Negro. About 1,500,000 of the rural youth are of this race. Serious as have been the problems of the nineteen-thirties for all this age group, they have weighed more heavily on the Negroes than on the whites because of the relatively disadvantaged position of the former race.

Depression reduced migration. We have seen that the lack of economic opportunity in the cities sharply reduced migration from farm to city, especially of youth. Melvin estimates that as a result the number of rural youth on farms increased by almost one million between 1930 and 1935.[9] The industrial recovery of 1937 and 1939-40 apparently corrected this condition somewhat. From the

[9] Melvin, B. L., *Rural Youth: Their Situation and Prospects*, p. 12. Washington, D.C.: Government Printing Office, 1938.

1940 ·Census results it appears that the age group fourteen to twenty-four years was increased by only 427,000 during the nineteen-thirties, or 7 per cent, although the total farm population remained practically unchanged. The rural non-farm group of these ages increased 740,000. Since migration to the cities becomes noticeable after age sixteen rather than at fourteen or fifteen years of age, there was apparently a slight gain in the farm youth group, and a gain of perhaps half a million in the rural non-farm youth group up to April 1, 1940. The war industrial program and military service unquestionably changed this situation, but, varying with the different census divisions, even in March, 1940, from 14.6 to 35.8 per cent of the males, and from 9.6 to 30.4 per cent of the females, of these ages who were in the labor force in rural non-farm areas were seeking work. The proportions among the farm group were very much smaller.

For the entire decade 1930 to 1940 the Bureau of Agricultural Economics estimates a net decline in the rural farm population of 200,000 youths between the ages of fifteen and nineteen years, because of migration, and an additional 448,000 between twenty and twenty-four years of age. These two age groups account for almost one half of the total net decline due to migration.[10] In some regions the net migration loss in these age groups, or in these and the ten- to fourteen-year-old group, more than accounts for the total net loss by migration.

Results of the rural-urban migration. The great movement to the city had far-reaching results in both city and country. Those who left their rural homes, quite naturally, took their mental furniture with them, and the influence of the frontier lingered in their blood. Although the city liberalized them, provincialism was not entirely eradicated. Consider, for example, their churches which remained, according to many studies by H. Paul Douglass (mentioned in another chapter), nothing but oversized country institutions. Our city school term, to take another instance, is that of the farmer, the vacations coinciding with the time when the farmer's children are most needed in the fields. Our taxation system, too, is still largely of agrarian origin. If, then, there has been urbanization of the country, there has been also ruralization of the city, and that to such an extent that some authorities believe that the rural heritage is a fundamental determinant of our national psychology.[11]

[10] Bennett, E. H., *Volume and Composition of Net Migration from Rural-Farm Population, 1930-40.* Washington, D.C.: United States Department of Agriculture, January, 1944 (mimeographed).

[11] Cf. especially, J. M. Williams, *Our Rural Heritage.* New York: Knopf, 1925.

We are most concerned, however, with some of the rural results of this migration, which were in some cases unfortunate, but more often beneficial if we look at the picture as a whole.

The city profits. The migration obviously contributed to the economic and social wealth of the city, both directly and indirectly. Its youth — most of the migrants were between fifteen and twenty-five — was a splendid addition to the manpower of the city. From one twelfth to one tenth were between twenty-five and thirty-five. The city thus obtained a horde of people whom it did not have to educate, for they were already educated in their places of origin. Another third of the migrants were under fifteen, but a majority of these had had some schooling. The cities probably bore less than half the cost of educating, providing medical service, and feeding and clothing the young men and women who went to work in their commerce and industries between 1920 and 1930. O. E. Baker estimated that in the nineteen-twenties the rural contribution to the city from the three causes amounted to $1,400,000,000 a year.[12] He also estimated that between $300,000,000 and $400,000,000 left the country for the city in the settlement of estates.[13] These sums are equivalent to about 20 per cent of the annual net farm income, and therefore lend cogency to the argument for the equalization of educational opportunity and costs by means of state or possibly federal subsidies. This matter is discussed further in another chapter.

The influx of so many people stimulated urban building trades and raised land values. If, however, the six million migrants had remained in the country, and thereby added that many people to rural population and to agricultural laborers, artisans and shopkeepers, standards of living would perforce have decreased and farms become smaller.[14] From this aspect, the migration was beneficial to the nation as well as to the city.

DISCUSSION TOPICS

1. Trace from census reports the contribution of other states to the population of your own. Do the same for the farm population.
2. Which group in your state, rural farm, rural non-farm, or urban, shows the greatest mobility? Is the balance in favor of or against your state? How do you account for this?

[12] Baker, "Rural-Urban Migration and the National Welfare," *Annals of the Association of American Geographers*, June, 1933.

[13] *Ibid.*, p. 87.

[14] Of course, if industry had decentralized, and these persons performed in the rural areas substantially the same work they did in the cities, the reverse would be true.

3. What were the causes of the rural-urban migration?

4. Select one community of which you know. Where have families gone who have left this community? Did they sell or rent? Who took their places? Trace young people who left when unmarried. Where did they go? Why? Education? Present occupation? Trace, if possible, effect of these changes in population on one or two social institutions.

5. Trace the moves of your family, or some family well known to you, as far back as you can. Give the motives for each major change in location.

REFERENCE READINGS

Anderson, W. A., *Mobility of Rural Families*. Ithaca: Cornell Agricultural Experiment Station, June, 1934.

Annals of the American Academy of Political and Social Science, "World Population in Transition," 237, January, 1945.

Baker, O. E., "Rural Urban Migration and the National Welfare," *Annals of the Association of American Geographers*, June, 1933.

Baker, O. E., "Utilization of Natural Wealth," *Recent Social Trends*, chap. II. New York: McGraw-Hill, 1933.

Brunner, E. de S., and J. H. Kolb, *Rural Social Trends*, chap. I. New York: McGraw-Hill, 1933.

Brunner, E. de S., and I. Lorge, *Rural Trends in Depression Years*, chap. III. New York: Columbia University Press, 1937.

Dorn, Harold F., *The Effect of Rural Urban Migration upon Death Rates. Population*, vol. I, no. 3, November, 1934.

Galpin, C. J., and T. B. Manny, *Interstate Migrations*. Washington, D.C.: United States Department of Agriculture, 1934.

Gist, N. P., C. T. Pihlblad, and C. L. Gregory, *Rural Migrations*, vol. 6, no. 1, March, 1941.

Goodrich, C., B. Allen, and M. Hayes, *Migration and Economic Opportunity*. Philadelphia: University of Pennsylvania Press, 1936.

Goodrich, C., B. Allen, and M. Hayes, *Migration and Planes of Living*. Philadelphia: University of Pennsylvania Press, 1935.

Hill, George W., and Harold T. Christensen, "Cultural Factors and Occupational Mobility," *Rural Sociology*, vol. 7, no. 2, June, 1942.

Hobbs, A. H., "Specificity and Selective Migration," *American Sociological Review*, vol. 7, no. 6, Part 2, December, 1942.

Janow, Seymour J., "Migration to the Far West," *Land Policy Review*, vol. IV, no. 10, October, 1941.

Lively, C. E., and C. Taeuber, *Rural Migration in the United States*. Washington, D.C.: Government Printing Office, 1939.

McMillan, R. T., *Migration and Status of Open-country Families in Oklahoma*. Stillwater, Minnesota: September, 1943.

Problems of a Changing Population. Washington, D.C.: National Resources Committee, Government Printing Office, 1938.

Sixteenth Census of the United States, 1940, Population, Internal Migration.

Sorokin, P. A., and C. C. Zimmerman, *Principles of Rural Urban Sociology*, Part V. New York: Henry Holt & Co., 1929.

Stanbury, V. B., *Migration into Oregon*. Eugene: Oregon State Planning Board, 1938.

Thompson, Warren, and P. K. Whelpton, *Population Trends in the United States*, chap. II. New York: McGraw-Hill, 1933.

Williams, B. O., *Occupational Mobility Among Farmers*, Part I. South Carolina Agricultural Experiment Station, Clemson College, South Carolina, June, 1934.

Zimmerman, C. C., and O. D. Duncan, "The Migration to Towns and Cities," *Journal of Farm Economics*, vol. X, no. 4, October, 1928.

4

Changing Patterns of Fertility, Residence and Age

THE TWO PREVIOUS CHAPTERS have discussed the origins and distribution of our present rural population and the great migratory movements of people within our boundaries affecting that population. But nothing has been said of the characteristics of that population so far as determined by the census. It is to this subject that the discussion now turns.

To the uninitiated it is sometimes surprising how many important clues the forbidding statistical tables of the census volumes on the characteristics of given population groups furnish the sociologist seeking to explain social behavior. Sharp variations in divorce rates, for instance, are evidences of varying mores in regard to this mooted subject. An area with a large proportion of its population under twenty-one years of age is likely to have problems and attitudes in educational matters different from those of a community or section with fewer children and more older people. Where males outnumber females in the population the whole social situation is different from where the reverse is true. The discerning student of census reports has, then, an exciting exploration ahead when he turns to them for indications that help him either to explain or discover revealing facts about people. Like many explorations, however, the way is none too easy.

As noted, the term rural population as used by the United States Census included all those who live on the farm and in places of less than 2500 population. In other words, farmers and villagers were enumerated together. In 1926 studies by the Institute of Social and Religious Research, based on special tabulation of census data for 177 agricultural villages, proved what had been surmised, but never before measured, that there were very significant differences between the rural farm and non-farm population groups. In 1930 the census provided data on this point for the first time.

VARYING TRENDS OF RURAL FARM AND NON-FARM POPULATION

It will be recalled that in Chapter 3 it was shown that the rural population had been furnishing an increasingly smaller proportion of the national total up to and including the 1930 Census. When the farm and non-farm are considered separately for 1920 and 1930, it develops that the decline, in this decade at least, resulted from the loss in the farm population, a loss incidentally entirely due to the decrease in the number of Negro and foreign-born farmers. In this decade, the rural non-farm group recorded a numerical gain of two points in excess of the national rate of growth — 16.1 per cent. Between 1930 and 1940 this group's gain was 14.5 per cent — double the national rate for that span. The increase was from 20,000,000 in 1920 to 27,000,000 in 1940; some of this increase was in suburban localities. It is significant that almost three fifths of this gain came in the nineteen-thirties. In the same decades the rural farm population dropped from 31,300,000 to 30,000,000, and from 29.7 to 22.9 per cent of the nation's total population. Both numerically and proportionately it has of course declined further since then. In June, 1945, the Census and the Bureau of Agricultural Economics estimated that the farm population of fourteen years of age and over had suffered a net loss of 5,160,000, because of migration and entrance into the armed services. In October, 1945, the Bureau of Agricultural Economics estimated that the farm population on January 1, 1945, was 25,190,000, 16.7 per cent less than five years earlier.

Rural non-farm population of increasing importance. As Table 8 shows, this changing position of the rural-farm and non-farm groups was consistent for all census divisions, though the trend was especially marked in the South Atlantic states, where it was doubtless due to the increase in rural industrial developments, notably in textiles, and in the East North Central, Middle Atlantic, and Pacific divisions.

It is entirely possible that by 1950 or 1960 the rural farm and non-farm groups will be approximately equal. The farm group that for nearly a century of our national life comprised more than half the total population may then not even be the major element in the rural population.

Implications of rural non-farm growth. The rapid increase in the numerical and proportional importance of the rural non-farm groups compared to the farm population raises several questions. Should the schools of county, village and town agricultural areas, for in-

TABLE 8. RURAL FARM AND RURAL NON-FARM POPULATION, BY DIVISION

Census Division	Number (in thousands)						Per cent Total Population						Per cent Rural Non-Farm in Total Rural		
	Rural Farm			Rural Non-Farm			Rural Farm			Rural Non-Farm					
	1920	1930	1940	1920	1930	1940	1920	1930	1940	1920	1930	1940	1920	1930	1940
United States	31,359	30,158	30,151	20,047	23,663	27,094	29.7	24.6	22.9	18.9	19.3	20.6	39.0	44.0	47.3
New England	535	499	528	1,000	1,355	1,488	7.2	6.1	6.3	13.5	16.6	17.6	65.1	73.1	73.3
Middle Atlantic	1,861	1,674	1,729	3,727	4,192	4,663	8.4	6.4	6.3	16.7	16.0	16.9	66.7	71.5	72.9
East North Central	4,887	4,453	4,584	3,539	4,049	4,598	22.8	17.6	17.2	16.5	16.0	17.3	42.0	47.6	50.1
West North Central	5,153	5,036	4,679	2,664	2,705	2,845	41.1	37.9	34.6	21.2	20.3	21.0	34.1	34.9	37.8
South Atlantic *	6,398	5,879	5,977	3,254	4,217	4,924	45.7	37.2	33.5	23.3	26.7	27.6	33.7	41.8	45.2
East South Central *	5,175	5,084	5,273	1,724	2,024	2,340	53.2	51.4	48.9	19.4	20.5	21.7	25.0	28.5	30.7
West South Central *	5,211	5,308	5,051	2,061	2,441	2,810	50.9	43.6	38.7	20.1	20.0	21.5	28.3	31.5	35.7
Mountain	1,153	1,124	1,101	968	1,120	1,276	34.6	30.4	26.5	29.0	30.3	30.8	45.6	49.9	53.7
Pacific	869	1,101	1,228	1,110	1,559	2,149	17.7	13.4	12.6	19.9	19.0	22.1	53.0	58.6	63.7

* Thus, in the South the Negro rural non-farm population is 43.2 per cent, the rural farm, 56.8 per cent of the total Negro rural group.

Source: *Fifteenth and Sixteenth Censuses of the United States,* 1930 and 1940, *Population Bulletin,* second series.

stance, expand their vocational education curriculum for boys beyond the agriculture now being offered? If this is necessary, how shall such expansion be financed? Should the extension services of the colleges of agriculture serve farm people or all rural people? In other words, should this program become national, following the lead of a few states in which especially the home demonstration agents and boys' and girls' club leaders are already enrolling considerable numbers of non-farm women and youth? If this is done what changes need to be made in the programs of agricultural extension services and in the training of their personnel? Will the growing co-operation of farmers and villagers in their social and economic life, and the increasing tendency for all rural life to be organized around villages and towns be accelerated or hindered? In either case what will be the political implications? Will the farm bloc become an all rural bloc? Will the village, especially if industry decentralizes, throw in its lot with the city or will it become powerful through holding the balance of power, under leadership not yet developed? In view of this situation what is the best policy for the city, the state, or the nation to follow in relation to proposals affecting public policy and emanating from either or both of the great rural population groups? Should the United States Department of Agriculture or Commerce and possibly Labor develop sections that would give attention to the rural non-farm aspects of their major divisions in some such way as the Department of Interior has already done in the rural section of the Office of Education? [1]

With the growing importance of the rural farm population, socially and economically, to places of 2500 to 10,000 population, will such centers, at least those that are not chiefly suburban or industrial, become more or less rural in their economic and social services, their attitudes, and their sympathies in the future? If they become more rural, should the Census of Population change its dividing line between rural and urban from 2500 to 5000, or restore the former division at 8000, or even adopt the Census of Distribution practice of including together as "rural and small town" everything under 10,000 population? [2] These and other similar ques-

---

[1] For instance, does the magnitude of rural retail trade, noted in Chapter 13, warrant a rural section in the Bureau of Foreign and Domestic Commerce of the Department of Commerce?

[2] There were 1332 places of between 2500 and 5000 population in 1930 and 851 of between 5000 and 10,000. In 1940 there were 1422 places of between 2500 and 5000 population and 965 of between 5000 and 10,000.

tions are matters that will be of increasing concern in the next fifteen or twenty years. Their importance is made manifest by the census revelation of the growth of the rural non-farm, or village, population, and by the research and sociological analysis, summarized in Chapter 13, that indicate the growing inter-relationships of the rural farm and non-farm groups. Clearly, then, the fact that the rural farm and non-farm populations show varying trends is important both in itself and because of the questions it raises.

Rural farm and non-farm population contrasts. It must be remembered, however, that the rural non-farm population has no such single occupational interest as has the farm group, diverse as agriculture is. It is made up of many elements with sharply different economic backgrounds. The bulk of it is, of course, found in villages, of which there are about 19,000, 55 per cent of these being incorporated in 1940. The total number of incorporated centers reported in the 1940 Census was 13,288. Of these, about 2700 were hamlets; that is, places with less than 250 population. The total population of all rural incorporated places in 1940 was 9,342,677, of which about 500,000 lived in hamlets. Over 4,000,000 more lived in the 7500 to 8000 unincorporated centers; 3092 of these had from 500 to 2500 inhabitants.[3] Therefore, between 13,000,000 and 14,-000,000 of the rural non-farm population live in villages or incorporated hamlets, which is about half of the 27,030,000 in this census category. Between 4,000,000 and 5,000,000 more reside in more than 35,000 unincorporated hamlets.[4] This leaves about 5,000,000 persons to be accounted for. Probably hundreds of thousands, possibly a million or more of these, reside in territory immediately adjacent to villages, towns, and small cities. They belong, to all intents and purposes, to these municipalities.[5] Other large numbers live in the uncounted crossroads centers with fewer than twenty-five persons, a number too small to list in an atlas. Others are lumberjacks, tearoom and roadhouse proprietors, and clergy of the open-country churches, teachers and many persons who commute

[3] Cf. *Sixteenth Census of the United States. Unincorporated Communities.* Washington, D.C.: Government Printing Office, 1943. Of these places 18.7 per cent were in New England.

[4] Estimate based on an atlas count in 1921-22 by the Institute of Social and Religious Research. Cf. Morse and Brunner, *The Town and Country Church in the United States* (New York, 1923) and Fry, *American Villagers* (New York, 1926).

[5] In ten cases where house-to-house community surveys were made by the Institute of Social and Religious Research the number of such persons ranged from 2 to 10 per cent of the population of the incorporated village.

to villages, town or cities. Some of them are part-time farmers.[6] It
will be interesting to discover in the following pages whether these
differences in the population groups are associated with differences
in the composition of population as revealed by the census. Chapter 13 gives a more extended discussion of this situation as it affects
villages. Here the purpose is simply to recall the general situation
as a background for the comparisons of rural farm and non-farm
populations which follow.

Rural non-farm population older than farm. Not only are there
sharp differences in rates of growth and diversity of location between the rural farm and non-farm populations, but there are also
many diversities in the make-up of their populations. Rural non-
farm people are, on the average, older than those on the farms. In
every age grouping above twenty years the proportion in the total
population for the rural non-farm exceeds that of the farm. For
instance, although the former has only 47 per cent of the total rural
population, it possesses slightly over one half of the 3,111,000 rural
persons sixty-five years of age and over. The percentage of the age
distribution of the rural farm and non-farm groups is given in
Table 9.

TABLE 9. AGE DISTRIBUTION FOR RURAL FARM AND RURAL
NON-FARM POPULATION

| Age Group | Rural Farm | | | Rural Non-Farm | | |
| | Per Cent | | | Per Cent | | |
	1920	1930*	1940	1920	1930	1940
Under 5 years............	12.7	11.1	10.0	11.6	10.5	9.3
Under 1 year.............	*2.5*	*2.1*	*2.1*	*2.3*	*2.0*	*1.8*
5– 9....................	13.1	12.5	10.4	11.2 ·	11.1	9.1
10–14...................	12.7	12.4	11.2	10.0	9.8	9.3
15–19...................	10.4	11.3	11.1	8.6	8.9	9.2
20–24...................	7.9	8.1	8.3	8.4	8.5	8.6
25–29...................	6.8	6.0	6.9	8.2	7.8	8.5
30–34...................	6.0	5.5	6.0	7.3	7.1	7.9
35–44...................	11.2	11.4	11.3	12.8	12.9	13.1
45–54...................	8.9	9.8	10.4	9.4	9.9	10.5
55–64...................	5.8	6.6	7.8	6.4	6.9	7.4
65–74...................	3.1	3.7	4.7	4.1	4.5	5.0
75 and over............	1.3	1.5	1.9	2.0	2.1	2.3

Source: *Fifteenth Census of the United States,* 1930, Table 20. *Population Bulletin,* Second Series and
Sixteenth Census, release, pp. 5–9.
  * One tenth of one per cent, unknown.

  6 There were about 70,000 places for which incidental agricultural production schedules were returned in 1930, which qualified as farms, but which
were not included in the agricultural census reports for 1930.

This aging of the population is a national phenomenon, but is especially marked in the rural non-farm group. Within this group it is the agricultural villages that produce the result. They are service stations, to be sure, but they are also the home of an increasing number of retired farmers and their widows. In every region the proportion of those over sixty-five and especially over seventy-five increased more rapidly than the population as a whole between 1920 and 1940.

The median age of the rural non-farm population, which was 25.8 years in 1930, advanced in 1940 to 27.7 years, which was 1.2 years over the national average. In contrast, the median age of the rural farm population in 1940 was 24.4 years. The median age was older than in 1930, when it was 21.6. The average age in the cities meanwhile advanced from 28.4 to 31 years. In terms of numbers this trend is startling. The number of persons sixty-five years of age and older in the rural non-farm population increased from approximately 1,500,000 in 1930 to almost 2,000,000 in 1940, or at a rate of 26.2 per cent. This was almost twice the rate of growth for the rural non-farm group. The gross numbers in these age groups in the farm population were practically identical with those in the rural non-farm group. The rate of growth was 28.2 per cent, despite the fact that the total farm population was practically unchanged between 1930 and 1940.

The same trends were operating among the Negro group, although its median age was younger than the whites'. Between 1930 and 1940 the median age of rural non-farm Negroes rose from 23.6 to 25 years, and of the farm group from 18.6 to 19.8 years.

The war, of course, changed these proportions. Seasonal movements of population have to be considered. For example, between April and July, 1944, there was an estimated gain of 350,000 persons in the farm population, followed by a drop to 25,190,000 by January, 1945. Comparing the census month of April, 1940, with the same month in 1944, a joint Census-Bureau of Agricultural Economics estimate [7] gave the following proportionate declines within this period:

Males under 14	13.2	Females under 14	13.7
Males 14 years and over	21.9	Females 14 years and over	10.5

Probably these changes have raised, at least temporarily, the average age of the farm population still further.

[7] Series Census, Bureau of Agricultural Economics No. 5, July 2, 1945.

Social significance of age. This aging population of the nation as a whole, as well as in rural America, has certain rather important implications. In census terms, at least, our young nation was built by youth. It was the adventurous and the youthful who followed the westering sun to the Pacific, who grappled with the frontier, settled and exploited the Mid-West, conquered the Rockies and tamed the Far West. As a population ages, it loses some of the traits of youth. It becomes conservative, less hospitable to new ideas, and it values security above all else. An aging population amidst the problems of the postwar world may then be a disadvantage unless its normal results can be combated by adult education, which is discussed in Chapter 20. The aging of the population is also responsible for the interest in legislation for old-age security through pensions.

In terms of the agricultural village this picture is reduced to miniature scale. A considerable portion of the inhabitants must conserve their resources. They seek peace, not opportunity; quiet, not life. They are likely to dwell in the past. They see little necessity for change or improvement. They are frequently out of sympathy with youth. Moreover, their relative financial security and their greater leisure give them sometimes a disproportionate voice in the affairs of the community and its social organizations.

Rural farm population has more children. The lower average age among the rural farm people proves that children make up a larger share of the whole group than among the rural non-farm group. Taken together, however, these two groups, comprising our total rural population, possess more than half the nation's children under fifteen years of age. This fact has great significance for the nation and its educational systems and gives to rural education a significance often underestimated. This matter is discussed in another chapter.

During the nineteen-thirties the rural farm population produced over 160 per cent of the number of children needed to sustain this population group at the 1930-40 level. The comparable figure for the rural non-farm residents was 115 per cent. In contrast, the urban rate was less than 75 per cent. In these figures lie the proof of the familiar statement that rural America is the seed-bed of the nation. Indeed, the urban deficiency was so great that in 1940 the net reproductive index for the nation was only 98 per cent. There was a spurt in the birth rate during the earlier years of the war, but inevitably there will be a decline, and it is probable that within a few years after the war's end the century-old decline in the birth rate will be re-established. Some measure of this decline is given in Table 10, which gives the data on the net reproductive index

TABLE 10.   ADJUSTED NET REPRODUCTION RATE BY REGIONS
AND PERIODS

	1935–40			1930–35			1905–10		
	Rural Farm	Rural Non-Farm	Urban	Rural Farm	Rural Non-Farm	Urban	Rural Farm	Rural Non-Farm	Urban
U.S.....	1661	1150	726	1632	1150	747	2022	1499	937
N.E....	1406	1035	715	1349	1049	756	1426	1439	1033
N.C....	1452	1146	753	1425	1115	759	1834	1451	963
South ..	1812	1211	712	1802	1250	742	2199	1591	764
West...	1559	1174	726	1473	1116	690	1848	1459	807

Source: *Sixteenth Census of the United States*, 1940, *Differential Fertility 1940 and 1910*, Table 7.
Adjusted rate of 1000 is equivalent to the maintenance of a stationary population.

for 1905-10. This stood at 133.6 for the entire United States, which was more than a third above the rate of the next generation. Even then the urban rate had dropped below 100. The reasons for this and the necessity of rural-urban migration, are made clear by Table 10. If all the children born in rural America remained there, farms would grow steadily smaller and standards of living would fall. The failure of city populations to reproduce themselves furnishes opportunity for the "surplus" rural population, especially the youth, who migrate cityward in considerable numbers, as a previous chapter showed.

Table 10 also shows the net reproductive rate by regions. It reveals a sharp decline in all regions by all three major population groups since 1905 to 1910. Proportionately, this drop has been less for the rural farm group than for the others. There are greater variations in this group, however, than for either the urban or rural non-farm population. The rural South is the most fertile among the regions, although the urban South is the lowest. It is interesting to watch the slight increase in the rate of the rural farm population in all regions during 1935 to 1940, as compared to 1930 to 1935, and the checking of the decline among the rural non-farm group in these periods. This happens in only one region for the city population. Whether this means that the decline has been checked, or that the intensity of the depression from 1930 to 1935 affected the rural and farm population birth rate, is an interesting but unanswerable question. From the point of view of sustaining the population of the nation, it is important that the net reproductive index should fall no lower. There is no evidence that the decline has been permanently checked.

This is especially apparent from Table 11, which employs the measurement of children under five years of age per one thousand women of fifteen to forty-nine.

TABLE 11. NUMBER OF CHILDREN UNDER 5 YEARS OLD PER
1000 WOMEN 15 TO 49 YEARS OLD, BY REGIONS,
1940 AND 1910

Region	1940			1910		
	Rural Farm	Rural Non-Farm	Urban	Rural Farm	Rural Non-Farm	Urban
United States........	462	344	238	623	488	357
Northeast...........	391	312	244	379	432	380
North Central.......	398	339	238	554	466	345
South..............	509	367	236	712	546	353
West...............	422	338	227	557	459	297

Source: *Sixteenth Census of the United States*, 1940, *Differential Fertility, 1940 and 1910*, Table 6.
Necessary to maintain stationary population, 368.

The data here, as in the previous table, are standardized for marital status and adjusted for under-enumeration. The pattern is the same. There are proportionately more young children in the rural farm than the rural non-farm group, and both exceed the urban population by large margins. There is also far less variation among the regions in the urban population than in the two rural groups. The stake of the nation, and especially of the cities, in rural children is again apparent. At the same time, the larger educational and health responsibilities of rural America are clear.

When distributed on the base of occupation of husband, it appears that the decline in fertility for farmers, measured by standardized rates, exceeds that of five of the eight other occupation groups.

Basically the reason that the rural population still has a larger proportion of children is that women marry earlier in rural than in urban America, as is clear from Table 13.

Negro pattern differs. The data given concern the total popula-

TABLE 12. CHILDREN UNDER 5 YEARS OLD PER 1000 NATIVE
WHITE WOMEN OF AGES 15 TO 49 MARRIED ONCE AND
LIVING WITH HUSBAND, ACCORDING TO MAJOR
OCCUPATION GROUP OF HUSBAND, UNITED
STATES, 1940 AND 1910 *

Major Occupation Group of Husband	Children Under 5 Years Old per 10,000 Women		Per cent Decrease, 1910–1940
	1940	1910	
Farmers and farm managers.......	629	836	24.8
Farm laborers and foremen........	618	745	17.0
Laborers, except farm and mine ...	622	705	11.8
Operatives (semiskilled)..........	476	643	26.0
Craftsmen, foremen..............	446	602	25.9
Service workers..................	402	524	23.3
Proprietors, managers, officials.....	368	525	29.9
Professional and semiprofessional..	361	468	22.9
Clerks, sales and kindred.........	359	459	21.8

Source: Quoted from the *Statistical Bulletin*, Metropolitan Life Insurance Company, June, 1945.
* The rates were standardized for age on the basis of the age distribution of the total female population at ages 15 to 40 in the United States, 1941. The source for basic rates was the United States Bureau of the Census, *Population, Differential Fertility, 1940 and 1910 — Women by Number of Children Under 5 Years Old* (Washington, D.C., 1945), Tables 41 and 42.

TABLE 13. PER CENT OF NATIVE WHITE WOMEN WHO HAD
EVER MARRIED, ACCORDING TO AGE; FOR THE UNITED
STATES AND ITS GEOGRAPHIC REGIONS, WITH
REGARD TO SIZE OF COMMUNITY, 1940

Region; Size of Community	Age						
	15–19	20–24	25–29	30–34	35–39	40–44	45–49
United States..........	11.1	51.9	77.1	85.1	88.2	89.5	90.2
Cities of							
250,000 and over......	6.3	42.6	70.0	80.4	84.0	85.1	86.1
25,000–250,000.......	9.9	48.3	74.1	82.8	86.4	87.7	88.2
2,500– 25,000......	9.9	49.5	76.5	84.7	87.5	89.0	90.1
Rural non-farm.......	15.1	62.6	84.2	89.7	91.5	92.3	92.2
Rural farm...........	13.6	58.6	82.9	89.1	92.2	94.0	94.8

Source: Quoted from the *Statistical Bulletin*, Metropolitan Life Insurance Company, June, 1945; United States Bureau of the Census, *Population, Differential Fertility, 1940 and 1910 — Women by Number of Children Under 5 Years Old* (Washington, D.C., 1945), Tables 5 and 61.

tion. In the South a considerable proportion of the residents in both rural and urban territory are Negroes. Among the urban and rural non-farm populations of this group the number of children under five years of age for every one thousand women fifteen to forty-nine

years of age is less than for the whites. This is to a considerable
degree a reflection of the much higher infant and child mortality
rate among Negroes than among whites. It is significant in this
connection that this ratio of children to Negro women of child-
bearing age was lower in 1910 than in 1940, despite the serious
economic depression of the nineteen-thirties, which bore down with
especial severity on the Negro group. This change is probably due
to an improvement in health conditions. The data on this point
are given in Table 14.

TABLE 14. NUMBER OF CHILDREN UNDER 5 YEARS OLD PER
1000 SOUTHERN WOMEN 15 TO 49 YEARS OLD
1940 AND 1910

	1940	1910
Urban white	234	349
Urban Negro	192	233
Rural farm white	434	647
Rural farm Negro	472	559
Rural non-farm white	383	591
Rural non-farm Negro	326	471

These tables make clear that during the last generation a profound change has occurred in the attitude of Americans in city
and country alike toward the desirable number of children for a
family to have. The figures given in these tables, the data in this
chapter, and the facts presented in *Problems of a Changing Population* warrant two generalizations on the subject. First, that the
cities have produced less than half their present population. The
rest has come from rural America and from immigration. Second,
that if normal rural-urban migration trends discussed in the last
chapter are restored, the time is not far distant — perhaps another
thirty or forty years — when the majority of the urban population
will have been born and reared in rural America, in both farm and
rural non-farm communities. Already this is true in some cities.
Certainly a considerable proportion of what will be the urban population from 1950 to 1970 are now rural residents.

It seems clear, from a study of the age distribution of the rural
population previously given, that the long-time rural decline may
continue for a while, barring an easing of immigration laws or other
unforeseen events. If this happens, and if the large cities are no
longer able to sustain their present population, the period of the
nation's maximum population is evidently not far distant. Recent
estimates place the peak year as between 1960 and 1980, and the

maximum population at 150,000,000.[8] Such an eventuality will have far-reaching consequences in a nation that has always looked forward to having more persons to feed and clothe tomorrow than it has today. Some economists and business analysts have already pointed to the slackening rate of population increase as one of the reasons for the delay in recovering from the Great Depression.

Youth at peak numbers. As a result of long-operative population trends the United States has reached its peak of population for the age years sixteen to twenty-four. In 1940 there were just under 24,000,000 persons fifteen to twenty-four years of age in the country, 1,500,000 more than in 1930. However, there were only 22,400,-000 in the age five to fourteen years group, over 2,000,000 less than in 1930. Obviously the youth population has passed its peak. This was largely an urban phenomenon. Despite migration, the number of five- to fourteen-year-olds in the farm group exceeded the fifteen- to twenty-four-year-olds by over 600,000, and was only slightly below the older group in the rural non-farm population.

The youth who fought and won World War II were highly valuable to the nation during that conflict. But it is well to remember that the youth who came into the years of potential employment from 1929 roughly equaled in numbers the number of unemployed from 1937 to 1939. It is quite clear from the data just given that with good economic conditions there will be more opportunity for rural youth in cities after the war than before. It is also clear that, if there should be a depression, farm youth especially would be in a difficult situation, for migration is an economic necessity for a considerable proportion of them. Rural America produces more individuals than it can absorb.

During the depression, a rough proportion of two and one-half males were reaching maturity in the rural farm population for every farm made vacant by the death or retirement of the operator. The Bureau of Agricultural Economics estimated in December, 1944, that in the decade 1940 to 1950 there would normally become available only three fifths as many farms as there would be young men reaching twenty-five years of age. In other words, the replacement ratio is 167. The Negro rate is 174, that for the whites 165, but in every state in the South the replacement ratio is higher for whites than for Negroes, the regional averages being 195 and

[8] Baker, O. E., "Rural-Urban Migration and the National Welfare," *Annals of the Association of American Geographers,* June, 1933; Thompson and Whelpton, *Population Trends in the United States.* New York: McGraw-Hill, 1933. *Problems of a Changing Population.* Washington, D.C., 1938.

175 respectively. The lowest replacement ratio rates — 123 — are found in the Pacific states, and in New England, which are 124; higher rates — 192 — are in the South Atlantic states — and in the East South Central states they are 190. In Utah, and eight Southern states, the rate is over 200. New Hampshire is the only state where the ratio is as low as 100. Even with the heavy demand of the armed services for youth, there is enough youth left on farms to fill the "vacancies" likely to occur between 1945 and 1954. The return of a majority of young men from the armed services will again make migration necessary.[9]

Marital status. The marital status of the population also bears on the situation discussed in this chapter. The proportion of single persons fifteen years and over in the United States seems to be slowly but surely declining. In the United States as a whole, 33.1 per cent of the white males and 26.2 per cent of the females fifteen years of age and over were unmarried in 1940, while in the rural farm population 37 per cent of the males of this age group were single, but only 25 per cent of the females. This contrast between the national and the rural farm population figures is directly related to the ratio of males to females, 111.7 to 100. In the cities, where the comparable ratio was 95 to 100, proportionately more white females, 27.8 per cent, and fewer males, 32.5 per cent, were single.

The proportion of persons who admitted that they were divorced when interviewed by the census enumerator in 1940 was small: 1.3 per cent of the males and 1.7 per cent of the females. In the rural farm census, the proportion for males was about half this figure, and for females about one third. This probably reflects a more conservative attitude toward divorce among farm people than among urban people.

It is likely that variations in the rate of population change influence all these population characteristics. Few if any studies on this point for the smaller political units exist, though it would be a simple matter to assemble the data from unpublished census reports. An indication of what may happen is found in an analysis made on the basis of the 177 villages. Thirty-eight of these increased more rapidly than the national rate between 1920 and 1930. Twenty-five lost more than 10 per cent of their population in this census period. When these two groups were compared it was found that the growing villages had a higher birth rate, a larger proportion of children and of adults of both sexes up to forty years of age, as well as a

---

[9] Taeuber, Conrad, *Replacement Rates for Rural-Farm Males Aged 25 to 69 Years, by Counties, 1940-50* (mimeographed).

higher ratio of males to females,[10] despite the fact that migration of population accounted for a considerable portion of their gain.

Rural population more homogeneous. Another significant characteristic of the rural population is its greater homogeneity as compared with the urban. Only 3.6 per cent — somewhat less than 1,000,000 persons of the farm population — were foreign-born. Of the rural non-farm population, 5.5 per cent, or 1,370,000, were foreign-born. The urban percentage in 1940 was 13.4. The farm foreign-born, moreover, come largely from northern Europe, have been in this country a considerable time, and are, therefore, well assimilated into American life.[11] Rural America, except for some industrial villages, has no counterpart to the Little Italys, the Ghettoes, and the similar foreign communities of the cities. Therefore, its social organization and political life is less divided by racial lines than is the case in cities.

The Negro. In the South the Negro is an important element in the rural population, although he is almost never foreign-born. Over one half of the 13,000,000 Negro population is rural and approximately one half of these people are on the farms. All but about 2 per cent of this figure are in the South. They comprise, in fact, about one fourth of the farm population of the South. Similarly, about 90 per cent of the Negroes in the rural non-farm population are in the South and account for about 20 per cent of the population of this group in this region.

In this region the Negro population is more separate in its social organizations than are the foreign-born in the cities. They have their own schools, churches, and social organizations. Space is lacking to analyze in any detail the census records for this one race, but such an analysis would show somewhat distinctive population characteristics, a few of which run counter to popular supposition; it would record a great cityward and northward migration; and it would reveal the struggle of the Negro toward security through land-ownership, and the disproportionately crushing losses of the depression, as well as the steady building-up of a business and professional group from its own race to serve its own people. In comparison with the social and economic institutions of the white race in the South, those of the rural Negro appear poor and inadequate. In view of the status of the Negro seventy years ago the progress has been indeed considerable.

[10] Cf. Brunner and Kolb, *Rural Social Trends* (New York, McGraw-Hill, 1933), p. 31, for the detailed statistics of this comparison.

[11] Cf. Brunner, *Immigrant Farmers and Their Children* (New York, 1928), for a study of this population group and their social organization.

The farm population, then, as compared to other groups has proportionately more children, more males, more single men, fewer single women, and more homogeneity.

DISCUSSION TOPICS

1. Compare the growth or decline since 1920 of the urban, the total rural and the rural farm and non-farm population in your state. Account for the results you discover. (*United States Census of Population*, 1940 and 1930, State Tables.)
2. Make a list of the states and census regions which have gained and of those which have lost farm population since 1920.
3. Make a simple chart showing the proportion of farm, of village, and of urban population in each of the following age groups: under 15 years; 15 to 44 years; 45 years and over. (See Truesdell, L. E., *Farm Population of the United States*, p. 83.)
4. Discuss two or three important social implications of the age and sex distribution, first of the farm and second of the village population as contrasted with the urban.
5. Compare net reproduction rates and number of children ever born to women 15 to 49 years old for rural farm, rural non-farm, and urban groups in your state or region. (See Census References under Reference Readings.)
6. Trace the trends in the size of farm family by census regions, states, or counties and explain this trend.

REFERENCE READINGS

Anderson, W. A., *Population Trends in New York State, 1900-1940*. Ithaca: Cornell Agricultural Experiment Station, 1942.

Baker, O. E., "Rural-Urban Migration and the National Welfare," *Annals of the Association of American Geographers*, June, 1933.

Brunner, E. de S., and J. H. Kolb, *Rural Social Trends*. New York: McGraw-Hill, 1933.

Clark, C. D., and R. L. Roberts, *People of Kansas*. Topeka: State Planning Board, 1937.

Fry, C. L., *American Villagers*. New York: Harper & Bros., 1926.

Goodrich, C., et al., *Migration and Economic Opportunity*. Philadelphia: University of Pennsylvania Press, 1936.

Goodrich, C., et al., *Migration and Planes of Living*. Philadelphia: University of Pennsylvania Press, 1935.

Harter, W. L., and R. E. Stewart, *The Population of Iowa, Its Composition and Changes*. Ames, Iowa: Agricultural Experiment Station at State College of Agriculture, November, 1930.

Mangus, A. R., *Rural Children and Youth in Ohio*. Ohio Agricultural Experiment Station, Columbus, 1945 (mimeographed).

Rossiter, W. S., *Increase of Population in the United States, 1910-1920*. Washington, D.C.: Government Printing Office, 1922.

Sixteenth Census of the United States. Washington, D.C.: Population, vol. 4, *Characteristics by Age*, Part I, U.S. summary, 1940.

Thompson, W., and P. K. Whelpton, *Population Trends of the United States*, chaps. I, X, XI. New York: McGraw-Hill, 1933.

Truesdell, Leon C., *Farm Population of the United States*. Washington, D.C.: Government Printing Office, 1920.

United States Census, *Differential Fertility 1940 and 1910* (2 vols.), Washington, 1943 and 1944.

Vance, Rupert B., *All These People: The Nation's Human Resources in the South*. Chapel Hill: University of North Carolina Press, 1945.

Whelpton, P. K., *Iowa's Population Prospect*. Ames, Iowa: Agricultural Experiment Station, State College of Agriculture, October, 1934.

Woodson, C. G., *The Rural Negro*. Washington, D.C., 1930.

See also population sections of any standard rural sociology and population censuses of the United States, especially 1920, 1930, and 1940.

Population studies by departments of rural sociology in state colleges of agriculture will be especially valuable. About thirty such departments have published approximately one hundred such studies, of which the first reference is a sample.

5

Psychological Characteristics

BECAUSE OF THE POPULAR BELIEF, among city people at least, that rural people are in some way inferior to their city cousins, it might not be impertinent to inquire at this point into the matter of rural and urban intelligence and characteristics, and try to analyze first, the scientific data now existing with regard to this question, and secondly, certain matters of common observation.

That the rural population is in a measure distinct from the urban has been reiterated in the course of this book; but the distinction has been projected almost entirely from the point of view of economics and sociology. This chapter will try to focus the attention on the psychological aspects of the differences between the farmer and the villager, and between them both and the city resident.

Conditions make such comparisons difficult. It is important at the outset to warn the reader against the pitfalls of such a discussion. The most minute observation, and the most voluminous tests can give us sufficient data on which to base only the largest generalities. American culture in the present century has shown a steady progress towards standardization. As a result of the amazing achievements in the sphere of locomotion and communication, the continent has been narrowed to the extent that the Pacific is now only twelve hours away from the Atlantic by plane, and that a radio broadcast can be heard simultaneously in California and on the eastern coast. Time has been annihilated and space has been materially diminished. Both rural and urban people are responding to a greater number of stimuli than ever before. They listen to the same coast-to-coast broadcasts, ride in the same automobiles, witness the same movies, have the same advertisement thrust at them in their daily papers, from posters, or from barn walls. They eat the same breakfast food, buy the same coffee, smoke the same cigarettes, and what is more, wear clothes of the same cut and style. There is now no such cleavage in much of the United States between the provincial and the urbanite as in any European country.

In the very matter of language alone, our dialects have tended to run together, so that the rustic and the spohisticate, Westerner and Easterner, not only as a rule read the same literature but understand each other readily. Contrast with that a pocket-sized country like England, or a larger one like Germany, where the man from the North understands with difficulty the man from the South, and where the provincial with his peculiar dialect speaks what amounts almost to a foreign language in the eyes of the townsman. The chasm between rural and urban in more backward countries like Hungary and Italy is even wider: there the peasant affects a particular mode of dress, speaks a dialect distinct from that of the city, and the amenities of his daily life are far removed from those of his town or city cousin.

Are Americans all alike? In a democratic country such as ours the tendency has always been toward a leveling of all classes, a fact which is proved by the usual taunt thrown at America by visitors when they say, "Your land is all alike. Every town is like the next. Every Main Street resembles every other Main Street." Far from being a taunt, this statement is an illustration of the fact that we have leveled out at least the material aspects of our civilization; our towns, villages, and cities are alike — the town is only the village multiplied, and the city is only an expanded town — because we have spread the good things of life to a great extent all over the country. For example, our concrete roads and the widespread use of electricity, to mention only the most obvious instruments of civilization, penetrate many rural areas as well as the wealthy cities. All classes, the pauper who accepts relief in the crowded tenement and sometimes the farmer as well may enjoy steam heat and have the benefit of inside plumbing and running water.

Similarities apparent. Our enormous natural resources, our relative prosperity, have tended to equalize rural and urban, so that no longer is the distinction as clear-cut as in the days of William Dean Howells or Mark Twain, whose uncivilized country types are now remote and antiquated. If you read a novel of farm life like *As the Earth Turns,* which depicts the process of assimilation of foreign-born farmers in so Americanized a section as New England, you are at once aware of the amazing equalization of our racial and economic groups, and you notice especially how much our farmers, particularly the younger ones, resemble our city residents. Their scheme of life duplicates, more than is possible in other lands, that of their city relatives. They do the same things — go to the same kind of dances and parties, indulge in the same social games, and conduct their domestic or commercial affairs in much the same fashion as the townsman, villager, or cityman.

The chief reasons for the *rapprochement* between urban and rural, as before intimated, are our educational system, our facilities for communication and transportation and the mobility of our population. Our country schools follow the lead of our city schools and disseminate generally the same type of information; even many of their extra-curricular activities are similar. Our newspapers tend to print the same news in city and country — a scandal like the Lindbergh kidnaping receives the same exaggerated treatment in the paper of Pumpkin Hollow as in the New York dailies. Again, the farmer's son goes to the city, acquires some of its veneer, and when he returns for a visit or protracted stay, leaves it with his rustic family. In what ways, then, are rural and urban psychological traits different?

In spite of these centripetal forces of standardization, certain traits and qualities peculiar to rural people have not yet been ironed out nor, perhaps, will they ever be. Although the appellation "farmer" no longer has the same precise, almost contemptuous meaning it had twenty-five years ago, when the heroes of all rustic novels ran off to the city to get rid of their opprobrious characteristics, the word still stands for more than an occupational class. Certain traits peculiar to the farmer have remained, and as we shall indicate, they are the traits which the cityman, so amenable to change and alteration, might very well admire.

Measuring Rural Intelligence

Many psychologists have attempted to prove that there is a visible objective difference between the rural and urban mind. They have conducted innumerable tests for the past thirty years to bring out the fact that the native intelligence of the country resident not only differs from but tends to be inferior to that of the cityman. These investigations are fraught with so many dangers — since intelligence is the most difficult of all human characteristics to isolate — that we must study the results with great care and try to indicate wherein they are fallacious.

Defining intelligence. Probably few persons under twenty-one in this country have escaped having their intelligence measured. Tests purporting to do this have been printed and used by the million in our public and private schools, colleges, and universities. The result has been that the I.Q., the Intelligence Quotient, has become one of the most widely used scientific terms. From this the reader might gather that doubtless the psychologists have discovered an infallible technique for the precise evaluation of each individual's intelligence. Such a conclusion should be held in abeyance for the nonce, at least, until the psychologists are better able to isolate and define *intelligence.*

Strange as it may seem, some textbooks give enormous space to intelligence testing and its results but do not define intelligence. Others remark that there are different kinds of intelligence, such as social and intellectual and mechanical, and give theories about and criteria for judging intelligence.[1] Some admit that intelligence is not easily defined and attempt several definitions, as Dashiell does.[2]

The psychologists themselves are beginning to recognize the dilemma. George Stoddard in 1942, writing of "New Light on Intelligence,"[3] pointed to the evidence, now indisputable, that the I.Q. score can change, and it can differentiate between "potentiality and actual delivered power." It is only the latter that can be measured. Doctor J. L. Anderson's presidential address for the 1944 meeting of the American Psychological Association stressed the importance of knowing the environment of the subjects of psychological studies, its quality, force and uniformity, and to what extent the subject had reacted or responded to it.

Sociologists, who have to deal with people in the mass, who must take account of individual intelligences and try to apprehend group intelligence as well, will perhaps prefer the simple and workable definition of Sorokin and Zimmerman: "Intelligence is that combination of mental factors which the individual is supposed to use in achieving some aim or goal in life or the ability to adjust himself adequately to a new situation."[4] They point out that there is disagreement as to the respective contributions of inherited and environmental factors in intelligence, and conclude that "it is probably a composition of the two certain innate abilities polished by the environments both mental and social." In essence, the best definition of intelligence is that it is the ability to learn.

[1] Cf. for instance, Trow, W. C., *Educational Psychology,* pp. 137 ff. Boston: Houghton Mifflin Co., 1931.
[2] *Fundamentals of General Psychology,* p. 342. Boston: Houghton Mifflin Co., 1937. Dashiell's conclusion is eminently worth remembering: "*That* the methods of examination [of intelligence] get at some ability has been abundantly shown, even if *what* they get at remains in doubt. The ability can be isolated in fact if not in words. And, in any case, there is some point to the claim that 'measurements should precede definition.'"
[3] *Proceedings Iowa Academy of Science,* vol. 49, pp. 51-60.
[4] *Principles of Rural-Urban Sociology,* Part III, p. 234. New York: Henry Holt & Co., 1929.

Beyond question, the so-called intelligence tests, as Dashiell says, are measuring important capacities, and are the closest approximate measure of intelligence yet devised. Their results have a high correlation with school achievements and with certain types of success in life, although, of course, this correlation can be interpreted to mean either that the tests simply measure school achievement in a different way or that intelligence is responsible for the scores made in both tests and school subjects. But though of great practical value in the schools, they are far from infallible in all cases. Our concern with them is to discover what they reveal when rural and urban people are compared.

Prerequisites for comparative testing. In order to attain some degree of accuracy in measuring two groups it is necessary to equalize as many factors as possible and reduce the number of variables, some of which are, considering that the subjects are usually children, the chronological age, social and economic status, environment, language, amount and type of schooling, size of family and order of the subject's birth, and the occupations of their parents. For instance, a comparison of rural and urban intelligence based on New York City school children and the children in an all-rural county in Mississippi introduces many more variables than a comparison of these rural children with the children of Jackson, Mississippi's largest city. In other words, the scores obtained in these tests are largely invalidated for purposes of group comparison when the environment of any one group varies sharply from that of the other. This seems self-evident, but has often been somewhat overlooked, especially in some of the earlier attempts to compare rural and urban intelligence.

Rural and urban intelligence test scores compared. Most of the studies have been carried on with school children. There are two reasons for this: first, measurements are of great value to the schools in the general study of their students, in many problems of grading, program guidance and adjustment; second, the younger the subject, the more pristine his intelligence and the less he is likely to be influenced by variable environmental factors.

In the twelve or fifteen years prior to 1929 about two score studies were made, important because of the standing of their authors, the techniques they used, or the results obtained, in which the intelligence of rural people, almost exclusively children, was measured and compared with similar urban scores. More than two thirds of these tests place rural children below urban, and a large majority of the investigators believe that the difference is a measure of difference in the native ability or intelligence of the two groups, a difference many of them explain by the assumption that the rural-urban migration deprived the country of many of its more intelligent children. In view of the huge size of the rural-urban migration, to say nothing of the causes and consequences of it, discussed in preceding chapters, this is a vulnerable assumption. When we examine it critically, a number of questions arise, which, in the judgment of the authors, seem to throw doubt on, if not entirely to vitiate, the conclusions of the psychologists as to the innate differences in rural and urban intelligence.

What is rural and urban? It is shown, for instance, in Part III that rural and urban are no longer clear-cut divisions. Rural characteristics vary markedly according to the distance from the city, as measured by concentric tiers of counties. Furthermore, during the nineteen-twenties, when these tests were being made, rural-urban migration was at its height and at least some of the city schools tested had had a considerable infiltration of rural migrants. Strictly speaking, the latter should have been separated from older residents in the scoring. Such a procedure was actually followed, in a small Iowa city, by Hornell Hart, who procured a difference in the score of 248 children from the farms compared with 447 from the city of $2.3 \pm .6$. This difference may have been influenced by several variables. Nothing is known of the reasons why the families of these rural children moved to town. If they migrated in order to get better educational opportunities, the chief variable would then be the type of school from which the farm children came. But they may have migrated also because of their failure on the farm, in which case another important variable would be introduced, rendering the difference of 2.3 of little significance in the main problem of determining whether, as a generality, rural children are inferior in intelligence to urban children.

Moreover, some psychologists have no adequate definition of the terms rural and urban. One study took all places over 1000 as urban, although in places up to 10,000 there are a considerable proportion of open-country children in the schools, as Chapter 18 shows. In several others, places of from 2000 to 3400 were included in the urban category. This confusion of terms resulting in the introduction of varying proportions of farm children in the urban enrollment, invalidates the results for comparative purposes.

Importance of homogeneity. One of the important factors in group intelligence testing is that of homogeneity. The rural farm population, having relatively few foreign-born, and outside the South, few Negroes, and hardly any Orientals except in California, is far more homogeneous than urban population in general. This homogeneity extends in great measure even to the rural non-farm element, which can be classified in fewer occupational groups than urban workers. The meaning of all this is that stimuli arising from such variables as environment and occupation are less diversified among rural than urban children. As will be shown later, however, the urban population undoubtedly contains more persons of distinction than the rural.

Influence of occupation. When tests are given in bona fide rural and especially open-country schools, the comparison with urban scores resolves itself into a comparison of the children of one or a few occupational groups with those whose parents belong to many occupational groups. Perhaps the fairest and most scientific method would be to divide both rural and urban children according to the occupations of their fathers, comparing, for example, the offspring of farmers with those of laborers, professional men, and so on. But even such a separation would not get rid of the fact that a majority of rural and urban test scores do not take into account differences in the efficiency of the schools attended by the children of both groups, as well as differences in their experiences and cultural opportunities.

Differences in schooling. For example, the urban school term, as noted in another chapter, is on the average ten working days longer than that of the village school and about a month longer than that of the one-room school. Urban teachers are older, more experienced, and better trained than rural. It seems quite likely that these phenomena influence the intelligence test scores even when, within the rural group, one-room and consolidated schools are compared. Such variations in educational opportunity clearly affected the measurements in the study conducted by Baldwin, Filmore, and Hadley, who gave the Stanford-Binet Tests to 253 children in one-room schools and to 425 of comparable ages in consolidated schools with the following results: [5]

	I.Q.	Below Av.	Percentage Av.	Above Av.
1 room school	91.7	.43	.47	.10
Consolidated	99.4	.23	.54	.23

The authors' commentary follows:

The differences between the main I.Q.'s on the first examination of the one-room and consolidated school children, analyzed statis-

[5] *Farm Children,* pp. 238 ff. New York: D. Appleton & Co., 1930.

tically by age groups, six to fourteen inclusive, are found to be significant at all ages except seven and eight. This likeness among the school children continues the similarity found among the pre-school children at all ages in the two communities and suggests that rural children are much alike in the pre-school and early school years, but with the advance in age some influence that produces differences begins to operate. . . .

It is obvious that there are a number of variables at work here and that the differences in scores cannot safely be attributed to the single factor of intelligence. This agrees with the conclusion of a study of nearly 5000 rural children located in two Eastern and two Middle-Western states.[6]

Environment influential. If this conclusion is sound when rural children are measured and compared according to type of schooling, it seems clear that when the rural and urban groups are compared for general intelligence the variables are multiplied and the difficulty of measuring pure intelligence increases. But since, as indicated, environment begins to become increasingly important with age, some clue to the solution of the problem may be had by measuring children of a younger age. Acting on this assumption, the Iowa Child Welfare Research Station tested seventy-two rural and seventy-two city babies matched for chronological age. No significant difference was found in the results, but on these tests there were five sub-tests in which rural children succeeded earlier than city children, and seven sub-tests in which city children succeeded earlier than those living on farms.[7] The authors of this exhaustive study conclude that at no age do rural children in one community differ strikingly from those of another, or from the general mental level, while rural and urban children seem to be equal in intelligence until the age of five.[8] This suggests a bias in those cognate tests of children of a higher age level where differences between rural and urban develop.

Testing experiences. On the whole, the tests often measure acquaintanceship with types of experience which are more largely urban than rural,[9] and with, on the whole, book knowledge rather

---

[6] Cf. Brunner, *Immigrant Farmers and Their Children*, chap. III. New York: Harper & Bros., 1929.

[7] Baldwin, Filmore, and Hadley, *Farm Children*, pp. 233-34.

[8] *Ibid.*, pp. 234-38.

[9] An interesting case of bias comes from a test made by a university in a fishing village known to the authors. Among others, the word-association technique was used. Following the word *rain* the pupil was supposed to write *umbrella.* Practically all put down instead the word *slicker,* signifying oil-skins, which offers almost complete protection from wet weather. This reply was scored wrong.

than experience. The alleged inferiority of any group over another may, therefore, perhaps be laid to the instruments used in testing rather than to any innate differences in the groups themselves, a conclusion which was reached by M. E. Shimberg, who conducted an *Investigation into the Validity of Norms with Special Reference to Urban and Rural Groups*, in which two information tests, A, scaled to the experience of rural children, and B to that of urban children, were taken by both rural and urban subjects. Some questions overlapped. On the urban-scaled test, rural children, as compared with urban, were about one year retarded; on the rural-scaled test, the opposite situation was found. The author concludes:

> Test A is more specialized in favor of rural children than Test B (or any standard test) which is specialized in favor of the urban children.
>
> From the same analysis we produced evidence that questions "fair" to a certain group cannot be selected *a priori*. This was also affirmed by submitting our questions to 14 rural superintendents who, despite their unusually rich experience, were unable to designate correctly (in a fairly large percentage of the cases) which questions favored the rural children.
>
> An analysis of current standard group tests shows that a large part of the material required is informational in character. So, our results may be said to have some application outside the narrow sphere of individual information tests.[10]

Some of the items in the rural test follow:

> Name the young of the sheep, cow, horse.
> Name *three* states in the United States where cotton is raised.
> Why is it necessary to limit the hunting season?
> In what part of the day are the shadows longest?
> How can you tell poison ivy by looking at it?
> How many pecks are there in a bushel?
> Of what use are insects to flowers?
> Name *five* wild flowers.
> Why does seasoned wood burn more easily than green wood?
> Tell one way of finding out the age of a tree.
> From what does maple sugar come?
> Name *two* birds that stay North in the winter.
> How can you keep milk from souring?
> Give one reason for the rotation of crops.
> Name *five* crops.

[10] For a full report of this study see *The Archives of Psychology*, nos. 99-104, vol. XVI, chap. VII.

What kind of dairy cow gives the richest milk?
Why are crops hoed?
Name *two* differences between the barks of birch and oak trees.

The army tests. It is necessary to consider the army tests in passing because they have often been used to support the contention of the backwardness of rural intelligence. These tests have unfortunately been misused in many ways by scientific popularizers ever since their publication. The army tests were narrowed to a search for prospective officers. Farmers rated "low average" on them, while officers of the engineering corps, with just such a background as the tests would favor, rated highest with a classification of "very superior intelligence," an inevitable conclusion. Moreover, probably the less efficient farmers and farm laborers took the test in disproportionate numbers, since most of the owners and tenants were exempted from the draft in order to raise food.

School paces. There have been numerous studies for both scientific and practical purposes of retardation and acceleration among school children which show that there is somewhat more retardation in rural than in urban schools. This, however, contributes little or nothing to solving the problem of differences in rural and urban intelligence. It simply shows that the conditions well known to be handicapping many rural schools, such as lower average attendance chargeable to weather, short terms, ungraded classes, poorly trained teachers, and other things described in another chapter, tend to retard rural pupils.

Achievement scores. For the reasons mentioned above, grade achievement in rural schools usually lags behind that of the city in some of the traditional subjects by as much as a year and a year and a half. This has been proved by numerous studies, but again it casts no reflection on rural intelligence *per se.* Progress made even in numerous one-room schools under the best conditions and methods; gains of two or three years in a single school year, as shown in another chapter, are sufficient reproof to those who blame rural intelligence rather than inferior schools for retardation.

It may be granted that rural and especially farm children take from one third of a year to a year longer to finish the first eight grades. But the census figures on school attendance show that rural boys and girls stay in school longer than those in the city. At least up to 1929, as Sorokin and Zimmerman indicate, the farm population of the United States, despite its larger proportion of children, had a higher ratio of high-school students, especially seniors, than the city.

The net result of this discussion is not meant to indicate that rural children are more intelligent than urban, but that accepted measurements of intelligence by achievement tests underrate the average mental ability of the rural and especially the farm children, and that, therefore, to conclude from these tests that rural children are innately inferior to urban is wholly unwarranted, especially in view of the proven equality between rural and urban children of pre-school age.

This discussion of tests has been interpolated at length, for many people have only a vague conception of the subject because of the incompleteness of these early studies. But what of more recent studies? To answer this question, all studies bearing on the subject of rural-urban intelligence listed in *Psychological Abstracts* from 1940 to early 1945 were examined. It would appear that the methodology used was more refined than those of earlier studies. But still the results are inconclusive, as perhaps should be expected. In several studies there were positive, but very low, correlations between intelligence and size of community of residence. The authors give as explanation the interpretations stated in the earlier discussion. Other studies, such as the one by Doctor D. S. Oberlin, which is based on general information possessed by Delaware school children,[11] find no significant differences between rural and urban children.

In this connection it is important to refer to an urban study. In 1922 Professor E. L. Thorndike, of Teachers College, Columbia University, began a study of nearly nine hundred boys who graduated from the eighth grade of New York City schools in that year. These same boys have co-operated in frequent periodic follow-up studies for twenty years. Among other significant findings, the check included a sub-group of individuals with I.Q.'s which were approximately equal in 1922. Of this group, those who never went beyond the tenth grade of schooling scored 103 in 1943. Those who completed the junior year of college or better scored 115. Education apparently made the difference, not in the innate ability of the individuals, but in the release and use of those abilities.[12]

Mental illnesses. Many pages on this subject have been written about insanity and feeble-mindedness in the rural and urban populations, and for that reason the subject is included here. The crude data indicate far less such illness in rural than in urban areas, but

[11] *Delaware State Medical Journal*, 1941, vol. 13, pp. 133-135.
[12] Cf. Lorge, Irving, "Schooling Makes a Difference," *Teachers College Record*, May, 1945, pp. 483-92.

even so, the data are contradictory and are not sufficiently precise to warrant generalizations. For example, among draftees rejected for military service by the army during World War I, mental deficiency accounted for 1.5 per cent of all rejections among the urban men but 3.9 per cent among the rural. Comparable results were obtained from the examination of draftees in World War II. These data are discussed in the chapter on rural health.

It should be remembered, however, that while the cause of rejection was entered as a single item, actually more than one cause may have operated. Flat feet or fallen arches also disqualify for military service and are easily detectable. This is a difficulty far more common among urban than among rural people. No one knows how many men rejected for flat feet as a result of the initial physical examination may have also had some "mental defectiveness." There is no data regarding the incidence of mental illness after enlistment. Several medical officers have stated to the authors, on the basis of observation only, that rural men endured the agonizing stress of overseas service better than their city brethren.

Again, the census of *Feeble-minded and Epileptics in Institutions* inclines toward the conclusion that mental deficiency is more common in cities than in the country. The rate of first admissions of such patients to institutions was about 85 per 100,000 population in the city and 40 to 45 in the country, according to recent censuses. Moreover, the more rural a region, the lower the rate. But these data must be considered in the light of the fact that rural people seem to be less likely than urban to seek institutional care for the less difficult cases of mental disorder, and that in many states, especially some of the more rural ones, institutional facilities for the mentally disabled are wholly inadequate for the demand made upon them, and therefore many are robbed of such care.

The testimony of Who's Who. In the last ten or fifteen years a number of investigators have studied the biographies of distinguished Americans as presented in *Who's Who in America* to determine whether the rural areas are producing their share of eminent figures.[13] The conclusion has been that the city has given birth to a disproportionate number of talented people — Visher, taking 1870

13 Cf. especially, White, C. R., "The Cityward Drift of Population in Relation to Social Efficiency," *Journal of Social Forces*, November, 1923; Visher, S. S., "A Study of the Place of Birth and of the Occupation of Fathers of Subjects of Sketches in *Who's Who in America*," *American Journal of Sociology*, March, 1925; and Cattell, J. McK., "The Distribution of American Men of Science," *Science*, vol. XXIV, pp. 658-65, 699-707, 732-42; vol. XXXII, pp. 633-48.

as the nearest census year to the birth of persons listed in *Who's Who* for 1922-23, found that cities, towns, and villages had 30 per cent of the population but contributed 74.1 per cent of the celebrities. The rest were born on farms.

This fact is interesting and valuable as far as it goes, but it contributes little to the problem of separating urban and rural intelligence. *Who's Who* inevitably selects those whose type of achievement puts them in the public eye, and perhaps specifically the eye of the urban public. For example, a Middle-Western farmer who developed a new, highly valuable and much used variety of corn, who has been an officer of one of the largest state farmers' organizations, and is now prominent in the Agricultural Adjustment Administration in his state, was not listed in *Who's Who* for 1922-23. Many similar examples could be produced from a perusal of *RUS* — the rural *Who's Who*.[14] It seems safe to conclude with the eminent psychologist, Professor E. L. Thorndike, "That cities give birth to an undue proportion of great men does not in the least prove that city life made them great; it may prove that cities attract and retain great men, whose sons are thus city born." [15]

The whole problem of innate mental capacity, as we have attempted to suggest, is shrouded in mist. Trustworthy evidence has not yet been produced to prove that rural and urban people have marked differences of cerebral ability; where such differences ostensibly appear they can be traced to environmental and particularly to occupational sources, to acquired rather than inherited attitudes and thought-patterns.

If this be true, it is time to turn to the second phase of our problem, and seek to discover in what respect, despite the cyclopean forces for standardization and equalization in America, rural and urban people differ, and deduce the social significances of such variations. Precise terminology cannot be used in such a discussion, for social psychology is in its infancy, and wholly adequate group measuring tools have not been forged.

TRAITS OF RURAL PEOPLE

At the outset it must be recognized that an analysis of rural traits is difficult not only because of the paucity of reliable studies in the field, but also because in few other realms is generalization in terms of all rural people more dangerous. The experience of the truck

14 Compiled by L. H. and E. Z. Bailey. Ithaca, New York, 1930.
15 *The Bookman*, vol. XXIV, p. 290.

farmer of the Eastern states, in frequent and often daily contact with storekeepers, middlemen and commission merchants, who transports his perishable produce daily by automobile, who operates his acres on the basis of intensive cultivation, is quite different from that of the wheat-grower, whose single, non-perishable crop comes slowly to maturity, who handles it by machine and not by hand, who sells it in one or at most a few transactions, ships it by railroad, and rarely comes into frequent contact with the whole machinery of marketing. Both of these persons have widely different experiences from the Southern Highlander, coaxing a precarious existence from the rocky hillside, consuming much of what he raises and selling little, whose contacts with the "outside" are few and far between. The attitudes and many of the traits of these types would vary almost as much as their economic experiences; yet all are farmers.

The investigator who knew only the last type might announce that farmers are highly individualistic, and in terms of his experience, he would be correct. The investigator whose experience was limited to the citrus-fruit growers of Southern California would, on the other hand, conclude that farmers were highly co-operative.

In any study of rural attitudes or traits, case histories must be considered. The farmer who declared in 1924, when asked to join a flourishing co-operative, "I'll be blanked if anybody's going to tell me when to sell my berries," was voicing the virile individualism that had characterized his forbears for three centuries in their struggle against the wilderness and the sea. The same man, when he capitulated to the co-operative in 1934, had changed none of his innate, inherited characteristics. He was simply bowing to experience. Certainly part of the equipment of the rural sociologist, teacher, or social servant should be to understand the motives and histories of the traditions and attitudes he seeks to change.

Some traits measurable. Efforts to reduce general observations about rural psychological traits are proving to be significant. Thus, in his *Experience Worlds of Southern Mountain People* [16] Taylor Matthews showed clearly that there were differences in attitudes, knowledge, and experience between those in the village center and those in more isolated pockets of the valleys leading into the villages. Leland Sttot's interesting findings in his *Personality Development in Farm, Small-Town and City Children,*[17] are based on careful research procedures. One important observation follows:

[16] Teachers College Bureau of Publication, New York, 1937.
[17] Agricultural Experiment Station, Lincoln, Nebraska, 1939.

The farm home setting appeared at a disadvantage in the area of social relationships. Two of the personality variables, namely, resourcefulness in group situations and ethical judgment, had particularly to do with facility and discrimination in social relationships. The farm group ranked lowest in both of these variables. The city and town groups averaged about equally but both were significantly superior to the farm group. These differences, however, were almost wholly contributed by the girls.

Effects of different types of farming. It is possible to trace from the behavior of groups of farmers over periods of years changes in attitude, at least in regard to agriculture itself. The traditional American farm was once as self-sufficient as it could be made, but now, in many parts of the country, a single money crop is the main objective. This change has produced psychological attitudes largely unknown before. It has converted the farmer into something of a speculator and mercantilist, an attitude which sometimes begins to color other types of behavior. Diversification of money crops in turn brings other experiences and traits. It is possible that types of agriculture are related to the temperamental qualities in the devotees they attract.

The effect of differences in types of farming can be frequently seen in the public opinion polls. Farmers in the big cattle-raising states, like other farmers, are for international co-operation as an abstract concept. However, they would register strong opposition if it were proposed to import beef from the Argentine Republic. On the other hand, the dairymen, poultry producers, orchardists, and vegetable growers of the eastern seaboard would welcome such beef, but in a poll the dairymen, for example, would register large majorities against importing butter or cheese free of duty from Denmark, Holland, or New Zealand.

Rurality itself is probably responsible only to a slight degree for rural attitudes on public affairs, as a forthcoming study by John Bovingdon shows. Despite new material on attitudes, the samples used, contrasted with the size of the totality of the farm population, are so small that he is a brave man indeed who declares, "Thus the American farmer thinks." We know that there are factors in the farmer's occupation which influence his behavior and attitudes. This is inevitable, and the same principle holds true for all other groups.

Influence of weather. There is also a possible relation between weather or climate, which plays so large a part in agricultural life, and the temperament or philosophy of the peasantry. Perhaps this is one reason why the peasants of such countries as China and India are so fatalistic in some of their attitudes. Again, agrarian life, linked so closely to the primal mysteries of Nature, of wind and weather, sky-changes and earth-changes, tends to bring out man's primordial instincts, his superstitiousness and leanings toward the supernatural. Perhaps that is why in some regions of the United States rural people are more religious and orthodox than city dwellers. It may also explain the lack of enthusiasm which the less informed farmer often evinces for scientific methods: he knows that capricious Nature too frequently upsets the best-laid plans of men.

Co-operative attitudes. The American farmer has often been described as highly individualistic; yet now, as will be shown in another chapter, a majority of the commercial farmers are members of co-operatives and considerable percentages of all farm products sold are marketed co-operatively. If such a record had been achieved by industry perhaps the "co-operative commonwealth" and the "new social order" of some of our social prophets would be nearer than they seem. The great progress of agricultural co-operation since 1915 certainly represents a marked change in attitude, a process in which it is possible to detect some of the formative elements. There was originally resentment against middlemen and processors, a tendency to unite against their menace, a growing understanding of the weaknesses of the old marketing procedures. Then came organization and education by the leaders to stir the great mass of unaroused farmers. Time was given, though sometimes not enough, to effect necessary modifications in the old, stubbornly persisting individualism. But the sense of need for collective action grew. Those with common interests, such as citrus-fruit, apple, milk, and butter producers, were the first to capitulate; and the success of these and of the movements toward combination among employers and laboring men in industry accelerated the general co-operative movement, which, although it still leaves much to be desired, is an excellent illustration of how attitudes are changed and how the alleged rural resistance to change was overcome by rural people themselves, frequently against outside opposition.

Religious attitudes. There appear to be certain distinctive rural religious attitudes, such as the orthodoxy just alluded to, though again generalization is dangerous. While rural church members are doubtless more orthodox than urban, this probably holds true only within certain regions. Judging by indirect evidence only, the rural people of the Pacific Coast, and more certainly of New England, are further from the traditional beliefs and interpretations of Christian Scripture than is true, for instance, in the urban South.

Rural religion is also more puritanical than urban, at least in many denominations, an evidence of which is to be found in the divorce statistics issued by the Census Bureau. The proportion of those enumerated as divorced people in rural America, as pointed out earlier, is about one half that in the cities, and probably is actually less than that because a smaller number of rural divorcées apparently remarry. Perhaps one reason for this is the fact that the farm is an economic as well as a family unit, but the necessities of this arrangement have been rationalized on religious grounds.

The Methodist prohibitions against dancing, theater-going, and card-playing became dead letters in the city churches long before the denomination as a whole allowed the issue to be settled on the basis of principle and the conscience of the individual. The old-fashioned evangelistic or revival campaign, while declining even in its stronghold, the South, began to lose popularity and efficacy in the city before it did in the country, and is still stronger in rural areas than elsewhere. Possibly, therefore, rural religion and even rural people are more emotional than others. There is some evidence that the individualism attributed to rural people, because of their relatively greater degree of isolation, has made rural religion more clannish in its denominational allegiances. Certainly councils of churches arose in cities before they did in states, and in the more urban states, or those whose religious administration was controlled by urban agencies, before the others. This, however, may have been a matter of a greater need for co-operation since, as shown in another chapter, the majority of local church co-operative experiments are rural in origin and location.

Other rural traits. Other rural traits can be deduced from the behavior of rural people which may not necessarily coincide with their expressions of values. Except among share-croppers and in areas of high and shifting tenant operation, attachment to the land is a characteristic of farm, and even village, people. Among some groups this is apparent even in the everyday idioms of speech. The patterns of exchange of work, or borrowing tools and supplies, discussed elsewhere in the text, give practical evidence of the value which rural people set on neighborliness. A helping hand is usually offered to a family in need, and any who withhold such assistance are subject to neighborhood criticism. It is possible that such behavior was becoming less common prior to World War II. It was interesting and significant that in areas where the neighborhood leader plan was successfully operated during World War II, many rural people expressed gratification at the resurgence of neighborliness, and expressed the hope that it would continue. Finally, as is shown in the chapter on the family, rural people place great value on family cohesion and loyalty. This is true throughout the Western world, and is even more true of the Orient.

On the other hand, rural people often claim to possess attitudes and beliefs which their behavior contradicts. Rural people frequently assert that "every man's as good as another around here," yet their behavior toward each other indicates a recognition of differences in status. The plantation-owner's daughter would not think of "dating" a share-cropper's son, although her brother might go 'possum hunting with him.[18]

Changing social attitudes. This text has already given evidence and will give more, of changing social attitudes. Thus the growing co-operation of farmer and villager and the increasing importance of the village and town as the center of the twentieth-century rural community, described in the discussion of the modern rural community, are evidences that the old antagonistic attitudes between these groups are passing. With growing acquaintanceship and mutual experiences these are being replaced more and more by co-operation. Moreover, social attitudes have been changed in other particulars, notably in education. Once school work always gave way to farm work if the children were needed at home. Today this is the exception, not the rule. Similarly the changes in social organization described in another chapter indicate changing attitudes and fashions as to the objectives of organized social life.

In January, 1931, *Farm and Fireside* published the results of an "opinion questionnaire" sent to its readers. Replies were received from 13,431 persons living in all parts of the country, of an average age of slightly less than forty years, of whom 70 per cent live on farms, 28 per cent in small towns, and 2 per cent in cities. Answers to a few of the questions reveal the extent of rural acceptance or rejection of urbanizing influences. Among the summaries published are the following:

Twenty per cent of those replying would "welcome large-scale corporate farming," while the other 80 per cent believe the "family farm" is a "sounder proposition."

[18] Cf. West, James, *Plainville, U.S.A.* New York: Columbia University Press, 1945, for a full discussion of what he calls the class system in a Mid-Western community.

Eighty-one per cent were opposed to any steps which would make "divorce easier to obtain."

Seventy-two per cent said that farm magazines should not publish cigarette advertising.

Sixty-seven per cent would favor legislation permitting "doctors to impart birth control methods to married couples who apply jointly."

Farm and Fireside regards the vote on birth control as the "most astonishing departure" from older standards. It believes there are economic and technical factors which have produced a change of opinion. The increasing mechanization of agriculture means that the labor of children is not used as extensively as before. It is also thought by some observers that changing living standards may be bringing about a "competition between children and other expenditures," already evident for some time in urban families.

Replies to a question which asked (of rural people) for "the thought that most needs to be emphasized throughout America at this time" reveals a significant difference "between the generations." Those over thirty seem to show much more concern about religion and conventional moral standards. Taking the group as a whole, however, 37 per cent say, in substance, "Hold fast to God and the old moralities." As to where chief emphasis should be placed, 85 per cent were distributed among such matters as law enforcement, better schools or roads, standards of citizenship, world peace, child training, improved human relations or "a closer spiritual relationship with God."

A subsequent check-up more than two years later, in which the same issues were presented in story form and the readers were asked to pass judgment, showed a further swing to more liberal attitudes.

Similar but later studies by the *Ladies' Home Journal* showed much higher proportions of farm women in favor of divorce, rather high proportions in favor of birth control, with a tendency for the village women to incline more in this direction than the farm women and the urban women slightly more than those in the village, except in cities with a large Roman Catholic population. The maximum spread between rural and urban on these items was only seven points. Religious principles rather than rurality might well explain such a difference.

Rural-urban comparisons. Differences in rural-urban social attitudes have already been extensively noted. We shall now advance some hypotheses which may account for the psychological and empirical separation between the two groups.

To begin with, the city resident has a broader range of experience than the country man, He sees more people, is thrown into more situations, and exposed to a far greater number of environmental action-patterns which leave their mark on his reflexes and habits. Consider the amount of transportation he endures — subways, buses, trolleys, automobiles; he has greater access to information and knowledge through libraries, lectures, museums, theaters, concert halls, art galleries, and the like. On the other hand, his direct, occupational experience is more limited than that of the farmer or villager. He is confined, perhaps, to one or a few mechanical operations, to a counter in a store, a desk in an office.

Thus, rural people may have fewer non-occupational or worldly experiences, and therefore a narrower basis for judging them. On the other hand, their wider range of occupational activities might make them more eager for facts, more resistant to superficial theories or propaganda. Moreover, the outdoor nature of their work makes the farmer, and to some extent the villager, sterner, more virile, persevering, and patient than those in many urban occupations.

These hypotheses could be illustrated with case histories, but even illustrations must be used with discretion and in terms of the background and experiences of particular groups. It is evident, however, that the lives of rural people, as indicated at the beginning of this chapter, are more and more bending to common national forces.

Rural people have been put into instant touch with the stream of world events. Isolation has been almost eliminated. Some rooted habits have been changed, others acquired especially in villages; as for example, the remodeling of old one-family houses into apartments, and the appearance of rural beauty parlors, unknown before 1925. Sales of labor-saving devices have multiplied; seasonal comestibles, for example, are now carried all the year round in many rural stores.

Some observers proclaim that rural life, especially village life, is being completely urbanized. This is true only to a certain extent. In the superficialities of life, such as dress, and other matters earlier enumerated, urban fashions set the pace in rural communities; in more intangible matters, morals, ideals and religion, such a conclusion cannot yet be accepted.

Differences exist and will continue. The country is zealous of its identity, and although it bends before exterior cultural forces, it always does so reluctantly. It is doubtful, indeed, if country and city, urban and rural, will ever be so completely leveled as to lose their group identities, even in the face of the annihilation of space, time, and castes. In the questionnaire alluded to, the suggestion that rural people were blindly accepting urban habits met with a storm of protest. Ruralites felt that those who believed this had "a very limited understanding of rural America," or were "unable or too provincial to conceive of the advanced conditions of the average village." [19]

From education to luncheon clubs, rural America insists on fashioning urban social devices to its own taste. That apostle of urban superiority, Carol Kennicott, seems to be no more popular on any Main Street than she was in Sinclair Lewis's Gopher Prairie, but, like Gopher Prairie, the average village seems to be improving itself in its own way.

The conclusion of the matter seems to be that so far as evidence exists, the psychological traits of rural people are not inherited but molded and perhaps created by their experiences. Rural psychology is distinctive in great measure from urban, despite a great leveling force at present operating in our country; it differs from region to region, from community to community. Yet there is a good deal of similarity between city and country: people move from one to the other with ease and adjust themselves without undue disturbance. The basic human qualities are doubtless practically the same wherever folk live, move and have their being.

DISCUSSION TOPICS

1. Summarize the psychological characteristics which Sorokin and Zimmerman attribute to rural people.
2. Discuss these characteristics in terms of your community presenting evidence for or against the conclusions of Sorokin and Zimmerman.
3. Write either the affirmative or negative brief for a debate on the question: "Resolved — that city people are more intelligent than rural."
4. Trace evidences of urbanization (or ruralization) of attitudes you have observed in your community.
5. Report any of the results of any studies made by the Department of Psychology in your institution on the comparative intelligence or achievement of urban and rural school children.
6. Account for any changes in the attitudes of your community on one

[19] Cf. a survey in 1930 of *The Small-Town Woman's Reactions to Urban Customs,* by a class in Sociology at Teachers College, Columbia University. Chicago, Colonial Press, 1930.

or more specific issues, paying special attention to the influences of communication.

7. Examine a rural population group (*a*) as to ancestry; (*b*) as to the demonstrable persistence of ancestral ideas.

REFERENCE READINGS

Books:

Baldwin, B. T., E. A. Filmore, and L. Hadley, *Farm Children.* New York: D. Appleton & Co., 1930.

Brunner, E. de S., *Immigrant Farmers.* New York: Harper & Bros., 1929.

Rice, Stuart A., *Farmers and Workers in American Politics.* New York: Columbia University Press, 1924. Especially chapter VII.

Schwesinger, G. C., *Heredity and Environment.* New York: The Macmillan Company, 1933.

Sorokin, P. A., and C. C. Zimmerman, *Principles of Rural-Urban Sociology,* Part III. New York: Henry Holt & Co., 1939.

Williams, James M., *Our Rural Heritage.* New York: Knopf, 1925.

Williams, James M., *The Expansion of Rural Life.* New York: Knopf, 1926.

Articles and pamphlets:

Armstrong, Clairette P., "A Study of the Intelligence of Rural and Urban Children," *Journal of Educational Psychology,* vol. IV, pp. 301-15. 1931.

Bickersteth, M. E., "The Application of Mental Tests to Children of Various Ages," *British Journal of Psychology,* vol. IX, pp. 23-73. 1919.

Cattell, J. McK., "The Distribution of American Men of Science," *Science,* vol. 24, pp. 658-65, 699-704, 732-42; col. 32, 633-48.

Duff, J. F., and G. H. Thomson, "The Social and Geographical Distribution of Intelligence in Northumberland," *British Journal of Psychology,* vol. XIV, pp. 192-98. 1923.

Jones, H. E., H. S. Conrad, and M. B. Blanchard, "Environmental Handicaps in Mental Test Performances," *University of California, Publications in Psychology,* vol. V, pp. 63-99. 1932.

Matthews, Taylor, *Experience Worlds of Southern Mountain People.* New York: Bureau of Publications, Teachers College, Columbia University, 1937.

Oberlin, D. S., "Social Background as a Factor in the Acquisition of General Information," *Delaware State Medical Journal,* vol. 13, pp. 133-35. 1941.

Olcott, M. T., *Rural Psychology: A Partial List of References*. Washington, D.C.: Bureau of Agricultural Economics, 1939.

Pressey, S. L., "A Study of Country Children in a Good and a Poor Farming District by Means of a Group Scale of Intelligence," *Journal of Applied Psychology*, vol. III, pp. 283-86. 1919.

Pressey, S. L., "The Influence of Inadequate Schooling and Poor Environment Upon Results With Tests of Intelligence," *Journal of Applied Psychology*, vol. IV, pp. 91-96. 1920.

Rosca, A., "Intelligenta in Mediul Rural-urban," *Review Psihol*, 1939, vol. 2, pp. 131-141.

Shepard, E. L., "Measurement of Certain Non-Verbal Abilities of Urban and Rural Children," *Journal of Educational Psychology*, vol. 33, pp. 458-62. 1942.

Shimberg, M. E., "Investigation into the Validity of Norms with Special Reference to Urban and Rural Groups," *Archives of Psychology*, nos. 99-104, vol. 16, chap. 7.

Smith, M., "An Urban-rural Intellectual Gradient," *Sociology and Social Research*, vol. 27, pp. 307-15. 1943.

Stoddard, G. D., "New Light on Intelligence," *Proceedings of Iowa Academy of Science*, vol. 49, pp. 51-60. 1942.

Sttot, Leland, *Personality Development in Farm, Small-town and City Children*. Lincoln, Nebraska: Agricultural Experiment Station, 1939.

Terry, Paul W., and Verner M. Sims, *They Live on the Land*, chap. X, Bureau of Educational Research, University of Alabama, 1940.

Thomson, G. H., "The Northumberland Mental Tests," *British Journal of Psychology*, vol. XII, pp. 201-22. 1921.

United States Census of Feeble-Minded and Epileptics in Institutions. Washington, D.C.

Visher, S. S., "A Study of the Place of Birth and of the Occupations of Fathers of Subjects of Sketches in *Who's Who in America*," *American Journal of Sociology*, March, 1925.

Wellman, Beth L., "Some New Bases for Interpretation of the I.Q.," *Pedagogical Seminary and Journal of Genetic Psychology*, vol. XLI, pp. 116-26. 1932.

Wellman, Beth L., "The Effect of Pre-School Attendance upon the I.Q.," *Journal of Experimental Education*, vol. I, pp. 48-69. 1932.

West, James, *Plainville, U.S.A.* New York: Columbia University Press, 1945.

White, C. R., "The Cityward Drift of Population in Relation to Social Efficiency," *Social Forces*, November, 1923.

Worbois, G. M., "Changes in Stanford-Binet I.Q. for Rural Consolidated and Rural One-Room School Children," *Journal of Experimental Education*, vol. II, pp. 210-14. 1942.

PART TWO

MAKING A LIVING
IN RURAL SOCIETY

6

The Agricultural Enterprise — Social Implications

MEN'S LIVES are greatly influenced by their means of livelihood which affect and mold their social contacts, their personal habits and condition, community attitudes and social organization. The farmer mingles with farmers more than with other occupational groups. He joins a farmers' organization, not a labor union. He looks at issues from the point of view of their effect upon agriculture. For all these reasons, we must consider the social contributions of agriculture, and the social implications of the business of farming.

This and the three following chapters will be devoted to this theme. This chapter will discuss the size and importance of the agricultural enterprise and also give some attention to the non-agricultural occupations of rural America. Land and land tenures with the related factors of taxation and credit will then be reviewed. Co-operation and problems of adjustment will follow. Finally, the adjustments made to national and war conditions will be considered. Throughout, the emphasis will be upon the social implications of these economic factors.

AGRICULTURAL DEVELOPMENT

Agriculture, of course, is a highly diversified industry. Farms vary in size from a square mile to the few acres of a subsistence homestead; they vary in type from the intensively cultivated irrigated tracts of the Pacific Coast fruit-grower to the grazing lands of a Montana rancher. Crops grown in one section of the country may be unknown to another. Wheat and cotton are not neighbors and citrus fruit is a stranger to Maine potatoes. Moreover, the capital invested in farms varies, as do the operator's tenure, his attitudes about and participation in agricultural co-operation, and his credit needs. All these factors have reacted upon him in the social organization of rural life.

The remainder of this chapter, therefore, attempts to catalogue briefly some of these essentially economic factors, to point out a few of their social implications, and to indicate significant differences among the various regions of the nation that are associated with differences in agricultural procedures.

THE AGRICULTURAL ENTERPRISE

Number of farms. But first of all it is important to gain some idea of the magnitude of the agricultural enterprise. More than half the total area of the United States is farm land. In some regions more than four fifths is so utilized. In only three regions is the fraction less than one half. Even in the industrialized Mid-Atlantic States over 50 per cent of the land is in farms. Taking the nation as a whole, in 1945 our over six million farms included over a billion acres. In every census region the proportion of land in farms increased between 1930 and 1935. Changes in this situation were slight between 1935 and 1940. Between 1920 and 1930 the number of farms decreased somewhat in the nation and in six of the nine census regions. Then the depression stimulated urban-rural migration. The 1935 Agricultural Census reported the number of farms as 6,812,350. This is an increase of 524,000, or 8.3 per cent over 1930, and is the largest number of farms the United States has ever had. The largest proportional increases were shown in the industrial East. By 1940 a reverse trend had set in. Every state reported a smaller number of farms in that year than in 1935, although only twenty-six had fewer farms than in 1930. The small 1930 to 1940 loss in number of farms is more than accounted for by the decline in the southern regions.

It is officially estimated [1] that by April 1, 1944 the number of farms in the United States had declined to 5,500,000, or about 10 per cent. However, the number of operators engaged principally in farm occupation, which stood at 4,750,000 or 77.9 per cent in 1940, declined 6.3 per cent to 4,450,000 by April, 1944, or 80.9 per cent of all farms. Almost half of the net decline was in the group of farmers sixty-five years of age and over. The preliminary 1945 census of agriculture returns given in Table 15 show a much smaller loss.

Size of farms. These six million farms range in size, of course, all the way from little tracts of three acres, or even smaller if producing a net return of over $250 annually, to holdings in the Far West that include more than 100,000 acres.

[1] Series Census, Bureau of Agricultural Economics, no. 3, May 7, 1945.

TABLE 15. NUMBER OF FARMS BY DIVISION

(In thousands)

Division	1910	1920	1930	1935	1940	1945	Per cent Increase 1920–1930	Per cent Increase 1930–1935	Per cent Increase 1930–1940	Per cent Increase 1940–1945
United States	6,361	6,448	6,288	6,812	6,097	6,006	− 2.5	8.3	− 3.1	− 1.5
New England	189	156	125	158	135	167	−20.2	26.7	8.2	23.7
Middle Atlantic	468	425	357	397	348	359	−15.9	11.2	− 2.6	3.1
East North Central	1,123	1,085	966	1,083	1,006	970	−10.9	12.1	4.1	− 3.7
West North Central	1,110	1,097	1,113	1,170	1,090	1,038	1.4	6.0	− 2.0	− 4.8
South Atlantic	1,112	1,159	1,058	1,147	1,019	1,070	− 8.7	8.4	− 3.7	5.0
East South Central	1,042	1,051	1,062	1,137	1,023	991	1.0	7.1	− 3.7	− 3.2
West South Central	943	996	1,103	1,187	964	908	10.7	3.1	−12.6	− 6.2
Mountain	183	244	241	271	283	214	− 1.1	12.5	− 3.2	− 8.1
Pacific	190	234	262	299	276	291	11.8	14.5	5.3	− 5.4

Source: *United States Censuses of Agriculture, 1930, 1935, 1940,* and preliminary estimates, 1945.

In the statistics dealing with the size of farms can be traced, from one point of view at least, the fascinating history of the development of the American continent. The first Europeans, their backs to the Atlantic, met and seized the opportunity to slake their immemorial thirst for land. It was to be had for the taking and clearing. The pioneers pushing westward took two centuries to reach the Pacific. The sizes of farms meant little in those early days, but as the pioneering period ended, the changing size of farms began to be reflected in changes in farm management. At the turn of the century the average farm included 146 acres. It remained almost stationary for the next twenty years, being 148 acres in 1920, but rose to 157 acres in 1930. This increase was shared by forty of the forty-eight states. Seven of the eight whose average acreage declined were in the South. Between 1930 and 1935, the average farm declined to 154.8 acres, which is in part due to the newer farms resulting from the urban-rural migration, the gains are an evidence in part of consolidation of holdings. The 1940 Census reported the highest average size farm in our history, 174 acres. All states increased their average over 1935, 30 states over their 1930 average.[2] By 1945 there was another sharp gain in average farm size. The data are detailed in Table 16.

It is obvious from the preliminary figures of the 1945 agricultural census that the war accelerated the growth in average acreage per farm. In the Mountain states and in Florida the sharp changes came as a result of the inclusion of grazing land not previously included in farms, but fenced since 1940. This, of course, is a continuation of a century-old trend. The gain in farm acreage in Florida in the 1940 to 1945 period was so great that the South Atlantic region shows a small increase in the average size of farms despite the fact that all other states in this region registered declines.

The preliminary nature of this 1945 Census of Agriculture report used in the text should be emphasized. On December 1, 1945, the Census Bureau issued an analysis of the preliminary census results and stated that the editing of the two thirds of the enumerators' reports thus far reviewed indicated that the final figures on the number of farms will be about 60,000 below the preliminary count. In other words, the number of farms in 1945 dropped below 6,000,000 for the first time in decades and stood at about 5,950,000.

Even so this figure was raised by a large number of Victory gardens. The definition of a farm includes an agricultural enter-

---

[2] A change in classification of grazing land in farms in 1940 as compared with 1930 affected this result somewhat.

TABLE 16. AVERAGE ACREAGE PER FARM BY DIVISION AND BY
TYPE OF OPERATOR

Census Division	1920	1930	1935	1940	1945 *
United States..........	148.2	156.9	154.8	174	190.1
New England..........	108.5	114.3	97.7	98.9	90.6
Middle Atlantic........	95.4	98.0	91.7	96.6	97.1
East North Central.....	108.5	114.7	107.9	113.0	119.5
West North Central.....	234.3	238.6	231.4	251.6	273.7
South Atlantic..........	84.4	81.6	83.7	90.8	93.0
East South Central.....	75.0	68.6	69.6	75.3	77.9
West South Central.....	174.1	166.7	176.8	267.9	228.4
Mountain..............	480.7	652.5	640.7	821.9	1,091.1
Pacific.................	239.8	231.2	208.6	280.6	246.4
Type					
Owner................	162.2	173.3	168.4	124 †	
Tenant...............	107.9	115.0	117.2	132	
Manager.............	790.8	1109.1	1261.7	1830	

Source: *Fourteenth Census of the United States*, 1920, vol. V, Table 12, p. 37. *Fifteenth Census of the United States*, 1930, "Agriculture, Summary for the United States, 1929 and 1930," Table 3, p. 24, and Table 7, p. 30; and *Census of Agriculture*, 1935, vol. I, *Census of Agriculture*, 1940, and preliminary estimates for 1945.
* Data for 1945 not yet available.
† Figure for owner. Part-owner operates 235 acres.

prise of more than three acres or smaller tracts with an annual production of $250 or more. As a result of war-induced high prices for
many agricultural commodities, Victory gardens that reached or
exceeded this $250 had to be counted as farms, though they would
not have been so counted at the 1939 level of prices.

This fact must be borne in mind in making comparisons with
previous censuses. When released, the tabulation of farms by size
will probably show a considerable increase in the number of farms
in the categories of under three and under ten acres. These, of
course, are part-time farms. Conversely, the number of commercial,
full-time farms appears to have declined a little more than the
census data thus far available indicate. Moreover, because the
vast majority of the 60,000 farms eliminated by the editing of the
schedules are in the Victory garden class, the average size of farms
in the United States is probably nearer to 192 acres than the 190.1
acres shown by the preliminary census results.

Regional differences. Table 16 also shows wide variations in size
of farms among the nine regions. New England's average of less
than one hundred acres is an indication of the preponderance of

truck and fruit-farming. The low averages of the South bear witness to the large number of small farms operated by Negroes and
poor whites. The better than square-mile average of the Mountain
states indicates the huge tracts used for stock-raising and those cul-
tivable only by the methods of dry-farming. The great gain in the
average acreage operated by employed managers is clear proof of
the possibilities of large-scale farms, often run on the corporation
plan, which mechanize their procedures as much as possible.

It should be remembered also that the size of a farm is one indication of population density, which is obviously low in a region
where single farms average more than a square mile. Small farms
mean compact rural communities, large ones, the reverse. These
differences indicate also great differences in the size, strength, frequency, accessibility, and administration of schools, churches,
libraries and similar social institutions. Transportation of pupils is
obviously a problem in an area of huge farms and low population
density. Churches, as will be seen later, are weak and at a disadvantage under such conditions.

Small farms gain. The average size of farms into which this huge
agricultural area is divided, even on a regional basis, conceals many
significant trends. When the farms of the United States are broken
up into size groups, it becomes apparent that American agriculture
is tending toward smaller as well as larger units. Nearly three
fifths of all our farms, 58.7 per cent, have less than one hundred
acres. In 1900 this percentage was 57.4 The farms of less than
twenty acres account for this increase. In the 1920-35 period, the
proportion of this size rose from 12.3 per cent to 18.4 per cent of
all farms, but declined to 17.5 in 1940. These smaller farms in all
regions are in large part located near the large towns and cities.
As Chapter 16 shows, there is a definite relationship between size
of farm, type of agriculture, and distance from the city; and the
farming area near the city partakes of more urban characteristics
than that farther away.

Large farms increasing. On the other hand, just as the proportion of small farms increased, so did those of 500 acres or more.
This group which constituted 2.6, 3.3 and 3.8 per cent of all farms
respectively in 1900, 1920, and 1940, though only 264,217 in number, comprised 45.2 per cent of the total farm acreage of the nation
in 1940, an increase from 33.6 per cent in 1900, when there were
217,200 of such farms. Other sizes of farms declined proportionately. Those of from 20 to 99 acres comprised 41.2 per cent of the
nation's holdings in 1940 as against 46 per cent in 1930. The num-

ber of farms between 100 and 499 acres also increased but continued the slow decline in proportion that began in 1900. Thirty-six and nine tenths (36.9) per cent of all farms are in this size group, 4 points less than in 1900. Most of this decline was in the 100 to 174 acre group. The trend is obviously, though slowly, toward small, intensively cultivated tracts and large mechanized holdings. A disproportionate concentration of these large farms is in the Mountain and Pacific census divisions. In the former 88, and in the latter 74 per cent of all farm land is in units of 500 acres and over. These two divisions have over 45 per cent of the farm land in units of this size in the entire United States.

These tendencies raise two questions which have become increasingly important during the late nineteen-twenties and early thirties, one relating to part-time farming, the other to large-scale farming.

Part-time farming. Many of the small farms are interesting also because their operators, while maintaining connection with the soil, seek to augment their income by non-agricultural employment. There seems to be a clear relation between type of farming, and rurality, and the proportion of farmers engaged in non-agricultural pursuits. For example, in Ohio only 8 per cent of the heads of farm families in the most rural areas studied had outside employment, while in the most industrial farm sections 27 per cent had non-agricultural occupations.[3] In a central New York community 17.8 per cent of open-country males were similarly engaged.[4] In some Massachusetts and Connecticut towns the proportions ranged from one half to two thirds.

The total number of farmers who worked elsewhere than on their own farms for pay or other income in 1939 was nearly 1,750,000, or 28.7 per cent of all farmers, almost the same proportion as in 1929. There was only a slight difference between owners and tenants in this respect, but marked variation among the regions. Though the number of farmers earning wages elsewhere declined 8 per cent between 1934 and 1939, the total number of days worked increased by nearly 20 per cent. The number and proportion not working on their farms one hundred days or more increased sharply, from 11 per cent in 1929 and 1934 to 15.5 per cent in 1939. Changes in the number employed on relief projects, and the increase in

[3] Lively and Beck, *Movement of Open Country Population in Ohio.* Columbus: Bulletin 467, Experiment Station, College of Agriculture, Ohio State University, 1930.

[4] Melvin and Kensler, *A Partial Sociological Study of Dryden, New York.* Ithaca: New York College of Agriculture, Cornell University, 1930.

farms under ten acres are probably explanations. The Mountain and New England states were considerably above the national average; the South slightly below. It is important to note that practically 30 per cent of the whites, but only 21.8 per cent of the non-whites, mostly Negroes, were able to obtain part-time employment. The discrepancy between the two races widened as the number of days worked off the farm increased, despite the fact that the Negroes operated smaller farms.

Conclusively, the average farmer who worked away from his farm in 1939 was so employed for 137 days, 40 more than in 1934, but there was an increase of more than 25 per cent in the number who had 250 days or more of such employment. It seems safe to conclude that part-time farming is a correlative of industrialization, and that it was stimulated by the depression.

The sources of such employment were varied. Only about 28 per cent were employed on other farms. Many farm homes put up "Tourists Accommodated" signs. Some opened roadside markets, gas stations, or eating places. Other farmers drove school buses, hauled local milk, operated city or town milk routes, ran sawmills, did road work. A number, as in the past, were preachers, some of whom supplanted ordained clergymen whom the churches could not afford to keep. A few took summer boarders. Since 1940 many farmers have done off-farm work in war industries and in army camps. In some of the New England states supplementary work has grown to such an extent that it has become the main source of income for many farmers who might be more accurately characterized as part-time farmers than as farmers doing part-time work.[5]

Some measure of the increase in off-farm employment during the war has been made available by the Census and the Bureau of Agricultural Economics, covering the year 1943.[6] One third of the total farm population ten years of age and over worked off their farms in that year. This involved 54.2 per cent of the farm operators and 24.4 per cent of other members of farm households. Slightly more than half of all those who worked off the home farm labored on other farms; slightly less than one half were engaged in non-farm work. Whether listed by sex, or by farm operators or other members of the household, it was true that the larger the number of days worked off the home farm, the greater the likelihood that such work was non-farm employment. Thus, of 850,000 farm oper-

5 For the most complete data on this subject, cf. *Part-time Farming in the United States.* Washington, D.C.: Bureau of the Census, 1937.
6 Series Census, Bureau of Agricultural Economics no. 6, October 15, 1945.

ators who were employed for 250 days or over in 1943, 630,000 did non-farm work, almost three quarters of the number. For the 660,-000 non-operators, the proportion in this category was over 80 per cent. On the other hand, more than two thirds of both the operators and the members of their families who worked less than fifty days off their own farms, were employed only on other farms. Over 1,200,000 operators shared work in this way. It is significant that in 1943 the proportion of farm operators working off their own land almost doubled, as compared with 1939, when it was 28.7 per cent. The great bulk of this increase was among those who worked less than fifty days in the year away from their own farm. Much of this was probably war-induced assistance to neighbors. However, the proportion working one hundred days or more rose from 15.5 per cent in 1939 to 20.5 per cent in 1943. Those who did non-farm work averaged 172 days off their farms in 1943, 13 more than in 1939; those working only on other farms 68 days, 7 more than in 1939. Significantly, however, so many more farmers helped out in this way that four times as many man-days, 122,000,000, were worked than in 1939, as against an increase of 36 per cent in man-days on agricultural work.

It is quite possible that the end of the war will reduce the amount of off-farm employment to near the 1939 proportions. This is a factor which needs to be recognized in connection with the full picture of income for the farm population.

Large-scale farms. Large-scale farms are often treated as synonymous with corporation farms, though such is not the case. Kansas, for instance, has a number of family holdings of 2000 to 6000 acres, highly mechanized as to operation. Some of the operators of these holdings are called "suitcase" farmers because they can use motors to transport their farm machinery many miles from their homes. Such trends account for population decline in areas of mechanized farming and for the difficulties of social institutions like schools and churches organized on the assumption that the pattern of wheat farming in the first decade or two of the twentieth century was permanent.

Mechanization is now spreading beyond the wheat belt. The cheaper, all-purpose tractor is revolutionizing some areas, especially the Southwestern cotton area. In some counties the proportion of farms with tractors has increased in the last half-decade from one fifth to four fifths. Tenant farmers and croppers, white and Negro alike, as well as farm laborers, are being swept from the land. Two illustrations are typical: A cotton planter in the Mississippi Delta had 160 share-cropper families. He purchased 22 tractors and 13 four-row cultivators, let 130 families, about 700 people go, retaining only 30 and these on a day-labor basis. On another much smaller holding of about 2200 acres, 35 tenant families were evicted, 180 persons, and the farm was operated by a few able-bodied single men and machines. In the latter case the families moved to the trade-center village and applied for relief. In the former some followed this policy, many others headed for California.[7]

Paul Taylor, of the University of California, in an address in April, 1938, reported an all too typical incident:

> On a Sunday morning last June I stopped at a tenant's house near the Texas Panhandle. There I found seven sturdy young men gathered together for the morning. These Texans are all displaced tenant farmers, victims of mechanized farming. The oldest man in the group is 33. All are on W.P.A. They support an average of four persons each on $22.80 a month. All are married and have families except one, who supports his mother and father. These seven Texans represent and support 29 persons. Native Americans all, none of them can vote, for Texas levies a poll tax of $3.50 on man and wife. These men, like hundreds of others, find nothing they can turn to on the Plains where they were born. They search for 200 miles in every direction and find no places which they can rent. With mechanization, the size of farms is increasing, and little is left for the tenants but sub-marginal land, relief, or flight.[8]

Under such conditions rural schools and churches decline, village institutions are weakened. The rise in the standard of living of the remaining farm operators does not compensate for the community losses. Lowered standards for the victims of mechanization increase class consciousness and bitterness. Health conditions grow worse. Even those still living under the older arrangements keep constant company with stark fear of the same fate. The problem is little recognized except in the local communities affected. Those states receiving the migrants are affected directly, but so are the states losing population and the nation that pays the social cost through relief and in other ways. The expansion of war industries in the Pacific region of course gave this people useful employment, but this is no guarantee that the problem is permanently solved.

[7] About 200,000 distressed migrants entered California from 1936 to 1940. Despite the breaking of the drought the flow of these people barely slackens. "The drought undermined them, mechanization finishes them." Cf. chapter on "Population Mobility."
[8] Paul S. Taylor, "What Shall We Do With Them?" Address before Commonwealth Club of California, San Francisco, April 15, 1938.

Corporation farms. One aspect of large-scale farming is that which is conducted by corporations. The census gives no data on these farms as such. The only clue is in the number of farms operated by managers, which, however, includes many estates. The number of such farms has fluctuated widely. The high point was in 1920 when there were 68,449. During the first period of the depression there was a decline to 40,700 in 1925. More than half this loss was regained by 1930, after which there was a further decline to 36,351 in 1940, during a time when the total number of all farms was increasing. Acreage in such farms, however, has increased steadily, except for a slight dip between 1930 and 1934. About 6 per cent of all farm land belongs to manager-operated holdings, but proportionately only one third as much of their acreage is in crop-land, as is the case with other farms. In 1930 less than one per cent of all farms and two per cent of all crop-land were operated by managers.

Again, the situation under discussion is especially important in the two western divisions. They had 8.3 per cent of all farms in 1940, but almost 19 per cent of the farms and 46 per cent of all acreage operated by managers. However, of the total land in managed farms in 1939 only 13.5 per cent was crop-land harvested in the Pacific division, and only 2.6 per cent in the Mountain division. This was from one fourth to one eighth the proportion in other tenure groups in these divisions. Probably agriculture on managed farms in these states is somewhat comparable to that of all farms of over five hundred acres. The difference between the two western divisions in this particular is undoubtedly a reflection of the much larger amount of stock-raising and dry farming in the Mountain states as compared to those on the Pacific Coast. The latter region also has many more acres under irrigation.

There have been many prophecies that large-scale farming, probably on a corporation basis, was coming. When it does come, the problem in the community is acute. An Iowa village paper thus describes the operations of a 24,000-acre corporation farm:

> Each tract in the group is operated as a single field and is planted to a single crop in a rotation program. In the working of its present holdings, the company employs seventy-five general purpose tractors, nineteen combined harvesters and threshers, fifteen two-row harvesters, seventy-five plows, forty grain drills, and associated equipment. This machinery is transported over a hard surfaced state-road system by means of ten motor trucks with semi-trailers capable of hauling three tractors to a load. Field machinery is entirely equipped with electric lighting system to permit twenty-four hour operation when necessary.

This company uses no livestock, has removed boundary fences, groves, and often the buildings from its holdings, and employs only unmarried men. Village hardware and implement dealers and repairmen feared the ruin of their business. Village social institutions would also be greatly altered if this procedure became general.

On the other hand, one of the oldest corporation farms in the United States has found it profitable, after years of experimentation, to employ only married men and to make both the conditions of operation and of living as similar to those of normal farming as possible.

Other problems of giant farms. The alarm of the villages and of the displaced farmers whose foreclosed acres made up the holding of the corporation described are not the only problems of large-scale farming. Heavy capital expenditure for equipment is required, and new techniques must be learned. Moreover, problems of industrial relations arise, for often the agrarian is not a docile employee, as was proved in the mills of Elizabethton, Tennessee, and Marion, North Carolina, in 1929 and 1930. Moreover, even in 1928, according to the United States Chamber of Commerce, corporation farms were earning only a slightly higher return on their investment than the family size farms with which they were compared. A number of these giants have not weathered the depression. The increase in large-scale farming will doubtless continue, though not so rapidly as some have imagined, since it is not a demonstrated panacea for the ills of American agriculture.

The issues of large- versus small-scale farming go deeper than these considerations, as has already been intimated. The Bureau of Agricultural Economics recently studied two California communities with approximately the same acreage and devoted to the same crops. One had large-scale, the other small-scale farms, the average acreage being 497 for the large and 57 for the smaller farms. The gross dollar value of farm production for the two was almost equal, the large farms having $40,000 more, the small farms an equal sum less, than $2,500,000. Average gross farm income was $18,000 and $3300 respectively. Other differences were most significant. In the large area about 20 per cent of the farm population were independent operators, and 80 per cent were wage hands. In the other area the distribution was fifty-fifty. The large farm community had poor, badly crowded houses, few recreational facilities, and a fairly serious delinquency problem. The other community had small, but generally adequate, better constructed houses on larger lots. The trade center of the small farm area was incorporated, had two banks, four well-located elementary schools and one high school. The center of the larger farm community was unincorporated and had no local government; it had only one grade school and no bank. It had 60 stores compared to 156 in the small-farm area, although its population of 6300 was only 1550 below that of the other center.

In every category of retail sales, except liquor, the families of the small farm community spent more than was spent in the larger community — often twice as much as was spent for important items such as household goods and furniture. Although the difference in population was only 23.8 per cent, and the difference in value of farm production was very little, the total value of retail sales in the small farm community in 1943 was $4,320,000, or 70 per cent more than the $2,530,000 of the larger farm area. In a more intangible sphere the testimony of businessmen and professional workers indicated that there was a much finer community spirit in the small-farm area than in the larger one. Comparisons of these two communities in terms of agricultural efficiency favor the large-scale farm by a small margin, but in terms of social factors and many economic factors, such as the level of employment, the comparison is all in favor of the small-farm community.

Facts on the size of American farms do, however, indicate a growing specialization in agriculture. Small farms, intensively cultivated and given over largely to truck and fruit or to part-time farmers will doubtless stay and probably increase. The very large farm, also slowly gaining in numbers and acreage, will be used for those crops that lend themselves to machine cultivation. Finally, the old type of medium-size general farm, though slowly declining in relation to the total number, is not likely to disappear in any predictable future. The first two types, wherever they appear in force, are working changes in the traditional pattern of rural social organization, and they will continue to do so.

Value of Farms

Total investment. Not only is agriculture, judged by the proportion of the nation's area devoted to it and by the number of its separate units, a major enterprise, but also, when judged by its capital values, it is our most important industry. The total value of farm lands, buildings, and equipment was over $73,000,000,000 in 1920, of which $57,300,000,000 was in land alone. In each decade from 1900 to 1920 the value of farm land doubled. In the first of these years it was $16,000,000,000; in 1910, $34,000,000,000. Even this rapid advance failed by about 25 per cent to keep pace with the decline of the purchasing power of the dollar which occurred during the period of high prices caused by World War I. The agricultural depression carried total valuation of land and buildings back to about $48,000,000,000. In other words, between 1920 and 1930 the capital values of agriculture declined 27 per cent, according to the census. This decline continued to 1935, when the census showed a further loss of 31.4 per cent to $32,800,000,000, or more than 50 per cent below the 1920 valuations. The 1940 figure was $31,700,000,000. This terrific deflation was one of the chief concomitants of the depression. It brought great suffering to agriculturists and their families, and vitally affected the credit system, as will be shown later.

Since the 1940 Census there has been a considerable increase in the value of farms. In part, this is a reflection of good prices for agricultural products and therefore higher farm income, more in some regions than in others. In some states the rise in values reflects a certain amount of speculative buying. As Table 17 shows, neither the decline nor the recent rise have been uniform among the regions. If the official estimates are correct, however, the 1945 Agricultural Census will show the capital value of American agriculture to be over $40,000,000. Whether this rise has gone too far, or will prove to be justified by postwar conditions, cannot now be determined, but at this writing there are elements of danger in the situation in some states.

It will be seen from Table 17 that the decline in the per acre

TABLE 17. ESTIMATED VALUE PER ACRE OF FARM REAL
ESTATE, BY DIVISION (1909–14 = 100)

Census Division	1920	1925	1930	1932	1935	1940	1945*
United States	170	127	115	89	79	84	142
New England	140	127	127	116	104	106	140
Middle Atlantic	136	114	106	96	85	90	128
East North Central	161	116	96	73	68	78	134
West North Central	184	126	109	81	68	65	106
South Atlantic	198	148	128	96	93	107	189
East South Central	199	141	128	97	93	112	212
West South Central	177	144	136	97	91	99	154
Mountain	151	105	102	82	70	78	134
Pacific	156	146	142	118	101	108	194

* Preliminary.
Source: Bureau of Agricultural Economics, March, 1946.

value of farm real estate was most drastic in the areas devoted to export crops and to general farming. Regions engaged in dairying, and in raising truck, fruit, and other specialized products, grown for the most part in proximity to cities and in the more industrialized areas, suffered least. Comparably, the rebound has been stronger where values were most depressed. This indicates the vulnerability to disaster of one-crop and export-crop areas. Such drastic changes obviously have their social effects on the communities concerned. One of the most important of these effects is related to a cultural trait — the urge for the possession of land and ever more land. It goes back to the hunger of the agrarian for a stake in the land. The result in our society has been to capitalize increased farm income in increased land values. This puts the purchase of land into competition with another possible policy; namely, the use of larger profits to procure a higher standard of family and community living. It tends to reduce the percentage earnings on capital invested and makes farms with a high or overcapitalized value vulnerable to depreciation when the price level for farm products declines.

Values per farm. It is important next to imagine what these huge totals mean in terms of the individual farm. Here again care must be taken to analyze the total figures. As Table 18 shows, the average value per farm in the United States dropped from $12,084 in 1920 to $9103 in 1930. In 1925 it stood at $8945. The increase from 1925 to 1930 was due entirely to gains in the investment in implements and machinery and livestock. Land and buildings alone declined steadily from $69.38 an acre in 1920 to $53.52 in 1925 and $31.16 in 1935. By 1940 the large size of farms had raised per farm valuations from 1935, but the difference on a per acre basis was slight — 55 cents. Table 18 also shows that the trends were not nation-wide. The greater stability of the eastern United States, already alluded to, stands out clearly, and is related there to the growth of cities and industrialization. Conversely the table shows that the deflation was most severe in the Central States, north and south.

Table 18 yields no information on two other important items; namely, the trend in values from 1940 to date, and the relation of farm values to the proximity of farms to a metropolitan center. As already noted, values declined sharply from 1930 to the end of 1933. As Chapter 16 shows, the loss in value was proportional to the distance of the farm from a city; the farther away it lay, the greater the average loss in value.

TABLE 18. AVERAGE VALUE OF FARM LAND AND BUILDINGS
PER FARM AND PER ACRE

Division	Average Value per Farm			Average Value Land and Buildings per Acre		
	1940	1930	1920	1940	1930	1920
United States............	$5,518	$7,614	$10,284	$31.71	$48.52	$69.38
New England............	5,478	7,530	5,860	55.38	68.56	54.00
Middle Atlantic..........	5,858	7,880	7,061	60.62	80.40	73.99
East North Central.......	7,289	9,660	13,371	64.53	84.20	126.87
West North Central......	8,065	13,623	22,307	32.05	57.10	95.22
South Atlantic...........	3,099	3,639	4,488	34.14	44.60	53.20
East South Central.......	2,272	2,528	3,484	30.16	36.88	46.44
West South Central......	4,388	5,263	6,316	21.10	31.57	36.27
Mountain...............	7,623	10,188	12,958	9.27	15.61	26.96
Pacific.................	11,720	18,431	19,941	50.82	79.70	83.16

Source: *United States Census of Agriculture*, 1935, vol. III, Table 12; *ibid.*, 1940.

Factors affecting farm values. Various factors affect the value of individual farms, even though the size and soil fertility of two given tracts may be approximately equal. Farms near markets are more valuable than those farther away. This is true not merely in connection with the major sources of consumption, the cities, as shown in Chapter 16, but also within communities where, as a rule, farms near the village and town center and located on good roads, especially hard-surfaced ones, are more valuable than those farther away and on poorer roads. Obviously, also the better the soil the higher the value. It frequently happens that there are important social correlations to this fact. Numerous field surveys have shown that the farms well located as to the community center, roads, and soil are more likely to be represented in the membership of churches, farm bureaus, co-operatives, and other social and economic organizations than are those not so well located. So, too, children from the better located farms more often attend high school.

Again, farms in the older and better established areas, and those devoted to highly specialized or well diversified products, such as fruit and truck, are usually more valuable, at least on a per acre basis, than farms in more recently developed areas, in one crop or general farm regions.

Erosion a serious difficulty. A final factor of increasing importance needs to be mentioned; namely, erosion. It is easy to assume that land is a permanent factor. This is not true with respect to top soil, which can be washed or even blown away. The geographer, Russell Smith, has even raised the question as to whether or not this is a permanent country.[9] In North Carolina, county agents, for instance, have reported that in fifteen years after the timber has been cut from the lumbering areas of that state, this land, which has produced some of the finest forests, must be abandoned for agricultural purposes because of erosion. Soundings made along railway rights of way and in adjoining fields in Iowa show that an appreciable proportion of its fertile soil has disappeared — some of it blown clear to the Atlantic as in the dust storms during the drought of 1934. The Land Planning Committee of the National Resources Board, in a preliminary report in January, 1935, estimated that "the usefulness for farming of 35,000,000 acres has been completely destroyed, that the top soil has been nearly or quite removed from an additional 125,000,000 acres, and that another 100,000,000 acres are starting" in the direction of depletion. Here is a factor that can utterly destroy not only land values but communities as well. It is encouraged, according to H. H. Bennett, Director of the Federal Soil Erosion Service,[10] by careless farming and deforestation.

According to Mr. Bennett, much of the subhumid grazing country of the Great Plains and countless sloping sections of the more humid areas must be used for perennial growths of trees or grass if the nation wishes to avoid the huge economic and social loss of allowing expanding deserts to arise in our midst. In some areas this may "involve redistribution of population" and thus become a problem for those who are struggling with this issue as a part of President Roosevelt's program for our submarginal lands. There is no greater threat to land values than the factor of erosion, a problem created largely by human behavior. Fortunately considerable progress has been made in the last decade or more in soil conservation. In some areas, but fortunately not in all, there has been a new overdraft on soil resources during World War II, but it is to be hoped that the soil conservation program will be fully resumed when possible. This is an important item on the agenda of postwar rural adult education.

The importance of this point is not adequately recognized. The phrase "mining the soil" is often used in discussions about soil conservation and tenancy. This practice, the failure to sustain the productivity of the land, eventually is reflected in changing land values.

[9] Cf. *Survey Graphic*, September, 1928.
[10] Cf. *New York Times*, June 17, 1934. Feature Section.

But for the most part farm management and farm accounting take no account of the slow deterioration of soil productivity. In short, the dollar gain to a landowner in using land values may be partly or wholly fictitious if the productive potential of his land is being gradually reduced.

This issue may be presented to the American public in a dramatic way. We have a huge synthetic rubber producing capacity developed during World War II. There are those who go so far as to say that we should buy little or no natural rubber in the future. Instead, they say, we should grow grain, turn it into alcohol, and the alcohol into rubber. But grain crops are hard on the soil. Apart from the effect of such policies on the standard of living of millions of persons in areas where rubber grows naturally, persons who were allies of ours in the world struggle, it cannot be asserted that synthetic rubber will be "cheaper" than natural rubber until the cost to the soil of the grain areas from such a policy is determined. Soil is, but should not be, taken for granted. Large social issues, as well as economic, emerge at this point — issues that affect not only rural society, but also the nation and the world.

FARM INCOME

Farm values represent a capital investment. It is natural next to ask what income is earned from this investment. It was pointed out in the last chapter that the increment of land values, far exceeding the increase in the prices of farm crops, gave the farmer for decades a source of wealth quite apart from the results of his management and toil. With the beginning of the agricultural depression in 1921, this stopped. Indeed, as just recounted, a reverse process set in. The matter of farm income therefore becomes of real importance. National figures are given in a subsequent chapter. The uses to which income is placed are discussed in the chapter on "Standards of Living." This section will deal simply with returns per farm.

The rate of return. Between 1921 and 1933 the average rate of return on invested capital varied from less than nothing per farm in the worst years of the depression to nearly 5 per cent in 1925. Translated into the reward for the average farm family for labor and management, after deducting interest, rental cost and value and expenses of operation, the figures vary from a deficit in 1932 to $903 in 1925. These figures are, of course, in terms of all farms.

It has already been shown that some farms are on little more than a subsistence level and that more than one sixth have less than twenty acres. This national average, therefore has, as usual, all the limitations of a single national figure. Two attempts have been made to break up these averages into more meaningful terms. One of these takes the average annual cash income per farm for the eleven years 1920-21 to 1930-31 inclusive by states. The results of this computation are given in Table 19, together with comparative figures for the single years 1940 and 1942. In the second attempt, Doctors Baker and Elliot of the Bureau of Agricultural Economics tried to estimate the value of all farm products by groups of farms.

Significance of income groups. They found that it shows that the least productive three tenths of our farms, over 1,500,000, produced for the commercial market less than 4 per cent of all our farm products; 1,250,000 additional farms added only 7.5 per cent more to the total. Thus only slightly more than one half the farms accounts for eight ninths of our agricultural production.

There was not much change in this situation in the following decade. The 1940 Census of Agriculture classed 1,942,729 of our farms — practically one third of the total — as subsistence; that is, as a major source of income for the farm family. Just over 1,250,000 farms, one fifth of the aggregate, had a total value of farm products of under $250 in 1939. This was four times as many as in 1929. Over 1,667,000,000 more raised from $250 to $600 worth of products. Only a few over 2,000,000 farms realized $1000 or more profit — about one third of the total. In all but the three Southern census divisions the proportion of farms producing more than $1000 worth of income in 1939 ranged between 41.2 per cent in New England to almost 50 per cent in the East and West North Central states. In the East South Central division this proportion was only 12 per cent, and in the other two Southern groups about 25 per cent. Every region experienced the great increase in the proportion of farms falling into all categories below $1000 production as compared with 1929. This, of course, is a reflection of the depression of the nineteen-thirties from which agriculture had not made a complete recovery even by the end of 1939. Since then there has been a steady improvement. The 1944 records, when given in the 1945 Agricultural Census, will doubtless show a better record than in 1929. It is well to recall this situation, however. It indicates the hazardous economic position of a large proportion of our farms. It explains the efforts of the American farmers in the war years to protect the favorable position they attained during the conflict.

But even counting income from non-farm work, the lowest rank-ing third of our farms receive about 12 per cent of the total income of all farm families; the top third, 62 per cent.[11] The smaller farm-ers accounted for a disproportionate share of war-induced increased production. The situation described has improved slightly since 1941, but even assuming that a farm family raised its income from $250 to $500 a year between 1939 and 1943, its share in the vaunted "American standard of living" would be nothing to enthuse about. Moreover, costs of living have also advanced. The gain in real in-come — that is, purchasing power — would be less than the gain in dollars.

These facts and the data in Table 19 exhibit the range of indi-vidual agricultural enterprise. They indicate the great complexity of conditions facing schools in utilizing local situations in their teaching, especially agriculture, and the difficulties of the extension service in planning its programs for farmers. This is equally true of other social agencies. These facts show the importance of the Farm Security Administration and its work with low-income farm-ers which is told about in Chapter 24. If, as seems clear, many of the 48 per cent of farmers who produced less than $600 worth of products in 1929, and consumed practically all of it at home, are to be found among the Negroes, the Southern mountaineers, and others on sub-marginal lands, it follows that the problem of deal-ing with sub-marginal population and removing them elsewhere is colossal. With this problem the Department of Agriculture is concerned. If, in addition, most of the rest of this 48 per cent are part-time farmers, it follows that the real problem of surplus con-trol — should such a policy again be adopted — is with barely half of our farms, and that since nearly three million farmers contracted to co-operate in the Agricultural Adjustment Administration pro-gram, this program had, in 1933-34, the clear support of a vast majority of the responsible farmers of the country. In other words, it had a nearly unanimous backing. Never before has agriculture been as united, and it is noteworthy that the farmers agree on a program that is little short of revolutionary. When we stop to con-sider the traditional attitudes and behavior of American farmers, the sociological implications of the Farm Act of 1933 take on addi-tional significance. Even with the changes occurring since 1935, the achievement of such a close approach to a national mind and

[11] From a radio address by Louis Bean, Economic Adviser to the Secre-tary of Agriculture, January 24, 1941.

TABLE 19. Average Annual Cash Farm Income per Farm 1920-21 to 1930-31, inclusive, and in 1940 and 1944

Rank			State	Average Cash Income per Farm		
1920-31	1940	1944		1920-31	1940	1944
1	1	1	California............	$4,236	$4,960	$12,824
2	3	4	Nevada..............	3,862	3,892	6,768
3	5	6	Arizona.............	3,519	3,436	6,674
4	6	5	Iowa................	3,048	3,370	6,768
5	14	16	Nebraska............	2,856	2,281	5,082
6	2	3	New Jersey..........	2,814	4,124	7,232
7	4	7	Wyoming............	2,621	3,871	6,095
8	23	12	Washington..........	2,512	1,858	5,508
9	18	11	North Dakota........	2,493	2,131	5,530
10	19	18	South Dakota........	2,486	1,926	4,620
11	8	9	Colorado............	2,425	2,775	5,841
12	22	22	Kansas..............	2,389	1,880	4,338
13	13	8	Idaho...............	2,332	2,291	5,900
14	9	10	Montana............	2,318	2,774	5,656
15	11	17	Connecticut.........	2,289	2,651	4,627
16	10	15	Illinois.............	2,237	2,700	5,211
17	20	19	Oregon.............	2,171	1,898	4,536
18	16	24	New York...........	2,077	2,223	3,982
19	24	28	Vermont............	2,073	1,850	3,207
20	12	21	Massachusetts.......	2,072	2,392	4,403
21	28	25	Wisconsin..........	2,072	1,717	3,982
22	17	23	Minnesota..........	2,017	2,144	3,984
23	7	13	Rhode Island........	1,988	3,361	5,445
24	21	19	Utah................	1,854	1,897	4,536
25	25	14	Florida.............	1,666	1,814	5,404
26	15	2	Delaware............	1,634	2,246	8,499
27	27	26	Maryland...........	1,602	1,742	3,881
28	33	32	Texas...............	1,595	1,409	2,980
29	32	30	Maine..............	1,589	1,413	3,077
30	30	27	Indiana.............	1,505	1,622	3,494
31	29	31	Pennsylvania........	1,477	1,670	3,029
32	31	33	Ohio................	1,471	1,448	2,946
33	35	35	Michigan............	1,406	1,312	2,605
34	34	36	New Hampshire.......	1,397	1,330	2,459
35	26	29	New Mexico.........	1,369	1,774	3,148
36	37	37	Oklahoma...........	1,330	1,141	2,424
37	36	34	Missouri............	1,292	1,150	2,667
38	39	38	North Carolina.......	994	790	2,197
39	43	39	Virginia.............	871	728	1,801
40	42	43	Louisiana............	850	763	1,565
41	38	40	South Carolina.......	785	843	1,779
42	41	42	Arkansas............	749	769	1,566
43	45	45	Tennessee...........	711	570	1,272
44	40	41	Georgia.............	678	774	1,748
45	48	48	West Virginia........	674	433	853
46	44	44	Kentucky...........	664	630	1,406
47	46	46	Alabama............	629	502	1,126
48	47	47	Mississippi..........	605	497	1,097
				No data	1,416	

Source: Bureau of Census, United States Department of Agriculture. The figures for 1940 and 1944 include government payments.

collective action among American farmers is a sociological phenomenon of prime importance.

Some general considerations. In terms of the entire nation gross farm income has varied since 1929 from about $6,400,000,000 in 1932 to $22,700,000,000 in 1943. From 1934 to 1939, the figure averaged around $10,000,000,000, counting benefit payments. These last in 1944 exceeded $715,000,000. Net income over farm operations, however, gained more, going from a low of $1,800,000,000 in 1932 to about three times as much in 1937 and over six times as much in 1943, or $12,040,000,000. In 1944 there was a slight rise to $12,482,000,000. This net income is the amount left over for family or for capital expense. The preliminary estimates for 1945 indicate further gains for that year with a probable total of $24,-200,000,000 of gross, and $13,000,000,000 net income from farming operations. From this, the highest level ever reached by American farmers, a decline of from 10 to 15 per cent is expected in 1946. Even that, however, would keep the farmers' returns at levels never reached until after the outbreak of World War II.

Interestingly enough, for over twenty years, through good and bad years, agricultural income and total industrial wages have shown practically a one-to-one correspondence. While no causal relationship has been demonstrated, this fact is at least another indication of the interdependence of our society.

THE OCCUPATIONS OF FARM PEOPLE

Agricultural employment less important. Agriculture is, of course, the chief occupation of farm people, but it has steadily decreased in relative importance. Before presenting the 1940 data, however, it is interesting to note the steady decline in the importance of agriculture among the major occupations, as measured by the proportion of all gainfully employed in it. In 1870, when there were half as many farms as in 1930, 24 per cent of the gainfully employed were farmers and almost as large a proportion, 23.1 per cent, were farm laborers. Thus nearly half the gainfully employed were agriculturists. There was a very slight increase in the proportion of farmers by 1880, but from then on a steady decline set in. By 1940 only 18.5 per cent of the gainfully employed were classed as farmers or as farm laborers. In other words, in seventy years the proportion of those employed in agriculture declined by more than half, despite a numerical gain of nearly five million persons in the farm population. None the less, when males alone are considered, over one person in every five of those employed in the United States in 1940 was engaged in agriculture. The only larger group was that engaged in manufacturing and mechanical industries.[12]

Agriculture is a man's work in our culture. The 1940 Census found only 144,334 women operating farms as owners, tenants, or managers among the six million farms in America. Over 288,000 more were listed as farm laborers, over 75 per cent of them unpaid [13] and therefore family workers.

It has already been indicated that agriculture, though the chief, is not the only occupation of the farm population. Not only are there thousands of part-time farmers with other occupations, but some members of farm households are wholly employed in nonagricultural pursuits. In terms of the total income of the farm population and of the farm household it is necessary to gain some understanding of the importance of this situation. It has a bearing on the farm family's standard of living, discussed in Chapter 17. This supplemental income also needs to be taken into account in computing the share of the farm population in the national output, and also in comparing the economic status of farm and non-farm families.

The importance of this factor is shown by a study of the National Industrial Conference Board.[14] It estimates that, excluding rental and benefit payments under the Agricultural Adjustment Act, these non-agricultural sources raised the total income of the farm population by 40 per cent in 1929. Though this figure may be unduly high, it indicates the importance of these secondary sources of income.

Farm group a working population. One characteristic of the farm population is the high proportion of its male members fourteen years of age and over who are in the labor force. In 1940 the proportion was 81.3 per cent as against 79.6 per cent for urban and

[12] Cf. Hansen, Alvin, "Industrial Class Alignments in the United States and Industrial Classes in the United States in 1920," *Journal of the American Statistical Association*, December, 1920, and December, 1922, and also in vol. 77, pp. 199-203, of the same, a note by Sogge, T. M., on "Industrial Classes in the United States in 1930." See also Fry, *American Villages* (New York: Institute of Social and Religious Research, 1926), Appendix B, pp. 135-40, and chapter VII for a socio-economic classification of the gainfully employed in agricultural villages in 1920.

[13] This is clearly an underenumeration, due to the fact that the census was based on employment during the last week of March, 1940. The proportion of unpaid workers, however, is significant.

[14] Martin, Robert F., *Income in Agriculture: 1929-1935*. New York, 1936.

74.9 per cent for rural non-farm males.[15] Moreover, only 4 per cent of the rural farm members of the labor force were wholly unemployed and seeking work at the time of the census, which was the last week in March 1940, compared to slightly over 11 per cent for both of the other two groups. In no state did the proportion of the farm population in this category equal the national averages for the other two groups. Indeed, in only fifteen states, seven in the Northeast and seven in the West, did this proportion exceed one half the national averages of the others.

As of April 1, 1940, 1,426,836 males in the farm population were gainfully employed in non-agricultural occupations and 164,622 more were seeking work. Obviously in these non-farm jobs the unemployment ratio was roughly equal to that in the cities and villages. Among women, just under 638,000 of the farm residents were non-agriculturally employed, and 52,238 more were seeking work. In total, therefore, over 2,000,000 farm persons had nonfarm jobs in 1940, and the total labor force available for such work was over 2,250,000. It is obvious that the wages from such a group would amount to an impressive sum. These figures do not, of course, include seasonal non-agricultural employment, as in canning factories. In some sections of the country there is much canning activity for short intensive periods. In 1936 about half of the 464 industries in 140 representative village-centered agricultural communities employed over 9000 seasonal workers, about one fourth of them from farm homes. Of the year-round full-time workers, just over one fifth came from the open country.[16]

All major occupational groups represented. The total non-agricultural employment of the farm population, except on emergency work, is given in Table 20.

While many of the non-agriculturally employed members of the farm population work in the open country, such as some miners, lumbermen, teachers, clergymen, and others, it is interesting to note that this group equals almost one fourth the size of the employed rural non-farm male group, and is over one third as large as the rural non-farm employed female group.

The large groupings given in Table 20 conceal many interesting facts, as is inevitable in such over-all national summaries. Over 80

[15] The figures for females were in reverse order: 12.1 per cent for the farm, 20.7 per cent for the rural non-farm, and 33.2 per cent for the urban population.

[16] Cf. Brunner, E. de S., and I. Lorge, *Rural Trends in Depression Years,* pp. 117-118. New York: Columbia University Press, 1937.

TABLE 20. OCCUPATIONS OF NON-AGRICULTURALLY EMPLOYED
PERSONS BY SEX AND BY MAJOR CATEGORIES FOR RURAL
FARM POPULATION: 1940

Occupation	Males		Females	
	Number	Per cent Total	Number	Per cent Total
Professional and semi-professional	73,346	5.1	136,856	22.2
Proprietors, managers and officials	138,183	9.7	17,981	2.9
Clerical and sales	129,141	9.0	92,384	15.0
Craftsmen, foremen, etc.	280,598	19.6	3,246	0.5
Operatives	420,137	29.4	93,783	15.2
Domestic service	12,290	0.9	214,011	34.7
Protective service	16,222	1.1	135	
Other service workers	34,027	2.4	48,900	7.9
Laborers	322,892	22.6	8,529	1.4

Source: Computed from *Sixteenth Census of the United States*, 1940, vol. III, *The Labor Force*, Part I, Table 59. Agriculturally employed persons and small numbers reported as employed but occupation unknown eliminated.

per cent of the professionally employed women in the farm population are teachers. Teachers are also the largest single group among the males in this category — 44 per cent. No other single sub-group contained as many as 10 per cent, though clergymen neared this proportion. Retail trade establishments were the largest sub-group among the proprietors of both sexes in the non-agriculturally employed farm population. This outlet also took the largest proportion of the clerical workers. The largest proportion of machine operators for both sexes was found in the various textile-worker sub-groups. The use of the automobile brought about great changes in rural employment as shown by the fact that one fourth of the farm females employed in the "other service group" were waitresses, as with the rural non-farm group. In addition, over 10 per cent were cooks in restaurants, inns, or other public eating places. So other details reflect the changing social customs and conditions of the American scene. Some of these will be commented on later in the analysis of the rural non-farm village population and its functions.

This summary of the non-agricultural employment of the farm population makes clear the fact that there is much economic opportunity available to farm dwellers who are not needed on the land. This employment is in the village and town center of the farming community, or in unincorporated centers, such as the mill villages of the South or the mining villages which are found in many states. The farm people are distributed among the various non-agricultural sub-occupational groups in much the same pattern as the villagers are. However, it is also clear that agriculture, especially among males, is still the primary occupation of the farm population.

DISCUSSION TOPICS

1. Conduct a class debate on the question, "Resolved, that corporation farming will benefit American agriculture and rural life."
2. What changes in farm practice have taken place in your home community within the last generation? How were these changes brought about? Were they part of any well-defined social movement, local or national? Were they related to changes in transportation facilities, or to the growth of cities?
3. Trace the changes in the average size of farms in your county or state since 1910 and explain the changes.
4. Explain the divergencies in average income per farm between the six highest and the six lowest states. Are these differences "natural"? Defend your opinion.
5. Report on the procedures and results of some soil-conservation measures in a district known to you.

REFERENCE READINGS

Brunner, E. de S., and J. H. Kolb, *Recent Social Trends*. New York: McGraw-Hill, 1933.

Brunner, E. de S., and Irving Lorge, *Rural Trends in Depression Years*. New York: Columbia University Press, 1937.

Chase, S., *Rich Land Poor Land*. New York: McGraw-Hill, 1936.

Dowell, A. A., and O. B. Jesness, *The American Farmer and the Export Market*, chaps. I, II, VI, VIII, XI, XII, XIII, XVII. Minneapolis: University of Minnesota Press, 1934.

Dummeier, E. F., and R. B. Heflebower, *Economics with Applications to Agriculture*. New York: McGraw-Hill, 1934.

Hullinger, Edwin W., *Plowing Through, the Story of the Negro in Agriculture*. New York: William Morrow & Co., 1940.

Johnson, G. W., *Wasted Land*. Chapel Hill: University of North Carolina Press, 1937.

Kuznets, S., *National Income and Capital Formation, 1919-1935*. New York: National Bureau of Economic Research, 1938.

Lord, R., *Behold Our Land.* Boston: Houghton Mifflin Co., 1938.

McWilliams, Carey, *Factories in the Field.* Boston: Little, Brown & Co., 1939.

Martin, P., *Income in Agriculture: 1929-1935.* New York: National Industrial Conference Board, 1936.

Rapier, A., *Preface to Peasantry.* Chapel Hill: University of North Carolina Press, 1936.

Social Problems in Agriculture. Geneva and Washington, D.C.: International Labor Office, 1938.

7

Man and His Land

THUS FAR the discussion has proceeded without mention of the arrangements by which farms of a given size, value and productive power are operated. Land is valuable, of course, only because on it men find shelter and employment, and because from it food and fiber can be raised and minerals extracted. It is the foundation of life. Under everything is the land, but on the land are people, and land has value only in its relation to people. Land, is, of course, owned. To be useful it must be operated, which means labor. Because it is wealth, it can be taxed for certain purposes. For the same reason, it is a capital resource which can be used as security for borrowing money. This very recital indicates the importance both of the social uses of land and social policies with respect to land. Mankind has evolved two major devices by which human beings are associated with specific plots of land from which they can produce needed agricultural commodities. The *owner* possesses his acres, controls them, and is the sole beneficiary of their productivity after his expenses are met. The *tenant* lives upon and cultivates land that belongs to another individual with whom he shares both the proceeds of his toil and usually the responsibility of management.

The hunger for land. There are few races that do not display a desire for land, and the more rural they are the stronger this desire usually is. To the peasant, land represents ultimate security. Agrarian unrest has often developed where the growth of commercialization caused the tillers of the land to lose their complete control of it. Land hunger was an important factor in both the Mexican and the first Russian revolution; and in the former's new constitution, as well as in that of Czechoslovakia, there are provisions making land available to the peasants at the expense of the great estates.

Causes for rise of farm tenancy. The American tradition has always been one of land-ownership, largely because so much land was available for so little money for nearly three centuries after the first settlements on the Atlantic seaboard. Even yet there is no pressure of population on the land such as one observes it in the Orient. The so-called tenancy problem did not present itself in this country until after the Civil War; and when it came it was, of course, directly associated with the declining quantity of good land available for homesteading under federal grant.

But there was at least one other cause for the rise in farm tenancy in the United States. Young men desiring to be farmers and not possessing sufficient capital to buy a farm, at once sought one they could work on shares. Conversely, elderly farmers desiring to retire sought to rent their farms, often to their own sons or nephews. The blood tie, therefore, was prominent in early tenant arrangements, and though its importance decreased, even in 1930 one fifth of the tenants were related to their landlords. This national average was brought down by the South where the proportion is less than one tenth. In the Middle West, Middle Atlantic, and New England states it was nearly one third. There are no data on this point for 1940.

It was the prevalence of the kinship factor in the early development of farm tenancy, along with a few other factors, such as the tenant's desire to be free to climb the agricultural ladder from tenancy to ownership when opportunity offered, that is responsible for the short lease, usually for only one year, which prevails in many sections. It is frequently judged to be socially disadvantageous when the tenant is unrelated to the landlord, since the necessity for an annual renewal of the lease makes for insecurity and removes some of the incentive to conserve the soil and property.

In the matter of farm tenancy, then, three rural sciences meet. To the soil scientist, tenancy has become almost synonymous with "mining" rather than cultivating the land. To the economist, tenancy means the problem of having a farm support more than one family. The sociologist is interested in the effect of tenancy and its arrangements on the tenant and the social life and institutions of his community.

Growth of farm tenancy uneven. The growth of farm tenancy in the United States has been uneven. When first measured by the census in 1880, it was found that one fourth, 25.6 per cent, of the farms were tenant-operated. Ten years later the proportion had risen to 28.4 per cent.

During the closing decade of the nineteenth century began the rapid rise in the price of farm land which lasted for thirty years.

Tenancy also rose apace, among many other reasons because it then took longer for a prospective owner to accumulate capital sufficient to purchase a farm. The proportion of tenant-operated farms increased by more than one fourth, and stood in 1900 at 35.3 per cent of the total.

Many felt that this was an alarming portent in American life. Tenancy was increasing most rapidly in the most prosperous agricultural areas. It was pointed out that owner-operators supported community organizations and that tenants did not. Tenants were found to have a lower standard of living than owners. There were prophecies that the American farmer, like the European, would become a landless peasant.

But with the new century the rate of increase in tenant-operated farms slackened. In 1910, 37 per cent of the farms were so managed; and in 1920, 38.1 per cent. Despite the early years of the agricultural depression, the special agricultural census of 1925 found only a slight increase in tenancy, 38.6 per cent. In 1930, however, the rate had increased to 42.4 per cent. This was a sharper increase within five years than occurred in any ten-year period in the present century. By 1940 the proportion of tenant-operated farms declined slightly to 39.7, practically the 1925 figure.

These national data conceal, especially in the years 1930-40, some very important diverse regional trends. Tenancy has always been higher in the sixteen Southern states than elsewhere because of the high concentration of Negroes and of share-croppers. These states have about one half the nation's farms, but over three fifths of the nation's tenants. Yet in this area, despite the depression of the nineteen-thirties, the rate of tenant-operation declined from 55.5 to 48.2 per cent of all farms. Moreover, in the four most northerly of these sixteen states, tenancy increased or declined slightly and for the group gained 7.1 per cent. The decline in the other twelve states is therefore slightly more than eleven points. In the thirty-two states outside the Southern group, the proportion of tenant-operated farms rose from 28.5 to 29.5. This small rise was the result of an increase in tenancy in about two thirds of these thirty-two states, although changes in some of the states were slight. The most notable increases were in four of the six New England states and in Wisconsin and Michigan, which brought their tenancy percentages nearer the Mid-West average. Tenancy increased in all the Pacific states. Even in the New England and Middle Atlantic states there were substantial increases of tenancy, despite a previous steady decline which had lasted for several decades.

The reverse of tenancy is, of course, ownership, but the statement that 60.3 per cent of the farms of the United States were owner-operated in 1940 again conceals an important difference between white and non-white, mostly Negro, farmers. Of the former, nearly two thirds, 65 per cent, owned all or part of their land in 1940. Of the latter, only 28 per cent were owners. For the Negroes alone the proportion of owner-operated farms was 25.5 per cent, slightly above the 1930 record. There has been little variation in the proportion of non-whites owning farms since 1900 except for the dip to 22.1 per cent in 1930 as a result of the depression.

There is a further difference between the farmers of different color. Non-white farm owner-operators, renting no additional land, have slightly larger acreages than the whites of the same group — 127.5 acres compared to 123.7, but white tenants operate an average of 157.8 acres each, and non-white tenants only 40.6 acres. This trend holds even for the share-croppers, the whites operating an average of 59 acres, the Negroes of 30 acres. Moreover, in the South, full owners who are whites operate an average of 122 acres, but the Negro full owners, 60.4 acres — slightly less than one half as much.

Causes of changes in tenancy, 1930-40. The explanation of these two trends is quite simple. In the thirty-two Northern and Western states many persons who had been owner-operators were forced back into tenancy by foreclosures of mortgages, which was a frequent occurrence during the depression. In a special sample census it was disclosed that one eighth of the tenants interviewed had been owners at one time. In the South, while foreclosures also occurred, the decline in tenancy was largely a result of the displacement of cotton share-croppers thrown out of employment by the reduction of cotton acreage under the Agricultural Adjustment Act, and the introduction of mechanization. The four states, Georgia, Arkansas, Oklahoma, and Texas, in which this mechanism was most generally used, account for almost two thirds of the decline in the number of share-croppers in the South between 1930 and 1940, though these states had less than two fifths of the South's croppers in 1930. The percentage decline in the number of croppers in these states between 1930 and 1940 is as follows:

State	White	Negro
Georgia	— 38.4	— 40.8
Arkansas	— 50.8	— 27.1
Oklahoma	— 76.0	— 77.9
Texas	— 63.8	— 58.9

Those displaced were forced into the lower status of laborers and huge proportions had to depend more than ever on relief.

In 170 of the most important cotton counties in the South, located in eleven states, that contained in 1930 more than two fifths of all the South's share-croppers, Frey and Smith [1] found a loss of 18.2 per cent in the number of white and of 7.6 per cent in the number of Negro share-croppers between 1930 and 1935. Two thirds of the decline in the number of white and two fifths of the loss in the number of Negro share-croppers took place in these counties.

It seems clear, therefore, that the trends and causes of the decline in tenancy in the South are rather localized, but the trend will probably spread as crop diversification and the increase in mechanization spread over the South. It is conservatively estimated by the National Research Project [2] that when the mechanical cotton-picker is perfected half a million persons will be displaced within five to ten years.

King Cotton is sick. The troubles of the Southern tenant were not caused by the AAA and the all-purpose tractor. Indeed, several studies in three states show that those *tenants who were retained* were better off under the AAA than they had been before. There has always been high mobility among share-tenants and share-croppers in the South. Forty-four per cent of all Southern tenants had been on the farm where they were enumerated in 1935 for less than a year. Those permanently displaced were the poorer workers, the discontented, restless, and otherwise undesirable persons. There have been periodic crises in cotton for decades. There was growing competition from abroad in India, Egypt, and to some extent in Brazil and later from Russia, long before the AAA. The lot of the plantation owner was not a uniformly happy or prosperous one, as the record of farm foreclosures in the South from 1921 on shows. Ten per cent of the plantation land in the South was in the hands of mortgagees and 25 per cent of individual holdings in 1934 had been acquired since 1929.[3]

The study of over two hundred representative cotton plantations in both 1934 and 1937, directed by Doctor T. J. Woofter, Jr., gives an excellent picture of the complexity of socio-economic problems

[1] Cf. *Rural Sociology,* December, 1936, vol. I, no. 4, pp. 483-515.

[2] Horne, R. L., and E. C. McKibben, *Mechanical Cotton-Picker.* Philadelphia, 1937.

[3] Woofter, T. J., Jr., *Landlord and Tenant on the Cotton Plantation,* chap. V. Washington, D.C.: Works Progress Administration, 1936. See also Holley, W. C., E. Winston, and T. J. Woofter, Jr., *The Plantation South, 1934-1937.* Washington, 1940.

associated with cotton culture, and the land-tenure arrangements associated with that culture. In terms of the nineteen-thirties, both years were relatively good and they compared favorably with 1929. Yet the net income per plantation in these two years was $5689 in 1934 and $7673 in 1937. This income, of course, was the aggregate for both the plantation-owner and his tenants and croppers. The operator took 44 per cent in 1934 and 46 per cent in 1937 of the total net income for the individual plantation, an average of $2528 and $3590 respectively. Allowing for interest on his investment at 6 per cent, which is a conservative estimate of commercial interest rates on agricultural loans in the South, the "salary" for supervision and management of the plantation-owner averaged $635 in 1934 and $1340 in 1937. In contrast, the net income for those years of tenants and share-croppers averaged $263 and $300 respectively. Roughly, one third of this amount each year was in the form of subsistence advances to tide the cropper's family over the winter, and the balance was cash. More than half the landlords had to borrow an average of $2300 for current expenses each crop year, at between 10 and 16 per cent interest, and combined interest on short- and long-term loans almost equaled the landlord's labor income. When the tenant moves before he "makes" the next crop, this advance is lost. Seldom is there a written contract between the landlord and tenant, least of all the cropper, and this opens the way to exploitation and misunderstanding.

The average tenant's home is a two- or three-room shack with a single thickness of rough boards, usually unscreened, and with half or more of the houses without window-panes or watertight roofs. Medical care for these people is all but non-existent, illiteracy rates are high, schools and churches poor. As indicated in the last chapter, there is not much resemblance between such conditions and "the American standard of living." Yet there are over 700,000 share-croppers in the South, almost equally divided between Negroes and whites and over a million cash and share tenants.

Uncle Sam to the rescue. In 1937, Congress set up the Farm Security Administration which among other things was given an appropriation of $10,000,000, rising to $50,000,000 a year in 1940 and thereafter, to finance able and selected tenants in the purchase of farms. Low interest rates and repayment of principal in between twenty and forty years are provided together with some guidance in farm management. This administration was also charged with the care of about 650,000 farm families, rehabilitation clients, whose farm management they are supervising and whose family standards of living their social workers are guiding. The amazing success of this program is discussed in the chapter on social welfare. The tenant-purchase program is akin to comparable programs in several other countries, notably in Ireland, where over a period of some decades the proportion of owner-operators among the total farm population was increased from 3 to 97 per cent.[4]

The Farm Security Administration program for aiding selected tenants to become owners is in the nature of a demonstration rather than an ambitious program to eliminate tenancy among American farmers. Thus far it has reached only about thirty thousand farm families, and is financially assisting over four thousand additional tenants each year. To date, 98 per cent of the payments have been made when due, and only six of the first ten thousand purchase loans have been defaulted. This compares favorably with the general farm credit situation discussed later in this chapter.

Several organizations, notably several insurance companies, have adopted the plan in financing the large number of farms it was necessary for them to acquire by foreclosure during the agricultural depression.

Broader aspects of the problem were attacked by a presidential tenancy committee, reporting in 1937. It planned in some detail for a Farm Security Corporation to assist tenants toward ownership and made suggestions as to the rehabilitation work. Other recommendations were designed to discourage land speculation, to improve lease contracts and landlord-tenant relations, to relieve small homesteads of taxation, to safeguard civil liberties. The need for improved educational and health services was also stressed.

These proposals have not been translated into effective operation; in fact, they have been ignored by Congress save for the important exception of the tenant-purchase program of the Farm Security Administration. But the fundamental fact is that no long-time national policies for agriculture can wholly succeed, whether they relate to prices, soil conservation, or production adjustment, unless some of the basic problems of tenancy are solved. Such policies would be handicapped by a pattern of land tenure that promises little security, and therefore little incentive, for millions of farm families. This condition makes migration from the land inevitable. Certainly some of these youth should migrate, but if the present situation continues, the more able children of tenants will be forced

[4] Cf. Hooker, Elizabeth, *Readjustments of Agricultural Tenure in Ireland.* Chapel Hill: University of North Carolina Press, 1938.

to seek opportunity elsewhere, away from the farm land which needs their vitality.

There is no possibility of expanding the tenant-purchase program to enable eligible tenants to become farm-owners. The cost to the government would run into billions. The answer appears to be not only in the proposals of the Presidential Committee on Farm Tenancy, but also in new legislation that would protect tenants. Such legislation might provide for longer terms for leases, compensate tenants for making improvements to land and buildings, and protect him from undue control in his farm-management program. Such provisions are written into law in a number of countries, notably England, which for over sixty years has had agricultural legislation which is far in advance of that which exists at present in any state in the Union. On the basis of the experience of these other countries, it is safe to claim that such legislation, adjusted to the American situation, would prove a powerful incentive for the tenant to conserve rather than mine the soil, would induce more farmers' sons to remain in agriculture, would result in a more careful selection of tenants by landlords, and would improve the level of the community itself by giving security and therefore stability to the tenant and his family.

Tenants help themselves. One interesting development has been the formation of the Southern Tenant Farms Union which claims thirty-five thousand members. For a while it was associated with the C.I.O. but withdrew. It has asked for wages of one dollar a day for cotton-picking, has sought to prevent flagrant exploitation, has helped tenants to use federal agencies, and has constantly tried to keep the plight of the cropper before the nation. Both whites and Negroes are members. There have been several strikes and in more than one place it has achieved somewhat improved conditions.

In summary. Conditions in regard to tenancy vary greatly among the regions but nearly two thirds of the nation's tenants are in the South. Elsewhere the tenant is usually on the road to ownership or remains a tenant by choice. He often owns some livestock and equipment. His income may compare not unfavorably with the owner's. He is still less secure, moves more often than an owner, and is not so well rooted in the community. But in the sixty years from 1880 to 1940, the United States has seen the number of farms operated by owners decline from three in every four to just over three in every five. In the South, by 1930, owners controlled barely one in every two farms. In the Middle West the proportion of owners to tenants is approximately two to three. In the other regions owners are on four of every five farms or better. In New England, on the other hand, the proportion is more than 90 per cent. The Middle West approximates the national average. The Southern record is, of course, a reflection of the difficulty which the Negro or the "poor white" has in securing land. But 1940 saw 137,000 more owners than in 1930 in this region, an 11 per cent gain.

Factors associated with tenancy. Tenancy is associated with a number of rather definite factors. It is low in new, rich areas, such as the irrigated sections of the Far West. It is low also in areas of poor or, at least, below average fertility, such as much of New England, where it is obviously more difficult for a farm to support more than the operator's family. This factor seems to be true even within states. The fertile limestone counties of Pennsylvania have the highest tenancy ratios in the state. Tenancy in the most fertile fourth of the counties in Illinois, measured by value of crops per acre, is more than half again as high as in the least productive fourth of the counties. Since topography is often associated with soil, it is not surprising to find hilly acres with lower tenancy ratios than level ones.

Tenancy is also associated with some crops more than others. Cotton and tobacco, with their Southern locale, are peculiarly crops cultivated by tenants. In the more specialized products tenancy is lowest. Race is another factor. In some states the proportion of Negro farmers who are tenants is practically 90 per cent. On the other hand, tenancy among foreign-born whites, especially northern Europeans, and of their native-born children, is considerably lower than among native stock. Finally, the tenant is younger than the owner, as would be expected, since the normal procedure up the agricultural ladder is from laborer, to tenant, to owner.[5] Of late years, farm ownership ratios have been rising near cities, though declining elsewhere, which reverses a previous trend.[6]

In 1920, 44 per cent of all farm operators had once been tenants and, outside the South, a large proportion of tenants expected to become owners. The long agricultural depression produced an unmeasured degree of change in the traditional procedure and attitude toward farm ownership. With taxes at a high level, with the

---

[5] For further discussion of factors related to farm tenancy, cf. Goldenweiser, *Farm Tenancy: 1920.* (Washington, D.C.: Government Printing Office, 1926.) On the foreign-born, see also Brunner, *Immigrant Farmers and Their Children* (New York: Institute of Social and Religious Research, 1929), chap. II.

[6] Cf. Brunner and Kolb, *Rural Social Trends,* pp. 135 and 340. New York: McGraw-Hill.

difficulty in borrowing money on farm land, and the even greater difficulty of repaying it with interest out of the low price levels, an increasing number of tenants came definitely to feel that they would be better off to remain tenants.[7] With the better, indeed prosperous times beginning in 1941, there has been a considerable increase in the purchase of farms. The 1945 agricultural census will show a further decline in the proportion of tenant operated farms to perhaps 36 or 37 per cent.

Social effects of tenancy. If tenancy is a function of industrialism and therefore an inevitable phenomenon of the present state of development in the Western world, those who maintain that land-ownership is one of the strongest bulwarks of national safety probably face inevitable defeat. But the United States has in the past placed powerful assistance at the disposal of those who crave their own stake in the land, and it may do so again, not only by advancing credit, but possibly by carrying out some of its embryonic policies for land utilization. Moreover, the increase in the ratio of farm ownership near cities must be considered in any argument on this point, though it may be due to the specialized type of agriculture required near cities.

Whether an unavoidable accompaniment of industrialism or not, areas of high tenancy differ from areas of high ownership in certain respects. The social scientist is interested in these differences, and the conditions they create are frequently problems for the rural educator, social worker, and clergyman.

There have been numerous studies of this point. As the chapter on standards of living shows, tenants are likely to have a somewhat lower standard of living than farm owners, at least as measured by the respective proportions possessing telephones, automobiles, musical instruments, bathtubs, electric lights, furnaces, and other conveniences. In these respects the tenant who is related to the owner of the farm makes a better record than the tenant who has no such tie.

These facts do not necessarily discredit either tenants or tenancy. The tenant is younger than the owner. He has not had an opportunity to acquire all the conveniences of life. He is perhaps trying to save for a first payment on his future farm. Moreover, he is more likely than the owner to have young children.

Effects on community usually adverse. When all allowances are made, however, it is clear that the social consequences of a high

[7] For a case illustration of this, see Brunner and Kolb, *Rural Social Trends,* pp. 327-28. New York: McGraw-Hill, 1933.

proportion of tenant-operated farms in a community are unhappy. Studies by the Institute of Social and Religious Research seem to show that such effects begin to appear when the ratio of tenant- to owner-operated farms exceeds one in five.

Up to this point, for instance, the proportion of tenants belonging to church and social organizations is approximately the same as that of owners similarly connected. Beyond this point, the differences become more pronounced. For example, in Middle-Western counties where 50 per cent or more of the farms are tenant-operated, there are only one third as many tenants as owners listed as active church members. Although these figures may vary with the type of organization, the trend is the same for lodges, farm bureaus, and all important types of social organizations.

An obvious corollary follows. In tenant-dominated communities all types of social organizations tend to be weaker and less progressive than in localities in which owners preponderate. One obvious reason for this lies in the insecurity of the renter's tenure. If he operates under a short-term lease he is not sure how long he will remain in the community. He hesitates to form ties until he feels more certain of permanence. Eventually, perhaps, he habituates himself to living more apart from organized social life than does the owner who, because of his capital investment, is likely to be more securely anchored to the locality and, therefore, more interested in its social life.

Another reason for the less satisfactory condition of social organizations where tenants form a considerable fraction of the population frequently lies in the phenomenon of absentee landlordism. Inevitably absentee landlords become interested chiefly, if not exclusively, on the return from the farm. Community betterment, especially if it raises taxes, is definitely unwelcome and hence opposed, as many a schoolman has found out to his sorrow. In times when taxes consume such a large part of the landlord's income, such an attitude is understandable.

The unfortunate social consequences of farm tenancy are especially noticeable in the South, where the problem is also complicated by the large number of share-croppers as already noted. But even elsewhere class distinctions between tenants and owners occur, since the two groups often belong to different churches, lodges, and social organizations.

FARM LABOR

Regardless of tenure status, obviously farms cannot be operated without labor. The great bulk of this labor is supplied by the farm operator himself and the members of his family. Approximately 83 per cent of over six million farms reported a family labor force of just under eight million persons during the last week in March, 1940, and 80 per cent were using 8,100,000 family workers six months earlier. In other words, there were from one and one half to one and two thirds family workers per farm, on the average, at these two periods. The actual number on any given farm was, of course, governed by the acreage and the number of family workers available. There was little variation in the averages according to tenure status except that managed farms greatly exceeded the others. Non-whites, according to tenure status, averaged from one half to two thirds more persons as family workers than whites.

Hired labor subject to many fluctuations. Just under 900,000 farms and just over 1,100,000 reported the use of hired labor at the two periods named. This was 14.6 and 18.2 per cent respectively of all farms. They employed 1,750,000 in the spring of 1940 and 3,120,000 in the fall of 1939. Ducoff, in his *Wages of Agricultural Labor in the United States,*[8] places the extremes of employment at January, July, and October, with 1,600,000 employed in the first month and just twice that number at the time of the summer and fall peaks. The difference is clearly due to the sharp variation in work between the opening of the crop year and its close. Harvesting requires more hands than preparing the soil and planting. This factor of seasonability in farm labor demands is one of the serious problems of agriculture. It came dramatically to the fore during World War II, and necessitated many emergency arrangements.

The census enumeration was, of course, made before war conditions had seriously affected either the demand for workers or their wages. Thus, at the two periods farms employing hired help averaged respectively about two and two eighths hands each.

The nearest approach by the census to a measurement of full-time continuing employees is its count of those who are hired on a monthly wage. At both periods about 500,000 farms had such workers and at both periods they numbered about 740,000 persons. Of these, 77.1 per cent had only one laborer; 14.6 per cent had two; and 7.6 per cent had from three to nine. In terms of the entire year, however, 625,000 farms — 10.3 per cent — employed workers

[8] Bureau of Agricultural Economics, Washington, September, 1944.

on a monthly wage at one time or another through the year. The effect on employment of the season in the crop cycle is shown very clearly in the count of workers employed by the day or week. There were 839,258 of these workers in March, 1940, but 1,560,000 in September, 1939.

The total cash wage bill of American agriculture in 1939 was $782,000,000, distributed as follows:

To workers hired by the month .... 37.5 per cent
To workers hired by the day or week .... 41.5 per cent
To piece and contract workers .... 20.9 per cent

The value of board, room, or other perquisites, such as land for a garden, is not included in these figures. Only 2,260,000 farms, 37.1 per cent, had cash expenditures for labor in 1939. The more favored position of white, as contrasted with non-white operators, is reflected also in average acreages and farm values. This is shown by the fact that 39.8 per cent of the former employed some labor during 1939, but only 16.3 per cent of the latter employed help. The place of the manager-operated farms in the farm labor situation is indicated by the fact that the average manager-operated farm spent $2841 for labor in 1939, while owner- and tenant-operated farms using labor averaged only $309 for wages.

These paragraphs summarizing census findings on farm labor do not show state and regional differences, nor do they reveal the history of many of the confused problems of this phase of rural life. Indeed, many of these problems are relatively new, and have grown out of the advances in agricultural technology in the last three decades. Some have been accentuated by World War II.

Regional differences reflect other social problems. Many regional differences revealed by the census are consistent with what would be expected from other data. Thus, the average number of family workers per farm in the three Southern census divisions is somewhat larger than in the rest of the United States. This is a reflection both of the larger family of the rural South and of an economic situation which has reduced the number of hired hands. The proportion of farms using hired workers and the number employed are obviously related to such factors as size of farm and the type of crops. Thus, about 90 per cent of the farm wage bill in 1939 was paid by the 35 per cent of the farms which totaled a gross production of over $1000. Almost one third of the wages were paid by the one per cent of the farms which had a total production of $10,000 or more.[9]

[9] *Op. cit.*, p. 20.

The regional variations are given in Table 21.

TABLE 21. PERCENTAGE OF FARMS HIRING LABOR AND
REPORTING WAGE EXPENDITURES, UNITED STATES AND
MAJOR GEOGRAPHIC DIVISIONS, FOR SPECIFIED PERIODS

	March 24–30, 1940		Sept. 24–30, 1939		Percentage of Farms Reporting Expenditures for Hired Labor During 1939
	Per cent of Farms Reporting Hired Workers	Average Number of Hired Workers per Farm Reporting	Per cent of Farms Reporting Hired Workers	Average Number of Hired Workers per Farm Reporting	
United States..........	14.6	1.96	18.2	2.81	37.1
New England..........	20.1	2.05	24.8	3.05	39.1
Middle Atlantic.......	21.9	1.80	28.3	2.53	43.2
East North Central....	15.5	1.46	20.5	1.77	38.9
West North Central....	13.5	1.45	17.6	1.91	42.1
South Atlantic.........	17.2	2.29	19.5	2.83	35.7
East South Central.....	9.9	1.96	11.5	2.79	23.0
West South Central....	12.6	2.34	15.4	4.39	35.8
Mountain.............	16.0	2.30	22.2	3.43	47.9
Pacific...............	18.3	2.94	22.2	5.10	53.8

Source: *Census of Agriculture*, 1940.

Types of farm labor. There are several clearly defined types of farm laborers. Traditionally, the "hired man" was a year-round employee, living and eating with his employer's family, and often the son of a neighboring farmer. This type of worker is still found, especially in the Northeast and North Central regions and on dairy farms. There are also the seasonal workers employed at periods of peak load, such as harvest time. Some of these workers originate in the trade centers of the immediate area of need. Some come from near-by cities. There are many examples of informal social patterns developing over the years through provision for this farm-labor need.

Industries in a number of smaller cities in the Northeast arrange their production schedules or inventory periods in order to release employees for farm labor when crops mature. The same people often return to the same farm year after year under such arrangements. Other seasonal workers travel longer distances, and some make a practice of following a crop from South to North as it matures. Under such conditions there is no personal acquaintance between the farm operator and his worker. Living conditions are often extremely unsatisfactory. Finally, there are the employees of the larger farms, sometimes corporation owned, who labor under conditions aptly described by Carey McWilliams as "factories in the field."

Farm wage rates low. Wages of farm laborers, whether paid by the month, week, day, or on a piece-work basis, have almost always been low compared to industrial pay, even when the value of board and room available to some workers is included. Between 1910 and 1914 the average wage of a farm hand was about $22 a month with board, or $29 without, the day rates being $1.16 and $1.42 respectively. There were pronounced differences in wages among the regions, even in the war year 1943, as Table 22 shows.

TABLE 22. ANNUAL AVERAGE FARM WAGE RATES, UNITED STATES AND MAJOR GEOGRAPHIC DIVISIONS, 1943

Area	Per Month		Per Day	
	With Board	Without Board	With Board	Without Board
United States......................	$61.91	$72.85	$2.87	$3.27
New England......................	69.54	103.65	3.55	4.56
Middle Atlantic....................	60.09	89.81	3.34	4.26
East North Central................	58.25	79.25	3.24	4.04
West North Central...............	66.25	85.75	3.63	4.56
South Atlantic................\.....	31.91	45.36	1.72	2.20
East South Central................	30.61	42.16	1.58	2.02
West South Central...............	42.75	58.70	2.27	2.74
Mountain.........................	80.14	107.57	3.86	4.77
Pacific...........................	112.89	148.10	5.23	6.57

Source: Ducoff, Louis J., *Wages of Agricultural Labor in the United States.* Washington, D.C.: Bureau of Agricultural Economics, United States Department of Agriculture, September, 1944.

In terms of 1939 the average annual cash wage per worker, as derived by Ducoff from 1940 census data, amounted to $329, with a range from $152 in the East South Central states to $659 in the Pacific. It must be remembered that many of these workers were also part-time farmers, and the figure given does not necessarily include the total income per worker or per family.

For migrant workers, however, the situation has been very difficult. Apart from the social problems obviously related to the low wages of farm labor, the chief concerns relate to the large numbers of migrant laborers. There are thousands of families whose labor makes possible the harvesting of fruit, vegetables, hops and other crops, who travel from locality to locality and are employed for periods of from several weeks to several months and then dismissed. Their total employment averages only six months a year. They live in camps often under unsanitary conditions. They have no connections with organized community life. The schooling of their children is at best seriously interrupted. Lack of medical care menaces the community as well as the migrants. They are welcome nowhere after their short-time jobs are over. The group is composed of predominantly native white Americans largely between the ages of twenty-one and forty-five years. The migration of these workers from place to place is largely unguided or illy directed. Earnings though difficult to determine average about three hundred dollars a year for single men and four hundred dollars for families. Public relief, dependent upon legal settlement as it is in most communities, is therefore not available. The problem is most acute on the Pacific Coast and in a few of the Eastern seaboard states.[10]

The whole situation, covering the years during which the Department of Agriculture has gathered data, is summarized in Table 23.

It is apparent that the farm wage rates do not fall as rapidly in a depression as net farm income does, but it is equally clear that they do not rise as rapidly as the income of the farm operator increases when times improve. Between 1939 and 1943, cash farm income gained 144 per cent, but composite monthly farm wages went up only 114 per cent. The span was greatest in the South Atlantic and East South Central states. Wages rose 108 per cent in the former region, but cash farm income rose 220 per cent; in the East South Central region the wages rose 91 per cent, and cash farm income rose 157 per cent. In the majority of the other regions, except the West North Central, the two rates were more nearly equal, the differences ranging from six points in two census divisions to seventeen in two others. In the Middle Atlantic states the increase in wages was slightly more than the gain in income.[11]

Ducoff presents another measurement of the relation of wage rates to the net returns of all labor from farming, or of wage rates on hourly basis, related to the operator and his family when they are the farm's total labor force. This comparison, given in Table 24, shows clearly the effect of wartime prices on total labor returns,

[10] Cf. *Migration of Workers*. Washington, D.C.: United States Department of Labor, 1938, mimeographed, especially vol. I, chaps. IX, X, XIV, XV, and XVI. Also an excellent summary of the whole situation in *Fortune* for April, 1939.

[11] *Op. cit.*, pp. 84-87.

TABLE 23. COMPOSITE FARM WAGE RATES, UNITED STATES
AND MAJOR GEOGRAPHIC DIVISIONS, 1910–39 PERIOD
AND 1943 *

Area	Composite Farm Wage Rate, 1943		Composite Monthly Farm Wage Rate, Average 1910–39	Highest Average Composite Wage Rate During 1910–39†		Lowest Average Composite Wage Rate During 1910–39‡	
	Per Month	Percentage of 1910–39 Average		Per Month	Percentage of 1910–39 Average	Per Month	Percentage of 1910–39 Average
United States.......	$65.45	189.6	$34.52	$59.88	173.5	$21.10	61.1
New England......	88.00	180.8	48.68	69.80	143.4	29.40	60.4
Middle Atlantic....	74.23	177.0	41.94	64.60	154.0	26.40	62.9
East North Central.	68.30	181.9	37.54	62.70	167.0	20.80	55.4
West North Central.	72.90	196.2	37.16	70.20	188.9	19.20	51.7
South Atlantic......	40.10	159.2	25.19	44.60	177.1	15.40	61.1
East South Central .	37.80	159.3	23.73	43.10	181.6	13.90	58.6
West South Central.	52.70	183.4	28.74	55.40	192.8	17.40	60.5
Mountain..........	84.50	197.5	42.79	73.90	172.7	25.80	60.3
Pacific.............	126.50	233.0	54.28	87.70	161.6	34.90	64.3

* The composite rate is the weighted average monthly wage of the rates per month and the rates per day converted to a monthly equivalent.
† Relates to the 12-month average of 1920.
‡ Relates to the 12-month average of 1933 except in the New England and Middle Atlantic divisions, where the lowest rate was in 1910.
Source: Ducoff, Louis J., *Wages of Agricultural Labor in the United States.* Washington, D.C.: Bureau of Agricultural Economics, United States Department of Agriculture, September, 1944.

and the lag in hired labor wages. It shows also that in a more normal year, 1939, the two rates are quite close. Indeed, in three of the eleven types of farming that Ducoff selected for this comparison, hired farm labor was compensated at a higher hourly rate than all farm labor, including the operators. This throws some light on the low wages consistently available to hired farm labor.

Many factors affect farm labor wages. The income of employing farmers, as indicated, is one of the factors determining the wages paid to hired help. The level of non-agricultural wages is another directive. Although many rural residents prefer the country to the city, they will go cityward when enough inducement is offered. This is one of the explanations of the extreme farm labor shortages in some areas during World War II, and is the reason why farm wages rose most where there was the greatest competition for workers. However, in terms of relationship trends, the wartime rise

TABLE 24. FARM WAGE RATES AND NET RETURNS FROM FARMING TO ALL LABOR,* SELECTED TYPES OF FARMS, 1942 AND 1939

Area and Type of Farm	1942		1939	
	Returns to All Labor per Hour (cents)	Wage Rate per Hour† (cents)	Returns to All Labor per Hour (cents)	Wage Rate per Hour† (cents)
Winter wheat — wheat........	165	37	40	21
Winter wheat — wheat, grain-sorghum...................	129	30	45	17
Corn Belt — cash-grain........	102	32	42	21
Winter wheat — wheat, corn....	74	36	05‡	20
Dairy — New York dairy......	48	37	24	23
Dairy — Wisconsin dairy.......	47	32	22	20
Corn Belt — hog-dairy........	45	31	19	21
Corn Belt — hog-beef-raising ...	43	30	14	20
Cotton — Mississippi Delta.....	40	13	20	10
Cotton — 2-mule Georgia......	24	12	10	9
Cotton — Black Waxy Texas...	26	19	14	13

* Net farm income after deducting all production expenses except wages to hired farm labor, and after allowing a return on capital investment.
† Based on the rate per day without board.
‡ High-risk area; comparatively low yields in 1939.
Source: Ducoff, Louis J., *Wages of Agricultural Labor in the United States.* Washington, D.C.: Bureau of Agricultural Economics, United States Department of Agriculture, September, 1944.

in farm wages in 1943 was still 20 per cent less than if the 1910-14 ratio of farm wage rates to net farm income had obtained, or 25 per cent under the 1924-29 rates. Wages of farm laborers in normal times are held down by the considerable number of under-employed farmers, those whose gross production is less than $1000 a year. The farm population, mainly the youth, which remained on the farms during the nineteen-thirties as a result of the depression also kept wage rates unduly low, since a surplus labor force was created. Also the progress of mechanization has reduced demand below previous levels in some areas.

Farm-labor wages less than industrial. There have been several indications in this section that farm laborers earn less than industrial employees. The comparison needs to be clarified. The operator on the farm performs managerial and skilled labor functions. His hired hand approximates the unskilled or common laborer of industry. The farm laborer is often a casual worker who shuttles back and forth between agricultural work, road-building, or unskilled industrial jobs. The fairest comparison wage rate is therefore on the basis of the unskilled categories. For this reason Ducoff [12] bases his comparison of agricultural and industrial wage rates on common labor engaged in road-building, using hourly rates converted to an eight-hour-day basis. The essence of these comparisons is given in Table 25, in which farm wage rates are expressed as percentages of wages in road-building.

TABLE 25. AVERAGE HOURLY EARNINGS OF FARM WORKERS *
EXPRESSED AS PERCENTAGES OF THE HOURLY EARNINGS OF
COMMON LABOR IN ROAD-BUILDING,† UNITED STATES
AND GEOGRAPHIC DIVISIONS, FOR SPECIFIED PERIODS,
1925–1943

Area	Annual Averages				Five-year Averages		
	1943	1942	1941	1940	1935–39	1930–34	1925–29
United States....	.46	.43	.40	.35	.37	.39	.59
New England....	.51	.58	.57	.52	.56	.60	.71
Middle Atlantic .	.46	.53	.50	.44	.46	.59	.79
East North Central......	.43	.43	.40	.34	.36	.45	.78
West North Central......	.58	.57	.51	.43	.43	.47	.79
South Atlantic...	.38	.36	.39	.41	.40	.46	.67
East South Central......	.36	.37	.34	.31	.35	.41	.62
West South Central......	.51	.46	.39	.33	.36	.41	.65
Mountain.......	.55	.50	.46	.41	.39	.42	.69
Pacific.........	.62	.51	.45	.40	.43	.47	.67

* Obtained by dividing the farm wage rate per day without board by the average length of work day.
† Federal Works Agency, Public Roads Administration.
Source: Ducoff, *op. cit.*, p. 119.

Table 25 shows that farm laborers who earned wages by road-building were paid less in all regions in 1943 than they were in 1925-29. Hourly wages of farm labor increased 110 per cent for the nation as a whole between 1939 and 1943, while there was only a 69 per cent increase for common labor in road-building. This is because of the depressed levels of wages in 1939. If the comparison is made in terms of 1929, farm wages had increased only 45 per cent by 1943, but road-building wages had increased 82 per cent.

Serious social effects of low wages.[13] The last twenty years have

[12] *Op. cit.*, pp. 114-21.
[13] Since the above was written the Bureau of Agricultural Economics of the United States Department of Agriculture has issued a further study prepared

brought an increased realization of the fact that the lot of the farm laborer is not only hard, but that it has resulted in social wastes and problems of real magnitude. This is especially true of migrant and other seasonal workers not employed in their home communities. The farm hand with reasonably steady employment had an average return of $910 in 1941, including perquisites, as compared to $1344 for farm operator families.[14] But other categories of farm labor were not nearly so fortunate. The intensive eleven-county farm-labor survey by T. Vasey and J. C. Folsom for the Farm Security Administration and the Bureau of Agricultural Economics, covering the crop year 1935-36, showed average annual earnings of $226.92 from farm and $34.96 from non-farm work; with $5.75 additional from relief agencies, a total of $267.63. Only one county located in California showed a total average income of over $500; four others ranged from $304.84 to $355.32. The four lowest counties' income per worker were from $126.75 to $191.00.

Employment is intermittent. A crop is harvested and the workers move on, often guided only by rumor as to where the next jobs may be had. Arriving at such a place, the crop may not be ready, and the prospective workers have to wait until it is. They are needed to get the crop in, but are looked at askance by residents. When the work is done, they are expected to move out of the neighborhood as quickly as possible.

Many of the migrants are in family groups. The constant movement interrupts the education of the children. If not employed in the fields, at best they stay briefly in a local school and then must move on with their families. Even in areas where farm labor is more settled and is concerned only with some one crop, the children who work frequently lose two or three weeks at the beginning or end of the school year. Their education is retarded, as a result, which has its obvious cost to society. In one North Carolina county the rural school supervisor discovered that retardation, plus the loss of state aid, which was then paid on the basis of days of pupil attendance, cost the county more than the children earned by their work.[15]

by Louis Ducoff and Margaret Hagood, *Wages and Wage Rates of Hired Farm Workers, United States and Major Regions, March, 1945* (Washington, D.C., October, 1945). This shows relatively slight changes as compared with the data given in the text, though the trend in wages was still upward. Two later studies of 1945 conditions are still to be issued.

[14] *Ibid.*, p. 160.

[15] An unpublished research term paper by Ann Cherry, done at Columbia University, 1929.

Sanitary and housing problems are created by large numbers of people moving into a community for a few weeks in a year. Knowing that their hands will be needed but a short time, farmers do not bother with adequate housing. Some farms have no housing provision at all, and squatters' camps result. Paul S. Taylor's *Survey of Migratory Labor Problems in California* is one long indictment of conditions. He says:

> Migrants are homeless and are at the mercy of whatever quarters may be available. In the increase of squatters' camps by the roadside, in the creek bottoms, or "no man's land," depression has dealt them a heavy blow. The California Division of Immigration and Housing describes these social pockmarks: "Groups of persons arrive at any given community and start a camp. No provision is made for sanitation, water supply, or even general camp cleanliness. Such housing accommodations as they may have is eked out by wood, tin, or such cast-off material as can be obtained in the vicinity. A sorry picture is presented of a condition that threatens to be a serious menace to those communities where squatter camps exist."
>
> At a Sacramento Valley squatters' camp there were only two privies, both filthy, for 500 people, and the water supply was contaminated. At a camp in Kern County, water was obtained only from the nearest service station, at five cents a bucket. The United States Special Commission on Agricultural Labor Disturbances in Imperial Valley in its report dated February 11, 1934, stated: "Living and sanitary conditions are a serious and irritating factor in the unrest we found in the Imperial Valley. . . . This report must state that we found filth, squalor, an entire absence of sanitation, and a crowding of human beings into totally inadequate tents or crude structures built of boards, weeds and anything that was found at hand to give a pitiful semblance of a home at its worst. Words cannot describe some of the conditions we saw. During the warm weather, when the temperature rises considerably above 100 degrees, the flies and insects become a pest, the children are fretful, the attitude of some of the parents can be imagined, and innumerable inconveniences add to the general discomfort. In this environment there is bred a social sullenness that is to be deplored, but which can be understood by those who have viewed the scenes that violate all the recognized standards of living. . . ." [16]

In addition to these problems, the unsanitary conditions often produce dysentery. Usually there are no medical facilities avail-

---

[16] Quoted from a synopsis of the study issued by the Resettlement Administration. Cf. also Taylor, Paul S., "Migratory Farm Labor in the United States," *Monthly Labor Review,* March, 1937.

able, nor have these ill-paid workers money to pay for doctors. They resort to home remedies. Working in the fields often causes permanent injury to the immature physique of the children, adding to the high cost to society of migratory labor.

Remedial measures few. These conditions have disturbed observers who are aware of their implications. Certain church missionary organizations have tried for years to bring spiritual, recreational, and health services to migrant workers. Growers have learned to appreciate these efforts and to co-operate, but the total amount of such work done in relation to the need has been small. On the Pacific Coast the Farm Security Administration has had an extensive program. It has included both portable and permanent camps for housing workers, with very low rental charges. Some health service has been given, and in some camps there have been recreational and even educational programs.

Labor unions have attempted organization. With the necessity farmers have for extra help at the moment a crop is ready for harvesting, and the risk of losing the crop if it is not gathered in time, one might imagine that the strike would be a potent weapon for improving conditions. However, the workers are so close to the danger line of starvation that they have no margin to tide them over even a short strike, and in the nineteen-thirties the available labor supply almost always exceeded the demand. The Bureau of Labor Statistics does have a record of 216 strikes in the nineteen-thirties, 35 of them in 1933, when 34,012 workers were involved and over 500,000 man-days were lost. About half as many days were lost in 1934 during 27 strikes and in 1936 during 28 strikes.

The two labor unions, the A.F. of L. and the C.I.O., have not been successful in their efforts to organize farm laborers. The reasons, apart from the one already given, are not far to seek. The "hired-hand" type of worker regards himself as on the first rung of the agricultural ladder, and is not interested. There has been great heterogeneity in language, color, and race among workers on many corporation farms. Labor-union dues were high for agricultural workers. Urban labor-union members have had little actual interest in rural wage-earners. Traditional labor-union techniques, designed for dealing with skilled, immobile, industrial workers, were not applicable to unskilled, highly mobile rural laborers. Nevertheless, some steps in this direction have been taken. One study made in the late nineteen-thirties found ninety-eight local agricultural worker unions; fifty-four of them, including most of the larger ones, were affiliated with the American Federation of Labor. Southern Tenant Farmers' Unions were organized in Alabama in 1931, and in Arkansas in 1934. These were aided financially and otherwise by sympathetic outsiders, and did gain some improvements in the lot of the share-croppers.

In July, 1937, the United Cannery, Agricultural, Packing and Allied Workers of America (U.C.A.P.A.W.A.) was formed and affiliated with the CIO. The Southern Tenant Farmers' Union was part of this group for two years. But the inclusion of all types of agricultural workers, with all fruit, fish, and vegetable canning and packing, all horticultural, and all workers in allied fields, was a confused attempt to combine groups with widely diverse, and sometimes even opposed, interests. The large majority of U.C.A.P.A.W.A.'s membership is in non-agricultural occupations. It made some progress among the migratory workers in California and the sugar-beet workers, but at the end of 1940, only 71 of its 168 largest locals composed of farm workers, were in good standing. On the other hand, 68 of the 77 non-farm locals were in good status. In three years of work, U.C.A.P.A.W.A. had spent three times as much on its farm locals as it received.[17]

The war improved conditions. It is obvious from the preceding discussion that the war has improved both the stated and the actual wages of farm laborers. Farmers and communities have also found that they had to improve living and working conditions in order to attract workers. Farm laborers were imported from Mexico, Newfoundland, Jamaica, and the Bahamas, and the governments of these countries and British colonies required wage, living, and health conditions that met adequate standards. Interestingly enough, Congress stipulated in the Farm Labor Act of 1942 that federal agencies could not apply such standards where American workers only were concerned, and in some instances Victory Farm volunteers from high schools, and other urban workers who offered to help in the emergency, labored under conditions worse than those of the imported foreign farm hands. Generally, however, the war has considerably improved the situation.

Improved farm-labor policies formulated. Out of this war experience and the studies of the nineteen-thirties has come a consensus as to an improved farm-labor policy. The importance of adopting definitive and improved practices for the farm-labor force is clear

[17] Cf. Schwartz, Harry, "Organizational Problems of Agricultural Labor Unions and Recent Developments Among Farm Labor Unions," *Journal of Farm Economics*, May and November, 1941. Also his *Seasonal Farm Labor in the United States* (forthcoming), New York, Columbia University Press, 1945. Much of the material for this section has been drawn from Doctor Schwartz's studies.

from the foregoing. At least part of each year four million people work for wages on our farms. Twice that number depend wholly or in part upon the wages paid for this work. Because the bulk of these workers is concentrated on the larger farms, one fourth to one third of our total farm production is dependent upon them. The record of the twentieth century up to the World War II is one of exploitation and neglect, and the result is a serious social cost.

The first step to betterment of conditions is to remove the legal discrimination against farm laborers. At present they are excluded from the benefits of the Social Security Act, which means no unemployment insurance and no old-age pensions for them. They have no protection under the wage and hour legislation, except employees of growers who receive benefits from the government under the Sugar Act. The existing wage and hour legislation, as it stands, would be difficult to apply to farm labor, but the experience of other countries shows that such laws can be adapted to agricultural conditions. The very fact that the bulk of the farm laborers are concentrated on relatively few farms should make such adaptation possible.

During World War II great strides were made in the efficiency with which seasonal and migratory farm laborers were placed. Lost time while waiting for crops to mature was reduced to a minimum by a system of reports to a central headquarters on the maturation of crops, and the number of workers needed for harvesting. Farmers learned to co-operate with federal agencies in this system. While a new Farm Labor division has been set up in the Extension Service to facilitate this work, in most states there has been effective co-operation with the United States Employment Service. This service in turn has learned a great deal about the peculiar problems of agriculture.

Adequate living and housing and safe health conditions must be provided. In California and a few other states there has been inspection and supervision of farm labor camps, and an effort made to enforce certain minimum standards. The experience with foreign workers during the war has been valuable. Such programs need to be perfected and applied to all groups of migrant farm workers.

What can be permanently accomplished is dependent upon what happens to farm income in the postwar period. But American agriculture must recognize the fact that to gain parity with industry its wage hands must have parity with industrial workers. Otherwise agriculture will have hidden profits against which society sooner or later will rebel.

8

Man and His Land (continued)

THE PREVIOUS CHAPTER has discussed the arrangements under which a man can operate land for agricultural purposes and the situation of those whom he employs to assist him. This chapter turns to the burden that both the man and his land carry in securing the necessary capital to operate the farm and in meeting financial obligations to society. Finally, the facts are centered in a discussion of the social uses of land.

TAXATION

Mention has already been made of the recent growth of a feeling among tenants that, despite its handicaps, under certain conditions the position of the tenant operator is more secure, economically speaking, than that of the owner. One of the most important reasons for this attitude lies in the matter of taxation.

Taxation is almost the oldest device by which society pays for its collective activities. For centuries, land as the basic source of wealth has had to bear the burden of supporting those enterprises which society has decided to conduct. The tax base and the income derived from it, therefore, influences directly the support and scope of various social utilities such as education, public health, welfare, and also fire and police protection, road-building and upkeep, and many other essentials of modern living. As such, taxation has sociological importance, although it is primarily an economic subject.

The rise in taxes. Rural America spent generously of its income in the nineteen-tens and early nineteen-twenties for improved schools, roads and other social services, and through bond issues by local municipalities and counties mortgaged its future profits as well. As a result taxes mounted rapidly, almost doubling between

1917 and 1930.[1] Since then there has been a decline, but taxes are still above the 1914 level. With the decline in commodity prices, increased taxation meant that it took more bushels of wheat or corn, more bales of cotton, more quarts of milk to pay a dollar's worth of taxes; in fact, several estimates for 1930 and 1931 concluded that between one third and two fifths of the net income of the average farm was absorbed by taxation. With the coming of World War II this situation improved markedly. This rise in farm income, however, together with lowered exemptions, has introduced the farmer to the federal income tax. In 1940, only 5 per cent of our farmers were liable for these taxes and paid but $15,000,000. In 1943 over 18 per cent paid $375,000,000.[2]

The farm share of the tax dollar. Even before the nineteen-thirties the National Industrial Conference Board of New York City estimated that the farmer was paying one fifth of the tax bill of the nation, in spite of the fact that his share of national income was only one tenth. About a score of the colleges of agriculture have made taxation studies in the last two decades.[3] It has been found, for instance, that in 1928 in Indiana farm taxes absorbed two fifths and the city taxes one fifth of the rent. In Michigan between 1919 and 1925, even if the so-called upper peninsula is excluded, farm taxes took 52 per cent of the net income of the average farm. In Pennsylvania, the farmers spent a 13 per cent larger share of their earnings for taxes than did the state as a whole, including the farmers.

Taxation is, therefore, a practical problem for the school superintendent, the librarian, or social worker, all of whom are concerned with the task of keeping such social utilities at maximum efficiency. Studies by the Institute of Social and Religious Research have revealed numerous instances where the enthusiasm for a new school building, community house, or other public building has resulted in

[1] In terms of index numbers the rise in farm taxation, using certain significant years, is as follows:

1913	100	1929	281
1917	129	1932	220
1918	137	1934	178
1919	172	1937	187
1920	244	1940	183
1921	259	1943	178
1925	270	1944	184

Source: Bureau of Agricultural Economics, Washington, D.C.

[2] *Agricultural Finance Review*, vol. 6, November, 1943.

[3] For a summary of fifteen of these studies, cf. *Taxation of Farm Property*, by Whitney Coombs. Washington, D.C.: United States Department of Agriculture, Technical Bulletin 172, February, 1930.

saddling the community with so large a debt that all other social improvements had to be postponed indefinitely.

Taxes: How much and what for. During the "parity" years, 1909-14, taxes on farm real estate averaged $184,315,000, and including personal property taxes totaled nearly $213,000,000. By 1924, the taxes on real estate had passed $500,000,000 and personal property added $63,000,000 more. The peak was reached in 1929, when the total levied from these two items exceeded $640,000,000, 9.7 per cent of the net farm income before taxes. The next five years saw a steady decline of almost one third, with only slight fluctuations since. The 1942 total was $440,000,000. However, in the meantime, motor fuel taxes, both state and federal, and licenses and permits of various kinds were increasing. The Department of Agriculture estimates that the farmers' total tax bill in 1942 was $614,000,000, or 6.6 per cent of net income before taxes. Tax levies on farm real estate, to use another measure, which took the twenty years from 1890 to 1910 to go from 13 cents to 19 cents an acre, went to 51 cents in the following decade. The peak by this measurement was 58 cents in 1928. Measured by taxes per $100 of value, the increase has been from 47 cents in 1910 to $1.54 in 1932, which was the peak, and now in 1945 stands at $1 per $100 of value. Regional and state differences are considerable. In Massachusetts taxes per acre in 1942 were $2.68. In four of the Rocky Mountain states they were less than 10 cents. There is far less difference in taxes per $100 of value, the spread between high and low regions being less than threefold.

Combining state and local revenues, property accounted for 54.1 per cent of the taxes raised in 1938; motor, fuel, and vehicle taxes for 13.5 per cent; sales and all excise taxes for 15.4 per cent; and state income taxes for 6.4 per cent. More than one fifth of this money was spent for education, about one seventh each for roads or streets and debt service, one eleventh for welfare, more than one twentieth each for protection and health.[4] In normal communities, of course, education is the major item of expense.

It is obvious that in many areas, in relation to income, farm taxes have been high.

Results of high taxation. High taxes were, in many cases, responsible for the actual loss of farms. In a rural county in North Carolina, part of which was surveyed in 1924 and again in 1930, the property of 58 persons was advertised for tax sale in 1915, the total amount due being less than $500. In 1925, 800 persons were

[4] Washington, D.C.: United States Department of Agriculture, *State and Local Government Finances in War Time*, 1942.

similarly involved, and in 1929 about 1400 who owed $52,630, or an average of $37.60 each, allowed their property to go to tax sale. In this case, and in many others uncovered in the investigation, much of the property attracted no bidders and reverted to the local government.

The Bureau of Agricultural Economics of the United States Department of Agriculture estimates that between March 15, 1925, and March 15, 1931, 109 of every 1000 farms in Montana were sold for taxes. In North Dakota, the number per thousand was 86; in South Dakota, 66; Virginia, 70; Kansas, 17. Nationally, the proportion, 1926-35, was 78.7 farms per 1000. In 1936, with the improvement in farm net income, this rate began to decline and except for one year has steadily dropped. Only 3.3 farms in every 1000 suffered tax sale in 1940. In 1944 the rate was 1.8. Even so, the situation was not normal in some states. The rate in Oklahoma, Maine, Montana, and South Dakota ranged from 5.8 to 7.6, and in North Dakota it was 12.7.

What this means in specific areas has been shown by a number of studies. In 17 counties in northern Wisconsin, said by the United States Department of Agriculture to be "illustrative of a widespread tendency in many parts of the United States," nearly one third of the land in one county was sold at tax sale in the single year 1927, more than 30 per cent in three others, and 20 per cent or more in twelve. In all, 2,600,000 acres were disposed of, 73 per cent of which had to be bought by the counties under a law that provided that tax certificates not otherwise purchased must be acquired by the county.

One of these counties was studied in 1921 and again in 1930 in the present investigation. In the first year the county was enthusiastically battling the stumps left by the lumbering interests. Settlers were pouring in, many of them foreign-born. Everything pointed to the development of a stable and reasonably prosperous agricultural county within a few years. In 1927 more than one fourth of the area of this county was put up at tax sales. In 1930 only 5 per cent of the land was in crops, 8 per cent in lumber, and the rest, except for village sites, railroad rights-of-way and the like, was idle. Emphasis is laid upon this situation because it indicates the necessity of wise handling of the entire tax structure. Only in recent years in the last quarter-century, prices of farm products have been at or above so-called parity. A decline of any magnitude would cause a recurrence of many difficulties.

The effect of such a situation on social institutions, schools and churches, and even on the local government, is, of course, adverse. Tax revenue obviously declines and tax-supported activities suffer. Furthermore, where huge acreages have become tax delinquent, serious problems of public policy are involved. Should delinquent land be allowed to remain idle, and produce inferior species of trees? Should it be reforested, and if so, by what agency? Should still other farmers be allowed to occupy land that has failed to produce even its taxes? What policies should be adopted to maintain roads and schools for farmers who are still struggling on here and there, surrounded by large areas which no one wants and where no one lives? [5]

Taxation problems deeply rooted. Recent taxation problems are not the product of the agricultural depression alone. The roots lie deeper, and one of the longest and most tenacious of these roots is the so-called general property tax. The bulk of the income for local and county government is raised by a tax assessed on the value of land and buildings. This tax is very ancient and was devised and worked well when the world was largely agricultural. It was not onerous when the nation was 90 per cent rural. But as wealth came to be more and more a matter of stocks, bonds, savings accounts, and other forms of less tangible and readily concealable property, non-concealable assets like land and buildings began to bear an increasingly disproportionate share of the tax burden. Moreover, the property tax cannot be shifted to the consumer as can taxes on coal, gas, long-distance telephone calls, and the like.[6] The retention of the present general property tax on the present basis long after the conditions that called it forth have changed is an interesting if not irritating example of the well-known lag between changing conditions and entrenched or traditional social practices.

Assessors inexpert. Further difficulty lies in the fact that the property tax is inexpertly assessed by local officials who have had little or no training, and the result, naturally enough, is great variations and irregularities. Differences of over 100 per cent in per acre assessed valuations on nearly identical farms lying within the same township are not unusual. Every study has shown a tendency for the assessment on small properties to represent a higher proportion of full value than on large ones. Similarly, the poorer the land, the higher the ratio of assessed to true value. In poor land areas the

[5] Wisconsin now has a law permitting counties to exchange county-held land for privately owned land if such action will result in more advantageous location of isolated farm families.

[6] In some states the problem is further complicated by assessing an added sum based on the potential value of possible sub-soil minerals.

reason for this is obvious. Government services are becoming increasingly standardized, at least, as to minimum requirements, and it costs more per family and in proportion to wealth to support them in a poor county than in a rich one. As we shall see later, the same problem confronts the church.

Expanded functions need more money. That the Government requires larger funds for operation now than a generation ago is obvious. School enrollments are much higher, their terms are longer, and children stay in school for a greater number of years. Better qualified teachers have been demanded and secured. All public services, including government services, cost more when population density is low. As the country is now organized, a multiplicity of units and small-scale operation is required. This multiplicity, a legacy from the period of pioneer agriculture and relative isolation, creates by itself a huge problem as will be seen elsewhere.

State aid. Because of these and other aspects of the situation, there has arisen a demand for the support of a number of social utilities on a state-wide or federal basis. Roads are now recognized as a state and national obligation. Increasingly, states rather than the counties, have assumed responsibility for bridges. But children are also a national asset and there is an increasing demand for the state to assume a larger share of educational costs. In Delaware and North Carolina there are now state-wide systems of education with little or no local support. There is state aid for schools in a majority of the other states and state aid in a few for libraries. Policies like this have resulted in the decline in the total amount of taxes levied against farm real estate.

The reason for this trend, which is discussed further in relation to education, in another chapter, is made apparent by a typical case in a West North Central state. The poorest fifth of its counties had less than $6000 of assessed value for each child of school age. The least wealthy of the top seventh of its counties had more than $12,000.[7] Obviously, equality of educational opportunity is hardly possible if the costs are to be assessed against the smaller government units. Some sort of aid from without must be provided. We are assuming, of course, that equality of educational opportunity is a function of a democracy, and that the poorer areas needing help justify such aid both economically and socially, an assumption which raises questions about the social uses of land. This point will be discussed later.

[7] Figures for 1928-29.

As the nineteen-thirties proceeded, rural communities, like urban, began organized campaigns for lower taxes. Taxpayer leagues frequently secured drastic reductions. It is symptomatic of human behavior in such situations that the bulk of such effort was directed toward securing reductions by dispensing with services and reducing salaries. Little or no effort was made to secure economy through greater efficiency, such as the consolidation of offices and of small, adjacent municipalities. Nor was much attention paid to introducing strict budgeting and accounting, to strengthening the weaknesses in the assessment and the collection of property tax. Tax pronouncements by the national farm organizations have dealt largely with the federal and state aspects of taxation.

FARM CREDIT IN THE UNITED STATES

The wealth represented in land is not only the basis for raising the tax monies which society needs to carry on its business. It is also the basis or security by which the landowner can obtain borrowed money for capital expenditures. Furnishing the farmer with both long- and short-term credit has long been a major problem in the rural world. The cost of credit has become a primary concern of those who are seeking to raise the farmer's standard of living in all lands. In Korea, for instance, the average farmer pays from 30 to 36 per cent per annum for the money he must borrow. In China the ratios are about the same. In India the situation is even worse, rates of from 60 to 300 per cent being not unusual, although above average.

What this means can be shown from a few illustrations drawn from one country. In a group of 4400 families in Tozen, Korea, the average indebtedness was found to approximate the annual gross income per farm. In other communities interest about equaled the total expense of farm operation or one eighth of the gross receipts from all income sources per family.[8] Interest rates of 24 to 36 per cent were common and in India they often reached 48 to 60 per cent. The situation in the United States has never been as serious as in the Orient, but it has been, nevertheless, a perennial difficulty. Th farmer felt that the banking system and credit machinery of the United States has never, since the days of Alexander Hamilton, taken agriculture sufficiently into account.

A store or an industry offers not only its property as a security, but, what is more important, its goods and products which can

[8] Cf. Brunner, *Rural Korea*, p. 27 ff. New York and London, 1928.

readily be converted into cash. Many types of farming, on the other hand, such as wheat, corn and hops, and cotton, have no steady source of income throughout the year. Their receipts are concentrated in a short period. If payments of interest fall behind, the creditor has only the farm as a security. Because this cannot be sold as readily as store goods, or a corporation bond listed on a stock exchange, it is said, therefore, that farm loans are "non-liquid."

As the nation grew older, however, farmers needed more credit. Free land through homesteading came to an end and, as we have seen, the price of land increased. The prospective farm owner had to borrow. Moreover, as agriculture became mechanized the farmer needed to purchase machinery which was usually so expensive that he could not pay cash for it. Hence the increased need for credit in addition to the perennial necessity of borrowing for current expenses when funds ran low between crops. The need was supplied by mortgage companies, insurance companies, and later by banks. Costs to the farmer frequently ranged from 8 to 12 per cent and there was constant agitation for lower charges.

The Federal Land Banks. Finally, in 1915, over bitter opposition, a federal credit agency was set up called the Federal Land Bank. Its twelve regional banks lent to farmers through local associations of ten or more members. Capital was raised by selling bonds secured by mortgages on the farms of borrowers. The average interest charge was 5.6 per cent. Repayment could be made at the rate of 5 per cent a year. During the nineteen-twenties there was an average of 4600 of these local credit associations with an average unit membership of about 100. The ordinary loan was for a little over $3000.[9] This system is quite generally credited with having equalized and reduced interest rates. It did not, however, eliminate other lenders from the field.

The rise of mortgage indebtedness. The following paragraphs describe in briefest detail the credit situation of the nineteen-thirties, but before examining the changes wrought by the depression it is important to glance at the increase in farm mortgage debt in the United States.

On owner-operated farms it amounted to $1,700,000,000 in 1900, rising to $4,000,000,000 in 1920, to $4,500,000,000 in 1925, the peak,

---

[9] In addition there was a smaller system, the original financing provided by the United States Treasury through the purchase of shares to be redeemed locally, called the Joint Stock Land Bank. Intermediate Credit Banks, designed to loan to farmers' co-operative organizations, were also set up.

and dropped to $3,140,000,000 by 1940. The average indebtedness per farm jumped from about $1700 in 1910, to $3356 in 1920, to $4004 in 1925, and then declined to slightly less than $2700 for full owners and $3329 for part owners in 1940. Although the value of mortgaged owner-operated farms was three times the debt in 1920, it was not much over twice the debt in 1940. A debt of this size is a threat to the stability of rural society as the paragraphs immediately following show. This explains the advice to farmers to use the higher income of the nineteen-forties to reduce debts. Meanwhile, the proportion of mortgaged owner-operated farms increased from 27.3 in 1910, to 42.5 per cent in 1940. If we add the $817,000,000 mortgage debt on the owned portion of partly owned farms, and the debt on mortgaged tenant-operated farms, it is probable that the farm mortgage debt burden of American agriculture is in excess of $5,000,000,000.[10]

Wide regional and state differences. There are wide differences among the states and census divisions in the proportion of farms mortgaged, and in the ratio of debt to value. Every division shows sharp increases in the percentage of mortgaged farms as compared with 1890. Fifty years ago less than 5 per cent of the farms in the East and West South Central divisions and only 7.3 per cent of those in the South Atlantic were mortgaged. The proportions in 1940 were from four to nearly eight times as large. The West North Central states had the largest proportion of mortgaged farms, 54.4 per cent; the South Atlantic division the lowest with 27.9 per cent. One half or more of the farms were encumbered in nineteen states, with North Dakota the highest, reaching two thirds. On the other hand, the percentage of mortgaged farms in twenty states was under 40.

Comparably the ratio of debt to value fluctuated, though not so widely. Again the West North Central division was high, debts averaging 51.3 per cent of total value. In this division were five of the six states in which the owners' equity in his land was less than one half. The three Southern and two far Western divisions were all low, ranging from 35.5 per cent in the Pacific states to 38.8 per cent in the Mountain division.

Depression problems. The steady increase in land values from 1890 to 1920, already alluded to, made it relatively easy for the farmer to borrow since it gave lenders increasing confidence in the

[10] These data from the census do not agree with estimates by the Department of Agriculture, which estimated the total farm mortgage debt as of January, 1943 at $6,350,000,000.

security of such loans. But with the rapid decline which began in 1921 the situation changed. Security was impaired. Many of these loans had been contracted when the dollar had a low purchasing power. As the price of agricultural commodities declined, even though the farmer maintained or expanded his production, it took an increasing proportion of his crops to meet mortgage payments and taxes. Many failed to do so, thus affecting the local country banks which held mortgages, so that in the nineteen-twenties more than 6000 failed, bringing a $2,000,000,000 loss to over 7,000,000 depositors.

Increase of foreclosures. Naturally, foreclosures on farm property increased. Farm bankruptcies, which had been a rarity in the United States in the early nineteen-hundreds, mounted. In the year ending March 15, 1932, 13.3 of every 1000 farms suffered foreclosure, and in the ten years 1926-35 the equivalent of almost 22 per cent of all farms were foreclosed. When the tax sales already noted are added, the seriousness of the situation becomes even clearer. The United States Bureau of Agricultural Economics estimated in 1932 that 7 per cent of all farms were mortgaged at more than their depression values. In Minnesota the College of Agriculture study showed that the average foreclosure sale netted only 4 per cent more than liabilities plus charges. Farms sold by the Federal Land Banks in the winter and spring of 1933-34 failed by a fraction of one per cent to cover the incumbrance. In other words, the debtor was wiped out.

In passing, it may be pointed out that from the financial point of view — that is, that of the security-holder — this is by no means a bad record, hard as it was on the debtor. In these years the bonds of many of America's major corporations were selling at huge discounts. Those of important metropolitan real estate companies upon foreclosure very often involved the creditor in the loss of large proportions of his investment.

It must be remembered that when a farmer loses his farm he also loses his home, that increasing debt and interest payments are taken directly out of money available for family living unless income increased by the same amount and that when agricultural prices fall while payments on interest and principal of debts remain stationary or increase the standard of living falls. In few if any other businesses are economic and social considerations so intimately interwoven as in farming.

The higher farm income of the first half of the nineteen-forties greatly improved the situation. Both long- and short-term debts have been reduced considerably despite the increased sale of farms at the sharply higher prices mentioned earlier. Transfer of farms by foreclosure or bankruptcy proceedings dropped to 12.6 per 1000 farms in 1940, to 4.4 in 1943, and 3.1 in 1944.

Federal action in the emergency. It is not surprising that in many states agrarian unrest increased in 1932 and 1933. In many places there was organized resistance to sales, which were sometimes actually stopped. In other instances, ridiculously low bids were made by neighbors and other bidders were escorted from the sales.[11] Laws were discussed in some states and passed in a few, declaring moratoria on farm-mortgage debt.

To meet this situation Congress reduced the interest rates on the loans in force through the Federal Land Banks, temporarily waived annual payments on the principal of outstanding loans, authorized additional loans, set up machinery for equitably adjusting and refinancing the indebtedness of hard-pressed farmers to save them from foreclosure.

Stabilizing land values. The scaling-down of the farmer's obligation in such cases represents the judgment of the Farm Credit Administration in regard to the *normal* value of the farm. The action of Congress in directing that Federal Land Bank loans be based on normal value has aroused interest. On this point the Land Bank Commissioner stated that the intent was to base valuations on long-time conditions, to be governed neither by the extremely low figures to which the depression has carried the price of land, nor by such inflated valuations as developed in the land boom of 1919-20. It was hoped that this action would introduce a stabilizing factor into the values of farm property. The intent of the law was to retard both deflation and inflation, but on a rising market private lenders, not governed by the legal directive to the Farm Credit Administration, could, and might, again lend freely. Certainly up to this writing the war-induced rise in land values has continued.

It is clear that the liquidation of mortgaged farms due to the depression has ended. In this connection, it is interesting to note that, although government agencies, notably the Farm Credit Administration, held 37.5 per cent of all mortgage loans as of January 1, 1941, foreclosed properties in their possession at that time were only 14.3 per cent of the total number of farms in that category.

---

[11] One such incident has been dramatized in a one-act play, *These Lean Years*, by Fred Eastman. New York: Samuel French, 1934. See also Brunner, E. de S., and Lorge, I., *Rural Trends in Depression Years*, pp. 40-44, for illustrations of resistance to foreclosure sales and off-farm strikes.

Interestingly enough, Australia and New Zealand passed credit legislation closely resembling our own and a number of other countries in both Europe and Asia took legislative measures to assist indebted farmers. This is another evidence of the world-wide character of some rural problems.

This fact may be comforting in that it shows the problems faced by the Uinted States are not due to special inefficiency on the part of our economy. But it is also disquieting both from the point of view of the farmers of the world and because the agricultural economists declare that the long-time world trend is for private credit to break down, for governmental credit and eventually controls to take its place and for the equity of the farmer in his holding to decline. This some believe is a threat to the stability of both economic and democratic institutions.

Who are the debtors? The farm borrowers have certain well-defined characteristics. Part-owners, who operate larger holdings than either owners or tenants, have larger loans and a larger ratio of debt to total value, 47.8 per cent, as against 42.6 per cent for full owners. For both groups of mortgaged owners, the whites have a smaller equity in their farms than non-whites, the difference being three points for full owners and nine for part owners. For those reporting both their ages and mortgage status, the group with the largest proportion of mortgages was that thirty-five to forty-four years of age, representing just less than half. The twenty-five to thirty-four, and the forty-five to fifty-four age groups, in order, had slightly less. These are the years when, traditionally, persons who have risen from the tenant group, or who otherwise are attempting to own a farm, must pay off such indebtedness as has been incurred. Of the farmers sixty-five years and over, 72 per cent were debt-free.

There is one important factor regarding farm debtors about which no data exist save in a few special studies of restricted areas. This factor is the degree, if any, of blood relationship between debtor and creditor. Several small studies found that up to two thirds of the owner-operated farms were acquired within the family group, but of these only from one fourth to one third were unencumbered. As is seen in the sections on population and the family, there are likely to be several heirs when the parents of a farm family die. Often one son who desires to operate the ancestral farm must go into debt to satisfy the claim of brothers and sisters for their share of the inheritance. Presumably intra-family debt, while just as much of a debt as any other, is less hazardous to the debtor, though there is little difference in the proportion of debt for farms between operators purchasing from relatives or from strangers.[12]

Does the land give security? It is clear that the device of credit is a social invention of great importance. Rurally it has been used to help persons toward farm ownership which many Americans believe represents the acme of security. During the depression, when thousands of urban unemployed were fleeing from the cities to what they felt was the security of the land, the very security which land had represented to agrarian people the world over was being undermined. Certain studies, beginning in 1924 — including one by a former chief economist of the Federal Land Bank system, now part of the Farm Credit Administration — have raised doubts as to the ability of the average farmer, under the economic conditions prevailing after World War I and until 1940, to achieve ownership unless his mortgage represented a smaller percentage of the value of his farm than it would represent under usual economic circumstances. But the socio-psychological attachment to the idea that land means security is very strong. It is responsible for the legislation concerning farm credit in our own and other lands. It is also a social justification for that legislation. The laws passed indicate an acceptance by society of the principle that farmers should have credit on terms roughly comparable to those available to other businesses. Furthermore, it is an indication that in time of stress relief measures should be instituted for agriculture comparable to the setting-up of the Reconstruction Finance Corporation which aided banks, insurance companies, railroads, and industries.

SOCIAL USES OF LAND

Most of the matters discussed in this chapter raise fundamental questions of long-time social policy, especially as to the use of available agricultural land resources. Tenure practices too often have resulted in anti-social exploitation of the soil, just as there has been sometimes anti-social exploitation of labor. Comparably the tax system, ideally suited to the period when the great proportion of all wealth was land and the buildings erected upon it, has now become less suited to a period when other and less visible sources of wealth have come to represent the larger share of our national assets.

[12] Leonard A. Salter, Jr., *Land Tenure in Process.* Madison: Agricultural Experiment Station Research Bulletin 146, University of Wisconsin, 1943.

So, too, as already suggested, there have been credit policies which, because of their pressure upon the debtor, have similarly resulted in the abuse of his fundamental asset, the soil. But this asset is also the basic asset of the nation. Except for the Homestead Law, which after the Civil War made the public domain available to settlers under easy terms, the United States had no national land policy for more than forty years. Development was in private hands, and areas have been boomed and settlers have been exploited purely for profit, sometimes in ways which created problems because the land was not adapted to the uses to which its promoters put it.[13] The matter gained urgency during the depression when titles to millions of acres reverted to the government; often when they were put up at tax sales they found no bidders. Increasing attention began to be paid to this problem during the administration of President Hoover. The Roosevelt administration gave it further consideration. Proposals were made for the removal of population from poor land to more fertile areas.

State policies. Prior to this proposal, two states, Wisconsin and New York, had formulated land policies beyond any previously attempted. They recognized that if certain land uses result continually in family poverty, in rural slums, in uneconomic costs for mediocre schools, roads and public services, a public danger or even a social menace is created. In Wisconsin land is being zoned, much as cities are, for particular purposes. Stranded families have been removed to better locations, and the state compensates the counties to some extent for areas converted into state forests.

National policies. During the depression of the nineteen-thirties the federal government made a number of attacks on this problem. Some soil conservation and much soil and forest improvement work was done by the Civilian Conservation Corps. The Resettlement Administration, formerly Subsistence Homesteads, and now the Farm Security Administration, resettled about twenty thousand families, largely from sub-marginal lands, on good soil.

But the problem is far wider than this essentially relief measure. As a result of various programs in soil conservation and land utilization the Department of Agriculture has purchased several million acres of land and has more millions under option. This is sub-marginal land. Some of it is used to help farmers to shift from wheat to stock farming and to prevent over-grazing. Here

[13] Cf. Brunner, *Immigrant Farmers and Their Children* (New York: Institute of Social and Religious Research, 1929), for examples of both good and bad development; cf. especially pp. 31-40 and 138-54.

the aims are agricultural adjustment and soil conservation. Other projects involve building dams for water conservation, reforestation, and the creation of recreational facilities. The lastnamed developments have meant the building of picnic shelters, bathhouses, bathing beaches, fireplaces, parking areas, park roads, docks, and similar facilities. Through construction of dams, several large lakes have been created for the run-off of water and to provide the surrounding population with long-needed recreational facilities. These latter projects have often necessitated the removal of all or part of the population of the surrounding country side.

No longer is all non-industrial and non-residential land conceived of as potential farm land. It is being used increasingly for private and public recreational purposes, as, for example, the national and state parks and the beginnings of county parks. Reforestation, not merely for commercial purposes, but to prevent erosion and for flood control, is another important use of land and one too long neglected in a country which is paying a heavy price for the planless destruction of its timber.[14] The problem of land utilization is enormous, and any public policy concerning it cannot ignore its broader social considerations and values.

The Program Planning Division of the Agricultural Adjustment Administration recognized some of these problems, and in its program looked far into the future, taking into account land use in relation to human welfare, the national needs for food, fiber, wood, water, recreational spaces, population growth, and the maintenance of our standards of living. On the basis of such data, a program is to be proposed which should be carefully studied as it develops, particularly as to its social implications. For there cannot be too much emphasis upon the human aspects in all this program-building. If the land of our nation cannot provide adequate social as well as economic life for rural people, no land policy can succeed. It may even be that these desiderata can be supplied only by an effort to regulate the number of farmers to the needs of the nation and its overseas customers for food and fiber. The great advances in agricultural technology indicate that eventually such questions may be raised. If that be so, then the long-range program of agriculture is but the first of a series of similar efforts. Industrial reorganization becomes involved, including occupational planning. For agriculture and rural life cannot come to full fruition in the national economy independent of all else.

---

[14] In many countries timberland is most carefully guarded. In Japan, for instance, no tree can be cut unless another is planted and not more than 5 per cent of a stand can be cut in any one year.

Such statements go beyond the realm of immediate policy, but it is likely that the questions raised will come to the fore eventually. The concept of regulating the number of farmers to the needs of the nation and the world is no more radical than adjusting the crops raised by farmers to the nation's and the world's needs, a procedure we have tried. Indeed, it is a concept which is even more considerate of the national welfare both in human and economic terms, for it proposes the maximum use of human capacities throughout our increasingly interdependent society. It challenges policies which seek solutions to problems in narrow terms, regardless of the relation of those problems and their proposed specific solutions to related areas of the national economy.

This is also related to problems of population policy. It was pointed out earlier that in some areas farms are small, the number of children large, and that this made migration desirable. But even so, in many sections, not only in the South, the average size of farms is uneconomic. It cannot support "an American standard of living." In these sections, schools are poor, other social utilities are conspicuous by their absence, and, to a considerable degree, unsupportable without subsidy. Permanent poverty or extremely painful adjustments loom. There is no theoretic reason why society cannot accelerate social processes for its own benefit, and in democratic fashion.

An illustration of this is in the matter of farm tenancy. As stated earlier, the American ideal has been one of land-ownership. To accomplish this a large segment of the farm population has burdened itself heavily with debt. To close estates, often ancestral acres are sold into slavery again. Possibly there are better ways. When one sees the hundreds of millions of dollars subtracted from farm income through interest charges, flowing mostly to the cities, the question arises as to whether, after all, every family in each generation should acquire full title to its farm by the usual purchase procedures. The arrangements in certain European countries by which farms remain in the same family for generations might be studied with profit. Do they offer any suggestions for America? The Farm Security Administration tenant-purchase plan should also be studied; at very low interest rates on federal loans it assumes a two-generation process before full ownership is achieved.

So, too, our tenancy arrangements might be challenged. They grew naturally out of our social situation. Once they made sense, but the situation has changed. It comes as a shock to an American to discover that in New Zealand a very efficient and prosperous agriculture is more than one half operated by tenants and that few, if any, of the social and economic problems attendant upon tenancy in much of the United States are present. This is because a very large proportion of the tenants are operating crown lands. Their acres belong to the state. They have life tenure if desired. Their sons can succeed to the leasehold. The leases safeguard the fertility of the soil, encourage initiative and enterprise on the part of the operator.

In the United States state-owned lands and the federal public domain are usually not the best lands for agricultural purposes. But the New Zealander or Australian from his experience would see no reason that the state should not acquire good land for agricultural purposes. Indeed, the Rural Commission of the Australian Ministry of Post-War Reconstruction proposes just such a procedure with many safeguards for the state and the settler alike, growing out of bitter experience with their land-settlement program after World War I. The whole focus of their report is to raise the rural standard of living. New Zealander and Australian alike would emphatically reject the charge that this was socialism. It simply grows out of their long experience with crown lands.

The point is, that many of our policies, good in themselves, and perhaps once effective, are not producing the results we greatly desire. This raises questions. Other democracies facing similar problems have attempted different solutions. As the social importance of our basic resource, the land, becomes clear, so does the stake of society, both rural and urban, in land policy. And there is no economic policy which does not have social results, nor is there any social policy which lacks economic implications.

DISCUSSION TOPICS

1. If possible, get estimates from local officials of the amount of unpaid taxes on farms since 1930. Record these figures and explain what you have found out about them.
2. Conduct a class debate on the question, "Resolved: that corporation farming will benefit American agriculture and rural life."
3. What social problems are involved in situations of high tenancy?
4. What are the causes of tenancy?
5. Should farm labor be unionized? Defend your opinion or conduct a class debate.
6. How were farm labor problems handled in your community during the war? Will such procedures have any effect on future plans? If so, what do you expect to happen? Why?
7. How is the tax dollar spent in your home county or municipality?

REFERENCE READINGS

Land and land tenure:

Bercaw, Louise, *Farm Tenancy in the United States.* A selected list of references. Washington, D.C.: Bureau of Agricultural Economics, 1937.

Land Committee, Public Works and Rural Land Use. Washington, D.C.: National Resources Planning Board, 1942.

Reports of the Land Planning Committee to the National Resources Board, Parts I, II, III, V, VII. Washington, D.C.: 1935 to 1937.

Schuler, Edgar A., *Social States and Farm Tenure.* Washington, D.C.: Bureau of Agricultural Economics, 1938.

Farm Labor:

Ahearn, Daniel J., Jr., *The Wages of Farm and Factory Laborers, 1914-1945.* New York: Columbia University Press, 1945.

Collins, Henry H., Jr., *America's Own Refugees.* Princeton University Press, 1944.

Cullum, R. M., F. C. Folsom, and D. G. Hay, *Men and Machines in the North Dakota Harvest.* Washington, D.C.: Bureau of Agricultural Economics, Federal Security Administration, April, 1942.

Daugherty, M. M., *Part-Time Farming in New Castle County.* Newark, Delaware: Agricultural Experiment Stations, April, 1936.

Ducoff, Louis J., *Wages of Agricultural Labor in the United States.* Washington, D.C.: United States Department of Agriculture, September, 1944 (mimeographed).

Gee, Wilson, *The Social Economics of Agriculture.* Chapter IX. New York: The Macmillan Co., 1942.

Grigsby, S. E., and H. Hoffsommer, *Cotton Plantation Laborers.* Baton Rouge, Louisiana: Agricultural Experiment Station, February, 1941.

Hoffsommer, Harold, *The Resident Laborer on the Sugar Cane Farm.* Baton Rouge, Louisiana: Agricultural Experiment Station, November, 1941.

Hood, Kenneth, *An Economic Study of Part-time Farming in the Elmira and Albany Areas of New York, 1932 and 1933.* Ithaca: Agricultural Experiment Station, April, 1936.

International Labor Office. *Collective Agreements in Agriculture.* Geneva: International Labor Office, 1933. (United States Distributor, World Peace Foundation, Boston.)

Johansen, Sigurd, *Migratory-Casual Workers in New Mexico.* Agricultural Experiment Station, State College, New Mexico, March, 1939.

Johnson, Elizabeth S., *Welfare of Families of Sugar Beet Laborers.* Washington, D.C.: Children's Bureau, 1939.

Landis, Paul H., and M. S. Brooks, *Farm Labor in the Yakima Valley.* Pullman, Washington: Agricultural Experiment Station, December, 1936.

Reuss, Carl, P. H. Landis, and R. Wakefield, *Migratory Farm Labor and the Hop Industry on the Pacific Coast.* Pullman, Washington: Agricultural Experiment Station, August, 1938.

Reuss, Carl, *Social Characteristics of Part-Time Farmers in Washington.* Pullman, Washington: Agricultural Experiment Station, July, 1939.

Sanderson, Dwight, Editor, *Farm Income and Farm Life,* chaps. II, X, XI, XII, XIII. University of Chicago Press, 1927.

Schwartz, Harry, *Seasonal Farm Labor in the United States.* New York: Columbia University Press, 1945.

Taylor, Paul S., and Tom Vasey, *California Farm Labor.* Social Security Board, California, January, 1937.

Thaden, J. F., *Migratory Beet Workers in Michigan.* Lansing, Michigan: Agricultural Experiment Station, September, 1942.

Wakeley, Ray, *Part Time and Garden Farming in Iowa.* Ames, Iowa: Agricultural Experiment Station, December, 1935.

Taxation:

Coombs, Whitney, *Taxation on Farm Property.* Washington, D.C.: United States Department of Agriculture, Technical Bulletin 172, February, 1930. See also the state studies by colleges of agriculture reviewed and summarized in this book.

Hibbard and Allin, *Tax Burdens Compared* (Farm, City, Village). Madison: University of Wisconsin, Bulletin 393, 1927.

Lancaster, L. W., *Government in Rural America,* chap. VI. New York: Van Nostrand, 1937.

National Planning Resources Board, N.R.P.B., *Tax Delinquency and Rural Land Use Adjustment.* Washington, D.C., 1942.

Credit:

Black, A. G., "Some Current Problems in Agricultural Credit," *Journal of Farm Economics,* February, 1941.

Horton, Donald C., "Credit and Mortgages," *Land Policy Review,* fall, 1943.

Kuznets, S., *National Income and Capital Formation,* 1919-1935. New York: National Bureau of Economic Research, 1938.

Martin, P., *Income in Agriculture: 1929-1935.* New York: National Industrial Conference Board, 1936.

Murray, William G., "How Should Agriculture be Financed?" *Journal of Farm Economics,* February, 1940.

Young, E. C., "Farm Credit and Government," *Journal of Farm Economics,* August, 1938.

9

Co-operation: Rural Society's Middle Way

WE HAVE FOUND in the previous chapters that rural society in its economic aspect is not a static thing. It changes, and the changes force adjustments. In this chapter attention is directed to one adjustment attempted by the farmers themselves. It is called the co-operative movement, and it has a history in the world of more than a century. It has existed in the United States for over eighty years. The co-operative movement is sometimes called "the middle way." It has proved to be a desirable alternative to corporation agriculture and collectivized agriculture as practiced in Russia. It gives the strength and the economic power and efficiency of huge combinations, but at the same time it preserves the traditional family-operated farm.

Mutual insurance companies the first co-operative effort. The first manifestation of economic co-operation in the rural United States was in the farmers' mutual fire insurance companies. The earliest of these were organized soon after the beginning of the eighteenth century, and many of them are still functioning. There are now about two thousand such companies with over $11,000,-000,000 of insurance in force. Their average net rates are lower than those of the regular insurance companies, and their experience with losses is more favorable.[1] Losses paid annually run into several hundred million dollars. At the time of the Valgreen study the premium income annually exceeded losses by an average of over 75 per cent. Reserves, therefore, were very high.

These companies were not purely co-operatives in the sense that they observed all the principles of the famous Rochdale pioneers who founded the first consumers' co-operative in Rochdale, England, in 1844, with a capital of $140. These principles provide, among other things, that each member of a co-operative shall have

[1] Very little study has been given to this phenomenon. Though out of date in some of the statistical data, the best account of the history, growth, and operating principles of these mutual companies is Valgreen, V. N., *Farmers' Mutual Fire Insurance in the United States.* Chicago: University of Chicago Press, 1924.

one vote, regardless of the number of shares he holds; that dividends shall be based on patronage and not on investment; that dividends on shares shall be nominal and limited; that membership shall be open to all without restriction.

Among farm co-operatives, in recent years there has been a very large expansion in the insurance field, promoted by various state Farm Bureaus, notably in Ohio. Most types of insurance are now written, including life, automobile, and accident insurance. These modern co-operative companies have had a phenomenal growth, and are substantial concerns in the insurance field of today.

Credit unions develop. A second area for co-operative effort has been the credit union organized for the purpose of supplying short-term small loans at low cost to farmers. This movement is also growing rapidly in the cities, but all unions holding a federal charter are supervised by the Farm Credit Administration, regardless of location. The use of local associations of ten or more farmers, as the local agencies of the Federal Land Bank was, of course, an extension to the credit field of the co-operative principle. However, the co-operative credit unions are in some ways more interesting to rural society than are these associations.

Even more interesting has been the recent development of credit unions. This movement is well known in India, China, and Japan, and to a lesser extent in Europe, as will be noted later. In the United States its growth dates from the depression of the thirties. The members of a credit union make small payments, usually monthly, to its capital and lend the funds in small amounts at reasonable interest rates to members for approved purposes. About forty states have laws which permit the organization of credit unions. In 1934 a Federal Credit Union Act was passed which makes it possible for such an organization to be incorporated in any state. Over four thousand unions now have a federal charter and the number is increasing steadily.

All told, there are now over 10,600 credit unions in the United States, not all of them rural, with close to 4,000,000 members. The average membership is 225, with savings by members of over $10,000 or more than $40 per member. The average loan is less than $100. There have been very few failures of credit unions and the per member loss in these cases was very small. It is significant that at a time of great economic and financial stress the co-operative features of credit unions have attracted such wide interest and support from people of small means.

But co-operation as practiced by farmers is far broader. It has been applied to marketing and buying and is a far-flung enterprise. Moreover, it is in essence social, based on mutual trust of the co-operators and is largely, though not exclusively, governed on the principle of one man one vote, regardless of the number of shares an individual may hold in a given co-operative enterprise. Most of the marketing co-operatives deal with one crop, such as citrus fruit, cheese, cotton, and the like. Any producer who cares to may join, but joining involves the obligation to market his crops through the co-operative organization, which acts as the sales agent for each member, pooling the products received and thus having more power in dealing with purchasers.

Development of the co-operative movement. The co-operative movement among farmers in the United States began soon after the Civil War in a time of disturbed conditions, new needs and problems arising out of postwar deflation. It was at the start, and for some decades, largely a neighborhood matter. A few farmers would combine in the manufacture of cheese, or a community group would finance and manage its own wheat-elevator or creamery. With the coming of the twentieth century the movement gathered momentum. The first successful large co-operative, that of the citrus-fruit growers of California, gave promise of organizing a considerable number of farmers on the basis of a single crop and over a considerable area. The small local co-operatives were federated into large powerful organizations. By 1915 there were over 5100 co-operatives engaged in marketing and purchasing products with a volume of business exceeding $635,000,000. During World War I and in the following years there was a remarkable expansion, with great campaigns and enthusiastic membership drives. Some of these co-operatives failed as a result of too hasty organization and an uninformed membership. The next forward step came under the Federal Farm Board, organized early in the Hoover Administration. The statistics of the movement are summarized as follows by the Farm Credit Administration:

Year	Number of Associations	Volume of Business	Memberships*
1915............	5,149	$ 635,839,000	651,186
1925............	10,803	2,400,000,000	2,700,000
1930............	12,000	2,500,000,000	3,100,000
1934†............	10,900	1,365,000,000	3,156,000
1938............	10,900	2,400,000,000	3,400,000
1943............	10,300	5,160,000,000	4,400,000

*Gross figures. It is generally thought that, correcting for duplications, over 2,000,000 are members of co-operatives, a majority of the farmers engaged in commercial production on any scale. However, the 1940 Census reports only 1,364,000 as claiming to do business through co-operatives.
† Lowest year of depression.

The United States Department of Agriculture has a record of 26,192 co-operatives being organized between 1863 and 1939, less than two thousand of them in the nineteenth century. The difference between the present total and the total number organized does not by any means represent the number of failures. Failures have been relatively few since 1910, when the gathering of careful annual statistics was begun, as will be noted later. Rather, in the last quarter-century there have been many consolidations. The small neighborhood groups mentioned were federated on a county, often a state or district, basis. Evidence of this and of the strength of the movement is to be seen in the table, which indicates that although the number of co-operatives has been declining since 1930, the actual membership has been increasing steadily. In the troubled depression years of 1930-39 the number of discontinuances of co-operatives averaged less than one in twenty per year, including those which were absorbed through consolidation. Moreover, about one half the present associations are a quarter of a century or more old.[2]

There is evidence that the federal count of the number of co-operatives is low. Both in 1930 and 1936 field workers studying the 140 village-centered agricultural communities alluded to in this book found about 25 per cent more co-operative associations than reported for these same communities by the United States Department of Agriculture. These were largely of two types, marketing or purchasing associations that had failed to answer the government inquiries or had escaped the notice of the government, and consumer co-operatives in which the purchasing of farm supplies was a minor or nonexistent element in the total business.

Regional differences in co-operative membership considerable. Table 26 shows that the Middle-Western census regions account for over one half of the co-operative business and that the Pacific Coast comes next. It also shows that the movement has spread from these two regions outward, and that though the number of associations and amount of business has grown, other regions are growing more rapidly. These figures must be further evaluated in terms of the number of farmers in each region and the size of their agricultural production. In these terms, for instance, it is clear that the co-operative movement is stronger in New England than it is in the East South Central states.

[2] The data in this paragraph are largely drawn from Elsworth, R. S., and Grace Wanstall, *Farmers' Marketing and Purchasing Co-operatives, 1863-1939.* Washington, D.C.: United States Department of Agriculture, 1941.

TABLE 26. FARMERS' MARKETING AND PURCHASING ASSOCIATIONS:
PERCENTAGE OF ESTIMATED BUSINESS BY GEOGRAPHIC
DIVISIONS FOR SPECIFIED PERIODS,* 1913 TO 1942–43

Geographic Division	1913	1921	1925–26	1930–31	1935–36	1942–43
New England.............	2.1	1.9	3.5	3.8	3.9	3.6
Middle Atlantic..........	4.9	7.5	6.4	10.2	10.5	8.8
East North Central.......	16.5	18.1	23.3	21.8	25.1	24.0
West North Central......	45.1	42.5	34.9	32.5	27.2	27.8
South Atlantic...........	5.7	4.0	6.3	5.0	4.1	6.1
East South Central.......	3.0	.8	4.9	2.5	3.4	2.8
West South Central....,..	3.1	5.5	5.4	5.5	5.8	6.8
Mountain................	2.9	2.8	2.9	4.1	4.8	4.5
Pacific.................	16.7	16.9	12.4	14.6	15.2	15.6
Total................	100.0	100.0	100.0	100.0	100.0	100.0
Number of associations....	3,099	7,374	10,803	11,950	10,500	10,450

* Most statistics pertaining to farmers' marketing and purchasing co-operatives are now compiled on the basis of the marketing season which includes the period during which the farm products of a specified year are moved into the channels of trade. Marketing seasons overlap.
Source: Washington, D.C.: United States Department of Agriculture, Bulletin 547, 1917, pp. 14–25, and United States Department of Agriculture, Miscellaneous Bulletin 83, October, 1945.

Tenure also affects co-operation. It is apparent from the 1940 Census data that the tenure status of the farmer has an influence on co-operation. Owners in every region are more likely to do business with co-operative associations than are tenants, and among owners, in every region it is the part owner who uses the co-operatives more than the full owner. It will be recalled that the part-owner also controls more land than the full owner. He is seeking in every way to expand his operations, and rents when he cannot buy or until he can buy. It is perhaps significant that proportionately he makes the greatest use of the co-operatives of any tenure group.

The tenant lags behind in every region, especially in the South. However, it must be remembered that under the Southern system the share-cropper turns over his crop to the landlord, who may market it through a co-operative, but the cropper may know nothing of this arrangement, nor does he profit from it. It is often alleged also that Southern landlords are opposed to co-operatives, to a greater extent than elsewhere, and will not permit tenants to join them.

Whether one accepts the United States Department of Agricul-

TABLE 27. PROPORTION OF FARMERS REPORTING ANY BUSINESS WITH CO-OPERATIVES, 1919–1939 BY TENURE

Division	All Farmers*			Full Owners 1939	Part Owners 1939	Tenants 1939	All Farmers All Types 1939
	1939	1929	1919				
United States............	17.1	18.1	9.7	23.7	34.8	13.3	22.4
New England............	17.1	13.6	6.5	19.4	39.4	16.7	20.6
Middle Atlantic..........	24.6	16.2	10.6	29.4	48.0	22.0	30.2
East North Central.......	26.3	22.4	16.0	33.2	45.0	26.4	34.9
West North Central.......	32.9	29.0	25.9	38.8	47.6	31.3	39.3
South Atlantic...........	5.7	3.5	1.6	12.3	13.7	2.9	9.5
East South Central.......	5.1	2.8	1.5	11.3	13.3	3.7	8.8
West South Central	6.3	4.3	1.9	11.2	19.8	5.2	10.6
Mountain................	21.8	18.0	8.1	23.7	33.7	21.5	28.2
Pacific..................	32.0	25.2	16.5	37.3	45.4	25.0	36.8

*The percentages for all farmers refer only to business with marketing or purchasing co-operatives, and are therefore not comparable to the 1939 data by tenure, which include all co-operatives. The United States figure for all co-operatives is 22.4, as noted in column farthest to the right.
Source: Washington, D.C.: *Sixteenth Census of the United States, 1940, Agriculture,* vol. III, chap. VI, pp. 22–23.

ture data on co-operatives or those of the census, it is apparent from both that the movement is growing steadily, even in the South where the proportion of members is less than one quarter of that in other regions. Since 1919 the proportion of farmers who are members of co-operatives has doubled according to the census. In the South it has more than tripled.[3]

Types of co-operatives. Many of these 10,450 co-operatives are still local organizations. Others are organized on two bases: (1) federations of locals through which the large organization keeps in touch with its membership, and (2) those organized from the top down, with no local agency. Contact between the member and the co-operative is direct but largely impersonal. Rural sociologists early pointed out that this was a dangerous procedure because it was in essence less democratic than the federation. More of this type than of the first have run into difficulties or failed. A few of them have constructed local organizations to meet this problem.

There is further significance of the co-operative movement and its advantages to grower and consumer alike. Co-operatives in this country are now beginning to follow the European example and to include adult educational programs in the theory and practice of co-operation. This helps to strengthen the organization. Some co-operatives have formed special youth and adult groups, and have developed recreational programs.

The significance of the data given earlier lies not so much in the membership figures as in the volume of business. It should be noted, however, that while the 1925 figures represent less than one fifth of the total volume of agricultural crops raised, including those consumed on the farm, the 1938 figures comprise more than one third of the total production. These fractions would be higher if based only on products sold commercially.

The volume of products handled by the co-operatives has gained over 50 per cent over the last decade. The gain in dollars has been over 100 per cent. Gains have been especially striking in co-operative purchasing of farm supplies and some consumers' goods. Total purchases through farm co-operatives in the year 1940-41 amounted to over $450,000,000, practically triple the amount of two

[3] There are reasons for believing that the census figures represent an under-enumeration. Census enumerators work close to home. With the feeling against co-operatives in some places many farmers may not wish to admit membership in such an organization. In at least one state the number of co-operators reported by the census is less than the actual number of client-members for whom a state-wide co-operative handled products and who paid dues.

years previously. It reached $730,000,000 in 1944, and is growing rapidly.

There is another way of looking at the various types of co-operatives; namely, in terms of the functions and services they perform. A partial but reasonably complete summary on this basis is given in Table 28.

TABLE 28. FARMERS' CO-OPERATIVES: TYPES, NUMBER, AND MEMBERSHIP

Type	Associations	Estimated Members or Participants
Production:		
Mutual irrigation companies (1936).................	2,442	177,392
F.S.A. machinery co-operatives (1943).............	10,145	90,000
F.S.A. sire associations (1943).....................	3,489	50,000
F.S.A. marketing and purchasing (1943)............	963	100,000
Dairy herd improvement associations (Feb., 1944)....	954	20,825
Dairy bull associations (Jan., 1943)................	306	5,981
Co-operative dairy-cattle artificial-breeding associations (Jan., 1943)................................	99	23,448
Grazing associations (1943).......................	40	1,954
Indian enterprises (Dec., 1943)....................	437	207,300
Marketing and purchasing:		
Marketing (1942–43).............................	7,708	2,580,000
Purchasing (1942–43)............................	2,742	1,270,000
Financing:		
National farm loan associations (Dec., 1943).........	2,805	448,000
Production credit associations (Dec., 1943)..........	523	275,196
Banks for co-operatives (Dec., 1943)...............	13	*1,158,525
Farmers' mutual fire insurance companies (1941).....	1,885	3,300,000
Public Service:		
Mutual telephone companies (1942).................	5,000	330,000
Electric power and light associations (1942)..........	850	1,210,000
Farmers' burial associations (1942).................	41	27,500

* Membership of 1362 associations having loans outstanding.
Source: Washington, D.C.: United States Department of Agriculture, Farm Credit Administration Miscellaneous Report 70, Wanstall, Grace and Elsworth, R. H., *Statistics of Farmers' Marketing and Purchasing Co-operatives, 1942–43 Marketing Season*, January, 1944.

Some advantages of co-operative marketing. Through co-operation, the farmer has sought to secure some of the middleman's profit for himself, to reduce marketing costs, to control the flow of non-perishable products to market and thus to avoid dumping, to create new markets for certain products both by research and by advertising, and to improve standards of production. Brand names have been adopted and products reaching market have been properly graded, thus protecting the consumer. In short, associated groups of farmers have sought the advantage and profits of the corporation through co-operation.

Opposition met. This growth has not been without great opposition. Co-operatives were fought in the courts, attacked by powerful financial institutions and charged with increasing the cost of living, and as interfering with legitimate private enterprise. Today some of the agencies, once opposed, are proclaiming co-operation as a panacea for the ills of agriculture, and are chiding the farmer for his too tardy acceptance of the principle. State and federal courts, moreover, have adopted a liberal attitude toward co-operatives.

In 1944 and 1945, opposition to co-operatives arose from the premise that they held an unfair competitive advantage because of "freedom from taxation." This, of course, is not true in terms of town, county, and often state taxation. The contention is based on the co-operative principle of patronage refunds. It is contended that in a non-co-operative business the amount of these refunds would be classed as profits, and subject to income tax. They are, of course, subject to taxation as a part of the farmer-member's income. In Pennsylvania this issue was pressed legally on the grounds that the state law did not give authority to the co-operatives to operate on the basis of patronage refunds. In 1945, the state legislature passed by large majorities three laws safeguarding this right.

Legislation has helped. Congress, like the states, has shown a benevolent attitude. Co-operatives have been exempted from federal anti-trust laws and from the federal income tax. This latter provision, of course, is deemed legitimate because, after setting up adequate reserves, as any business does, the income is distributed to members in proportion to their patronage. In 1926 and 1929, Congress set up machinery to aid co-operatives in their development and expansion, and loans were made available to them through governmental agencies in 1921, 1924, and 1929.

Failures among co-operatives. Failures among co-operatives compare very favorably with other business failures. Causes of failures and voluntary liquidations were chiefly friction among members, failure to educate or cultivate the members, overexpansion, insufficient capital, and too liberal dividend or credit policies. Unfair competition by commercial organizations, while frequently cited, is responsible for only 2 per cent of the failures.

The co-operatives and the community. An indication of the status of the co-operative movement in terms of the local community is given by the survey of the 140 village communities alluded to again and again in this text. In 1936, 93 of these places had an average of 2.16 co-operatives each as against 120 with an average of 2.2 each in 1924. This was a loss of 62 or 23.6 per cent from the total of 263 co-operatives found in 1924. But against this there was a gain of 14.1 per cent in membership.

The explanations of this trend toward a smaller number of local co-operatives, but a larger aggregate and average membership, are three. A few of the weaker co-operatives were liquidated during the depression years, usually with little or no loss. There were a few local consolidations. But the chief explanation reflects an adaptation to changing conditions, specifically to greater ease of transportation. The "local" unit of the co-operative was changed from a social community to a county basis or to some other unit larger than a local trade area.

As would be expected from the national data already given, the number of purchasing and consumers' co-operatives increased, indeed by more than 50 per cent, and there was also an increase of 40 per cent in the number of co-operatives which both marketed members' products and sold farm supplies and some consumers' goods. The total volume of business for both types of co-operatives in 1935-36 was $113,000 per organization, which exceeded tenfold the volume of the average mercantile establishment in the 140 communities in the same year.

Consumer co-operation growing rapidly. Consumer co-operation has been growing by leaps and bounds in the United States since the Great Depression and in this growth rural America has been leading. There are now a large number of central or regional wholesales. In some states the co-operatives have entered into the processing field. They own a number of refineries and before the war began shipments of petroleum products to co-operatives in Europe. The butter given the highest score by a consumers' research agency for a number of years was processed by a large chain of co-operatives. In wholesaling, in processing and retailing, the rural co-operatives began with farm products and supplies, but are increasingly enlarging to include the entire consumer field. The business of the co-operatives in all these lines has been increasing rapidly, even in the worst of the depression. In several of the Mid-Western states public schools now teach both consumer and marketing co-operation.[4]

---

[4] Cf. the publication, *Cooperation*, Cooperative League of America, Chicago, and its weekly news release for up-to-the-minute news of the movement.

SOME CASE ILLUSTRATIONS

Many of the co-operatives that purchased supplies and goods for resale to members had greatly increased their business. Typical of these was a concern called Farmers, Incorporated, in a medium-sized Virginia village. Half of the 500 farmers in the community belong to this organization. In the inter-survey period, 1924-30, the business increased about 50 per cent to total nearly $170,000 annually. By 1935 there were 400 members and consumer business alone had increased to $244,000. Since its founding in 1919, the dividends to member-stockholders had more than equaled the stock investment. Consumer co-operation among farmers is growing nationally and significantly.

The case of Rockwell, Iowa. Behind each unit of the statistics assembled finally in this chapter on co-operatives in local communities lies a story of agitation, leadership, education, of action, and often of struggle. A glimpse of what co-operation means in these terms is given in an account of the oldest grain co-operative in Iowa,[5] written by one connected with it as member and officer for thirty years.

In Rockwell, Iowa, by 1889 there was evidence that grain buyers were acting in unison and not competitively, thus holding down the price paid the farmers. There happened to be in the community two men of energy with some experience elsewhere with co-operation. After ceaseless agitation they finally gathered in a granary a group that, after much discussion in the flickering light of a lantern, decided to form a co-operative elevator society.

The businessmen of the town were confident that the step would mean ruin for the community, and the grain trade fought the enterprise by offering higher prices to sellers. This infant co-operative, however, showed from the first the sagacity which has made for its success for more than two score years. It was democratically organized. Any farmer with ten dollars for a share of stock could join and no matter how many shares he held he cast but one vote. Competition from the grain trade was met by requiring members to pay the usual commission to the co-operative even when selling to a private elevator, upon pain of losing their other privileges in the society.

These other privileges soon became important, for the society

[5] Holman, Reuben A., *Forty Years of Co-operation.* Rockwell, Iowa: Farmers Elevator, 1931.

began to handle machinery and then lumber and gave its own members discounts on such business. In ten years this ridiculed co-operative, that had begun business with barely $1000 capital, showed a business volume of over $300,000 a year, which, in turn, was doubled within another half decade.

Then a new threat arose. Efforts were made to shut off the urban outlet for co-operative marketed grain, but some thirty similar societies that had sprung up, following Rockwell's example, combined in a state co-operative association and were powerful enough to overcome this danger.

In Rockwell itself hogs and livestock were added to the marketing activities and coal, shoes and clothing to the products purchased for the community. By the end of forty years — that is, 1929 — the society had paid individuals 68 times the original investment. Since then, under a new charter, cash dividends have been limited to 5 per cent annually and other profits have been distributed on a pro rata patronage basis.

There have been several factors contributing to the success of this enterprise, which is still functioning successfully. The management has been almost from the start in the hands of one family, father and sons, men of integrity who refused to be swayed by offers of positions or profits from the grain trade. Other leadership has also been continuous. There were but four presidents and two secretaries in the first forty-odd years of its history. These leaders, as Holman shows in his delightfully simple and human history, have been men of fundamental integrity, and repeatedly in times of crisis their appeal to essential moral principles carried the day. Scripture was often quoted in their meetings. Finally the co-operative has been a stabilizing influence in the community itself, which has seemed to suffer less from migration than many, and which has built up a co-operative spirit in many of its other relationships.

Some co-operative problems. The co-operative movement has produced some problems within its own structure which reflect stress and differences in social attitudes among groups within the movement. This is inevitable. In the first place, in some of the largest marketing co-operatives there is an observable tendency for some of the problems of big business to appear. One of these tendencies is the growing importance of the managerial function and the difficulty of preserving democratic controls which are the essence of the philosophy of the movement. With this goes also the intricacies of employer-employee relationships. Again, it has happened that executives of the large co-operatives have displayed attitudes more characteristic of industry than of the co-operative movement. Also, marketing co-operatives have not always willingly concurred with consumers' co-operatives, fearing that their own profits would be adversely affected. Happily, while this problem has not been solved, the two types of co-operatives are developing mutually advantageous arrangements. As consumer co-operatives grow in number and strength, these instances of commercial amity will doubtless increase.

Finally, there is a tendency to push back into processing and even manufacturing. This trend has gone farther in England and Scandinavia than in the United States, and appears to be a constructive development. Here it has progressed farthest in the petroleum field, where co-operatives own processing plants, pipe lines and oil fields.

Agricultural co-operation elsewhere. Co-operation is strongly rooted among farmers in most of the world. It has perhaps reached its peak in Scandinavia and Czechoslovakia. It has spread rapidly in Canada, the situation in Nova Scotia being especially interesting. As long ago as 1913, Woodrow Wilson sent large official deputations to Europe to study the co-operative movement among farmers. A similar study was made at President Roosevelt's direction in 1936. Japan, with a million fewer farmers than the United States, had 15,000 rural co-operatives including credit unions in 1940. All of these are closely supervised by the Government. The movement is growing also in Korea, where some results of great social significance have been achieved.[6] India has more than 12,000 organizations. In this country co-operative credit unions have had the greatest development. Co-operation has begun to grow also in China, especially since the Japanese attack in 1937. There are reputed to be over 170,000 co-operatives in China as of 1945, five times as many as in 1938 and sixty times as many as in 1930. The membership is well over 15,000,000 persons. Chinese co-operatives generally fall into seven categories — credit, supply, producers, consumers, markets, insurance, and public utilities. Most of them, however, are credit societies, with agricultural producers and consumers' co-operatives next. Agricultural and handicraft enterprises handled by co-operatives include general farms, animal industries, tea cultivation, cotton-growing, vegetable and fruit-raising, irrigation, textiles, and paper making.[7]

Attitudes toward co-operation. While the success of farmer co-

[6] Cf. Brunner, *Rural Korea*, pp. 37-38. New York and London, 1928.
[7] *Chinese Agricultural News Letter*, vol. II, no. 1, January, 1945.

operatives has been considerable, the progress of the movement is, according to surveys by the late Doctor Theodore Manny, of the Office of Population and Rural Life Studies of the United States Department of Agriculture, conditioned by a number of factors, largely social in character. He found that entrenched habits, especially individualism, hindered the movement in local communities. In some instances, farmers will sabotage their own organization if they think it to their immediate profit; this usually happens, however, only when the co-operative has not sufficiently educated its members as to its objectives, methods, and ideals. The co-operatives are more successful in enlisting the better educated, the more experienced, wealthier farmers than the others, and farm owners will join more readily than tenants. Tenants especially hesitate to subscribe to its stock, since they do not know how long they will reside in a community. In the main co-operators belong to more organizations like churches, farm bureaus, lodges, and have a higher standard of living, more conveniences and more equipment than non-co-operators.[8] These facts in themselves suggest some of the obstacles the co-operative must overcome in order to progress. Numerous studies seem to show that the anti-co-operation attitudes of many farmers grow out of ignorance concerning what co-operation is and impatience with mistakes, coupled with the failure of some of the co-operatives to consider the sociological aspects of their problem and to use their locals as social as well as economic groups.[9]

Quite apart from these phenomena, co-operatives, wherever they are local organizations or units, provide a mutual interest and face-to-face contacts. The co-operative at Rockwell, Iowa, just described, was not a social organization in the strict sense of the term, but no one can read the history of its forty years without realizing how it has woven itself into the warp and woof of community life. Through it, leadership was developed, class distinctions broken down, and mutual trust and democratic processes encouraged. These beneficial results have appeared again and again.

[8] Cf. Manny, *Some Ohio Trends in Membership Relations, Some Social Factors in Membership Relations* (Washington, D.C.: United States Department of Agriculture, 1929 and 1930); and Howell, *The Relation of Economic, Social and Educational Advancement of Farmers in Their Membership in Organizations,* i.e., Cotton Growers' Associations (Stillwater: Oklahoma Agricultural and Mechanical College, 1929).

[9] These observations are based on field-work reports and newspaper clippings secured in a number of the 140 villages where the survey was fortunately in process during the annual meeting or annual membership drive of a local co-operative or its overhead organization.

Nationally and locally the co-operative movement is a social as well as an economic force, and it is significant that despite their reputed individualism one third of the American farmers and a majority of those producing commercially have joined one or more co-operative enterprises. Henry A. Wallace has written and has frequently said that a good country church is a great asset to a co-operative even though it cannot be counted on the balance sheet, and that the reverse was also true. He says that Christians and co-operators have learned that the good things of life come by mutual effort. Co-operation is not a panacea for the ills of agriculture; it is a definite help in any situation. It is an association of individuals who combine their capital and work power in a self-help organization which also has social tasks and aims, especially to improve the standard of living through lowering costs and increasing returns. Co-operatives are social groups, and, though instruments of economic progress, they tend to help integrate the communities or groups they serve. They work within the existing framework of society and its regulations *for* their members, not *against* anyone. The individual by his voluntary connection multiplies his own powers by association with a like-minded group.

DISCUSSION TOPICS

1. Find out the proportion of farmers who belong to farm co-operatives in your county.
2. What values has the Danish co-operative movement for the United States?
3. Contrast the co-operation principle with the individual sales principle and the private corporate principle of merchandising farm or other products. (This discussion topic can be arranged in the form of a three-cornered debate by members of the class.)
4. Report on the organization, procedures, problems, and accomplishments of some one co-operative.

REFERENCE READINGS

Farm credit:

Brunner, Edmund de S., *In Relief of Debtors*. New York: Teachers College, Columbia University, Bureau of Publications, 1933.

Brunner, E. de S., and J. H. Kolb, *Rural Social Trends*. New York: McGraw-Hill, 1933.

Brunner, E. de S., and I. Lorge, *Rural Trends in Depression Years.* New York: Columbia University Press, 1937.

Clark, Evans, *The Internal Debts of the United States,* chap. II. New York: The Macmillan Co., 1933.

Journal of Farm Economics. Various authors, pp. 276-98, April, 1934.

"Long Term Credits in a Depression," *Journal of Farm Economics,* October, 1932.

Wiecking, E. H., "Farm Real Estate Values," *Journal of Farm Economics,* April, 1933.

Co-operation:

Brunner, E. de S., and J. H. Kolb, *Rural Social Trends.* New York: McGraw-Hill, 1933.

Brunner, E. de S., and I. Lorge, *Rural Trends in Depression Years,* pp. 58-64. New York: Columbia University Press, 1937.

Childs, M., *Co-operation: The Middle Way.* New Haven: Yale University Press, 1935.

Christensen, Chris L., *Agricultural Co-operation in Denmark.* Washington, D.C.: Department of Agriculture, 1924.

Coady, M. M., *Masters of Their Destinies.* New York: Harper & Bros., 1939.

Cowling, Ellis, *Co-operatives in America.* New York: Coward-McCann, 1938.

Elsworth, R. H., *Agricultural Co-operative Associations, Marketing and Purchasing, 1936.* Washington, D.C.: Farm Credit Administration, 1937.

Elsworth, R. H., and Grace Wanstall, *Farmers Marketing and Purchasing Co-operatives, 1863-1939.* Washington, D.C.: Farm Credit Administration, 1941.

Elsworth, R. H., *The Story of Farmers' Cooperatives.* Washington, D.C.: Farm Credit Administration, 1939.

Fowler, B., *Consumer Co-operation in America.* New York: Vanguard, 1936.

Galla, K., *Sociology of the Co-operative Movement in the Czechoslovak Village.* Prague: Spolek Pece o Blaho Venoka, 1936.

Howell, *The Relation of Economics, Social and Educational Advancement of Farmers to Their Membership in Organizations.* Stillwater, Oklahoma: Agricultural and Mechanical College, 1929.

Kallen, H., *The Decline and Rise of the Consumer.* New York: Appleton-Century, 1936.

Kress, Andrew, ed., *Introduction to the Co-operative Movement.* New York: Harper & Bros., 1941.

Landis, Benson Y., *A Co-operative Economy*. New York: Harper & Bros., 1943.

Manny, T. B., *Some Ohio Trends in Membership Relations, Some Social Factors in Membership Relations*. Washington, D.C.: United States Department of Agriculture, 1929 and 1930.

Turner, Howard Harris, *Case Studies in Consumers Co-operatives*. New York: Columbia University Press, 1941.

Wanstall, Grace, and R. H. Elsworth, *Statistics of Farmers' Marketing and Purchasing Co-operatives, 1942-43*. Washington, D.C.: Farm Credit Administration, 1944.

10

Agriculture Adjusting to National and World Economy

THE PREVIOUS CHAPTERS have discussed certain facts of American agriculture, their social significance in terms of situations existing in specified areas and at definite periods of time. There have been changes over the years and these changes have produced difficulties and have made adjustments necessary. What happens in the great "out-back" of Australia, on the steppes of Russia, and the pampas of the Argentine in these modern days is often more important to the American farmer and his family than what happened in the next county was to his grandfather. This became very apparent after World War I, and it is even truer today. Therefore, this chapter begins with a quick review of the development of our agriculture up to the opening of World War I, and then turns to a discussion of the adjustments that were attempted during "the long armistice" between it and World War II.

AGRICULTURAL DEVELOPMENT

Early agriculture was self-sufficient. In early American history agriculture was self-sufficient. The pioneer built his house of logs from the trees which he cleared from his land. He raised his own food, butchered his own meat, churned his own butter, made his own soap. His womenfolk converted the wool from his sheep into homespun clothes. He counted his wealth in acres, buildings, and livestock. He had little use for money. What goods he could not produce, such as coffee and sugar, he often obtained by barter with the nearest storekeeper. Only cotton and tobacco farmers exported their products for cash, and hence for decades these people were closer to the current of world affairs than any other agrarian group. But specialization began to take place. The farmer ceased grinding his own grain and took it to the miller, who converted it into flour for a cash consideration. He sold his wool and bought clothes in the store. A community creamery took the place of the household churn.

Changes began with the nineteenth century. With the startling technological changes of the nineteenth century, agriculture began to change rapidly. The railroad opened up the rich lands of the Middle West, and thither, as we have seen, the population streamed. Eastern cities grew, and needed more food for their population. Western acres yielded abundant crops, and food was transported East at such low prices that it was impossible for the New England farmer to compete, since yields from his relatively inferior soil were too low and production costs too high. The rural-urban migration which was discussed earlier was accelerated by these forces.

The West beckons. But the West beckoned always more seductively. Land was to be procured for little more than hard labor. Moreover, the young nation needed capital to build railways and factories — capital it was not producing as rapidly as required. Huge sums were imported from Europe, and payment was made in rapidly multiplying bushels of grain and bales of cotton, coaxed from the soil by the multiplying hordes of farmers. Every spike fastening rail to tie in the expanding web of railroads which were opening territory after territory, first to the plow and then to the world market, was a blow to general farming in New England. The social problems of depopulation began to arise in this region. America spread a bargain counter in food and fiber before world buyers. Frequently, production, growing by leaps and bounds, especially as agriculture began to abandon the hoe for the machine, outstripped consumption. Prices were then depressed, and out of such depression grew the Populist revolt, the Bryan demand for free silver in the 1896 presidential campaign, and the national farmers' organization, Patrons of Husbandry, better known as the Grange, which is yet, incidentally, a powerful agency. This was the first important agrarian movement of the modern era.

From 1860 to 1910 our farmers increased from 2,000,000 to 6,000,000, and from 1870 to the turn of the century our agricultural exports gained more than fourfold to $1,250,000,000. By 1895 we were exporting about 500,000,000 bushels of cereals — over three times the 1870 figure.

Transportation changes help expansion. The perfection of long-distance transportation of non-perishable agricultural products and the establishment of an agricultural export trade are vital facts in American history. Farming thereby ceased to be largely a self-sufficing way of life, and became instead a business, acquiring something of the nature and spirit of capitalistic enterprise. Gradually it acquired, too, some of the techniques of capitalism. It learned to profit from co-operation and combination. It revised its commercial manners according to the best capitalistic standards. Its credit arrangements, as worked out in the Federal Land Banks, imitated corporation finance.

Specialization changes social arrangements. This shift from a largely self-sufficient type of agriculture to a more commercial one completely revised the social arrangements of farming people. It required specialization, and therefore made the farmer more and more dependent on the rest of society for primary needs. The farmhouse became less self-contained; it dispensed with its butcher shop, creamery, soap factory, and tailoring establishment. Distribution of specialized crops brought the farmer into contact with world markets. Developments of communication widened not only mental horizons but community boundaries as well. Schools, churches, and other social organizations responded in varying degree to an expanding world. Social and economic factors are inextricably interwoven in the tangled web of forces which changed the farmer's principal market from his own home to the world, and moved the center of his world from the neighborhood to the village or town.

Agriculture experiences a painless revolution. In the early years of the twentieth century, the agricultural structure underwent marked changes. In the crop year ending July 30, 1914, our cereal exports were only one third the 1900 figure, or only about one ninth our total production as against more than one third in the years 1891-95. There were four reasons among others for this:

(1) Foreign countries were competing with us more and more; especially Canada, Australia, Russia, and South America.

(2) Our tariffs on European goods were being raised, thereby making it more difficult for Europeans to purchase our cereals.

(3) We had come practically to the end of our free land, and the value of a single acre had therefore increased tremendously. This in turn raised costs and prices.

(4) Urban population began to multiply even more rapidly than agricultural, especially because of the flood of European immigrants, attracted by (and imported for) our increasing industrialization. Thus, some of our European customers became our inhabitants.

Moreover, because of the approach of the end of new land,

the rate of agricultural production slackened. The farmer, however, became more prosperous, because the domestic market grew, accompanied by a rise in prices and in land values. Per acre valuation was $11.14 in 1850, almost twice that in 1890. Between 1890 and 1900 there was little change, but between then and 1920 unearned increment in land, though fluctuating, averaged over 12 per cent a year. The average value per acre was $21.31 in 1890, $19.81 in 1900, $39.60 in 1910, and $69.38 in 1920. We had gone through a gradual and painless, even profitable, revolution, despite the loss of a large fraction of our European trade. Some have, in retrospect, called the period from 1900 to 1914 the golden age of American agriculture. Agricultural and industrial products were exchanged on a remarkably stable basis. This prewar parity the Agricultural Adjustment Act of May, 1933, sought to regain.

Social and economic progress keep step. In the first decade of our century there was great stimulus on the human side of agriculture. President Theodore Roosevelt appointed a Country Life Commission. Agricultural education expanded enormously. The movement for consolidation of rural schools began. There was agitation on behalf of the country church. Economic gains of the period were reflected in improved family and community standards of living. Few, if any, noticed, in those years, that the price of land was rising out of proportion to the productivity of that land, and to the price indexes of agricultural commodities. The seeds of the economic and social agricultural travail of the nineteen-twenties and thirties were being slowly sown, obscured in large part by the European war which soon engaged the whole world. For the value of the land increased far more rapidly than its productivity or than the price of the commodities it produced.

World War I and after. The war stimulated American agriculture tremendously. The slogan "Food Will Win the War" echoed throughout the land and the American farmer responded to it. Thirty million acres were added to our agricultural domain. Land already tilled was handled with increasing efficiency and per acre yields climbed speedily upward. We surpassed all previous export records.[1]

After the war, European demand fell off rapidly because Europe strove for agricultural self-sufficiency for reasons of national defense, and for reasons of economic security. After 1929 Europe

[1] About ten pages of material between this point and the end of the chapter are quoted without further reference from Brunner, *The Farm Act of 1933* (New York, 1933), by permission of the publishers, the Teachers College Bureau of Publications.

expanded her agricultural operations beyond prewar levels,[2] not wholly because she wanted to stop purchasing from us, but because she was in our debt. There are only three ways in which international debts can be paid, and none of these ways was open to her. She could not pay us in gold; there is not enough gold in the world to pay even her war debt to us. She could not pay us in goods; we wanted to sell, but not to buy, and raised our tariffs to prove it. A third possibility was for her to borrow money to pay for the goods which she wanted and which we wanted to sell her. For some time after the war this third expedient was tried, but when we stopped lending to her she had nothing with which to buy, and in consequence our farmers were raising food to sell to people who could not pay for it.

We become a creditor nation. Before World War I the picture was exactly reversed. We were a debtor nation and were paying our foreign debts largely in farm products, about two hundred million dollars a year in interest alone. After the war other nations owed us half a billion in interest, and by 1929 the sum had risen to a billion. The result was inevitable. For twenty years prior to 1930 we had sold to other nations more than one sixth of our farm, but only one twentieth of our non-agricultural products. Consequently, when European buying collapsed and we sold abroad in 1930 only 12.2 per cent of our production and in 1931 and 1932 less than 7 per cent, it was especially hard on agriculture.

Producing for vanished markets. Yet the American farmer went on producing for this vanished market. Moreover, instead of planting fewer acres he sowed more. The total net production of agricultural commodities in the United States in 1932, despite unfavorable growing conditions, was 4 per cent above the average for the period of 1919 to 1927.

This was not sheer perversity. The farmer had to meet fixed charges such as freight rates, taxes, interest, which remained stationary or increased. Each individual farmer argued, as one told the United States Department of Agriculture, that, "A man has to raise twice as many hogs at three cents as at six cents to stay in business." With six million farms in the United States, each trying its best to stay in business, this attitude is understandable, even though it contradicts the old theory of supply and demand. Theoretically, when prices fall from six to three cents, consumers will take more, thus eliminating the surplus, and at the same time the

---

[2] The world surplus of wheat in 1933 just about equaled the total increased production in Europe.

farmers, discouraged by the low price, will reduce production. But things did not work out that way after World War I so far as the export crops were concerned.

Causes of agricultural difficulties. The difficulties of agriculture began in 1920-21 with the postwar depression. Industry recovered in 1922-23, but agriculture did not, partly for reasons already noted; namely, the falling-off of the export market, and the high fixed charges such as interest and taxes. But there were other reasons. The food habits of the nation were changing. Our annual consumption of cereals, for instance, declined nearly 100 pounds per capita between 1909 and 1930. The number of acres required per person per year for food dropped from 3.2 to 2.7, a drop of more than 15 per cent. Our rate of population increase had also slowed down. The number of mouths to feed was not increasing as fast as formerly.

Moreover, farmers used more machine, less animal power. We have approximately 11,000,000 fewer horses and mules than twenty years ago. These vanished animals ate the product of about 15,-000,000 acres of corn land, not to mention 20,000,000 acres of hay and oats land. Human beings, from choice, and hogs, because farmers have learned to feed them more efficiently, needed together about 9,000,000 fewer acres of corn land than formerly. New uses for corn offset this decrease by not more than 2,000,000 additional acres. Thus, although consumers were better served, the farmers sold less.

Again mechanization and greater scientific knowledge have tremendously increased the efficiency of agriculture. In the decade 1922 to 1931 agricultural production per worker was about 22 per cent greater in volume than in the decade 1912 to 1921. Between 1870 and 1920 the volume per acre doubled. Canada, Argentina, Australia, and the Soviet Union have been similarly influenced. Surpluses became a world phenomenon.

Agricultural adjustment has, for all these reasons, been a difficult process. Powerful forces let loose in agriculture cannot be changed as easily as a factory can be shut down. For example, between 1929 and 1931 steel production was cut 85 per cent, but agriculture cannot act so abruptly. Its production problems are unique. Plant and animal biology and the care of soil are involved. The farmers, however, seemed about to succeed in their quest for readjustment to the new situation when, in 1929, the world-wide depression appeared and agriculture, along with other basic industries producing raw material, suffered tremendously, its previous problems still unsolved.

Measuring the damage. To do so, of course, applies to agriculture the techniques used by industry when the markets of manufactured products is smaller than had been anticipated.

In the years before World War I the prices the farmer received and those he paid maintained a remarkably stable relationship. This relationship is referred to as prewar parity, upon which much emphasis is laid in the Farm Act of 1933. This relationship, or ratio of the prices received by the farmer to those he paid, can be represented by 100 and an index can be constructed to measure the fluctuations in this relationship — that is, in the purchasing power of the agricultural producer.

This index of the Department of Agriculture has varied as follows:

	Revised Index		Revised Index
1909-14	100	1930	87
1915-16	94	1931	70
1917	117	1932	61
1918	115	1933	64
1919	105	1934	73
1920	105	1935	86
1921	82	1936	92
1922	89	1937	93
1923	93	1938	78
1924	94	1939	77
1925	99	1940	80
1926	94	1941	94
1927	91	1942	106
1928	96	1943	119
1929	95	1944	115
		1945	116

In passing, it is well to note that the agricultural depression was world-wide and that it was especially severe in nations which, like our own, were largely industrial. If reduced to index numbers, the curve of the price of rice in Japan somewhat resembles that of wheat in the United States, and early in the nineteen-twenties the Japanese government began to attempt to support the price of rice by purchases. Farm relief was the most important domestic issue before the Japanese Diet in 1927 and in 1934, and from 1921 onward there have been thousands of farmers' strikes in Japan, many of them violent. Most of these strikes were rebellions of tenants against their landlords. In 1926 and 1927, the number of these strikes exceeded two thousand, and by 1939, despite the dissolution of political parties and labor unions and other restrictive measures, the government admitted over six thousand tenant strikes. It is not too much to say that the aggression of Japan against China in 1937, and against the United States and others of the United Nations in 1941, cannot be wholly understood without taking into consideration the distress of the Japanese farmer, whose average holding was less than three acres, and without realizing the strangle-hold of ten thousand principal landlords upon several million tenant operators. Agrarian problems will be acute, and radical agrarian reforms demanded in the new Japan which is emerging from World War II.

Three phases of the agricultural depression. The table makes quite clear the three phases of agriculture's long postwar depression. First there was the severe shock of the collapse of European demand and the recession of industrial activity in 1921-22. The second period, from 1923 to 1929 inclusive, was characterized both by a vain struggle to regain the prewar price relationship between industry and agriculture, and, toward the end, by the beginnings of a new stabilization. The third is that marked by the world-wide economic cataclysm — the depression, which covers the years 1930 to 1933. In the last-named year a fourth period began with the coming of a new national administration. In the table above, the parity index turned upward. A new chapter in the history of American agriculture opened because of the vigorous and completely new program on which the national administration embarked in an effort to re-establish agricultural prosperity and, through it, to aid the nation. This program will be discussed later in this chapter.

Farm and urban dollars out of step. But first, by way of summary, an illustration of the working of the parity index may be given. In short, the farmer in March, 1933, was receiving only 50 cents for goods that he sold for $1 before the war, but he was paying $1.03 for what then cost $1. A pair of nationally advertised women's shoes could be bought for four bushels of wheat in 1920. Despite a 50 per cent cut in price, such a pair required eleven bushels in January, 1933.

Expressed in terms of prices, equally startling changes were occurring. Take, for instance, the story of wheat and bread. In 1928 the wheat producer's share of the retail price of a loaf of bread in New York City was 1.9 cents; that of the bakers, millers, transporters, and retailers, 7.2 cents. In 1932 the producer's share was 0.6 cents, a drop of 68 per cent. The others received 6.1 cents, a drop of 15 per cent, less than one fourth the decline suffered by the producer. Or, to take another instance, between 1929 and 1933 the price of sausage, pork chops, and other products from 100 pounds of live hog dropped from $16 to $10. Practically none of this drop was suffered by the meat packer, the railroad, or the butcher. All of that $6 drop came out of the pocket of the producer. And so with other agricultural products.

Serious results. What the situation meant can be read in terms of economic statistics and human experience. It caused a drop in farm income from about $12,000,000,000 in the later nineteen-twenties to just over $5,000,000,000 in 1932. Return on investment disappeared, land values dropped sharply, farm bankruptcies and tax sales rose sharply.

The indirect results were also serious. All this meant real suffering for tens of thousands of farm families and serious social and economic dislocation in thousands of rural communities. In the school year 1932-33 nearly ten thousand rural schools were opened for only part of the usual term or were closed altogether. In other communities teachers were not paid in full, or essential educational services were dispensed with. Other community institutions suffered, such as churches, the agricultural extension service, and those agencies of social welfare that had just begun in the nineteen-twenties to remedy their patent neglect of rural America.[3] The farmer and his wife made fewer purchases, and as a result it has been conservatively estimated that between six and seven million workers were unemployed either directly or indirectly because of the collapse of the farmer's purchasing power, approximately between one third and one half the total number of unemployed in the spring of 1933. Obviously, the merchant and the manufacturer suffered as well. The nation discovered that it could not prosper with agriculture prostrate.

One may well wonder what the historian of another century will say of the early months of 1933. In the world's richest nation perhaps one quarter of the able-bodied wage-earners of four years previous were eager for work that was not to be had. Thousands of them, their reserves gone, shuffled in city bread lines. Meanwhile, great piles of grain were rotting in the Middle West, fruit went unpicked on California trees, and heavy-hearted farmers were pouring milk into rivers, all because there was no one with the price to buy.

Because of this situation, because farmers, as was noted in another chapter, were losing their farms and homes by mortgage

[3] Only one third of the rural counties had a social worker resident within their borders in 1932, according to the American Country Life Association.

foreclosures and tax sales, sporadic violence broke out in many farming areas in 1932 and especially in 1933. The best known of these attempts was that of the Farmers' Holiday Association which sought to force higher prices by withholding goods from market and preventing shipments of food and milk from reaching urban markets.

The Agricultural Adjustment Act

Because of this situation President Franklin Delano Roosevelt and his administration decided, almost as soon as they assumed power, that the so-called Farm Act of 1933 was a national necessity to meet what the President termed "a national emergency." This law has introduced such vast changes into American farm practice and has such important sociological ramifications that a discussion of it is of prime importance. It represents, too, our first nation-wide effort to exert social control over a highly individualistic industry — agriculture; and as such, it will probably always have historic significance.

How the law operated. This act empowered the government to adjust production with effective demand in order to restore the farmer's buying power; to finance and readjust farm mortgages and interest payments; and to bring about controlled inflation. The heart of the law was the first provision.[4] The goal was to restore the relationship between the prices the farmer received and those he paid that existed between 1909 and 1914. This is the "parity price." Behind all our complicated modern price system, we are still bartering one thing for another, bushels of wheat and corn, quarts of milk, or pounds of rice, for shoes, radios, or medical care. When we exchange on even terms, trading goes on steadily. But when trading gets too one-sided, agriculture and industry together head for trouble.

The Secretary of Agriculture was to arrange with individual farmers of seven specified crops to reduce their acreage or production by a predetermined amount and to compensate them either by rentals or by direct benefit payments. The land not used for these seven crops was to be fallow or be planted to soil-conserving crops. The amount of these payments was supposed to be such as to give the farmer the buying power for his produce he would have received for it in the five years before World War I. This meant, if

---

[4] The Second Section became the responsibility of the Farm Credit Administration discussed elsewhere.

the law achieved its objective, that the farmer would receive as much in exchange for a bushel of wheat or corn or a bale of cotton as he did in the years 1909 to 1914. The funds for the payments were raised by small taxes on the processing of the crops included; wheat, cotton, hogs, field corn, rice, tobacco, and milk and its products. Crop plans were put into operation only after approval by the farmers concerned. The act was broadly conceived and gave wide powers to the Secretary of Agriculture so that, as conditions changed, changes could be made within certain limits. The wisdom of this was shown in the terrible drought of 1934. If 35,000,000 acres of the 40,000,000 taken out of production in that crop year had not been planted to soil-conserving forage crops, the damage to our livestock industry would have been a national calamity. The reductions arranged for in crops for which a plan was approved by the growers, applied *only* to the export portion of the crops. This was to prevent the risk of famine or high prices in the United States.

Farmer participation voluntary. The participation of any farmer in this plan to utilize or reduce food and fiber was voluntary and remained voluntary under subsequent legislation. It is important to stress this point, not only because of the charges of "regimentation" made against the Agricultural Adjustment Administration, but also because in practically all the other democracies of the world that have experimented with marketing or production controls, such as Great Britain, Denmark, the Union of South Africa, and Australia, the plan proposed became mandatory on *all* producers as soon as a given proportion of growers or the acreage had been committed to the plan. To give a single illustration, the Australian Cane-Sugar Law not only made an acreage reduction of 20 per cent mandatory on all but the smallest growers, but also forced the cane farmers not to grow cane on any of their acres except those used for the purpose when the law went into effect. Under our law, however, the government could exercise no compulsion, but by reimbursing the participants it made it possible for them to cut their production.

The law declared unconstitutional. In January, 1936, the Supreme Court, by a vote of six to three, declared the act unconstitutional on the ground that it violated states' rights. Washington was immediately flooded with demands from farmers and townsmen alike for a substitute law. As a stopgap measure, parts of the program were included in a Soil-Conservation Act in which control features were largely absent and the benefits of which applied to all farmers.[5] In 1938 a new act was passed, but, before summarizing it, a word must be said about the results of the first act.

Results of the first Agricultural Adjustment Act. The economic results of the act are a subject of debate among economists so far as its benefits to the nation as a whole are concerned, though there is no doubt but that the act increased farm purchasing power.[6]

In the local communities the results were quite significant. In 96 of the 140 investigated in the series of rural trends studies, farmers and villagers alike agreed that the act had been invaluable or had helped considerably. Ten more approved it, but felt the help had been slight. One in seven were opposed, the rest neutral. Opposition came almost entirely from areas where the first law did not apply, either because their crops were not included under the law or, as with dairying, because the producers failed to agree on a plan. Merchants in places where the act operated reported greatly increased sales and large payments on indebtedness. In the drought area there was great enthusiasm for the act. "It saved us from complete ruin," was a frequent comment by both farmers and villagers. Two instances are typical of many:

> In one village which had suffered from both low prices and drought, one merchant had carried farmers for two years, especially for purchases of food and gas. The Agricultural Adjustment Act saved him from bankruptcy. Within a few weeks after the receipt of the checks, farmers paid off $40,000 on their charge accounts, an equivalent of almost a year's average business. . . .
> . . . In one community, the banker traced the results of the first check to come in, a fairly large one. The farmer paid the hardware merchant, grocer, doctor, dentist, and tax collector. Both doctor and dentist turned over the farmer's checks to others in the community whom they owed, including again the tax collector, who was able thereby to make an overdue payment to the School Board, which forthwith made a two weeks' payment on back salaries due teachers, who in turn immediately put the money into circulation. As other checks arrived, there was a general circulation of the

[5] The ground of the Supreme Court decision aroused a storm of debate among farmers, the press of the nation, and constitutional lawyers. Much of the attack centered on the application of a "legal fiction" to an economic issue that transcended state lines. In a public address the late Lee McBain, Professor of Constitutional Law at Columbia University, called the decision one of the most important and most harmful ever made by the Supreme Court.

[6] The best sources of information on these points are to be found in the study by the Brookings Institution of Washington, entitled *Three Years of the Agricultural Adjustment Administration*, and in the *Journal of Farm Economics*, especially volume XVII, nos. 1, 2, and 3, and volume XVIII, nos. 1 and 2.

funds, wiping out old obligations and securing much-needed consumer goods, which cleared up the whole credit situation and stabilized the entire community.[7]

The law of 1938. The second Agricultural Adjustment Act, among other things, continues the soil-conservation program; provides for attempting to build up foreign markets for farm products and widen domestic distribution; grants loans on various farm commodities to prevent both price collapse and scarcity; sets up regional laboratories to find new uses for farm commodities and the by-products thereof; increases the share of payments to small farmers and tenants; secures greater protection for tenants with reference to payments and provides that the farmers by a two thirds vote may establish marketing quotas to be effective only when there are surpluses above what the domestic and foreign markets will absorb. If more than one third of the farmers under such conditions oppose such quotas, they cannot be put in effect.

Sociological considerations important and neglected. Too little attention has been paid to these. In the first place, huge proportions of the farmers concerned co-operated in the program. In the referenda held in the months before the Supreme Court decision nearly three million farmers voted on whether or not to continue specific crop programs, probably 90 per cent of the full-time farmers concerned. The favorable majorities were larger than in the first vote and ranged by crop from about 9 out of 10 to 49 out of 50. The 1938 act was not as popular, but still commanded overwhelming support in 1939.[8] The significant thing here was the unanimity of farm opinion and also the high degree of interest evidenced. American farmers may be, as is often claimed, individualistic, but, from whatever motives, they acted practically as a unit in this matter. This is significant and may become more so. If agriculture should begin to speak as a unit in national affairs, as business frequently does, or as labor did and may again, it will unquestionably become more powerful and more vocal in agricultural as well as in nonagricultural policies.

Again, the Department of Agriculture has tried to administer the

[7] Brunner, E. de S., and I. Lorge, *Rural Trends in Depression Years.* New York: Columbia University Press, 1937.

[8] About 85 per cent, or nearly 6,000,000 of all farm families, received AAA payments in 1939. Approximately 92 per cent of the cotton farmers, 80 per cent of corn and wheat growers and dairymen, and between 70 and 80 per cent of the tobacco, rice, and potato growers participated in the 1939 program. Cf. Statement of the Secretary of Agriculture before the Agricultural Sub-Committee of the Senate Appropriations Committee, April 13, 1939.

act democratically. The local and county administration was wholly in the hands of farmers elected by their fellows. They were paid a small per diem only for days worked. The five state committeemen, also elected, had to spend much more time on administrative business. This was a truly significant effort to tie the operation of the act close to the people concerned, who had voted to approve the programs. It also brought the federal government into a closer relationship to the individual farmer than ever before, through the medium of a neighbor. This was a device new to political science, and its significance is not as yet fully appreciated. However, these local committeemen have been brought into closer relationship with Washington than they ever had been before. The sociological effects of this organization and its contacts should not escape attention. Will these groups become a potent force in marshaling rural public opinion and thus constitute themselves a political power? Will they and the Agricultural Adjustment Act permanently change the ethical concepts of the farmer, and develop in the agrarian group the demand for the permanent assumption of the rôle of Santa Claus by the federal government? If so, may not class antagonism increase?

There are many who think that the answer to these questions is in the affirmative. They have observed that the feeling of farm solidarity has been strengthened. They point out that Congress continued benefit payments to farmers well into World War II and long after the original need had disappeared under the impetus of war prices.

Others are interested in the effect of the last decade and a half upon the social or institutional organization of agriculture. They point out that a new group of professional farm workers has arisen from the ranks of the farmers themselves, and that this is comparable to the development within the ranks of labor. A quarter of a century ago this group was small, represented only by the few persons on the staffs of the large state or national farm organizations. Not only are these staffs larger today, and their organizations more powerful, but they have been joined by farmers selected to represent their fellows in the multiplying new relationships of farmers and government. Inevitably, the processes of building a new social institution began. In some regions the process went further than in others and had to be restrained by administrative edict from the office of the Secretary of Agriculture, commanding the farm committeemen to stay within the law.

Other criticism of the act. The act has also been attacked on the grounds that it contravenes the law of supply and demand; that its objectives as they work out in dollars and cents would if achieved under present conditions create new problems; that it favors the farmer against the rest of the nation; that it was unethical to destroy cotton and reduce production when millions lack food and clothes; that the farmers by intensive cultivation on smaller areas raise as much as before; and finally, that the act will destroy initiative and undermine American traditions. There is also a real and far from groundless fear that since acreage has been sharply reduced, many tenants, especially the croppers in the South, will be dispossessed entirely. The experience thus far provides an effective answer to some but not all of these points.

Another problem that may prove increasingly difficult to cope with and which is beginning to raise critical questions arises from regional or crop variations in economic well-being. In 1938 the purchasing power of the farm cash income compared with 1929 on a percentage basis varied sharply among the states. West of the Mississippi River there were only two states that slightly exceeded 1929. One state had only 55.5 per cent as much as in 1929. Eleven others had less than 85 per cent. East of the Mississippi, on the other hand, two thirds of the states had a higher purchasing power of farm cash income than in 1929. The cotton states were prominent in the one third that fell below that level.[9] Variations of this sort were cared for under the first Agricultural Adjustment Act, invalidated by the Supreme Court, by extending aid only to depressed products and withdrawing aid when parity prices were established.

Another criticism relates to the use of any base period for an indefinite length of time. There were very few soya beans grown in the United States in 1909-14. What years are to be used for such new crops? Again, advances in technology have greatly reduced production costs of some crops, somewhat less of others, and very little of the costs of still others. Progress in efficiency has been uneven. Therefore, it is charged that some producers earn undue profits and the benefits of lowered costs are not passed along to the consumer.

Of course, the mere setting of a parity price does not guarantee that the farmer will get that price. As already noted, it took almost a decade after the passage of the first Agricultural Adjustment Act before farm prices as a whole crossed parity. It took the war to bring that about. This consideration has force at the moment,

[9] *United States News,* April 17, 1939.

however, because Congress has guaranteed the American farmer 90 per cent of parity, 92.5 per cent in the case of cotton, for two crop years after the end of World War II. This is defended because many farmers altered farm practices radically and at some cost to meet war needs.

However, this illustrates another difficulty; namely, the tendency of Congress to order changes in the formula. Its validity as a comparative basis is thereby further impaired. Men can obey laws, but economic facts are not subservient to any legislation. This same difficulty arose in connection with the administration of the guaranteed price law in New Zealand.

The war and parity. The war demands have held farm prices above parity for some years. The total agricultural production of the nation has broken all records despite lacks of labor, fertilizer, and machinery from 1938 to 1945. Aided by good weather, the farmer has worked miracles despite the handicaps. As with industrial production, questions have arisen as to the future of agriculture after the war if such production is maintained. It should be noted that the present act provides both for expansion and reduction. Will we again resort to reduction? Ideally, the destruction of food and fiber in a needy world is unjustifiable. The technique of industry applies to agriculture, of course, when there are few purchasers for its products. For instance, at one time in the depression steel production stood at 13 per cent of normal capacity despite needs for housing, rails, and other items. So with other industrial products. In short, this law is defended as a necessity in the sort of society which men have built for themselves. Its defenders admit that to challenge the law on this point is to challenge society.[10]

Part of the discussion of agricultural policy overlooks a very fundamental point. It is one thing to declare that "policies to limit output must be reversed all along the line," as the Land Grant College Association postwar policy report did. It is another to demand that farmers should be protected or subsidized in raising unlimited quantities of any crop beyond the capacity of the nation or world to absorb the production. Thus, at the insistence of senators and congressmen from the cotton states, the price of American cotton has been held above world prices for some years with legis-

[10] How this appears to one from a civilization still largely agrarian may be seen from the comment of a Chinese farmer's son studying in this country in 1932. Said he: "I do not understand America. In my country when people starve from famine, it is because we have not the railroads to take them the food. In this country you have the food and the railroads and still you let city people starve. Why don't you take food to them?"

lative help. This has encouraged the production of cotton else-where, and also the use of synthetic fiber. At this writing, the carry-over of cotton in the United States amounts to well over an entire year's crop, with another crop soon to come.

North America and Australia similarly have more improved acres per worker in agriculture than any other areas of the world. Especially in cereal crops they are therefore a dependable source of food in war, but normally they are surplus-producing areas. The solution for such surplus-producing farm groups would appear to be freedom of trade and perhaps subsidies to export their products to needy countries, as, for example, the United States sent wheat to China during the nineteen-thirties. But if, as seems likely after a few crops, there would still be unusable surpluses, there will be need for controls. There is no social sense in producing what is not needed when other commodities are needed much more.

For instance, the South could profit much by diet containing more of the so-called protective foods. As the Selective Service records show, there were many rejectees bcause of physical conditions caused by bad nutritional habits. This was not at all peculiar to the Southern region, though the incidence was greater there. Millions of people in the nation are ill-fed.

Just as land taken from unsalable crops in the nineteen-thirties was sowed to other crops which were more needed and more soil-conserving, so it may be wise to make comparable shifts in our farm management. There is nothing sacrosanct about the present patterns of our agriculture. They must be molded to the needs of society as based on the newer findings of science.

Can we raise enough? In 1929 the United States Department of Agriculture conducted a study to learn if the United States could raise enough to give its people a nutritionally adequate diet if the average yearly per family income should be raised to three thousand dollars, twice what it was in that prosperous year. It found that only in cereals and potatoes were we producing enough to meet the demand under such conditions. The study was ridiculed as theoretical and useless. But in 1943 and 1944, with average per family incomes at over four thousand dollars, America resorted to food-rationing. True, there were war and relief demands and war wastages. Many people blamed lend-lease exports of foods for these shortages. Actually, in the case of many products, we exported no more through Lend-Lease than we often exported in peacetime. The dramatic fact is that for the first time in our modern industrial history Americans had enough money to buy the diet they craved, the protective foods and proteins often denied to the poor. Statistically, America was better fed in the war years than from 1935 to 1939. High incomes produced the scarcity of wanted foods.

Many implications are to be had from this. One is that the farmer has a high stake in industrial prosperity. It has brought him good income in the same way that industry prospers when the fifty million people on the farms and in the service-station hamlets, villages, and towns have money with which to buy industrial products.

Another is that Americans will, if they have the means, buy the costlier and better foods.

A third is that with our interdependent society it is essential for agriculture, labor, and industry to join hands in maintaining a prosperous postwar America.

A fourth is that under such conditions it is far wiser to adjust farm management to demand than to subsidize less valuable and less nutritious crops. That is the best type of agricultural adjustment. It may require some subsidy while the change-over is being made. It is simply an agricultural equivalent of industrial reconversion.

The classical economist will say that the laws of economics will bring this about. Perhaps; but this cannot be taken for granted. "Agriculture is a way of life" is a well-worn phrase, but it is not an empty phrase. In the cotton country, school terms and vacations, church revivals, primary elections, and countless other events are fixed by the rhythm of the cotton year. A former president of the American Cotton Association once confessed to the writer that he had plowed up asparagus, which had netted him over two hundred dollars an acre, and put back cotton. He admitted that such a procedure made no sense from an economic point of view, but stated, "You see, the Lord meant this country to grow cotton. It's grown cotton for nigh on to three hundred years. You just can't quarrel with the Almighty."

Just as no policy of farm management or economics is without social results, so no type of agriculture is without its cultural roots which help hold in place the soil of tradition. Education or government, or both, must stimulate and inspire the needed action.

If depression comes. Postwar prosperity cannot be assumed. Then what of the problems of agricultural adjustment? In considering this question it is essential to take into account the historical review in the earlier portion of this chapter. It shows the terrible cost to American agriculture and the farmers of the long-continued agricultural depression. It was a cost measured in drastic reductions of purchasing power, resulting not only in lowered standards of living on the farm, but also in greatly increased unemployment in the cities. It was a cost measured in hundreds of thousands of evictions of farm families from their lands and homes, in disrupted communities and the spending of hundreds of millions of dollars in direct relief or remedial measures of various types. It was a cost measured in ten thousand bank failures and the wiping-out or impairment of the savings and equities of the more prosperous and stable portion of the farm and rural non-farm population. It was a cost measured in the closing of thousands of rural schools, depriving children of education and contributing to a lowered educational status for our population. It was a cost measured in the abandonment or reduction of the work in agricultural and home economic extension services, in public health, and other social fields. The social and economic costs are incalculable. Therefore, the stake of the nation, city and country alike, is very high in agricultural prosperity.

A retention of the parity principle is a solution which will obviously receive much support. It has been with us for over a decade. It was enacted to help agriculture, but also to help the nation by helping the farmer who is such a large segment of society. There will be other proposals, such as announcing in advance of the crop a price which the government will support or guarantee, as is done in New Zealand. This would enable farmers to plan and businesses to have some assurance as to the probable spending ability of the farm and the village people. Such a device could also become an instrument of social policy. By putting attractive "forward prices" on needed crops and less attractive prices on surplus crops farmers would have a powerful incentive to shift to the former crops, which are more in demand. Government subsidies to consumers in the form of aid for school lunches and a revival of the prewar food stamp plan could support either of these policies. There are those who advocate a government bounty paid on exports. This is regarded by many as "dumping." The United States will not permit foreign lands to "dump" surpluses on it, and such a proposal would arouse opposition abroad, bring retaliation against our products, induce trade wars, and have a serious negative effect on international relations in general and on such specific efforts toward international co-operation as the international Monetary Fund and the International Bank proposed by the Bretton Woods Conference.

It is not for the authors to advocate any specific solution or solutions. It is highly important to point out these issues, to stress the inevitability of adjustments, whether prosperity or depression follows World War II, and particularly to emphasize that, though the policies to be adopted are economic in nature, the profits or losses accruing must be measured in social terms as well, for they have social results of great magnitude. Man was not made for money. Rather money was invented by man as a tool for use.

DISCUSSION TOPICS

1. If benefit payments have been made in your community, how has the money been used and how has the community benefited? Ask your banker, storekeeper, the tax collector, and others about this matter.

2. From the agricultural census secure information as to quantities of chief crops raised in your state for 1900, 1910, 1920, and 1930. If possible, compare with prices received. Interpret the results.

3. Compare over a series of months the prices of various kinds of goods the farmer sells (such as cattle, cotton, vegetables, etc.). Are prices of farm commodities going up as fast as prices of manufactured commodities?

4. Make a study of your own or some near-by neighborhood to see how much it has been affected by the agricultural depression and the Agricultural Adjustment Act.

   a. Interview men and women engaged in various types of work in order to determine their attitudes toward the agricultural situation. Go through local newspaper files and study the Farm Act in relation to what local people have had to say about it.

5. Trace the exports on a given crop, the prices received on the farm in your state and the total production by five-year periods from 1900 to 1935. Graph your results and interpret them.

6. Conduct a class debate on the subject of the Agricultural Adjustment Act, such as, "Resolved: that the Agricultural Adjustment Act has retarded national recovery," or, "Resolved: that the Agricultural Adjustment Act is unfair to urban America."

7. Contrast the functions performed by the pioneer and the modern farm family in order to gain a livelihood.

REFERENCE READINGS

Achieving a Balanced Agriculture. Washington, D.C.: Department of Agriculture, 1934.

Agricultural Adjustment: 1933-35. Washington, D.C.: Department of Agriculture, 1936.

Baker, O. E., "Agriculture and Forest Land," in *Recent Social Trends,* vol. I, pp. 90-121. New York: McGraw-Hill, 1933.

Beard, C. A., *The Rise of American Civilization,* chap. XXII. New York: The Macmillan Co., 1927.

Black, John, *Parity, Parity, Parity.* Cambridge: Harvard University, 1942.

Blaisdell, Donald C., *Government and Agriculture.* New York: Farrar and Rinehart, 1940.

Brandt, Karl, *The Reconstruction of World Agriculture.* New York: W. W. Norton & Co., 1945.

Brunner, E. de S., *The Farm Act of 1933.* New York: Teachers College Bureau of Publications, 1933.

Brunner, E. de S., and J. H. Kolb, *Rural Social Trends,* chap. II. New York: McGraw-Hill, 1933.

Ezekiel, Mordecai, and Louis H. Bean, *Economic Bases for the Agricultural Adjustment Act.* Washington, D.C.: Government Printing Office, 1933.

Nourse, E. G., J. Dewis, and G. Black, *Three Years of the Agricultural Adjustment Administration.* Washington, D.C.: The Brookings Institution, 1937.

Reports of the Secretary of Agriculture, 1934-39. Washington, D.C.

Schafer, J., *The Social History of American Agriculture.* New York: The Macmillan Co., 1936.

Schmidt, Carl T., *American Farmers in the World Crisis.* New York: Oxford University Press, 1941.

Schultz, Theodore W., *Redirecting Farm Policy.* New York: The Macmillan Co., 1943.

Schultz, Theodore W., *Agriculture in an Unstable Economy.* New York: McGraw-Hill Book Co., 1945.

PART THREE

GROUP RELATIONSHIPS

11

Rural Families

FAMILIES remain the firm foundation of our American society. This is true despite all the population changes detailed in previous chapters, the general downward and recent upward trend of birth rates, increase of divorces, world wars and depressions. The latest census reports from which materials are drawn for this chapter make this quite clear. Families are important groups in any society, but especially in rural society. The farm family is the working unit as well as the living unit. Any country scene is convincing evidence of this, for there in one cluster stand the house and the barn surrounded by smaller buildings and yards, with the fields beyond. The whole layout is called the "homestead" and it has a social connotation which means far more than such terms as "farm," "factory," or "store." These family groups are more isolated physically than are urban families, although they may not be more isolated socially, as some have assumed. Many intimate contacts are maintained with neighbors and with relatives.

The village family resembles the farm family in many respects. Its dwelling and place of business are not far apart; they may even be in the same building. Both home and business are located near neighbors and relatives with whom associations are personal. Judged by various characteristics, the village family stands between the country and the city family.

The family can be defined as a genetic group bound by kinship and marital ties. It is a group consisting of father, mother, and children, living together under one roof. Many times rural households are not so simply composed. A grandfather or maiden aunt may be living there also, or perhaps a younger family is living with the parents. There may be hired help or summer boarders also, and consequently it is necessary to distinguish between the immediate natural family and the larger household.

The younger family may live in a separate house on the same farm, on an adjoining farm, or in the same village as the parents. There may also be married brothers or sisters, aunts or uncles. In this case it is the "great family" of relatives and kinsfolk. Frequently the great family is of more importance than is the individual family, in matters of social control, in perpetuating attitudes and forming opinions. This is especially true if its members live in the same locality and thus form the neighborhood group.

Family groups, like other groups in society, have their own social institutions such as home, standards of living, household systems, marriage, and divorce. Some of these will be considered in later chapters, but it is the family as a social group to which attention is given here. In common with other groups, families are not static but dynamic, always changing, adjusting and readjusting to their own internal as well as to their external environments.

THE EARLY AMERICAN FAMILY

As a background against which to view changes in the more modern rural family, a brief sketch of the earlier or pioneer family is drawn. Longer perspectives are useful in periods of seemingly rapid and radical changes. Literature abounds with stories of early settlement. A sort of "myth" has been built, sometimes deliberately, about the "early American family." It has its variations, from region to region, from New England to Southern plantation and Western pioneer, but in essentials it is much the same.

Land — private property in land — stands out in dramatic fashion as one of the important features of early American agricultural and family life. Questions of land, its utilization, taxation, and possession, continue to be dominating issues, as, for example, the land-planning policies of the New Deal. In the settlement days before and after the Homestead Act of 1862, ownership of land was the symbol of a domestic economy, whether for the Pennsylvania farmer, the Western pioneer, or the Southern planter. As Doctor Wilson has phrased it, "the household farmer owned his home. He built upon his farm a homestead which represented his ideal of domestic and family comfort. He built for permanence. So far as his means permitted, he provided for his children and for generations of descendants." [1] This relationship of land, family, and home is the background for many writers' interpretations of country life. It may be Whittier's *Snow-Bound;* Hamlin Garland's *Son of the Middle Border;* Gladys Carroll's *As the Earth Turns;* or Louis Bromfield's *The Farm.* This relationship represents the "social origins" of the rural family.

[1] Wilson, Warren H., *The Evolution of the Country Community*, Rev. Ed., p. 22. Chicago: Pilgrim Press, 1923.

Self-maintenance with a sense of isolation is another characteristic of the early rural family. The importance of this fact to agriculture and the business of farming will be detailed in a later chapter, but for the family and its household, it is the tradition which
has been passed on in such stereotypes as "independence," "individualism," "integrity," and the like. Without doubt the roots of
this tradition extend back into the Old World. Stories of the
struggle of pioneer families attempting to maintain themselves economically, socially, and religiously, serve as contrasts for those who
today are striving to remake rural society by such means as co-operative marketing, community organizations, or larger parish churches.
How strange it sounds to hear Mr. Wright telling of his early family experiences in Otsego County, New York, in 1848. "Our new
home was in a comparative wilderness; not a house was in sight.
The nearest neighbors on the south and east lived over a mile from
us. On the west, the nearest lived three fourths of a mile, and on
the north over one fourth of a mile; and a thick dark forest inter-
vened." [2] Today these would seem like near neighbors, too near
perhaps for some kinds of commercial agriculture. The swing away
from the idea of self-maintenance in some quarters of highly specialized production has been very wide, but like so many extremes,
it has swung back again until one finds that "subsistence homesteads" are one emphasis within the present planning for agriculture. There can be little doubt that the early isolation and the
sense of independence did much to magnify the importance of the
family and to intensify its relationships.

Kinship, with a sense of solidarity, was another important bond
in the framework of the early family. This feature stands at least
in partial contrast to the former, but it is questionable whether
such complete independence or such entire isolation as some writers
have suggested really did exist. A sense of kinship, of continuing
a line of common descent, must have been a sustaining force in
those pioneering experiences. Moreover, kinsfolk tended to settle
in small clusters or neighborhoods as will be described in the next
chapter. The pioneer family of Footes in Vermont, for example,
sent some of its branches to New York, or "York State," as it was
called. They, in turn, sent younger members to Ohio and to Wisconsin; and so on to Iowa and to California. No one individual
family went alone; it was always in company with others, aunt or
uncle, brother or sister, or cousin. Communication and contacts

[2] Wright, H. C., *Human Life: Illustrated in My Individual Experience.*
Boston, 1849.

were relatively frequent. Letters flowed freely, and annual or semi-annual visits were made, even though it did take almost a week to return by team and buckboard from Iowa to Wisconsin. Fealty to kinsman, then, is one of the great heritages of the early rural family. This bond of the great family was a strong influence. To what extent it is a factor which can still be counted upon, and to what extent it has been dissipated by the greater mobility and by what may even be termed the larger independence of the modern family is a problem for the student of modern rural society to consider.

CHARACTERISTICS AND CHANGES OF RURAL FAMILIES

Present-day rural families need to be considered against the background of the early American family. This is true because one who would understand rural society or would endeavor to change it must know not only those forces and processes related to the past, but also those which can be utilized for the future. The rural family, of course, must be considered as a usual family, not as something different and distinct; yet it does possess certain characteristics which can be identified and which are useful for our study. Five of these will be considered here.

In the midst of its occupation. A striking characteristic of the farm family, and to a lesser extent of the village family, is that it lives in the midst of its occupation. Its residence is as fixed a part of the layout as are the barns, fields, or fences. The family and its homestead, together with the farm and its farmstead, make up the living and the working unit. This, then, is the physical and the social setting or environment in which the farm family group lives and works.

The village family included in the term "rural," is not so different in its setting. As is the case with so many village characteristics, the village family stands midway between farm and city families, partaking of the nature of each, but having traits of its own. It is not uncommon for a village retail or repair business to be conducted as a family responsibility and for the living quarters to be in the same or in an adjoining building. It is common indeed for the family to own its own land on which is found its house, its garden, and even its business establishment.

The occupational environment puts all the members of the family group into close contact with each other. It is in this world that the group develops and builds up its modes of behavior and

its institutions and traditions. Acquaintance with this world is best
gained by contact with those who live in it. Brief extracts from case
stories, written by college students, of their own home are therefore given.[3]

> I believe my father should be considered an average father,
> judged by the standards of his community. He always seemed to
> me to put far more thought on having the best corn crop, the
> largest potatoes by the Fourth of July, etc., than he did on dispos-
> ing of them to the best advantage. The income for the family was
> not adequate for the standards which were my mother's goal. There
> were times when I wonder how she contrived to manage as she did
> and give us the opportunities she did. We always had plenty of
> good food, but my mother's ingenuity, industry and instilling the
> necessity for care of materials into us were the factors which for
> years solved the problem of comfortable and attractive clothing for
> her large family.
>
> My mother and the girls in our family did very little work in
> the fields, which was rather singular, since there were so many
> girls and only one boy, and since it was customary for women to
> work in fields. We, the girls, helped pick up potatoes, and pick
> sweet corn several summers when my father had contracted some
> for a canning factory. My mother did much work in the garden,
> always raised many chickens, and helped milk until brother as-
> sumed the task. My mother was always opposed to the girls learn-
> ing to milk and none of us did. We thought it a lark to ride on the
> hayload, get a chance to lead the horses to water, etc. This was
> probably because we were not required to do so.

It is this sort of family life which has influenced students of the
family to conclude that rural families have developed characteristics of their own. LePlay, the great French scholar of family life,
places a great deal of stress on what he terms "successful families,"
upon the sentimental attachment or relationship which exists between the family group and its homestead or its "hearth." Thus, at
least one of the backgrounds of the early family seems to have extended its influence through the years to the present, namely, the
organization of a family occupation about the utilization and possession of land.

As a matter of fact, agriculture is the last of the great industries
to be operated on the individual family plan. Although it must be
recognized that there are variations among the various types of
farming, such as cotton, grain, dairy, and fruit and truck farms,

---

[3] Lively, C. E., *Readings in Rural Sociology*, vol. I, "Life in the Farm
Family." Mimeograph by H. L. Hedrick, Columbus, Ohio, 1933.

essentials of the family pattern are found in them all. Of course, the question of future trends arises. If the Industrial Revolution completely overtakes agriculture, what will become of the rural family? Will it become just like urban families and lose its distinguishing characteristics? There was some evidence pointing in this direction just prior to 1929. Since then other trends have appeared. For example, the difference in size between urban and rural families widened in the decade 1930 to 1940. This is partially explained by the migration of city families from large urban centers to their suburban fringes. Farm families also continue to be significantly larger than urban families.

As an earlier chapter has shown, the proportion of small farms increased to 1930, and even though there was a tendency toward consolidation into larger operating units in certain regions during the war years, at least three fifths of the farms can be considered family farms. In addition, there has been an increase in the number of part-time farms; also in what might be called "residence" farms, especially in those areas adjoining industrial centers. There is little to indicate that the family farm will not remain a dominant pattern in many sections of the United States for a long time.

During the depression years, government policy encouraged the family farm as an offset to widespread unemployment in cities. Credit and financing plans were introduced to check the inconsistency of taking farms away from those families who really wanted to farm. Many programs are being promoted by public and private agencies to make farms available to those returning from military and industrial services. The number that will take advantage of these arrangements, of course, cannot be predicted.

More family units in terms of adult population. The early American family was part of a domestic economy, and the rural family, in its close contact with its occupation, has continued this system to a greater degree than have families in other sections of our society. It is to be expected, therefore, that in terms of the adult population, relatively more family units are found in rural than in other sections of society. This is true because country people marry earlier in life; the union is less frequently broken, and there is a tendency for the unmarried and those left by broken marriages, either by divorce or death, to migrate. The latter is especially true of country girls and women. The country simply does not serve as a hospitable place for single persons, especially for unmarried girls and women.

Family is the law of the land. In 1940, 7,000,000 of the 35,000,000 families were on farms and another 7,000,000 lived in rural territory and were known as "non-farm" families. While the size of all families has declined, the marriage rate has held even. Therefore, there has been an increase in the proportion of all families to population. Total population increased 110 per cent from 1890 to 1940, but the number of families increased much more, namely 175 per cent.

More rural people than urban marry in the age groups fifteen years and over. The percentage of farm men who are married, as shown in Table 29, seems to be an exception to this generalization.

TABLE 29. MARITAL STATUS OF POPULATION 15 YEARS OLD AND OVER, EXPRESSED IN PER CENT BY SEX, RURAL AND URBAN, 1940

Rural and Urban	Per cent Married	
	Males	Females
Total United States............	61.2	61.0
Urban......................	61.8	58.1
Rural non-farm...............	62.7	64.5
Rural farm....................	58.3	66.3

Source: *Sixteenth Census of the United States*, 1940, *Population*, vol. IV, Part I. Characteristics by age, marital status, relationship, education, and citizenship.

However, when the age group fifteen to twenty-four years is considered separately, the difference between farm and urban males is not significant, but the difference between farm males and farm females of this age is significant: it is 2 per cent for males compared with 15.3 per cent for females. The number of males in this age group is relatively larger in the open country, and the marriage rate is lower than for the females. Even in the next age group, twenty to twenty-four years, nearly twice the number of farm girls are married as are farm boys.

The family group, once formed, is less likely to be broken in rural than in urban areas, or if broken, is more likely to re-form, or the remaining members will migrate. A little more than one sixth of the families in the nation as a whole were reported in 1940 as being headed by persons widowed, divorced, or separated. The most frequent cause was the death of husband or wife, accounting for 71 per cent of the cases, or 12 per cent of all families. The difference between rural and urban society is significant. Only 4.5 per cent of males and 8.8 per cent of females, fifteen years old and over, on farms, were widowed, while for the rural non-farm females the rate was 16.6, but for males only 4.6 per cent. The urban rate was 12.4 for women and 4.2 for men.

TABLE 30. MARITAL STATUS OF THE POPULATION 15 YEARS OLD AND OVER, EXPRESSED IN PER CENT, BY COLOR AND SEX, RURAL AND URBAN, 1940

Rural and Urban	Per cent Males Married		Per cent Females Married	
	White	Non-white	White	Non-white
Total United States.......	61.3	60.0	61.2	58.5
Urban..................	61.9	60.8	58.3	56.2
Rural non-farm..........	63.1	58.6	65.0	58.8
Rural farm.............	58.2	59.5	66.9	62.6

Source: *Sixteenth Census of the United States*, 1940, *Population*, vol. IV, Part I. Characteristics by age, marital status, relationship, education, and citizenship.

TABLE 31. MARITAL STATUS OF POPULATION 15 YEARS OLD AND OVER, EXPRESSED IN PER CENT BY REGION AND SEX, 1940

Total United States	Per cent Married	
	Males	Females
United States..................	61.2	61.0
North Eastern States...........	59.3	57.6
North Central States..........	61.5	62.0
The South....................	63.1	62.3
The West....................	60.2	63.2

Source: *Sixteenth Census of the United States*, 1940, *Population*, vol. IV, Part I. Characteristics by age, marital status, relationship, education, and citizenship.

Conclusions from special studies which are reported in a succeeding chapter suggest that villages and small towns become the haven for separated family members, especially if the family group is broken by the death of the father. Those divorced, especially women, seek opportunities in towns and larger cities. In general, it can be said that broken families are found twice as frequently in the city as in the country.

Although death rates have fallen, increased divorce rates have completely offset their effect as far as the general family situation is concerned. Divorces accounted for 9.3 per cent of all broken families in 1940, but when those separated (19.6 per cent) were added, it meant that three out of every ten families were headed by a person divorced or separated. For all families the proportion was one out of every twenty. Among the farm population about one half as many males and one third as many females were recorded by the census as being divorced, as in the general population.

In a special study of the Chicago metropolitan area in 1930, it was found that one in every ten homes was broken by separation or divorce. In Chicago itself, it was one in every seven or eight, while in the rural territory surrounding the city the rate was one in twenty-three, despite the fact that divorce was increasing in rural areas.[4] Families with children are less likely to be broken by divorce, and this has peculiar significance for rural society.

In summary, the selective factor of migration has much to do with the population characteristics of rural society and certainly with its family comparisons. City conditions and opportunities attract certain kinds of people, which is only another way of saying that farm or country life is unfavorable to some people. Girls, for example, leave farm homes more frequently than do boys and about two years younger. Those who remain marry earlier than the boys. Likewise, children of tenant farm families and of owner families with lower incomes are more likely to leave than others. A large majority of single, widowed, and divorced women are quite sure to leave the country for village, town, or city.

Also, during the depression years of the nineteen-thirties, population movements or lack of such movements toward cities made it evident that the age distribution of the farm population shifted somewhat toward lower age levels. Some young people in cities sought refuge in the country from disillusionment and unemployment. With the coming of the war and war-boomed industrial opportunities in urban centers, the whole migration process was again reversed. Many sections of the farm population are now in the upper age brackets.

What the postwar period holds in store cannot be predicted with certainty, but it seems certain that many rural youth returning from military and industrial services will remain in the country to form their own families, and urban families with children or those in the younger age groups themselves will continue to be found in larger numbers among the rural non-farm population than before the war. It is certainly safe to say that rural society will continue as a society of families and of children.

[4] Ogburn, W. F., *Recent Social Trends*, chap. 13, p. 680. New York: McGraw-Hill, 1933.

Children, the distinguishing characteristic. Discussion of family occupation and distribution lead to questions of family composition. Children are most characteristic of rural families; in fact, they are the most distinguishing thing about rural society itself. The country produces children, the city consumes them. This is one of the fundamentals in rural-urban relationships. It is at the basis of rural to urban migration and its many attendant and necessary readjustments.

Before the war, slightly more than three fourths of all families were units consisting of husband and wife living together with or without children. A little more than 6 per cent were families with a single head. In spite of the rapid rise in marriage rates and in birth rates, too, during the years following the outbreak of the war, and despite the undoubted increase when the armed forces and those in military-industrial centers are demobilized, the general trend of the family pattern is quite certain to continue its long-time downward trend through the postwar period.

While the size of the family may continue to decline, it is not without its consequence for the future that in 1940 more than one half of all the men at heads of families and living with their wives were under forty-five years of age, and that three fourths of these were providing for one or more dependent children under seventeen years of age. Among those households with husbands over forty-five years of age, about two fifths had children under eighteen.

One hundred and fifty years ago, in 1790, the size of the family household in the United States was 5.7; a hundred years later it was 4.9, and fifty years later, in 1940, it was 3.8. This means, of course, fewer than two children per household, while under present rates of mortality, it is necessary for the average number to be at least three in order to maintain a stationary population. For all urban places, the average family size in 1940 was 3.6 persons, while in all rural areas it was 4. Since 1930 the decrease in metropolitan centers was more rapid than in the general urban classification. This again is partially explained by movements of families to suburban areas.

Comparison of fertility ratios given in an earlier chapter makes the consequence of this family trend even more dramatic. In the period 1935 to 1940, for example, the net reproduction rate for the urban population was only 74, while the farm rate was 144, that is, 44 per cent in excess of what was needed to maintain itself. The rural non-farm rate stood between, at 114 per cent, but it should be observed that it was closer to the farm than to the urban rate.

If this general trend should continue in the postwar era, then one would expect the urban population to decline by one fourth in each generation, and the farm to increase by almost one half in the same period, surely a very unbalanced condition.

General averages, however, do not reveal the whole situation. In that study of Chicago and its metropolitan environs to which reference was made, it was found that the size of the family itself, not the entire household, in the city center was 2.8 in 1930, a decrease of 11 per cent in thirty years. The number of farm families in the area had increased 63 per cent in the same period, while the small towns increased 39 per cent. Expressed in slightly different terms, if the size of the farm family in this situation were to be expressed by 100, the size of families in the small towns would be represented by 86, those in the small cities by 79, but those in the metropolitan center itself by 66. These are significant differences.

Composition of households can be compared from the census summaries as illustrated in Table 32. In the chart it is family rather

TABLE 32. POPULATION IN HOUSEHOLDS BY RELATIONSHIP TO HEAD, EXPRESSED IN PERCENTAGE, RURAL AND URBAN, 1940

Relationship	Total U.S.	Rural Farm	Rural Non-farm	Urban
Total	100.	100.	100.	100.
Head (no. private households)	27.2	23.6	27.8	28.5
Wife	20.7	19.3	21.4	21.0
Child	39.9	46.2	40.8	37.1
Grandchild	1.9	2.6	1.8	1.6
Parent	1.7	1.6	1.5	1.9
Other relatives	4.3	4.1	3.5	4.6
Lodger	3.5	1.6	2.6	4.6
Servant or hired hand	0.8	1.2	0.6	0.7

Source: *Sixteenth Census of the United States*, 1940, *Population*, vol. IV, Part I. Characteristics by age, marital status, relationship, education, and citizenship.

than household which is made the basis for comparison. As in all other comparisons, it is clear that children are the distinguishing characteristics of farm families.

There are significant differences, however, among various types of families. For example, families of farm owners decreased 19 per cent in size in the thirty years following 1900, while those of farm renters increased 5 per cent; those of farm laborers increased 13 per cent. When families with wives of the same age group, thirty-five to thirty-nine years, were compared, it was found that farm-owner families declined somewhat in size, while farm-laborer families did not. Among urban groups during the same period, the greatest decline in size was found among the professional group, about 10 per cent. In the proprietary group the decline was 6 per cent, in the clerical, 5 per cent; in the skilled and semi-skilled, 3 per cent, and in the unskilled, 11 per cent, the same as in the farmer-owner group.[5]

It is interesting to find that the non-farm family units take their usual place between the farm and city family groups, and that growing villages have a higher ratio of children than villages with a declining population, as will be shown in greater detail in Chapter 13. Therefore, questions arise as to how to provide for the education and the health of this disproportionate number of farm and village children. There are also questions respecting child labor, since agriculture is an occupation in which children live and work during school age. The experience may be a useful apprenticeship or it can be turned into exploitation. Some of these questions will be dis-

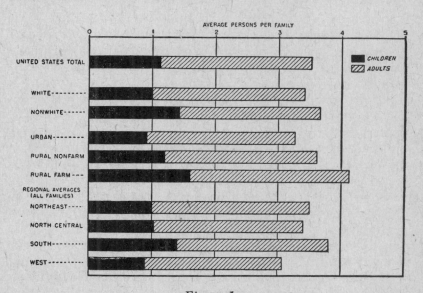

Figure 1

AVERAGE NUMBER OF PERSONS PER FAMILY, BY
COLOR, RESIDENCE, AND REGION, 1940

[5] Woofter, T. J., "Children and Family Income," *Social Security Bulletin,* vol. 8, no. 1, January, 1945. Washington, D.C.: Social Security Board.

cussed in other chapters, but the next point to consider is that the family is a changing group; it moves through a recognized cycle.

Rural families have a distinctive life cycle. The family group must not be considered as a static thing. A family made up of a wife, husband, and one or two children, does not necessarily stay just that way. Family groups are formed of two original members; children are born and grow up; some leave temporarily, some permanently, so that sometimes the group is reduced to its original two members. More concisely stated, families go through life cycles. They experience periods of formation, development, augmentation, and decline. In rural families the cycle ordinarily requires about twenty-five years. Each period entails different requirements, diverse relationships, and to some extent, varying characteristics.

In order to secure a better understanding of some of the differences in family relationships in the various periods of development, 267 farm families were chosen for special study from a total of 900 families, representing all of the major farming type areas of a Mid-Western state.[6] The periods or stages of development were defined primarily in terms of school ages of the children. Four stages were considered: the pre-school, with children under six years of age; grade-school, with children six to thirteen years; high-school, with children fourteen to eighteen years; and the all-adult, with children nineteen or more years of age.

For the majority of all farm families, the pre-child period was found to be short, since the family usually increased in size within the first or second year. The post-child period is reached after all the children have left home and the family is again composed of the operator and homemaker. Most farm families of the post-child period, however, were found to contain at least one grown son or daughter who was helping with the farm or home work. Such families were thus classed in the all-adult group. The average size of family increased from 4.1 persons in the pre-school stage to 5.1 persons in the high-school age and returned again to 4.1 persons in the all-adult.

(1) *The pre-school family* is a young family in a double sense: it has existed a relatively short period of time, and usually its operator and homemaker are between twenty-five and thirty-five years of age. Pre-school families, in contrast to those in other stages of

[6] Kirkpatrick, Tough, Cowles, *The Life Cycles of the Farm Family in Relation to Its Standards of Living.* Madison: Research Bulletin 121, Agricultural Experiment Station, University of Wisconsin, September, 1934.

development, spend more time in reading and listening to the radio, and they are usually more interested in community affairs.

In the depression period, many farm families were unable to meet interest and tax payments. Children's illnesses went without professional medical care or doctors' bills went unpaid. This became a major family problem, not only from the standpoint of the future health situation of the children, but in family relationships, because mothers of pre-school children made it very clear that in their minds children were more important than unpaid interest or delinquent taxes. When money became more plentiful in the war period, the greatest expansion in family expenditures was for medical care, especially among a group of relatively low-income farm families, as will be detailed in the chapter on home and standards of living.

(2) *The grade-school family* is similar in many respects to the pre-school family, although, of course, the operator and homemaker are older. It, too, is making sacrifices to climb the "agricultural ladder," is finding it difficult to meet interest and tax payments, and has relatively high expenditures for medical care.

In talking about plans for the future, homemakers and operators in this stage of development are primarily concerned with education for the children. The family will have to make provision for these future educational needs at the sacrifice of many other things including even immediate housing improvements, as was indicated in a conversation with Mrs. Roth, who is the mother of children in grade school. Her ambition for her two children is a high-school education. In addition, she wishes her son to go to college to learn to be a "real farmer." She stated that neither Mr. Roth nor she went to high school, but "no matter what happens, the children are going because they need it and must have it." This story is a good illustration of the projection upon the children of the unfulfilled educational desires of the parents. Such projection is more likely to be characteristic of the family with younger children.

(3) *The high-school family* presents a decided contrast to the two earlier stages. In this period the family is larger than at any other stage, reaching its maximum size of 5.1 persons and, obviously, children or adolescents constitute three fifths of this family. In this group the labor of the boys and girls is a substitute for hired help. Wants in the high-school stage are many and varied. They make themselves felt in expenditures for clothing, and advancement goods and services for the children. In rural areas it is necessary for the children to go to the neighboring village high school

and this involves either expenditures for transportation or for board and room. In addition, expenses for advancement goods take the form of relatively high outlays for reading materials, for organization dues, and for recreation. Hours spent in reading and listening to radio programs at home drop for this group as compared with the others.

Since the amount of cash available for family living in this group is not necessarily more than that at the other three stages of family development, the relatively large amounts spent for clothing and advancement must result in curtailment of expenditures for other goods and services. This reduction occurs in such items as furnishings, household operation, maintenance of health, and insurance.

(4) *The all-adult family* has greater expenditures for family living than any other group. This indicates not only that the wants in this group are greater and more diverse than those at the other stages of development, but also a greater tendency to gratify them. Relatively large expenditures are made by families in this stage for clothing, furnishings, schooling, reading matter, church support, recreation, and personal goods.

Often the all-adult stage of development is a period when anticipated wants on the part of the parents for the children are fulfilled, at least in part. The children are educated, have positions, have been married and very often are beginning another family cycle. The child who has fulfilled the family's desires is a source of satisfaction to his parents.

Closer family relationships. Composition and cycle of families as described above has, of course, a direct bearing on their whole internal, social relationships. An interesting formula of family interaction has been devised which holds that with the addition of each person to the family group, the number of persons increases in simple, whole numbers, while the number of personal interrelationships within the group increases in the order of triangular numbers.[7] For example, the first child increases the number of persons in the family by one, but it increases the number of personal relationships by two; that is, from one to three. Another member would increase the number of persons to four, but the personal relationships from three to six; that is, increased by three. This has important implications for the larger rural families.

The increased diversity of household with distinct differences between those on the farm and those in urban centers has been

7 Bossard, James H. S., "The Law of Family Interaction," *American Journal of Sociology*, January, 1945.

shown in a general way. The point can be detailed by considering the natural family rather than the household as a whole; also by breaking down urban figures into the metropolitan centers and into the smaller cities classified as urban. This was done in the special study of the Chicago area to which reference has been made. Two and a half times as many unbroken farm families had children as did those in the metropolis. In the farm group, 35 per cent of the families with husbands and wives living together had more than two children; in the city center only 6 per cent. When taken together, there were about three and a half times fewer husbands living alone and wives living alone on farms than in the metropolitan center. The family situation for the towns and for cities of about 100,000 population fell between the two extremes. The family type with husband, wife, and four or more children, presented a strong contrast of 19 per thousand in the metropolitan center compared with 214 on the farms. For the nation as a whole, only 2.7 of city families had four or more children under ten years of age, compared with 4.8 per cent of rural non-farm families and 7.7 per cent of the rural farm families.

The presence of children is, therefore, a primary consideration in the social relationships of families. These relationships appear to have characteristic solidarity and cohesion among families in rural society; there are various means of studying and observing them. Interesting illustrations are found in family case stories written by college students and quoted here from sources to which previous reference has been made.

> When I look back now, I am sure she, mother, was overburdened. I think she was so busy caring for the physical needs of her children, that she did not have time to enjoy them. Much of her care of the younger children fell to me, since I was the oldest and a girl. Even yet I feel a deep responsibility for the other children, and find myself eternally planning and deciding for them, when there is no need and they would many times prefer that I did not.
>
> Father had the greater say-so. He did not consider mother his inferior. She belonged in the house and he over the place in general. He didn't consider her his equal in some cases for the reason that he did transact most of the business. Furthermore, mother wasn't interested in details. Mutually, they both decided to make things go, and they did go. Mother did not feel inferior to father and she never felt that he expected her to feel so. She knew that he knew what he wanted and both were interested in making things go. So they worked together. Even with all the drudgery they enjoyed working together and going places together.

It is also significant that professional leaders in agriculture whose duty it is to assist farmers in their farm management and economic problems should have concluded that the wife's co-operation is a very important consideration. Even their measuring stick of profits points to the importance of the wife in the farm enterprise. They report that since no exact measure of her co-operation was possible, they chose for comparison seventeen families in which co-operation was evident and seventeen in which there was least evidence of it. The average labor earnings showed a difference of $915. This might seem too great a difference, but it is even more significant that farm operators themselves ranked the co-operation of their wives second on a list of fifteen items which they regarded as most important in the success of the farm.[8] At least it is evidence of the close relationship of family and farm. Farm management can be stressed and home management can be emphasized, but encompassing the two is family management; farming is a family affair.

The close relationship of the family in its farming and its home-making is becoming more generally recognized in many professional circles, but it is doubtful that the implications are fully realized. In a recent issue of the Agricultural Extension Service, a home economics worker stresses the point that during the early organization of this work there was a tendency to "carve up" the family into three parts: the farmer, the home-maker, and the children. "We lost sight," she says, "of the fact that the family is a social and economic unit with co-operative relationships. Certain things are to be done by the man, and there are certain things to be done by the women, but both are home-makers. So are the children."[9]

The closely knit relationships of the family carry over into the rural situation of which it is a part. Many studies and observations confirm this. For example, in a study of family resettlement it became evident that in the internal relations among the family members, their attitude toward one another and toward the farm, as well as the interfamily relations with neighbors, might easily become a handicap which would preclude successful adjustment of the family with the land.[10]

[8] Wilcox, Boss, Pond, *Relation of Variations in the Human Factor to Financial Returns in Farming*, Bulletin 288. Minneapolis: University of Minnesota, Agricultural Experiment Station, 1932.

[9] Barry, Maggie W., "Rededication to Truth," *Extension Service Review*. Washington, D.C.: United States Department of Agriculture, June-July, 1944; Milam, Ava B., "Strengthening Home Economics Stakes," *Journal of Home Economics*, vol. 36, no. 10, December, 1944.

[10] Hill, George W., Walter Slocum, Ruth O. Hill, *Man-Land Adjustment.*

Women are assuming a greater amount of leadership in rural organizations than in the earlier days. In some localities they now make up about 50 per cent of the officers, and incidentally, their education in terms of schooling is about two years more than that of the men in similar positions. But of even greater significance was a conclusion that the cultural backgrounds of the locality and of family relationships themselves were important factors shaping the future trend of rural social organizations.[11]

In New York similar conditions were found. Doctor Anderson reports that participation in organization activities is a characteristic of the family as a whole, and that the best approach in promoting such family participation would be through the mother, since she exhibits the trait more than other members of the family. This is to say that if the mother becomes a participant, her influence is likely to spread to other family members, thus encouraging their participation.[12]

It is in such terms, therefore, that family relationships need to be considered. They are vital to the members of the family group and to rural society itself. Professor Burgess of Chicago has emphasized repeatedly that the family is a group of interacting personalities. There are the husband-wife, the parent-child, the child-child, the family-farm, the family-neighbor relationships. All are important and all are constantly changing. The peculiar rôle of the family is that of helping to work out some semblance of consensus and harmony among these varied relationships. Whether experiences of the depression and of the war have strengthened or weakened the rural family is difficult to say without more studies than are now available. However, those who have worked closely with families, both urban and rural, seem to agree that well-organized families tend to remain well organized or even become stronger under stress, while the breaking-up of poorly organized families is hastened.

An opportunity as well as a challenge to rural society lies with this important social group, the family. Its early tradition, its land anchorage, and its more recent trends point in this direction. More family units and greater solidarity will not suffice in themselves, be-

Research Bulletin 134. Madison: Agricultural Experiment Station, University of Wisconsin, February, 1938.

[11] Kirkpatrick, E. L., J. H. Kolb, Creagh Inge, A. F. Wileden, *Rural Organizations and the Farm Family*, Research Bulletin 96. Madison: Agricultural Experiment Station, University of Wisconsin, November, 1929.

[12] Anderson, W. A., "Social Participation and Religious Affiliation in Rural Areas," Reprint from *Rural Sociology*, vol. 9, no. 3, September, 1944.

cause they may result in handicaps or even suppressions and frustrations, especially among the children. Much more needs to be done to populate rural society with happy homes which can carry on their important functions.

Three important family functions. The first great family function is preserving and protecting life. This involves the multiplicities of home-making, housekeeping, and family living. Though modified in many ways, as the chapter dealing with the home and its standards of living will show, they still remain dominant activities of the rural family. Changes recorded by families in urban society suggest that many of these household services have been shifted to other agencies such as bakeries, restaurants, laundries, and commercial canneries. Such conclusions, especially regarding housekeeping functions, can hardly be said to characterize the farm family. Tendencies during the depression and during the war would seem to point in the opposite direction. The family and its household has had to become more self-reliant and more self-assertive under the urge of necessity.

A distinguished English student of family trends and vital statistics, Doctor Enid Charles, once remarked in personal conversation that the real culture of a people was measured by its infant mortality rate. While the general infant mortality rate in the whole nation has been greatly reduced since 1923, yet the rural sections have not kept pace with the urban. As a result, in 1940 the rate for the urban stood at 42.3, while the rural rate was 50.7 per 1000 live births.[13] Such facts would suggest that in rural society there is still much to do in the realm of this first great function — preserving life. The chapter on health and medical care will explore the subject more fully.

Another situation must be taken into account when this family function is in question. Children are inversely correlated with family income; that is, the greatest number of children are found where there is the least family income. There is, in fact, a concentration of children in low-income families. Nearly half of the children are growing up in relatively few large families. This generalization holds with respect to urban and farm populations where, as has been pointed out, the majority of children are to be found. The farming sections with the largest families are those of the Cotton South, the Appalachian and Ozark Mountain areas, the

[13] *Fact Sheet on Rural Health and Sanitation.* Washington, D.C.: United States Department of Agriculture, Office of Information, January 3, 1945.

Lake States cut-over, and the Mexican border.[14] Among Oklahoma completed farm families, differences in number of children were found to be related, not only to socio-economic status, but also to education, migration, and residential backgrounds.[15]

If this function of protecting life is to be given primary consideration, the family must prepare in advance before swinging into that cycle where these responsibilities are heaviest. Unless this can be done to a much greater extent than at present, the wide differences in the economic and social situations of families can be offset only by some manner of group or public responsibility. Only in this way will it be possible for every child to be well born and guaranteed an equal chance in beginning life.

A second function is that of perpetuating the race and caring for the sex relationships. The rural family has certainly distinguished itself in the first part of this function as has been amply proved; no adequate basis for comment on the second part exists. Comparative studies on divorce may be of some little value, but certainly marital felicity goes much deeper than that. The rural family continues to have a real measure of stability, as has been shown. Field studies, however, indicate rather clearly that domestic tranquillity is not universal even in the country. Further studies are needed to show trends and to point ways and means for attaining a greater degree of "success in marriage." Studies have been made in some urban situations.[16]

Much has been done for rural people in the way of research and education regarding plant and animal production, household efficiency and farm management. May not the future trend lie in the direction of facing issues of marriage and family relations? Helpful suggestions are needed and will be welcomed by young people embarking in such ventures.

A third great function, or perhaps better a group of functions, has to do with personality in the cultural and affectional relations. Members of a family need some sense of security, of status or group solidarity, and, quite as important, they need to cultivate facility in relating themselves to other groups such as neighborhoods, communities, and to the Great Society itself. It is difficult to consider

[14] Woofter, Thomas J., Jr., "Children and Family Income," Reprint from the *Social Security Bulletin,* vol. 8, no. 1, January, 1945. Washington, D.C.: Social Security Board.

[15] Sewell, William, "Differentiated Fertility in Completed Oklahoma Farm Families," *American Sociological Review,* vol. 9, no. 4, August, 1944.

[16] Burgess, Ernest W., University of Chicago. Article in *The Family,* March, 1926.

this function unless some idea of goal or direction is introduced. It means raising the question of what values need fostering in rural life and what services the family can render to achieve them. The obvious answer would seem to be children. In adopting its Children's Charter, the White House Conference pointed out that every phase of child life affects the welfare of society itself. Similarly, the Committee on Recent Social Trends concludes that the future of the family will depend more and more on the strength of its affectional bonds. As we have seen, the farm family is distinguished by children. Children are the prime objects of affection; thus, the circle would seem complete.

There is evidence of a growing recognition of the importance of this personality function in family life. It is most readily observed in the fields of education and research. In magazines such as *Parents' Magazine*, there is a notable increase in the articles dealing with family life. In schools and colleges the number of courses which deal with marriage and the family is increasing. In an index of research projects the emphasis is shown to have shifted from economic and legal problems of the family to those of its human relations, interaction of husband and wife, parents and children.[17]

Gunnar Myrdal, the Swedish authority on population matters who was called to this country to study interracial problems, suggests that children are the central clue to individual and to family happiness, a means to the healthy development of personality in the various members of the family, including the children themselves.[18] The implications of such a premise are far-reaching. If children were really considered basic and were given a position of high value in both personal and social plans and in both private and public measures, some of the inconsistencies facing a society threatened with a general declining birth rate might be resolved.

THE GREAT FAMILY IN RURAL SOCIETY

Individual rural families and more especially farm families, live in a degree of physical isolation. This need not and more frequently does not mean social isolation. As personalities are the basis of the family group, so individual families are closely knit by threads of kinship and marriage with other families. A whole philosophy or

[17] Nimkoff, Meyer F., "The Family," *American Journal of Sociology*, May, 1942.
[18] Myrdal, Gunnar, "Population Problems and Policies," *Annals of the American Academy of Political and Social Science*, May, 1938.

analogy of the family has been built up about the idea of "trunk" and "branches." It is to the effect that an individual family sends out branches when its children marry and in turn have their own offspring. The whole network of relationship is known as the "family tree." This interesting line of thought cannot be followed here, but the point for emphasis is that families are not family units by themselves; they cannot be considered complete integers. On the contrary, they are part and parcel of a larger kinship organization — the great family. This is one of the significant legacies of the early family and one of the important characteristics of the modern rural family.

W. I. Thomas and his collaborator, Florian Znaniecki, in their study of the Polish peasant in America, found that this larger family group — the great family — "had an integrity and a self-sufficiency providing the materials out of which personalities and careers of its members were built." [19] "We found," they said, "that land hunger and status were the drive within this group, and accounted for the intensity with which pursuits were directed and carried on. That is to say, the individual was predetermined by the habits of this group." No one familiar with rural society can doubt the importance and the influence of this larger group of relatives by blood or marriage, to the third and fourth generations. The great family is the custodian of the culture, the traditions, and the ideals of its members.

One simple and practical illustration of the implications of this principle was pointed out by Doctor Galpin in 1918, when he studied the occupancy of five hundred farms in one locality over the preceding ten years.[20] Almost 50 per cent of the 125 rented farms were occupied by tenants who were related to the owners. Over 30 per cent of the transfers in titles during that period were from fathers to sons. "It is worth noticing as a piece of rural sagacity in the climb up the 'agricultural ladder' that sons who purchased farms, kept close to the father as advisor or landlord and presumably received the father's material backing when it came to purchase."

Neither small family nor the great family, however, is adequate for the needs of personalities in modern times. Other contacts and

[19] *Proceedings, Conference on Family Relations*, Merrill-Palmer School, Detroit, Michigan, December, 1928; Thomas and Znaniecki, *The Polish Peasant*. New York: Knopf, 1927.

[20] Galpin, C. J., *Farm Tenancy*, Research Bulletin 44. Madison: Agricultural Experiment Station, University of Wisconsin, 1919.

other intimacies are needed. This leads to a further exploration of the group organization of rural society.

DISCUSSION TOPICS

1. List and describe briefly five distinctive characteristics of the farm family as compared with, first, the village family and, second, the urban family.
2. Compare and contrast the manner of early farm family settlement in New England, in the Old South, in the Middle West, and in the Far West.
3. Does a greater proportion of rural or city people marry? Which marries younger? Which has more children per family? Give your explanations.
4. How does the life cycle of farm families differ from that of village or city families?
5. Study the trends in rural divorce in your county or state, either from the census or from local court records. What accounts for the upward swing?
6. Explore the idea that family success and happiness are based on companionship and affection, and that children have cultural and psychological importance. How are these ideas related to the principle of democracy? If put more fully into practice, how might they influence divorce rates, birth rates, public health and housing policies?
7. Give the best example you know of a "great family." What influences does it exert upon individual families and upon the personalities of younger members?

REFERENCE READINGS

Arensberg, Conrad, *The Irish Countryman*. New York: The Macmillan Co., 1937.

Baber, R. E., *Marriage and the Family*. New York: McGraw-Hill, 1939.

Baldwin, Fillmore, and Hadley, *Farm Children*. New York: D. Appleton & Co., 1930. An investigation of rural child life in selected areas of Iowa.

Becker, H. F., and R. Hill, *Marriage and the Family*. Chicago: D. C. Heath & Co., 1942.

Burgess, E. W., and L. S. Cottrell, *Predicting Success or Failure in Marriage*. New York: Prentice-Hall, 1939.

Burgess, E. W., and H. J. Locke, *The Family*. Cincinnati: American Book Co., 1945.

Frazier, E. Franklin, *Negro Family in the United States.* Chicago: University of Chicago Press, 1939.

Goodsell, Willystine, *A History of Marriage and the Family.* Rev. Ed. New York: The Macmillan Co., 1934.

Goodykoontz, Bess, and Beulah Coon, *Family Living and Our Schools.* New York: D. Appleton-Century Co., 1941.

Groves, E. R., *The American Family.* New York: Lippincott, 1934.

Kirkpatrick, Tough, Cowles, *The Life Cycle of the Farm Family in Relation to Its Standards of Living.* Madison: Research Bulletin 121, Agricultural Experiment Station, University of Wisconsin, 1934.

Mowrer, E. R., *The Family.* Chicago: University of Chicago Press, 1933.

Ogburn, W. F., *Recent Social Trends,* chaps. XII, XIV. New York: McGraw-Hill, 1933.

Reuter, E. B., and Jessie R. Runner, *The Family.* New York: McGraw-Hill, 1933.

Sanderson, Dwight, "Sociological Analysis of the Family," Reprint from *Social Forces,* vol. XII, no. 2, December, 1933; and "Changes in the Farm Family," Reprint from *Religious Education,* February, 1924.

Sorokin and Zimmerman, *Principles of Rural-Urban Sociology,* chap. 15. New York: Henry Holt & Co., 1929.

West, James, *Plainville, U.S.A.,* pp. 57-58. New York: Columbia University Press, 1945.

12

Country Neighborhoods

OUT BEYOND THE FARM FAMILY lies the country neighborhood. The question, "What is the name of the neighborhood in which you live?" often brings an answer such as, Wheeler Prairie, Spring Valley, Pierceville, or Pumpkin Hollow, which is just as definite and full of meaning as the family name. Neighborhoods are localities where country people live; they are groups of neighbor families whose members know each other by their first names. Frequently these neighbors are relatives; usually they are associated in school, church, or social activities.

In stricter phraseology, a neighborhood is that first group outside the family which has social significance, and which has some sense of local unity. It is conditioned both geographically and psychologically. It is an area of local association and it is a group of primary, personal, or face-to-face contacts. In rural society propinquity continues to make a difference and as elsewhere, primary groups are very important to the lives of individuals. It was Charles H. Cooley who gave this primary group concept its puissance and its clarity so that it is sure to be useful for a long time in studying human society.[1] By primary groups he meant those groups which are personal, intimate, or face-to-face in character. They are primary because they are fundamental in forming the social nature and the ideals of the individual. In fact, Professor Cooley said that personality cannot exist without such association or fellowship. Human nature is but a trait of primary groups, he insisted. Among the more important phases of this kind of group life, he enumerated the family, the neighborhood, and the play group. It is the country neighborhood to which attention will be given in this chapter.

The neighborhood has played its part from the time when country people first formed themselves into more or less permanent settlements and established themselves on some specific piece

[1] Cooley, Charles H., *Social Organization*, chap. III. New York: Scribner, 1925.

of land. In the European rural society which formed the cultural background of the early American settlers, the agricultural village was the center for settlement and group activity. In Russia it was the mir; in Scandinavian countries, it was the family estate; in Norman England, the manor. Familism was characteristic of these types of rural social organization quite as much as of the separated farm system which developed later in this country.

EARLY NEIGHBORHOOD SETTLEMENTS

In New England the village form of local social economy was continued. Residences were clustered around "the common." At the center were the squares for church, school, and town hall. Barns and sheds were on the home lot with the house. The tillable lands were adjoining, but extending back into the open, often in rather narrow strips. Beyond lay the meadow land and frequently the wood lots.[2] In many ways the New England town with its town meeting and village-centered social life was the primary group. Its influence is widespread, for many of its social institutions and ideals were carried westward, almost "bodily" by the settlers, although for many reasons the centralized village pattern was not transplanted. Coupling it with the powerful religious concept of the four-square "City of Zion," the Mormons, however, took it west and made it their dominant type of settlement and social organization.

In the South the plantation was to all intents and purposes the primary locality group. Its origins can be traced more or less directly to the old English manor of lords and country gentlemen. The plantation plan lent itself to large-scale, single-crop farming, to a slavery system of labor, and subsequently, to tenants and croppers.[3] Both the social and the economic life of the area were organized about the plantation and carried on as a unit enterprise. It might range in size from six or eight families to more than a hundred. There were the plantation buildings, the commissary, often the school, the large dwelling house, and the coterie of small cottages and cabins. The planter and his family were, of

[2] For full description, see MacLear, Anne B., *Early New England Towns*. New York: Columbia University Studies in Economics, History, and Public Law, vol. 29, no. 1.

[3] Brennan, C. O., *Relation of Land Tenure to Plantation Organization*. Washington, D.C.: United States Department of Agriculture, Bulletin 1269.

course, the dominant figures in the group and represented the aristocracy of Southern society.

In the Middle West and Far West the separate-farm, neighborhood settlement was most common. Individual farms were settled by families who went out to get land and to seek their fortunes. They settled in groups on adjoining farms and were bound together by such ties as kinship, common nationality, the same educational, social, or religious purposes. When the neighborhood was composed largely of a kinship group or of the great family as described in the preceding chapter, a very closely knit organization was formed. Topography and crop or forest cover were also important. Some of the earlier settlers sought the "oak openings," or moved directly into the timber so that they might have building material and fuel. They looked for springs or streams to supply water for themselves and their livestock. Mutual aid, exchange of work, building bees, social affairs, schools, and churches soon became the organized ways of these groups. If adjoining settlements were made by those of different cultural backgrounds, or nationality, and unlike purposes, group lines were drawn a little closer. School district boundaries were gerrymandered so as to include only the in-group. Only the arbitrary township lines laid off by the surveyor and carefully executed on the checker-board pattern would not yield to the social or group design. Herein may lie at least some of the reasons for the impotency of local government organized on the township basis.

Country neighborhood settlement and social organization went on quite independently and often prior to small-town settlement. The latter sprang up to render certain special types of services which the neighborhood could not organize for itself, such as transportation, banking, merchandising, and certain forms of manufacturing. Villages or towns were often populated by a more heterogeneous group, unrelated in blood or ideal to those of the country neighborhood. These differences became the basis for some of the lack of understanding between town and country, and even for conflicts which developed a little later, when mutual relationships became more important and when the newer transportation and communication systems tied town and country more closely together. Unlike the New England plan, Mid-Western and Western villages were incorporated as municipalities, thus withdrawing from the township unit and leaving the country group to its own plans.

In the pioneer fringes neighborhood settlement continues ever

westward and northward. C. A. Dawson describes the process in
the Peace River district of Alberta and British Columbia.[4] He tells
about the individual settlements of Fairview and Grande Prairie;
he describes how they preceded the railroad; how they set up one-
room schools, with a six-month term; how whole families go to
all-night dances, putting the small children to sleep in a space set
aside for the purpose, and how informality and kindliness prevail. These two settlements are simply examples of the old neighborhood primary group formation process. Dawson goes on to
point out that the next stage is soon reached when there is a greater
diffusion of culture, when urban influences are felt, and when the
later settlers demand greater accessibility to the town with its
stores, clubs, theaters, hotels, and athletic teams. With a division
of interests there is a realignment in primary group organization
and the beginning of secondary forms of contact. Very similar
situations were found in Beaverhead County, Montana, and in
Union County, New Mexico, when they were studied in 1920.

Neighborhoods Persist

One of the most important discoveries made in the various restudies of rural localities is the persistence of country neighborhoods. Many persons predicted that this form of local group organization was a thing of the past because of increased facilities for
communication and travel, greater mobility of both country and
city people, and the loosening of kinship and nationality ties. To be
sure, some changes have come in the numbers as well as in the
character of these groups. The many studies made in the period
1924 to 1936 show that there was a rather heavy mortality of
neighborhoods.

The depression period brought discouragement which could not
be overcome; therefore, many neighborhoods ceased all forms of
local activities. On the other hand, economic difficulty and social
insecurity in this period made many such groups more active and
more determined to satisfy their social necessities in their home
localities. Families bound themselves together more firmly by
mutual aid and exchange of work. They joined in home talent
effort such as music, drama, recreation, and group discussion.

The war came, and many neighborhoods sprang into renewed
activity all along the home front. Under local, voluntary, and Agri-

---

[4] Dawson, C. A., *Pioneer Settlement*, chap. 6. New York: American Geographical Society, 1932.

cultural Extension Service stimulus, they became the farmers' units for civilian defense, for rapid circulation of information and services, for stepping-up production, and for better utilization of existing food, machinery, and labor supplies. To be sure, the response was uneven throughout the country, and the extent to which such resurgence will carry into the postwar period is a matter of debate. It appears rather doubtful that the long-time trend will be greatly changed. One can be quite safe in saying that those country neighborhoods which do persist will be more the result of deliberate action and social readjustment, of kindred interests and of organized activities than of mere locality, propinquity of residence, or of pioneering traditions. This is not to suggest that locality and the proximity of living and working no longer influence local primary group association. They do, but they must be accompanied by other social functions.

Extent of neighborhood persistence. The number of neighborhoods found in the 140 town-country communities in 1924, in 1930, and in 1936 declined about 36 per cent during the whole period. The net loss between 1924 and 1930 was 23.5 per cent. Some new groups were found in the course of time and some considered inactive at one period were definitely active in another.

There were variations from region to region. The net loss for the last period of study in the Middle West was 20.8 per cent; for the Middle Atlantic, 23.5 per cent; for the South, 26.6 per cent; and for the Far West, 31.6 per cent. The percentage of decline in the Far West during the earlier period was only 4 per cent, but throughout the whole period it was 20.8 per cent, which was the lowest for any region.

Various elements of change were more active in the South than in other regions. Better roads were considered a factor in the majority of cases where neighborhoods had disappeared. The road-improvement program in the South was initiated later than in other sections, and consequently its effects upon country neighborhoods were delayed; in other regions this element was effective in only one fifth of the cases. Adjustments had already been made, since any innovation necessitates group changes and considerable time is often required.

Intensive case restudies of special areas reveal much the same conditions with regard to the persistence of country neighborhoods. In Boone County, Missouri, for instance, a preliminary check showed that forty of the original fifty-nine neighborhoods located in 1924 were still in existence in 1931, while fifteen new ones were in evidence. Continuation of informal social and neighboring contacts was frequently apparent in this county. In Otsego County, New York, the movement from the neighborhood to the town-country community form of rural organization had proceeded farther than in many other sections, yet the restudy in 1931 showed that of the twenty-two neighborhoods described in 1921, ten were still active, five were weaker, six had given up their activities, and one had been absorbed into the life of an expanding city.

In Dane County, Wisconsin, neighborhood organization, which had grown up in early settlement days as a result of such factors as topography, nationality, and religious organization, was strong when first studied in 1921. Neighborhoods in the county seem to have reached their peak by 1931 with a total of ninety-four actives, within one of the original total. Seven neighborhoods located in 1921, but considered rather weak and inactive at that time, were clearly in the active ranks in 1931. While there was a difference of only one in the number of active neighborhoods between 1921 and 1931, this does not reveal the actual changes during the decade. Thirty-two neighborhoods, active in 1921, became inactive; twenty-four were discovered for the first time, while seven had been considered inactive in 1921 but became active by 1931.

The seventy-six neighborhoods considered active in 1941 represent a loss of about 20 per cent compared with 1931. This is approximately the same reduction found in the Middle-Western states between 1930 and 1936.[5] Reasons for what may seem rather an unusual situation will be given consideration as the discussion proceeds.

The hamlet-centered neighborhood. A type of neighborhood which merits special attention is the one centered about a small residence cluster, usually not over two hundred and fifty people and having one or more local institutions. This type of center is commonly known as a hamlet. In all of the areas studied this type of neighborhood was found among those classed as "new." Although population changes were not great in the interval between the studies, the relationships of these small centers to the surrounding country areas were different. In the earlier studies they had frequently been classed as centers for a village-country community, but in the interim they had slipped down into another classification. They could not possibly be considered the center for a town-

[5] Kolb, J. H., and D. G. Marshall, *Neighborhood-Community Relationships in Rural Society*, Research Bulletin 154. Madison: Agricultural Experiment Station, University of Wisconsin, November, 1944.

country type of community group. They were usually to be found within the service areas of some larger center and to all practical purposes were similar to such open-country neighborhoods as were centered about one or two local institutions, such as school, church, or store.

In summary, then, the types of neighborhood that exhibit the greatest tendency toward persistence are: first, local groups characterized by visiting, informal sociability and various forms of organized social activity; second, locality groups integrated about one or more local institutions, groups whose continuity was not insured until such institutions were developed; third, the hamlet type which by reason of better educational systems or more modern service institutions has come to be a country neighborhood type of center rather than a town-country community center.

Characteristic activities. Activities, organizations, or local institutions are the things which hold together country neighborhoods more generally now than they did a decade ago. This is only natural, because in the earlier settlement days or during the first period of a neighborhood group's existence, effort was directed toward building up forms of common life which would persist. Many of the earlier settlers did not rest until their ideals had been embodied into a school district and a schoolhouse, a church society and a church building, or a social organization and a constitution. They often built the school and the church with their own hands and presided over many of their functions in the absence of professional leadership.

Activities characteristic of neighborhoods, in the 140 community areas to which reference has been made, have changed very little during the periods of study. Among those activities which acted most forcefully as factors in holding country people together in neighborhood groups, the following may be listed, either singly or in various combinations: school, church, social or economic organizations, store, racial bands, and great family. Variations among the four geographic regions are frequent. For example, in the Far West, church neighborhoods were not found as frequently as elsewhere and racial groups were not as important in the settlement of this region as they were in the Middle West. On the other hand, in the Far West two thirds of the neighborhoods were characterized by combinations of school and some social or economic activity, by social or economic activity alone, or by school, church, and trade.

In the Middle West and South some forms of organization or

society, such as an agricultural extension project, a mothers' club, or social activity, had grown to a place of greater importance in binding the group than the fact of living in close proximity. Often special activities were organized or special interests were appealed to in order to compensate for the decline of the simple neighboring tradition. Activities were often found together, some supplementary, others competitive. The Wisconsin county gives further evidence that activities are often found in combination, that is, neighborhood life is not uni-centered, but moves about common or overlapping interests.

In this county the following combinations were found:

COMBINATIONS OF FOUR	NUMBER OF NEIGHBORHOODS	
	1931	1941
Public school, mothers' club or P.T.A., 4-H club, county federation	13	9
Public school, mothers' club or P.T.A., 4-H club, store	12	9
Public school, mothers' club or P.T.A., church, store	10	16
Public school, mothers' club or P.T.A., club, church	4	7

COMBINATIONS OF THREE	NUMBER OF NEIGHBORHOODS	
	1931	1941
Public school, mothers' club or P.T.A., 4-H club	32	17
Public school, mothers' club or P.T.A., county federation	24	18
Public school, mothers' club or P.T.A., store	23	28
Public school, church, store	19	23
Public school, mothers' club or P.T.A., church	18	29
Mothers' club or P.T.A., church, store	10	16

The combination of activities in a neighborhood group suggests that there is a process of cumulation or a piling-up of the factors making for group solidarity. Such groups, then, are characterized not only by a single dimension of lateral or geographic extent, but also by a second dimension of depth or intensity.

Ranking of functions holding neighborhoods together. Another way of showing the relative importance of certain influences at work in group continuity and the extent to which changes are taking place was to rank the functions which tend to hold neighborhoods together. Obviously, not all functions have an equal influence in a combination. Some are of major and some of minor importance. Therefore, a value of one was assigned to a major and one half to a minor emphasis. Thus, a single score could be given each neighborhood for each period of study. As can be observed from the ranking, the religious and educational functions changed places with the educational and social from 1931 to 1941, thus restoring them to their early 1921 positions.

RANKING OF FUNCTIONS FOR ACTIVE NEIGHBORHOODS

Functions	1941	1931	1921
Religious	1	3	1
Educational	2	1	2
Economic	3	4	4
Social	4	2	3

The story of Rogers Hollow neighborhood. To give a clearer and more vivid picture of neighborhood activities and of how the various influences work together, a case story is given from the Otsego County study. Rogers Hollow is an open-country neighborhood in the west-central part of Unadilla Township. The activities of the neighborhood center around the schools, a Grange, and a Friends Church, the latter being probably the most important in giving the neighborhood its identity. The neighborhood fair, which has been held each fall for the past eleven years, includes the school districts of Idumes and Unadilla Center on the north and the Meeker district on the south, in addition to the two school districts in Rogers Hollow. The Grange is stronger than it has been for several years. About five years ago interest in it declined to such an extent that the meetings were held at the homes of the members. Under the present leadership, however, interest has again revived. There are now fifty-three members meeting twice a month at the Grange hall with an average attendance of twenty-five to thirty people. In addition to the regular meetings, dances and parties are held in the hall about once a month.

The Friends Church is the center for most of the life of the neighborhood, due to the able leadership of the resident pastor. The church has slightly more than one hundred members with an average attendance of about fifty persons at church and an enrollment of forty to forty-five people in the Sunday School. The membership is well organized, having two young people's societies, the Penn Helpers and the True Blues, each of which holds a regular monthly meeting; a Missionary Society which meets every month at the homes of the members, supplemented by an annual public meeting and entertainment in the community house; a Ladies' Aid Society, at present combined with the Home Bureau unit, which also meets regularly. There are also monthly church nights. The

4-H Club for boys and girls, directed by the minister, has about twenty-two members, and usually meets once in four weeks at the community house. In 1929, Rogers Hollow united with Rockdale, Guilford, and East Guilford, all of which are in Chenango County, in the formation of a larger parish, a movement which will undoubtedly strengthen all the churches of the area. Every child in the neighborhood is a member of the Sunday School and nearly every family is represented in either the church or Sunday School.

There is a young people's branch of the Woman's Christian Temperance Union and a Loyal Temperance Legion for the school children. Both the Farm Bureau and Dairymen's League have a local organization which holds about two meetings annually. As a result there is a social party or meeting of some kind every week in the year, and often two or three meetings in the same week. This is by far the most active neighborhood in the county and is an excellent example of what a country church with a resident pastor can contribute to the life of its people.

Westville, a hamlet neighborhood. Located in Cherry Creek Valley, it is halfway between Middlefield and Milford. At the center there are nineteen houses, a garage, a general store, two sawmills, a Grange hall, a grade school, and two churches, one a Baptist with a resident minister, and the other a Methodist, served by the minister at Milford. Milford, about four miles south, has the high school, and is the trading center except for drygoods and women's ready-to-wear, most of which are bought in Oneonta. The only organizations connected with the churches are the two Ladies' Aid Societies; neither church has a young people's organization. The average attendance at church services is about twenty people. The Home Bureau has a local organization with twelve members, but interest in the work is not very strong because most of the members belong to one of the Ladies' Aid Societies or to the Grange. The only organizations for the young people are the Boy Scout troop, with six members, organized by the minister, and the local 4-H Club with twenty-two members.

The Grange is probably the most important factor in the life of the neighborhood. It has one hundred and twenty-six members and meets every two weeks in the Grange Hall, with an average attendance of approximately fifty. It recently organized a degree team which has been instrumental in maintaining the interest of the younger members. During the winter social parties are held after the regular meetings and each member is allowed to bring one guest. The Grange membership area is somewhat larger than the immediate neighborhood, extending as far as Middlefield on the north and Milford on the south. Westville is the most active of the hamlet centers of the county and is a good example of that type of neighborhood.

The rôle of institutions. As is definitely shown in the cases of Rogers Hollow and Westville, established institutions are among the strongest forces holding neighborhood groups together. As has also been suggested, one of the early ambitions or objectives of many country groups was to establish a local school, church, or social organization. Once established, the institution has great power in keeping people together. It furnished common objectives. It is tangible evidence of group achievement. It is only natural, therefore, that in the earlier years neighborhood boundaries frequently determined the size of school districts, church parishes, and organization or trade areas, and in later years were themselves fixed by the radius of the institution's influence.

In this New York county where Rogers Hollow and Westville are located, it is quite evident that churches and Granges are typical of the older institutions in both open-country and hamlet neighborhoods. Organizations such as Home Bureau, social club, and 4-H Club, are most characteristic of the recent years.

Interfamily visiting and exchange-of-work patterns. Further evidence that farm families have a tendency to cluster together in neighborhoods for their essential living purposes is shown by a recent study of those primary group functions which include neighborly visiting, mutual aid in time of emergency, and exchange-of-work habits. Such primary culture patterns are limited in area and produce some of the most compact and cohesive neighborhoods to be found anywhere. The extent of such interfamily relations determines in many cases the degree of success that a family has in converting income into goods and services essential for living and thus for maintaining its independence and self-respect. These interfamily ties are often overlooked by agencies seeking to rehabilitate families which have succumbed to the economic and social pressure of the depression period.

Patterns can be drawn indicating the kind and extent of such family interdependence. They may be used as a measure of the second dimension of group intensity to which reference has been made. One illustration is the exchange-of-work pattern of the Garden Valley families. Twenty-one families lived in this neighborhood and, as can be observed from the accompanying chart (Figure 2), a highly developed exchange-of-work pattern exists among them.

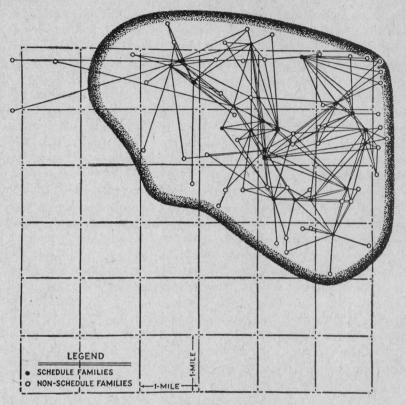

LEGEND

• SCHEDULE FAMILIES

○ NON-SCHEDULE FAMILIES

1-MILE

1-MILE

Figure 2

MOST GARDEN VALLEY FAMILIES EXCHANGED
WORK WITH SEVERAL NEIGHBORS

Source: Hill, Slocum, Hill, *Man-Land Adjustment,* Research Bulletin
134, University of Wisconsin, February, 1939.

Patterns of mutual aid in times of stress were not quite so highly
developed, but with few exceptions the families visited with each
other as well as with some of the families of Almond Center, the
near-by village.

Three neighborhoods in emergency times. The importance of
interfamily relationships, especially in emergency times, can be observed in two other cases which are in contrast with Garden
Valley, although located in the same general land area. The first of
these is Komensky, a Bohemian settlement of fifty-six families, living in the trade and service area of Black River Falls, a county-seat
village of about two thousand people. A very high degree of social

life, both formal and informal, was found in this neighborhood. There were picnics, dances, birthday celebrations, and folk festivals. The chart used to show the visiting, exchange-of-work, and interdependencies in times of trouble, is a veritable network of interconnected lines. The houses in which the families lived were of good construction, but were without many of the modern conveniences. When family incomes and expenditures were balanced for the year 1935, only seventeen families had deficits; none of the deficits were over one hundred dollars. Twenty-five families had supplemented their farm income from other sources, but only five had turned to relief.

The second is the South Brockway settlement of sixteen families, also in the Black River Falls trade area. Very few inter-family contacts were found; many social maladjustments were evident. These families were not closely united by cultural or mutual interests. There was a greater tendency for them to move about than in the Komensky neighborhood. The chart showing contacts for emergency help is almost a blank, but the visiting lines do connect most of the families with the near-by village families. The standards of housing and family living were low, and when earnings and operating costs were compared, only two families had been able to make their expenses for the year, even though some had secured work off the farm. The others relied on loans, gifts, and relief. Twelve families were receiving some form of public assistance.

It is important that families have a land base, as the previous chapter has shown, but it is also evident that families cannot live successfully when socially and economically isolated. Inter-family relations are a condition of success when measured in terms of self-dependence and social security — terms which are to be considered in a later chapter. The Komensky and South Brockway settlements are extreme cases, to be sure, for opposite reasons. Garden Valley is the more usual. It is a mixed neighborhood as far as nationality is concerned. Its family contacts are not as frequent nor its interdependencies as great as in Komensky; nevertheless, it has worked out a definite plan of inter-family relations. They are characterized by friendly social contacts, by relatively high standards of living, and by a farm economy which rendered it unnecessary for any family to go on relief during that year. Seven of the families did have to borrow, secure credit, or draw on savings, but they maintained their self-dependence, an achievement far beyond the average socially isolated family in that general area and beyond the grasp of most of the families in the disintegrating neighborhood of South Brockway.

Neighborhoods Change

Despite the evidence cited and the implications drawn concerning the persistence of neighborhood groups, their relative stability, the continuance of their local institutions, and the formation of new ones, changes are, nevertheless, taking place. In pointing out the tendency to continue or to persist, we have repeatedly called attention to the tendency to change. In fact, the latter is a condition of the former. Unless there are changes, adjustments, or adaptations, growth stops and life goes out. Persistence itself is a kind of change or process.

We shall now turn our attention to some of the elements which enter into the changes in neighborhood life, and summarize briefly the more characteristic of these changes.

Population changes. Among the most important elements affecting neighborhood groups ánd making readjustments necessary, are population increases or decreases and shifts in the composition of the population, as for example, in the major age groups or in the proportion of foreign-born. This is well illustrated in the case of the Wisconsin county. During the latter part of the ten-year period there was a continued northward movement of the Swiss in fan-shape formation, with New Glarus as the focal point. The county has experienced such wave-like motions of population from its beginning. First, there were the New Englanders or "Yankees," then the Germans and Scandinavians, and now in the southwestern part of the county, the Swiss. Each time a wave moves over an area, readjustments in the social arrangements have to be made. Churches are the first to come and the last to go. In more recent years population migration was a cause for the lapse of neighborhood activities, both in drought-stricken areas which lost population and in those areas which received an influx of people that they could not assimilate. The former circumstance was particularly noticeable in the Middle West, while the latter played an important rôle in the Far West.

Transportation changes. Automobiles and hard-surfaced roads are another means of disturbing the social groups. Many things are now possible which were quite out of the ken of the pioneering fathers. Federal and state aids, together with campaigns and contests to bring "a good road to every farmer's gate" have opened new opportunities to country people. Some have prophesied that these improved facilities for travel would mean the ultimate dismantling of all rural groups, organizations, and institutions. Changes have

COUNTRY NEIGHBORHOODS 239

taken place, to be sure, but as we have shown, many local neighborhoods and social institutions still have a surprising vitality. Whenever new ways of making contacts or making them more frequently are instituted, rearrangements in social and group affairs are necessary. Farm-to-market roads built during the depression proved a disturbing element to neighborhoods that had experienced a degree of isolation. Thus there was a heavy decline of neighborhoods in Pennsylvania where the state administration attempted to keep its promise of "getting the farmer out of the mud." Results were akin to those of earlier years when hard-surfaced roads upset the life of neighborhoods that lay in their paths.

Increased facility for moving about does not necessarily mean disintegration of all local or all primary groups, however. It may even strengthen them by permitting greater selection of members, larger variety of activities, and wider contacts with other similar groups. In a word, rural groups in the modern régime are more voluntary associations than formerly. An illustration of this was found in the Missouri county which was restudied. In a careful recording of all social contacts for the people of a village center and each of the surrounding eleven school districts, it was found that the annual per capita visiting contacts for the village was 170; for districts adjacent to the village, 108; and for districts not adjacent, 126. Furthermore, it was pointed out that the local visiting or neighboring contacts were 2.7 times as numerous as were the special-interest or organization contacts, both inside and outside the district; and that special-interest or special-activity contacts are more likely to be outside than inside the district in a ratio of 3 to 2. Therefore, as has been suggested, locality and special organization or interest-group arrangements may develop together. Modern facilities for communication and travel may increase outside contacts, but they may increase the local contacts at an even greater rate.

Direction of important changes. The general direction of changes in country neighborhoods may be briefly summarized thus: First, some groups do disappear or lose those elements found in the definitely active groups. In Dane County roughly one third fell out of the recognized active class. In the New York county the proportion was greater. In the 140 village-country communities there was a net decrease of about 16 per cent in the number of neighborhoods. Disappearing neighborhoods may retain their form; they may even appear active. But they tend to take the direction of decadence.

Second, new groups appear or old ones become active again. They assume characteristics which by all the refinements of analysis make them comparable to the older and the more readily recognized groups. These newer groups, however, are more often the result of deliberate organization, promotion, or voluntary association. They are centered generally about certain interests such as social activity, drama, or club programs. They are less dependent upon tradition, nationality, locality, or religious purpose than the older ones.

Third, there is a tendency for neighborhoods to retain or to assume only certain kinds of functions. They are less self-sufficing than some were at the time of the earlier studies, whose traditions carried back to settlement days, and whose strong nationality or kinship bonds were often sheltered from outside influences by the topography of the country. Open-country neighborhoods retain their schools and churches, but also take on certain social activities and give up certain economic services. Specialization has set in, although this trend has been somewhat checked in more recent years.

Fourth, neighborhoods in the immediate vicinity of small towns or villages tend to give way first. Their functions are slowly assumed by the larger town-country community unit. Because of freer and more frequent contacts this larger group becomes more primary or personal in character, whereas formerly it was likely to be largely of a secondary order.

Fifth, the number of hamlet class of neighborhoods tends to be augmented by the addition of village-centered groups that have not been able to maintain the standing of a village community. Distances measured in time units have shrunk. In the process some village centers have settled back to a hamlet status. As was pointed out earlier, they are not essentially different from the more nearly open-country groups centered about two or more local institutions. This trend was very evident in the case of the New York county, and in the 140 town-country communities distributed over the nation.

Measures of neighborhood change and persistence. Activities or functions, essential as they are, are not sufficient in themselves to keep neighborhoods active; there are impersonal factors related to activeness and therefore to persistence. In the last Dane County restudy, 1941-42, out of some twenty factors, three were found to be especially significant in differentiating between active and inactive neighborhoods. They were length of residence, tenure status, and nationality background of the families within the neighborhoods. It must be emphasized at once that these three factors were correlated; that is, they act together as a sort of social complex. It became evident in the course of analysis that a greater or a lesser proportion of any given factor would tend to accelerate certain neighborhoods toward activeness or inactiveness.

Toleration points were, therefore, worked out for each of the three factors. This is only another way of saying that active neighborhoods can "tolerate" a certain proportion of tenants, of families with short periods of residence, and families with a certain degree of similar nationality background. A change in any one factor may not be sufficient because it may be offset by a higher proportion of another. However, if all three tend toward their toleration points, then the neighborhoods in question are likely to show signs of inactiveness. Under conditions of the restudy, neighborhoods could expect to remain active, provided their tenancy rate was no higher than 28 per cent, the proportion of their families less than twenty-five years in residence no larger than 42 per cent, and provided the families of similar nationality background represented not more than 64 per cent of all their families.

It seemed especially significant that neighborhoods in which at least 36 per cent of the families had mixed or indefinite nationality backgrounds were more likely to be active than those with 64 per cent or more of their families with similar and recognized backgrounds. This is contrary to some popular opinion, but it points to interesting possibilities for future neighborhood development and change. It should be added that if an active neighborhood had families of similar nationality background, it was more apt to remain active if those backgrounds were German rather than Scandinavian. The chart (Figure 3) gives the comparisons.

Full explanation of the differences shown in the chart cannot be given because they are not known, but apparently during periods of settlement and in early stages of group formation similar nationality backgrounds may help to hold groups together. In later periods, when other cultural values and different group tenets are being taken over, too much similarity of nationality may be detrimental to keeping groups active. Preliminary findings in the studies of nationalities in the state indicate that different nationality groups react differently, both in the character of their adjustments and in the time required to make them.

Such findings suggest that a certain amount of social change within a neighborhood is compatible with activeness — persistence.

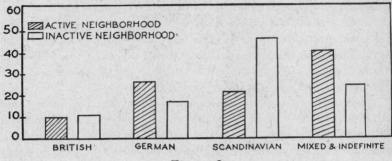

Figure 3

COMPARISON BY PERCENTAGES FOR NATIONALITY
BACKGROUNDS OF ACTIVE AND INACTIVE
NEIGHBORHOODS

Tenants can become owners; nationalities can intermingle; new families can take up residence. This should be of practical importance to those interested in the future of country neighborhoods.

NEIGHBORHOODS IN THE WAR EFFORT

Farmers and their neighbors often meet in their homes, schoolhouses, churches, stores, and town halls to discuss their common problems. This has been an accustomed way to arrive at group decisions in rural society, as the chapter has attempted to show. It is only to be expected, when problems of national moment arrive, that such local action should be taken. State and federal agricultural agencies have frequently depended upon local leaders and neighborhood meetings to help to promote various programs of work.

One such plan was the "Land-Use Programs" organized through local committees representing the numerous local interests involved. In many states the neighborhoods and communities were mapped and land-use plans drawn.[6] Although this program did not carry over into a continued national program, it did help to gain experience and to pave the way for the so-called Neighborhood-Leader plan which developed so rapidly once the war began. The Agricultural Extension Service, under the slogan, "Reach the last farm

6 Holt, John B., *Rural Neighborhoods and Communities of Lee County, Alabama, and Their Significance for Land-Use Planning*. Washington, D.C.: Bulletin United States Department of Agriculture, Bureau of Agricultural Economics, 1941.

down the last road," helped to stimulate a nation-wide movement. Original stimulus also came because farm people were faced with the prospect of reduced gasoline supplies, shortage of labor, and stepped-up quotas for production. Local meetings were therefore shifted from county or community back to the neighborhood basis. This proved to be less of a handicap than expected, especially when care was taken not to duplicate or unduly expand the number of local meetings. By October, 1942, reports showed that over 90 per cent of the more than three thousand counties were organized with 648,000 neighborhood leaders in 260,000 neighborhoods.[7]

The plan of organization and the effectiveness of the program differed from state to state and from locality to locality. In general the work was carried on by personal contacts, distribution of printed material, and by local meetings. Projects receiving special attention were scrap collection, ordering feeds and fertilizers, using enriched flour, checking machinery repair, planting Victory gardens, harvesting and storing fruits and vegetables, controlling fires, stimulating production, promoting better health and nutrition.[8]

The conclusion drawn from the numerous reports is that the greatest success was achieved when there was co-operation with local existing agencies and organizations and in neighborhoods which were active and well organized. Here the war effort was carried on easily and effectively. In other situations committees sometimes resorted to artificial units for organization, such as a school district when a school was closed; or they held to school-district lines when a country church congregation was the strong local group. In some localities the township has very little group significance; therefore is a weak unit for organization purposes. One farmer, a township leader, reported that families within his township were divided three ways with respect to trade, high school, and church. Therefore, he was having real difficulty in organizing on the township basis civilian defense, food production and preservation, as well as Red Cross work. In such a situation it would have been better to make the country-village community the basis for such committee activity.

[7] Brigham, Reuben, *Shoulders Together*, Extension Service Circular 380. Washington, D.C.: United States Department of Agriculture, 1942; *Highlights of the Neighborhood Leader Conference*, Extension Circular 402, March, 1943.

[8] *Evaluation Study of the Neighborhood Leader System, Berkshire and Essex Counties, Massachusetts*, May, 1942; *Influence of Neighborhood Leaders in Waldo, Maine*, Extension Service Circular 389; *Orange and Lee Counties, North Carolina, Demonstrate How Neighborhood Leaders Can Help in Securing Participation of Rural Families in Agriculture's Wartime Program*, Extension Service Circular 387.

Other wartime projects were carried on through school-district or neighborhood organization. Teachers helped with ration programs, school directors promoted bond sales, neighborhood and community committeemen helped to determine farm labor needs, encouraged exchange of work and machinery, guarded against fires, sabotage, and theft. Such shared experience is certain to have convinced farm people that they do have common concerns and responsibilities, either on a neighborhood or community basis, even though their individual and selfish interests are frequently made the objects of strong appeal. Their professional leaders should also have gained more respect for human relationships in rural society and greater knowledge of how to work with them.

NEIGHBORHOODS RELATED TO OTHER GROUPS

A final important question to be considered in this chapter is that of changing relationships of neighborhoods with other rural groups, especially with the larger community consisting of town or village and country people. This rural community becomes the subject for a later chapter.

The 1936 restudy of the 140 rural communities showed that neighborhoods had greater vitality at some distance from the growing and larger village or town centers. It was significant to find that thirty-three communities had no active neighborhoods within their boundaries, compared with only three in 1924. This is evidence of closer village-country integration. Neighborhoods are also likely to appear at a distance of four to six miles from towns of 8000 to 10,000 population. Such local centers, often hamlets, had lost many of their services to the cities, but some industrial regions had gained commuters.

Distance continues, therefore, to play a part in neighborhood affairs. As a growing village or larger city draws more and more of the secondary services to itself, a demand seems to arise from country people for some kind of local and convenient centers, close at hand, to supply some of the more primary social services. In a number of the Far West communities studied recently it appeared as though some farm leaders had definitely decided upon what they wanted supplied at the village center, and what they determined to keep in their own neighborhoods. One such leader urged that farmers must maintain "a real sense of possession and control" over at least the services of recreation for both youth and adults, religious education for the youth, some forms of adult education, and co-operative marketing of produce and purchasing of supplies. If this could be done advantageously with the villages, this leader would be satisfied, but if distances were too great and the "possession or control" was to be lost, he would insist that the services be organized on a neighborhood basis, with such co-operation with villages or other neighborhoods, as was required.

Three cases will now be described to show how changes in neighborhood life occur, and to indicate how larger group relationships develop. Local cases are, after all, a lively and interesting way to study rural society, or any society for that matter.

The case of Pleasant Hill, Oregon. The most clearly defined, and in many respects the most interesting open-country community in Lane County, has its center on Pleasant Hill, twelve miles southeast of Eugene, between the Coast Fork and the Middle Fork of the Willamette. Here the five neighborhoods of Evendale, Coastfork, Enterprise, Trent, and Pleasant Hill join in supporting the oldest open-country high school in Oregon.

There is no feeling of diversity of interests between the people at the center and those on the outskirts of the high-school district; the church, the hall, the cemetery, and the high school border the road at dignified distances which make it clear that here is no thought of an organized town. Until recently the store was a mile and a half from the blacksmith shop.

The Pleasant Hill neighborhood grew up about the farm of Elijah Bristow, first settler in Lane County. Bristow, a veteran of the War of 1812, was a sturdy pioneer, a member of the Disciples of Christ, father of fifteen, and a native of Kentucky, who came to California in 1845 as an emigrant from Illinois. In 1846, he came to Oregon and in 1848 took a donation land claim, built the first house in Lane County, and later asked the Legislature for permission to name his farm Pleasant Hill.

Bristow and his family entered upon this fertile land and possessed it with a thoroughness which must be considered the most significant factor in establishing the unity of the Pleasant Hill community. They initiated and for many years controlled the religious and educational activities of the community. For more than fifty years, the center of the Pleasant Hill community remained where Bristow made the first settlement. The stones of the chimney of his house are now preserved in a memorial watering trough in front of the post office, only a few hundred yards from the site of the original building. In the spring of 1910, when the site of the Union

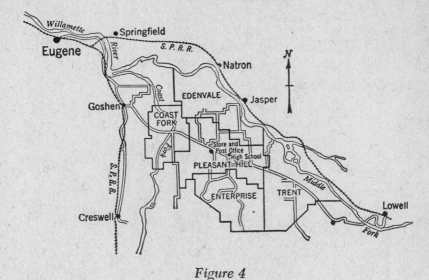

Figure 4

MAP SHOWING LOCATION AND EXTENT OF
PLEASANT HILL COMMUNITY

Source: *A Rural Survey of Lane County, Oregon.* Country Church
Work Board of Home Missions, Presbyterian Church in the United
States, 1916.

High School was definitely fixed, the real center of the district may
be said to have moved somewhat.

The high school was established in 1907. When the proposition
was made by the County Superintendent and some members of the
faculty of the University of Oregon, to organize the first open-
country high school in Oregon, the five districts comprising the
neighborhoods of Evendale, Trent, Coastfork, Enterprise, and
Pleasant Hill voted without any serious opposition to make the
experiment.

Union High School Number One is the strongest force now operating to hold the Pleasant Hill community together. It was established just in time; otherwise, the community would even now be
breaking up, following a tendency toward disintegration that becomes more noticeable as the farms fill up with people who knew
not Elijah and who owe no allegiance to the Christian Church.
From the first the high school has offered four years of work. For
six years it has graduated at least seven students annually, and
holds within its student body practically the entire high-school
population of the district, some forty young men and women.

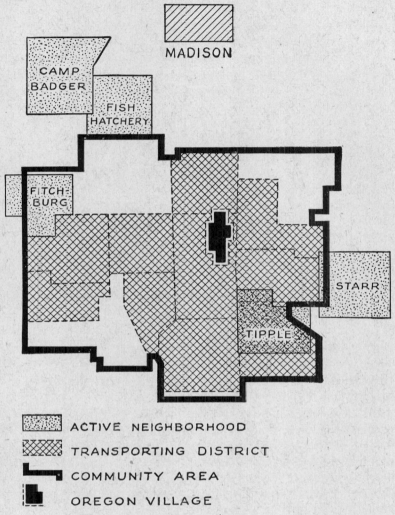

ACTIVE NEIGHBORHOOD

TRANSPORTING DISTRICT

COMMUNITY AREA

OREGON VILLAGE

Figure 5

THE OREGON COMMUNITY AREA WITH ACTIVE
NEIGHBORHOODS AND COUNTRY SCHOOL DIS-
TRICTS TRANSPORTING PUPILS TO OREGON

Nothing but the high school could have preserved the integrity
of the community against the influence of the small towns by
which it is surrounded. Each of these towns has a logical claim to
some part of the Pleasant Hill territory, but none can at present
effectively enforce its claim because not one can offer to the coun-

try people any social or educational advantages superior to those at present available in the open country.[9]

The case of Otsego County, New York. The tendency toward the organization of rural life into larger units is shown by the organization of central rural school districts in this county. This case is cited because it is almost a perfect illustration of a tendency found in many sections of the country, and one which is made the basis for a plan of community organization described in Chapter 14. Nine central school districts were organized in the ten years between the two studies. These schools are located in the villages. In addition, five other similar district plans are proposed, the formation of which, together with those already in existence and those formed in adjoining counties, will mean that the majority of the common-school districts of the county will be included in some larger unit plan. Depending on the wishes of the people, the local country school may be maintained for the first six grades; but beginning with the junior high school or seventh grade, all pupils will be transported to the central school. A striking similarity was found between the community service areas of the fourteen larger centers in the county and the high-school areas. In fact, with two or three exceptions, the areas of the central school districts already established coincide very closely with the service areas of the larger village centers in which the school buildings are located. This is additional evidence of the importance of the high school in modern rural life, to which repeated reference will be made.

In this larger school arrangement, country children are sure to form friendships that in time will tend to weaken neighborhood activity and strengthen the connection of country and village centers. Organizations serving young people tend to be located in such centers also. For example, fourteen of the twenty-four Grange halls in the county are located in villages, as are twenty-three of the thirty Home Bureaus, and thirty-one of the forty-two Farm Bureaus. Similar tendencies were discovered in many of the 140 village communities. With such a concentration of educational and agricultural life, it seems logical to anticipate the decline of the neighborhood and the increase of the larger community plan of rural group organization in counties of the type of Otsego.

The case of Oregon, Wisconsin. The most striking change in the case of the Oregon community is the "social" consolidation of ten near-by country school districts with the village grade school. The

[9] Morse, H. N., *A Rural Survey of Lane County, Oregon,* in co-operation with Extension Division University of Oregon, Eugene.

"legal" consolidation is far from a reality. This tendency for social action to precede legal sanction is an important process in rural society and one which local lay leaders as well as professional workers need to understand more fully; hence, the inclusion of this case story. Each of the ten districts has its annual school meetings and votes to request the village school to teach their children for a tuition remuneration. They also vote to pay for the transportation to the village. The concreting of the state highway Number 13 had much to do with forwarding this plan. Leaders in the local districts were nearly unanimous in their praise of the plan, but they were equally united in their determination not to consolidate legally with the village. They emphasized the things they might have to give up rather than the things they might have to gain. Tradition apparently still lays a heavy hand upon many shoulders.

Many organizations and social activities are now on the larger community basis. Neighborhoods within the area have felt this tendency. Of those fairly close to the village center only Fitchburg remained active in 1931, mainly because of its small post office, store, feed mill, and church. This does not mean that all social or group life has gone from the open country. There are still informal and special interest-group activities on the neighborhood basis such as the social club in the old Tipple district, the cemetery association at Rutland Center, and the mothers' clubs at Oak Hall and Stoner Prairie. It does mean, however, that the larger community in this particular locality is on the ascendency for certain types of social activities. Some of these activities centered in the village of Oregon and others in Madison or beyond. For those centering in Oregon, there is little or no distinction made between village and country youth. The experiences in the high school obliterated what differences there may have been. This is a factor of much importance in the future of town and country relations.

In conclusion, it can be said that country neighborhoods come into being; some become inactive; many live on. Changes and readjustments, however, are characteristic of those that remain active. The evidence is clear that country neighborhoods can maintain their activeness, and by the same token, inactive neighborhoods can be revived or new ones formed. Primary personal contacts can be made; families can meet, discuss problems, and determine what they will do. Tenants can be helped to the ownership of their farms; new families can be encouraged to move in; those of similar nationality backgrounds can be given opportunity for meeting freely with those of other backgrounds.

Young people can be introduced to the ideals and attitudes of a primary group and to the cultural values of the society of which the group is a part. This can be done directly by personal association or by means of the expressive arts — drama, music, folk dancing, literature — " . . . man consciously . . . hands over to others, feelings he has lived through, and other people are infected and also experience them." [10] This is important. An emotional continuity "from one generation to the next is one of the outstanding features of man's life in society." [11] It gives society a certain "toughness" so it does not break apart readily, and so is not swayed by every gust of passing opinion.

The evidence also showed that neighborhoods are related to other groups in society. The purpose of neighborhood integrity is not to keep people hemmed in or protected from the rest of society. Rural groups are not hedged about by mutually exclusive boundaries; they are intermeshed and connected. Moreover, the only group culture which can have vitality is one which is poured out — given away.

Furthermore, primary contacts are not confined to country neighborhoods. "In our kind of society, being little bound by place, people easily form clubs and fraternal societies based on congeniality which gives rise to real intimacy." [12] Such relations are readily formed in school, at work, or at play. Work exchange and family visiting patterns have been described. Other groups discussed in a following chapter, known as "interest groups," abound in rural society. They may, and very many do, become primary, personal in nature.

Personal contacts of farm families with village families are also multiplying so that the web of group relationships in rural society enmeshes, not only country families and neighborhoods in its design, but also villages and communities, even cities.

DISCUSSION TOPICS

1. Draw an outline map of a rural or an urban situation with which you are personally acquainted, locating the following:
   a. The home with which you are acquainted.

[10] Tolstoy, Lev Nikolaevich, *What is Art?* New York: Oxford University Press, 1930.
[11] Young, Kimball, *An Introductory Sociology*, Rev. Ed. New York: American Book Co., 1939.
[12] Cooley, Charles H., *Social Organization*. New York: Scribner, 1925.

b. The boundaries of a recognized neighborhood.

c. The location of the important social and economic institutions with which this home has regular contacts.

2. List in their order of importance the factors which have created the neighborhood you have outlined above, or if there is no such recognized grouping, the factors which have prevented such an arrangement.

3. Characterize and give reasons for changes which are taking place in primary or personal groupings in present-day society, first rural and second urban.

4. What forces are tending to integrate, and what to disintegrate, country neighborhoods?

5. Why do neighborhoods with local social institutions such as church, school, or club tend to persist longer than those without institutions?

6. What functions do you think country neighborhoods may well render in the future?

REFERENCE READINGS

Cooley, C. H., *Social Organization.* New York: Charles Scribner's Sons, 1912. See early chapters for an excellent statement and definition of primary social groups.

Hoffsommer, Harold, Herbert Pryor, *Neighborhoods and Communities in Covington County, Mississippi.* Washington, D.C.: United States Department of Agriculture, July, 1941.

Kolb, J. H., *Trends of Country Neighborhoods.* Madison: Research Bulletin 120, Agricultural Experiment Station, University of Wisconsin, 1933. A restudy of rural primary groups.

McMurray, J. Donald, Fred R. Keeler, Donald F. Rehl, *Rural Neighborhoods and Communities of Ross County, Ohio.* Agricultural Extension Service, Ohio State University, and United States Department of Agriculture, co-operating, August, 1941.

Nichols, Ralph R., John S. Page, *Community and Neighborhood Areas Lincoln County, Oklahoma.* Washington, D.C.: United States Department of Agriculture in co-operation with Oklahoma Joint Land-Grant College — B.A.E. Committee, May, 1941.

Nichols, Ralph R., *Locating Neighborhoods and Communities in Red River Parish, Louisiana.* Washington, D.C.: United States Department of Agriculture in co-operation with Louisiana State Extension Service, April, 1941.

West, James, *Plainville, U.S.A.,* pp. 69-75. New York: Columbia University Press, 1945.

Winchester, Frank, *Rural Neighborhoods and Communities in Thirteen*

Kentucky Counties, 1941: Size, Population, and Social Structure. Kentucky Agricultural Station, Bulletin 450, June, 1943.

Reports of the five original studies of country neighborhoods:

Baumgartel, Walter H., *A Social Study of Ravalli County, Montana,* Bulletin 160, Agricultural Experiment Station, University of Montana, 1923.

Kolb, J. H., *Rural Primary Groups.* Madison: Research Bulletin 51, Agricultural Experiment Station, University of Wisconsin, 1921.

Morgan and Howells, *Rural Population Groups.* Columbia: Research Bulletin 74, Agricultural Experiment Station, University of Missouri, 1925.

Sanderson and Thompson, *Social Areas of Otsego County.* Ithaca: Research Bulletin 422, Agricultural Experiment Station, Cornell University, 1923.

Taylor and Zimmerman, *Rural Organization.* Bulletin 245, Agricultural Experiment Station, North Carolina, 1922.

13

Agricultural Villages and Small Towns

BETWEEN THE COUNTRY AND THE CITY are the villages and small towns, sharing the nature of each, but having distinguishing characteristics of their own. Rural society has been divided into two parts, farm and non-farm, as the chapter on rural population points out. The non-farm portion represents an increasing element and one frequently neglected in discussions of rural society. About two thirds of the rural non-farm population is made up of people in villages and hamlets. It also includes those part-time farmers living on acreages which do not come within the census definition of "farm," and others who live in rural territory, although they may work in cities.

Strictly speaking, a village is a population center ranging in size from 250 to 2500 population. A hamlet is a smaller center. Villages and hamlets may or may not be legally incorporated, but unless they are, they will not be enumerated separately in the census, unless their population is 500 or over. Towns are centers of 2500 to 10,000 population and therefore are included in the "urban" classification of the census.

Will the village and small town come back? is a question often raised. The facts indicate that they have never been away. They have continued to play their part in rural society, and not only maintain, but increase, their proportionate share of the population. Apparently they do have a chance in a modern society of improved highways and automobiles, radios and newspapers, chain stores and national advertising. Unless they did have a degree of stability and power to hold their own, it would be idle to talk about their place in rural society, and as rural community centers. But before considering the question of the extent to which they are holding their own and taking a part in rural life and agriculture, it is well to look into their origins and backgrounds.

HISTORICALLY CONSIDERED

Agricultural villages were more often than not the residence centers and the primary social groups of rural society in many Old World countries, as the previous chapter on country neighborhoods has suggested. In New England and in certain regions of the West, the plan was continued by the pioneer settlers, but in most other parts of the country the village or small town has other origins. Inasmuch as settlement was first made on individual farms in neighborhood groups, the small town came later as an adjunct to the agricultural enterprise, performing services of transporting, retailing, and financing. Or, as was often the case in Mid-Western and Western settlements, the town was deliberately projected and made the spearhead of railroad development into new territory in order to stimulate settlement and provide new business. It is reported that one railroad company whose track traversed a particularly fertile agricultural state actually "planted" towns at five-mile intervals along its right-of-way, so as to develop a volume of business for itself.

However started, the town soon became an economic or business center rather than a social or residence center for farm families. The enterprise may have been trading, manufacturing on a small scale, mining, shipbuilding, or fishing. For these and various other reasons, the nucleated agricultural village failed to make headway on American soil.

In this failure Professor Gras believes that America suffered a great social loss.[1] In Europe as elsewhere, he emphasizes, close proximity has meant the development of such daily social contacts as group singing or dancing, and various other forms of social activity. "Such things," he says, "lead to rural amenities and to rural art of which America has had all too little." In similar manner, he suggests that co-operation in social affairs prepares the way for co-operation in the business phases of agriculture, which in this country has grown slowly and with many set-backs. A very important cause of this was the fact that farms in America were too large to be compressed into a village form of organization. It is of interest, however, to find that in periods of emergency when farm families, because they have pushed too far out toward the margins, must be relocated, or when city workers, because they have no employment, are encouraged to move to the country, the

[1] Gras, N. S. B., *A History of Agriculture*, chap. II. New York: Crofts & Co., 1925.

question of the village type of settlement is again being considered by those who are guiding governmental policies.

Business rather than social enterprises and residence, then, can be said to be an important origin or background of the American rural village or small town. Small manufacturing, trade, and transportation were important early business enterprises and their importance has continued, as a later section of the chapter will indicate.

There is little possibility of succeeding in tracing the relative importance of these three types of business enterprise, and probably small value in doing so, but it should be pointed out in passing that the shipping or the transporting function, whether it consisted of sending grain or livestock away to city markets or of receiving merchandise for local retailing, was especially important in locating town centers. As Professor Cooley described the process, wherever any shipping or transporting service was needed, there a town or city usually appeared. It may have been a fork in a river where cargoes had to be divided; it may have been a place where transfers from water to land or land to water had to be made; or, it may have been a division point where carload lots were broken up for smaller shipments, or where train crews were changed. In any case, the great network of transportation and communication systems does tend to converge at centers and, as will be more evident later, the services or functions performed by the centers bear a recognizable relationship to their distances apart, as well as to the size and character of their populations.

There is also a political background or origin of the small town or village. In his description of A Hoosier Village, Professor Sims tells of a typical situation in the early history of Indiana in which two enterprising pioneers took up land and went about organizing a county seat for local government.[2] They divided their land into lots, made a town plan, and proceeded to see that a courthouse, jail, and other county political institutions were located there. Business establishments and residents soon accumulated: the store, the inn, the blacksmith shop, the abstract office, the country weekly newspaper, and so on, until a thriving political center was established. The influence of county-seat functions is still very important and is easily recognizable in the study of the 140 town-country communities which is detailed in the next chapter.

Still another feature to be considered is the physical layout of the

[2] Sims, N. L., A Hoosier Village. New York: Columbia University Press, 1912.

village or small town together with its organization or "legal incorporation," as it is termed. For numerous reasons, which in themselves would make an interesting study, very many of the "business" type villages or towns were laid out on straight lines, with square corners in checker-board fashion, with the business blocks featured, but often with little or no plan for future development. The square or rectangular effect can be seen in the accompanying diagram.

Other towns were strung along a main street, a railroad track, or a river. In marked contrast were the villages or towns, laid out in the East, as "social" or residence centers. They were frequently built about a "common" with prominent blocks given over to public buildings, schools, and churches. A simple plan illustrating the triangular type of town common is seen in the diagram (Figure 6). Other types, according to Professor Waugh, are the wide-street type as represented by Northfield, and the quadrangular type as represented by Amherst. Definite planning was done in advance and an

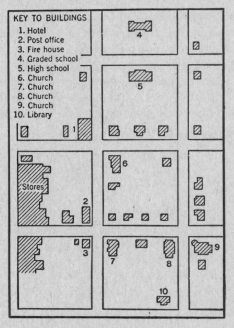

Figure 6

THE "BUSINESS" TYPE OF VILLAGE WITH STRAIGHT
LINES AND SQUARE CORNERS

Source: Paul H. Douglass, *The Little Town.* The Macmillan Company, 1921.

effort was made to make the village a pleasant and attractive place in which to live. More recently much has been done to beautify and improve some of the rectangular "business" centers by setting aside and fitting up parks and playgrounds, by such public improvement as lighting, and by encouraging private planting and landscaping.

Associated with the so-called "Western" and "business" type of village or small town, perhaps not by definite design, but certainly out of a similar traditional background, came the practice of incorporating, that is, setting the center off legally from the surrounding country. As described before, the strictly agricultural villages of New England and Utah did not so incorporate; politically, as well as socially, they remained part and parcel of the country. This physical, legal, and mental severance of the town from the country is one of the traditions and backgrounds of far-reaching consequence in any plan for improvement of town and country relations. In the early country neighborhood there was a certain assumption of self-sufficiency, and in the incorporated municipality there was a certain sense of superiority or completeness, a facing-away from the country, often toward the city.

In similar manner, certain social institutions have come to be associated with and to belong to villages or towns: high school, library, hospital, theater, park. Country people use them, but it is "by leave" of the village or town people. These institutions do not

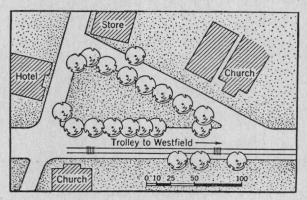

Figure 7

TRIANGLE TYPE OF TOWN COMMON, HUNTINGTON
TOWN COMMON, MASSACHUSETTS

Source: F. A. Waugh, *The Town Common*, Extension Bulletin 7, Amherst, June, 1916, Massachusetts State College and the United States Department of Agriculture co-operating.

"belong" to country people. Doctor Galpin pointed out the inconsistencies of the situation when he began to study village or town and country relations.[3] He called attention to the fact that all too often the banker, storekeeper, and blacksmith (now the garage man) knew the farmer as "the goose that lays the golden egg." His money was good and necessary, and his good will must be retained. But to incorporate him into the stream of village or town life was another matter. He did not share in the control and responsibility of the institutions he patronized. He even stood on "other people's streets." The embarrassment was on both sides. The farmer paid so much money into the town through trade that he felt he ought to have some consideration, yet he contributed so little directly toward some of the social institutions that the villagers did not consider his rights very compelling. And the legalized insulation of the village or town through its incorporation and separation from the township and the town government has added to the puzzling situation.

Greatly improved facilities for travel and communication — physical inventions of the modern age — have increased enormously the freedom of movement and thought for both farmers and villagers. They have also changed and improved details of the general situation, but they have not met the central problem. Social inventions are needed for its solution. Villages and towns continue to need the country and its agricultural wealth, and the country needs the village and town social and educational institutions even more than formerly. Country people are not so dependent upon any one center for business services as they once were. In fact, village and town business leaders generally recognize that today the range of choice has expanded and that retail trade, in the majority of cases, now follows high-school attendance, which is a recognition of the social function of rural centers. A rural community is therefore in formation, a collation of small town or village and country, arising out of their interdependences and their mutual needs, but not yet recognized in the legal structure of the day. It is time then to consider in detail the place of the village and town in our modern rural society and their power to survive and to perform needed services.

[3] Galpin, C. J., *The Social Anatomy of a Rural Community*, Research Bulletin 34, p. 25. Madison: Wisconsin Agricultural Experiment Station, May, 1915.

Villages and Hamlets — Their Place in Modern Rural Society

The place of the village in modern American life is not entirely typical, for, as has been explained, agricultural villages in the Old World were often residence centers for farm families as well as for villagers. In parts of Australia and in some South American countries the division of "rural" population is often between larger market centers and the open country. Intermediate small towns and villages have relatively less importance. In the United States rural society seems to need the village and the small town; they have made a place for themselves and constitute a definite group. They have certain distinguishing characteristics and they fall into certain recognized types.

Trends in number and population of all rural incorporated places. First of all, one should gain some impression of the recent trends of all incorporated places in rural society — that is, centers of less than 2500 population — their number and their population. In 1940, the United States Census reported 13,288 places of this description, while in 1930, 13,433 such centers were enumerated.

Table 33. All Rural Incorporated Centers

Year	Number	Population
1940	13,288	9,342,677
1930	13,433	9,183,453
1920	12,858	8,971,549

Sources: 1940, *Sixteenth Census of the United States, Population* vol. I, Table 10, p. 26; 1930, *Fifteenth Census of the United States, Population,* vol. I, Table 10, p. 7; 1920, Fry, C. Luther, *American Villagers,* Doran & Co., 1926. *Fourteenth Census of the United States, Population,* vol. I, Table 81, p. 50, reported 12,857 centers with a population of 8,969,241, but for some reason did not include Littleton, New Hampshire, with a population of 2308.

There would appear to be a loss of 145 centers between 1930 and 1940, but a gain of 430 in the twenty-year period. However, simply placing centers of any defined size into categories for any particular year does not tell the true story of trends. It can very easily lead to false conclusions. The reason, of course, is that village, hamlet, or even town populations do not stay put; they change from one census enumeration period to another. The changes may be sufficient to place them in different-size categories. Thus, to compare the number or the population of any one size group, one decade with another, gives an incomplete conclusion.

It must be kept in mind that the 1940 figure can be checked only by starting with the 1930 number, then adding new centers which may have been incorporated during the decade, subtracting those which passed over the 2500 mark, and therefore became towns and were classed as "urban," as well as adding any which might have slipped back from the urban classification. While the net loss was 145, yet the number passing into the urban exceeded those falling back, so that in reality there were 142 more incorporated rural centers and villages grown into towns in 1940 than there were in 1930.[4]

Regional differences in numbers were found by means of a special analysis of these rural incorporated centers.[5] Nearly 44 per cent of the new incorporations occurred in the three census regions known as the South. Elsewhere such changes did not exceed 8 per cent. The South, notably the "Old South," also accounted for 71 per cent of the centers which disappeared from the lists between 1930 and 1940. Probably this part of the country felt the influences of improved travel and communication later than did other sections of our rural society. While the net loss was great in the South, this was the region with only 32 per cent of all the incorporated centers of less than 2500 population in 1930, yet it furnished nearly 48 per cent of those which grew from villages to towns in the last decade, 1930 to 1940.

Incorporated villages only. A simple tabulation presents changes among incorporated villages, centers from 250 to 2500 population.

TABLE 34. INCORPORATED VILLAGES

Year	Number	Population
1940	10,441	8,879,112
1930	10,451	8,697,249
1920	10,422	8,556,387

Sources: 1940, *Sixteenth Census of the United States, Population,* vol. I, Table 5, by states; 1930, *Fifteenth Census of the United States, Population,* vol. I, Table 5, by states; 1920, *Fourteenth Census of the United States, Population,* vol. I, Table 5, by states; and Paul H. Landis, "The Number of Unincorporated Places in the United States and Their Estimated Populations," *Research Studies of the State College of Washington, Pullman,* vol. VI, December, 1938.

The number of villages in similar categories has not changed significantly in the two decades, yet it should be remembered that those centers which passed into the "town" and therefore the "urban" classification were, in the great majority of cases, the larger villages. The main sources of new incorporated villages are unincorporated villages and growing hamlets.

Incidentally, it can be pointed out that even though allowances are not made for such changes in classification, the population in

[4] Smith, T. Lynn, "The Rôle of the Village in American Society," *Rural Sociology,* March, 1942.
[5] Brunner, E. de S., and T. Lynn Smith, "Village Growth and Decline," *Rural Sociology,* June, 1944.

the villages so classified in each period increased nearly 145,000 in the decade 1930 to 1940. However, if the estimate of ten million is made to include those villages which did pass into the town category, then the increase would be 8.9 per cent, which is more than the rural rate of 6.4 per cent, or the urban rate of 7.2 per cent, but less than the rural non-farm rate of 14.2 per cent.

Population fluctuations were specially tabulated and expressed in percentages by size groups.[6] In every village population group — that is, excluding hamlets of less than 250 people — well over two fifths showed only a slight change, in fact, gaining or losing less than 10 per cent in the decade. This means an average rate of less than one per cent change per year, surely indicating a relative stability. It is significant, however, that in every category the number of villages growing up to the 10 per cent exceeded by a considerable margin those declining at the same rate. In total, exactly 50 per cent more villages gained up to 10 per cent than lost that proportion. Thus, the reason for any seeming loss of places in the village categories is because half of them are growing toward the town category. This is a trend which extends back at least to 1900, when about 43 per cent of the villages showed less than 1 per cent a year change in the ten years ending in 1920.[7]

Similar results were found by making comparisons by 100-person intervals. For example, if a village of between 450 and 550 persons remained in the same interval in 1940 as in 1930, it was placed in a zero group; if it moved up into the next class of 550 to 650, it was placed in a + 1 group, and so on. Table 35 gives the percentages of change by these intervals as well as the differences according to the various census regions. The most striking figure in the table is the 42.1 per cent of the villages which fell into the zero class; that is, remained in the same hundred interval in 1940 as in 1930. The most stable regions were the East and West North Central, where just under one half of the villages remained in the same hundred group in which they began the decade. The two Far Western regions showed the greatest tendency toward growth. The West Central census divisions, both North and South, showed the greatest percentage of incorporated places which lost one or more hundreds. These two regions, along with the small group of villages in New England, also showed the largest proportion of places declining one or more hundreds. On a state basis, however,

---

[6] Brunner and Smith, *op. cit.*

[7] Ratcliffe, S. C., "Population Changes of Hamlets and Villages," *Rural Sociology,* September, 1942.

Census Division	Number of Villages		Percentage Distribution by Units (Hundreds) of Change									
	Number	Per cent	−3 and over	−2	−1	0	+1	+2	+3	+4	+5	+6 and over
United States.........	9816	100	1.6	2.2	10.8	42.1	22.8	9.2	4.3	2.2	1.4	3.4
New England.........	60	100	1.8	3.5	14.0	45.6	26.3	5.3	3.5	0.0	0.0	0.0
Middle Atlantic.......	1041	100	1.6	1.9	10.4	44.0	28.5	7.5	2.8	1.0	0.8	1.4
East North Central....	2342	100	0.7	1.0	5.5	49.5	26.5	9.2	3.1	1.8	0.9	1.8
West North Central....	2356	100	0.7	1.8	14.0	49.8	20.0	6.9	2.6	1.3	1.0	1.2
South Atlantic........	1272	100	1.0	1.8	10.3	49.0	20.7	8.7	5.4	2.3	1.6	4.2
East South Central....	705	100	1.4	2.6	10.3	41.3	21.3	10.1	4.3	3.1	2.2	3.4
West South Central....	1061	100	4.4	4.7	13.8	39.8	16.9	8.2	3.5	2.1	1.2	5.4
Mountain.............	619	100	0.7	1.4	9.4	34.8	22.0	10.9	7.0	3.4	2.3	8.1
Pacific..............	360	100	2.2	2.1	6.1	35.0	21.3	13.0	8.6	4.2	1.4	6.0

Source: Brunner and Smith, *op. cit.*

the proportion of such declines was less than the national average of all villages for the decade, 1920 to 1930.

When the villages were analyzed according to size, it was again apparent that the larger places seemed to grow more rapidly than the smaller ones, but a larger proportion also declined one or more hundreds. This tendency was less pronounced in the decade just closed than in the previous one, as Table 36 shows. Apparently the greater growth in village population between 1930 and 1940 affected more communities than between 1920 and 1930. The forces that brought people into some villages kept more villages unchanged. Extreme fluctuations were reduced.

TABLE 36. PERCENTAGE OF INCORPORATED VILLAGES CHANGING ONE HUNDRED CATEGORIES, 1930-1940 AND 1920-1930, BY SIZE GROUPS

Type of Village	Declining One or More Hundreds		Remaining Same Hundred		Gaining One or More Hundreds	
	1930-40	1920-30	1930-40	1920-30	1930-40	1920-30
All villages........	14.6	27.5	42.1	34.2	43.3	38.3
Large.............	17.5	25.1	15.2	13.1	67.3	61.7
Medium..........	17.1	30.1	22.0	20.9	60.9	49.0
Small............	13.6	26.6	51.4	41.8	35.0	31.6

Source: Brunner and Smith, *op. cit.*

The trends just traced for the United States are similar to those in the state of Victoria, Australia. Between 1933 and 1939, of the 180 villages and towns (250 to 10,000 population), 46 per cent were stationary, 33 per cent were increasing, and 21 per cent decreasing. Of the 59 centers increasing, 63 per cent were over 1000 population and of the 39 decreasing, 92 per cent were below 1000.[8]

Unincorporated villages. Only estimates are possible. Unless a center is legally incorporated, or has a population of 500 or more, it does not receive enumeration by the census. Estimates must, therefore, be based upon recordings of other agencies, such as Dun and Bradstreet, a business organization which secures, tabulates, and distributes information regarding the type, location, and rating of all business firms; or atlases, such as Rand-McNally or Crams. In 1940 it was estimated that there were about 8900 unincorporated villages with a population of about 4,900,000 people. In 1930 the

[8] McIntyre, A. J. and J. J., *Country Towns of Victoria.* Carlton, N. 3, Victoria, Australia: Melbourne University Press, University of Melbourne, 1944.

estimates were about the same number of villages, but with probable population somewhat higher.

TABLE 37. UNINCORPORATED VILLAGES

Year	Number	Population
1940................	8,918	4,901,878
1930................	8,916	5,612,358
1920 { Fry.............	8,142	4,348,862
{ Landis.........	9,018	5,368,646

Sources: 1940, Special Census Release, *Unincorporated Communities, Population*, 1940, for places of 500 to 2500 population, and a special analysis by Douglas G. Marshall, Department of Rural Sociology, University of Wisconsin, of the Rand McNally Commercial Atlas, for places of 250 to 500 population, administrative release, Madison, December 1, 1945; 1930, Landis, Paul, *op. cit.*; 1920, Fry, C. Luther, and Landis, Paul, *op. cit.*

TABLE 38. UNINCORPORATED VILLAGES BY SIZE IN 1940

Size	Number	Population
Total................	8,918	4,901,878
250 to 500...........	5,828	1,868,139
500 to 1000..........	1,960	1,326,253
1000 to 2500..........	1,130	1,707,486

Sources: Special Census Release and special analysis of Rand McNally Atlas, *op. cit.*

Thus, the total for all villages, whether incorporated or unincorporated, for the year 1940 is 19,359; the population for these places is 13,780,990. This population represents 24.1 per cent of the total rural population and 51 per cent of the rural non-farm population. This means that one in four of the people in our rural society are villagers and that every second person in the rural non-farm population lives in a village.

What about the incorporated hamlets? By census count there were 2847 incorporated places of less than 250 population in 1940 and the population was 463,565.

TABLE 39. INCORPORATED HAMLETS

Year	Number	Population
1940................	2,847	463,565
1930................	2,982	486,204
1920 { Fry...........	2,619	461,890
{ Landis........	2,436	415,162

Sources: 1940, *Sixteenth Census of the United States, Population*, vol. I, Table 5, by states; 1930 and 1920, *Fifteenth Census of the United States, Population*, vol. I, Table 5, by states. See also Paul Landis, *op. cit.*, and C. Luther Fry, *op. cit.*

When submitted to similar analysis as those given the villages reported above, hamlets (incorporated places under 250 population) gave some evidence of increase and growth, but never to the extent of the villages. This was true for the 1930 to 1940 period as well as in the earlier decades. Of the 1959 hamlets incorporated in 1910, one fifth had become villages by 1920 and over one fourth by 1930. Again, of the 507 incorporated between 1910 and 1930, about one fifth had moved into the village class by 1930. The average size of all places which remained hamlets in this period decreased from 173 to 162, but the average for all centers which were hamlets in 1910 increased to about 250 by 1930.

And the unincorporated hamlets? Finally any estimate of places under 250 population and not legally incorporated will depend very largely upon definitions. Many of them are only cross-road centers which may or may not measure up to the hamlet definition recently proposed by the geographer, Professor Trewartha.[9] A special analysis of the 1943 edition of the Rand McNally Atlas gives the results indicated in Table 40, where comparisons can be made with esti-

TABLE 40. UNINCORPORATED HAMLETS

Year	Number	Population
1940	55,971	3,458,472
1930	34,221	2,029,819
1920	41,248	2,273,147

Sources: 1940, Special analysis by Douglas G. Marshall of the 1943 edition, Rand McNally Atlas, *op. cit.* In this analysis all duplicate entries were carefully eliminated and only those places with a stated population were included; 1930 and 1920, Landis, Paul, *op. cit.*

mates of earlier decades.

Again, the estimated total for all hamlets, whether incorporated or unincorporated, for the year 1940 is 58,818 places with a population of 3,922,037. The nearly four million people represent 6.9 per cent of the total rural population and 14.5 per cent of the rural non-farm population.

All incorporated and unincorporated villages and hamlets together. The final figures toward which we have been striving are 17,703,027 people in 1940, living in 78,177 places — villages and hamlets of less than 2500 population. This is a large number of people, 30.9 per cent of the total rural population and 65.5 per cent of the rural non-farm population. It is 13.4 per cent of the total population of the nation as of 1940. In 1930 the percentages were as follows: 31.3 per cent of the total rural population, 71.3 per cent of the rural non-farm, and 13.7 per cent of the total population. It is also a large number of places, and begins to explain that expanding rural non-farm element within our own rural society. How-

[9] Trewartha, Glenn T., "The Unincorporated Hamlet — One Element of the American Settlement Fabric," *Annals of the Association of American Geographers,* vol. XXXIII, March, 1943.

ever, it is not in the villages nor yet in the hamlets, whether incorporated or unincorporated, where major increases have come. Villages and hamlets are holding their own in the total population growth and have done so, at least since 1920, as the various tabulations clearly indicate. It is rather in the scattered areas and more especially in the vicinity of urban and industrial areas where the greatest gains in this rural non-farm population have taken place. This comparatively recent development will be discussed in the chapter on rural-urban relationships.

Agricultural villages show less growth but more stability. The question should be considered at this point whether the conclusions drawn for all centers in rural society apply to agricultural villages as such. The general answer is that they do, because the majority, at least of the incorporated centers of less than 2500, are agricultural, but some are also industrial, some mining, some fishing, and others are suburban or resort villages. Further evidence is secured by the special study of the sample of 140 strictly agricultural villages. The plan of plotting by 100-person intervals revealed that 28 of the 132 villages incorporated by 1910 stayed in the same class in 1930; 104 changed, 17 fell one or more classes; 11 of the medium size went into the next class below. Of the 87 which moved up, 21 went into the class just above; 22 went two classes; 15, 3, and 29 advanced still more. By 1940, 13 had "passed over" into the town category. Of the remaining 127, 9.6 per cent lost one or more hundreds; 34 per cent remained in the same class; 24.4 per cent moved into the next higher hundred category, and 32 per cent gained from two to six hundreds.

In terms of the actual rate of growth for the decade 1920 to 1930, and by regions, the percentages are as follows: for the total 140 an increase of 9.6 per cent; for the 28 Middle Atlantic villages, 11.0 per cent; the 30 Southern, 13.8 per cent; the 60 Middle Western, 2.4 per cent; the 22 Far Western, 15.5 per cent. In the next decade, 1930 to 1940, the same general trend is maintained, although with some variations according to regions, notably the Middle Atlantic and the Middle West. Table 41 gives the changes and in terms of size also. It can be readily seen that these agricultural villages follow the general trend line of all villages, the smaller ones tending to grow more slowly than the larger ones. The contrast is rather distinct between the small villages of less than 1000 population and those which have stepped up into the town class, a range of 5.8 per cent to 23 per cent.

Thus it is evident that agricultural villages manifest somewhat

TABLE 41. RATE OF GAIN, 1930–1940, OF 140 VILLAGES BY
REGION AND SIZE GROUPS

Region	Total	Small	Medium	Large	Town
Middle Atlantic............	4.1	6.7	5.3	−1.3	0.01
South....................	10.6	8.6	6.4	13.7	15.2
Middle West.............	11.8	5.1	10.1	14.0	25.1
Far West.................	20.6	4.5	16.3	15.7	28.8
All Villages..............	11.5	5.8	9.0	12.1	23.0

Source: Brunner and Smith, *op. cit.*

greater tendencies toward stability and toward maintaining their populations than do all villages. A close population relationship between the village center and the surrounding farm population is also maintained, as the chapter on community relations will indicate. This relationship is reasonably constant among the various crop areas. Doctor Douglass pointed this out in his early study of small towns in Iowa.[10] He suggested that rural people, especially farmers, have villages or small towns as their own numbers warrant and as they "can afford them," meaning the economic and social services they need and can pay for.

Answer to the question of growth or decline. Villages, especially agricultural villages, are achieving a greater relative stability. Villages with rapid change tendencies seem to be on the decline and those of a more steady and established character appear to be on the increase. Nevertheless, there has been a tendency for some to grow and some to decline in population. The smaller villages are likely to be found in the latter class, some having dropped to hamlet or even to country neighborhood status, becoming "convenience" centers for a limited clientèle. At the other end of the scale are those exhibiting steady growth tendencies, and that trait sooner or later carries them into another class — the small town.

Of course, irregularities have been introduced into the long-time trends by the changes and uncertainties of the depression and war periods. In the early years of the 1930 to 1940 decade, the larger villages and the towns grew disproportionately to the smaller ones. In certain regions there were migrations from farms to the villages, but fewer migrations from villages to cities. There were also likely to be more full-time farmers living in the villages. In some regions there was a movement from cities back to villages and towns, fam-

[10] Douglass, H. Paul, *The Little Town.* New York: The Macmillan Co., 1927.

ilies seeking lower living costs, trying to qualify for government work projects or at least for relief grants. In the South many forces were at work, such as mechanization of farm work, displaced cropper and resettlement projects. In the Middle West and the Far West, the droughts drove people into the villages or to specialized farming areas.

Better times for industry and for agriculture have changed much of this. Many villages and small towns are facing, some more and some less, radical readjustments in the postwar period. A study in Kansas may be pointing the way toward this future.[11] Its conclusion is that many rural centers are being subject to considerable strain, but that there is little to support the idea that those ready and willing to make readjustments are likely to lose population or to die out. This would suggest that a modified rural organization is emerging in which villages with stability and tendencies to steady growth may assume a somewhat different but still an important rôle in rural society. Those with more rapid growth tendencies are destined to become the small towns of rural America.

SMALL TOWNS, U.S.A.

During the first forty years of the century some two thousand of the more rapidly growing and larger villages increased their population beyond the 2500 mark and have come into the "town" classification. This number is equivalent to about four fifths of all the incorporated places of 2500 to 10,000 population, reported by the 1940 Census. In the decade 1930 to 1940, 316 villages moved into the town category.

TABLE 42. TOWNS-INCORPORATED AND UNINCORPORATED, 1940

Size class	Total		Incorporated		Unincorporated	
	Number	Population	Number	Population	Number	Population
Total..........	2826	13,646,383	2387	11,707,805	439	1,938,578
2500 to 5000....	1739	6,110,450	1422	5,025,911	317	1,084,539
5000 to 10,000..	1087	7,535,933	965	6,681,894	122	854,039

Sources: Incorporated, *Sixteenth Census of the United States*, 1940, *Population*, vol. I, Table 9, p. 25; Unincorporated, *Sixteenth Census of the United States*, 1940, special release, *Population, Unincorporated Communities*.

[11] Clark, Carroll D., and Roy L. Roberts, *People of Kansas*. Topeka: The Kansas State Planning Board, National Reserve Building, 1936.

TABLE 43. INCORPORATED TOWNS — TRENDS

Year	Number	Population
1940	2,387	11,707,805
1930	2,183	10,614,746
1920	1,970	9,353,530

Sources: 1940, *Sixteenth Census of the United States, op. cit.*; 1930, *ibid.*; 1920, *ibid.*, vol. I, *Population*, Table 10, p. 26.

In 1940, the 2826 towns with their over 13,500,000 people, represented a little more than 10 per cent of the total population and over 18 per cent of the "urban." Many, if not most, of these towns are still agriculture-centered to a high degree. This is especially true of the smaller ones and as such they extended the number and enlarged the scope of their services to the farming population and likewise to those villagers dwelling in the near-by smaller and more restricted service centers. Some of the larger towns may disown or forget their soil connections, but their many relations with country people are still certain, although such service relations may be of a somewhat less direct and less personal character than those of small villages. Both the economic and social services of the towns are more likely to be of a somewhat specialized order; some wholesaling, a central credit agency, a flexible processing plant for agricultural products, a daily newspaper, theater, hospital, vocational school, and perhaps the county courthouse.

In the absence of detailed studies of the town and its rural relations, it is in point to describe the thirteen agricultural villages in the sample of 140 which became towns by the time of the last restudy, 1936. They had more stores, by 25 per cent, than even the large villages, but they claimed quite comparable proportions of farmer trade. They had more industry, but it was more directly related to processing of agricultural products or other raw materials than was true of the villages. The 28 per cent of their elementary school enrollment from the open country was higher than the proportion for all villages in 1930, but 1.2 points under the average in 1936. The town high schools had 38.8 per cent of their enrollment from the open country. The proportion of church members from open country in town churches was six times that in 1920 and above the proportion for all villages in 1930.[12] The figures as detailed above would seem to indicate that the very growth of villages into towns enhanced their interdependence with farming people.

[12] Brunner, E. de S., and T. Lynn Smith, "Village Growth and Decline," *Rural Sociology*, June, 1944.

Who Villagers and Townsmen Are

One ready way of describing the population characteristics of any group is by comparison. Comparing the village population characteristics with those of the city and farm, we find they seem to represent a mid-point in many of their features; that is, a point toward which both city and farm population seem to be approaching. In certain respects villagers are more like the city population than the country; in others, the reverse is true. Yet between 1920 and 1930, both city and country became more like the village. This was true for the proportion of native and foreign-born whites, in ratio of children to women and in the percentages of many, although not all, of the age groups. In this sense the village population may be indicative of the nation's population characteristics as it approaches stability, which is predicted for about 1980 or 1985.[13] Such an hypothesis in no wise detracts from the observation that villages have been in existence in our American rural society long enough to have developed some of their own distinguishing characteristics.

Some characteristics of agricultural villages. In general, the smaller villages maintaining close contacts with the country have characteristics which resemble those of the farm population more closely than the urban. The larger villages, especially those over 1500 population, are more likely to resemble the urban patterns in a number of respects. Villages do not have the extremes of tenancy, of illiteracy, or the large portions of foreign-born found in the larger centers. In the ratio of children under ten years to women aged twenty to forty-five years, villages are higher than cities but lower than farms. This is true for every region.

The main differentiating factor of village populations is the high proportion of old people, so it may be suggested in none too gracious terms that the village is rural society's "old folks' home." Except in certain areas of the South where the population is fairly normal in age distribution, the disproportion of old people in villages is general. The excess is due in major part to older persons moving in from the country areas, since there is no significant difference in death rate at the various age levels between the two populations.

A comparison has been made between growing and declining

[13] Thompson and Whelpton, estimates quoted in United States Census Release, Series P-3, no. 15, July 23, 1941.

agricultural villages.[14] The conclusions as to the age structure were that the largest difference was in the age group under ten years; growing villages had a larger proportion than those declining. The second greatest difference was in the group twenty to thirty years of age: the growing villages had substantially larger proportions. In every age group beyond forty years the declining villages had the larger proportion.

Special report on all large villages. From a study of all incorporated villages with populations of 1000 to 2500, it was found that in 1930 the sex ratio was 97.8 males per 100 females. This is below the national ratio of 102.5 as well as below the urban and the rural rates. Thus, a high proportion of females is one of the significant features of village population. These larger centers follow the general trend respecting age distribution, namely much fewer children than the farm population, but more than the urban. They were more similar, however, to the city than to the farm. In the scarcity of working-age persons, these large villages were much different from the urban, but quite like the farm. They had the highest proportion of persons of advanced age.[15]

Small-town folk. Comparisons of items available from the Census of 1930 for all incorporated towns of 2500 to 3000 population were made with the large villages, 1000 to 2500 population. As was anticipated, differences were not wide. The sex ratios, for example, were 98.0 and 97.8, respectively. There were some differences from state to state. The greatest excess of females was found in the Old South, where the general sex ratio is low and where migrations northward have left a disproportionate number of women in the small towns. There was a scarcity of single men and an excess of females who were single. In fact, the most significant feature in relation to marital status was the concentration of widowed and divorced females in the towns. They outranked the farm population in this respect, and even the cities where those divorced and widowed are especially numerous. There was likewise a tendency for widowers and divorced males to be found here. The age distribution was in line with the larger villages, namely, a slight deficiency of children, a marked deficiency of the early working ages, and an excess of aged persons.

[14] Jenkins, David, *Growth and Decline of Agricultural Villages.* New York: Bureau of Publications, Teachers College, Columbia University, 1940.
[15] Smith, T. Lynn, "Village Demography," *Social Forces,* October, 1941.

What Villagers Do, Functions Villages Perform

Villages and towns are something more than aggregations of people, struggling to "hold their own" or to improve their positions in the census columns. Their ability to continue as centers depends in large measure upon services rendered to their own residents and to those of the countryside. It cannot be concluded from what has been presented that the future of all villages, or even towns, is secure. It is easy enough to classify and to characterize places in terms of their population changes. A more fundamental question is one of function — what do they do? There are, of course, correlations between function, size, and characteristics, as the next chapter will show. In this chapter, discussion will be largely about functions and services performed in the village and hamlet centers in terms of the occupations of the people and the kinds of business institutions and agencies found there. In the next chapter, emphasis will be upon the relation of the centers with their country constituencies, a relationship which is rapidly becoming the contemporary rural community.

Major occupations of all rural non-farm people. First, consider the general occupational distribution of all non-farm people in rural society as enumerated by the census in March, 1940. To be sure, this cannot be considered as representative of all village and hamlet situations, but the differences may not be too great for purposes of a general survey. A strictly village picture drawn from a special analysis will be presented in Table 44.

TABLE 44. PER CENT DISTRIBUTION OF EMPLOYED PERSONS BY MAJOR OCCUPATION CATEGORIES FOR RURAL NON-FARM POPULATION, 1940

Occupation	Males	Females
Total..............................	100.	100.
Operators............................	24.6	18.2
Craftsmen, foremen....................	17.3	0.7
Other laborers........................	13.7	1.2
Proprietors, managers, officials...........	12.4	5.8
Clerical and sales......................	10.0	20.7
Professional and semi-professional........	6.1	16.1
Farm laborers........................	5.7	1.2
Other workers........................	3.6	12.0
Protective service.....................	3.1	0.0
Farmers and farm managers.............	2.0	0.2
Domestic..............................	0.6	23.4
Others not reported....................	0.9	1.6

Source: *United States Census, "The Labor Force," United States Summary*, vol. III, Part 1, pp. 84–86.

Operators is the high ranking class for the males as Table 44 shows. This includes manufacturing, 7.3 per cent, and mining, 6.3 per cent. Within the manufacturing classification all textiles is 2.3 per cent. Among the female operators manufacturing is twice as high, 14.3 per cent, two thirds in the textiles. The second high class for men is crafts and foremen, mechanics being 3.3 per cent and carpenters, 2.7 per cent. When proprietors, managers, officials, clerical and salespeople are combined, the ranking for men is third, but for women it becomes first. Retail trade for men represents 5.4 per cent. Saleswomen are 6 per cent, stenographers, secretaries, and typists, 5 per cent, and other clerical, 4 per cent. All farmers do not live on farms as the table shows; some are in villages but manage farms or work as farm hands; together it is 7.7 per cent for the males.

Among the women, domestic service ranks first in the table, but second if a combination of clerical, sales, and proprietary is made. Operators stand third, a wide classification which includes 2 per cent beauticians and manicurists. The fourth rank among women is professional, with 16.1 per cent, including teachers, 10.9 per cent. Teaching for men is only 1.4 per cent.

Occupations of strictly villagers. Only by special tabulation and analysis can the occupational situations in villages, and in this case strictly agricultural villages, be observed. It is not possible at this time to present the 1940 figures. The previous decade, however, does give a definitive characterization of village functions in rural society. Measured in terms of total numbers, six occupations are of major importance and characterize agricultural villages rather definitely. They stand in the following order when the total numbers of gainfully employed men and women are considered: manufacturing, trade or merchandising, domestic and personal services, agriculture, professional service, and transportation. If professional, domestic, personal and clerical services are combined, surprisingly enough, the number so occupied almost equals the largest group, manufacturing, each having slightly over 26,000 persons. Tables 45 and 46 give the number gainfully employed in the agricultural villages specially studied, together with their distribution by sex, region, and type of occupation.

(1) *Manufacturing.* It may surprise some persons to find manufacturing at the top of the list of village occupations. This is at least partially accounted for by the rather inclusive census definition which includes such artisans as carpenters, masons, seamstresses, as well as those employed in industrial plants. The num-

TABLE 45. GAINFULLY EMPLOYED MALES AND FEMALES, BY PRINCIPAL OCCUPATION — 177 VILLAGES *

Occupation	Males			Females		
	Number Employed		Per cent of Change	Number Employed		Per cent of Change
	1920	1930		1920	1930	
All occupations..............	63,244	69,030	+ 9.1	17,626	21,332	+21.0
Agriculture..................	9,968	8,931	−10.4	480	488	+ 1.7
Manufacture†.................	22,041	23,519	+ 6.7	2,943	2,790	− 5.2
Transportation..............	7,447	8,713	+17.0	665	737	+10.8
Trade......................	12,736	14,872	+16.8	1,754	2,069	+18.0
Profession..................	3,965	4,668	+17.7	3,618	4,528	+25.2
Domestic and personal........	3,093	3,868	−25.1	6,098	8,205	+34.6
Clerical‡...................	2,216	2,484	−12.1	1,939	2,425	+25.3
All other..................	1,778	1,975	−11.1	132	95	−31.8

* Brunner and Kolb, *Rural Social Trends*. New York: McGraw-Hill, 1933.

† By census definition manufacture includes all artisans like carpenters, masons, seamstresses, and the like as well as those employed in industrial plants.

‡ The clerical category was abandoned by the United States Census in 1930, clerical workers being distributed over the other major categories. These figures were obtained in connection with the special tabulation made for the 177 agricultural villages.

TABLE 46. DISTRIBUTION OF MANUFACTURING INDUSTRIES, BY REGION AND BY TYPE OF INDUSTRY — 140 VILLAGES *

Type of Industry	Percentage Distribution									
	All regions		Middle Atlantic		South		Middle West		Far West	
	1924	1930	1924	1930	1924	1930	1924	1930	1924	1930
Total................	100.0	100.0	100.0	100.0	100.0	100.0	100.0	100.0	100.0	100.0
Food and beverages...	33.3	35.2	31.5	31.7	28.9	29.9	35.0	38.3	37.9	41.1
Textiles..............	3.4	4.5	7.6	7.2	3.4	6.6	1.7	3.3	0	0
Iron and steel........	3.7	4.3	2.7	3.0	3.4	3.7	3.7	4.5	5.8	7.4
Lumber..............	14.1	14.0	18.5	21.5	22.9	20.4	7.5	8.2	11.7	6.3
Leather..............	1.1	0.8	3.8	1.8	0	0	0.8	0.8	0	0
Paper†..............	27.8	25.5	20.1	19.8	23.7	20.4	34.6	30.2	30.1	30.5
Chemicals...........	3.1	3.6	1.1	2.4	6.8	6.6	2.9	3.3	2.9	2.1
Stone...............	3.6	4.2	2.2	3.6	1.7	1.5	5.0	5.3	4.8	6.3
Tobacco.............	1.7	1.1	3.8	1.8	0	0	1.7	1.6	0	0
Transportation ‡......	1.1	0.9	3.3	1.8	0.8	0	0	1.2	0	0
Miscellaneous........	7.1	5.9	5.4	5.4	8.4	10.9	7.9	3.3	6.8	6.3

* Brunner and Kolb, *Rural Social Trends*. New York: McGraw-Hill, 1933.

† Paper, according to census definition, includes newspaper and printing establishments as well as paper mills, of which there were only a few.

‡ Transportation includes equipment.

ber of those employed in manufacturing has tended to decline slightly, as the table shows; however, it does maintain a very considerable lead over the others and represents in a real way one of the main services of the village.

A distribution of the types of manufacturing industries in the agricultural villages is significant, as an examination of Table 46 will show.

Industries connected with food assume a major importance and, moreover, an importance which increased in every region during the period studied. When the food group is combined with lumber, tobacco, textile groups, and with paper mills, they total over 60 per cent, and hence their direct associations with and dependence upon agriculture and forestry is quite evident.

(2) *Trade or merchandising.* Trade showed the greatest tendency to increase its total number of employees, as well as its percentage when compared with the others in the decade 1920 to 1930. This is apparently some indication of growth and of the ability of villages to maintain themselves as retail trade centers in the face of greater urban competition. A later chapter will discuss the changes and trends in this merchandising function and in the institutions associated with it.

(3) *Domestic, personal, and professional services.* The increase in domestic, personal and professional employees is an important reflection of the increasing concentration within village centers of those institutions and services which are more and more needed by people living in the village and in its country community area. Schools, libraries, hospitals, and churches are, of course, examples of institutions that employ professional people, while the increase of such establishments as restaurants, beauty parlors, pressing and cleaning shops, and tourists' service places accounts for the definite increase of those in the personal services.

(4) *Agriculture.* The decrease of those employed in agriculture is probably not evidence that fewer farmers reside in the villages, but that there is a lessening demand for agricultural laborers because of the increasing use of machinery. In some regions it is probably due also to the fact that fewer farmers are retiring to live in the village and supervise the management of their farms from there. The difficulties arising out of the depression tend to keep families on their farms. Furthermore, it has been pointed out by those familiar with census materials that the 1930 counts were made in April, while the 1920 enumeration was in January; and, of course, more agricultural workers and operators are likely to be found in villages in January than in April.

(5) *Transportation.* Transportation is an excellent illustration of the function the village performs in rural society. Transportation agencies assemble for primary processing of food products and raw

materials destined for local or distant consumption and then transport them to other manufacturing centers or to city wholesalers and retailers. In reverse process transportation agencies bring to the village for distribution those things needed for local consumption or required in farming, merchandising, and manufacturing.

Variations and changes — A trend toward specialization. Many variations of the service or occupational relationships of villages are to be found; variations in size, growth, distance from cities, and geographic regions. Village functions are changing; they are constantly making imperative readjustments. The trend of the whole process seems to be toward specialization, each village finding it advantageous to discover its niche in rural society and then to organize its life accordingly.

Variations by size of village center and its location are noticeable. Many villages under one thousand population, except in the Far West, have fewer males employed in manufacturing and more in agriculture than formerly. For women there are fewer opportunities in domestic and personal services, except again in the Far West, but more opportunities in the professional services. As might be expected, the smaller places have more artisans than industrial employees.

Variations in the number and kind of service agencies in which villagers work is illustrated in the case of New York State centers of 1750 to 2000 and of 2000 to 2500 population as shown in the chart (Figure 8). It can be seen that, besides the stores and other service agencies usually found in smaller places, there is a furniture store, a paint shop, a florist shop, a bakery, and other specialized services. The chart introduces the subject of business institutions in villages. Manufacturing and merchandising, the two top ranking occupations of villagers, will now be considered.

INDUSTRY IN AGRICULTURAL VILLAGES

In considering the place of factories in rural America, especially the interrelation of industry and agriculture, a number of things must be kept in mind. As one of the authors says elsewhere:

> When one thinks of "rural" America, one habitually thinks in terms of agriculture — of the open country with its wide farmlands and of the agricultural villages whose chief function is to serve the needs of the surrounding farm population; one is likely to forget that all that is rural is by no means agricultural. The fact is that approximately one village out of every four classified by the United

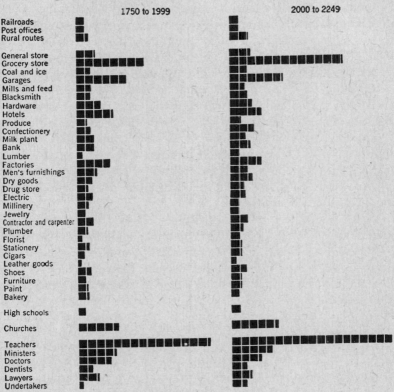

Figure 8

ECONOMIC AGENCIES AND PROFESSIONAL PEOPLE
IN TWO CLASSES OF VILLAGES, 1750 TO 1999
AND 2000 TO 2249

Source: Bruce L. Melvin, *Village Service Agencies,* New York, 1925.
Bulletin 493, August, 1929, Cornell University Agricultural Experiment Station, Ithaca.

States Census as "rural" has no connection with agriculture and no dependence upon it for a livelihood.

Statistically overwhelmed by the population of the farms and of agricultural villages are several million people who are in the country but not of it. In the places in which they live not corn and wheat but coal and iron are the gifts sought from Mother Earth. The technique employed is not cultivation that enriches while it produces, but the surgery of drills and steam shovels that wound the surface and, burrowing beneath, removes forever the prized veins of ore. Or perhaps the products of the fields and hills are here converted from standing timber into standardized lumber, from puffballs of snow-white cotton into piece goods of the newest shades and patterns.[16]

The absorption in a single manufacturing enterprise to the exclusion of almost all other economic activity differentiates the industrial from the agricultural village. There are approximately 3500 to 4000 of the former, inhabited, in 1929, by nearly 4,000,000 persons, devoted chiefly to the manufacture of textiles, to mining, lumbering or some specialized production of wide range, such as cosmetics, musical instruments, bricks, paper.

This does not mean that factory industries are lacking in agricultural villages, but that they are smaller, more diversified, more dependent for both raw material and labor on immediate locality and especially on local farmers. Some non-agricultural rural industries, the so-called cottager or handicraft type, are frequently found where agriculture is backward or handicapped by poor soil. Among these are weaving, woodworking and similar activities in the Appalachians,[17] or household industries, governmentally promoted as an added source of peasant income in the Orient, especially India, Japan, and Korea.[18]

How important is industry in agricultural villages? In 1930 the average number of industries for each agricultural village was between three and four, not counting job-printing plants. This was 10 per cent more than in 1924. Each village factory employed an average of *only* twenty-two full-time persons; more than three fifths of the factories, however, had less than ten full-time employees and only one in twenty more than one hundred. Thus, less than one sixth of the persons gainfully employed in agricultural villages were factory laborers. During the first six years of the depression the number of industries per village dropped from 4.2 to 3.7. The number of establishments with less than ten full-time employees rose to almost two thirds. Those with one hundred or more declined slightly both in number and proportion. About one plant in twenty was in this largest group. Thus the average number of full-time employees in these village industries dropped to twenty-one as contrasted with thirty-one in 1924 and twenty-five in 1930. Forty-

[16] Cf. Brunner, *Industrial Village Churches*, chap. I. New York: Harper & Bros., 1930.

[17] Cf. Nason, W. C., *Rural Industries in Knott County, Kentucky*. Washington, D.C.: United States Department of Agriculture, 1932 (mimeographed).

[18] Mukerjee, *Rural Economy in India*. (London and New York: Longmans, Green, 1920), chap. XIII, and Brunner, *Rural Korea* (New York and London, 1928), pp. 28 (Table V) and 61.

three per cent of the industries in agricultural villages were engaged in food processing and 7 per cent more worked with fiber products, such as cotton or lumber and with tobacco. This close association is important when we consider the enthusiasm for industrial decentralization. Thus far rural industries are closely related to the soil, especially many of the larger ones. Widespread decentralization must move against past trends and if successful will create a new industrial situation.

Although industry in these villages is intimately related to agriculture, the proportion of full-time employees drawn from farms appears to have fluctuated widely in the last fifteen years. In 1924 there was one such employee in every eight. Six-years later the proportion had dropped to one in thirteen, although in the seventy industrial villages studied at the same time the proportion was one in nine. During the depression years, however, persons living on farms competed successfully with villagers for available jobs. One in five of the employees in these industries in 1936 lived in farm homes. At least three factors help to explain this change. Some retired farmers living in the village center with children employed in village industries were forced to move back to their farms, reacquired because of foreclosures. Some village industries employed persons from farm homes when it was realized that the addition of a wage to the family income would save a farm from foreclosure. Sometimes such employment was at the expense of village youth.

Village industries have high death rate. Not only are industrial establishments in agricultural villages small, but their life cycles are apt to be short. By 1930 one of every four existing in 1924 had closed, although every defunct factory was replaced by 1.1 newcomers. Most newcomers (in the 140 agricultural villages) as well as the small net gain, are accounted for by a net increase of thirty-six factories in villages located more than fifty miles from a city of over 25,000. In villages less than fifty miles from such centers there was a net loss. During the depression this death rate increased and the birth rate declined. Two fifths of the industries existing in 1930 had ceased operating by 1936. There were only two births for every three deaths. Here, then, is another suggestion of urban influence on rural areas. Insufficient capital, poor planning and leadership, competition from newer and more efficient plants, and fires, caused most of the failures other than those caused by the depression. Villages seeking a payroll had often invested unwisely in some of the ill-considered schemes of outside promoters. It is manifest, then, that in our sample of agricultural villages, factory industries were not as important as trade, but unlike trade, they put money into the farmer's pockets by purchasing raw materials from him.

Successful rural factory industries are small. The average village concern was rather small and of uncertain future. But we must remember that there are some outstandingly strong industries in American agricultural villages, as is illustrated by a national survey in 1932 of 121 successful rural factory industries,[19] all but two of which were located in places of less than 6000 population and a majority in villages or hamlets.

This survey reveals the smallness of such enterprises (all but nineteen had plant valuations of $200,000 or less), and it also shows that, like those in the villages, they were directly dependent upon local products for their raw materials. Therefore, in addition to furnishing a market for these, they were a source of some support to many farm homes.

The first fact is proved by the fact that more than half of these industries used cotton for textiles. The others were connected with food, forest, clay, and leather products. In all, one half of the raw materials used were purchased from farms.

The industries were tied into the community also by investment. Quite naturally, perhaps, the farmers were more interested in food processing plants than in others. They furnished two thirds of the capital and an even larger proportion of the stockholders for this group of industries. Other local people held most of the rest. The only considerable investments by outsiders were in textile, leather, and clay products, where they supplied from two fifths to two thirds the capital.

The survey reports that such enterprises benefited home life, since young people were kept at home and added income made radios, books, magazines, telephones, and household conveniences possible. Similarly, community life improved in the average instance, roads were better, electricity was frequently made available at low rates, stores sold finer wares, school buildings improved, broader curricula were offered, and medical services were augmented.

Some of the details are of real interest. A successful vegetable canning company, co-operatively owned by farmers, not only canned local products but was paying mountain farm girls $1200

[19] Cf. Manny and Nason, *Rural Factory Industries.* Washington, D.C.: United States Department of Agriculture, Circular 312, 1934.

yearly for picking wild strawberries to be made into jam and packed into attractive earthern jars produced by local farmers. A chair factory, three miles from the nearest village, employed fifty-seven people, twenty-one from farms, and paid over $46,000 wages in 1931. It maintained an experimental woodlot; chairs were bottomed at some farmhouses. Farmers used the wood shavings for bedding down cattle, and eventually as fertilizer.

This special group of successful rural industries reveals several important things. The recruiting of an appreciable fraction of labor in farm homes, and the purchase of local raw materials, made the factory a potent influence in community life. Local investments, well distributed, and local control made for adherence to the industry rather than the opposite. As in the agricultural villages, no labor trouble was experienced, although the opposite was true in industrial villages, mentioned above. This government survey makes clear that as in the case of stores, these local industries were institutions of some social as well as economic importance. If industries increase in rural areas there will be an increase also of certain socio-economic problems such as wage rates, conditions of labor, employer-employee relations.

There are certain indications that American industry is slowly decentralizing. The depression, with its experiments in subsistence homesteads, discussed elsewhere, has stimulated the agitation for a union of agriculture and industry. The data thus far seem to warrant the conclusion that the merger is not progressing rapidly, that where individual cases succeed, at least in a social sense, the project must not introduce widely different social interest or population groups; it must utilize the assets of and contribute to community life, and management, if not local, must at least take local mores into account.

Industrial Villages

The industrial village is usually overlooked by those interested in the amalgamation of agriculture and industry, yet it is most important. Moreover, its history is valuable to those who would bring a payroll to the support of agriculture. For three quarters of a century industrial villages have been doing this very thing, evolving a distinctive type of community, in which population is younger, with more males and children and fewer widows than in agricultural villages. There is small contact with the hinterland, partly because of location, as in lumbering centers, and partly because of independent interests. The average trade area is only four square miles, with only half as many stores as in the agricultural village. Farmers do not frequent its churches, farm children do not attend its schools. One eighth of its employees come from farm homes. Life is ordered by the factory whistle and the decision of an often distant and unknown executive. Industry dominates the social organization of the community, in which there is often a high degree of paternalism, never found in agricultural villages. In the South, where textile mills have been imported into agricultural villages, a great gulf usually exists between the old population and the new who live on "the mill hill." Mill-workers and agrarians are served by different churches, although of the same denomination. So far from uniting industry and agriculture, the average case has bred social estrangement.[20]

VILLAGE MERCHANDISING

It has been shown earlier that the great majority of American villages, or places of less than 2500 population, are in the main service centers for agricultural areas, existing largely to serve the needs of farmers. If, then, chain stores, mail-order houses and city department stores succeed, as is often maintained, in eliminating much retail trading, village economic life, trade arrangements and community structure and social organization are profoundly altered. On the other hand, there are advocates of the decentralization of industry who would move most of our factories nearer to the sources of raw materials, that is, the villages; in this way, they argue, surplus farm labor would be absorbed, farmers could be employed in slack season, labor costs and taxation reduced, and with the development of superpower, it would be cheaper to transport electric current than raw material. Some persons have gone so far as to assert that such a program will save the American village. Decentralization would, at least, introduce a whole series of new problems and relationships. Population would increase, school and church enrollments gain, and social organizations grow and multiply. For this reason, the discussion now turns to an examination of rural retail trade and rural industrial life.

[20] For a full discussion of the problem based on a nation-wide field survey of 70 industrial villages, cf. Brunner, *Industrial Village Churches* (New York: Harper & Bros., 1930), especially chapters I to V and the Appendix, pp. 175-81. See also Woofter, J., and E. Winston, *Seven Lean Years* (Chapel Hill, North Carolina, 1939), pp. 113-16.

This subject is also important because merchandising, as conducted by these institutions called stores, is not merely an economic activity. It is social as well. It brings farm and village people into contact. It offers opportunity to exchange news and opinions. It is conducted on a personal basis to a far greater extent in rural than in urban America. It affords employment for local people who in turn support local churches and social organizations. It is the medium by which the pressing desires and needs of people for goods is met. This social function of merchandising has been too much neglected in the past.

This social function of merchandising is likely to receive increasing emphasis with the growing interest in consumer education and protection. As the efforts along these lines of the schools, the home economics extension service, the women's clubs, the consumer cooperatives, and other agencies become more general, the retailers will begin to feel pressure from their clients. It is possible that, because of the smaller numbers of people involved and the degree of personal relationship existing between buyer and seller in the rural community, the rural demand for improvement along lines advocated by consumer agencies will be an important factor in changing the national situation.

Number of stores in agricultural villages increasing. Any impartial examination of retail trade throws grave doubt on the conception that the small town "can't come back." In the main the data show that it has never gone away. It has already been pointed out that village population has been gaining rather than declining; that the proportion of villagers employed in trade has increased. It is not surprising, therefore, to discover that the number of village stores and other commercial enterprises has steadily increased between 1910 and 1930. In 1910 there was an average of 44.9 commercial establishments in each American village, in 1920, 49.3, and in 1930, 56.2. This trend is true for villages in all population groups and for every major region, and was due entirely to an increase of 43 per cent in retail trade outlets between 1910 and 1930 in the 140 villages surveyed. Chain stores are not included in these figures.[21]

Considering retail stores alone, as contrasted with all commercial

21 These comparisons are based on *Bradstreet's Book of Commercial Ratings*, whose figures in 1930 were checked by a field survey and the *United States Census of Distribution*. There were 7890 such enterprises in the 140 villages, 5476 devoted to retail trade, exclusive of 300 chain stores, as listed by Bradstreet. The *Census of Distribution* reports 5411 retail trade outlets inclusive of chain stores, and the field survey only a few less.

establishments, the increase in the number between 1930 and 1936, in the 140 villages was from 39.6 to 49.7, not counting the chain stores. The rate of increase was in inverse proportion to the size of the community. The largest gain was made in centers of 600 to 1000 population. All of it was in privately owned stores. The number of chain stores remained constant. Between 1910 and 1936 the increase was from 27.7 stores per village center to 49.7, again excluding chain stores, or 80 per cent in a quarter of a century. The growth of non-chain stores has been more rapid than that of the population. Deviations from the average among the regions were relatively slight, in no case as much as 25 per cent. In the main the South and Middle West were close to the average, the Middle Atlantic was below and the Far West above.

Interestingly enough, a multiplication of retail shops was observed even in villages which had lost 10 per cent or more population between 1920 and 1930, although this increase was not as rapid as in villages gaining population at a higher rate than the national figure. The ratio of population to number of stores was also larger in developing than in declining villages.

Village size was obviously a potent factor, not only in the total number of stores, but also in the type of commercial enterprise. Thus, two fifths of villages under 1000 had no furniture stores, and large villages had 6.5 apparel stores as compared with 1.5 for small centers.

Specialization. There are several reasons for this gain in the number of retail stores, even through the depression years. One is an increase in specialization. Automobile and accessory shops gained enormously, as did restaurants and soft-drink establishments. Most of the gain in these categories is due to the automobile, good roads, and the resultant increase in travel. The greatest increases were in the other retail group which includes beauty parlors, drug, novelty, and liquor stores, the last named obviously of recent origin. There was an average of one liquor store per village and 1.25 beauty parlors. Of this latter type there were almost none in 1924 and few outside the large communities in 1930. The details are given in Table 47.

This increase in stores offering specialized goods is a national phenomenon. The number of available services is increasing in rural as well as urban America, but the gain, despite the depression or perhaps because of it, is significant.

A village banker declared, "After our stores modernized, our village added two hundred farm families to our regular customers."

TABLE 47. RETAIL OUTLETS: NUMBER OF STORES PER VILLAGE
BY TYPE OF STORE

	Number of Local Stores per Village			No. of Local Stores per Village 1936	No. of Chain Stores per Village 1936	Total Stores per Village 1936
	1910	1920	1930			
All retail stores.............	27.7	32.1	39.6	49.7	2.8	52.5
Grocery*..................	2.4	3.1	4.3	3.9	1.0	4.9
All other food.............	2.5	2.1	3.3	2.5	.1	2.6
General...................	5.5	5.2	4.4	2.2	.2	2.4
Apparel*..................	3.7	3.6	3.7	1.7	.1	1.8
Automobile accessories.......	0.2	4.4	8.8	10.3	.8	11.1
Furniture	1.0	1.0	1.0	.9	.0‡	.9
Lumber...................	1.2	1.2	1.3	.5	.5	.6
Hardware.................	1.6	1.7	1.8	2.2	.1	2.3
Feed and farm supplies......	1.4	1.4	1.4	.6	.0‡	.6
Restaurants and soft drinks..	1.2	1.6	2.4	5.2	.0‡	5.2
All other retail†............	7.0	6.8	7.2	19.8	.3	20.1

* Does not include chain stores in 1910, 1920, or 1930.
† In 1936 this category included for the first time liquor stores, tourist camps, and boarding-houses.
‡ Less than .1.
Source: Brunner, E. de S., and Irving Lorge, *Rural Trends in Depression Years: A Survey of Village-Centered Agricultural Communities, 1930–1936*, Table 34, p. 102. New York: Columbia University Press, 1937.

Again, it was frequently stated, "People trade at home much more than they did two years ago." An editor summed up his local situation in these words: "When the automobile brought us into competition with the outside world, the town was dazed. Then stores modernized and prices were reduced. A couple of the inefficient places gave up. There was one consolidation. Now we're served by the optimum number of agencies and are holding our own against all comers." The president of a Farm Bureau declared: "Urban competition forced our merchants to become efficient. That stopped their exploitation of the farmer, and now we're all satisfied." In several villages, improvement began after trade surveys had been made, in one instance at the expense of the municipality. In four villages the chains were routed, but in most places there seemed to be room for both local merchants and chains.

One Southern village of 2200 widened the community area from 108 to 210 square miles. The Chamber of Commerce attributed this improvement to good roads and the automobile, modern merchandising, better transportation facilities, and the decline of a smaller competing center, a decline to which the aggressive policy of this village contributed.

The decay of places of from 100 to 300 or 400, or occasionally even larger centers, has been mentioned more than once, a decay attended by growing trade areas in contiguous villages, and sometimes accelerated by the removal of a prominent tradesman from a minor center to a larger village, who usually carried his clientèle to the new location.[22]

Retailers younger in the prewar period. Probably another reason for the ability of many agricultural villages to hold their own or improve their position during the nineteen-twenties, despite the agricultural depression, lies in the fact that a new generation of merchants was in command. In most villages which progressed during the decade field workers found stores operated by sons of former proprietors, with an aggressive merchandising policy and the newest selling technique. The special census of 140 villages and 37 others showed that the average village proprietor's age was 45.5 in 1930 as against 45.6 in 1920; despite a lapse of ten years, the 1930 generation were somewhat younger. Almost exactly half were under forty-five; many of those over forty-five were associated with the more skilled trades such as millinery, dressmaking, proprietors of "domestic and personal service" agencies.

Younger people also accounted definitely for a goodly amount of the increase in stores between 1930 and 1935. Recent college graduates especially showed considerable ingenuity in discovering opportunities for new merchandising services. The war changed this. Older men and the women, including wives of soldiers and sailors, carried on many village mercantile enterprises. Even before then, older persons who had previously retired, but who had capital, opened small stores, usually of the more conventional or general type.

Chain stores and results of their local competition. Interest in the chains was acute in the late nineteen-twenties and early thirties, about a dozen states levied special taxes on them, though the constitutionality of such taxes has been attacked. There was active press and radio propaganda against the chains.

The agricultural village has been invaded in the last decade,

[22] The absorption of territory resulting from the decline of minor places occurred frequently in former lumbering areas which failed to adapt themselves to the needs of farmers moving into cut-over land, and hence the nearest farmers' town profited accordingly. This agrees with the findings of the study of industrial villages by the Institute of Social and Religious Research, a study which proved that farmers seldom patronized stores in former lumbering communities. Cf. Brunner, *Industrial Village Churches,* pp. 21-24. New York: Harper & Bros., 1930.

and particularly in the last five or six years, by chains of all kinds; groceries, clothing, drugs, tobacco, gas, and even banking chains. Grocery and clothing units were most frequently found in agricultural villages. One or more chains were operating in 107 of the 140 villages; in all but two of the Middle-Atlantic and Far-Western villages, three fifths of the Southern, and seven tenths of the Middle-Western. Two thirds of those lacking chains were places under 1000. In all, there were 300 chain units in 107 villages, an average of nearly three, more than double the number in 1924. Significantly, however, the number of chain stores in the communities studied remained constant at 2.8 between 1930 and 1936.

What are the consequences? In some places local merchants who could not adjust themselves to superior competition were routed. In one Eastern county seat the number of chains increased from two to nineteen between 1921 and 1930, altering the town completely. Sons of former proprietors, who had expected to become themselves proprietors, were now working for the chains or had emigrated. Every malady logically chargeable to chains seemed to exist in this town, and in some few other villages in our survey, but not in the majority of them. On the other hand, many villages seemed less worried by the chains in 1930 than in 1924, when there were half as many of them, and still less in 1936.

There were several reasons for this surprising change of attitude: (1) local enterprises had increased despite the chains; (2) merchants in a large number of villages had joined independent co-operatives or voluntary chains — now numbering four hundred and operating, for instance, more grocery units than ordinary chains,[23] and in 1929-30 doing an annual business of nearly seven hundred millions. These merchants buy co-operatively, use group advertising and chain merchandising techniques. Some cover wide regions, others are county affairs. Voluntary chains and co-operatives have been successful in many villages and were approved by community leaders who spoke of lower consumers' costs, adequate retail profit and salvation from ruthless corporate chains as well. These villages considered the problem solved. Merchants again and again said, "If the chains beat us, it is our own fault."

Many independent operators explained their ability to hold their trade on the ground that there was strong local prejudice against chains, which were considered an urban assault on the community. Residents rallied to the support of local stores. When the chain

23 *The United States Daily*, Washington, D.C., July 3, 1931, and *Monthly Letter*, National City Bank, August, 1931.

abstained from participation in community affairs, antagonism was often intensified. One large chain, wherever found, was, however, locally commended for its civic spirit and generosity.

Another reason for lessened concern over the chain was that it attracted people to the village who patronized non-competing stores. Chains were also commended for retaining former owners as their managers.

In spite of all this, chains constituted barely five per cent of all retail shops in agricultural villages, although their share of business was probably one tenth. Nor must it be forgotten that, as explained, chains have not everywhere captured the trade of a community. A canvass of nearly fifteen thousand rural homes by *Woman's World* of Chicago showed that 62.8 per cent patronized local merchants exclusively, and 14 per cent used both chains and locals. Less than one fourth, therefore, employed chains exclusively.

Another reason for the failure of the chain stores to grow during the depression years was the successful competition from the growing number of consumers' co-operative stores.

There is to be seen operating in this situation a complex of social forces and attitudes as varied as effective co-operation against a common danger, local pride, self interest, community spirit. It is clear, too, as already stated, that merchandising is a social as well as an economic function, that trading with friends and neighbors of years standing, when on a satisfactory basis, is often more attractive than with outsiders. Where the local store extends credit, which chains never do, that also is a factor.

This is not to say that the chains have not brought grief to individual merchants and to some communities. This has happened. But the situation, for the time at least, seems to have stabilized. Rural communities have developed an unexpected and surprisingly successful resistance to chain stores and in so doing they have confounded the prophets of gloom of the middle nineteen-twenties. Certainly thus far the chains have been confined for the most part to a few specific types of merchandising.

Summary. Despite the depression, the birth rate of rural stores was considerably higher than the death rate, though with banks, social organizations, and churches the reverse was true. Perhaps this is an indication of the growing adaptability of retail trade. Rural merchants, the country over, realized something of the nature of their troubles and took steps to overcome them. They sought to improve relationships with their clientèle, especially farmers, and between village and country. They organized "buy-at-home" campaigns and sought, often with success, to enlarge their areas of service, turning improved roads to good account. They bettered their merchandising and rendered more specialized service. Some merchants, some communities failed; more did not. In the large the business situation has given evidence of the same vitality of rural America that is observable in other aspects of our study.

DISCUSSION TOPICS

1. Sketch the stages of development and changes through which some village or small town with which you are personally acquainted, has gone.
2. Account for the fact that village and open-country neighborhood settlement occurred separately in the Middle West.
3. Describe the New England and the Southern form of group settlement and organization.
4. Make a list of all incorporated places in your home county, indicate gains or losses in population of each for the decades from 1920 to 1930 and 1930 to 1940. Is there any tendency for growth or decline to be associated with certain sizes of places? Explain.
5. Which types of retail establishments are tending to leave, which to remain, and which to come into agricultural villages? Give your explanation.
6. Enumerate the factors which seem to influence where farm people trade. How do these differ from those influencing village people?
7. What problems and what benefits come to local communities by reason of chain stores or chain banks?
8. What types of industry are likely to come to agricultural villages and small towns? Give your reasons and cite evidences.

REFERENCE READINGS

Brunner, Edmund de S., *Village Communities*. New York: Doubleday, Doran & Co., 1927.

Brunner, Edmund de S., G. S. Hughes, and Marjorie Patten, *American Agricultural Villages*. New York: Doubleday, Doran & Co., 1927.

Brunner, Edmund de S., and Irving Lorge, *Rural Trends in Depression Years*. New York: Columbia University Press, 1937. A survey of village-centered agricultural communities, 1930-36.

Bunin, Ivan, *The Village* (authorized translation from the Russian by Isabel F. Haygood). New York: Alfred A. Knopf, 1923.

Douglass, H. Paul, *The Little Town*. New York: The Macmillan Company, 1927. An early study of Mid-Western villages in their country relations.

Fry, C. Luther, *American Villagers*. New York: Doran & Co., 1926. Report of census study of American villages and village populations and shows growing importance of the village in rural life.

Gillette, J. M., *Rural Sociology*, Rev. Ed., 1928, chap. 19. New York: The Macmillan Co. Growth and decline of American villages. Conclusions in contrast to the Fry study.

Kolb, J. H., *Service Relations of Town and Country*. Madison: Research Bulletin 58, Agricultural Experiment Station, University of Wisconsin, December, 1923.

Kolb, J. H., *Service Institutions of Town and Country*. Madison: Research Bulletin 66, Agricultural Experiment Station, University of Wisconsin, December, 1925.

Lorge and Brunner, *American Agricultural Villages: 1930*. American Statistical Association, Monograph no. 1. New York: Columbia University, 1933. An analysis of census data.

Melvin, Bruce L., *The Sociology of a Village and the Surrounding Territory*. Ithaca: Bulletin 523, Agricultural Experiment Station, Cornell University, 1931. A New York State study.

Miller, Elva E., *Town and Country*. Chapel Hill: University of North Carolina Press, 1928.

Nelson, Lowry, *The Mormon Village: A Study in Social Origins*, Studies no. 3, 1930, and, *A Social Survey of Escalante, Utah*, Studies no. 1, 1925. Provo, Utah: Brigham Young University Studies.

Vaile, Roland S. (editor), *The Small City and Town*. Minneapolis: University of Minnesota Press, 1930.

Vincent, George E., and A. W. Small, *An Introduction to the Study of Society*. New York: American Book Co., 1894. Chapters on Village and Town, tracing growth of community relations.

Williams, J. M., *An American Town*. Published privately, New York, 1906. An early study of a New England town.

Wilson, Warren H., *Quaker Hill*. Published privately, New York, 1907. A study of a New York country community from 1728 to 1880.

14

Rural Communities

EVERY FARMER'S GATE opens onto a road and that road leads to a
village or town. Because of this web of communication and transportation, there is an intermesh of town and country relationships.
Just as the country looks increasingly to the village or town for
many services, such as education, recreation, and merchandising,
and just as the village or town is more and more depending upon
the country for trade, raw materials, and patronage of its institutions, so the two in this reciprocal relation are becoming the town-
country community of modern rural society.

As a matter of fact, many social trends which are developing in
rural life today are closely linked with the whole question of village
stability or growth which was considered in the last chapter, and
with this growing interdependence of village or town with country.
The areas of social, business, and educational contacts are expanded
beyond neighborhood boundaries. Farmers and villagers are mingling as citizens of a larger community. This has fundamental importance for many of the movements which are to be discussed in
later chapters. We shall consider, for example, the consolidation of
country schools, the leadership of high schools, the reorganization
of retail merchandising through principles of specialization, and
the institution of the larger parish plan for churches by use of this
town-country community idea.

America is becoming an older country; the frontier escape is no
longer possible, and the result is a necessity for group organization
and social planning which will make that mature life more satisfying. This emerging community which encompasses both town
and country has many possibilities; hence we shall, in this chapter,
focus our attention on a careful analysis of community areas and
relationships. With the opening of the West under the Homestead
Act, the method of settlement was largely on separate farms in
neighborhood groups, as explained in a previous chapter. Villages
and towns sprang up as business and institutional centers. Finally
the integration of these two elements of rural society began.

THE COMMUNITY IDEA

It was some little time after the actual formation of such communities that students of rural society began to study and talk about this community idea. Writers in the general field of sociology had used the term "community" in the more general sense of association or solidarity or identification of interests. For example, Doctor Small used "community" and "solidarity" practically synonymously. It is "the common relation of all parts," he said.[1]

Park and Burgess, on the other hand, define the concept more nearly in the terms to be used in this chapter. "Community is the term," they say, "which is applied to societies and social groups where they are considered from the point of view of the geographical distribution of the individuals and the institutions of which they are composed."[2]

One of the first, if not the very first, student of rural society to write about this emerging rural community of country and village or town was Doctor Warren H. Wilson. He described the community in terms of a "team haul."

> People in the country think of the community [he said] as that territory with its people, which lies within the team haul of a given center. . . . Social customs do not proceed further than the team haul. Imitation, which is an accepted mode of social organization, does not go farther in the country than the customary drive with horse and wagon. . . . The team haul which defines the community is a radius within which men buy and sell. . . . It is the radius of social intercourse. Within this radius of the team haul families are accustomed to visit with ten times the frequency with which they pass outside the radius. . . . The community is the larger social whole outside the household; a population complete in itself for the needs of its residents. . . . It is a man's home town.[3]

The idea of self-sufficiency assumed in many definitions led to an over-emphasis upon the community as a sort of mutually exclusive group. Doctor Butterfield, for example, warned against a possible confusion of "neighborhood" and "community."

[1] Small, A. W., *General Sociology*, p. 582. Chicago: University of Chicago Press, 1905.
[2] Park and Burgess, *An Introduction to the Science of Sociology*, p. 161. Chicago: University of Chicago Press.
[3] Wilson, Warren H., *The Evolution of the Country Community*. Pilgrim Press.

A neighborhood [he said] is simply a group of families living conveniently near together. . . . A true community is a social group that is more or less self-sufficing. It is big enough to have its own centers of interest — its teaching center, its social center; its own church, its own schoolhouse, its own Grange, its own library and to possess such other institutions as the people of the community need.[4]

It remained for Doctor Galpin to invent a method for locating and mapping the rural community area, to coin the term "rurban" for its description, and to present an analysis of the community group as an interrelationship of town and country people together with their institutions. The following paragraph is recognized as a classic statement of the community idea in rural society:

It is difficult, if not impossible, to avoid the conclusion that the trade zone about one of these rather complete agricultural civic centers forms the boundary of an actual, if not legal, community, within which the apparent entanglement of human life is resolved into a fairly unitary system of interrelatedness. The fundamental community is a composite of many expanding and contracting feature communities possessing the characteristic pulsating instability of all real life.[5]

Doctor Galpin made his first community study in Walworth County, Wisconsin, but the origin of the idea goes back to an earlier survey of Belleville, Jefferson County, New York. When, as a young man, he was teaching in the academy there, he undertook a survey of the surrounding agricultural community. In reporting this study before the first Wisconsin Rural Life Conference in the spring of 1911, he said:

This stretch of land impressed me with its solid social front, with its variety of social activities, with its real progress made by the voluntary association of many small amounts of surplus labor and capital, and I decided to map the social topography of this whole community, at least as far as it was definitely organized, in order that I might discover the clue to its solidarity.

It was found that twenty-seven organizations center in the village. . . . No organizations except district schools were found in the open country. Village and open farming country form a community of homes which seems to be a sort of social drainage basin

[4] Mobilizing the Rural Community, Ex. Bulletin 23, Massachusetts Agricultural College, 1918; p. 6 of Introduction.
[5] Galpin, C. J., The Social Anatomy of an Agricultural Community, p. 18. Madison: Research Bulletin 34, Agricultural Experiment Station, University of Wisconsin, 1918.

beyond whose border every home drains off into some other basin.

The big discovery of this survey is the fact of a real rural community and also pretty clearly the area of this community with its bounding lines. It appears that this community takes in parts of four townships, and ignores in its social dealings the voting precincts set by law.[6]

The beginning of this idea of spatial arrangements of social phenomena can thus be seen in the early Belleville study, but the technique for presenting it was revised and greatly improved in the Walworth County study, in which the publication of striking maps, showing the community relations of the twelve centers, attracted wide attention.

The growth of the "trade area" idea, so far as I see it now, was something like this [Doctor Galpin said later in personal correspondence]. Belleville, a country village of 500 population, was a center of store trade since 1815. Farmers were constantly coming to town to buy and sell. In 1828, when the farmers established an academy, they wanted a convenient place for it. What was more natural than the place their roads led to, and to which they constantly drove? In 1870, when they established a Grange, what was more natural than to have it where they traded and where they schooled their high school children. In 1880, when they established a co-operative creamery (largest then in the United States, I believe), what more natural than to place this also in Belleville. I observed the magnetic relation of trade, barter, buying, selling. I came to believe that trade was a primary relationship which determined many other relationships. And, I always said that the Academy strengthened all these trade relationships. Naturally the spatial element came to the fore, as the large majority of social contacts of the farmers radiated to one center.

Thus, the map became the means for analysis, and "rurban," a contraction or amalgam of "rural" and "urban," a graphic descriptive term. But perhaps a point which is implicit in the foregoing description will bear re-emphasis; namely, that in studying any rural community, we must consider not only its physical boundaries, or locality, but also the functions which gives it its life as a group. It is the fusing of the geographic or ecological and the psychological or functional elements which gives the community idea its real power and usefulness. To follow this in analysis is not always easy for, unlike the village, the town-country or rural

[6] *Country Life Conference.* Madison: Bulletin of the University of Wisconsin, Series no. 472, General Series 308, February, 1911.

community does not have such an easily recognizable physical base or a definite corporate boundary. Nor are its social functions integrated and united by political organization to the same extent as in the village. In the rural community, associations and social contacts are more voluntary; that is, people are drawn together by common interests of trade or education, recreation or religion. It is a community of interest, but all interests need not be coterminous. Despite the process of specialization detailed in the previous chapter on the village, there is, nevertheless, a coincidence or a grouping of functions and interests, as the next section of this chapter will demonstrate. Similarly there is a central core which can be considered the community group. The most recent and satisfactory definition arising out of careful analysis of modern rural life as well as a detailed tracing of the older forms of group living, reads as follows: "A rural community consists of the social interaction of the people and their institutions in the local area in which they live on dispersed farmsteads and in a hamlet or village which forms the center of their common activities." [7]

The locality phase and the interest phase are thus brought together. It may be a little more or a little less of the one or the other. One community may represent an area easily recognized and well defined, with the social interactions of its people rather weak or sluggish. Another may have a high degree of social integration, but its boundaries may be none too clear. Patterns of service areas and the activities which take place within them will be the order of further discussion in this chapter.

PATTERNS OF RURAL COMMUNITY AREAS

The service and institutional relations of a country population include the village or town as the center of a community; when traced on a map this includes a fairly definite land area. The country people in this area are more closely bound to the center, and more definitely related to its people than they are to the country groups beyond the community area or to more distant centers. Thus, the general pattern of the village or town-country community is circular; the relation of the land to its center is similar to that of wheel to hub. It is more than mechanical, however; the currents of life within the community relationship constantly flow together.[8]

[7] Sanderson, Dwight, *The Rural Community*, p. 481. The Natural History of a Sociological Group. Boston: Ginn & Co., 1932.

[8] Galpin, C. J., *Rural Social Problems*. Madison: Fourth Wisconsin Country Life Conference, Serial no. 711, General Series 515, University of Wisconsin, 1914.

A few examples of community areas will be given by the use of maps; then a summary will be presented in terms of types of centers and their services, together with a generalized formula of the factors involved in the patterns.

Community areas indicated by services and institutions. The first maps to call definite attention to the growing interdependence of village or town and country were those of Walworth County, Wisconsin. The generalized trade area map (Figure 9) is presented.

In the original study of 1913, a series of maps was made showing the various areas for such services as banking, newspaper, milk-marketing, the church, high school, and library. Some of the maps were grotesque in appearance because certain portions of the near-

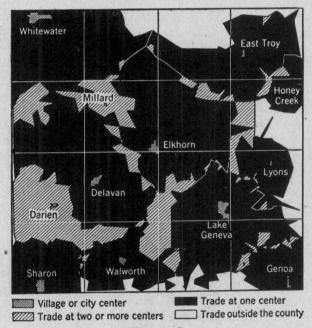

Figure 9

TRADE COMMUNITIES

Twelve villages and small cities in the county serve as trade centers for farm homes precisely as for villages and city homes trading at the same center form a trade community. Township lines six miles apart indicate distances.

Source: C. J. Galpin, *The Social Anatomy of an Agricultural Community*, Research Bulletin 34, May, 1915, Agricultural Experiment Station, University of Wisconsin.

by country were not included in the service areas, and at other points, the boundaries were extended to include only a few family farms. The map of high-school areas, for example, shows that some farms were not included in the areas of some centers, either because of farm children not attending high school or because some of the centers did not have high schools of their own. Even in the early trade-area map overlapping boundaries were indicated. The influence of differentiation or specialization which will be stressed in the summary can be observed.

Sixteen years after the original study was made, a restudy was undertaken. Expansion was found to mark the general trend of the changes in service areas when the seven services for each of the twelve centers were carefully compared. No one center, of course, expanded all of its areas, but the general expansion took place because of three things: first, there was a more complete coverage of the county, suggesting a greater use of village services and insti-

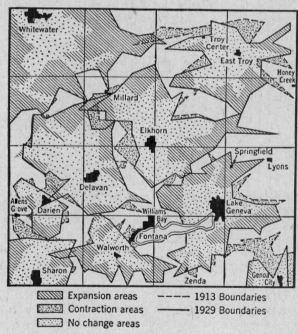

Expansion areas — — — — 1913 Boundaries
Contraction areas ———— 1929 Boundaries
No change areas

Figure 10

CHANGES IN THE HIGH-SCHOOL SERVICE AREAS

Source: Kolb and Polson, *Trends in Town-Country Relations,* Research Bulletin 117, September, 1933, Agricultural Experiment Station, University of Wisconsin.

tutions by country people; second, there were encroachments of the larger centers into territory formerly served by small village or hamlet centers; and third, there was a very appreciable increase in the overlapping of service areas of two or more centers. The library area increased most while banking and drygoods areas expanded least.

An examination of the whole set of Walworth County maps shows that many service areas are not greatly different in total area from what they were sixteen years before. The majority of changes appear at or near the borders of the old areas, as may be observed on the high-school map (Figure 10), leaving the comparatively large central portions around the larger centers practically unchanged.

A Southern county-seat town and community is St. Matthews, South Carolina, a relatively large center with a large community

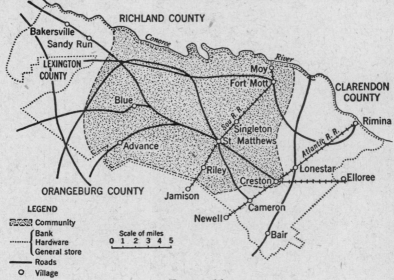

Figure 11

A SOUTHERN COUNTRY-SEAT COMMUNITY

Large population and possession of the county seat has given St. Matthews a large community area. Its banks exceed even this area and serve the entire county. County lines are, however, effective barriers. Though a neighboring county forces a wedge into St. Matthews County, its banks do not draw many people from the other side of the county lines. Note how all roads lead to the village.

Source: Brunner, Hughes, Patten, *American Agricultural Villages.* New York: Doran Company, 1927.

area. The banking area, however, extends even beyond the community area. County boundaries are important in setting the limits of the community area, and highways converging at the center do much to extend as well as to consolidate the area.

Exceptions to the wheel or circular pattern can be found in certain regions where farms, roads, and county lines are laid out on the gridiron pattern with straight lines and right angles because there are few topographical interferences. The case of Alta, Iowa (Figure 12), is an illustration in point.

Small and large areas show different patterns. Two types of centers and service areas in southeastern Whitman County, in the State of Washington, are indicated on the accompanying map (Figure 13). The small areas are those of smaller centers, and it should be observed that they lie entirely within the areas of the larger centers.

The general community area and changes in its pattern. In the studies of the 140 agricultural villages, the general community boundary in each case was drawn to include that area from which a majority of the country people came for a majority of their services, such as retail trade, education, or marketing. The boundary line did not necessarily represent exactly the area of any one or more services. Rather, it indicated what could be regarded as the model area with which any particular service area could then be compared.

Changes in community areas drawn according to the "majority" definition were found in the restudies. Nearly one third of the community areas had increased significantly between 1930 and 1936. In the Middle-West region the increases were above this average; in all of the other regions they fell below it. The larger villages expanded their areas rather more than did the others.

Trade areas were more difficult to determine in 1936 than in the former years of study, except for such special services as hardware or banking. General retail trade tended to be more scattered, and the economic areas for specific villages were less definite. Areas for regular social and recreation services were more clearly defined than in the earlier years, but they continued to be somewhat smaller than the general trade area. The high school was increasingly important as a determinant of the community area. More than any other single service, its area was likely to coincide with the general community boundary. The importance of this for community organization will be discussed later in the chapter.

In summary, the American village or small town is in possession

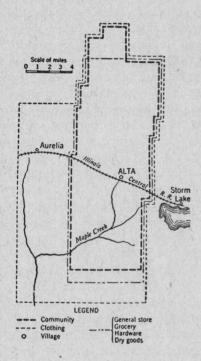

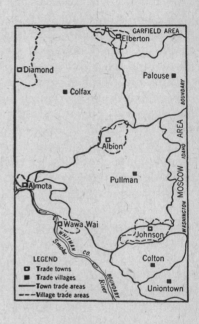

Figure 12

COINCIDENCE OF COMMUN-
ITY AREAS AND SERVICE
AREAS

Alta, Iowa, in its various service
areas, illustrates how closely these
areas can correspond to the community boundaries. The map shows the
rectangular type of community common in the Middle West, where farms
are laid out by quarter sections and
most roads run due north and south
or east and west because of the absence of topographical features.

Source: Brunner, Hughes, Patten,
American Agricultural Villages. New
York: Doran Company, 1927.

Figure 13

TRADE AREAS, SOUTHEAST-
ERN WHITMAN COUNTY

It will be observed that smaller trade
areas lie completely within those of
the larger centers.

Source: Taylor and Yoder, *Rural
Social Organization in Whitman
County,* Bulletin 203, June, 1926,
State College of Washington, Agricul-
tural Experiment Station, Pullman.

of the major patronage of rural people for staple groceries, farm machinery, work clothes, hardware, certain types of furniture and clothing, banking, marketing, high school, library, the weekly newspaper, and some forms of recreation. In determining community areas, however, trade lines are less important than they were ten years ago, while the educational, organizational, social, and, to a lesser extent, religious relations, are more important. Tendencies for uniting town and country around certain types of functions and institutions, observed and recorded in earlier studies, have continued, but centers of reasonable size and completeness are becoming the rural community centers of today. This is not to say that there is evidence of complete self-sufficiency of any one type of rural community, because the village center is giving way to city centers for such services as ready-to-wear clothing and for specialized forms of recreation and hospital or medical care.

Generalized types of centers correlated with size and services. Just as variations exist in the functions of various centers in rural society, so these differences are also found to be related to the population of the center and to the pattern of the area itself. This is another way of saying that by processes of differentiation and specialization, possible because of greatly increased facilities for communication and transportation, the modern trend is toward the accumulation of certain utilities in certain types of centers. It is possible, therefore, to describe and to classify them on these bases.

(1) *The single, simple service type.* This type of center is usually an open-country neighborhood or hamlet center where single and comparatively simple or undifferentiated services are performed. The agencies in such centers may be school, church, general store, Grange hall, or repair shop. The centers usually fall into the hamlet classification; that is, places of less than 250 population.

(2) *The limited, simple service type.* This type of service center may range in size from about 200 to 400 or 500 people. Villages in this class fall short of providing what may be termed a "six-service standard"; that is, having agencies in all of the following groups of services: economic, educational, religious, social, communication, professional.

(3) *The semi-complete, intermediate type.* This type of center averages about 800 to 1000 people with a range from about 400 to over 1200. In certain Middle-Western states it is the most frequent type. It is intermediate because it stands between the type last mentioned and the larger centers, some of which are county-seat towns. It is semi-complete because it is frequently lacking in ful-

fillment of the six-service standard. It may have a bus line, but no railroad; a high school, but a small one; a market, but with inadequate processing agencies for raw products. Its trade area is relatively large and its merchandising agencies frequently draw as much as 75 per cent of their business from farm sources.

(4) *The complete, partially specialized type.* This type averages about 2500 or more persons and may range from 1200 to 5000, or just a little over. Its agencies are numerous enough to cover all the more common needs, and differentiated enough to take on specialized characteristics. Its services are often rendered on a less personal basis than in the small centers. Together with its tributary community area, it has some elements of functional self-sufficiency. If the population in the center ranged from 1000 to 2500, within limits and in regions of general farming, one would expect to find about an equal number of people in the tributary country area.

(5) *The urban, highly specialized type.* This type, which needs further sub-classification, is represented by the larger town and the city. The interests assume larger proportions and are divided into such functions as manufacturing, wholesaling, and financing. They are the centers in which farmers and their wives, as well as villagers, shop when quality, variety, and opportunity for a wide and discriminating selection are wanted. They cannot cater to general trade needs as the small town can; they specialize to a higher degree. The farmer does not look for spools of barbed wire on the city square, but his wife does shop there for some of her choice, ready-to-wear clothing — at least, she likes to do her window-shopping there.

Conventionalized pattern with the four factors involved. In order to generalize the situation still further, a graph was drawn to indicate the service areas surrounding the various types of centers. For the smaller places there was very little difference in size between the general community area and the specialized area, if indeed a specialized type of service area was present at all. By contrast, the larger city center does not have the primary or personal area, and its general area is relatively small, while its specialized area extends far out to include most of the areas of the smaller centers. Neighborhoods or hamlet centers appear near the periphery of the larger community areas, while they tend to cluster on the outskirts of the larger city.

It should be evident, therefore, that an association does exist in this pattern of service relationships which involves four factors: first, size of center in terms of population; second, type of center in terms of its aggregate institutions and agencies; third, size and conformation of the service areas; and fourth, distances between the centers.

A dotted hill-and-valley-shaped line connects the various types of centers in the graph (Figure 14). This line might be considered the "great American highway." As was suggested at the beginning of the chapter, every farmer's gate opens onto this highway, but, as can be seen, it extends beyond his "home town" to the other centers, large and small. Not only the farmer, but also the villager and the city dweller, are using this highway; the traffic is in two directions. The highway, then, becomes the symbol of the interdependence of service centers and tributary areas.

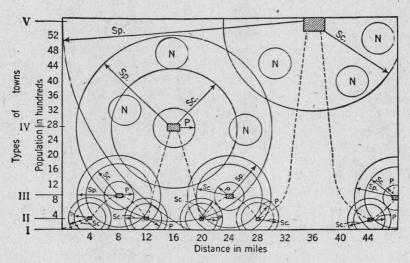

Figure 14

**A THEORETICAL GRAPH INDICATING THE INTER-
RELATION OF RURAL GROUP AREAS AND
TYPES OF SERVICE CENTERS**

Type I. Single service (neighborhood or hamlet). *Type II.* Limited and simple service (small village). *Type III.* Semi-complete or intermediate (village or small town). *Type IV.* Complete and particularly specialized (town or small city). *Type V.* Urban and highly specialized (city).

P. Primary Service Area; Sc. Secondary Service Area; Sp. Specialized Service Area; N. Country Neighborhood Area.

Source: J. H. Kolb, *Service Relations of Town and Country,* Research Bulletin 58, December, 1923, Agricultural Experiment Station, University of Wisconsin.

RURAL COMMUNITIES THE WORLD AROUND

Patterns of similar design but with variations are found in other countries the world around. Unlike the isolated country neighborhoods unique to the Americas, villages and their relations with agrarian people within or outside their borders are nearly universal.

In England. The retail shopping areas of Leeds and Bradford, England, are of a similar pattern to those of Whitman County, Washington. In Leeds there are the market-day customers' areas and the seasonal customers' areas, arranged in concentric circles about the center. Bradford is a smaller center and maintains a secondary position in the large area, but has a small area of its own.

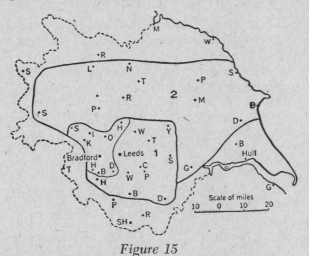

Figure 15

RETAIL SHOPPING AREAS OF LEEDS AND
BRADFORD, ENGLAND

1. Market-day customers' area. 2. Seasonal customers' areas, mainly shopping at Leeds.

Source: R. E. Dickinson, *The Regional Functions and Zones of Influence of Leeds and Bradford.* Reprinted from *Geography,* September, 1930.

In Australia. A recent study of the country towns of Victoria shows that the town (and village by our definition) and the surrounding farm land can be considered as a social and economic unit. The pattern, however, is irregular and inconsistent as in other parts of the world. "The delineation of districts [areas] was complicated by the illogical distribution of towns and the consequent tendency for districts to overlap; for example, Dronin and Warragul are only four miles apart; Dronin is evidently used by part of the district which also uses Warragul, and people living in Dronin do much of their shopping in Warragul."[9]

The authors point out that the war has complicated the situation even more, and they suggest that growth and necessary adjustments will not be a smooth, automatic, painless procedure, but must come as the result of careful planning and effective public education and action.

In New Zealand. Littledene is the story of a real New Zealand rural community, though that is not its real name. It is typical of the country, especially North Island, and charmingly written, and it leaves no doubt about the actual social and economic interrelationships of town and country people. This is fully demonstrated in the occupation pyramid (Figure 16) showing how Littledene earns its living.[10]

One of the discriminating insights in this community study is found in a very brief chapter titled, "The Great Society and the

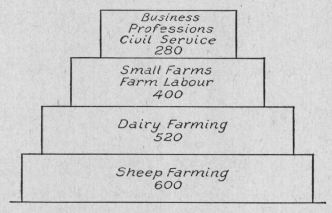

Figure 16

THE OCCUPATIONAL PYRAMID: HOW LITTLEDENE
EARNS ITS LIVING

Drawn to scale, showing the numbers supported from each type of occupation.

[9] McIntyre, A. J. and J. J., *Country Towns of Victoria*. Melbourne University Press and Oxford University Press, 1944. University of Melbourne, Carlton N. 3, Victoria, Australia.
[10] Somerset, H. C. D., *Littledene — A New Zealand Rural Community*. New Zealand Council for Educational Research, 1938.

Little." The economic depression and the experience of the war have brought "the Great Society into closer co-operation with the Little in some unexpected ways." The young people are learning that intolerance with the ways of others is to show lack of knowledge. One of the interesting ways this is being learned is through correspondence clubs in which half the pupils in the upper classes of the local school correspond with children in other parts of the world, particularly in the United States.

In China. Residences are clustered in the small villages, but, as the map shows (Figure 17), there is the market town with its large market and trade institutions, its large temple, its new school, and its railway station. Yao Hwa Men, the market town, is the community center for seventy-two small farm villages. Farmers bring their eggs to the center each market day and exchange them for the goods they need. Grain is sold for money at the grain shop. Each farm village has its own worship place and the local temples are the centers for religious activities. The large worship area covers a radius of twenty-one li, and the villagers make an annual pilgrimage to the larger temple at the community center.

In the Orient. The general pattern of China holds for much of the rest of the Orient. It grows out of the extreme pressure of population on land, and the consequent small areas of the farms. It is also influenced by the fragmentation of holdings. The area of a single farm operator may consist of from three to six or seven small fields in various parts of the farming area of the village. Under such conditions there is no problem of determining community areas. The farmers live in a cluster of houses at the center. They go out to their fields in the morning, returning home in the evening. In a majority of these Oriental communities the only cattle are work animals, so there is no need for grazing land. The available soil resources cannot support human beings and cattle. The exceptions are in the relatively small areas of low population density, such as southeast Asia and parts of Manchuria. As in the United States, there is a direct relationship between population density and community area, and, in the parts of Asia mentioned, between cattle population and area.

In Japan. On northern Hokkaido, the least populated island, farms average five to six times the two and one half acres of the other islands. There is more dairying on Hokkaido than elsewhere, community areas are larger, and the villages have more services, resulting in less dependence upon the market town.

In Thailand (Siam). As the result of a study in 1930, it was re-

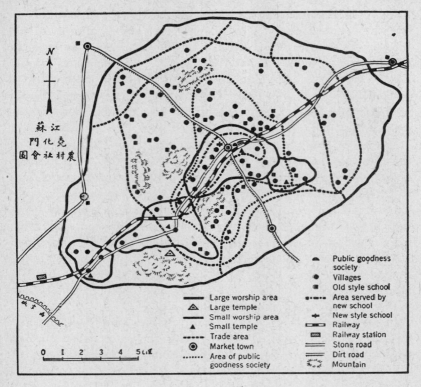

Figure 17

SERVICE AREAS OF YAO HWA MEN, NEAR
NANKING, CHINA

The scale of the map is indicated by Chinese li. By using this scale, the distances may be measured from the market center to the different villages.

Source: Chiao Chi Ming, *Mapping the Rural Community*, Miscellaneous Series 4, December, 1924, University of Nanking, College of Agriculture and Forestry, Nanking, China.

ported that, as a rule, the people are grouped into units which may be described under several headings. The first of these is the village along a stream or river bank; the second is the village scattered among fruit farms on which are homesteads with rice lands beyond; the third is the grouped village of people who farm the surrounding rice fields; the last and least prevalent is the isolated farm.[11]

[11] Zimmerman, Carle C., *Siam — Rural Economic Survey, 1930-1931*. Bangkok: The Times Press, Ltd., October, 1931.

In Korea. Before the Japanese domination, there were about twenty-six thousand villages, which were very important in the whole scheme of social organization. They formed the central units for communal activities, and were the most characteristic feature of Korean rural life. They were democratic, largely self-contained, and in them family life was deeply rooted.[12] The result of detailed studies of thirty-five carefully selected villages showed that fifteen of the thirty-five contained no employed persons except farmers and an occasional policeman, teacher, or preacher. The others had some beginnings of trade, but each one made up a social community. The areas of these communities, comprising the village and its fields, varied according to region and population.

> The commercial and professional services which an American village offers to the farmers in its contiguous territory are performed in Korea by the market town. There are about 1300 such towns in Korea, in each of which itinerant peddlers every fifth day spread their wares on the sides of the main street for people from villages for miles around to view and buy. Market day is a social institution of great vitality. It takes the place of the newspaper and the lodge. Its frequent recurrence is an economic detriment, as attendance usually means the loss of an entire day's work. The area which these market towns serve is considerable, and quite comparable to the trade area of agricultural villages in the United States, ranging in those visited from 50 to 210 square miles.

In the Pacific islands. The situation, at least among the more primitive societies, and in parts of Africa, is similar to that of the Orient, except that the institution of the market town is less well established, and often is nonexistent. Thus, in larger islands like Fiji or New Guinea, there are many communities in the interior whose only contacts outside the village are with near-by villagers. Where there has been some contact with Western life, the port towns or cities of the island serve as market towns in varying degrees. In some parts of Africa the location of the village is not fixed. When the soil begins to show signs of exhaustion under the unscientific methods of cultivation, the whole village moves to a new site. Some Indian tribes in North America had this custom.

In some areas of commercialized agriculture, as in the rubber plantations of the Malay States, Africa, and the Dutch East Indies, or the sugar and pineapple plantations of Hawaii, the workers live

[12] Brunner, Edmund de S., *Rural Korea.* New York: International Missionary Council, 1928.

in village communities under rural conditions, but the plantation usually supplies the function of the market town, and the degree of social organization and sometimes the social utilities available are more complex and more numerous than elsewhere. Western contacts have brought great changes, and some communities are more analogous to the rural industrial communities in the United States.

Two neighbors to the south. In the Argentine, Doctor Taylor reports that locality groupings range all the way from geographically isolated, highly cohesive groups which are easily identifiable as communities or neighborhoods. An even greater number can be classified merely as neighborhoods, and are so transient that an attempt to describe them would be of little value.

Early settlements in the Argentine, unlike those in North America, were not colonies of ethnic groups seeking homes on the land; they were little more than squatters' camps. Immigrants did not come in family groups, but were usually single men. Each new settlement was formed with indigenous Indian groups as nuclei and gradually realigning the groupings into semi-agricultural communities. This was facilitated by the rapid mixing of the two racial groups. However, today over 90 per cent of the country's population has its ancestral antecedents in persons who came to the country after 1850. Much good land was allotted before the great tide of these later immigrants arrived; it was not in family-size farm units, however, but in great holdings running to thousands of acres. Local group patterns had to work against this *estancia* form of farm organization.

Against this historic background, however, the present objective is said to be for the family-size, owner-operated farm. This means a transition from certain types of locality groupings to other types, and there are many variations among the major types of farming areas. In the livestock areas, the large *estancias* do not fit into any neatly patterned locality groups. Such local organization as there is is not for purposes of neighborliness nor for community social action, but for convenience of work administration. School, church, and generally town trade centers, are not a part of the *estancia* organization.

In the cereal mixed farming area, locality groups as known in the United States are more or less diffused. The pampa, in which almost the whole cereal belt is located, is an almost flat, unbroken plain with few barriers to communication. Furthermore, none of the nationalities form cliques or retain their old folk-cultures. They have made their adjustments to agronomic requirements of the area.

The uniformity of these adjustments and the flat, evenness of the pampa have, as it were, flattened out the social life of the people who live on it.

In other areas where settlement has a fairly long history of family-size farms and where more or less continuous ownership prevails, the usual locality group patterns found elsewhere have developed. Likewise, in areas of geographic isolation, as in the desert oasis settlements like the Eldorado in Misiones, also among the Jewish colonies or in the government-sponsored colonies, local group formation is hastened and highly developed. Especially on the larger oases where population density is great, all three locality groups of neighborhood, local community, and urban centers exist and function as complements each to the other.[13]

In Brazil, Doctor Smith reports there are many similarities between the locality groups of that country and those of North America. One of the reasons for this is that, in the colonization of Brazil as in the settlement of the United States, extensive use was made of single farmsteads. Therefore, the farm or *fazenda* stands out as an entity in Minas Geraes as it does in Iowa. Then, the country neighborhood is made up of a relatively small number of families, who live on adjacent farms. The Brazilian village or town, as in parts of the United States, was almost an "afterthought" so far as the early agricultural economy was concerned. It came later to care for the multiplying social and economic needs of rural people. Residences and business places for tradesmen, moneylenders, men skilled in the professions, and workmen of all types are found in the village or town. Here, too, are schools, churches, and recreation institutions. The church is said to be especially important. The farm families who live in surrounding country areas make the village their trading and social center, and in many cases they maintain a "town house" for use on week-ends, holidays, and on occasions of marriages or funerals. The North American expression "go to town" is counterpart of the Brazilian's *"ir ao commercio"* (go to do business).

There are also differences in relations of rural groups on the two continents. For example, in Brazil the service of the church is more important than trade is, in delineating the community boundaries; therefore, the religious areas coincide more closely with those of the general community. As in certain southern portions of the United States, so in Brazil, the village-centered community may embrace

[13] Taylor, Carl C., "Rural Locality Groups in Argentina," *American Sociological Review,* vol. 9, no. 2, April, 1944.

large estates, *fazendas,* or plantations which by themselves may be almost large enough to qualify as a community. Often the proprietors have "town houses" in the community center, in addition to their manor houses on the land. It is obvious that the social horizons of these landowners are quite different from those of the laboring classes.

Finally, an increasing tendency is observed for the *municipio,* the Brazilian administrative government unit which would correspond to the North American county, to function as a larger or urban community. Especially in southern Minas Geraes and in Sao Paulo, the local seat of the *municipio* is becoming the economic and social center for rural communities. The fact that Brazil does not allow the *cidade* to separate itself by incorporation from the open country contributes directly to this trend.[14]

An interpretation. Briefly stated, the design and character of rural communities wherever found, are functions of (1) pressure of population on the land, including systems by which family and farm are interrelated; (2) agrarian practices and traditions, including type of crops and farm management; the factor of crops being related to size of farm. (In the wheat belt, the area of the rural community is seven times greater than that of a community in a fruit-growing region, while the density of population in the fruit area is six times that of the wheat.) (3) the degree of impact of industrialization and commercialization upon agricultural and other phases of life, together with proximity of cities; and (4) the region, characterized not only geographically but culturally.

Professor Frederick J. Turner was one of the first to stress this last point in his vivid analysis of the westward movement of the American Frontier. Later anthropologists emphasized the whole nexus of value systems which hold groups together, and determine what is important, right and wrong. The social psychologists and educators gave the community its personality attributes. Viewed against its cultural background, "the community has a pattern. In each of these the individual member can find meanings for his own guidance."[15]

Thus, similar conditions produce situations similar to rural community patterns and organizations the world over, and it is possible to distinguish various types ranging from the primitive isolated communities of Africa and the larger islands of the Pacific to the

[14] Smith, T. Lynn, "The Locality Group Structure of Brazil," *American Sociological Review,* vol. IX, no. 1, February, 1944.
[15] Hart, J. K., *Mind in Transition,* p. 107. New York, 1938.

rather highly organized service-station villages and towns of the more densely populated areas of the United States.

COMMUNITY RELATIONS AND SOLIDARITIES

Reference to cultural and personal matters leads directly to a consideration of the internal relations and solidarities of rural communities as groups. Do various persons in such communities identify themselves differently with the group? Are there likely to be differences along class or status lines? The answers to such questions are obviously yes, but to measure such differences and to give reasons why they exist, is a more difficult assignment. This is a phase of the study of rural society which has not been explored as fully as others, and it is a comparatively recent emphasis.

Number and kind of contacts multiplied. What goes on within its area determines, at least to some extent, the character and solidarity of the rural community. It must be kept in mind that this community is an emerging, developing group. In the past, rural society was characterized by its country neighborhoods and its village or town settlements, many of which set themselves off by legal incorporation as was explained in the previous chapter. Now common interests and concerns are bringing the two together.

Many group activities in rural communities may not lend themselves to exact measurements; they are, nevertheless, the very things which give significance to map-making and to tabular analysis. It must be recognized, first of all, that improved travel and communication facilities have enabled country and village people to multiply their contacts manyfold — contacts of trade, education, recreation, and sociability. Some of these contacts are of the day-by-day character which occur in the market-place, in the school-room, on the street-corner, or in social affairs. Others are contacts of a more fundamental kind, as represented by a condition found in one Middle-Western village of about 1200 population, where more than 150 village families were retired farmers. In some instances the older children were left on the farm; in others, the younger ones accompanied the parents in order to attend the village school. The retired farmers usually became home-owners in the village, and therefore, interested voters, although sometimes reluctant taxpayers. Consequently, lines of cleavage were not so easily found within the village group or between the village and country elements of the community. A further reason for this was that a number of businessmen had spent their childhood on the ad-

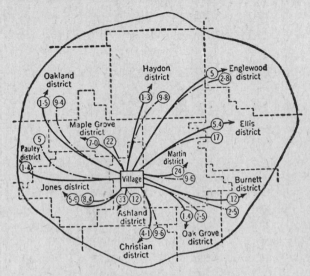

Figure 18

PER CAPITA EFFICIENCY OF THE VILLAGE IN PRO-
DUCING CONTACTS FOR THE OTHER AREAS,
AND VICE VERSA

Solid lines indicate contacts per capita of village population for each
district. Broken lines indicate contacts per capita of the district
populations for the village.

Source: H. J. Burt, *Contacts in a Rural Community*, Research Bulletin 125, August, 1929, Agricultural Experiment Station, University
of Missouri.

jacent farms. Other villagers owned farms and rented them to
grown sons of neighboring farmers. So complete had the solidarity become in this community that in 1931 a country neighborhood
church, very strong and quite isolated in 1921, had merged with
the village church of the same synod, to form one congregational
organization. Services were continued in the two places, but the
congregations were one. Other local community situations are
quite different and "problems" arise.

Problems of status and solidarity in rural communities. The popular way of explaining the problem is that not everyone in a community "counts" the same. This is only another way of saying that
not everyone plays the same rôle, has the same influence, assumes
the same responsibilities, participates in the same activities. The
extent to which social stratification does disrupt or threaten the
solidarity of rural communities cannot be definitely asserted, but a

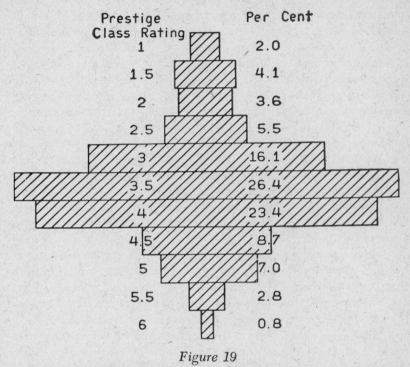

Figure 19

THE CLASS STRUCTURE OF THE MACON COMMUNITY

number of most interesting studies of the problem have been made recently.

A "prestige" class rating-chart (Figure 19) was constructed for a New York State rural community. Eleven classes were made on the basis of detailed tests within the community.[16] The characteristics which seemed to distinguish the members of the various classes were (1) nature and extent of participation in formal and informal activities, (2) attitudes regarding certain social questions, and (3) occupation, education, and level of living.

One of the most significant conclusions drawn from a comparison of persons in the various classes was that the concentration of both formal and informal leadership appeared in the upper classes. Fifty-one people were in a position to control most of the formal organizations of the community. The majority of individuals in the

[16] Kaufman, Harold F., *Prestige Classes in a New York Rural Community.* Ithaca: Memoir 260, March, 1944, Cornell University Agricultural Experiment Station.

lower classes had no organization connections. They had their informal contacts within their kinship groups or in their neighborhoods. It is of importance to note that the social stratification was in terms of social participation and social attitudes, many of which were not of a predominantly economic or political nature.

Similar importance was given the place of organizations in rural community relations in other studies. As a result of analyzing the personnel of land-use planning committees in a Kentucky county, the hypothesis was ventured that greatest receptivity to organization programs is found among the "middle" groups of farm people; those on medium-size family farms who engage in a moderate amount of activity in community enterprises are neither apathetic nor highly aggressive in their economic activities, neither wholly detached from family and neighborhood activities nor completely absorbed in them.[17]

Lack of community integration in a Virginia community was attributed to the fact that country neighborhoods were not closely related with the larger community group, that many families, especially those with low incomes, did not participate in activities, and that factionalism was almost a tradition in the community.[18]

Finally, a generalization from such studies of the internal relations of rural community groups should be of great help in better understanding them and working in them. No single factor or set of circumstances determines the responsiveness of persons to the community and its associations. Rather, it is a "network of social influences" among which leadership, organization, and group morale are very important.[19] But leadership, as we shall see in the next section, is but one of many group processes — a way of interacting with others.

Similarly, as the result of studying the effects of status on attitudes in a New York rural community, it was concluded that people's attitudes and their group affiliations do not exist in isolation, but in "related patterns" — a pattern of attitudes which appears to concur with certain patterns of group identification. For example:

[17] Beers, Howard, *et al, Community Land-Use Planning Committees — Organization, Leadership, and Attitudes, Garrard County, Kentucky, 1939.* Lexington: Bulletin 417, Agricultural Experiment Station, University of Kentucky, 1941.

[18] Edwards, Allen D., *Beaverdam: A Rural Community in Transition.* Blacksburg: Bulletin 340, Virginia Agricultural Experiment Station, May, 1942.

[19] Hoffer, C. R., and D. L. Gibson, *The Community Situation as It Affects Agricultural Extension Work.* East Lansing: Special Bulletin 312, Michigan State College Agricultural Experiment Station, October, 1941.

Mr. Jones was conservative in his attitude toward the rights of labor; he believed in a high protective tariff; he was a member of the Republican Party and the local Episcopal church.[20]

Informal grouping arrangements within rural communities. Group solidarity and unity need not be the result of attempts at uniformity or quiescence in any one plan. Persons assume varying rôles in the community as has just been shown, but this process is not simply one of separate individuals relating themselves to the various organizations or activities of the one larger group, the community; they may, and many often do, form themselves into smaller affiliations which in turn may or may not contribute to the solidarity of the whole. One does not attempt to add together these smaller or more informal groupings to arrive at the total larger group. The relationship is much more complex than that. It is a network of interrelations, and unity may be achieved by an emphasis upon the unique rather than the uniform character of the various group relations. This is the formula which Louis Adamic urges as the American contribution to the social culture of the future age. It will be illustrated in the case of the Norwegians in the Prairie community, which follows.

Furthermore, the single person does not acquire his place in the larger community group by climbing up through an imagined hierarchy of small groups, such as the great family, neighborhood, or informal visiting group; he is in fact a participating member of all of these group identifications at one and the same time. To be sure, he may not reconcile all such interests into a unity for his own personality or for the groups concerned. This is involved in the problems considered in the previous section.

Three illustrations of small and informal groupings within rural communities will be presented briefly. First is a visiting pattern of families in a neighborhood in Charles County, Maryland.[21] Of the visiting relationships by the forty-four white families living in the neighborhood, nearly one third were with families outside the neighborhood, 12 per cent within the Waldorf community, and 20 per cent in Baltimore, forty miles away, or Washington, D.C., twenty-five miles distant. Of those who visit outside the neighborhood, three fourths visit relatives. This would indicate that kinship

[20] Bee, Lawrence S., *The Effect of Status on Attitudes in a New York Rural Community.* Ithaca: Department of Rural Sociology, Mimeograph Bulletin no. 6, Cornell University Agricultural Experiment Station, October, 1942.

[21] Dodson, L. S., and Jane Woolley, *Community Organization in Charles County, Maryland.* College Park: Bulletin A21, Agricultural Experiment Station, University of Maryland, January, 1943.

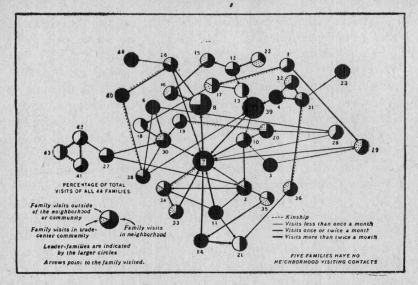

Figure 20

VISITING AMONG FAMILIES OF WHITE PLAINS
NEIGHBORHOOD, CHARLES COUNTY, MARYLAND

ties draw people rather long distances to visit. It is reported that
real visiting between white and Negro families does not take place.

Second is the interrelation of families in neighborhoods and
communities. Some family contacts are via the neighborhood itself,
as, for example, when its country school is closed and the officers
arrange with the village school board to have the children transported to the village center; or when its country church is yoked
with a village church. Other contacts of country neighborhood
people with village or small-town people are direct and personal
in nature, as through enrollments in the village high school, membership in the village churches, or officerships in co-operative business enterprise. Thus the rural community cannot be considered
an accumulation of country neighborhoods, nor can neighborhoods
and communities be considered as opposing types of relationships;
they can be complementary.

In the case of West Koshkonong, first ranking active neighborhood in the Dane County restudy of 1941-42, when the one contact
of retail trading was traced, 33 per cent of the families of the neighborhood did much of their trading at the store within the neighborhood boundary, and 54 per cent did most of their shopping in

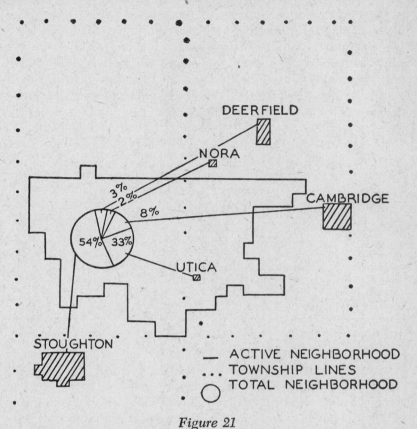

Figure 21

THE WEST KOSHKONONG NEIGHBORHOOD SHOWING
TRADE CENTERS PATRONIZED

Stoughton, the rural community center. These contacts tended to integrate both the neighborhood and the community.

Third is the case of an ethnic group, first and second generation Norwegians in a prairie town and farming community.[22] Although a minority group, they were not persecuted, but found themselves free to develop their own social organizations, maintain an in-group unity, at the same time achieving a working relationship with both their own cultural heritage and the ways of living in the contemporary societal scene.

Tendencies toward community co-operation and conflict. Finally,

[22] Useem, John, and Ruth Hill Useem, "Minority-Group Pattern in Prairie Society," *American Journal of Sociology*, vol. L, no. 5, p. 377, March, 1945.

an effort was made to measure the tendencies leading toward co-operation and toward conflict within town-country communities, by the combined use of all materials gathered in the study of the 140 rural communities in the twelve years from 1924 to 1936. Each local community was classed in one of three categories for each period, namely, "co-operative," "neutral," or "in conflict," as Table 48 shows.

TABLE 48. VILLAGE AND COUNTRY RELATIONS, BY REGION — 140 VILLAGES

Region	No. of Villages	Co-operative			Neutral			Conflicting		
		1924	1930	1936	1924	1930	1936	1924	1930	1936
All regions.......	140	27	100	85	89	34	42	24	6	13
Middle........										
Atlantic.......	28	5	19	17	20	8	7	3	1	4
South..........	30	4	26	14	22	4	9	4	0	7
Middle West...	60	9	41	38	37	16	20	14	3	2
Far West......	22	8	14	16	10	6	6	3	2	0

Source: Brunner and Lorge, *Rural Trends in Depression Years.* New York: Columbia University Press, 1937.

Even if all due allowances are made for personal bias in such a classification, the table points toward a significant trend — that of greater co-operation between village or town and country. More frequent contacts made possible by improved highways are without a doubt an important contributing factor to this. The village had also become a center for many types of activities. Furthermore, farmers had moved into villages, and villagers in many regions, had become farm-owners by purchase, inheritance, or foreclosure. The distressed condition of agriculture had done much to create a new sense of relationship and a keener understanding of farmers' problems by the villagers than ever before. Farmers, too, seemed more intelligent regarding problems of readjustment being faced by many businessmen. They had "talked things over." A feeling of mutual interdependence had emerged. This was the explanation given by local community leaders.

Co-operation, however, was not complete. The communities classed as "neutral" left much to be desired, although their number had decreased. Ordinary routine was being followed in the "neutral" communities — going to town, to trade, to market, to church or school — but little was being done to quicken a sense of community interdependence. Things were just taken for granted. In other communities there appeared a tendency among some to guard one's own interests against encroachments, but to remain inactive or neutral in community issues. This might be interpreted as incipient conflict.

Conflict had not disappeared from some of these town and country situations, but it had assumed other forms and features. Sometimes the failure of an attempted mutual enterprise, such as consolidation of town and country schools, produced a serious ruction. Bank failures, bankruptcy proceedings, or business crises following the financial crash of 1929 exposed old cleavages. More recent conflicts arose over consumer co-operation, rural electrification, relief grants, and demands of hard-pressed farmers for credit.

In still other situations, tendencies toward conflict were no longer on the older personal basis, but had passed into more impersonal relations, more remotely controlled. For example, the increasing financial and administrative control of local institutions by outside agencies. For stores and banks it was the chain or affiliated organizations; for the marketing agencies it was the co-operative or corporate terminal association; for the newspaper it was the syndicate; for the schools and churches it was the centralized authority of general boards. There were instances where a local representative of the centralized agencies could not seem to true his decisions and actions with what local people considered to be their local needs. Chain-store managers were charged with a lack of interest in local problems of credit, unemployment, or community organization. School principals were thought to be more sensitive to state or national standards than to local requirements.

Rural communities composed of villages or towns and their surrounding countrysides are in process of developing. They are relationships capable either of fine integration or of controversy. They may constitute the "line of scrimmage" [23] between what is termed the rural and the urban cultures, but they also are a field of rapprochement, as the evidence presented here has amply shown. Conflict need not and often does not lead to disruption, but to closer unity, because issues are clarified and faced. But whether in co-operation or in conflict, rural communities are increasingly fabricating their various strands of life within our present-day rural society.

[23] Smith, T. Lynn, "The Rôle of the Village," *Rural Sociology*, vol. 7, no. 1, p. 21, March, 1942.

RURAL COMMUNITY ORGANIZATION — CONSENSUS AND ACTION

Community fabrication requires a degree of agreement-consensus and effort-action. The Australians conclude their report of the social survey of country towns by suggesting that community effort is a sort of medley — a mixture of kindliness, bitterness, generosity, meanness. The end is to dispel the antipathy which so frequently exists between the good of the few and the good of the many, and the harm that the many may be indirectly causing in refusing to unite and plan for their own benefit.

It must be emphasized that community organization in present-day North American rural life is almost entirely dependent upon the voluntary, deliberate effort of leaders and citizens. This is in sharp contrast to the village type of economy, described earlier, characterizing much of the rural life of the Orient, Europe, and New England. As has been shown, the modern rural community is permeated with separate institutions and agencies of many kinds and purposes, such as education, religion, recreation, agriculture. Some measure of local organization and co-ordination is needed.

The issue is squarely before rural people today, farmers and villagers alike, as to whether they will organize a community of sufficient size and solidarity to give them the social utilities and institutions which they feel they need, and at the same time develop a point of view which will be recognized in larger political, educational, and religious spheres. National and state politics, as well as urban educational and religious interests, have used disorganized rural society too long as a pawn in issues in which local rural interests are little concerned, if at all. If democracy is to be preserved in government as well as in the other great functions of life, rural local opinion and action must be made more effective. Citizens must assume greater part in public policy.

The argument runs even deeper. Some leaders of social thought raise serious question as to whether a civilization can be built apart from local, primary, or personal groups. They claim that social stability does not develop without it and social control is not effective apart from it.

General "lay-out" of the community. The general structure or lay-out of the community must conform in workable measure with the functions to be performed. It was pointed out earlier in the chapter that three factors were associated with service functions in the patterns of group relationship, namely, population, area, and distance. The implication is, that to perform essential minimum functions, any community must have sufficient people living in a center and the surrounding accessible area. If one factor is limited — for example, if the population in the center is small — then there must be compensation in the extent or population density of the tributary area. If centers are too close together, they must either combine for certain functions or services, including institutions, or deliberately bulge their areas in opposite directions in order to gain the required expanse. This is the principle of unit requirements, and simply means that that community must consider its terms of reference in order to organize and maintain certain service agencies and social institutions. In agricultural circles it is necessary to know how large a volume of business is essential to the effective operation of a creamery. It is equally essential that rural communities know what basic requirements must be met in order to constitute a community in contemporary rural society.

Illustrations of such unit requirements are readily available. Some years ago it was determined that within counties of central and southern Wisconsin, at least 1250 people would be required to maintain a minimum enrollment of 100 pupils in high school, assuming that all those of high-school age actually would attend.[24] That number would probably have to be increased because of present trends, but it was calculated that the 1250 people would require an area of about 41.7 square miles when all the centers of 3000 population were excluded, an area slightly larger than the conventional township.

Or, one could start from some other premise, as a committee on postwar agriculture did. Its report states that, as a measure of size and strength, a rural community must be large enough and strong enough to provide not only elementary, but secondary or high-school, education, and also some adult education for all its people.[25] The high school, the report insists, must have at least six or seven teachers in order to offer a course of study varied and vital enough to match the backgrounds, interests, and future needs of all rural youth. Teachers, the committee believes, are the important desiderata in regard to schools. With such a minimum, a locality can readily determine required enrollment by a pupil-teacher ratio, population constituency, yearly budget, tax rate, evaluation of dis-

[24] Kolb, J. H., *Service Institutions for Town and Country*. Madison: Research Bulletin 66, Agricultural Experiment Station, University of Wisconsin, December, 1925.

[25] *Rural Communities of Wisconsin*. Circular 353, Extension Service, College of Agriculture, January, 1945.

trict, and building requirements. If it is unable or unwilling to provide these minimum requirements, it cannot lay claim to being a full-fledged community in its own right; it will need to join with another, do its part, but not attempt to "go it alone."

Internal readjustments. Even in those studies to which reference has been made, where the focus of attention was upon different classes and status, the conclusions are unanimous that there is need of wider participation to increase community identification and consciousness. To neglect this is to miss the whole lesson of our democratic traditions. Moreover, if group experiences and interactions have the power of therapy, as Doctor Moreno [26] attests for those disturbed or in conflict with themselves or with others, they should also strengthen those normal individuals who would achieve stronger and healthier communities by the ordinary day-to-day and week-to-week associations within their own localities.

Unfortunately, such high ideals are yet to be realized in many a local rural community. On the debit side, some researchers report that even churches and schools perpetuate class lines and accentuate differences, thus setting children and their families apart from each other and the common life of the community.[27]

"Generally speaking, the church has lagged in the realignment of smaller centers to form larger and stronger community groups." [28]

"The school occupies an interesting place in this course of events; despite its rational curriculum, it was not the effective cause of change. Indeed, careful perusal of school records shows that there have been no major curriculum innovations in perhaps fifty years."[29]

Opportunity still knocks at the door of the high school. A unique opportunity for leadership in this emerging village or town-country community presents itself to the high school. Ten and twenty years ago retail trade was a ready means for determining boundaries of rural communities. Today retail trade is broken up in its distribution between village or town center to city center, but the high school rises to a place of significance, not only in delineation of community areas, but in determining trade and social contacts. May

[26] Moreno, J. L., *Who Shall Survive?* Washington, D.C.: Nervous and Mental Disease Publication Company, 1934.

[27] Freeman, Edith Jeffers, *Social Class as a Factor in the Family Group Relations of Certain New York Farm Families.* Ithaca: Cornell University Abstracts of Theses, 1943.

[28] Hoffsommer, Harold, "The Relation of Rural Churches to Other Social Organizations," *Social Forces*, December, 1941.

[29] Passin, Herbert, and John W. Bennett, "Changing Agricultural Magic in Southern Illinois: A Systematic Analysis of Folk-Urban Transition," *Social Forces*, October, 1943.

not the high school, with its courses in agriculture, home economics, commerce, music, drama, and the arts, as well as its regular academic work, become the focalizing institution for both youth and adult in a round-the-year program for the rural communities of tomorrow?

Readjustments will have to be made, but they are on the way in many quarters. In the study of Charles County, Maryland, already referred to, the high school was found to be definitely at the community center, because of both geographic location and leadership exerted.

In New York State, the policy for centralizing rural schools is posited on the theory that they should be community-centered. Doctor Dwight Sanderson, of Cornell University, emphatically stated that if school consolidation is effected on the sole basis of so-called efficiency, either as to cost or curriculum, the importance of the community relation tends to be ignored. He argued that placing the school outside the community setting alienates community interest and control, and that the pupil is in much the same relation to it as the rural patron is to a city department store — he goes to a school which is outside his area of experience and his natural ties, to buy a certain type of schooling.[30]

Formal community organization can help. Consensus and action, the goals of community endeavor, can be enhanced, not only by informal means, but by tested social mechanisms of organization and promotion. Professor Wileden defines rural community organization as the deliberate and voluntary co-ordinating, integrating, and at times subordinating of various interests, activities, even classes within the community, by fixing the emphasis upon common ends and the attainment of satisfactions for all.[31]

Permanent organization is not always necessary. There may be special means for particular objectives. Rural communities in many states have set up planning committees, meetings, or temporary organizations to prepare postwar programs. Formal community organization, on the other hand, may proceed either by direct or indirect methods.[32] The direct method is for all members of the

[30] Sanderson, Dwight, "Criteria of Rural Community Formation," *Rural Sociology*, December, 1939; Stromberg, E. T., *The Influence of the Central Rural School on Community Organization*. Ithaca: Bulletin 699, Cornell University Experiment Station, 1938.

[31] Wileden, A. F., Class Notes, *Rural Community Organization*. Madison: College of Agriculture, University of Wisconsin.

[32] Sanderson, Dwight, and R. A. Polson, *Rural Community Organization*. New York: John Wiley & Sons, 1939.

community to participate as individuals, in meetings, committees of the whole, or in an organized association with constitution and officers. The traditional form for this direct means is the New England town meeting. The indirect method is framed on the principle of a representative democracy in which a community council is composed of representative groups concerned. The representatives in question may be selected on an area basis, from special-interest organizations, social institutions, age groups, or some agreed combination.

A more formal definition of a community council geared to exigencies of the postwar situation is the following:

> A community council is a body of responsible citizens representing the organizations, agencies, and major interests of the community. Its chief functions are to co-ordinate, to plan, to inform, and to act in the interest of the total community. Through a successful council a community can often do for itself what an agency cannot accomplish alone. A good council also increases the amount of social participation and develops leadership. Morale is built by the successful functioning of a council.[33]

Organization presupposes what is popularly recognized as leadership. In a more careful reference the two are but aspects of the same relationship. Stable organization is dependent upon recognized responses among those individuals who compose it. This recognition may depend upon personal qualities, social position determined by means of prestige described earlier, or it may be determined by affiliations or other relations which have thus far defied isolation and accurate measurement. In any case, there must be some agreement as to what qualities are to be regarded as "high" or "low," what values or goals are to be sought.[34] This is at the very basis of group organization. In an organization system different persons represent different rôles; some have authority over others; some have obligations toward others, and so on. Leadership, therefore, as was suggested earlier, is a group process in which persons interact with other persons within a recognized relationship of social values.

[33] Brunner, Edmund de S., *The What and How of Community Councils.* Washington, D.C.: Extension Service Circular 403, United States Deparment of Agriculture, March, 1943. Brunner, Edmund de S., *Community Organization and Adult Education.* Chapel Hill: University of North Carolina Press, 1942.

[34] Loomis, Charles P., and Douglas Ensminger, "Governmental Administration and Informal Local Groups," *Applied Anthropology*, January-March, 1942.

Local communities dependent upon intercommunity connections.
Not only does the Great Society have roots in "Littledene," New
Zealand, but in every other rural community and urban community as well. No local group exists by itself, apart from society;
we need no more Pearl Harbors to demonstrate that fact. Its application, however, will require much trial and error in organization
plans as rural communities face toward the future. There are many
practical examples; programs instituted at "higher" or more remote
levels can completely nullify local efforts, or selfish local blocs can
neutralize much of generalized good intent.

Finally, it is possible that the modern rural community and its
deliberate organization as described may be the meeting place toward which two trends appear to be moving. One trend is the
centralizing of smaller rural groups and institutions — centralized
schools, reorganized local co-operatives, enlarged recreational facilities. The other is the decentralizing of larger urban units and
agencies — branch mercantile establishments, family housing projects, electrically driven industrial projects.

This is but another way of attempting to summarize and to emphasize that rural community organization is not for purposes of
limiting or fencing in, but rather for introducing and relating
groups and their members to the larger society. Herein lies the
function of the rural community if it regards the principles of
comity and co-operation. Comity means courtesy between equals;
co-operation means acting jointly. Some community relations must
be on the basis of comity, some must follow the principle of co-
operation. For example, in religious matters, where church bodies
are of widely differing cultural and theological backgrounds, obviously common ground can be gained only by comity. On the other
hand, in great enterprises of marketing and buying, where volume
of business is essential and large overhead agencies are needed,
the co-operative or joint-action principle must be employed. In
both relationships the rural community has a responsibility. Community means having in common; communication means making
common. Therefore, through principles of comity and co-operation,
and by means of communication, community life may become a
social reality and a part of the general society.

DISCUSSION TOPICS

1. Consider again a household, rural or urban, with which you are well
acquainted. Indicate its location and then, by use of six arrows drawn

so as to indicate the direction and distance, show the location of centers to which members of this household go for each of the following services: (You may have to split some arrows if more than one center is used for some services.)

a. Economic — marketing, merchandising, financing.

b. Religious — church, religious education, organizations.

c. Education — school, high school, library.

d. Social — sociability, recreation, welfare.

e. Communication — mail service, telephone, newspaper.

f. Professional — doctor, lawyer, dentist.

2. Are "trade" areas and "social" areas for villages or towns coincident? Explain why.

3. Draft in general form the general community or service area of the "home town" village you have described in the previous chapter. Sketch the areas of each of the six services listed in the previous exercise if they differ from the general community area. (The general community area shall be defined as that area from which a majority of the families come to the village for a majority of their services.)

4. What does Doctor Galpin mean by "rurbanism"? State your agreement or differences with this idea.

5. What difficulties and inhibitions need to be overcome in drawing farmers and villagers into larger community arrangements? Illustrate.

6. Describe in detail an effective plan for rural community organization which you have observed or read about. What are its chief elements of strength, and what are its deficiencies?

REFERENCE READINGS

Arensberg, C. M., *The Irish Countryman.* New York: The Macmillan Co., 1937. An anthropological study.

Brunner, Hughes, and Patton, *American Agricultural Villages.* New York: Doran & Co., 1927. A report of field research of 140 agricultural village communities made in 1924.

Bureau of Foreign and Domestic Commerce, *Small-Town Manual for Community Action.* Washington, D.C.: Industrial Series no. 4, United States Department of Commerce, 1942.

Chapin, F. Stuart, *Community Leadership and Opinion in Red Wing (Minnesota).* Minneapolis: University of Minnesota Press, 1945. A study of the impact of war, Bulletin 3 in the series, *The Community Basis for Postwar Planning.*

Galpin, C. J., *Rural Life,* chap. 4. New York: Century Company, 1918. Original study of Walworth County, in which was developed the concept of the rurban community.

Kolb, J. H., *Service Relations of Town and Country*, Research Bulletin 58, 1923; *Service Institutions for Town and Country*, Research Bulletin 66, 1925; *Trends in Town-Country Relations*, Research Bulletin 117, 1933. Madison: Agricultural Experiment Station, University of Wisconsin.

Leao, A. Carneiro, "Rural Brazil," *Rural Sociology*, June, 1944.

Loomis, Charles P., "Extension Work at Tingo Maria, Peru," *Applied Anthropology*, vol. 3, no. 1, December, 1943.

Lynch, Russell W., *Czech Farmers in Oklahoma*, Bulletin vol. 39, no. 13. Stillwater: Oklahoma Agricultural and Mechanical College, 1942.

Morgan, Arthur, *The Small Community*. New York: Harper & Bros., October, 1942. A most interesting and important statement of the place of small communities in our contemporary society by an engineer and administrator.

Pearse and Crocker, *The Peckham Experiment*. Yellow Springs, Ohio: Community Service, Inc.

Sanderson, Dwight, *The Rural Community*. Boston: Ginn & Co., 1932. Note particularly chaps. 1 and 2, 10, 11, and 12, 15 and 16. This is a thorough study of the rural community as a population group.

Sanderson, Dwight, *Leadership for Rural Life*. New York: Association Press, 1940. A very good beginning analysis from both practical and theoretical aspects.

Sarkar, Benoy Kumar, *Villages and Towns as Social Patterns*. Calcutta: Chuckervertty, Chatterjee & Co., Ltd., 1941. A study in the processes and forms of societal transformation and progress.

The State Education Department, *Problems Confronting Boards of Education*. Albany: The University of the State of New York, 1944. A Manual for community participation in educational planning.

West, James, *Plainville, U.S.A.* New York: Columbia University Press, 1945. A detailed study of a local rural community in Missouri. All names including the author's are fictionalized.

Wilson, Warren H., *The Evolution of the Rural Community*. Pilgrim Press, 1923. A very good discussion of the development or evolution of rural society.

Young, Hsin-Pao, "Agricultural Planning with the Chinese," *Rural Sociology*, March, 1945.

Zimmerman, Carle C., *The Changing Community*. New York: Harper & Bros., 1938. A summary of modern trends with excellent case studies of individual communities.

15

Special Interest Groups

RURAL SOCIETY is made up of many different kinds of groups. Neighborhoods, villages, and communities all have their places, but within their boundaries or cutting across them are to be found such other groups as farmers' clubs, homemakers' clubs, 4–H clubs, spray rings, parent-teacher associations, choral and dramatic clubs, young people's societies, breeders' associations, co-operative buying or selling organizations, informal social groups, and many, many others. These groups are not characterized so much by their location as by their activities, and the purposes or the interests which they represent. Although there is a very wide variety of such groups in rural society, it is possible to bring together some of the more readily recognized types and to study them from the point of view of interest.

Interest groups arise out of likenesses and differences in age, sex, occupation, tradition, experience, choice, propensity, intent, and so on. They may be contrasted with locality groups. Locality groups have lateral or geographic dimensions. Interest groups have perpendicular or voluntary dimensions. Locality groups depend upon common life, proximity, residence in a specific physical area. Interest groups depend upon polarity, promotion, special concerns, leadership, deliberate effort. This polarity implies fields of magnetic influence. When thus released from locality restrictions certain people are attracted to certain of these poles of interest. In popular parlance, the phrase, "Birds of a feather flock together," conveys the idea very well indeed. Then, some wag has added, "And they sit a long time," which simply means that when people are thus drawn together into groups of congenial interest, the tendency is for them to want to continue and to hold together.

Origins of Rural Interest Groups

Americans have a penchant for organizations and associations, at least so say many foreign critics. A gibe of one such critic is to the effect that whenever two or three Americans get together, they soon organize, elect officers, adopt a constitution, and appoint committees. Although this is obviously an exaggeration, it does suggest something of the part which organized groups of many kinds have played and continue to play in this country.

A very brief excerpt from just one foreign writer will serve as an illustration. The Frenchman, de Tocqueville, was greatly impressed by the many organizations and societies which were common to the early periods. He writes:

> Americans of all ages, all conditions, and all dispositions constantly form associations. They have not only commercial and manufacturing companies in which all take part, but they have associations of a thousand other kinds — religious, moral, serious, futile, general or restricted, enormous or diminutive. The Americans make associations to give entertainments, to found seminaries, to build inns, to construct churches, to diffuse books, to send missionaries to the antipodes. . . . Wherever, at the head of some new undertaking you see government in France, or a man of rank in England, in the United States you will be sure to find an association.[1]

It may well be that this tendency to join hands in the prosecution of common interests is an essential part of a democratic society. The great historian of the American frontier was quick to see the rôle which such voluntary groups played in the opening and the developing of new territory by the pioneers. In a characteristic paragraph, Professor Turner says:

> From the very first, it became evident that these men had means of supplementing their individual activity by informal combinations. One of the things that impressed all early travelers in the United States was the capacity for extra-legal voluntary associations. This power of the newly arrived pioneers to join together for a common end without the intervention of governmental institutions was one of their marked characteristics. The log-rolling, the house-raising, the husking-bee and apple-paring, and the squatters' associations whereby they protected themselves against the speculators in securing titles to their clearings on the public domain, the camp meeting, the mining camp, the vigilantes, the cattle-raisers' associations, the "gentlemen's agreements," are a few of the indications of this attitude.[2]

[1] de Tocqueville, Alexis, *Democracy in America*. From a translation by Henry Reeve, vol. I, p. 242. 1876.

[2] Turner, F. J., *The Frontier in American History*, p. 343. New York: Henry Holt & Co.

This tendency toward many forms of organization did not decline with the recession of the frontier. It is a factor of importance in rural society at the present time for, as Professor Turner emphasizes, its origin is not one of tradition and custom, but of initiative and of voluntary action. He continues:

> It is well to emphasize this American trait, because in a modified way it has come to be one of the most characteristic and important features of the United States today. America does through informal association and understanding on the part of the people many of the things which in the Old World are and can be done only by governmental intervention and compulsion. These associations were in America not due to immemorial custom of tribe or village community. They were extemporized by voluntary action.[3]

Groupings like the neighborhood which characterized earlier society as Professor MacIver points out, tend to break up into associational units and to assume associational character in a more modern life.[4] In the earlier neighborhoods there were so many common interests that group organization could be quite simple, differentiations few, and practically everyone was included in the general plan. As has been shown in an earlier chapter, the more active neighborhoods of the present are characterized by activities, institutions, and special interests more than by locality, nearness of residence, or traditional ways of life. It must be said, however, that many of the newer forms of group alignment have sprung from the soil of the older neighborhoods.

INTEREST GROUPS IN MODERN RURAL LIFE

Facilities for travel and communication are freeing country and village dwellers from former restrictions of locality and residence so that they can seek their satisfactions in group arrangements of their own choice or design. One might expect this trend in the newer sections of the country, but it is true even in New England. From the study of the rural town of Lebanon, Connecticut, the conclusion was drawn that similarity of interests is a more workable basis for most rural group life than is mere geographical juxtaposition.[5]

[3] *Ibid.*
[4] MacIver, R. M., *Society, Its Structure and Changes,* p. 55. R. R. Smith, Inc., 1931.
[5] Hypes, J. L., *Social Participation in a Rural New England Town,* p. 99. New York: Bureau of Publications, Teachers College, Columbia University, 1927.

This transfer from locality groups to interest groups and from organic forms to contractual forms of association, whether by voluntary means or through skillful promotion, is a significant trend and one which explains many of the rural social movements of the present time. This is not to say that neighborhood and community groups have entirely lost their influence, but simply that interest groups are of increasing importance.

Interests about which country groups form. Even though there is a wide variety of interests about which groups in rural society form, certain types can be selected for study. For the purposes of this chapter some of the more easily recognized country groups will be chosen. They are the ones which are rather deliberately formed and have officers, programs and procedures. Of course, there are other types which are more informal and transient, and there are also those which bring together country and village people and, in some cases, even rural and urban people.

In a sample area of five counties in central and southern Wisconsin, 351 country groups of the type described were found.[6] They included organizations with seventy-five different names, but Table 49 shows that about 75 per cent of them can be grouped into

TABLE 49. SPECIAL INTEREST ORGANIZATIONS IN THE ORDER OF FREQUENCY OF OCCURRENCE IN FIVE WISCONSIN COUNTIES

	Organizations	
Professional Forms	Number	Per cent
Total...	351	100.0
Parent-teacher Associations...........................	47	13.4
Farmers' Clubs.......................................	46	13.1
Community Clubs.....................................	43	12.0
4–H Clubs...	34	9.7
Homemakers' Clubs...................................	20	5.7
Co-operative Associations.............................	20	5.7
Spray Rings...	14	4.0
Breeders' Associations................................	10	2.8
Horticultural Societies................................	8	2.3
Cow Testing Associations.............................	7	2.0
Shipping Associations.................................	7	2.0
Milk Producers' Associations..........................	5	1.4
Miscellaneous (63 names).............................	91	25.9

twelve classes or kinds. It is evident that such forms as parent-teacher associations, farmers' clubs, community clubs, 4–H clubs, homemakers' clubs, and co-operative associations are among the

[6] Kolb, J. H., and A. F. Wileden, *Special Interest Groups in Rural Society*. Madison: Research Bulletin 84, December, 1927, Agricultural Experiment Station, University of Wisconsin.

most popular groups. The 91 organizations included under the miscellaneous item, include mothers' clubs, boys' clubs, farm bureaus, fair associations, equity societies, and cemetery associations. The names, however, are often more indicative of the form which the organization takes and may not be a reliable cue to the real activity or the central interest of the group. For example, it was found that a group called a farmers' club was actually a choral society; that a parent-teacher association was a women's social and sewing group, and that a community club was a cemetery association. Because the name did not always designate the interest, the 351 groups were studied at first hand and then classified according to their real interests.

The twelve major interests or functions about which the groups formed are shown in Table 50. It is quite evident from the table

TABLE 50. INTERESTS ABOUT WHICH GROUPS FORMED IN THE ORDER OF FREQUENCY OF OCCURRENCE

Interest classes	Organizations	
	Number	Per cent
All organizations *	351	100.0
Social enjoyment	252	71.8
Better farming	115	32.8
Help school and teacher	84	24.0
Better business	59	16.8
Young people's interests	59	16.8
Health and social welfare	41	11.7
Home improvement	40	11.4
Public and civic affairs	15	4.3
General community betterment	13	3.7
Unite locals	5	1.4
Mutual improvement	5	1.4
Help church and preacher	5	1.4

* Obviously the sum of the organizations in the various interest classes greatly exceeds the total number of organizations, because any one organization may fall into more than one of the classes.

that social enjoyment is an important interest, for it was found to operate in over 71 per cent of the cases. Better farming comes second; the most significant fact, however, is that these groups are not single in interest; the majority of them have two or more interests. This is one of the outstanding characteristics of this type of country organization. Many have interests which are not highly specialized; that is, several interests are closely associated. Some interests, such as the social in the sense of sociability, are seldom found alone.

Preliminary analysis has been made of the changes in these country special interest groups over a fifteen-year period, 1925 to 1940.

It indicates that the total number of groups has increased nearly 60 per cent, but with a rather wide variation among the localities and among the types. The more specialized women's and youth groups have increased most, while those of the general family type and the men's groups have declined slightly. The latter include local farmers' clubs and country parent-teacher associations. The greatest increase came in those groups organized or sponsored by public agencies, such as 4–H clubs and homemakers' clubs, under the sponsorship of the Agricultural and Home Economics Extension Services. There were also more Future Farmer Associations promoted by high-school vocational agricultural departments. The interests which showed most expansion, in addition to those concerned with youth, were those devoted to health and welfare, and to public and civic affairs. The war undoubtedly accelerated this trend, as has been traced in other chapters, notably the chapters on the neighborhood and on health.

Similar types of groups organized about similar poles of interest are found in other states. An Illinois study is summarized in Table 51, where the kinds of organizations and their purposes are com-

TABLE 51. ORIGINAL PURPOSES FOR WHICH 230 GROUPS OF ILLINOIS FARM PEOPLE WERE ORGANIZED

Type of Organization	Number of Groups	Educational Purposes Per cent	Social Purposes Per cent	Better Farming Per cent	Community Development Per cent	Improvement of the School Per cent
Community clubs........	47	27	54	13	31	8
Farm bureau units........	46	70	26	60	13	13
Parent-teacher ass'ns......	45	30	27	0	20	70
Home bureau units.......	31	84	3	41	16	0
Subordinate granges......	24	44	60	20	20	0
Community units.........	15	60	40	27	20	0
Others *.................	22	39	48	9	18	0
Total..................	230	49	35	25	20	17

* Includes 9 farmers' clubs, 4 4–H clubs, 4 women's clubs, 3 community councils, and 2 farmers' unions.

pared. In the 230 groups of farm people, the educational and the social or sociability interests rank very high. The social purposes most frequently mentioned by the leaders were as follows: developing acquaintanceship and fellowship, providing opportunity for the exchange of ideas which would in any way contribute to the social welfare of the community, and satisfying purely recreational needs through games, dances and the like. Granges, community units, and community clubs were more likely to emphasize social than educational purposes.[7]

In a Southern state, Virginia, the interests about which country groups have formed are classified under three general heads: educational societies, farm organizations, and commodity marketing associations.[8] Among the educational societies are found the Co-operative Education Association, the parent-teacher association, farmers' institutes, homemakers' associations, farmers' evening classes, and numerous educational councils, such as agricultural advisory councils, home advisory councils, 4–H club councils, and high-school advisory councils. An analysis of the work of these societies reveals a wide variety of activities and purposes. Although of a special interest character themselves, some of the societies are broken down into highly specialized committees or groups. For example, the Co-operative Education Association has ten standard committees, among them being health, child welfare, roads, agriculture, and citizenship.

Among the more general farm organizations are listed the Farmers' Union, the Farm Bureau, the Grange, and very many independent farmers' clubs. The commodity marketing associations are reported to be on the increase in the state of Virginia. They are local in character, but many attempt to cover the state by means of federations or co-operative agreements. The whole development of the marketing associations, especially those organized on the co-operative principle, is a movement of great importance in rural society. In many ways it becomes a first-class illustration of the tendency toward the interest or functional type of organization which is being considered in this chapter. The co-operative form of organization becomes a principle or a pole of interest which attracts some farmers and repels others. The different types of commodities also become a selective factor which draws certain producers together. The following are but a few examples, indicating the extent to which specialization has grown: Valley of Virginia Co-operative Milk Producers' Association, Coon River Tomato Association of the Northern Neck, Rockingham Co-operative Farm Bureau, Inc., Eastern Shore of Virginia Produce Exchange and Rockbridge Co-operative Livestock Marketing Association.

[7] Lindstrom, D. E., *Local Group Organization Among Illinois Farm People.* Urbana: Bulletin 392, Agricultural Experiment Station, University of Illinois, June, 1933.

[8] Garnett, W. E., *Rural Organizations in Relation to Rural Life in Virginia.* Blacksburg: Bulletin 256, Virginia Agricultural Experiment Station, 1927.

In this state, furthermore, another whole set of country interest groups and organizations is found. They are Negro organizations,[9] and they, in turn, can be classified into three large types of interests, as follows: agricultural organizations, educational societies, and fraternal or secret orders. In many respects the agricultural and educational organizations parallel those which have previously been described, for there are farmer conferences, 4—H clubs, agricultural extension societies, school improvement leagues, and county fair associations. The fraternal and secret orders have many interesting and unique features. The interests to which they cater are evidently a feeling of brotherhood, a desire for security, which takes the form of insurance and mutual-aid plans, and a sense of the religious, which expresses itself in ritualism. Organizations of a fraternal nature are, according to the bulletin, most numerous among rural Negroes. A list of the names of the organizations in the one community of Fairfields, Northumberland County, may convey some idea of a local situation. In this community there are thirteen adult organizations, as follows: Knights of Jerusalem, Court of Queen Esther, Good Samaritans, Lone Star, Edwardsville and Ophelia; Odd Fellows, Bay View and Tranquillity, Household of Ruth, Pride of Lilian, Masons and Eastern Star, and Rock Lee Home Society. It is not unusual to find a half dozen or more such organizations in a single community. Although they bear a variety of strange names, their objectives are practically identical.

Interest groups involving country and village. As has been indicated elsewhere, the restudy of community relations of the 140 agricultural villages showed the growing interdependence of country and village people. There was an increase in the participation of country people in the special interest organizations centered in the villages and towns.[10] This means closer and more intimate personal contacts between the two major classes in rural society — farmers and villagers. Increased country enrollments were also observed in the educational organizations, largely the Parent-Teacher Associations, a corollary of the increased use of village schools by country people, and likewise a compensation for the falling off in such country groups as just noted.

A graphic representation of this interest or functional organization, involving both country and village, given in the accompanying chart (Figure 22), illustrates a situation in rural Illinois. It shows

[9] Ellison, J. M., *Negro Organization and Leadership in Relation to Rural Life.* Blacksburg: Bulletin 290, Virginia Agricultural Experiment Station, 1933.
[10] Brunner and Kolb, *Rural Social Trends.* New York: McGraw-Hill, 1933.

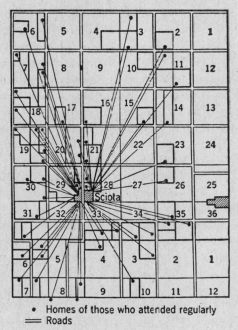

• Homes of those who attended regularly
═ Roads

Figure 22

AREA OF INFLUENCE OF THE SCIOTA COMMUNITY
CLUB OF McDONOUGH COUNTY, ILLINOIS, 1930

Source: D. E. Lindstrom, *Local Group Organization Among Illinois Farm People*, Bulletin 392, Agricultural Experiment Station, University of Illinois.

the selective membership of the Sciota Community Club. The homes of the country members are scattered over two townships, some are as far as five miles from the village center.

A significant relationship was found between the numbers and types of special interest groups and the size of village or town centers. Another aspect of this situation has been described in the chapter dealing with recreation, namely that the smaller villages had fewer organizations and the larger ones had more, but the average number seemed to level off at about twenty per village. Their mortality rate increased as the number increased above that figure. In New York State a correlation was found between the population and the number of socio-educational organizations, especially in the dairying and in the fruit-raising counties.[11]

[11] Melvin, B. L., *Village Service Agencies in New York*. Ithaca: Cornell University Bulletin 493, 1929.

Similarly in the Australian study of the country towns of Victoria, it was found that a larger number of women's organizations were likely to be found in places of less than one thousand population than in the larger centers. Men's and youth organizations, on the other hand, were somewhat more characteristic of the larger villages and towns.[12] Women's organizations, the report states, are the most numerous and the most hardy of all. These organizations have for their main purpose the helping of some cause, interest, or institution, such as overseas mission, hospital, or school, and even those which exist primarily for the benefit of the members usually have some helping activity as a secondary function, a characteristic quite like that of the American groups described earlier. Men's organizations in the Australian towns were less numerous and meetings were usually held at night. They were rather a contrast with the women's groups, since the majority of them existed chiefly for the benefit of the members themselves, although their activities were varied and many of them "do good works." Lack of vitality characterized the youth organizations. This, it was thought, was due to the fact that they were so largely founded on the idea of doing good for the young people and training them to social conformity, rather than for their enjoyment.

Some general characteristics. Diverse and varied as those special interest organizations are, they do possess, nevertheless, certain general characteristics. First of these is their dependence upon leadership and promotion. In the five counties the organizations of which were described in the previous section, the responsibility for starting and promoting was shared about equally by local leaders and by leaders from outside the community. The original motivation or urge for those organizations concerned with the farm, the home, the educational and the young people's interests, came, in the majority of cases, from outside leaders, representing such agencies as the agricultural or home economics extension service, the parent-teacher association and school officials. In getting the organization started, these outside promoters worked usually through local leaders. In organizing the educational interests local teachers played an important part.

Locally elected officers were given practically the entire responsibility for keeping the organization active. Those groups concerned with young people's interests were sometimes an exception, for adult sponsors or leaders were usually present. The quality of

[12] McIntyre, A. J. and J. J., *Country Towns of Victoria*. Melbourne University Press, 1944.

the local leaders — their abilities, training and outlook — is, therefore, very important. If this fact is overlooked, too great emphasis may be given to the organization itself and too little to the continuity of its leadership, an oversight which accounts for the relatively short life of many local organizations. The election of officers is not enough; their subsequent training and work is what counts in the long run.

A second general characteristic is that most interest groups depend upon a program of activities to accomplish their objectives. Meetings are held, their nature and frequency depending upon what the organization is trying to accomplish. For those groups organized about the social, the educational or the young people's interests, the meeting usually consists of four parts: an educational program, a social period, a business session, and refreshments. To attempt a general meeting of country people without refreshments would be like trying to run a car without gasoline. Eating and visiting together are prime requisites in the programs of many a congeniality group. Co-operative organizations, of course, give more time and attention to business features, but even they do not completely neglect the occasional picnic or social affair. Activities other than the regular meetings are many and varied, such as poultry culling and tree spraying demonstrations, health clinics and exhibits, plays and pageants, parties and picnics, community and county fairs, debates and discussions, or games and field days. Such activities become the center of attention for the group itself, and they also provide an opportunity for displaying or dramatizing its work before other members of the community. The accompanying chart (Figure 23) shows which type of activity is likely to be associated with the several kinds of organizations and which ones are peculiar to one or two. Picnics, for example, are found with each of the seven kinds of organizations included in the chart, while clinics are confined largely to the health interest groups, and sales agencies to the co-operative business organizations.

Now and then an activity may be fostered which is quite out of line with the main interest for which a group has been organized, in fact, it may be done to divert attention from the central purpose. The story is told of a co-operative creamery which was not doing very well in a business way. The directors conceived the idea of holding a dance once a month for their members, hoping that they would have such a good time that they would overlook the financial difficulties. It came to be known as the "dancing creamery."

A third characteristic of interest groups is that by their very

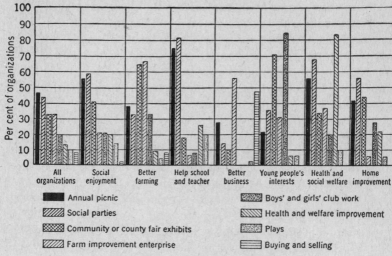

Figure 23

PRINCIPAL PROJECTS

Characteristic projects are of a social nature, such as picnics and social parties.

Source: Kolb and Wileden, *Special Interest Groups in Rural Society,* Research Bulletin 84, December, 1927, Agricultural Experiment Station, University of Wisconsin.

nature only certain kinds and numbers of people are attracted to them. It may be redundant to say that interest groups need people who are interested, but the practical implication is important. Leaders are likely to go to one of two extremes. They will either generalize their programs in order to hold a larger group, and in this way lose the support of the persons most deeply interested, or they will hold too strictly to their original objectives and thus fail to attract sufficient numbers to carry on their enterprise. In other words, there is an appropriate size and kind of organization for certain types of interests. In the business or co-operative field the principle is known as "sufficient volume of business." There is also an appropriate "volume of people," neither too large nor too small, needed to carry on a mothers' club, a choral society or a subordinate Grange. It is not an accident, for instance, that college or university fraternities and sororities average approximately twenty-five or thirty members. A larger unit might be more economical to house, but the limiting factor is the number who can be truly congenial and who are enough alike in interests and propensities to work out a closely-knit, primary, functioning group.

Observation soon reveals that certain numbers do tend to become associated with certain interests. A good example is the 4—H club. At one time there were those leaders who sought to increase general county or state enrollments by enlarging local clubs. It did not take long to discover, however, that wider differences in age and more varied interests soon altered the desired character of the organization. Therefore, relatively small groups are maintained, and when more boys and girls can be interested, other units are formed and other leaders are sought. This principle is sometimes difficult to appreciate, since the ambition for large numbers is often very compelling. The executive of a certain local farm organization could not be content until he "signed up" his two hundredth member. For some weeks after the "membership drive" everything seemed to go along very well. A general program with a high proportion of sociability and entertainment seemed to hold "the crowd." As cold weather set in, however, the distances to travel seemed too great for some of the members. When the real program of work was announced, others were not interested, and when it became apparent to those most interested that their opportunity for participation would be limited because of the large membership, they too lost their original zeal.

A fourth characteristic of interest groups and organizations is their tendency to federate. As the chapter dealing with recreational and social agencies will indicate, the modern tendency is for groups of like kind to federate. This is often undertaken in an attempt to unify the efforts and activities of a series of local organizations within a district or perhaps a county-wide plan. The county organization may even precede the locals and then promote and establish them. At other times the federation is the result of already established locals, which combine in a desire for united action and for wider outlets of group endeavor. The tendency to federate may also be considered one form of reconciliation for the overlapping and conflicting loyalties which arise in a local situation where there are many interest groups. The process may take place on a community basis, in which case it becomes one of the steps in social integration or "community organization," as it is termed, a problem with which a later chapter will concern itself.

In his discussion of the social organization of the rural community, Professor Sanderson summarizes this characteristic as follows:

Inasmuch as these associations frequently represent interests which are common to similar groups in other communities, they federate in the same manner as did the early villages and for the same reasons, that is, to promote their common purposes, for defense of their organization, and to secure the greater social control of the individual association through the sanctions of the federated groups. Herein is one of the pressing problems of the rural community today: How may it maintain its autonomy against powerful national organizations which seek to establish local branches? Competing associations may go their way in the larger cities without opposition, whereas in the rural community undue competition of organizations is soon seen to be a waste of social resources, which are none too adequate at best. Hence many rural communities are seeking some sort of community organization which will bring together the various interest groups in a common effort for community progress, a tendency which is an inevitable result of the specialization of interest groups, if the social organization finally tends to result in their better integration in the interest of the welfare of the locality group.[13]

The life cycle of interest groups. Like other living things, groups follow cycles. These cycles consist of rather definite stages through which they pass, the periods being of long or short duration, according to the nature of the group, its central interest, and its surrounding conditions. The rise and decline of groups and organizations, in the abstract, may be taken for granted by many persons, but when a group with which they are personally associated is involved, it is quite another matter. Students of rural society will do well to watch the cycles of change carefully, not only within those groups of which they are members, but other special interest groups as well, for such changes are becoming very common. Many such organizations have a comparatively short life cycle, and this is a problem of much concern both to their leaders and to their members. This section presents a sort of composite narrative of what happens in the various periods in the life cycle of rural interest groups. Four periods may be observed. They are: stimulation, rise, carrying-on, and decline.

(1) *Stimulation.* The period of stimulation may come about by direct action, or it may be by indirection. In the first instance the purpose is stated openly. This is the rationalized procedure. When sufficient sentiment has been aroused, a union of kindred spirits takes place. Like the chemical reaction, it may be either a rapid or a slow process. It may come quickly at some promoted meeting where definite organization was not anticipated, even by the

[13] Sanderson, Dwight, *The Rural Community*, p. 539. Boston: Ginn & Co., 1932.

leaders; suddenly the idea "takes hold" and the movement rises like a wave, carrying the originators far past their channel markers. It may take more time when a certain amount of capital stock must be sold, or when a certain original quota of membership must be signed. Even then there usually is some kind of "drive" or campaign with a certain amount of emotional excitement.

The indirect method of forming an interest group may have its origin in a social gathering which was greatly enjoyed. The desire for more occasions in the near future is voiced. A loosely formed organization results. In this case the purposes or interests remain veiled for a time, but gradually take form and become the axis around which further activities revolve.

(2) *Rise*. During the period of rise people who have never thought of organization approve it; they do more; they ask for admission and offer help in getting it started. There are frequent meetings and large crowds. Special meetings are called to decide upon such important matters as a constitution and the election of officers. Enthusiasm runs high. Everything is new and there are plenty of ideas. "Everybody" joins, that is, everyone at the organization meeting who is eligible. There are fewer who join at the next meeting and finally there are no new members.

Meanwhile, the structure of the organization is becoming "set." A constitution is accepted. This specifies that this organization shall meet once a month during the school year. It shall meet at the school house. It shall have four officers: a president, vice-president, secretary, and treasurer, to be elected annually at the first meeting in January. Anyone who is "truly interested" may become a member. A two thirds vote is necessary to change the constitution, which means that it is the fixed code or method of procedure for the organization from that time on.

After the first few meetings, however, the officers must "go it alone." Occasionally they assume the responsibility regularly, but more frequently they cast about for a method of assistance, and decide upon the plan of appointing committees. The organization has its select group of officers, committee chairmen, and volunteer speakers from the floor who virtually run it. The officers may change about, and new committees may be added, but this inner circle remains practically the same. Radical changes in the inner circle usually mean equally radical changes in the nature of the organization, and vice versa. The problem, from the beginning, then, becomes one of creating loyalty of the leaders and through them to the organization. This process is well under way by the time the organization reaches its peak. Ideals and purposes have become codified, and even custom has begun to play its part. In other words, precedents have been established.

(3) *Carrying-on.* The crucial time for every organization comes after the promotion period is over and the newness has worn off. This is the period of "carrying-on." By this time the outside promoters have disappeared almost entirely from the scene, and the burden must be shouldered by local people, usually by the officers. From this time on, disillusionment may begin, for often certain promises were made and objectives held forth by the promoters that apparently are not and frequently cannot be fulfilled. Factions develop within the group and conflicts arise.

It may also be discovered at about this time that the group is conflicting with the ideals of other groups, or institutions, such as the school or church. Consequently, they may be denied the use of the school building, or the clergy may forbid their young people to take part. On the other hand, this new group may be trying to do almost the same things as an older group in the same locality. Adjustments are necessary and methods of establishing working relations with these other groups must be devised. If this necessity is ignored, the results are often fatal to both groups.

During this carrying-on period, the changing demands of the membership must be carefully watched. There are seasonal fluctuations in the programs and activities to be considered. People tire after a while even of pie, although it may be the much-coveted pumpkin pie. Likewise, debates and plays run their course, and something else must be supplied. Suggestions for change are brought before the organization. About half of the time, however, the constitutionalists or the fundamentalists win, and the proposed change is not made. If the group will accept the change, it may secure a new lease on life.

Added to the difficulties of this period is the tendency for an organization to grow up with its members. As a new organization, it begins life with people unfamiliar with its ways. They gradually mold it to conform to their ways of doing things. Amateur leaders gain confidence gradually and their efforts become more and more successful. New people coming in later cannot experience this same "give and take" process. They must take things more largely as they find them. This they occasionally refuse to do, particularly those of a younger generation. Thus, it is not unusual to find separate organizations for the various age groups, and to see a new organization cycle start with each succeeding generation.

(4) *Decline.* When decline once sets in, there are but two
avenues open, other than demise. One is specialization. The old
generalized club may become a strictly social club; it may become
a women's welfare organization, or a farmers' discussion club. The
present tendency is toward more specialized groups. The other
avenue is a complete reorganization. For example, women's clubs
which were practically inactive have reorganized and become active homemakers' clubs; community clubs have become parent-
teacher associations, and equity societies have become co-operative
shipping associations.

If disintegration begins in earnest, it is difficult to check without
rather drastic measures. An attempt may be made to revive the
organization, but revivals are rarely successful during this period.
In the minds of many of its members the organization is not really
dead, because they still have the constitution, the records, and some
money in the treasury. It is simply "inactive." There does not seem
to be a thoroughly respectable ritual of demise for organizations,
and therefore many of them continue far beyond their span of usefulness and after the purposes or interests for which they were
originally intended have completely disappeared. The officers say
in great anxiety, "Why, we can't have it die on our hands."

(5) *"The road an organization travels."* If presented diagram-
matically, the life cycles just described would appear as drawn in
Figure 24. In this chart the time units must not be construed in
terms of years, although in some cases they might indicate years.
Superimposed on the first curve may be the stimulation and rise
periods of other groups. Another group can be expected to appear
on a local scene as the first shows a tendency to decline. This dia-

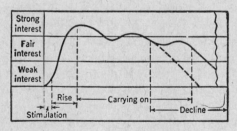

Figure 24

THE ROAD AN ORGANIZATION TRAVELS

Source: Kolb and Wileden, *Making Rural Organizations Effective,*
Bulletin 403, October, 1928, Agricultural Experiment Station, University of Wisconsin.

gram might carry the designation, "The Road an Organization Travels." The question which an organization leader or officer, or, for that matter, a member, may well ask himself is, "Where are we on this road just now?" Each period brings certain problems, and if one's location can be fairly well established, much can be done to anticipate and therefore to cope with the difficulties lurking in the next valley. The skillful leader, like the modern highway engineer, may find that he can fill up the low places by cutting down the hills.

UNEVEN RESPONSE OF PEOPLE TO GROUP ORGANIZATION

Another side of the shield, frequently not examined in this whole question of interest groups in rural society, is that of the uneven response of people to such groups. While some people in any local situation may identify themselves with many organizations, there are others who have no such affiliations. They simply do not belong; they are not "joiners." There is likewise a tendency for this unevenness to appear when one family or one locality is compared with another.

Students of rural society need to concern themselves not only with its group organization, but also with the response which people living in that society make to its groups. They need to stand off now and then and view the situation through the eyes of the local people; they need to ask such questions as the following: When is a community well organized? What is the capacity of a rural family for affiliation with and support of organizations? How is the development of personality related to its identification with social groups?

Variations in organization affiliation. Three measures can be employed to compare organization affiliations: locality to locality, family to family, and person to person. In order to have a concrete situation as an illustration, the results of a study in the five counties whose special interest organizations have been described will be very briefly reviewed.[14] The first evident variation was from locality to locality. Apparently there is something about a local situation which fosters or frowns upon organizations. Six school districts were found which averaged nineteen organizations per district, while six others averaged but eleven per district. The first

[14] Kirkpatrick and Kolb, *Rural Organizations and the Farm Family.* Madison: Research Bulletin 96, Agricultural Experiment Station, University of Wisconsin, November, 1929.

set might be called "high" organization districts and the second "low" organization districts. The variations from family to family are even more striking. All of the 282 families in the twelve districts were visited, and the results are brought together in Table 52. It is significant that over 28 per cent of the families were with-

TABLE 52. NUMBER OF ORGANIZATIONS WITH WHICH FAMILIES ARE AFFILIATED

Organizations with Which One or More Members of Family are Affiliated	All Districts (282 Families)		High Organization Districts (151 Families)		Low Organization Districts (131 Families)	
Number	Number	Per cent of Total	Number	Per cent of Total	Number	Per cent of Total
None	81	28.7	25	16.6	56	42.7
One	57	20.2	28	18.5	29	22.1
Two	63	22.4	32	21.2	31	23.7
Three	31	11.0	24	15.9	7	5.3
Four	15	5.3	11	7.3	4	3.1
Five	15	5.3	12	7.9	3	2.3
Six	8	2.8	8	5.3	...	...
Seven	5	1.8	5	3.3	...	...
Eight	6	2.1	5	3.3	1	.8
Nine	1	.4	1	.7	1	...
Average per family	2.0	....	2.6	....	1.2	....

out any organization affiliation; in the "high" districts it was only about 16 per cent, while in the "low" districts it was over 42 per cent. The organizations with which one or more members of the family were affiliated range from one to nine, the average being two.

Since the size of the family makes a difference, the comparison is made person to person. There were 924 persons ten years of age or over, in the families. About one fourth of these persons were without affiliations in the "high" districts; over two thirds, in the "low" districts. In positive terms, the average number of organizations in the "high" districts was 1.4 per person, while in the "low" districts it was but .4 per person.

A final comparison brings the families and the persons together. It was found that 34 per cent of the families had every member ten years of age or over affiliated with one or more organizations; these might be called "100 per cent families." At the other extreme, there were eighty-one families or over 28 per cent of the total,

which had no member affiliated with any organization. They might
be designated as "zero families." Again the variation between
"high" and "low" districts was significant. For example, the "low"
districts had nearly half (42.7 per cent) of their families in the zero
classification, while the "high" districts had over half (53.0 per
cent) of their families in the "100 per cent" group. On the whole,
women and girls were affiliated with more organizations than were
men and boys.

Such wide variations in the affiliations of rural people with organizations have many practical applications. For example, if a person
were to attempt to introduce a new organization, should he go to
"high" or to "low" organization districts, to "100 per cent" or to "zero"
families? This is a general problem, for similar variations are found
in all states where investigations have been made. The Illinois situation, for example, is well summarized in Table 53. Variations in

TABLE 53. EXTENT TO WHICH PERSONS ANSWERING THE
QUESTIONNAIRE WERE AFFILIATED WITH RURAL ORGANIZATIONS

(Localities represented, 306; counties, 60)

Organization	Number of Persons	Percentage of Total
Community clubs................	55	13
Farm bureau units..............	54	12
Parent-teacher associations.......	48	11
Home bureau units..............	40	9
Subordinate granges............	29	7
Community units................	28	6
Farmers' clubs..................	12	3
Miscellaneous..................	18 *	5
Total affiliated persons........	284	66
Non-affiliated persons..........	149	34
Total all persons reporting......	433	100

* Includes 7 members of women's clubs, 5 members of 4–H clubs, 4 members of community councils,
and 2 members of farmers' unions.

the extent to which persons are affiliated with various types of
organizations are shown to range from 13 per cent in the case of
community clubs to 3 per cent in that of farmers' clubs.

The Virginia study to which reference has been made concludes
that the majority of rural people, when questioned, seem to believe
in local organizations, but less than 20 per cent give them their
active support. In Madison and Union counties, Ohio, it was found
that in 610 farm families, 24 per cent had members belonging to
lodges, 16 per cent to Granges, 28 per cent to Farm Bureaus, and
33 per cent to 4–H clubs. The question is, why such variations?

Reasons for variations in response to groups. One is sure to be impressed with the wide variations in the response of people to group organization, and in their behavior with respect to group activity, which the situations described above display. Why there are such variations and what difference they make in communities and in people are still open questions, calling for more study and thought. People themselves recognize the condition but do not seem to go far in the explanation of the underlying reasons. One hears characterizations of this or that neighbor in such phrases as the following: "He belongs to everything," "She is always there," "He really supports his club," or, "She is a natural leader."

Careful analysis does reveal certain factors which are somehow related to or at least associated with this matter of group relationships. In the study of the 282 families, it was found, for example, that higher proportions of farm owners, higher proportions of native born heads of families, larger gross incomes, more periodicals taken, more books owned and borrowed, greater tendency to vote, more hours of radio auditing, of reading, and more kinds of recreation are apparently associated with high organization affiliations of families. Other factors, including the composition of the family, the possession of an automobile, a telephone, central heating system, central lighting system, and running water in the home, seem to have little positive relation to organization membership. Church affiliation and attendance and size of farm business resources do not appear to be significantly related; in fact, there is some evidence of a negative relationship.

According to all methods of analysis the factors pertaining to education and to cultural advancement, including periodicals taken, books owned, books borrowed, schooling of the operator, and time spent in radio auditing and in reading, apparently are among the most significant. But these things are merely related to or associated with organization behavior and cannot be regarded as causal factors in the situation. They may be the effects of other more basic causes. For example, a large number of periodicals taken and a high organization affiliation per family may both be results which go back to other parent reasons. There can be little doubt, however, that the whole cultural background and experience of a locality and of a family have much to do in shaping the patterns of organization response on the part of the people concerned.

Mutual influence of group and personality. In the introduction to the neighborhood chapter, Professor Cooley was quoted as saying that personality cannot exist without association or fellowship, and that human nature itself is but a trait of primary groups. Obviously, therefore, it is important to realize something of the mutual influence of the group and the person. One cannot exist without the other. The more important spheres of primary group life, Professor Cooley points out, are the family, the neighborhood, and the play group.

Some people have become concerned with recent tendencies in modern rural life, saying that the drift from primary or personal to secondary or impersonal forms of contact and from local neighborhood to the many different kinds of voluntary associations, or special interest organizations, endangers personality. They fear it will become distraught, pulled apart, by the many and diverse demands of widely different and separate group fealties. May it not be, however, that the presence of various interest groups offers an opportunity rather than a danger? Professor Cooley recognized that interest groups as well as locality groups can be either primary or face-to-face in character, else why did he include the play group in his classification? Various facets or sides of personality can be burnished and brightened by varied group contacts. Fortunately all of life need not be confined to one locality in days of rapid transit. Problems there will be, but there were personality and group problems in the days of the pioneer neighborhood. Different times bring different problems but also more opportunities for rural organizations. This idea finds expression in Miss Follett's call for group organization as a basis for new methods in politics. She says: "The reason we want organization is not to keep people within their neighborhoods, but to get them out." [15]

Professor J. K. Hart describes this mutual relationship which may exist between different interest groups and personality in the following fine statement: "Every membership in a new group brings some distinctive new touch to the personality of the individual. If he can find his way around the range of humanizing groups, he will thus find his way around into all the distinctive phases of humanity and he will become a complete human being." [16]

It is entirely possible, however, that the tendency toward multiplication of special interest groups which has been traced in this chapter may swing to an extreme. Some persons say that it has already done so.[17] Extreme specialization and division of labor

[15] Follett, M. P., *The New State, Group Organization the Solution of Popular Government*, p. 249. New York: Longmans, Green & Co., 1918.

[16] Hart, J. K., "Belonging to Too Many Groups," *Survey*, March 15, 1924.

[17] Taylor, H. C., *Proceedings of the American Country Life Association*, 1936, p. 144, "Education for Democracy." Chicago: University of Chicago Press.

may result in such complexity that common ground will be difficult
to find. Conflicting loyalties within the same individual, or overlapping authorities of special *ad hoc* governmental districts may
lead to confusion. An accumulation of highly specialized and pro-
fessionalized services in small rural communities may "bog down"
their whole financial structure. These are problems which will be
dealt with in the chapters on rural communities and local government.

INTERRELATIONSHIPS OF RURAL GROUPS

Finally a brief summary is presented of the interrelationships of
the various groups in rural society which have thus far been
studied. The family is the point from which to start.

First there are genetic groups, the individual family and the
great family, which trace back to natural origins. The family group
is difficult to classify because, for the adult members it is, in origin
at least, a voluntary association, while for the younger members
who are born into it, it is a genetic or natural group. Second, there
are locality groups, neighborhoods, villages and communities,
which occupy a territorial area and which have an ecology or
"mutual relation with their environments," as the biologists would
phrase it. And third, there are special interest groups.

Two significant changes in the relationships of families with these
various groups have taken place. First is the transfer in emphasis
from locality to interest as a major basis for group formation and
solidarity. In the settlement days nationality and kinship coupled
with isolation, due to restricted travel, laid the foundation for the
neighborhood as a primary locality group. Then, special interests
became recognized and could be satisfied only by the establishment of some organization, the formation of some association, or
the promotion of some activity. Locality, however, continues to
play its part, since certain types of special interest groups still form
in certain local areas. For example, 4—H clubs, homemakers' and
mothers' clubs are more likely to be found on the neighborhood
scale. Size and proximity are important factors because such
groups tend to be small and restricted in membership to neighboring families; they are also personal or primary in nature.

Local interest groups may become the axis about which the life
of the family group turns, provided there is sufficient identity of
interest. If not, then members of the family seek their satisfactions
in more scattered groups, non-localized or non-neighborhood in

character. In this event the older locality influence wanes and the newer, special interest waxes stronger. In some cases, therefore, locality as represented in neighborhood and interest as represented in activity or organization are co-ordinate. In other cases they are divergent. This accounts for the rise and the fall, the little more or the little less, as well as the interplay of these two main influences.

The second important change in interrelationships of rural groups is the more frequent and the more intimate association of members of the family with groups outside its local neighborhood and beyond its own immediate interests. Local, personal or primary groups are not enough. Farm families are aligning themselves with other families to form the larger rural community of town and country and the wider interest of a modern society. This wider movement is taking place on a locality as well as on an interest basis as the discussion has amply shown.[18] The wider locality contacts are in town-country communities and in rural-urban areas, while the wider interest associations are seen in such activities as breeders' associations, county health committees and in numerous voluntary associations, some organized on the community scale and others on the still wider scale of rural-urban relationships.

The practical implications of such changing relationships are many and they are of great importance to rural society and its leaders. Groups are always in process of change, some in short and some in long-time cycles, depending on many factors. Leaders who resist instead of taking advantage of the changing desires of their group members and of the more general trends of the times, soon find themselves in trouble; they may be bitter because, as they say, "the world is all against us," and, as a matter of fact, it is. Organizations and societies may easily outlive their usefulness, but still attempt to persist. On the other hand, if readjustments are continually attempted, new methods sought, new causes espoused, new group alignments made, then rural society, through its primary locality and its primary interest groups, as well as through its larger community and urban connections, may become dynamic, articulate, and group-conscious in the constructive sense, to the end that its interests, its objectives, and its future may be respected and made serviceable in the larger drama of national life.

[18] Kolb, J. H., *Family Life and Rural Organization*, p. 146. Adapted with permission from the *Publications of the American Sociological Society*, vol. XXIII, 1929.

DISCUSSION TOPICS

1. Write a case history or life story of some special interest group or organization which you know by first-hand contacts, such, for example, as a social club, a parent-teacher association, a co-operative marketing organization, a young people's society, a fraternity or sorority. Give special attention to the following points.

   a. Reasons and circumstances surrounding its origin.

   b. How members are recruited.

   c. What kind of leaders are chosen.

   d. Plans for keeping members loyal.

   e. Difficulties with other groups.

   f. Conflicts within the group.

   g. Readjustments made to overcome difficulties.

   h. Evidences of permanence or decline.

2. Make a list of all the social organizations such as community club, Grange, Union, Farm Bureau, parent-teacher association, 4–H Club, etc., which have members in a rural locality, with which you are acquainted. Do you think there are enough, too many or too few such organizations there? Give reasons for your answer.

3. Outline the social and the organization plan and policy of one of the national farmers' organizations, as the Grange, Farmers' Union, Farm Bureau, or of a state or national breeders' association.

4. Outline the rural and the organization plan and policy of one educational, social, or fraternal organization, as the parent-teacher association, the Kiwanis, Rotary, or other service club, the Royal Neighbors, P.E.O., or any other state or national organization of these types.

5. Enumerate and discuss briefly the social forces which have given rise to special interest groups in rural society.

6. What problems do interest groups create for a local community?

REFERENCE READINGS

Brunner, Edmund de S., and Irving Lorge, *Rural Trends in Depression Years.* New York: Columbia University Press, 1937. Chapter X, "Social Organizations."

Buck, S. J., *The Granger Movement.* Cambridge: Harvard University Press, 1913.

Butterworth, J. E., *The Parent-Teacher Association and Its Work.* New York: The Macmillan Company, 1928. The story of an organization movement.

Edwards, G. T., *The Farmers' Union Triangle.* Jamestown, N.D.: Farmers' Union Education Service, 1941.

Hibbard, B. H., *Marketing Agricultural Products*. New York: D. Appleton & Co., 1921. Part II has a brief statement of the origins and development of the various farmer organizations as Grange, Alliance, Equity, Union, Farm Bureau.

Kile, O. M., *The Farm Bureau Movement*. New York: The Macmillan Co., 1921.

Kirkpatrick, Kolb, Inge, and Wileden, *Rural Organizations and the Farm Family*. Madison: Research Bulletin 96, Agricultural Experiment Station, University of Wisconsin, 1929. Report of a study of rural organizations from the standpoint of the family and its individual members.

Kolb and Wileden, *Special Interest Groups*. Madison: Research Bulletin 84, Agricultural Experiment Station, University of Wisconsin, 1927. Report of a research study of special interest groups in five Wisconsin counties.

Lindstrom, D. E., and W. M. Dawson, *4-H Club Work: Effect on Capability and Personal Quality*. Urbana: Bulletin 451, University of Illinois, Agricultural Experiment Station, 1939.

Lively, C. E., and R. B. Almack, *Some Rural Social Agencies in Missouri*. Columbia: University of Missouri, Bulletin 307, 1931.

Manny, Theo. B., *The Ohio Farm Bureau Federation from the Farmers' Viewpoint*. Washington, D.C.: United States Department of Agriculture, Bureau of Agricultural Economics, in co-operation with the Ohio State University and Federal Farm Board. Preliminary Report, April, 1931.

Smith, C. B., *Boys' and Girls' 4-H Clubs*. Washington, D.C.: United States Department of Agriculture, 1926. A popular description of a widely distributed organization.

Wing, D. C., *Trends in National Farm Organizations*. Washington, D.C.: 1940 Year Book of Agriculture, United States Department of Agriculture.

16

Rural - Urban Relationships

OUT AT THE END of the road stands the city with its smokestacks and its jagged sky line. The traffic on that great American highway moves in two directions — toward the city and toward the country. Moreover, it is not simply a physical highway for the transport of goods and people, but an open channel for the interplay of ideas and attitudes. Ten and fifteen years ago students of rural society were not so conscious of urban influences upon rural life; they were more concerned with the great cityward drift of country people. Present-day studies of rural social organization, however, cannot fail to recognize the importance of the city.

Farmers, villagers and their families have many direct contacts with urban centers, and conversely, city dwellers are in closer touch with rural affairs than they were formerly. Indirect contacts between city and country, more subtle in character, have likewise multiplied greatly, and they are determining more and more the form and content of rural life and agriculture. Among these indirect forces are not only the radio, the moving pictures, the daily newspaper, the weekly or monthly magazine with national advertising, but also those other forms of control and policy-making which are inherent in plans for linking local institutions such as stores, banks, churches or schools with centralized agencies whose leadership and headquarters are located in distant city centers.

Finally, the great flow and ebb of millions of country people into the cities and back again has made profound changes in rural-urban relationships. This action and reaction of mobility and of contacts have continued long enough to make many general differences between rural and urban centers less pronounced. Changes and adjustments have been made in merchandising practices, in type of agriculture, in forms of social activities and even in those population characteristics by which rural and urban were formerly distinguished. Now many differences may be found within urban or within rural populations which are greater than those existing between the two. Hence, the old dichotomy of society into rural and urban has less and less meaning as a method for comparison and study. Rural and urban are becoming more relative terms which can be scaled by gradients out from a city center.

THE RISE AND FALL OF CITY CENTERS

A background for viewing the changing rural-urban relationships in long-time perspective is necessary. This can be found in the great dynamics of population mobility described in an earlier chapter, and in the dramatic story of the rapid rise of great American cities with their metropolitan areas. In the half-century, 1880 to 1930, the proportion of the nation's population classed as urban nearly doubled. For each of the decades in that period there was an ever-increasing concentration of people in city centers and their immediate environs. The Sixteenth Census of the United States, 1940, reported that the 140 metropolitan districts, each with a city center of at least 100,000 population, contained 47.6 per cent of the total national population; in 1930 the proportion was almost exactly the same, namely, 47.5 per cent. To be sure, there was included in these districts or zones, ranging from twenty to fifty miles, a large population which by regular census definition would be termed "rural," but which possessed characteristics neither strictly rural nor urban in the traditional meanings of those terms. Later sections of this chapter will describe this situation.

The rapid rise of cities and the concentration of people and socio-economic activities within and around them was not a matter of haphazard geographic arrangements. There was the tendency for such concentrations to occur at the waterfronts, especially along the Atlantic seaboard, and in the Great Lakes region, as well as along other transportation routes, particularly wherever there were necessary "breaks" in the systems. The breaks would come at assembly and distribution points, where there were transfers from water to rail routes or the reverse, where car lots had to be broken, and at division points.[1]

Reversal of trend in city concentration. The population movement toward the deep-water rim, of course, did not spread evenly over the whole bordering territory, but concentrated in large cities. Such concentrations were impressive during the two decades, 1910

[1] Cooley, C. H., "The Theory of Transportation," *Publications of the American Economic Association,* vol. IX, May, 1894; and Edward Ullman, "A Theory of Location for Cities," *American Journal of Sociology,* vol. XLVI, no. 6, May, 1941.

TABLE 54. POPULATION CONCENTRATION IN A ZONE EXTENDING APPROXIMATELY 50 MILES INLAND FROM THE SEABOARD AND THE GREAT LAKES, 1900–1930 * †

Census Year	Population within Zone	Per cent of Total U.S. Population within Zone	Increase within Zone Since Preceding Census	Per cent of Total U.S. Increase within Zone
1900........	27,842,288	36.6	5,495,234	42.1
1910........	35,633,796	38.7	7,791,508	48.8
1920........	43,865,221	41.5	8,231,425	59.9
1930........	55,413,567	45.1	11,548,346	67.7

* Compiled from *United States Census Reports.* The table is computed on county units by the author, R. D. McKenzie, "The Rise of Metropolitan Communities," *Recent Social Trends,* chap. IX.

† The area of the zone is 435,863 square miles, or 14.65 per cent of total land area of the United States. It may be defined as a region approximately fifty miles wide which skirts the salt-water rim of the country and the southern shores of Lakes Ontario, Erie, and Michigan.

to 1930. The great Empire State Building in New York City, with its shaft reaching skyward a quarter of a mile, is a symbol of the age of city building, as well as a masterpiece of construction engineering.

Then came the industrial *débâcle* of 1929 and the nineteen-thirties, when cities literally spewed back into the country their accumulated millions. Some of the results of this reversal of population movement are recorded in the census reports for 1940. Central cities within the metropolitan districts grew only 6.1 per cent during the decade, 1930 to 1940, a fraction of a per cent less than the total rural increase (6.4) in that same period. But for the first time in American history, 29 per cent of the large cities of 100,000 or more people experienced a population decline.[2] Five of the ten largest cities actually lost population, and a sixth remained practically stationary. The reverse trend can in no sense be interpreted as the beginning of the end of urban growth and development, but rather as a forerunner of new patterns of population distribution and concentration, two of which will be briefly described in following paragraphs.

The urban population situation in 1940 can be observed from Tables 55 to 57. In that year there were 1140 cities of 10,000 or more population; 63 of them, with over 1,000,000 people, were unincorporated. In the regular census reports some of these people would be classed among the rural non-farm. The total population of 63,767,269 represented 85.7 per cent of the urban population

[2] Gillette, J. M., "Some Population Shifts in the United States," *American Sociological Review,* vol. 6, no. 5, October, 1941.

TABLE 55. INCORPORATED AND UNINCORPORATED CITIES OF
10,000 OR MORE POPULATION, 1940

Size Classes	Total		Incorporated		Unincorporated	
	Number	Population	Number	Population	Number	Population
Total..............	1,140	63,767,269	1,077	62,715,897	63	1,051,372
10,000 to 100,000...	1,048	25,779,280	985	24,727,908	63	1,051,372
100,000 to 1,000,000 .	87	22,077,123	87	22,077,123	0	..
1,000,000 or more...	5	15,910,866	5	15,910,866	0	..

Sources: Incorporated, *Sixteenth Census of United States*, 1940, vol. I, *Population*, Table 9, p. 25. Unincorporated, *ibid.*, special release, *Population of Unincorporated Communities.*

TABLE 56. INCORPORATED CITIES OF 10,000 OR MORE.
NUMBER AND POPULATION BY DECADES, 1910 TO 1940

Year	Number	Population	Increase in per cent
1940.............	1,077	62,715,897	7.5
1930.............	982	58,340,077	30.2
1920.............	752	44,804,443	31.6
1910.............	597	34,053,318	...

Source: *Sixteenth Census of United States*, 1940, vol. I, *Population*, Tables 13 and 14.

TABLE 57. POPULATION OF METROPOLITAN DISTRICTS, 1940 AND 1930

Metropolitan Districts	Population		Increase	
	1940	1930	Number	Per cent
Total (140 districts)...........	62,965,773	57,602,865	5,362,908	9.3
In central cities...............	42,796,170	40,343,442	2,452,728	6.1
Outside central cities..........	20,169,603	17,259,423	2,910,180	16.9

Source: United States Bureau of the Census, *Sixteenth Census of the United States*, 1940, *Population: Number of Inhabitants*, United States Summary, First Series, p. 71. Washington, D.C.. Government Printing Office, 1941.

and 48.4 per cent of the total population. These percentages changed very little from those of 1930. There was a significant change, however, in the rate of increase. The increase in the incorporated centers was about 30 per cent between 1920 and 1930 and between 1910 and 1920, but it fell to only 7.5 per cent between 1930 and 1940, which is evidence of decentralizing tendencies.

Since 1940 there have been many "irregularities" in population trends. The Census of the United States, from sample analyses, estimates an increase in the total urban population of about 7,286,000 from April, 1940, to January, 1945 — a gain of 5.5 per cent. Much of this gain is attributable to the large numbers of people moving to cities to work in war industries, the increase in the number of females, and in the number of children under fourteen years of age living in urban areas.[3]

"Metropolitan Constellations." The late Professor McKenzie explained that large cities seldom appear isolated or alone, but nearly always surrounded by clusters of smaller centers of varying sizes with which they are closely related in a sort of complex. These he called "Metropolitan Constellations." Table 57 compares populations of the metropolitan districts in 1940 with 1930. One interesting figure is the 16.9 per cent increase in population outside the central cities. It is a larger increase than for the total rural non-farm population, 14.2 per cent, and indicates a trend away from cities. It means that a third of the people were living in the outlying areas of the metropolitan districts, not in the city centers.

The commercial interdependence of the central city and its satellites can be shown from reports of the Census of Distribution. If we take Chicago as an example, three zones can be marked off: the first, with a twenty-mile radius from the loop, contains twenty-one smaller cities; the second, twenty to forty miles out, has six centers, and the third, forty to eighty miles away, includes ten cities. A comparison of the average number of persons per store and the average expenditures per store for food, wearing apparel and general merchandise, indicates that the influence of the central city gradually tapers off.

The tendency to form large metropolitan clusters is not wholly inspired by commerce and industry. Certain other advantages accrue to a center of high specialization and great division of labor. Such centers attract those types of social institutions, and those leaders in the professions and in the arts and the sciences who contribute to and benefit from highly differentiated services. Large cities possess almost unlimited opportunities for diversification and specialization, not only for business and commerce but for amusements and for social and professional contacts. This constitutes an important corollary attraction or "lure" of the city.

Metropolitan influences, however, extend beyond immediate

[3] *Census of the United States, Population,* series P-S, no. 4, April 28, 1945, and P-45, no. 5, May 22, 1945.

circling cities to rural areas, and this is an important reason for knowledge of city development and influence on the part of students of rural society. One means of showing the more general zones or regions of metropolitan influence is by mapping daily newspaper circulation areas. This is done in the full-page map (page 361), and changes between 1920 and 1929 are shown.

Cities used as centers in the newspaper circulation map include the Federal Reserve Banking Centers, both headquarters and branches, together with six others, making a total of forty-one regions. Each region is an area in which one half or more of the newspaper circulation comes from the particular center.

Other services determining metropolitan regions of influence are those of trade, including wholesaling, of industry, and of financing. Because of motor transportation, with truck and delivery service, there is apparently a tendency for certain functions to cumulate in the dominant centers and for others to gravitate to the sub-centers. Thus, there is a sort of regional economy evolving, whereby certain self-sufficiency or independence is being sought in such matters as industries, markets, and financial control. Small cities tend to fit into the region of which they are a part, or, if they are too far removed from large centers, attempt to assume functions similar to those of the intermediate cities. Professor Gras describes the process as follows:

> Just as the development of towns in town economy displays steps or phases, so does the growth of metropolitan economy illustrate certain steps which stand out more or less clearly. In the first part of the growth we see the prospective center reach out its tentacles by land and sea to secure supplies and to sell goods. It creates a situation and a feeling of dependence, although its means of exploitation are strictly limited. In short, it begins to organize the market. Then comes the development of manufacturing and transportation. In many parts of America these two grew up hand in hand, and with them, but lagging a bit behind, came the close financial knitting together of the whole area.[4]

There are those who would argue that this slowly forming metropolitan region may become a rival in economic administration and control to the present political system based upon federal, state, and county units. The city is more than a congeries of streets,

[4] Burgess, E. W., *The Urban Community*, p. 183. Chicago: University of Chicago Press, 1926.

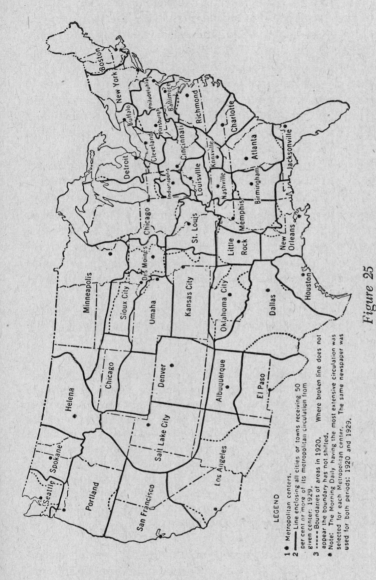

LEGEND

1 ● Metropolitan centers.
2 ── Line enclosing all cities or towns receiving 50
     per cent or more of its metropolitan circulation from
     given center: 1929.
3 ∙∙∙∙ Boundaries of areas in 1920.   Where broken line does not
     appear the boundary has not shifted.
● Note: The Morning Daily having the most extensive circulation was
     selected for each Metropolitan center. The same newspaper was
     used for both periods: 1920 and 1929.

Figure 25

METROPOLITAN REGIONS IN THE UNITED STATES AS DEFINED BY DAILY
NEWSPAPER CIRCULATION: 1920 AND 1929

Source: *Recent Social Trends*, McGraw-Hill, 1933.

buildings, telephones, people and service institutions, as Professor
Burgess well points out. He adds:

> The city is rather a state of mind, a body of customs and tradi-
> tions, and of the organized attitudes and sentiments that inhere in
> these customs and are transmitted with this tradition. In other
> words, the city is not merely a physical mechanism and an artificial
> construction. It is involved in the vital processes of the people who
> compose it; it is a product of nature, and particularly of human
> nature.[5]

If this "state of mind" and "organized attitude" does follow the
mechanisms of trade, market and finance out into the larger metropolitan regions already described, then rural society will soon
assume vastly different aspects. The mutual impacts of rural and
urban ways of life will be considered in the next section, but the
point of the present argument is that rural and urban are not
separate entities, and that students of rural society need to famil-
iarize themselves with the rise, the development, and the influence
of cities and metropolitan areas.

"*Rural-urban fringe.*" A second relatively recent pattern of population concentration, in addition to the constellation of a number
of smaller centers around the large city center, is what the late
Professor Wehrwein termed the "fringe" or zone surrounding any
large city. He said that it was an area of transition between well-
recognized urban land-uses and the area devoted to agricultural
purposes.[6] This interpretation represents a different conception
of rural-urban relationships from that of the early German writer,
von Thunen, whose scheme of land-use was a series of concentric
circles surrounding a city. All the land beyond the boundaries of
the city, he declared to be agricultural. He made no provision for
a transitional zone between the rural and the urban. Some recent
students of society have also assumed a dichotomy of either "rural"
or "urban." This, together with the arbitrary population limits set
by the census reports, has tended to obscure recent developments
in the rural-urban scene.

Improved communication and transportation facilities, together
with the expansion of electrification and other public utilities, have
encouraged settlements of people in areas contiguous to cities. The
movement is a two-direction affair. It is an "escape" from con-

[5] Park and Burgess, *The City*, p. 1. Chicago: University of Chicago Press,
1925.
[6] Wehrwein, George S., "The Rural-Urban Fringe," *Economic Geography*,
July, 1942.

gested city centers, a thrusting-out into country areas of certain urban activities or land-uses, some unwanted or "condemned" by city ordinances, and often the result of suburban development or subdivision promotion. On the other hand, it is a movement of farm and village people in toward urban opportunities for employment, markets, education, and other social services. For example, in the Madison fringe area, to be described presently, six out of every ten adults were reared on farms or in villages. A third of the families had never lived in the city.

Reports of recent studies make it quite clear that the force of these two movements coming together is making for a new pattern of living which is different from the traditional urban or rural forms. In times of industrial curtailment, for example, the "fringe" or "satellite" areas tend to absorb the shock; families step up their part-time farming activities. In periods of expanding employment opportunities, the city draws more heavily upon this area for workers, and non-farm activities of the families approach full-time proportions.[7]

Many problems arise in this transition area because neither the urban nor the rural social institutions or habits of social life are fully adjusted to the new situation. There are increased demands for more and better school facilities, thus increasing the already heavy tax load on real estate — farms, acreages, lots. Land values rise and the former ways of farming cannot survive. Certain commercial recreational activities are promoted over which local town governments fail to exercise adequate control. City authorities, thinking the solution to be in the direction of expanding the city limits, seek to incorporate adjoining areas. People in those areas resist the attempt, organize their own public service; they even incorporate as villages. Then, between or surrounding such organized sub-units there are likely to be disorganized areas — slums and untoward conditions — endangering the entire rural-urban relationship. There is great opportunity for some political inventions by which the whole situation can develop, the urban center assuming its portion of responsibility and the fringe areas having freedom to assume some local direction and control for certain of their group interests. Families with small children have little concern for "downtown" schools or playgrounds.

[7] Conklin, Howard E., "The Rural-Urban Economy of the Elmira-Corning Region," *The Journal of Land and Public Utility Economics*, February, 1944, vol. XX, no. 1; Gordon, W. R., *Satellite Acres*. Kingston: Experiment Station Bulletin 282, Rhode Island State College, March, 1942.

The clashes and tensions that develop in the fringe area are well illustrated in a recent study of what, in 1923 when first surveyed, was an agricultural service station village and its rural community, Webster, New York.[8] Today it is the fringe of Rochester, New York. The process began when the overcrowded condition of the city's high schools resulted in towns within the metropolitan area sending pupils to Webster High School. Soon people from the city began to move to this attractive village. Taking up citizenship, they soon tried to accomplish "reforms," especially in the schools. In a short time there were three distinct groups, villagers who "belonged," the farmers, and the newcomers, known locally as "commuters." The farmers resented interference with their schools, the commuters having inspired a movement for consolidation. The "superior attitude" of the new population, together with their failure to conform to the local mores with respect to exchange of work and borrowing, soon set them apart. The villagers feared for their political dominance, in local government, in the village social organizations, and even in their churches. The commuters complained of the conservatism of the community and resented their exclusion from personal fellowship with "the natives," especially since they had come to Webster because of the importance they placed on rural living and rural values.

The situation can be further illustrated by a brief review of a study of the fringe area of Madison, Wisconsin.[9] In the decade, 1930 to 1940, the city itself increased by 16.5 per cent to a population of about 67,000; the metropolitan area, exclusive of the city, increased 69 per cent in the same period. The "fringe" was delineated by use of three indices: (1) proportion of non-farm families to all families, (2) density of non-farm population per square mile, and (3) assessed valuation of land and buildings per acre. The forty-nine township sections thus selected were found to contain a total of 3700 non-farm families. The most striking characteristic discovered about these families was their large number of children. Children under five years represented 20 per cent of the total population, while those under fifteen years were 40 per cent. Only 3 per cent of the people were sixty years of age or older.

Table 58 and Figure 26 show the population distribution by age

[8] Koos, Earl L., and Edmund de S. Brunner, *Suburbanization in Webster, New York*. New York: University of Rochester, 1945.
[9] Rodehaver, Myles W., adapted from an unpublished thesis, Department of Rural Sociology, University of Wisconsin, and an administrative release to the Madison Area Planning Council, June 28, 1945.

TABLE 58. DISTRIBUTION BY AGE OF MADISON FRINGE, CITY. AND FARM POPULATION OF DANE COUNTY

Place	Per cent under 5 Years	Per cent under 15 Years	Per cent 25–39 Years	Per cent 60 Years and over
Fringe................	20.1	40.0	30.4	3.1
Madison.............	6.6	20.1	26.4	10.5
Rural-farm (Dane County)	8.8	28.1	18.7	10.2

classes and give comparison with the city of Madison and with the farm population of the county. The actual size of the immediate family, comprised of head, wife, and children, for the fringe families was 3.8; for the city of Madison, 2.9; for the rural non-farm population of the state, 3.2; and for the state's farm population, 3.7. Such comparison suggests the importance of more discriminating studies of rural and urban population fertility. They might show that the urban population is not "dying out," but those families with

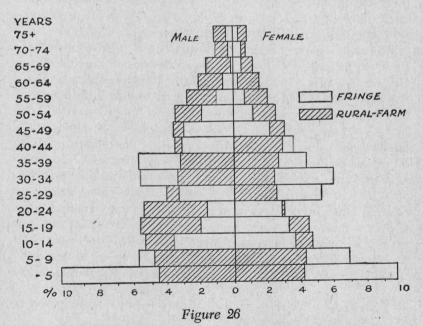

Figure 26

AGE-SEX DISTRIBUTION FOR FRINGE AND FOR
DANE COUNTY RURAL-FARM

children and going to have children are "moving out" from city centers.

The intermediate or transitional character of the rural-urban zone is further attested by the record of social and economic contacts of the non-farm families in the Madison fringe. Three fourths of the breadwinners were employed in the city. An equal proportion of the families did their "grocery" shopping in the city, not necessarily "on the square," but often in the secondary shopping centers near the city limits. Nine out of ten families used the Madison banks and commercial recreation places. Only six out of ten went to Madison for church services. Seventeen per cent had children in the city elementary schools and 13 per cent in high schools. Thus, for many social activities and institutions, such as education, religion, and non-commercial recreation — picnics, outings, parties, children's games — the fringe families focused their efforts outside the city, and in many instances joined with the so-called rural farm families also living within the fringe area or near-by.

Similar conditions prevail elsewhere. For example, Professor Butterworth of Cornell University reports that there were seventy-six one-, two-, and three-teacher schools around Ithaca, a city of about 20,000 population in 1940, which are not included in the prevailing central rural community school systems. About forty of them contract with the city for most of their grades, nine through twelve. The rest are carrying on in an independent manner. It is a sort of educational "no man's land" to which neither the rural nor the urban systems are adapted.

The Changing Design of Rural-Urban Relationships

It thus becomes evident, as we examine numerous current situations, that a city does not really end at its legal or corporate limits nor even at the edge of the rural-urban fringe; it influences, and is influenced by, the characteristics and activities of people who live and work in areas beyond. This is the result of common and continual readjustments, the urban center adapting its functions to a wider circle, and both village and country accommodating themselves to greater conformity with the city. A design or pattern of rural-urban relationships is therefore finally formed which can be mapped and studied.

In order to examine such relationships a plan was devised for the analysis of the concentric zones extending out from cities.

Eighteen medium-sized cities, scattered throughout the nation, were studied.[10] The county containing the city was called the "city county" and was treated as a whole, that is, the city figures were included in the county totals. In all 347 counties, about nineteen to each urban center were involved. Counting the cities, 10.2 per cent of the national population was included. In practically all indices used, the regional and national totals in this sample differed little, if at all, from regional and national totals as given in the United States Census. For convenience, zones were plotted on a county basis, counties contiguous to the urban centers being chosen to represent areas of tributary influence. Wholesale grocery areas mapped in a supplement to the *Market Data Handbook*[11] were used as guides in selecting counties and in forecasting the points where the influence of other cities might appear. All counties immediately bordering the city county were designated as Tier One Counties; counties bordering the first tier were called Tier Two Counties, and so on, until the concentric character of the entire design was traced.[12]

This section of the chapter will present first, two measures of rural-urban relationships as they were discovered in a single city, Des Moines, Iowa, in order to make the plan of the entire study more clear. Secondly, a few of the more significant measures for all of the eighteen areas will be grouped under such headings as population, agricultural, trade, and educational relations. To show the changing character of the design, it is necessary to examine not only the situation in 1930, the last year for which complete information is available, but also conditions which prevailed in earlier

[10] The population of these cities in 1930 ranged from 20,760 to 634,394. Three were less than 50,000 population. Six had between 50,000 and 80,000; five between 110,000 and 183,000 and four over 300,000. The cities were: Binghamton, New York; Columbia, South Carolina; Des Moines, Iowa; Fargo, North Dakota; Fort Worth, Texas; Harrisburg, Pennsylvania; Lincoln, Nebraska; Milwaukee, Wisconsin; Montgomery, Alabama; Nashville, Tennessee; Pine Bluff, Arkansas; Portland, Oregon; Richmond, Virginia; San Francisco, California; Springfield, Illinois; Toledo, Ohio; Wichita, Kansas; Williamsport, Pennsylvania. With the exception of San Francisco, all large metropolitan groups such as New York, Chicago, or Boston, were omitted to avoid, as far as possible, complicating the story of rural-urban relationships by interjecting the factor of suburbanism.

[11] United States Bureau of Foreign and Domestic Commerce, *Domestic Commerce Series* no. 30, 1929.

[12] For a more complete statement regarding the method used, the location of the areas and for many more measures than can be included in the chapter, see chapter V and Appendix D in Brunner and Kolb, *Rural Social Trends*. New York: McGraw-Hill, 1933.

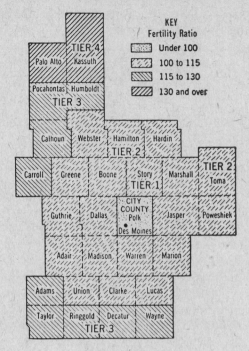

Figure 27

FERTILITY RATIOS IN THE DES MOINES AREA,
BY TIERS OF COUNTIES, 1930

Source: Brunner and Kolb, *Rural Social Trends.* McGraw-Hill, 1933.

decades. Comparisons are therefore made for 1910, 1920 and 1930,
when possible.

The case of the Des Moines area; an illustration. For the purpose
of illustrating the type of measurement and the twofold comparison
made in a single area, one item has been selected from population
data, fertility, and one from agricultural data, value of field crops
per acre.

Fertility may be measured by taking the ratio of children under
ten to all women twenty to forty-five. The data for Des Moines
show that this ratio is lowest in the city county and increases with
each succeeding tier. There appears to be a relationship in any
measured unit of population between the birth rate and the distance from the city. This is illustrated in Figure 27. Furthermore,
as may be seen in Table 59, this same relationship existed in both
1910 and 1920. It is also clear that in the city county, and in all the

TABLE 59. RATIO OF CHILDREN UNDER 10 TO WOMEN 20 TO 45
YEARS OF AGE IN THE DES MOINES AREA, BY TIERS OF COUNTIES

Year	City County per cent	Tiers of Counties			
		First per cent	Second per cent	Third per cent	Fourth per cent
1910	87.2	119.7	120.1	131.9	153.9
1920	80.9	115.4	116.0	123.2	142.5
1930	78.9	107.4	109.6	118.9	135.4

Source: *Thirteenth Census of the United States, 1910, Population,* vol. II; *Fourteenth Census of the United States, 1920, Population,* vol. III; *Fifteenth Census of the United States, 1930, Population,* vol. III, Part I.

others, the ratio has been falling during the two decades prior to
1930. The points of difference between 1910 and 1930 are greater
in the city county than in any other tier of counties except the
fourth, but even here the proportionate decrease is not so great
as in the city itself. This comparison suggests a graduated influence
in the operation of forces controlling birth rate as one moves from
the urban county to rural counties surrounding it.

Values of field crops per acre may be followed in Table 60. In

TABLE 60. VALUE PER ACRE OF FIELD CROPS IN THE DES MOINES
AREA, BY TIERS OF COUNTIES

Year	City County	Tiers of Counties			
		First	Second	Third	Fourth
1910	$11.33	$ 9.58	$ 8.73	$ 7.67	$ 6.84
1920	31.85	27.78	27.24	25.76	26.63
1930	17.70	14.29	13.59	12.58	15.12

Source: *Thirteenth Census of the United States; 1910, Agriculture,* vol. VI; *Fourteenth Census of the United States: 1920, Agriculture,* vol. VI; *Fifteenth Census of the United States: 1930, Agriculture,* vol. I.

this Des Moines area the per acre value of crops is highest in the
city county, and decreases with distance in the first three tiers, as
is shown in Figure 28. The story of agricultural prosperity which
culminated in 1920 and the ensuing prolonged depression is told in
these figures, for the rise and the fall of values are certainly abrupt.

Other relationships, therefore, can be examined in terms of distance from cities and over periods of time. Other indices will now
be studied from these two points of view, covering the entire
eighteen areas selected for study.

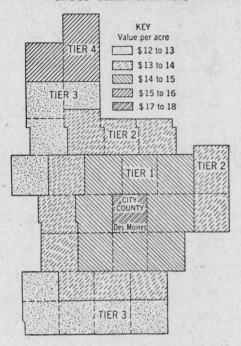

Figure 28

VALUE PER ACRE OF FIELD CROPS IN THE DES
MOINES AREA IN 1930, BY TIERS OF COUNTIES

Source: Brunner and Kolb, *Rural Social Trends.* McGraw-Hill, 1933.

Population relations. It is evident from the Des Moines area that
the design of rural-urban relationships has at least two important
features: first, a gradient character, that is, it tends to show gradual
variations as the distance from the urban center increases, and
second, a tendency to change with time. Population characteristics
vary rather definitely as one proceeds away from or toward the
city, but the differences seem to lessen with time.

(1) *Number of children varies directly with distance from urban
center.* Children have been the most distinguishing characteristic
of rural society, hence it is important, first of all, to compare the
changing fertility ratio or the replenishing power of rural and urban
population. The ratio of children under ten to women twenty to
forty-five increases definitely as Table 61 shows, as one goes away
from the city county to outlying tiers. This is true for the total
population, but is even more pronounced when the rural popula-

TABLE 61. RATIO OF CHILDREN UNDER 10 TO WOMEN 20 TO 45
YEARS OF AGE IN THE TOTAL AND IN THE RURAL POPULATION,
BY TIERS OF COUNTIES — 18 AREAS

Year	City County per cent	Tiers of Counties			
		First per cent	Second per cent	Third per cent	Fourth per cent
Total population					
1910........................	93.5	133.5	139.7	141.8	156.9
1920........................	90.8	125.8	134.1	136.2	142.8
1930........................	84.7	119.6	125.2	124.2	126.0
Rural population					
1910........................	138.1	144.3	148.2	152.2	163.5
1920........................	130.9	139.2	144.0	147.0	150.9
1930........................	123.4	131.8	136.3	137.4	134.5

Source: *Thirteenth Census of the United States,* 1910, *Population,* vols. II and III; *Fourteenth Census of the United States,* 1920, *Population,* vol. III; *Fifteenth Census of the United States,* 1930, *Population,* vol. III.

tion is taken separately. In both instances the tier one counties hold an intermediate position between the city county and tier two counties and those beyond. Proximity of city is related to the replenishing power of the population, and the gradient character of this design is evident in every region, although there are some variations from state to state.

Similar results are secured when the effective birth rate is calculated in terms of the number of children under one year of age for each one thousand population. Rural districts have a consistently higher proportion of such births, the figure increasing as the outer tiers of counties are reached. Thus, it is apparent that the farm is still the seed-bed of America, but it is equally clear that this function is not distributed equally among all country districts: their distance from the urban centers causes variations.

An interesting question arises at this point; namely, what is the relation between birth rates and population growth? The answer is that a negative relationship prevails between birth rates and the growth of population, and what is more important, this inverse relationship increases with the distance from the city.[13] This suggests that population growth in any area is, after all, more a matter of migration than natural rate of increase. According to this line of reasoning, those counties removed from urban centers may not

[13] See Brunner and Kolb, *Rural Social Trends,* p. 119. New York: McGraw-Hill, 1933. Series of correlations showing this relationship.

expect to grow by virtue of relatively larger families. Their function is to rear children to restock the city counties.

(2) *Birth rates begin to equalize between rural and urban.* Declining birth rates and fertility ratios are recognized national phenomena, but it has not been realized that the rate of decline is greatest in those counties removed from cities. Rates of decline calculated upon the basis of the fertility ratios given in the preceding table are brought together in Table 62 for both total and rural

TABLE 62. RATE OF DECLINE IN FERTILITY RATIOS FOR TOTAL
AND FOR RURAL POPULATION BETWEEN 1910 AND 1930

Year	City County per cent	Tiers of Counties			
		First per cent	Second per cent	Third per cent	Fourth per cent
Total population.............	9.5	10.4	10.4	12.4	19.6
Rural population.............	10.6	8.7	8.0	9.7	17.7

population in the eighteen selected areas. The greater rate of decline in fertility rates for the outer tiers of counties suggests that the general decline in birth rates which has been noted, probably began later in these outlying counties. If this continues, the future may see less difference between rural and urban groups, in which case rural America will be making a smaller proportional contribution to the population of the nation than it has in the past.

(3) *Age groups vary definitely from tier to tier.* Both birth rate and migration are closely related to and influenced by the changing age distribution of the population, in rural as well as urban areas. Two age comparisons are presented in tabular form, first the proportion under ten years, and second, the proportion of those twenty-one to forty-five, in the total and the rural population. These appear in Tables 63 and 64.

From these tables it is quite evident that there are graduated differences between rural and urban, depending again on proximity or remoteness to cities. Rural and urban are matters of degree. Age composition of the population is convincing evidence, since rural tiers of counties have a consistently larger proportion under ten years and under twenty-one years. At the other end of the scale, rural counties have a greater proportion of people over forty-five years than the city county. For the under-ten group the

TABLE 63. PROPORTION OF CHILDREN UNDER 10 YEARS OF AGE
IN THE TOTAL AND IN THE RURAL POPULATION, BY TIERS OF
COUNTIES — 18 AREAS

Year	City County per cent	Tiers of Counties			
		First per cent	Second per cent	Third per cent	Fourth per cent
Total population					
1910.....................	19.2	22.7	23.4	23.9	25.5
1920.....................	19.1	22.1	22.8	23.2	23.8
1930.....................	17.7	20.2	20.9	21.0	21.6
Rural population					
1910.....................	22.6	23.6	24.2	23.6	26.1
1920.....................	22.6	23.0	23.6	24.0	24.7
1930.....................	21.0	21.1	21.7	21.8	22.3

Source: *Thirteenth Census of the United States*, 1910, *Population*, vols. II and III; *Fourteenth Census of the United States*, 1920, *Population*, vol. III; *Fifteenth Census of the United States*, 1930, *Population*, vol. III.

TABLE 64. PROPORTION 21 TO 45 YEARS OF AGE IN THE TOTAL
AND IN THE RURAL POPULATION, BY TIERS OF COUNTIES
— 18 AREAS

Year	City County per cent	Tiers of Counties			
		First per cent	Second per cent	Third per cent	Fourth per cent
Total population					
1920.....................	40.0	33.4	32.9	33.4	34.2
1930.....................	38.9	32.6	32.2	32.7	34.0
Rural population					
1920.....................	34.3	32.3	32.0	32.3	33.8
1930.....................	34.3	31.3	31.0	31.3	33.2

Source: *Fourteenth Census of the United States*, 1920, *Population*, vol. III; *Fifteenth Census of the United States*, 1930, *Population*, vol. III.

gradation by tiers, both for total and rural population, is definite
as the distance from the urban centers is increased, especially for
1910 and 1920. When rural population is divided into its two component parts, farm and non-farm (the majority of which is village),
the trend for the farm group is consistent, as anticipated. The increase from the city county (20.7) to tier one (21.6) continues to tier
four (23.0), and the trend remains significantly uniform when the
national totals are slipped into regional divisions. Rural non-farm

population, however, shows no appreciable variation when passing from tier to tier; children are native to farms, not to villages.

The proportion of youth from ten to twenty-one years of age shows tendencies similar to those under ten, but in less marked degree. Here are seen the effects of the migration of youth to cities. In the group twenty-one to forty-five years, however, a reversal of this trend is apparent, the city county being high, with a sharp tapering off until tier four is reached, when there is some indication of an upturn.

Agricultural relations. Many comparisons were made for agriculture and its changing relations considered from the standpoint of proximity or remoteness to urban centers. Such comparisons show that the distance from the city is as potent in agricultural affairs as it proved to be in population characteristics, although it has probably received less recognition. Trends in such agricultural relations measured by tiers and by decades will be summarized under four headings: land in farms, its ownership, its value, and its uses.

(1) *Proportion of land in farms decreasing near cities.* The general tendency for the proportion of land in farms to decrease in the East and South and to increase in the Far West, between 1910 and 1930, was very evident in the eighteen groups of counties selected for special study. When all were combined (Table 65), an unmistak-

TABLE 65. PROPORTION IN FARMS OF ALL LAND, BY TIERS OF
COUNTIES — 18 AREAS

Year	City County per cent	Tiers of Counties			
		First per cent	Second per cent	Third per cent	Fourth per cent
1910........................	74.5	78.6	76.9	73.9	65.4
1920........................	70.7	76.0	75.8	73.4	65.7
1930........................	65.2	72.5	73.5	71.6	66.6

Source: *Thirteenth Census of the United States,* 1910, *Agriculture,* vols. VI and VII; *Fourteenth Census of the United States,* 1920, *Agriculture,* vol. VI; *Fifteenth Census of the United States,* 1930, *Agriculture,* vol. II.

able trend was found: the percentage of all land in farms decreased more rapidly near the city than far away from it. The city county was inclined to use more land for non-agricultural purposes, such as industrial or suburban development, and the land values were higher because of this urban expansion. Such land as was employed for farming was cultivated more intensively near the urban center. There was a tendency also for farms to increase in size with the distance from the urban center. The discussion of agriculture as an occupation will show that there has been a general trend for small farms and large farms to increase, but it is clear from these rural-urban comparisons that this is not simply a matter of Eastern industrialization and Western expansion, but also a question of distance from cities.

(2) *Trends in ownership of land reversed in terms of distance from city.* Nationally the tendency was for tenancy to rise, but in 1910, as Table 66 indicates, the proportion of owner-operated

TABLE 66. PROPORTION OF FARMS OPERATED BY OWNERS, BY TIERS OF COUNTIES — 18 AREAS

Year	City County per cent	Tiers of Counties			
		First per cent	Second per cent	Third per cent	Fourth per cent
1910....................	57.7	62.1	63.5	64.2	66.5
1920....................	57.6	60.8	61.2	61.6	60.4
1930....................	60.9	60.4	60.3	58.9	56.0

Source: *Thirteenth Census of the United States,* 1910, *Agriculture,* vols. VI and VII; *Fourteenth Census of the United States,* 1920, *Agriculture,* vol. VI; *Fifteenth Census of the United States,* 1930, *Agriculture,* vol. II.

farms increased consistently with the distance from the city. Between 1910 and 1920 the proportion remained the same in the city county, but declined in all tiers. Between 1920 and 1930, the proportion increased in the city county, but decreased in the tiers. Therefore, by 1930 the trend had reversed and owner-operation decreased as one moved away from the city.

(3) *Value of all crops and of dairy products by tiers suggests specialization.* The value of all crops considered from decade to decade continues the story of inflation and deflation, but when considered from the standpoint of the tiers of counties it suggests a trend toward specialization as one moves toward the city from the country. The increase in crop values was doubtless responsible for a wider utilization of marginal farm land and for the rise in mortgages, so that when the decline set in the farmers farther from the urban center found themselves saddled with heavier debt and with proportionally less opportunity for paying it.

When vegetable and cereal crops were analyzed by tiers for the three decades, specialization was again apparent. More vegetables were grown, as might be expected, in the city county, near the market. In 1930 this tendency seemed to extend into tier two. Conversely, the percentages of cereal crops increased through the rural tiers, although in 1930 tier two was relatively high. The trend toward specialization was even more evident in the comparison of dairy products per acre for the three periods. All areas taken together showed an increase of 167 per cent from 1910 to 1920 and 20 per cent more from 1920 to 1930, the change being reasonably uniform for all geographic divisions and all tiers. The analysis by tiers, however, reflects the concentration of dairy products within easy trucking distance from the city. The per acre value of dairy products by tiers and by decades, together with its per cent of increase, is given in Table 67.

TABLE 67. VALUE PER ACRE OF DAIRY PRODUCTS, AND RATE OF
INCREASE, BY TIERS OF COUNTIES — 18 AREAS

Year	City County	Tiers of Counties			
		First	Second	Third	Fourth
1910......................	$2.11	$1.23	$0.91	$0.74	$1.06
1920......................	5.34	4.07	3.00	2.65	3.03
Per cent increase............	153	230	230	258	186

Source: *Thirteenth Census of the United States*, 1910, *Population*, vols. VI and VII; *Fifteenth Census of the United States*, 1930, *Population*, vol. II.

Higher rates of increase for the first three tiers of rural counties may presage a gradual disappearance of the discrepancy between the city county and the rural tiers. Trucks lessen the necessity for having dairy farms concentrated very near to the city. A study of the value of poultry and eggs per acre indicates a significant similarity to this trend in dairy products.

In the South there was a sharp difference in the per cent of dairy products sold in the city and in the country, for each decade. Nevertheless, the increase in sales in 1930 was high and tended to indicate a change in southern farming, perhaps reflecting a growth of manufacturing.

Educational relations. Children from seven to thirteen years, the compulsory school ages, attended school in larger proportions in 1930 than in 1920. There was a tendency in 1920 for the proportion to decrease with distance from the urban county. Excluding the

South, this tendency had disappeared by 1930, so that the proportions of such children attending school tended toward a constant when the city county and the rural tiers were compared.

Passing from the compulsory to the voluntary school ages of fourteen and fifteen, sixteen and seventeen, and eighteen to twenty, we can see in Table 68 the trends for the whole nation.

TABLE 68. PROPORTIONS OF SPECIFIED AGE GROUPS IN SCHOOL, BY TIERS OF COUNTIES SURROUNDING CITY CENTERS, 1910-1930 *

Year	City County per cent	Tiers of Counties			
		First per cent	Second per cent	Third per cent	Fourth per cent
Age 14 and 15					
1920	85.2	83.6	84.7	84.6	84.1
1930	92.7	88.8	88.6	89.1	89.3
Age 16 and 17					
1920	46.8	49.1	51.4	52.2	54.3
1930	65.4	61.5	60.2	62.7	64.6
Age 18 to 20					
1910	15.3	18.7	19.8	19.1	21.0
1920	17.2	17.8	18.6	18.8	21.1
1930	25.5	24.3	23.1	24.1	28.8

* Data for 1910 not available for first two age groups.

In the fourteen to fifteen group the compulsory school age trend is maintained. The city county has a somewhat larger proportion in school, but the difference is not great. The four rural tiers maintain an almost constant ratio for both 1920 and 1930. The proportion of the sixteen to seventeen group in school for all areas in 1920 was 49.2; in 1930, it was 62.2, indicating the marked increase in secondary education. In 1920 the city county had a smaller proportion than the non-urban tiers; in fact, there was a tendency for the proportions to increase with distance from the city. By 1930, however, the urban tier had reversed its position, having the largest proportion in school, despite an increase in all tiers. In 1910 the ratio of the eighteen to twenty group in school was significantly less in the urban centers than in the rural tiers. Between 1910 and 1920 higher education increased in the city counties. In 1930 they had surpassed three rural tiers. Variations between urban and rural counties decreased sharply from 1910 to 1930, which indicates that rural-urban differences in higher education are gradually vanishing.

Social implications of the changing relationships. Rural-urban
relationships can now be summarized by tiers of counties or zones
of mutual influence as follows: City counties and tier one counties,
especially in 1920 and 1930, were likely to have smaller farms devoted to truck crops, fruit and intensive dairying. This necessarily
means more compact communities, relatively higher population
density, and more frequent contacts of all sorts with the city center.
The process has continued long enough so that such counties share
increasingly those population characteristics which have been associated with the city; namely, fewer children, more persons in the
productive age groups, lower birth rates, and so on, through the
list of comparisons which have been presented.

Beyond the first zone, dairying tends to appear accompanied by
its various influences. This tendency is especially clear in tier two
counties, and to a certain extent in tier three. The value of dairy
products increased 230 per cent between 1910 and 1930, and tier
three counties appeared to gain even more, because of an unusually
low figure in 1910. Tier three areas are naturally intermediate.

Tier four counties and beyond, until the influence of another
urban center is encountered, are the outer zone. (In some regions,
counties of the third tier have somewhat similar tendencies.) This
outer zone has larger farms but fewer acres per farm under cultivation. Cereal crops or cotton are grown by a population of lower
density, that is, in larger communities with fewer urban contacts.

Implications of changing rural-urban relationships. The story of
rural population and its particular characteristics revolves about the
tendency of families in the outer rural tiers to have more children.
This is evidenced by fecundity and birth rates, by age distributions,
and by sex and the marriage ratios. Children are a distinguishing
characteristic of farm populations removed from cities. The tendency was more pronounced in the last decade, despite the fact
that general differences in this regard between rural and urban
people were decreasing.

Although the country is likely to contribute fewer young people
to the nation in the future, its share will undoubtedly be disproportionately large for some time to come. The ratio of children to
persons twenty to forty-five years of age is greater in the outer rural
tiers than elsewhere. These persons may find it increasingly more
difficult to provide an education commensurate with the city
county's, which has a greater proportion of people in this productive
age group. This is a problem for consideration in the chapter on
rural education.

Evidence also pointed to the fact that these outer tiers experienced the most violent fluctuations in property values, both in the period of inflation, 1910 to 1920, and in the time of deflation, 1920 to 1930. Because of the city's equity in the benefits to be derived from country youth, it may well aid any plan which will equalize educational opportunities. The importance of this is emphasized when the tier analysis for various educational expenditures is extended through 1934. The more rural the area, the harder was public education hit.

THE INTERACTION OF RURAL AND URBAN

Certain characteristics or traits have traditionally been associated with rural and with urban populations. The question naturally arises, what will be the future results of the greater interaction of the two groups? With the freer contacts and the increased mobility, will the city urbanize the country or will the country ruralize the city? From the evidence of present trends, there seems to be little immediate likelihood that all differences will be obliterated. There can be no doubt, however, that many of them will be greatly modified. On the other hand, it should be pointed out that there are many common traits which are neither rural nor urban. In the great population movements described in an earlier chapter, first from rural to urban, prior to 1929, and then from urban to rural in the following five years, the question is, which traits have been sloughed off and which have been rendered more common? What will be the effects of efforts to decentralize industry and population, and to move city workers to "garden plots" and subsistence homesteads?

It has been suggested that rural and urban are now more relative terms than they were, which is only another way of saying that a process is under way which is modifying wide differences and distinguishing characteristics. Now that the changing design has been examined, the process itself should be studied a little more thoroughly. The implication is that it is a two-way action or process, which, at the risk of over-simplifying and over-popularizing, will be termed "urbanization" and "ruralization." These terms are widely used, but often with so little discrimination that it is important to examine their implications.

Urbanization. To urbanize means to transfer the characteristics of a city. Direct and indirect contacts have, without doubt, made country and city more alike in many respects, but to say that the city has deliberately, octopus-like, fixed its features upon the country, is an exaggeration. The city is not sufficiently organized and unified to do this, although it is quite evident that certain city groups and enterprises have proceeded with that aim. That both country and city are exposed on a grander scale to the influences of mechanical invention, mass production, and centralized control would be a more exact statement. Often the city acts as the earlier laboratory and then is used as the diffusion or propagation center. To say that an invention comes out of a city, however, does not prove that it is of the city.

The clearest evidence of direct rural contacts with urban centers is, of course, in the commercial field, where it is easy to observe and to record. For example, among 1328 Middle-West farm families surveyed in 1930 by *Successful Farming* of Des Moines, it was found that the average distances traveled to make purchases of hardware, farm machinery, groceries, and automobile accessories, varied from 5.9 to 7.8 miles. (The results of this study will be given in greater detail in a later chapter dealing with retail merchandising.) The average distance traveled for furniture, however, was fourteen miles, and for women's ready-to-wear, 19.5 miles. The last two items were procured by the greatest number of families (31 and 47 per cent) in places of from 2500 to 10,000. Cities of more than 10,000 secured the trade for these two items from one eighth and one sixth of all families respectively, although they attracted but one twentieth of the families for other goods. In other words, centers of various sizes attract to their stores only that proportion of the families who live within their primary sphere of influence, and the goods which are bought at such centers pertain directly to the farm or to daily living. When clothing and other specialties are purchased, then the larger places have a far greater attraction. In this way some of the apparent differences between the countryman and the cityman have partially disappeared; both buy their clothes at the same city stores.

Indirect contacts are more subtle in influence, as was emphasized before. The invasion of city practices, finance, and control into rural banking, rural storekeeping, and village manufacturing plants was evident over and over again when specific rural communities were restudied after a lapse of ten years. Social institutions and agencies were not immune to urbanization. Outside influences were playing upon rural schools, and within the local churches the force of administrative boards dominated by urban points of view was constantly felt. Similarly, luncheon clubs, parent-teacher associations, men's clubs and women's clubs, receive from their regional, state or national offices more and more suggestions new to the rural world. Such indirect influences are not limited to institutional and organizational contacts. Wherever tests were made, rural people were found to be subscribing to city newspapers twice as frequently in 1930 as in 1925.

The radio, too, is exerting an immeasurable influence. In 1925, 4.3 per cent of the farmers had radios; in 1930 the figure was 20.8 per cent. In that year two fifths of the villagers also possessed them. This simultaneous exposure of rural and urban people to the intruding radio, the city-edited newspaper, and the silver screen can hardly fail to iron out some of the mental curves of difference between the two groups.

The modulating effects upon population characteristics and upon agricultural practices have become evident in the last section of the chapter. Furthermore, the great backward flow of people from cities to farms and villages which began in 1929, is of significance. It reduced the average age of the country population because many younger people returned, and many others did not leave the country. Those who did return are sure to have brought with them modified ideas and attitudes regarding urban life.

Ruralization. To ruralize means to impart a rural character or aspect. If there has been urbanization of the country there has also been ruralization of the city. The urban movement reached its height during the first thirty years of the century. Those were the years of city building, the increasing use of the automobile, extension of mechanical power, and of telephone and radio improvement. It is estimated that in the decade 1920 to 1930 nearly twenty million, and from 1940 to 1945 another five million people migrated. Certainly these millions did not shed all of their ideas, attitudes and ways of living at the city gates, as some writers have implied in their great emphasis upon the urbanization of the country.

Even superficial observation, as for example from a roof-garden of a city apartment house several hundred feet above the ground, provides evidences of ruralization. The roof-garden itself is reversion to a country form of living. There over the ledge can be seen a front porch, a suspended line with drying clothes, flower boxes gay with color, formalized pines at an entrance across the street, a dog in his runway on another flat roof, and beyond, a cat sunning herself contentedly. In the outskirts, past the "downtown" districts, many other country scenes greet the understanding eye. The more trenchant implications of the rural-urban migration as a phase of rural-urban relationships which were discussed in an earlier chapter, have been summarized in a few sentences by Sorokin, Zimmerman, and Galpin. Regarding the cityward trend, they say: "The characteristics of the rural population are carried into the city by each new generation of migrants. The spiritual and moral convictions, the habits of life, and the personal traits of the rural population, whether good or bad, are constantly being injected into the culture that obtains in the city."

Then there is the reverse movement. Regarding this countryward trend these authors add, "a small stream of migrants continues to go from city to country. These representatives of the city carry with them the culture and characteristics, the good and the bad of the urban centers to the country." They conclude, "In the long run the city gains more by this process than it loses." [14]

There are various evidences of the reaction of rural culture upon urban life. An interesting example is that of the rural practices which carry over into the administration and conduct of city churches. By carefully devised measurements Doctor Douglass is able to identify city churches of rural origin and to determine the extent to which adjustments have been made to urban conditions. He suggests that city churches as a group vary all the way from extreme simplicity to great complexity of program, and the explanation is they are getting away more and more from a rural tradition and moving toward the urban. He estimates that 25 per cent or more of city churches which are least developed are no larger and no more highly organized than the average rural church. He concludes that the city church represents an evolution from a rural parent stock, although its immediate ancestor is the town church. [15]

Furthermore, just as the countryman has many direct contacts with city life, so there are an ever-expanding number and type of direct contacts for the cityman when he goes to the country: contacts of business, pleasure, hunting, fishing, touring, or the more extended associations of a country home, summer vacation, and rural relatives. It is also estimated that a perceptible amount of agricultural wealth migrates annually to cities through inheritances, as an illustrative study in Ohio shows. [16] Thus rural and urban are

[14] Sorokin, Zimmerman, and Galpin, *A Systematic Source Book in Rural Sociology*, vol. III, p. 534. Minneapolis: University of Minnesota Press.

[15] Douglass, H. Paul, *One Thousand City Churches: Phases of Adaptation to Urban Environment*, chap. IV. New York: George H. Doran Co.

[16] Tetreau, E. D., *Some Trends in Rural Social Organization in Four Ohio Counties.* Columbus: Ohio Agricultural Experiment Station, Bulletin 42, November, 1931.

bound by many ties. Communication inventions and the wider use of machines in country and city are important forces in this process.

Rurbanization. To rurbanize means to bring town and country together *en rapport.* This intermediary process is suggested as an explanation of a present trend. It is not merely a figure of speech to say that midway between country and city stands the village or small town, one hand extending toward the country and the other toward the city. It is rather a description of an actual situation. Likewise, the rurban community of town and country manifests many features of a reconciliation between extreme ruralism and extreme urbanism. And finally, the designation of the village or small town as the mid-point toward which the changing characteristics of both country and city populations are approaching, is a representation of present and probable future trends. Rural and urban societies already tend to resemble each other in many respects, a resemblance which may continue as the expression of modern relationships, and this without undue sacrifice of those unique qualities which have characterized their past and which are needed for their future.

Finally, implications following from the changing rural-urban relationships detailed in this chapter require the attention of the people who live in the country and those who live in the city. Traditionally farmers have had an antipathy to city dwellers. Some experiences of the depression and of the war have seemed to modify this attitude and give an increased realization of the interdependencies of agriculture and the business and industry of the city. On the other hand, issues have been raised regarding prices, wages, tariffs, and labor unions. There have been McNary-Haugen bills, export debenture plans, and the AAA. For the first time some villages have had an experience with organized labor. The employees of a small industrial plant in an eastern agricultural village were organized in 1934 by men sent out from union headquarters. A strike was called. In a Middle-Western farming community the state labor board exercised its authority in a dispute between the directors of a farmers' co-operative association and its employees. The political reverberations of this action are sure to be heard for many a year. Alignments of farmer and city wage-earners have been attempted, but they seem to fall apart rather easily. In New Zealand a labor party came to power by the votes of farmers, but there is ever the struggle to keep together in thought and attitude. It is very difficult for a farmer to understand a labor organizer's point of view, and it constantly tests the patience of a labor official to have a farmer stress the importance of land-ownership, low farm wages, and high prices for the food and fiber produced on the farm.

It is futile to think of turning back. The future lies, as Lewis Mumford says so well, in "intelligent participation and understanding at every stage in the process," and the "process" is sure to involve rather fundamental readjustments for both urban and rural society.[17]

The foregoing discussion of the group organization of rural society extending all the way from families and neighborhoods to rural-urban relationships should give greater point to considerations of population presented in earlier chapters. The most important elements of groups and societies are the people themselves.

DISCUSSION TOPICS

1. Draw or secure a general outline map of the United States indicating the location of cities of over 500,000 population in 1930. Indicate the percentage of growth or decline in each case since 1920.
2. Describe and give reasons for such direct contacts between rural and urban people, as shopping, visiting, recreation, which you think have increased most in the past five years.
3. Make a list of five city-centered agencies operating in country-village communities. Describe briefly the local system of organization and operation of each. Example: chain store, trade union.
4. Describe any variation which you have been able to observe in driving out twenty miles or more from a medium-sized city, in respect to density of country population, types of agriculture, frequency and size of villages, characteristics of the population.
5. How do you account for this gradient pattern of rural-urban relations? What are its practical implications for land-use planning? For curriculum building in high schools?
6. Give the best example of which you know where farmers and city wage-earners are successfully working together, or give an example of a conflict situation and suggest ways out.

REFERENCE READINGS

Douglass, H. Paul, *Suburban Trends*. New York: Century Company, 1925. The movement toward decentralizing cities and the growth of satellite cities.

Hauser, Phillip M., "How Declining Urban Growth Affects City Activities," *Public Management*, vol. XXII, December, 1940.

[17] Mumford, Lewis, *Culture of Cities*. New York: Harcourt, Brace & Co., 1939.

Hoyt, H., "Forces of Urban Centralization and Decentralization; Historical Review of Urban Development," *American Journal of Sociology*, vol. 46, May, 1941.

Lynd, Robert R. and Helen M., *Middletown*. New York: Harcourt, Brace & Co., 1929. A study in contemporary American Culture, life in a small city.

Lynd, Robert R. and Helen M., *Middletown in Transition*. New York: Harcourt, Brace & Co., 1937.

McKenzie, R. D., *The Rise of Metropolitan Communities*. New York: McGraw-Hill, 1922. A social trends monograph.

Mumford, Lewis, *Culture of Cities*. New York: Harcourt, Brace & Co., 1939.

Park and Burgess, *The City*. Chicago: University of Chicago Press, 1925. Studies of the areas of influence of cities and their growth formations.

Smith, Mapheus, "Rural-Urban Intelligence Gradients," *Journal of Sociology and Social Research*, vol. XXVII, August, 1943.

Sorokin and Zimmerman, *Principles of Rural-Urban Sociology*, Part I. New York: Henry Holt & Co., 1929. Fundamental relations of the rural and urban worlds.

Spengler, J. J., "Population Movements and Economic Equilibrium," *Journal of Political Economy*, vol. 48, April, 1940.

Thaden, J. F., *The Lansing Region and Its Tributary Town-Country Communities*. East Lansing: Experiment Station Bulletin 302, March, 1940, Michigan State College.

Tomars, Adolph S., "Rural Survivals in the American Urban Life," *Rural Sociology*, vol. 8, no. 4, December, 1943.

Whetten, Nathan L., and E. C. Devereaux, *Studies of Suburbanization in Connecticut* (1. Windsor: A Highly Developed Agricultural Area). Storrs: Experiment Station Bulletin 212, October, 1936, Connecticut State College.

Whetten, Nathan L., and R. F. Field, *Studies of Suburbanization in Connecticut* (2. Norwich: An Industrial Part-Time Farming Area). Storrs: Experiment Station Bulletin 226, May, 1938, Connecticut State College.

Whetten, Nathan L., *Studies of Suburbanization in Connecticut* (3. Wilton: A Rural Town Near Metropolitan New York). Storrs: Experiment Station Bulletin 230, February, 1939, Connecticut State College.

PART FOUR

INSTITUTIONAL
ARRANGEMENTS

17

Standards of Living and the Rural Home

SOME WRITERS begin their study of society with the great social institutions such as home, school, church, or government. These institutions seem so tangible and so permanent that they challenge attention at the outset. This procedure, however, seems to be "putting the cart before the horse," as the old agricultural adage expresses it, for it should be quite clear from the preceding discussion that social institutions spring from group experiences and backgrounds and from the desires and traditions of people. They are the results of evolution and change, since to survive, institutions must constantly make adjustments.

In introducing the social institutions of rural society, it should be emphasized at once that the house is not the home, the school is not the building, nor is the church the building with the steeple. The terms and the ideas for which they stand are easily confused. An institution is the more or less regular way a group does things. Habit and custom are important, since people tend to repeat methods of accomplishing their ends until the habit becomes definitely established. Such ways and methods are finally given the sanction of society. They may be society's plan for keeping certain groups in line with accepted social standards.

The school, for example, is the whole social arrangement of teachers and pupils, teachers and parents, and pupils and parents. It has its curriculum, its community relations, and its public policy. The school building is only an external evidence of internal activity. Similarly, the home with its ways of living, which is the subject of the present chapter, is something vastly more than a house. This truth was evidently in the mind of the popular writer who said, "It takes a heap o' livin' to make a house a home."

THE RURAL HOME AS SOCIAL INSTITUTION AND CONSUMER CENTER

Characteristics of the rural family group and its chief occupation, farming, have been discussed in other chapters. It is the purpose of this chapter to study the family's ways of living. Such institutional forms of behavior have an internal sphere in the home and an external phase in the community. Society has never given the family group an entirely free hand in its own internal ways of living. Standards of health, honesty, morality, and many other forms of conduct have been prescribed. Whether internally or externally conditioned, the home with its standards of living is a social institution of primary importance.

Standards of living as a component part of this institution, the home, are themselves social forms of behavior embracing not only consumption of the economic goods — food, clothing and shelter — but also the consumption or use of the wide range of non-material elements including those spiritual, esthetic, and social amenities which go to make up ways of living. These ways of living in the home can be observed or studied through actual budgetary expenditures, through socio-economic status as reflected in the possession of cultural goods or household conveniences, and in other forms of social behavior such as the participation in social groups or the use of time for recreation, education, religion, or other activities.

Broadly considered, consumption means the converting of gross profits into goods and services for human joy and living. The consuming takes place through the home, and the nature of the consumption is defined through the standards of living. In short, the rural home so conceived is as definitely a consuming institution as the farm is a producing institution, and together they become a mode of living quite as much as a means of livehihood.

"Socially desirable" standards, result of social processes. Standards of living from this focus of the home are obviously group products. They arise out of social experience, and what is finally considered necessary or proper — that is, "desirable" — emerges as regular and recognized. This is the social process of building up a social institution. To be sure, different families have different ways, and these ways are undergoing constant change and adjustment, but this is the dictum of society.

In rural society where the family group is so important, its ways of living are subjects of vital interest. Through studies of living, some of which will be described later in the chapter, it is possible to observe some of the changes and readjustments going on in the home and also to understand more fully the social processes involved. One may think of the matter as a game of choosing: so much food as compared with so much shelter, or so much recreation, in order to have the sort of home life one wants. This proportioning of the factors of consumption becomes a very complicated affair, and its analysis soon leads one into many questions which cannot be considered here. What are wants? What conditions them? Why do they differ for different people? These are problems with which social psychologists must wrestle.

Some of the results of the proportioning, however, can be seen from the studies. For example, it was found that for farm families within the same state, food costs ranged from 20 to 50 per cent of total expenditures. The explanation does not lie entirely in the amount of income available, but leads back to social customs, to size of family, to values placed upon food as compared with education or religion. The matter of valuing and choosing is one of the most fundamental in human relations. Professor Cooley suggests that all psychical life is in some sense a choosing.[1] He declares, "a system of values is a system of practical ideas or motives to behavior."[2] Behind the whole valuation process, therefore, is this effort of human beings to continue life and to work out their interests in a changing world.

The consumer emphasis in modern life. Thus the rural home and its standards of living are seen to be closely related to other aspects of rural society and to the "great society" beyond. Experiences during depression years have given practical demonstration of the importance of this consumption emphasis.

Consumption, according to Professor Gide, University of Paris, is the final goal or "consummation" of the whole economic process. He says, "The domain of consumption is infinitely rich and as yet half explored; it is from here probably that economic science will one day start anew."[3] Despite this strong statement, he and many other political economists develop their system of economic thought around the concept of production. In fact, as stated elsewhere, Americans have become well schooled in the production theory of economics, a theory born when recurring famines and other shortages of uncounted centuries pointed to the need for supplying sufficient food and shelter for mankind.[4] In early American life it fitted in with the whole pioneering spirit to which reference has been

[1] Cooley, Charles H., *Human Nature and the Social Order.* New York: Scribner, 1902.
[2] Cooley, Charles H., *The Social Process.* New York: Scribner, 1925.
[3] Gide, Charles, *Political Economy.* Authorized Translation from the third edition, 1913, of the *Cours d'Economie Politique.* New York: D. C. Heath & Co.
[4] Brunner and Kolb, *Rural Social Trends.* New York: McGraw-Hill, 1933.

made. Settlers sought to exploit and subdue the natural resources and to make them produce. There were always hungry mouths to feed in both country and city. The only problem was to produce sufficient quantities; the market seemed always to be calling for more. The government later, through extension service, urged farmers to increase per acre yields through use of more science and better technology. In recent decades such technology has multiplied many forms of production so that now that which was apparently impossible has happened. Production has outstripped consumption and finds itself caught in the web of a theory which never envisaged such a possibility. Hunger and want are still pressing their claims, but now in a land of plenty.

Rural people are directly concerned with consumption from a second angle. Consumption habits, which in many particulars have changed but little for centuries, can now be altered or even revolutionized in a few months. Production, then, cannot be regarded for its own sake, but for consumers' needs and wants, and consumption habits must be studied and even forecast. The science of consumption should be built up by students of society rather than by sales managers.

Finally, from the standpoint of public policy, consumption includes various uses to which wealth is put. It must be admitted that more than once wealth has been amassed where it is not of maximum social usefulness. The question has been seriously raised as to whether consumption, conditioning as it does so many phases of life, is not the next area to which government and private agencies need to turn their attention.

Doctor Galpin emphasizes the place of consumption in agriculture and rural life when he says: "The farmer's problem is far from being solely a problem of price for farm products and profits of agriculture. It is a problem also of consumption goods, and for the college to leave this problem untouched and unsolved is to invite a situation in agriculture in which farmers know how to make profits as farmers, but not how to spend their profits as consumers. Such an agriculture is neither stable nor prosperous nor well paid." [5]

Robert Lynd, after an extended study of "The People as Consumers" for the President's Research Committee on Social Trends, concludes his report with the two following significant sentences: "The primary concern is whether the government is prepared to

[5] Galpin, C. J., "Spending the Dollar Wisely in Home and Community." Address at Thirty-Eighth Annual Convention of the Association of Land-Grant Colleges, Washington, D.C., 1924.

give to the spending of the national income the same degree of concern that it at present bestows upon the earning of that income. Such coherent leadership is needed if schools and other agencies are to educate the consumer in the practice of the fine art of spending money." [6]

Importance of living recognized by rural groups. The practical implications of the consumption emphasis and of the necessity for recognizing standards of "desirable" ways of living are being increasingly appreciated by farm people themselves. There was a time when certain groups of families chose to delay much home consumption until the farm was paid for, or until "it could be afforded." Private property in land was a "motive for behavior," driving the pioneer westward, as was noted in the chapter on the rural family. The old motto of scarcity economy was, "You can't have your cake and eat it." More recently the living side of the farm has risen to a new recognition. The modernized saying is, "You can't keep your cake unless you eat it," which suggests simply that profits from farming should be converted into standards of living for home and for community. To use an agricultural metaphor, profits should be "plowed back" into the soil of family and community life, rather than into the physical soil simply to induce more production.

Necessity for protecting standards of living has been recognized by agricultural leaders. In the earlier days there was discussion of "eliminating the marginal producers" and now the dangers attendant upon sacrificing accepted standards of living by "marginal consumers" have been voiced. Probably as striking a statement of this as can readily be found is that in a discussion of "success" in farming by two English writers. They say:

> But ultimately there is no general success which is not measurable in human values, and most of the success in farming can eventually be measured by the standard of living obtainable and enjoyed by the family. This is not a plea for ostentation, for real standards of living are not to be measured by outside show. . . .
>
> Although the possibilities of the standard of living for individual families over the whole group are largely determined by the common standard of living, this imposes the general limitations on the competition for the requirements of production, especially land and labor, but it also has a great influence on the conditions under which capital is accumulated or obtained. Thus the individual who is

[6] *Recent Social Trends,* vol. II, p. 911. New York: McGraw-Hill, 1933.

willing to sacrifice the accepted standard of living in the competition for either, is a danger to his neighbor.[7]

Concern of society in rural levels of living. Various agencies of government have "stepped into" the rural home and influenced its living in the last decade. Many of the governmental programs are discussed elsewhere and need emphasis at this point only as evidence of the definite concern of society regarding the rural living functions of the home. One way in which the government affects living is through assuming more and more of the early functions of the home, such as education, health, and recreation. Another important means of helping consumers is standardization, labeling and sumptuary legislation, and the enforcement of various food and drug acts.

More recently governmental agencies have tried to work out minimum budgets, particularly for food. The value of these budgets has been questioned, but they have actually been used in planning for marginal family groups such as relief families.[8] The Works Progress Administration in 1935 established minimum standards for various commodities but found that 18 per cent of the American families were below the so-called "emergency" level and that 40 per cent were below the "maintenance" scale.

The Federal Housing Authority and the Rural Electrification Administration have undertaken large programs for the improvement of standards of living through better housing and household conveniences. The significance of these programs for the present discussion is the recognition from the standpoint of public policy and interest that there are certain levels of living below which rural families should not be allowed to go. With such extreme reductions comes the danger to public health and the burden of poor relief, which will be emphasized in the chapter on public health and welfare. It is likewise recognized that levels of living of rural families have a real relation to public policies for land use, credit, and taxation, topics which have been explored in other chapters.

[7] Ashby, A. W., and J. P. Howell, "Success in Farming; Its Nature and Determination," *Journal of Surveyor's Institution,* 1926. Reprinted in *Rural Standards of Living, a Selected Bibliography.* Washington, D.C.: United States Department of Agriculture, Agricultural Economics Bibliography no. 32, August, 1930. Mimeographed.

[8] Hoyt, Elizabeth Ellis, *Consumption in Our Society.* New York: McGraw-Hill, 1938. Stiebeling, Hazel K., and Medora Ward, *Diets for Four Levels of Nutritive Content and Cost.* Washington, D.C.: United States Department of Agriculture, Circular 296, 1933. Stecker, M. L., *Intercity Differences in Costs of Living in March, 1935, in 59 Cities.* Washington, D.C.: Research Monograph 12, Public Works Administration, 1937.

EARLY STUDIES OF LEVELS OF LIVING

Although detailed studies of levels of living in the rural home are of comparatively recent date in this country, knowledge concerning living conditions in general has grown through a series of systematic studies, mostly of urban laborers, dating back at least to the comparisons made by Gregory King for the years 1688 and 1699 for England, France, and Holland. Since that time hundreds of studies have been made. The methods employed have varied considerably, and no one of them singly deserves credit for providing complete help. There are, however, students whose contributions have proved particularly useful as a means of understanding the standards of living in the rural homes of America.

Studies of levels of living become a means or a "tool" for a better understanding, not only of the rural home, but of society itself. Budgets of income, expenditures, use of time or energy, have importance in and of themselves, but they have wider usefulness as a means of studying family organization, discovering social classes, and observing the interaction of family groups with other groups and with the institutions in society.

The Le Play case studies. As a professor in Paris, Le Play started his investigations of family living in about 1830, and for half a century carried on his studies in practically every country of Europe. He would arrange to live with families which he selected as representative of certain types and he would stay long enough to secure sufficient information to write a whole monograph, that is, a complete case analysis of the family.[9]

Le Play was concerned with the problems arising out of industrialization in the nineteenth century. It was evident to him that there was a close connection between the consumption habits of families and the social policy of a nation. In times of prosperity, if habits of waste and unwarranted expansion of standards of living were allowed, there was sure to be a reaction which would end in suffering. Society should, therefore, influence families to prepare for the rainy day rather than to hasten its coming. He pointed out that if society's leaders were willing and prompt to act, much

[9] The reports are published in a series of volumes called *Les Ouvriers Européens* and *Les Ouvriers des deux Mondes*, 1856-1930. The present summary of the early studies is adapted from interpretations made by Carle C. Zimmerman, "Development of Research in Family Living," Scope and Method Monograph; *Research in Family Living*, Social Science Research Council, J. D. Black, editor, pp. 48-56; and "Family Budget as Tool for Analysis," *American Journal of Sociology*, vol. XXIII, p. 901, May, 1928.

suffering caused by wars, industrial crises and famine could be avoided, and the consequent lowering of standards of living and the disruption of the social classes averted. He made the family his unit for thinking and for studying. Emphasis was placed on the mores, habits, and institutions which preserve the physical as well as the mental and social well-being of the family.

As was noted in the early chapter on the rural family, Le Play placed a good deal of stress upon the sentimental attachments which exist between the family group and its homestead or its "hearth," as he called it. Therefore, it is not strange that he should seek to analyze the ways of living of the family. He maintained that he who makes a complete analysis of the factors influencing the income and expenditures of a family, possesses a complete knowledge of that family. By the use of this case-study method he and his followers made classifications of societies according to their types of family organization, and gave explanations of the processes and changes in the society itself. The home, with its ways of living considered as a social institution, was the starting point for Le Play in his study of society.

The Engel statistical studies. In contrast with Le Play, Engel put his emphasis upon the accumulation of data regarding many families. His was a statistical study of what might be termed "mass" consumption. He used some of the original material gathered by Le Play and others, and also the studies of wage-earners in Belgium in 1886 and 1891. By statistical analysis he was able to show relationships between the distribution of the items of the budget and the rise of the family in the social scale. His statements of these relationships have come to be known as "Engel's Laws" of consumption. The statements took two forms. The first, which has received much the less attention but which has significance for the student of society, was that the importance of food in a budget was the best single index of the social position of the family. The second was that an increase in income was associated with declining proportions of the budget spent for food, with about the same proportions spent for clothing, rent, fuel, and light, and with increasing proportions for education, health, recreation and amusements.

Although the relationships suggested by Engel have been found in general to hold true for present wage-earner families, as well as for rural laborers and salaried people, some revisions and modifications have been made on the basis of more recent studies in this country.[10]

[10] United States Public Health Service Report 35, no. 48. Washington, D.C.: United States Treasury Department, 1920.

The influence of Engel's type of analysis has been direct in both rural and urban studies of standards of living. The method affords an opportunity for observing the changing behavior of families as they move up and down the income scale, and also for making limited comparisons between rural and urban families. It does not give the chance, however, for relating the home as an institution to its own immediate social environment. Therefore, both the Engel and the Le Play method can be used to very good advantage as complements to each other.

American farm family studies. Studies of farm families in America were much later in starting than those of wage-earners and low-salaried groups, but once under way they increased rapidly. Among the early contributions were the field studies of Warren in 1909, of Funk in 1913, and the writings of men like Galpin. These publications and the series of studies which followed have provided background knowledge regarding ways of living in American rural homes, especially farm homes.

One of the significant field surveys was a project of the Bureau of Agricultural Economics, United States Department of Agriculture, directed by E. L. Kirkpatrick. In this study, data were collected from 2886 white farm families in eleven states, for a one-year period during 1922-24. The results secured were believed to represent general conditions for the country as a whole. Although no other nation-wide surveys were immediately undertaken, agricultural colleges co-operating with the United States Department of Agriculture have made a great many local studies which contributed both to research method and to an understanding of how farm families live.[11]

Studies of the ways in which rural people spend their time also afford a clue to their standards of living. The use of time reflects the value attached to this or that form of activity. Such studies offer interesting insight into some of the traditional attitudes toward recreation, for example.[12]

Finally, the realistic portrayals of rural life through the novel

[11] Zimmerman, Carle C., *Consumption and Standards of Living.* New York: D. Van Nostrand, 1936; Williams, Faith M., and Carle C. Zimmerman, *Studies of Family Living in the United States and Other Countries.* Washington, D.C.: Miscellaneous publication no. 223, United States Department of Agriculture, 1935.

[12] Frayser, Mary E., *Use of Leisure in Selected Rural Areas of South Carolina,* Bulletin 263, Clemson Agricultural College Experiment Station, 1930. Wilson, Maud, *Use of Time by Oregon Homemakers,* Bulletin 256, Oregon Agricultural Experiment Station, 1929. Rankin, J. O., *Use of Time in Farm Homes,* Bulletin 230, Nebraska Agricultural Experiment Station, 1928.

and drama must not be overlooked. Only by making use of all available sources can we come to know how farm people live and what factors influence their ways of living.

RECENT STUDIES OF LIVING IN RURAL HOMES

Like any other social relationships in a dynamic society, ways of living in homes change. Generalized statements are therefore difficult to make because of changes over periods of time, differences from one region to another, and differences among various classes — tenants, racial or ethnic groups, and families of varying size and occupation. Nevertheless, some general impressions can be had by a brief review of some of the more recent studies of rural family living.

It should be borne in mind that there has not been complete agreement in the use of such terms as "cost of living," "level of living," or "standards of living." However, "level of living" is understood to mean the ways that groups actually live in a particular time and place, while "standard of living" is the broader term, implying social patterns in the institutional sense, also implying a general standard of norms. In the presentations to follow, levels of living described are in terms of the physical goods and services which particular families use or consume in given periods of time. It is difficult, if not impossible, to get a common physical measure of goods and services; therefore, the common practice is to express items of a family budget in monetary terms. Even this is far from satisfactory, since the buying power of a dollar is not a stable thing when considered in terms of hours of work or bushels of corn necessary to acquire it.

Fortunately for those interested in rural society, many recent studies of family living have considered not only items of expenditure, but have attempted to trace their relationships with other family concerns, such as mobility, social participation, source of income, housing, and even the use of time. Scales for measurement and comparison of levels of living have been devised. Some are long and complicated, others short and simple, but the purpose is to find measuring techniques with standardized and validated indices.[13] There are also attempts to study and measure the non-

[13] Sewell, William H., "A Short Form of the Farm Family Socio-Economic Status Scale," *Rural Sociology*, vol. 8, no. 2, June, 1943; "A Scale for the Measurement of Farm Family Socio-Economic Status," *The Southwestern Social Science Quarterly*, vol. XXI, no. 2; *The Construction and Standardization of a*

monetary items in family living. There is payment in kind, such as eggs, milk, and garden space for the farm laborer or the cash tenant, and there are many items produced by the family itself, whether living on the farm or in the village or town. Finally, there are the numerous factors which contribute to standards of living of families which do not yield to physical measurements at all — trustworthy traditions, attractive settings of woods or fields or mountains, and spiritual qualities attendant upon filial confidence and sense of security.

Family expenditures in the United States. A comprehensive study of consumer incomes and expenditures of families living on farms, in villages, towns, and cities was made by the National Resources Committee, the Bureau of Home Economics of the United States Department of Agriculture, and the Bureau of Labor Statistics of the United States Department of Labor, in co-operation with the Central Statistical Board and the Works Progress Administration.[14] Schedules were collected covering a one-year period from July, 1935 to June, 1936. Included in the survey were 66 farm counties, 140 villages, 29 cities, 14 medium-size cities, and 6 large cities, all selected to represent various cultural and economic groups of the country. As a "back-drop" against which to view the living of families in rural society, the summary picture of national income and consumption is given here. It was possible to consider the 29,400,300 families of two or more persons, and the 10,058,000 men and women living as lodgers or servants in private homes, rooming-houses, and hotels, or maintaining homes of their own as one-person families. These 39,000,000 "consumer units" included over 98 per cent of the total population and received nearly 99 per cent of the total consumer income. The consumption expenditures of the remaining 2,000,000 consumers — those living in institutional groups — were made, for the most part, on an institutional basis, and are not directly comparable with the disbursements of the rest of the population.

The total volume of income flowing into the hands of the nation's families and individual consumers during 1935-36 was approxi-

Scale for the Measurement of the Socio-Economic Status of Oklahoma Farm Families. Stillwater: Technical Bulletin no. 9, April, 1940, Oklahoma Agricultural College.

[14] *Consumer Incomes of the United States: Their Distribution in 1935-36,* August, 1938; *Consumer Expenditures in the United States, Estimates for 1935-36,* March, 1939; and *Family Expenditures in the United States,* Statistical Tables and Appendices, June, 1941. National Resources Committee Publications. Washington, D.C.: Government Printing Office.

TABLE 69. AVERAGE DISBURSEMENTS OF FARM, RURAL NON-FARM, AND URBAN FAMILIES, 1935-36

Category of Disbursement	Average Disbursements per Family			Percentage of Income		
	Farm Families	Rural Non-Farm Families	Urban Families	Farm Families	Rural Non-Farm Families	Urban Families
Current consumption:						
Food:						
Purchased............	$187	$352	$492	15.4	25.0	26.5
Home-produced.......	286	31	...	23.5	2.2	...
All food............	$473	$383	$492	38.9	27.2	26.5
Housing:						
Money expense........	$18	$127	$244	1.5	9.0	13.1
Imputed value........	114	60	70	9.4	4.3	3.8
All housing..........	$132	$187	$314	10.9	13.3	16.9
All household operation	$93	$156	$192	7.7	11.1	10.3
Furnishings, clothing, automobile, medical care, recreation and other personal and advancement items	$352	$472	$591	28.9	33.5	31.9
All consumption items	$1050	$1198	$1589	86.4	85.1	85.6
Gifts...............	23	44	54	1.9	3.1	2.9
Personal taxes......	3	11	36	.3	.8	2.0
Savings.............	139	156	176	11.4	11.0	9.5
All items...........	$1,215	$1,409	$1,855	100.0	100.0	100.0

Source: *Family Expenditures in the United States*, adapted from Table 40, p. 18, *op. cit.* See volume cited in note 14 for methods of deriving estimates of home-produced foods and other items. The estimates in this table include those receiving some relief during the year. The succeeding tables do not.

mately $59,300,000,000. Of this amount, $50,200,000,000, or about 85 per cent, was spent for current consumption; $2,200,000,000, or nearly 4 per cent, was used for gifts to relatives and friends, and for contributions to the church and to philanthropic agencies; and about $900,000,000, or 1.5 per cent, was paid out as income taxes, poll taxes, and certain minor personal property taxes. The remaining $6,000,000,000 — 10 per cent of total income — was saved.

Average expenditures, with the percentages of income, can be compared for farm, rural non-farm, and urban families. As Table 69 indicates, the proportion of incomes spent for various consumption items by all families is surprisingly similar. The actual amount spent by farm families is considerably lower, $1050 compared with $1589 for the urban families. The proportion for food, including both purchased and furnished, is significantly higher for farm families, namely, 38.9 per cent. Home economists suggest that when 40 per cent or more of family income must be spent for food, the budget is likely to be out of balance and other items are necessarily cramped.

Differences in expenditures are wide when comparisons are made by regions and by income levels. This comparison is made of farm families only, in Table 70.

It is significant that no budgets for any region were balanced at the $500 to $1000 income level. This was also true for non-farm and urban families. The effects of the depression were still felt, and such current deficits had to be met from previous savings, borrowings, or from relief, either direct or work relief.

Comparisons between white and Negro families in Southern rural communities by various income levels for the major categories of consumption — food, clothing, shelter, and other items — are given in Table 71. Expenditures for Negro families are significantly smaller for the majority of items at every income level. In the urban communities the same situation prevailed.

Food is the major item in all the budgets; therefore, it is of interest to observe the different proportions required at the various income levels. The farm family stands out in such comparisons because of the high proportion produced on the farm, especially at the lower income levels. This is further evidence of the household type of economy described in the earlier chapter on the rural family.[15]

"All food" does not fall below the 40 per cent level within the

[15] See Zimmerman, Carle C., "Engel's Law of Expenditure for Food," *Quarterly Journal of Economics*, November, 1932, for a discussion of the food item.

TABLE 70. AVERAGE OUTLAY OF FARM FAMILIES IN FIVE
GEOGRAPHIC REGIONS FOR CONSUMPTION, GIFTS AND PERSONAL
TAXES, AND SAVINGS, AT SELECTED INCOME LEVELS, 1935–36

Income Level and Region	Average Income per Family	Average Outlay per Family for		
		Current Consumption	Gifts and Personal Taxes	Savings
$500–$1,000:				
New England.............	$786	$917	$27	−$158
North Central...........	786	912	19	− 145
South...................	732	725	9	− 2
Mountain and Plains......	753	1,097	24	− 368
Pacific..................	774	926	20	− 172
$1,500–$2,000:				
New England.............	1,724	1,486	58	180
North Central...........	1,725	1,423	38	264
South...................	1,708	1,497	36	175
Mountain and Plains......	1,709	1,447	42	220
Pacific..................	1,740	1,492	52	196
$3,000–$4,000:				
New England.............	3,328	1,808	65	1,455
North Central...........	3,380	1,964	56	1,360
South...................	3,416	2,534	99	783
Mountain and Plains......	3,312	1,723	52	1,537
Pacific..................	3,414	2,075	90	1,249
$5,000–$10,000:				
New England.............	7,189	2,560	119	4,510
North Central...........	6,619	2,282	126	4,211
South...................	6,345	3,477	218	2,650
Mountain and Plains......	7,304	2,483	142	4,679
Pacific..................	6,574	3,347	216	3,011

Source: *Family Expenditures in the United States,* adapted from Table 45, p. 15, *op. cit.*

$500 to $1000 income class. This is true for all three types of families. When the size of families is compared, the food demand is greater in the larger farm families. In the $750 to $1000 income level for farm families of three to six persons, the food percentage stands 54.4 per cent. This condition of farm families where children are to be found must be constantly kept in mind when programs of rural welfare are considered. Experiences with nutrition programs during the war should contribute toward improvement.

Two other items in rural family expenditure are worthy of brief review here because of their bearing on topics to be considered in later chapters, namely, recreation and medical care. Among ex-

TABLE 71. AVERAGE EXPENDITURE OF WHITE AND NEGRO
FAMILIES IN SOUTHERN RURAL COMMUNITIES FOR MAJOR
CATEGORIES OF CONSUMPTION, BY INCOME LEVEL, 1935–36

Family Group and Income Level	Average Expenditure per Family for						
	Food	Shelter		Cloth-ing	Auto-mobile	Medical Care	Other Items
		Housing	Other Items				
White families:							
Under $500	$251	$42	$57	$42	$14	$20	$31
$500–$1,000	405	66	87	77	38	34	58
$1,000–$1,500	546	120	158	127	91	51	103
$1,500–$2,000	619	183	230	172	148	72	147
Negro families:							
Under $500	193	30	41	33	11	12	23
$500–$1,000	382	39	67	69	30	22	44
$1,000–$1,500	570	72	89	119	82	41	78
$1,500–$2,000	697	98	105	147	128	54	101

Source: *Family Expenditures in the United States*, adapted from Table 58, p. 19, *op. cit.*

penditures for recreation, radio purchases rank first and movies
second for farm families, but in the reverse order for the rural non-
farm families. Sports and games are a close third for the latter. For
medical care, physicians rank first for both farm and rural non-farm
families, followed by medicine and drugs, then dentists. Among
the urban families expenditures for dentistry follow those for
physicians.

*Comparisons with estimates of consumer spending in 1941 and
1942.* The figures in the tables which follow are estimates which
apply to the year 1941 and to the first quarter of 1942. When income in kind was added to the cash income, the 1941 amount was
$1550 and the 1942 amount was $1610, compared with the median
of $1070 in 1935-36.[16]

With such an increase in incomes it is interesting to watch what
happened to expenditure items for all families and for farm
families. In the case of food, the increase for all families was about
$500, representing an increase of 32 per cent over 1935-36. Among
families in the lower income brackets, total expenditures for food
were not above the 1935-36 levels, although the price level had

[16] *Agricultural Situation*, September, 1942. Washington, D.C.: Bureau of
Agricultural Economics, United States Department of Agriculture.

TABLE 72. FOOD: PERCENTAGE OF INCOME OF FARM, RURAL
NON-FARM, AND URBAN FAMILIES SPENT FOR VARIOUS CATE-
GORIES, AT SELECTED INCOME LEVELS, 1935–36 *

Income Level and Type of Community	Percentage of Income for			
	All Food	Purchased Food		Home-Produced Food
		At Home	Away from Home	(imputed value) †
$500–$1,000:				
Farm.............	57.4	19.6	0.6	37.2
Rural non-farm....	41.2	36.1	1.2	3.9
Urban...........	41.6	40.2	1.4	...
$1,500–$2,000:				
Farm.............	36.0	12.6	.9	22.5
Rural non-farm....	29.5	25.0	2.1	2.4
Urban...........	31.1	28.1	3.0	...
$3,000–$4,000:				
Farm.............	23.2	8.2	1.3	13.7
Rural non-farm....	20.9	15.8	2.9	2.2
Urban...........	23.0	19.2	3.8	...
$5,000–$10,000:				
Farm.............	13.2	4.9	1.6	6.7
Rural non-farm....	12.9	9.2	2.6	1.1
Urban...........	16.5	12.8	3.7	...

* Both the sample expenditure and the population weights used in preparing these estimates exclude families receiving any direct or work relief (however little) at any time during year. The farm group includes
families living on farms in rural areas only. The rural non-farm group includes families living in communities with population under 2500, and families living in the open country, but not on farms.
† Data on home-produced food were obtained from farm and rural non-farm families only.
Source: *Family Expenditures in the United States*, Table 136, p. 49, *op. cit.*

advanced nearly 6 per cent by 1941 and 16 per cent by 1942. With
rising prices, the family manager can alter, not only the items
within the budget, but also the quality and the quantity purchased,
and in the case of the farm family, the proportion purchased as
compared with the part furnished; that is, grown. Apparently families do not increase cash expenditures for food directly as incomes
rise, unless they have incomes permitting a relatively high level of
living. For both farm and rural non-farm families, outlays for food
did not follow price changes until approximately the $1500 income
bracket was reached.

Greatest differences were found in expenditures for so-called
durable consumer goods, such as household equipment, washing

machines, and refrigerators, which were already scarce in the early quarter of 1942. The increases in this department of the budget occurred in every income group. At the $2500 level these items averaged $140 in 1941 compared with $85 in 1935-36.

Expenditures for clothing went up 9 per cent; for housing the estimates for rents were 5 to 9 per cent above the 1935-36 levels, while in 1941 actual expenditures for housing and household operation in each income class were definitely below those for 1935-36. Luxury items which loomed large in popular opinion, at least during the spending period of World War I, do not appear in 1941 or in the early part of 1942.

This general situation for the farm family in 1941 is shown in an "Outlook" report. The estimated gross cash income from marketings, commodities placed under loan, and from government payments, stands at $1300.[17] The net family income is estimated at $1230, which includes $150 from non-farm sources and $420 of non-monetary income from the farm itself.

It is evident from comparisons made during the depression period following 1930 and during the early war period, 1941-42, that consumption lags behind income both on the upturn and the downward trend. Total expenditures for family living, income class by income class, were not substantially different in 1941 from those in 1935-36, as comparison of the tables presented will show. During the period of retrenchment, families held to their standards of living as long as possible. First, savings were used, shifts were made, among farm families at least, to more "furnished" rather than "purchased" items. There were minimum levels below which families could not go without real danger to the public welfare, so "relief" provisions were made.

The trend continued upward after 1942. By 1944, cash farm receipts had increased 6 per cent over the previous year, and 152 per cent above the prewar average. Net savings had increased six times. It was estimated that individuals invested one-third of their 1944 savings in war bonds. The remainder went to other savings, to retire debts, and "many other purposes." [18] The "many other purposes" will be of great importance, at least for rural society, since farm families were in an all-time "high" as far as money avail-

17 The Outlook for Farm Family Living, 1941. Washington, D.C.: Bureau of Home Economics, United States Department of Agriculture, October, 1940.

18 Ballinger, Roy A., "National Economic Conditions in 1944." The Agricultural Situation. Washington, D.C.: Bureau of Agricultural Economics, United States Department of Agriculture, April, 1945.

able for family living was concerned. How they utilize it to improve standards of living in home and community will determine their future and the future of rural society.

Special reports with special points of emphasis. Six counties in Virginia were selected as representative of the white population in the major farming areas of the state. Farm families reported an average of $1130 spent for goods and services consumed during 1935 as compared with $1332 for urban families. Forty-six per cent of the 1730 farm families and 44 percent of the 761 urban families included in the study reported a total cost of living during 1935 of less than $1000. Measured by the cost-of-living index, differences between the tenure groups were large. Farm-owners reported an average of $1249; renters, $946; and croppers, $719. Urban families who owned their dwellings reported an average expenditure of family living of $1558, while those residing in rented dwellings reported $1153.[19]

Food represented a relatively larger proportion of rural farm than of urban family budgets, 41 per cent in the former, compared with 29 per cent in the latter. But there was little difference in the total value of food consumed per capita by the two groups. In all residence and tenure groups the proportion of the total family budget allocated to food decreased as the total cost of living increased. The proportions allocated to maintenance and operation of the family automobile, to health, births, and deaths, and to advancement increased as the cost of living increased.

A greater proportion of urban than of farm families reported such household facilities and conveniences as radios, telephones, and running water. In the open country more owners than tenants reported these, and in both residence groups more were reported by families with a higher total cost of living than by those in the lower brackets.

There was a definite relationship between the duration of marriage and the total value of goods and services consumed. As the time of the marriage union lengthened and the ability to buy economic goods increased, it appeared that the families attempted to improve their status through greater emphasis in the family budget upon certain items that would give tangible evidence of this increase. There appeared to be a definite relationship between the duration of marriage, the tenure status of the farm operator, and the number of acres operated. Farm croppers and renters who

[19] Davidson, Dwight M., Jr., and B. L. Hummel, *Standards of Living in Six Virginia Counties.* Washington, D.C.: Social Research Report XV, March, 1940.

were related to their landlords were generally those who had been married for a relatively short time.

The average amount of savings and investments for farm families was $102; in the urban, $168. The owners reported an average of $118; renters, $79; and croppers, $36. Savings accounted for the largest proportion of total investments in both residence groups. Urban families placed greater proportions in insurance, stocks, and other investments than did farm families.

Urban families devoted more time to leisure activities than did farm families. Time allotted to these activities ranged from an average of 2.6 hours per day for the farm operator to 4.6 hours for the urban homemaker. Male heads of urban families, with slightly higher formal educational attainments, spent an average of six hours per week reading, or approximately two hours more per week than the male head of the farm family.

The special emphasis of a study made in Ohio and reported in 1941 was on the interrelations of level of living, social participation, and social adjustment of farm families. Social participation was measured in terms of the amount and kind of organized group activities engaged in by the members of the families. Social adjustment was measured on a five-point scale in terms of the attitudes of satisfaction or dissatisfaction expressed by farm people toward their social environment.[20] The results of the study showed that Ohio farm people are generally well satisfied, but the degree of their satisfaction depends upon the various circumstances in which they live. The three factors — level of living, social participation, and social adjustment — were found to be closely associated, but they were also dependent upon such things as age, place of residence, size of family, religion, education, and occupation status.

Some of the significant relationships among the three factors are the following:

(1) Families ranking high on the scale of living were much better adjusted than the lower-ranking families.

(2) The majority of farm people participate very little in organized groups, but those who did are better adjusted than those who did not.

(3) Those persons in families which rank high on the scale of living participate more actively in organized groups than do those among the low-ranking families.

[20] Mangus, A. R., and H. R. Cottam, *Level of Living, Social Participation and Adjustment of Ohio Farm People.* Wooster: Bulletin 624, September, 1941, Ohio Agricultural Experiment Station.

(4) The degree of social adjustment was about the same in the major areas of the state studied, but the level of living and social participation differed rather widely.

While the three factors studied were closely interrelated, each factor was also influenced by other elements. For example, farmowners were better adjusted, had a higher level of living and participated more in social organizations than did tenants. This is quite in keeping with the results found in the study of New York farm-family patterns reported in the chapter on rural families.

Ohio families comprised of five or six persons attained the maximum ranks on all three scales, and those families having children at home were better adjusted and participated more than did those without children. This is an interesting confirmation of the observation made in the family chapter, regarding the rôle of children in family living. The family cycle is also reflected in the fact that up to fifty or sixty years people participated increasingly in community organizations, but with subsequent older age came a sharp curtailment in such social activity.

Persons with the most education had the highest levels of living, yet those who had finished high school were less satisfied and took less active part in social groups than did those with eighth-grade or some high-school training. Those who had not completed the eighth grade were lowest on all counts. Those affiliated with churches were best adjusted, took most active part in organizations, and had highest levels of living, yet there were wide differences among those belonging to different church groups.

Social participation and group standards. The emphasis given to relating levels of living to the social situation leads to other interesting considerations. A study of clothing supplies and social participation of white farm families in twelve representative beats (districts) in Mississippi during 1940 provides another illustration. Table 73 gives the basic figures from which conclusions were drawn.

The average number of family members is lower for families ranked A or B in clothing than for those classed as C. Social participation figures show that the majority of families with A clothing ranks also have highest social participation. Of families with B and C clothing ranks over one half were in the average social participation group. However, a larger proportion of the C than the B clothing rank families had low social participation. The relationships between incomes or tenure and clothing rank are in line with expectations — low for tenants, high for owners.

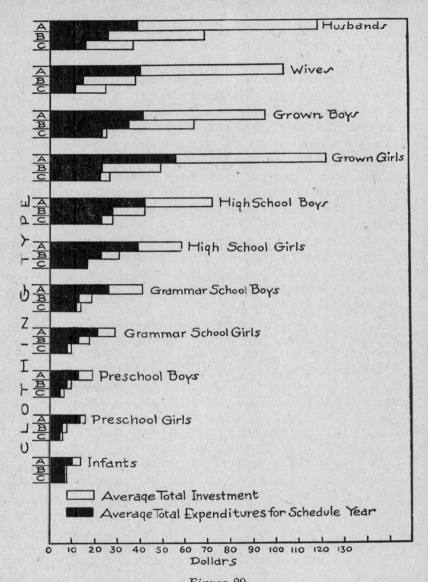

Figure 29

AVERAGE INVESTMENTS IN CLOTHING INVENTORIES
AND AMOUNTS EXPENDED FOR CLOTHING
DURING SCHEDULE YEAR, BY SEX
AND ACTIVITY GROUPS

Source: Alice Bowie and Dorothy Dickens, *Clothing Supplies of Socially Participating White Farm Families of Mississippi,* Technical Bulletin 30, June, 1942. Mississippi Agricultural Experiment Station, State College.

TABLE 73. FAMILIES' CLOTHING RANKS COMPARED WITH
SOCIO-ECONOMIC DATA

	Families' Clothing Rank			
	A	B	C	All
Total number of families......	46	117	24	187
Per cent of families...........	24.6	62.6	12.8	100.0
Average number of members per family....................	3.6	4.1	4.8	4.1
Social participation:				
Per cent high (A)...........	58.7	22.2	12.5	30.0
Per cent medium (B).......	37.0	55.6	58.3	51.3
Per cent low (C)...........	4.3	22.2	29.2	18.7
All......................	100.0	100.0	100.0	100.0
Incomes:				
$250 to $749..............	30.4	66.6	70.8	58.3
$750 to $1249.............	28.3	27.4	25.0	27.3
$1250 and over............	41.3	6.0	4.2	14.4
All......................	100.0	100.0	100.0	100.0
Tenure:				
Owners...................	78.3	60.7	45.9	63.1
Cash renters..............	15.2	17.1	20.8	17.1
Share renters.............	16.5	15.4	20.8	13.9
Sharecroppers.............	0.0	6.8	12.5	5.9
All......................	100.0	100.0	100.0	100.0

Source: Bowie, Alice, and Dorothy Dickens, *Clothing Supplies of Socially Participating White Farm Families of Mississippi.* State College: Technical Bulletin 30, June, 1942, Mississippi Agricultural Experiment Station.

From this type of study the important observation is made that clothing is a type of consumer goods which is not primarily used for physical welfare purposes, but rather for "psycho-social" welfare.[21] This means that clothing fulfills a social purpose and that a minimum amount of it is as necessary for social participation in church or school as is a minimum amount of food for adequate nutrition. The social importance cannot be the sole basis of judgment, to be sure, since there are questions of comfort and of difference because of age and sex. Finally, it may be suggested that personality can find expression in clothing through color and design, and through the social situations in which it is to be worn.

Practical implications regarding food also flow from this kind of

[21] Dickens, Dorothy, "Social Participation and Clothing," *Rural Sociology*, December, 1944.

social participation analysis. The same author, Miss Dickens, advises that women are more ready to adopt those food preparations and serving practices which are followed by their neighbors and relatives.[22]

This point of view has confirmation in other areas. In a study of food and culture in southern Illinois the conclusion is drawn that dietary changes are found associated with degrees of commercialization and contacts between groups such as German and Old American. It is said that differences in food habits as well as differences in resistance to change were closely related to the contemporary social scene.[23]

A study of nutrition among Spanish-Americans in northern Colorado reveals that there is a close relationship between local culture and environment and the food habits of people. This means that any recommendations for improvement in diet must be made in terms of the local situation and with an understanding of the ethnic hiatus between Americans of Spanish-Indian background and Americans of North-European origin.[24]

Families in resettlement communities compared with those in commercial and subsistence situations. It is often more revealing to study special types of family living rather than to spend too much time in analysis of general averages. Therefore, a brief description is given of families in seven resettlement projects and then compared with families in South Dakota and in an Appalachian area. The resettlement projects were the Raperville Farms in Hockley County, Texas; the Penderlea Homesteads in Penderlea County, North Carolina; the Dyess Colony in Mississippi County, Arkansas; the Cumberland Homesteads in Cumberland County, Tennessee; the Cumberland Mountain Farms in Jackson County, Alabama; the Bosque Farms in Valencia County, New Mexico; and the Ashwood Project in Lee County, South Carolina. Families in the resettlement projects were divided into three groups: first, those families that had

[22] Dickens, Dorothy, "Food Preparation of Owner and Cropper Farm Families in the Shortleaf Pine Area of Mississippi," *Social Forces*, vol. 22, no. 1, October, 1943.

[23] Passin, Herbert, and John W. Bennett, "Social Process and Dietary Change," *The Problems of Changing Food Habits*. Washington, D.C.: Report of the Committee on Food Habits of the National Research Council, National Research Council Bulletin 108; and Bennett, John W., Harvey L. Smith, and Herbert Passin, "Food and Culture in Southern Illinois — A Preliminary Report," *American Sociological Review*, vol. VII, no. 5, October, 1942.

[24] Pijoan, M., and R. W. Roskelley, *Nutrition and Certain Related Factors of Spanish-Americans in Northern Colorado*. Rocky Mountain Council on Inter-American Affairs, Denver, Western Policy Committee, Des Moines, Iowa, 1943.

lived on projects for at least a year and designed on the chart (Figure 30) as "Project." Second, were the families who had been on the projects less than a year, called "Prior-Year," and third, families living in neighborhoods close by the projects shown as "Neigh-- borhood."

The chart gives the expenditures of the three groups of families and indicates the proportions furnished and purchased. The striking thing is the high proportion of the total spent for food. In no instance is it less than 40 per cent. During the year preceding arrival on the projects, the range for food was from 43 per cent for the Penderlea families to 70 per cent for one group in the Ashwood and Dyess projects. During the first year on the projects, the average amount spent for food was $438, of which 54 per cent was furnished by the farms.

Levels of living are closely related with other aspects of family life as is shown in other sections; therefore, it is important to note that among the families in the settlement projects higher expenditures for family living were, with one exception, associated with the high ranks for social participation, years of schooling completed, homes having radios and current reading material. Likewise, families using smaller proportions of total expenditures for food were the ones in the highest ranks for other scores; they had money available for other items in the family budget. This should be added evidence (1) that family living and spending are not isolated activities, but are tied up with the other aspects of community life; (2) that if the total amount available for family living is too limited, the whole style of the family is cramped simply in order to have food.

Comparisons of the seven resettlement families with families in South Dakota and in the Appalachian region make these relationships even clearer. Families in the South Dakota group, for the most part engaged in commercial agriculture, consumed goods and services valued at $1111, while for the Appalachian families, largely subsistence or part-time farmers, the average was $584. Between these limits fell the Project families with $806, the Prior-Year families with $787, and the Neighborhood families with $732. Families in the Appalachian region, however, produced 50 per cent of their food, which, together with the purchased, meant 55 per cent of the total amount of family living. The proportion allocated for food by the South Dakota families was 44 per cent, still high by some standards.

Shelter — housing and household conveniences. No less than food

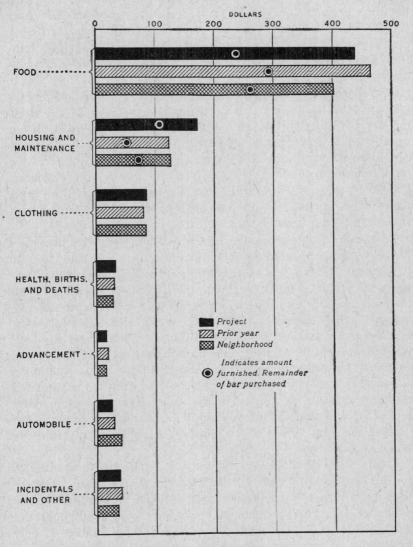

DOLLARS

FOOD

HOUSING AND
MAINTENANCE

CLOTHING

HEALTH, BIRTHS,
AND DEATHS

ADVANCEMENT

AUTOMOBILE

INCIDENTALS
AND OTHER

Project
Prior year
Neighborhood

Indicates amount
furnished. Remainder
of bar purchased

Figure 30

AVERAGE VALUE OF PRINCIPAL ITEMS OF GOODS
AND SERVICES CONSUMED, BY TYPE OF
RESIDENCE, SEVEN RESETTLEMENT
PROJECTS, 1935

and clothing, shelter — the family house with its furnishings and conveniences — is a part of the level and the standard of living of families. The house may be considered the symbol of the home, while its equipment and conveniences are the instruments which, in the hands of skillful homemakers, may greatly influence standards of living. Rural housing, from the standpoint of new construction, repair, or maintenance and the introduction of modern conveniences, suffered severely during the period of agriculture's distress. The national government worked diligently during the last two administrations to set plans in motion for the relief of too heavy indebtedness on homes and for the encouragement of new construction, repairs, and conveniences. However, the war demanded that materials necessary for such purposes be put to destructive rather than constructive uses.

Many comparisons of housing in rural society can be made from the United States Census data. An example is given in Table 74 of rural farm families by persons per room, region, and tenure, in 1940.

One item of convenience, frequently considered the most important, is electricity. It may be considered a kind of index suggesting the speed with which technology is reaching the farm. Only 10 per cent of the farms in 1930 were receiving central station electricity; the estimate for 1944 runs to 42 per cent for the rural farm population and 78.7 for rural non-farm.[25]

In the farm homes the Census for 1940 makes the report by regions, as carried in Table 75. According to this report Massachusetts ranked highest with 83.5 per cent of its farm homes supplied with electricity from a central station, followed closely by Rhode Island with 83.3 per cent; the lowest was Mississippi with 9.5 per cent.

The Rural Electrification Administration, now a unit within the Department of Agriculture, is responsible for bringing electricity to many farms. Private utilities have expanded their services to rural areas. In the ten-year period, 1935 to 1945, about two million more farms had electricity than before; about half the farms are still without the service. The REA has set as its goal 1,300,000 more farm families within three years after materials are available. The public agency advances its program on the expressed assumption that electricity on the farm can be a source of income and the basis for improvement of family living. With electricity come the many appliances which can keep the household abreast of the farmstead

[25] "Rural Electrification After the War," Rural Electrification Administration, St. Louis 2, 1945.

TABLE 74. RURAL FARM FAMILIES BY PERSONS PER ROOM, REGIONS, AND TENURE, 1940

	Number of Persons per Room					
	0.50 or Less	0.51 to 0.75	0.76 to 1.00	1.01 to 1.50	1.51 to 2.00	2.01 or More
All Families Reporting						
Total: 6,982,020	2,037,440	1,352,420	1,466,280	1,000,620	637,600	487,666
Per cent: 100.........	29.2	19.4	21.0	14.3	9.1	7.0
Owner Families Reporting						
Total: 3,729,840	1,409,300	784,240	724,760	427,940	222,700	160,900
Per cent: 100.0.......	37.8	21.0	19.4	11.5	6.01	4.03
Tenant Families Reporting						
Total: 3,252,180	628,140	568,180	741,520	572,680	44,900	326,760
Per cent: 100.0.......	19.3	17.5	22.8	17.6	12.8	10.0
Northeast States						
Owner, per cent....	55.1	22.2	14.4	6.0	1.8	0.5
Tenant, per cent ...	38.6	24.1	21.7	10.6	3.5	1.4
North Central States						
Owner, per cent....	46.1	22.5	17.1	8.5	3.6	2.3
Tenant, per cent ...	34.3	23.3	21.4	11.8	5.4	3.3
The South						
Owner, per cent....	27.1	19.8	22.4	15.5	9.0	6.2
Tenant, per cent ...	10.8	14.2	23.2	21.0	17.0	13.8
Non-White, per cent	11.3	12.8	22.3	19.5	17.9	16.1
The West						
Owner, per cent....	34.1	19.8	20.8	11.4	6.5	7.4
Tenant, per cent ...	20.8	16.1	25.9	15.4	11.4	10.3

Source: *Sixteenth Census of the United States, Population and Housing*, Table 3, pp. 79–81.

in this age of machinery — house lights, radio, washing machine, pump, vacuum cleaner, dishwasher, toaster, refrigerator, sewing machine, curling irons for the women and electric razors for the men.

Farms and small cities or towns were compared from data in the Pennsylvania-Ohio farming section in 1935-36, for $500 to $1000 and for $2500 to $3000 income levels. The percentage comparisons between cities and farms for the $500 to $1000 income level were as follows: running water: farms, 21 per cent, cities, 85 per cent;

TABLE 75. DWELLINGS ON FARMS LIGHTED BY ELECTRICITY,
BY DIVISION

Census Division	Per cent 1930	Per cent 1940
All divisions	13.4	33.3
New England	42.9	68.0
Middle Atlantic	31.9	65.3
East North Central	21.0	55.6
West North Central	13.2	26.9
South Atlantic	6.1	25.0
East South Central	3.0	14.3
West South Central	3.6	16.8
Mountain	20.4	45.0
Pacific	52.9	75.4

Source: Tabulations from the *Sixteenth Census of the United States*, 1940, 2d edition. Washington, D.C.: Bureau of Agricultural Economics, United States Department of Agriculture, October, 1941.

hot water in kitchen and bathroom: farms, 9 per cent, cities, 41 per cent; electricity: farms, 31 per cent, cities, 95 per cent; central furnace: farms, 18 per cent, cities, 40 per cent.

If the gauge for a so-called "modern" home is one equipped with electricity, running water, both hot and cold, and indoor flush toilet, then fewer than one tenth of the farmhouses in this country are modern, according to estimates made in the Consumer Purchase study in 1935-36 to which reference has been made. Surely here is an opportunity for utilizing savings during the postwar period.

The problem of rural housing is evidently not merely one of more rooms. Farm homes are large enough, at least for those families in the North Central states, according to conclusions of the Farm and Village Housing Committee which will be reported in a following section. Overcrowding is not so much in terms of floor space as of heating facilities during the cold and wet seasons, in order that all the family need not be confined to the kitchen; of lighting facilities, especially for children to do their reading and school work, of bathing and toilet facilities for the furtherance of good health. Beyond these are facilities for cooking, washing, and other cleaning. "The whole picture leaves much to be desired," according to the Consumer Purchases Study. Limiting factors are the prevailing low incomes in certain areas of high birth rates, tenant and laborer status, and the long period of depression and war, during which comparatively few repairs were made and little remodeling done.

The establishment of the United States Housing Authority in 1937 marks a change of public policy in respect to this area of family living. Funds and credit, provided for in the act, are to be used to assist the several states and their political subdivisions to alleviate recurring unemployment and to remedy housing condi-

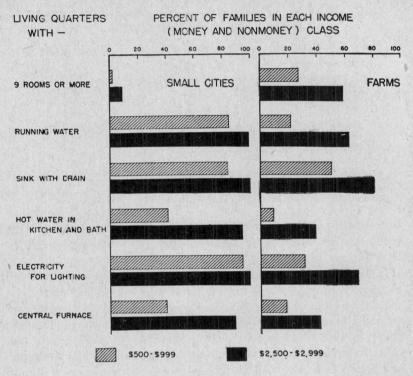

Figure 31

FACILITIES IN LIVING QUARTERS: NORTH CENTRAL
SMALL CITIES AND PENNSYLVANIA-OHIO
FARM SECTION, 1935-36

Source: The Outlook for Farm Family Living, 1941. Bureau of
Home Economics, United States Department of Agriculture, Washington, D.C., October, 1940.

tions and the acute shortage of decent, safe, and sanitary dwellings
for families of low income in rural and urban communities.

While in the first years this public agency gave attention mainly
to the urban situation, rural housing projects have been undertaken
recently. County Housing Authorities are set up by the states,
which in turn enlist the aid of the United States Housing Authority
and that of the Department of Agriculture. To secure such help,
farms must be approved by the Department of Agriculture as being
sufficiently productive, and legal title must be with the Authority.
Such plans call for a house costing about two thousand dollars, a
small orchard, fencing for garden and poultry, a sanitary privy, and

a covered well. The homes will rent for about forty to fifty dollars per year.

Helping farm families to improve their own homes with their own labor and private funds is a phase of service rendered by other public agencies, such as the Agricultural Extension Service, Farm Security Administration, the Forest Service, and vocational teachers of agriculture and home economics in the local community high schools.

Farm and village housing. A study of farm and village houses was made in 28 representative counties, well distributed over the country, on the basis of types of farm areas. From these investigations the following conclusions were drawn. There is little apparent need for more space (which has been a common need in urban housing) in most farmhouses, with the exception of instances in the Appalachian-Ozark Highlands, the Cotton Belt, and the Great Plains area. Generally, farm dwellings were built some years ago when costs of constructing and operating houses were low. In many cases, even in the Corn Belt and the Northern Dairy sections, not all the available rooms are in use throughout the year. There are exceptions, however, in the southern sections, the Great Plains and the Great Basin areas, where the need for more space is felt.[26]

Modern equipment and conveniences have received too little attention in all of the sections. There are many farmhouses in the different regions, the Appalachian-Ozark Highlands, the Cotton Belt, and the Great Plains areas particularly, where items of equipment which are indispensable to comfort, cleanliness, and the maintenance of health are not available, and where modern conveniences seem out of reason. Much is to be desired in all sections in the adaptations of the farmhouse to the purely physical needs of the family. There is also a field for unlimited development in farm housing from the esthetic point of view, in regard to the setting, the landscape planning and the planting, the room arrangement, the interior finish, furnishings and equipment, as well as additional labor-saving facilities for conserving the energy of the homemaker.

Although, according to this study, village housing problems are less acute than farm housing problems, they also merit further investigation and attention. There is need for the development of hous-

[26] Committee on Farm and Village Housing, A. R. Mann, chairman; report prepared by Bruce L. Melvin and edited by John M. Gries and James Ford. The President's Conference on Home Building and Home Ownership, Washington, D.C., 1932. In the paragraphs which follow there is literal and even *verbatim* use of this committee's report, as it is the best available source.

ing standards which are attainable by different groups in the village population. These standards should take into consideration the architectural design of the houses, and the methods of financing. They should be developed in the light of a growing interest in village planning for individual comfort and social efficiency in housing.

An interesting section of the report is devoted to the history of rural architecture in the United States. To the student of rural society it is much more than a record of plan and design of dwelling; it is the story of family ideals, and the culture of a new country made up of many groups of differing backgrounds, as represented by English, Dutch, French, and Spanish Colonial dwellings. It is also a record of the westward march of the frontier with the simple log cabin; the more substantial structure in Kentucky, Tennessee, and along the Ohio River; the frame house of the Mid-West with the constant influence of New England in its architecture, and finally some of the best designed and most artistic farm homes in the rich fruit areas of California, Oregon, and Washington.

After urging the need for more study of the problems, for adequate and recognized standards and for a greatly expanded program of education, the report concludes with the following significant paragraph:

It is clearly recognized that American agriculture and rural life are in process of reconstruction, but it is believed that to strengthen and enrich rural family life is a paramount function that can be partially performed by aiding home improvement. The house, as a physically conditioning factor, in any setting, makes easy or difficult the formation of habits of order, cleanliness, healthful living, and an appreciation of beauty. It may be an object of pride or embarrassment. It constitutes part of the objective environment in which happy or unhappy relationships within the family grow, and in which the child's personality — fully blossoming or dwarfed — evolves. It is believed that better planned homes, more modernized houses, and an increasing number of flower-and-shrubbery decked yards on our farms and within our villages will stimulate an idealism that can give new values to the economic motive in society, and in the midst of financial depressions hold rural living above the ravages. However, economic achievement cannot be the end for human effort; economic activities fluctuate; the longings of men and women reach for permanency in satisfactions — health, harmony within the home, physical comforts, beauty, and many tangible qualities that give zest to family and individual living.

As a conclusion to these comparisons, it must be emphasized that rural family living cannot be compared in any wholesale fashion with urban or village conditions. The surroundings and the plan of farm life differ from those of the city. The major satisfactions of farm life, and, probably to a lesser extent, village life, can come from many different sources, and may be less dependent upon direct financial income than the major satisfactions of city life. Many farmers have close at hand the things for which the villager or the urbanite is willing to pay well in time or money. On the other hand, the urban dweller may be envied by the farmer or villager for his readier access to many of the sources of advancement goods, and services. It is possible that with more small-farm machinery adapted to the family-type farm, and with more household conveniences, more young people will remain in or will move to the country. The so-called drudgery of farm life has driven many people away from farms in years past, but with science, machinery, and improved transportation many of the considered advantages of the city are now available to country people. In all comparisons one must keep in mind that farm, village, and city modes of living are different, and that mental and emotional reactions are not susceptible of measurement in a way to permit complete comparisons.

Standards of living have both material and non-material aspects; this is one reason why some people prefer farm life to city life. With the greater freedom of movement and contacts outlined in the chapter on rural-urban relationships, it should be easier in the future for those who prefer rural life to choose it. Significant contributions to American attitudes and values can be made by rural people in respect to the non-material but essential elements of home life.

Factors Influencing Rural Ways of Living

It is not possible, of course, to account for all the changes and differences in ways of living shown by the studies which have been presented, yet some of the factors influencing those ways can be pointed out. Illustrations will be drawn from cases so that ways of living among various types of rural families can be further described. It is well to point out again that actual figures for any one group of families, or for any one year may mean very little in themselves. They take on importance for the student of society only as they reveal important relationships in the home and in the various social groups of which the family is a part. The factors to be discussed should be thought of as forces or situations which help to determine standards in the home as a social institution and the levels of living in any given time or place. These factors or forces do not act singly, but in various combinations. One element in the complex may be strong or another weak, and they may change with the passage of time and with the cycle of family experience.

The family cycle. The description of cycles of family development in an earlier chapter shows that rural families are constantly in the process of change; the family forms with two persons, children come and eventually go. The period for this full cycle in an average farm family is about twenty-five years. In a study of a group of farm families in Ohio, the period was longer, but the maximum size was reduced after about eighteen years.[27] The demands on the family's budget change with the swing of the cycle. It is not only a question of the number of children to feed, clothe, and house, but of their habits of life, which change with age.

In a Wisconsin study, the proportionate value of food to the value of all goods increases from 39.6 per cent for families with no children, to 47.5 per cent for families with six or more children. Similarly, the proportion used for clothing increases from 11.1 per cent to 17.9 per cent. It is the clothing item which most clearly reveals the differences of age and sex. In a chart giving the average amounts of clothing purchased for persons of different sex and age groups, sons and daughters from nineteen to twenty-four years of age become conspicuous, almost doubling the amounts they required between the ages of twelve to fourteen years.[28] The same relationship is shown in the chart of the Mississippi families and the clothing requirements of their members.

During the high-school period there is a decided change in the behavior pattern of the family when compared with the earlier stage when the children are small and with the later, all-adult age. Radical adjustments have to be made in the spending budget and in the time-schedule of the family. Frequently income cannot be increased as rapidly as demands expand. The figures found in the study of the seven resettlement areas indicate that families reached their peak in total cost of living about fifteen to twenty years

[27] Lively, C. E., *The Growth Cycle of the Farm Family*. Columbus: Ohio Agricultural Experiment Station, Mimeograph Bulletin 51, October, 1932.

[28] Kirkpatrick, E. L., Rosalind Tough, and May Cowles, *The Life Cycle of the Farm Family*. Madison: Research Bulletin 121, Agricultural Experiment Station, University of Wisconsin, September, 1934.

after marriage, and when the children were near maturity and could aid in family tasks. It was in this period also when the largest proportion of the livelihood was furnished by the farm. In the Ohio situation the size of farm enterprise was only slightly related to size of family.

Consideration of the family cycle simply means that a family must anticipate and make preparation for the changing requirements of its members. This means good family management, as will be pointed out. It also means that those working with rural families, whether in programs to improve health, education, recreation, or husbandry, also need to understand these changes. Standardized approaches will not appeal to all families in every stage of their cycle. When the family is formed and the first children come, there are strong filio-centric bonds. Calls to community meetings or church services may be met with seeming indifference. At the other end of the cycle, when the family loses its driving force, when the children are grown and gone or are beginning their own family cycle, perhaps on the "home farm," then the motives of the original pair have changed. They are less likely to respond to suggestion of larger profits; they may want more flowers in the family garden or some provision for old age.

Family management. Just as the success of the farm or of a business is more than a matter of farm or business management, so is the success of the household as a consumer center more than a matter of home management in the narrow sense. Both are matters of family management. Different families may spend very different amounts to get approximately the same kind of consumption goods or services. Different items of the budget may give more satisfaction to some families than to others. Standards of living, therefore, become a matter of management quite as much as a matter of income. Making the most of home resources is an important consideration. The truth of this can be seen in the differences in distribution of purchased and furnished goods in the same relative income classes. Good management practices which the family should utilize are budgeting in advance, keeping accounts, knowing how to get one's money's worth in the market through knowledge of products and materials, and understanding the principles of personality development.

Skillful management and co-operation of members of the family are necessary in converting local resources to good advantage, such as improving the home grounds by planting trees, shrubs, grass, flowers, and vegetables. Many of these things can be had with little cash expenditure. Time may be used to better advantage if planned in advance or fully utilized for home-talent recreational and educational activity.[29] A sense of "home" may be achieved by a touch of the artistic, by good taste, which means appropriateness. The question is, Can the rural family make its house its home?

Interrelated with income. According to various measures which have been devised, there does seem to be correspondence between larger incomes and higher expenditures for family living. Yet there is no evidence that the relationship is a thoroughly automatic one; that is, one cannot reason directly from cause to effect. Larger incomes do not necessarily mean better expenditures for living, nor do greater expenditures imply actual higher standards of living; they only make them possible.

There is little doubt that greater attention given to spending and to improving home conditions in the last two decades has had important effects in actually improving levels of living. Groups of families have had conferences, as was described earlier; they have talked over their budgets and considered their essential needs for living. This has tended to vivify those needs as well as to create incentive to convert the resources of the farm to meet those needs. To be sure, many such hopeful efforts had rude shocks, and died natural deaths during the successive years of emergencies, depressions, and wars.

Changes in a family's ways of living fluctuate less suddenly and less violently with changes in general economic conditions than does income, as was demonstrated in the data presented earlier. Farm families, like other families, tend to hold to certain established standards. They attempt to maintain their accustomed ways of living, even though former sources of income have been cut off; savings are used or debts are contracted in order to carry on the family living. One mother asserted in no uncertain terms that she would see the farm go before she would deny her children the opportunity of an education.

The struggle to maintain standards in a period of decreasing buying power and declining prices has many serious consequences. The evidences were found in increased mortgage indebtedness, tax delinquencies, and lack of upkeep of farm buildings and fences,

[29] Frayser, Mary E., *Use of Leisure in Selected Rural Areas of South Carolina,* Bulletin 263, Clemson Agricultural College Experiment Station, 1930; Wilson, Maud, *Use of Time by Oregon Homemakers,* Bulletin 256, Oregon Agricultural Experiment Station, 1929; Rankin, J. O., *Use of Time in Farm Homes.* Madison: Bulletin 230, Nebraska Agricultural Experiment Station, 1928.

for, as one popular writer said, "Farm folks are eating their fences, their barns, and their houses." He meant, of course, that the income available was going toward the family living rather than toward the usual repairs about the farmstead.

These instances emphasize what was evident in the comparisons of expenditures and incomes. There becomes visible what can be considered an American pattern of family living. In it, the interrelations between income and expenditure are, with due allowance for fluctuations, remarkably stable. And this is true for all types of families compared — farm, rural non-farm, and urban. Income is a limiting factor to expenditures and to debts assumed for consumption purposes, as the figures indicate. The counterpart of the interaction is equally true. Standards of living, as they condition family relationships in their social, health, and spiritual aspects, have a definite influence upon the income-getting capacity of the family unit. As has been stressed repeatedly, the family is a working unit. Family units are not isolated things, however, as will be detailed later. They make up the general society, not through any process of addition, but in a more organic sense of vital relationships. Society is, therefore, concerned with the welfare of its units. For example, among poorer families a set of forces may be in operation over which the individual family has little control. Society must step in. At the other end of the scale there may be what has been called "conspicuous consumption"; that is, spending for effect, for ostentation, without regard to those standards which concern the welfare of the family or the social groups of which it is a part. Here, too, society exerts various forms of social control, such as taxation, social conventions, public opinion, or even ridicule.

Related to tenure status. Differences in ways of living in many areas in the homes of owners, tenants, and laborers are significant. A study of the social status and farm tenure of Corn Belt and Cotton Belt farmers compares the tenure groups, while attempting to control or hold constant, by statistical means, the racial and the geographic factors.[30]

A comparison of the median-size house in terms of number of rooms shows the following: Northern owners, 7.7; Northern tenants, 7.3; Northern laborers, 6.5; Southern white owners, 5.7; Southern white tenants, 4.4; colored owners, 4.4; Southern white laborers,

[30] Schuler, E. A., *Social Status and Farm-Tenure Attitudes and Social Conditions of Corn Belt and Cotton Belt Farmers.* Washington, D.C.: Social Research Report IV, United States Department of Agriculture, 1938.

3.9; Negro laborers, 3.8; and Negro tenants, 3.5. When these same groups are compared as to possession of three household conveniences — running water, kitchen sink with drain, and indoor toilet — surprising differences were found. Nearly three fifths of both owners and tenants in the North possessed these conveniences, while only about one fifth of the Northern laborers had them. In the case of Southern whites, the order was completely reversed, the owners reporting possession in only a little more than one fifth of the cases while of the tenants and laborers nearly two fifths had them. For Negroes, the proportion having the conveniences, regardless of tenure class, was negligible.

Racial differences. It is commonly known that there is variation in ways of living on farms between groups having different cultural backgrounds, but the extent of differences between the various racial and nationality groups in America is not fully known. Comparisons in the small but carefully selected samples of Southern white and Negro farm families were included in the study of tenure just described. It was found that the average number of rooms in Negro houses was 3.2, less than one room per person, while Southern whites had an average of 4.6, which was more than one room per person. For heating facilities, about two thirds of the Negro families and one half of the Southern whites had only fireplaces. For lighting, kerosene lamps were used by about eight out of ten Southern white, and about ninety-eight out of a hundred Negro, families. More than half of both Negroes and whites in the South were getting water from open wells. One of the most striking differences between the two races was the matter of sanitation.

Education of parents. Analysis of the many families described previously shows that the amount of education of parents, both farm operators and home-makers, makes a difference in the ways of living of the family. Several smaller and more recent studies have verified this conclusion, but they also point to the fact that the schooling of the home-maker is more closely associated with the ways of family living than is that of the farm operator. More education on the part of both parents is associated with greater total expenditure. The proportioning of the various items within the family budget also changes with increase of education. For those families whose home-maker has had more than average schooling, the percentage spent for food decreases noticeably, and the percentage for "advancement goods" almost always increases. It should not be argued that education can be measured by amount of schooling, since the character of experience is vastly important;

nevertheless, education, even by such comparisons, is a consequential factor in family living. The problem is, how best to educate rural youth for the great adventure of homemaking in modern rural society.

Farm and home — compete or co-operate? Attention to the factors of income, status, race, and education soon poses the larger question of interaction of farm and home; are they strengthening each other or may they be competing? Opportunity for competition seems greater in rural than in urban society, since a smaller proportion of city than farm families is in independent business undertakings. In this case, business would seem to compete less strongly for funds in urban than in farm households. There are many illustrations. Payments on mortgages often absorb more than the amount left from the total farm income after paying farm expenses and family living. Farms are frequently rented or sold on the basis of land rather than housing facilities afforded the family. In fact, in a recent bulletin offering advice in buying a farm, it was emphasized that the farm is the source of income and the house must be considered as of secondary importance.[31] Apparently it was overlooked that farm income, no matter how high, cannot stand alone. It must have family support to give it meaning and purpose, and the family must have an adequate and attractive house if it is to be made a home.

This is an age-old problem, and it has found its way into conventional drama plots. The story is in terms of the proverbial choosing between values. The farm boy, back home from his college of agriculture training, marries the country girl, but her college training was in the school of music. The first family crisis came suddenly when very unexpectedly they learned that the adjoining forty acres of land were for sale. Should they buy the forty or the new piano they had just priced? Well, the last scene presents the decision to buy both because the young man's father plays his characteristic rôle of helping them acquire the land. It also brings an announcement of the prospect of a family heir. Families and their homes are built generation by generation, and that continuity is one of the elements of stability in family life and in family living which has been the theme of this chapter and the earlier chapter on rural families.

A danger point may arise if farm families overemphasize the

[31] Wilcox, Walter M., and P. E. McNall, *Some Questions to Ask — When Buying a Farm.* Madison: Circular 347, September, 1944. Extension Service, College of Agriculture, University of Wisconsin.

advantages of increased income and place an overvaluation on their land, or attempt to overextend the margins of farming areas, or frankly to "mine" the soil and then move on to another farm. As was suggested early in the chapter, some of this income advantage must be plowed back into family and community standards of living if rural life is to offer continuing opportunities for families.

Granted that agriculture should be efficient and capable in productive capacity, a highly commercialized economy is vulnerable, indeed, unless it can perpetuate a household policy which will foster children — their health, education, and happiness. If it does not, it will not be more than a generation before its farms will be peopled, although perhaps not owned, by the more fecund, self-sufficing families.

Improvements in agriculture as in industry must proceed from, or at least be associated with, the urge for better standards of living.[32] An Interbureau Committee and the Bureau of Agricultural Economics of the United States Department of Agriculture, in a special report on Technology on the Farm, recognize this co-operative formula when they urge expansion of production in both agriculture and industry, because that would make possible a higher level of living for the entire population, and a more stable and satisfying rural culture. "That is our goal," the report concludes.[33] Much is to be done in the years just ahead to bring this ideal to reality.

Agitation of market and sales pressure. Agitation of the market through national advertising, direct-mail selling, and the constant pressure of salesmen is surely influencing the ways of living of rural as well as urban families. The extent and the character of this influence is still largely a matter of conjecture; studies have not extended far enough to tell definitely. There are also the modern devices of credit agencies and installment buying. Credit practices and instruments have been expanded. In a buying and selling economy, the family feels the impact of a set of forces quite different from those at work when it operated with its own individual spinning wheel, churn, and smokehouse. The availability of goods of recognized quality and reasonable price is a first-rate problem for the household consumption manager. Dependence upon mer-

[32] Taylor, Henry C., "World Social Structure," *Land Policy Review,* vol. VII, no. 3.

[33] *Technology on the Farm.* A special Report by an Interbureau Committee and the Bureau of Agricultural Economics, United States Department of Agriculture, August, 1940.

chandising is a major factor in the interdependence of town and country, as a previous chapter has emphasized. The problem for the home manager is, How can she be sure of her market, and how can she know when she is getting the most for her dollar?

Customs and demands of society. Another factor which influences levels of family living is that of custom and the demands of society itself. It may be well to emphasize again that families in their homes are not independent integers; rather, associated with other families in other homes, they are dependent upon them. Indeed, it is in this way that the structure of rural society is organized. Society has many different ways of making its demands felt. Some are direct; others indirect and subtle. There is that wide range of psychological and cultural factors known as custom, tradition, and conventionality. "It is the thing to do," or, "This is the way our folks have always done it," are powerful means of determining the direction that consumption shall take. They play their part in answering such questions as present versus future spending, or in determining the competition between land-ownership and consumption-goods, to which reference has been made.

Moreover, society has a way of imposing its demands upon families by legislation and taxation. Also, under the rationalization of public policy, general society is assuming more and more direction of the functions and services which in the past were largely assumed by the family itself, at least were in the pioneering days. As long as the family members as citizens continue to have a voice in the determination of those policies, family and society interests can be reconciled, although they may clash at times.

In the public welfare. This line of discussion leads directly to questions of public welfare; it is more than a one-way circuit. If society imposes its demands, it must also accept its responsibilities. Briefly, this would seem to mean that if there are farm programs, there must be corresponding family programs; if there are land-use planning policies, there must be correlated population policies. If, as is urged in some economic circles, the goal is increased average per capita productivity and therefore need for fewer and fewer people on the land (and the argument should also hold for industry), then there should be some plan made for the disposition of the so-called "surplus population." Surely another depression should not be necessary to demonstrate the havoc wrought by wresting families from their moorings. People should not be forced to go without food when many producers of food have "surpluses." Surpluses of food and of people at the same time, in the same country, are anachronisms. Correction of this state of things will put this generation to the test.

The subject of population and family living can be considered only partially here. It will be recalled that children are found in greatest numbers in certain types of agricultural areas. Here families require help in health, education, and sanitation measures. It may be necessary to zone certain marginal areas against agriculture, moving the families out and helping them to raise their own levels of living in their new environments. Depressed classes do not move automatically even in periods of dire distress. As has been shown by case studies, higher levels of living are correlated with fewer children.

Even in those farming areas where the size of family is near average — that is, two children — there must also be opportunity for choice unless the farm is to be divided. The principle of equalization, long recognized in education and health programs, needs to be employed to even greater extent in such situations. School curricula should be varied to permit occupational exploration and choice, and this at general public expense, since all the children will not remain in the local community. An ingenious suggestion has been made that if there is to be "subsidy" for agriculture, it should be given, not to individual families, but for the improvement of public services and the social amenities of the rural community.[34]

Problems may not be so acute among farm-owners with average-size families; however, some public measures are needed to encourage the numbers of larger-than-average families on the land, but only tenuously attached to it — tenants, laborers, croppers, seasonal workers. They have the children and the lower levels of living. They need help in securing basic standards for housing, working conditions, sanitation, education, and health. One answer might be greater opportunity for collective action, bargaining for income, co-operative housing, or consumer purchasing.

The trend of arguments often heard seems to assume continuation of the traditional increase in the population of the nation, but the analysis of population changes given in earlier chapters belies this assumption. If the reproduction rate should fall as low as in Sweden, for example, before the war, then the population-surplus argument might be thrown into reverse. It is already evident, even in rural society, that some groups and classes of families even now, are

[34] Smith, T. Lynn, and Ralph W. Roberts, "Sources and Distribution of the Farm Population in Relation to Farm Benefit Payments," *Journal of Farm Economics*, vol. XXIII, no. 3, August, 1941.

not replacing themselves. In another generation they will have died out; their farms will be for sale, and their particular types of social institutions will not be needed.[35]

In conclusion, food, clothing, shelter, articles for adornment, the flower garden, even the family car, are not only physical things. They all cost money and time, they are all items in a family budget. But they are vastly more than that; they are means for personality expression; they are the stuff, the artifacts, out of which cultures are made; they are objects of primary affection to which important values are given. The urge found in rural people to live well is a great social resource. The determination to improve family as well as community standards of living is clearly discernible to those who know rural America, and from the numerous study reports which have appeared through the years. This struggle may become a challenge as compelling as the conquest of the frontier; might it even become the moral equivalent of war?

All of living cannot be done in the home, however. The recognition of this fact leads to a consideration of those community institutions and agencies with which members of the rural family are increasingly associating themselves. They are subjects for the succeeding chapters.

DISCUSSION TOPICS

1. Give your own definition of consumption. What forces have been at work recently compelling changes in farmers' and villagers' standards of living? What have been the social and community consequences?

2. What items does your family trim first with a declining income? Which last? What items does it expand first with an increasing income? Which last?

3. How may a farm or village family improve its standards of living without increasing its income?

4. List in order of what you consider to be the four most needed home improvements in a community, rural or urban, in which you are acquainted. Give reasons for your choice.

5. Secure as accurate information as you can regarding the costs last year of operating the household which you know best. You will need to make estimates when definite amounts are not known. With this

[35] *Congregationalism in Rural Wisconsin,* Wisconsin Congregational Conference, Madison, in co-operation with Town and Country Department. New York: Church Extension Division, Board of Home Missions, Congregational and Christian Churches, 1942.

information in hand, make the calculations necessary to the construction of the table outlined below. (It is possible that the ease or the difficulty with which this exercise is done will illustrate the importance as well as the problems connected with the whole matter of family standards of living.)

Items of Consumption	Total of Furnished and Purchased		Furnished by Garden, Farm or Store (if Owned by Family)		Total Purchased	
	Dollars	Per cent	Dollars	Per cent	Dollars	Per cent
Total	·	100		100		100
1. Food...............						
2. Clothing...........						
3. Heat, light, fuel.....						
4. Rent (including taxes, insurance, depreciation on house)............						
5. All other operating expense..............						
6. Health.............						
7. Advancement.......						
a. education........						
b. recreation........						
c. religion..........						
d. savings...........						
e. all others.........						
8. Personal incidental items..............						

REFERENCE READINGS

Atkeson, Mary Meek, *The Woman on the Farm*. New York: Century Company, 1924. An account of the homemaker's problems.

Bureau of Agricultural Economics, U.S. Department of Agriculture, *Attitudes of Rural People Toward Radio Service*, January 1946, Washington, D.C. A nation-wide survey of farm and small-town people.

Chase and Schlink, *Our Money's Worth*. New York: The Macmillan Co., 1931. How consumers are exploited; some suggestions as to what can be done about it.

Cottam, Howard R., "Housing Scales for Rural Pennsylvania," *Journal of the American Statistical Association*, December, 1943.

Dickinson, R. E., *The Le Play Method in Regional Survey*, The Le Play Society, 58 Gordon Square, London, W.C. 1.

Freeman, Ruth C., and M. Attie Souder, *Living Expenditures of a Selected Group of Illinois Farm and Small-town Families (1929-30)*. Urbana: University of Illinois Agricultural Experiment Station, Bulletin 372, September, 1931.

Galpin, C. J., *Rural Life,* chapters 5 and 6. New York: Century Company, 1918. The rôle of the housewife and the child in home and community.

Hoflich, Harold J., Wm. H. Taylor, and Lauren W. Casaday, *A Study of the Incomes and Disbursements of 218 Middle-Income Families in Honolulu.* University of Hawaii, Bulletin 10, vol. XVII, October, 1938.

Hoyt, Elizabeth E., *Consumption in Our Society.* New York: McGraw-Hill, 1938. Contains an important section on consumption and choice.

Kirkpatrick, E. L., *Farmers' Standard of Living.* New York: Century Company, 1929. A comprehensive treatment of the subject and the first book of its kind.

Kirkpatrick, E. L., *Better Living in Home and Community.* Circular 247, July, 1931. Madison: Extension Service, College of Agriculture, University of Wisconsin. Popular summary of the National Country Life Conference on Standards of Living.

Kirkpatrick, E. L., *Standards of Living.* Circular 241, September, 1930. Madison: Extension Service, College of Agriculture, University of Wisconsin. Compilation and interpretation of available publications on standards of living.

Kyrk, Hazel, *A Theory of Consumption.* Boston: Houghton Mifflin, 1923. Statement of the theoretical and psychological backgrounds of consumption.

Mangus, A. R., and Robert L. McNamara, *Levels of Living and Population Movements in Rural Areas of Ohio, 1930-40.* Bulletin 639, March, 1943. Wooster: Ohio Agricultural Experiment Station.

Riemer, Svend, "Farm Housing Behavior," *Rural Sociology,* vol. 10, no. 2, June, 1945.

Rush, Donald R., and Olaf Larson, *Farm Resources and Farming Systems Needed to Meet Living Needs of Farm Families.* Washington, D.C.: Bureau of Agricultural Economics, United States Department of Agriculture, March, 1942.

Stewart, Maxwell S., *How We Spend Our Money,* Public Affairs Pamphlet, 18 (Revised), 1941. Public Affairs Committee, Inc., 30 Rockefeller Plaza, New York.

Terry, Paul W., and Verner M. Sims, *They Live on the Land; Life in an Open-country Southern Community.* Bureau of Educational Research, University of Alabama, 1940.

Zimmerman, Carle C., *Consumption and Standards of Living.* New York: D. Van Nostrand, 1936. Provides an analysis of the standard of living in all countries and in urban as well as rural society.

18

Education and the Schools

THE AMERICAN PEOPLE are noted for their interest in education and their belief that a democratic form of government makes education at public expense a social necessity. As early as the sixteen-forties the colony of Massachusetts passed two laws requiring that each town (township) tax its citizens for the support of a school. From this beginning public education for all children spread throughout the nation. At first, education for everybody did not go beyond the elementary school, but in the last sixty years the opportunity for high-school training has become almost universal in most states.

The school district as set up within our rural townships became the smallest tax unit. The land was dotted, before the nineteenth century was very old, with thousands of these districts, each with its school, consisting usually of only one room. The majority of the districts covered several square miles. Although the small school district and its one-room, ungraded school are now largely outmoded, as will be shown, it is well to pay tribute to the pioneers who succeeded in placing such an institution within walking distance of almost every six year old child.

THE RURAL SCHOOL SITUATION

It is important to note that the country school became a **neighborhood institution**. It was omnipresent. Neighborhoods might lack churches or any one or more of the other social institutions, but never a school. Each school district was administered by trustees or directors chosen from among those who lived in the tiny area inhabited by its pupils. Its teacher often boarded with the families of the neighborhood in rotation. Few were the families who were not in direct touch with the district school through the attendance of some child. No wonder that the "little red schoolhouse" lives on in the song and story of the nineteenth century.

Times changed. Farm families, as we have seen, grew smaller, farms enlarged, the population decreased. Educational standards were raised. The one-room, ungraded school, even if it had enough children to subsist, became increasingly unable, largely because of limitation in personnel and financing, to satisfy either school administrators or parents and was handicapped in meeting the demand for an enlarged curriculum and the entrance standards of the American high school. The automobile and good roads made accessible the village and town schools, which, it was assumed, usually offered better educational opportunities. The movement for a consolidation of country schools, described later, began. Nevertheless, one-room schools have persisted. There were about 107,000 such schools in 1944, 30,000 less than a decade earlier. Together with some 20,000 two-teacher schools, they comprised over two thirds of all rural schools and more than half of all the schools in the United States.

Rural and urban schools compared. Rural education obviously constitutes the major part of the nation's educational enterprise. In fact, this is a conservative statement. Over four fifths of the nation's grade schools and over three fourths of the high schools are rural. So are 482,000 teachers, 54 per cent of the total public-school teaching force. Fifty and seven tenths per cent of the nation's population of compulsory school age, six to fifteen years of age inclusive, lived on farms or in rural non-farm territory in 1940. Despite this fact, only $730,000,000 was being spent annually on rural education in the early nineteen-forties, 37 per cent of the support the nation gives to its public elementary and secondary schools. This proportion was about three points lower than in 1934.[1]

The average school term in the nation in 1940 was 175 days, the range from 146 to 188 days. Nationally the average term was 182 days in urban, 167 days in rural, schools, a difference of three school weeks between rural and urban. However, in 1926 the difference was thirty-three days. This is bad enough under the conditions to be described in this chapter, but these are average figures. There is far less fluctuation in the urban averages by states than in the rural. There are states where the rural child has two months less schooling than the average urban child. Therefore, there is not only poorer education in much of rural America; there is less of what there is.

Financial disparity great. The differences in educational opportunity between rural and urban America are high-lighted by the

---

[1] Data from various *Biennial Surveys of Education in the United States,* United States Office of Education, and from United States Census.

support given the schools. The President's Advisory Committee on Education reported a range among the states of from about $25 per pupil per year to $135, more than fivefold. The United States average was $74.30. Five out of six of the lower half of the states were considerably more rural than urban. In 1936, per pupil costs in rural America were $55.30, in urban, $92.68. In 1942, the respective amounts were $69.66 and $104.72. There has been some increase since then. On the basis of cost per classroom unit, the variation between the top urban schools and the bottom, all-rural schools is one hundred per cent. In both New York and California only about 10 per cent of the classroom units receive less than $2700 a year. In two highly rural states the top 1 per cent receive less than $2200; the bottom one third, $500 or less. The national median of school support per classroom unit is between $1600 and $1699. Nine states, all heavily rural, have a median of less than $1000.

These findings are illustrated by Figures 32, 33, 34 from J. K. Norton and E. S. Lawler's, *An Inventory of Public School Expenditures in the United States.*[2] These charts also make clear the inability of states to give equality of educational opportunity to whites and Negroes alike, because of a long social heritage which forces different systems of education for the two races.

Some educational implications. The implications of these and other facts to be given in this chapter will be discussed later, but certain generalizations should be observed here. The bulk of American education is rural; the problems of supervision, administration, and teacher-training are largely rural problems, and the fact that three fifths of the states are more rural than the nation as a whole is assurance that this condition will continue. Certain differences between rural and urban schools should be noted. The foremost is population density. The average urban elementary school has from seven to eight times as many pupils and five or six times as many teachers as the rural school. These facts explain why educators are agitating for differentiated training for rural teachers, supervisors, and administrators.

RURAL EDUCATION AND GENERAL WELFARE

Before considering country and village schools as social institutions in their neighborhoods and communities, it is important to

[2] American Council on Education, Washington, 1944.

pursue further the status of rural education as a whole and its bearing on the general welfare of the United States.

The starting-point for this discussion is the unchallenged conviction of the American people that democracy itself rests upon adequate education. How far is that ideal realized in our society?

Proportionately fewer rural children attend school. The first answer to that question is furnished by the 1940 Census. In every age category there were proportionately fewer farm children enrolled in school than village, and proportionately fewer of both than in the cities. Ages seven to fourteen inclusive are compulsory school attendance years in every state; about 97 per cent of urban children in this age group are in school, but only 90 per cent of the farm and 93 per cent of the rural non-farm children. At age fifteen the proportions are urban, 93.4; rural non-farm, 87.3; rural farm, 77.4 per cent.

Despite regional variations, the fact remains that the holding power of the country school on farm children is not as strong as that of village and urban schools on their children. Generally speaking, the lower the farm income and the lower per capita retail sales, the lower the proportion of children in school at any age, and the lower the educational status of the adult population. Actually, although rural America has over one half million more children of elementary-school age than urban America, it enrolls nearly one million fewer children in schools of the elementary level than do the cities. The detailed data on this point are given in Table 76.

TABLE 76. PROPORTION OF UNITED STATES RURAL FARM, RURAL NON-FARM, AND URBAN POPULATION IN SCHOOL BY AGE GROUPS

Age Group (years)	Rural Farm	Rural Non-Farm	Urban
6	56.5	64.5	79.7
7–9	90.1	94.7	96.7
10–13	91.8	95.8	97.4
14	86.1	92.9	96.0
15	77.4	87.3	93.4
16–17	56.8	67.6	75.6
18–19	23.9	27.5	31.7
20	9.2	10.7	14.5
21–24	3.3	3.8	6.1

Source: *Sixteenth Census of the United States,* 1940.

This is not a good situation. However, there has been some improvement over a period of years. Including all rural children, in the following list, the proportion in school by decades has been as follows:

Age Group	1940	1930	1920
7–13	92.9	93.3	87.6
14 and 15	85.4	85.0	79.4
16 and 17	61.8	51.1	no data

The urban age group, seven to thirteen years, has been practically unchanged at just over 97 per cent since 1930, but the urban proportion for the fourteen- and fifteen-year-olds had risen to 94.7 per cent by 1940, two points over 1930, and twelve points over 1920. For the sixteen- and seventeen-year-olds the urban proportion in school in 1940 was 75.6 per cent, as against 60.5 per cent in 1930. It is clear, then, that while there was increased high-school attendance in rural, as well as urban, America, over the last decades, proportionately the disparity between city and country increased. The rural child not only has a shorter school term than the urban, but he is less likely to attend.

One reason for this is inherent in the rural situation. Because of the low density of population, schools are not as available as in the cities. In a special study of twenty-two representative counties, Gaumitz found nearly one fourth of the country children living more than one and a half miles from their school, and nearly one in twenty more than three miles. Both attendance and enrollment declined noticeably, especially among younger children, as the distance from the school increased, unless transportation was available.[3]

There is one credit item that should be taken into account. In the early part of the century there was more retardation than now in rural schools, because of shorter terms and the more frequent interruptions of school attendance for farm work. Proportionately, more children fourteen years of age and over were still in the elementary school. The Office of Education estimated, in 1938, that rural high-school enrollment had doubled in the previous ten years. But making all allowances, it is clear from these data, as well as from those on the financial support of schools presented earlier, that the American ideal of equality of educational opportunity is, in practice, a myth.

Rural teachers adversely affected. Obviously the quality as well as the quantity of education received is a travesty on our prin-

[3] Cf. Gaumitz, *Availability of Public School Education in Rural Communities.* Washington, D.C.: Office of Education, 1931.

ciples of equality of opportunity. The younger, inexperienced, and/or poorer teachers gravitate to the rural school. The average salary of all rural teachers, including the better-paid ones in the villages, was only $959 in 1942-43, less than one half the urban average of $1955, and less than one half the salary of civilian employees of the federal government, or of employees in manufacturing industries.

Forty per cent of all teachers, most of them rural, were paid less than $1200 annually, which is the annual wage of the lowest classification of federal employees. Eight per cent of all rural teachers received less than $600. There are a number of predominantly rural states in which the average compensation of all teachers and educational administrators, rural and urban, was less than $1200. In the lowest state the average was $859. From 1938 through 1943, urban living costs increased about 21 per cent, rural about 34 per cent, but teachers' salaries gained less than 7 per cent. The heaviest increases in living costs took place where teachers' salaries were already lowest.

Small wonder, then, that nearly 200,000 public-school teachers were new to their positions in 1942-43, more than double the normal turnover. Small wonder that over 70,000 teachers in this one year of 1942-43, a disproportionate number rural and women, left for other positions. In this same year, 13,000 classrooms, almost wholly rural, had no teachers at all, depriving several hundred thousand children of any education. Emergency certificates in this year numbered 37,000, over nine times normal.

Rural educational status lower than urban. What this means is shown from new data in the 1940 Census on the median years of schooling completed by American adults. The median years of school completed by adults twenty-five years of age and over was measured by the 1940 Census of Population. Urban native-born whites on the average completed 9.6 years of school. For the rural non-farm population the median was one year less, 8.6 years. The farm population median was 8 years. For the Negroes the median years of completed schooling for urban, rural non-farm and farm groups were respectively 6.8, 5, and 4.1 years.

Not only is this true, but there is every indication, despite the progress made in rural education in the last decades, that there is more inequality in educational opportunity between rural and urban America now than there was at the close of the Civil War, and that the gap between the two has become progressively wider with each decade since 1920. One evidence of this inequality is the median years of school completed by adults in the various age groups. Less than a year separates the medians for urban, rural non-farm, and rural farm among all those thirty-five years of age and over; the figures being 8.8, 8.6, and 8.1 years respectively. However, for those twenty to twenty-four years of age, the medians are respectively 12, 10.7, and 8.8 years. Thus, in 1940 those in the first half-decade of adulthood in cities had on the average completed high school, but the comparable rural farm group had barely passed grade school. This serious lag first becomes noticeable in those under forty years of age and increases with each five-year period down to the twenty to twenty-four-year group. The full facts on this are given in Table 77.

TABLE 77. MEDIAN YEARS OF SCHOOL COMPLETED BY PERSONS 20 YEARS OLD AND OVER, BY AGE, FOR THE UNITED STATES, FOR RURAL FARM, RURAL NON-FARM, AND URBAN

Age (years)	Rural Farm	Rural Non-Farm	Urban
Total, 20 and over...	8.2	8.7	9.0
20 to 24..............	8.8	10.7	12.0
Total, 25 and over...	8.1	8.6	8.8
25 to 29..............	8.6	10.0	11.0
30 to 34..............	8.4	9.3	10.3
35 to 39..............	8.2	8.8	9.0
40 to 44..............	8.2	8.6	8.8
45 to 49..............	8.1	8.5	8.6
50 to 54..............	8.0	8.4	8.5
55 to 59..............	7.9	8.3	8.4
60 to 64..............	7.7	8.3	8.4
65 to 69..............	7.1	8.1	8.3
70 to 74..............	7.0	8.1	8.3
75 and over..........	6.5	8.0	8.2

Source: *Sixteenth Census of the United States*, 1940.

It may be said that this is simply the result of migration. But if so, it but emphasizes the problem, for agriculture has become a highly skilled occupation. The food supply of America and the conservation of our basic capital resource, the soil, cannot be left with safety to an ill-educated group. When one recalls the facts on the migration of rural youth to the cities, urban America's stake in good rural education and other social utilities becomes very plain.

It should be pointed out that there are sharp variations among states and regions in these particulars. Differences are small in the Northeast. Elsewhere they are larger. This again emphasizes the inequality of educational opportunity existent in the United States. The regional comparison is given in Table 78.

TABLE 78. HIGHEST AND LOWEST STATE MEDIAN YEARS OF SCHOOL COMPLETED FOR NATIVE WHITES 25 YEARS OLD AND OVER FOR RURAL FARM, RURAL NON-FARM, AND URBAN AREAS: 1940

Region	Rural Farm		Rural Non-Farm		Urban	
	High	Low	High	Low	High	Low
New England	9.8	8.6	10.4	8.6	10.7	8.8
Middle Atlantic	8.4	8.1	8.9	8.3	9.1	8.8
East North Central	8.2	7.9	8.8	8.5	9.4	8.9
West North Central	8.4	7.9	8.9	8.3	11.0	8.8
South Atlantic	8.0	7.2	8.9	7.7	11.3	8.5
East South Central	8.1	7.1	9.9	7.8	11.7	8.6
West South Central	8.0	6.3	9.3	8.1	10.6	9.1
Mountain	9.0	7.2	10.5	7.8	11.5	9.9
Pacific	8.8	8.6	9.6	9.1	11.4	10.8

Source: *Sixteenth Census of the United States*, 1940.

From the point of view of national welfare, as well as from that of rural America, these discrepancies are serious, especially when the findings in economics and in psychology, discussed in the chapter on rural psychology are considered. Educational status is lowest in the areas where school support per pupil or per classroom is lowest. The situation feeds on itself, as the relatively slower improvement in the educational status of adults in rural, as contrasted with urban, America shows. The tragedy lies in the fact that in proportion to their wealth the rural states are spending more on education than the richer, urban areas. They get less for their expenditure because they have more children. Some rural states have twice as many children of school age for every thousand adults as have the wealthiest urban states, as the section on rural population shows. Everywhere, in terms of population, the rural burden of educating and rearing children is heavier than the urban burden, for relative economic ability has not been taken into consideration.

The national stake in this situation is obvious. Rural America is the seed-bed of the nation. As of 1940, the cities were producing only three fourths enough children to sustain their populations. The rural non-farm group had a surplus of 11 per cent, the farm population of 44 per cent. Numbers of these children, however, will migrate to the cities. Rural youth must leave home or the rural standard of living would fall. In 1935 there were potentially 2.4 farm boys available for every farm becoming vacant through the death or retirement of the operator. Through the decades, about half of our rural youth have migrated to the towns and villages. If this half are to become city dwellers, it would seem incumbent on society to give them adequate educational preparation for the experience.

Rural youth concerned. Rural youth themselves are conscious of the situation, of the denial of democratic and equal educational opportunity. In a careful sampling study of nearly six hundred Iowa farm youth, 39 per cent of the girls and 29 per cent of the boys stated they disliked farm life because the schools were usually poor. About one fourth of each sex said they would like farm life better if the rural schools were as good as those in the city. Similar data emerge from the studies of the American Youth Commission and several other youth surveys by colleges of agriculture.[4]

RURAL SCHOOLS AS INSTITUTIONS

Against this background the discussion turns to a consideration of the rural school itself as an institution. Rural schools can be divided into two general groups, the one- and two-teacher schools so largely characteristic of the open country, and the open country consolidated and village schools, which are more comparable to the schools in the cities.

Small schools have some advantages. Where population density is not too low or enrollments too small, the small rural school has some advantages the urban institution lacks. There is far greater opportunity for intimate acquaintanceship among pupils, teachers, and parents and, if teacher-turnover is low, for a prolonged period of contact. This offers many possibilities for socializing experiences and for educational growth. The environment can be more readily utilized and there is more chance for the whole school to join in projects that will promote community betterment and the growth of desirable social traits.[5] Practical illustrations of some of these advantages are given later.

[4] A number of paragraphs in this chapter have been taken from a report prepared by one of the authors for a Committee of the Department of Agriculture.

[5] Cf. *Schools in Small Communities*. Washington, D.C.: *Seventeenth Yearbook*, American Association of School Administrators, 1939. Especially chapters I and II.

Villages and towns offer almost all the high-school education rural America has. More than half of the rural elementary-school enrollment is in village grade schools and this includes about one fourth of all open-country children. All told, about three fifths of all rural children attend village schools.

Village schools are larger, better equipped, have better trained teachers, longer terms, and spend more money per pupil than do those in the open country. Details on some of these points will be noted later.[6] In some states there is little if any difference between the village and city schools in many of these respects.

School buildings improved. On a state basis, the value of public elementary- and high-school property per pupil enrolled ranges from $80 in one largely rural state to well over $500 in a highly urbanized state. Nonetheless, since 1924 there has been an improvement in rural school buildings, especially those in villages. In that year nine tenths of the buildings in the village centers of the 140 communities rated fair or better. However, by 1939 the school plant in these villages had been almost completely rebuilt at a cost of about $15,000,000. Over one third of the new construction occurred between 1934 and 1936, a large part of it assisted by grants from the Public Works Administration.

The average cost of the schools built without federal aid was $67,650, $10,340 above the investment in the aided buildings. There is some evidence that federal participation and review of the plans held down costs at no sacrifice in the efficiency and quality of the building. The contrasts with the open-country schools is seen when it is realized that the average rural structure, including village and open country, white and colored, was assessed at less than $6000.[7]

RURAL SCHOOL FINANCING

Rural schools are financed in a number of ways. Local taxes usually bear the major cost, although state and federal aid is granted in considerable if varying measure. Naturally, when such aid increases — as it has been increasing in many states since the depression — state control of policies has often been extended also, in accordance with the proverb, "Who pays the piper calls the

[6] Cf. Brunner, E. de S., and Irving Lorge, *Rural Trends in Depression Years.* New York: Columbia University Press, 1937.

[7] Derived from Rural School Circular 27, Office of Education, Washington, D.C.

tune." In two or three states, notably Delaware and North Carolina, almost the whole burden of education is borne by the state. In seven more states, including West Virginia, California, and Indiana, from 1931 to 1934 the state agreed to guarantee an increasing share of the cost of education, although in some cases these increased appropriations meant divorce from state control.

State aid. State aid to schools has gone through two cycles. From 1890 to 1895 the proportion of public school revenue derived from federal and state sources was 23 per cent; it dropped to 16 per cent in 1925 and rose to 17.3 per cent in 1930, when the variation by states was from 87.9 per cent in Delaware to 1.7 per cent in Kansas. Since 1930 there has been a great increase in state aid, which in 1936 amounted to 29.4 per cent of the cost of public-school education. The local share in these years dropped to 63.5 per cent from 72.7 per cent. Since 1937 there has been a further small increase in state aid to education. Counties supplied the rest. In fourteen states less than 10 per cent of the school costs was secured from state and federal sources; in twenty-five, the average exceeded that of the nation as a whole. Sixteen states, nine of them in the South,[8] contribute more than 25 per cent of the total cost of their public education. These figures are for entire states and for both rural and urban schools. They indicate the great diversity of methods of financing rural schools.[9]

This state aid is given with a view to equalizing educational opportunity but a study by the President's Advisory Committee on Education found that "in fewer than one third of the states do equalization plans appear to provide for . . . a reasonably equitable distribution of aid to those areas that probably have the greatest need."[10]

In this respect practice in the United States seems to lag behind that in many other democracies. In New Zealand and Australia, for instance, as in other nations of the British Commonwealth,

[8] Mort, Paul R., *State Support for Public Education*, pp. 26-31. American Council on Education, 1933. This volume of 496 pages is the best study and discussion of the subject. It is part of a National Study of School Finance. According to the Office of Education, the amount of state aid to local schools increased 3.8 per cent throughout the nation, between 1937-38 and 1939-40, and 6.5 per cent more up to the school year 1941-42. In this last period there were increases in all but two states.

[9] For a discussion of methods to extend state aid, cf. Swift, Fletcher H., *Public School Finance*, and a summary by Brunner and Kolb, *Rural Social Trends*, pp. 179-80.

[10] Cf. Edwards, N., and H. S. Richey, *The Extent of Equalization Secured Through State School Funds*. Washington, D.C., 1939.

every effort is made to give the rural child just as good educational advantages as are enjoyed by his urban cousin.[11]

Pros and cons of state aid. This matter of increased state aid for schools is arousing much discussion. In some states the factions on this point are urban *versus* rural. In one Eastern commonwealth augmented aid to schools has been defeated in the legislature for fifteen years because of such a division. City people not unnaturally object to contributing to the cost of the education of farmers and villagers. The latter groups retort that a democracy means equality of educational opportunity, the cost of which should be spread equitably over the entire commonwealth if not over the nation, especially since a large proportion of rural children — approximately half of them in normal times — become urban residents. They point out that there are great inequalities in the type of wealth taxed for school purposes, which now consists chiefly of real estate. Thus even in one largely urban state, the assessed valuation per child in the eight most urban counties was well over double the figure in the eight most rural counties. On the other hand, as in Missouri, the state-aid program was the creation of the rural districts which controlled a majority of the legislative votes.

Increasing influence of state boards. The fear lest the state board of education dictate to local districts is another argument advanced against state aid. There is no question but that these boards have acquired more and more power in the last quarter-century. School administrators in every region testify to this. On the whole, this is a beneficial development, for the state often succors rural schools; but where the state board lacks an adequate understanding of the peculiar problems of the local system, it may create real hardship.[12] Some state boards are, however, ill-staffed and the potentialities of their leadership must wait upon the strengthening of such boards, as was recognized by the President's Advisory Committee on Education in its report in 1938.

Educators have quite generally come to favor state aid, an effort at equalization of costs and opportunity, and this seems to be the

---

[11] Cf. Kandel, I. L., ed., *Rural Education and Rural Society.* New York: *Yearbook,* International Institute, Teachers College, Columbia University, 1938.

[12] State control of rural education is exerted in the following ways: supervision of building plans and buildings so as to safeguard health and prevent fires while at the same time seeing that an efficient school plant is maintained; formulation of the qualifications for a teacher's certificate; standardizing and often raising local salaries; checking up on local educational finances, suggesting curricula and attempting in various ways to put expert service at the disposal of the community.

trend, although the depression compelled some states to reduce their grants, one state by as much as 60 per cent. Tax delinquencies running into hundreds of millions of dollars complicated the situation.[13] This, of course, raises the whole question of the ability of the states to support an adequate program of education. As pointed out elsewhere, there is a wide variation in their ability to support adequate systems of approximately equal efficiency. New York and Nevada, for instance, could raise from five to six times as much as Mississippi, and the six richest states, considered as a group, are four times as well able as the six poorest to meet the standardized measure of educational need.

Federal aid. Even before the depression, inequalities of wealth among the states had created a movement for federal support of schools in addition to the grants supplied for vocational education under the Smith-Hughes Law, the only form of federal aid to public-school education, except for some emergency grants during the depression and in behalf of war industrial communities during World War II. The eight wealthiest states in the Union average eight times the wealth per child, of the eight poorest.

Indeed, as pointed out earlier in this chapter, two or three states have practically twice as many children for each one thousand adults as have California and New York. This means that the burden of supplying equally good educational service, even if the resources were equal, would be twice as heavy in the former states as in the latter. The states with the largest proportion of children, nevertheless, contribute most to the restocking of the urban population. These figures make the agitation for federal aid for local education, based on democratic principles, quite understandable, and it was such sociological aspects that the President's Advisory Committee on Education stressed strongly in its program of federal aid for education. This program recommended that certain types of aid be given in proportion to the need of the states.[14]

Local rural school costs. The over-all average costs per pupil in rural and urban schools were given in the opening section of this chapter. The study of the 140 communities provides some in-

[13] See the various surveys of this problem conducted under the direction of Professor Paul Mort, of Teachers College, Columbia University. Among the more recent studies are those of Missouri, Ohio, New Jersey, and Maine. Cf. also the National Study of School Finance, *op. cit.*, chaps. VI, VIII, and IX. See also the *Relative Economic Ability of the States to Support Education*, by Leslie N. Chism. New York: Teachers College Bureau of Publications, 1935.

[14] Cf. *Report of the Advisory Committee on Education*, Sections A II and III and B IX. Washington, D.C., 1938.

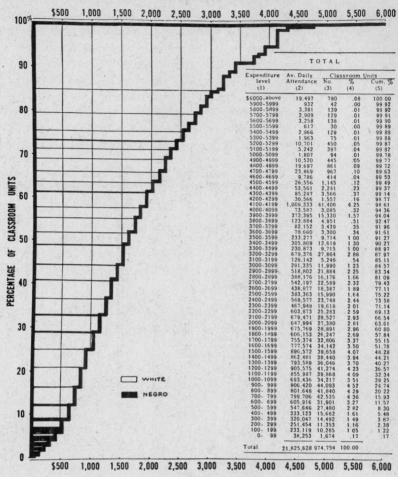

Figure 32

DISTRIBUTION OF CLASSROOM UNITS ACCORDING TO
LEVELS OF EXPENDITURE, UNITED STATES, CURRENT
EXPENDITURE PER CLASSROOM UNIT, 1940

Figures 32, 33, and 34
Source: Norton, J. K., and Lawler, E., *The Unfinished Business.*

sight into the local situation. Between 1930, the high point, and
1936, total operating and teaching costs declined as a result of the
depression. In the village centers this decline was 16 per cent in
total costs, but 20 per cent in teaching costs. In the open-country
schools both items declined almost 30 per cent. There were sharp
regional variations in these fluctuations. Per pupil costs in the
Middle Atlantic communities by 1936 were slightly above 1930

figures and stood at $57.83 for all pupils, high school and elementary. Southern white schools cost half as much. Southern Negro schools cost about $8 per pupil, only one third of that which was spent for white schools. This fact gives point to the proposal of the President's Advisory Committee on Education that, in states maintaining a dual system of education, federal funds, if appropriated, should be in addition to present budgets and should be distributed in proportion to the school enrollments of the two races. By the school year 1943-44, in the few villages resurveyed after 1936,

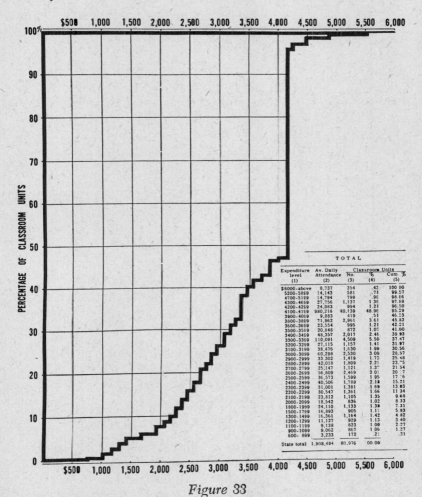

TOTAL				
Expenditure level (1)	Av. Daily Attendance (2)	Classroom Units No. (3)	% (4)	Cum % (5)
$6000-above	8,737	354	.43	100 00
5200-5899	14,143	581	.71	99.57
4700-5199	14,794	799	.98	98.86
4300-4699	27,756	1,137	1.38	97.88
4200-4299	24,083	994	1.21	96.50
4100-4199	980,216	40,139	48.96	95.29
3900-4099	9,883	419	.51	46.33
3800-3899	71,962	2,961	3.61	45.82
3600-3699	23,554	905	1.21	42.21
3500-3599	20,848	872	1.07	41.00
3400-3499	48,357	2,017	2.46	39.93
3300-3399	110,091	4,509	5.50	37.47
3200-3299	27,115	1,157	1.41	31.97
3100-3199	38,476	1,630	1.99	30.56
3000-3099	60,298	2,530	3.09	28.57
2900-2999	33,302	1,419	1.73	25.48
2800-2899	42,018	1,809	2.21	23.75
2700-2799	25,147	1,121	1.37	21.54
2600-2699	56,809	2,469	3 01	20 17
2500-2599	36,573	1,599	1 95	17 16
2400-2499	40,506	1,789	2.18	15.21
2300-2399	31,001	1,381	1.69	13 03
2200-2299	30,547	1,361	1.66	11 34
2100-2199	23,812	1,105	1.35	9 68
2000-2099	18,542	836	1.02	8 33
1800-1999	24,110	1,133	1.38	7 31
1500-1799	16,893	905	1.1	5.93
1300-1499	16,361	1,164	1.42	4.82
1200-1299	11,127	929	1.13	3.40
1100-1199	9,138	823	1 00	2 27
900-1099	9,062	867	1 06	1.27
600- 899	3,233	172	.21	.21
State total	1,908,494	81,976	00.00	

Figure 33

DISTRIBUTION OF CLASSROOM UNITS ACCORDING TO LEVELS OF EXPENDITURE, NEW YORK, CURRENT EXPENDITURE PER CLASSROOM UNIT, 1940 school budgets had reached an all-time high. One community was spending about $100 per pupil, or $84,000, 20 per cent more than in 1936, though there were no more children enrolled.

The size of a community had little or no effect on school costs within regions, but these were related to wealth as measured by per capita retail sales; in communities with per capita sales of under $200 per year, elementary-school teaching costs were $26.10 per pupil, rising to $42.80 where sales were between $400 and $500, after which there was a slight decline. Expenses varied according to place.

The pupils. The increase in school atendance for every age group was national and affected every region, although, as is the case in many school comparisons, the rural South lagged behind the other regions. The higher figures for urban areas doubtless reflect the stricter enforcement of attendance laws. The rural gain, apart from the prevailing American philosophy of giving every boy and girl as much education as possible, can be attributed also to more attractive teaching and more competent teachers, to improved transportation facilities, increase of consolidated schools, better rural health generally, and the lessening of child labor. The ratio of attendance to enrollment also increased, totaling 91 per cent in village high schools, nearly 95 per cent in village grade schools, and 80 per cent in country schools. Nationally the proportion of daily attendance to enrollment was 87.1 per cent for urban and 88.2 for all rural schools in 1941-42.

The gains made in this and other aspects of rural education mentioned later have been substantial, but it must be remembered, as shown in the opening pages of this chapter, that they have not kept pace with urban progress.

Elementary-school pupils decrease; high-school pupils increase. According to the Office of Education [15] the number of pupils in rural grade schools declined by 9.4 per cent between 1926 and 1934. In 1934 enrollment was 10,821,777 as against almost 12,000,-000 in 1926. This decline has continued. The 1940 Census reported 8,300,000 children of elementary school age in school. If the same proportion of rural as of urban children were enrolled, this figure would be nearly a million higher, in itself an indication of the weakness of the typical rural school district. In 1942, 12 per cent, or about 2,300,000, of these children were in one-room, one-teacher schools. Moreover, this group of children, who make up 12 per cent of the elementary-school children of the nation and who occupy the attention of 19 per cent of the teachers, have only 4 per

[15] *Op. cit.*

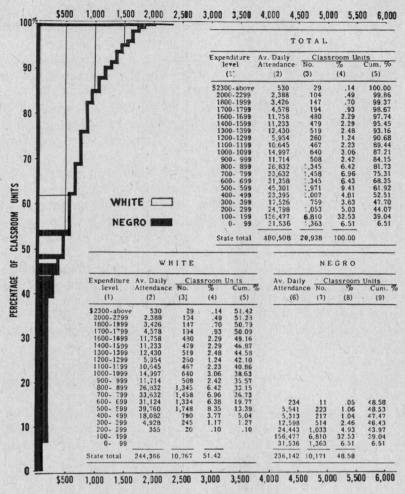

TOTAL

Expenditure level (1)	Av. Daily Attendance (2)	Classroom Units No. (3)	% (4)	Cum. % (5)
$2300-above	530	29	.14	100.00
2000-2299	2,388	104	.49	99.86
1800-1999	3,426	147	.70	99.37
1700-1799	4,578	194	.93	98.67
1600-1699	11,758	480	2.29	97.74
1400-1599	11,233	479	2.29	95.45
1300-1399	12,430	519	2.48	93.16
1200-1299	5,954	260	1.24	90.68
1100-1199	10,645	467	2.23	89.44
1000-1099	14,997	640	3.06	87.21
900- 999	11,714	508	2.42	84.15
800- 899	26,832	1,345	6.42	81.73
700- 799	33,632	1,458	6.96	75.31
600- 699	31,358	1,345	6.43	68.35
500- 599	45,301	1,971	9.41	61.92
400- 499	23,395	1,007	4.81	52.51
300- 399	17,526	759	3.63	47.70
200- 299	24,798	1,053	5.03	44.07
100- 199	156,477	6,810	32.53	39.04
0- 99	31,536	1,363	6.51	6.51
State total	480,508	20,938	100.00	

WHITE ☐

NEGRO ▓

	WHITE					**NEGRO**			
Expenditure level (1)	Av. Daily Attendance (2)	Classroom Units No. (3)	% (4)	Cum. % (5)		Av. Daily Attendance (6)	Classroom Units No. (7)	% (8)	Cum. % (9)
$2300-above	530	29	.14	51.42					
2000-2299	2,388	104	.49	51.23					
1800-1999	3,426	147	.70	50.79					
1700-1799	4,578	194	.93	50.09					
1600-1699	11,758	480	2.29	49.16					
1400-1599	11,233	479	2.29	46.87					
1300-1399	12,430	519	2.48	44.58					
1200-1299	5,954	260	1.24	42.10					
1100-1199	10,645	467	2.23	40.86					
1000-1099	14,997	640	3.06	38.63					
900- 999	11,714	508	2.42	35.57					
800- 899	26,832	1,345	6.42	33.15					
700- 799	33,632	1,458	6.96	26.73					
600- 699	31,124	1,334	6.38	19.77		234	11	.05	48.58
500- 599	39,760	1,748	8.35	13.39		5,541	223	1.06	48.53
400- 499	18,082	790	3.77	5.04		5,313	217	1.04	47.47
300- 399	4,928	245	1.17	1.27		12,598	514	2.46	46.43
200- 299	355	20	.10	.10		24,443	1,033	4.93	43.97
100- 199						156,477	6,810	32.53	39.04
0- 99						31,536	1,363	6.51	6.51
State total	244,366	10,767	51.42			236,142	10,171	48.58	

Figure 34

DISTRIBUTION OF CLASSROOM UNITS ACCORDING TO
LEVELS OF EXPENDITURE, MISSISSIPPI, CURRENT
EXPENDITURE PER CLASSROOM UNIT, 1940

cent of the expenditures allotted to them. This is not a rapidly disappearing problem. True, consolidation has reduced the number of one-teacher schools to 107,000, as stated earlier, but because of such factors as population density and topography, it is doubtful if the reduction can go below 60,000 to 75,000. These figures are an indication of the slackening in the rural birth rate which is discussed in the section on population.

On the other hand, according to the Office of Education, the enrollment in rural high schools slightly more than doubled in this same period, 1926-34. The population of high-school age in rural America in 1940 was 4,750,000; in the cities, 4,980,000. Of these, 3,500,000 rural, and 4,230,000 urban, youth attended school. If as high a proportion of rural as of urban youth attended, the rural enrollment would have been raised by 1,400,000, or 40 per cent. The Office of Education and the National Education Association believe that the census data quoted are an underenumeration. They point out that in some states the census was not completed until late in the spring after schools had closed, and that the question of school attendance in the preceding school year could have been interpreted in terms of whether the child was attending school at the moment of the census enumerator's visit.[16]

To the authors this appears to be a valid point, but it is also clear that rural high-school enrollment has increased, though proportionately not as rapidly as in the cities. Various causes account for this surge of rural youth into high schools, which parallels the urban trend and exceeds it in proportions. The lack of employment possibilities kept many in school. Again, school principals are reporting less retardation than formerly, with the evident tendency for more grade pupils to enter high schools and complete their courses. Rural four-year high schools rose in number from 9926 in 1926, to 12,360 in 1934, and to 17,600 in 1944. However, about three fourths of these high schools had less than one hundred pupils.

Since Pearl Harbor, high-school attendance, especially on the part of boys, has turned downward for obvious reasons, but there are good grounds for believing that the basic trends described will reassert themselves after the war. It is to be hoped that the courses will be sufficiently accelerated to enable rural America to make as much progress as the cities have.

Farm tenancy seemed to be an influential factor in school enrollment. In a survey of 43 of the 140 communities in which tenancy had increased between 1924 and 1930, the number of country children attending village grade schools increased 40 per cent, and high schools, 32 per cent. In 26 communities where tenancy decreased, these figures were respectively 70 and 100 per cent. Apparently farm-owners are more eager than tenants to send their children to the village schools. As the chapter on rural-urban relations shows, there seems to be a clear relation between the propor-

[16] Letter of July 23, 1945, from Doctor Frank Hubbard, Director of Research Division, National Education Association, Washington.

tion of children in schools and the proximity of the county of residence to a large city.

It is interesting to note that, while the village school systems reflect the trend toward a rapid increase in high-school enrollment, they show an increase in elementary-school pupils of 8.7 per cent over 1924, most of which took place prior to 1930. This departure from the national trend is partly caused by increases in enrollment because of the consolidation of open-country schools with those in the village, and is also an evidence of the stability or even growth of village population.

College attendance of rural youth has gained. The Office of Education, in its biennial survey, 1928-30, reported that more than two fifths of the rural high-school graduates were continuing their education. In 1937, the proportion was 45 per cent, three points higher than for the graduates of all public high schools, urban and rural.

Another indication of rising college attendance from rural areas is to be found in the 1930 Census. In 1920, only 15.6 per cent of the rural youth between eighteen and twenty years of age were reported in school; in 1930 it was 20 per cent; in the surveyed 140 villages alone, 33.2 per cent. In 1940 the proportion, after dropping sharply during the depression, came back to 20.2 per cent. While some of these students were doubtless in high school, most of them were in college. At the same time the proportion of rural inhabitants twenty-one years of age and over in school increased 135 per cent during the decade; that is, to 299,500 persons. Among Negroes this increase was fourfold: to 36,118 persons. The 1940 Census reported 3.3 per cent of the rural farm and 3.8 per cent of the rural non-farm population twenty-one to twenty-four years of age in school, against an urban proportion of 6.1 per cent. The total for the entire rural population of this age group in 1940 was only 134,662. This is a very large decline, which does not check with other available data. The effect of the depression may account for some of this decline, movement into war industry for some, and underenumeration for some.[17]

RURAL SCHOOL CONSOLIDATION

The discussion thus far has shown that the country schools have poorer physical facilities, a smaller clientèle, and slightly lower attendance; it will show in the next section that they are staffed by

[17] The fact that the period for the 1940 Census enumeration coincided with the spring vacation in the colleges, and that many farm boys were probably

fewer well-trained and more underpaid teachers than the city schools. It has been indicated, also, that village schools are superior to country schools in all these respects. One of the solutions advocated by many educators for bringing country schools up to the level of village and city schools is consolidation.

Consolidation defined. A consolidated school is difficult to define technically, but it may be considered a combination of two or more smaller schools brought together for the sake of greater efficiency and for the purpose of serving all the districts whose schools it has displaced.

Progress in consolidation. The nineteen-twenties saw real progress in school consolidation, the number of consolidated schools increasing rapidly from 9752 in 1920 to about 17,300 in 1934.[18] Since 1934 about five thousand more consolidated schools have been organized.[19]

A considerable number of all consolidations, especially where high schools were involved, centered in villages — another evidence of the increasing integration of the rural community around the village.

Advantages of consolidated schools. The advantages of the consolidated school are, in the first place, a large building which provides a room for each grade and space for laboratories and social and recreational facilities, which enrich the whole of community life. Larger school grounds often make possible athletic fields, school gardens, and demonstration plots.

In the second place, the tax base of the consolidated school makes possible better teachers than the old districts afforded, and provides not only the normal recitation period but some degree of subject-matter specialization among the faculty. In other words, instead of having a teacher for each grade, the consolidated school can hire a teacher for each subject. In some states there is special state aid for consolidated schools.

Thirdly, consolidation makes possible better administration and supervision than is attainable under the traditional type of rural school.

Finally, the pupils are benefited in many ways. There are

employed helping with spring plowing is a possible explanation of some under-enumeration. The consideration noted above in connection with high-school attendance as measured by the census also holds here.

[18] Figures corrected to make comparable with previous reports, eliminating thereby effect of changed definition of consolidated school. Cf. Biennial Survey of Education, 1934-36, *op. cit.*, pp. 50-55.

[19] Since 1920, as a result largely of school consolidations, as a result of population movements, the number of one-teacher schools in the United States has been reduced from 189,227 to 107,692, or 43.1 per cent.

enough children to carry through adequate grading, to develop group and project work, and to organize many socially significant types of extracurricular activities. Moreover, enrollment and average attendance usually increase.

The costs of consolidation. Consolidation is frequently opposed on the ground of its high cost, which is, of course, reflected in the tax bill. Where the area covered and the population served is adequate, however, there is some doubt as to whether costs are significantly higher except when a too expensive new building is required.

In this connection Arkansas provides an illuminating illustration. There careful surveys were undertaken in practically every county to formulate plans for county-wide consolidations on the basis of satisfactory local school units. In the main, this program resulted in increased elementary- and high-school attendance, a higher median average salary for teachers, and a raising of their qualifications. In one sample county, Pulaski, the number of schools was sharply reduced, those of one and two rooms being practically eliminated. Per pupil costs declined slightly, while the total budget dropped from $314,783 to $290,052 in one year of operation, despite increased transportation costs. Thus not only was money saved but education improved at the same time. Many similar examples could be given.[20] The Arkansas plan has been copied. Its soundness lies in the careful preliminary survey of the situation; consolidated school districts which ignore the natural social and economic patterns and have an insufficient population or tax basis are handicapped from the start.[21]

Sometimes consolidation means increased rather than decreased costs. Doctor Little studied 223 counties in fifteen Southern and Middle Western States to discover potential economies under consolidation. Only ten, however, showed potential increases up to 10 per cent; the other 213 showed a median decrease of 6.1 per cent and a range of from 0.13 to 27.52 per cent.[22] Consolidation,

[20] Cf. Dawson and Little, *Financial and Administrative Needs of the Public Schools of Arkansas.* Little Rock: State Superintendent of Education, 1930. Also, Dawson, *Satisfactory Local School Units.* Nashville: George Peabody Teachers College, 1934.

[21] It should be stated, however, that Arkansas has recently dropped the office of county superintendent of schools and is one of the two or three states that were forced to rely most heavily on federal emergency aid to keep its schools open. This retrogression was due more to the depression and the great droughts of 1932 and 1934 than to the reorganization described.

[22] Little, *Potential Economies in Reorganization of Local School Units.* New York: Teachers College Bureau of Publications, 1934.

however, often shifts the total burden, making it lighter in some of the former districts and heavier in others.

Opposition to consolidation. The real crux of occasional farm opposition to school consolidation, especially in states with large profitable farms, is the fact that the tax bill of the individual farmer is necessarily increased, since real-estate holdings are larger and more valuable than in the villages. As shown in the discussion of taxation, real estate is the chief source of school-district local tax funds. A recent investigation in one state, conducted in more than two thirds of all consolidated districts which include incorporated towns — 191 districts in all — has shown that the owners of farm property were paying 3.84 times as much per farm child as were the owners of town property per town child. In these 191 districts, farm-owners were paying $142.40 per farm child per year, while the owners of town property were paying but $37.12 per town child per year.[23]

Consolidation is opposed for other reasons. Parents object to having their children ride in school buses and wait in bad weather for the arrival of the bus. In some localities, where one- or two-room schools had an excellent community program and had become something of a community center, the closing of this school has meant a distinct social loss. Local people feel unwilling to enter as fully into the program of the consolidated school as they did in their own, but this strangeness and aloofness can be overcome in time by school officials.

A compromise plan. Doctor W. E. Sheffer, of Manhattan, Kansas, has proposed an extension of the consolidated plan in what is known as the co-operative school area.[24] He proposes "to close certain one-teacher schools and transport their pupils to those neighboring graded schools which could care for a larger enrollment. Such a procedure would result in the organization of what will be called . . . Co-operative School Areas, which are defined as areas consisting of one-graded school districts with one or more adjacent one-teacher districts whose pupils would be taught in the graded school for a payment made by the respective one-teacher district school boards to the graded school board." The value of this plan can be inferred from the fact that in the school year 1932-33, 1054 schools in Kansas had an enrollment of seven or less, in 2243 ten or less; four in seven Kansas one-room schools have 15 or less, while the average state enrollment in these schools is

[23] Cf. Lancelot, W. H., *Rural School Reorganization in Iowa.* Ames: Iowa State College, December, 1944.

[24] Sheffer, W. E., *The Co-operative School Area in Kansas,* Topeka: Kansas State Printing Plant, 1934.

steadily decreasing; in 1907-08 it was 22.6, in 1930-31, 12. Obviously, this situation is educationally uneconomic and inefficient.

Consolidation by social process. Consolidation is as important in the high schools as in the grade schools. In 1930, the 61 consolidated district high schools in the 140 villages drew 51.4 per cent, and the 79 village high schools not part of a consolidated district 47.2 per cent, of their students from the open country. By 1936 these percentages had risen to 53 and 50 respectively. Regional variations were slight. Even in the village elementary schools almost one third of the student body lived in the country. In other words, what is in effect consolidation by social processes is an important element in the picture.

How this works out in a specific state is shown in Iowa, where in the school year 1939-40, 45,121 rural children attended approved graded school systems with their tuition paid by a still-existing home school district.[25]

Such a process, however, often raises serious problems for the village or town high school, which perforce educates these country children, but in many states are allowed to charge the school districts from which the pupils come only the per pupil cost as based on current expenses with no allowance for capital costs. At best, this procedure is a makeshift. The goal is legal school consolidation, and the basic justification is found stated in the Iowa study. That state in 1940 had 386 consolidated school districts operating high schools. The percentage of children of school age who attended school was higher in these districts than in *any other* type of district in the state.

Some one-room schools must remain. As previously stated, it is estimated that, because of low population density and topography, it will be impossible to dispense with between 60,000 and 75,000 of one- and two-room schools, as long as people live in the area these schools serve. How, therefore, can these schools be made to yield the maximum social and educational fruit? An example of what can be done with the one-room school under determinative conditions is found in a four-year experiment conducted at Quaker Grove, New Jersey, under the general direction of the Department of Rural Education, Teachers College, Columbia University. In this old type, one-room school, with an unusually large enrollment of fifty, various educational methods, intended to produce the greatest educational benefit, were tried. As a result, very few children (and most of them had I.Q.'s below 90) made less than the

[25] *Ibid.*

year's normal progress per grade as measured by the Stanford Tests. The others achieved 1.4 to 4.25 years' advancement per grade.

The work done in this school is not exceptional, although it is unfortunately considerably above the average pupil achievement. The Porter School near Kirksville, Missouri, affords another classic example of excellent work under adverse conditions, an achievement that had favorable repercussions in the community. Vermont which, because of population and geographical conditions, must continue to have many one-room schools, instituted a campaign ten years ago to improve their conditions through the superior training of teachers, higher salaries, and better equipment and curricula. Certain assets of the one-room school are in this state being turned to good account; the lack of grading allows for more adequate individual attention; some of the school housekeeping is done by the pupils as lessons in home management and a development of a sense of responsibility, while the close association of children of various ages allows the older to help the younger ones.[26]

Sometimes it is helpful to distinguish between the attendance unit or area of a given school and the administrative unit. Schools can be consolidated for administrative purposes but remain undisturbed in their relationships and service to their community neighborhood. Under some conditions this plan works out quite successfully where complete consolidation is impractical or impossible. The unit of attendance, whether an administrative unit or not, should conform to the natural community as educators are increasingly recognizing. Indeed, this is an official recommendation of the New York State Survey of Education.[27]

It develops, therefore, that while increasing school consolidation is solving many problems, the handicaps of the one-room school can be overcome very successfully if necessary. In other words, the techniques exist for a great advance in rural education when the administrative, financial and teacher-training problems are solved. Since this is so, the discussion turns now to the teacher.

RURAL SCHOOL TEACHERS

Salaries low. Since instruction costs are such a large part of the current expenses of rural schools, it is worth while to inquire into

26 Cf. *Rural Vermont: A Program for the Future by Two Hundred Vermonters,* chap. XIV. Burlington: The Vermont Commission on Country Life, 1931.

27 *Education for American Life,* chap. IV. The Regents' Survey. New York: McGraw-Hill, 1938.

what teachers are paid. The Federal Office of Education gives the following figures as the average annual salaries of rural public school teachers:

	1925	1930	1935
Teachers in one-teacher schools	$761	$788	$517
Teachers in two-teacher schools	754	829	620
Teachers in three or more teacher schools (open country)	*	980	*
Teachers in consolidated schools	*	1037	*

* Not given.

In 1942-43, the average salary of all rural teachers, including the better-paid ones in the villages, was only $959, which makes not difficult to understand the shortage and high turnover of rural teachers described in the introductory section of this chapter.

In the villages, salaries were slightly higher, averaging $1373 in 1930 and $1147 in 1936. The 1936 salaries averaged slightly lower than in 1924 or 1930 in every region except the Middle Atlantic States. The National Study of School Finance found that the salary of all rural white elementary-school teachers in the lowest 10 per cent of the nation's counties in 1930 was less than $621, the top 10 per cent more than $1167, and the median fourth ranged from $788 to $952.[28]

Training. The rural school, it has often been observed, is handicapped by poorly trained, as well as underpaid teachers. Mort, in the National Study of School Finance,[29] presents figures relative to years of training beyond the *elementary school* based on the records gathered in 1930-31, of 120,000 rural elementary-school teachers. He used rural in the census sense; that is, including communities of less than 2500 in the open country and villages. The 10 per cent lowest counties employed teachers who achieved 4.84 years beyond elementary school, or barely more than a high-school education. The next 23.3 per cent of the counties in the scale employed teachers who had from 4.84 to 5.42 years' education beyond the grammar school; in the middle fourth the range was from 5.43 to 6.03 years, or just around junior college or normal school. The next 23.3 per cent contained teachers with from 6.04 to 6.52 years of higher education. The top 10 per cent exceeded 6.52 years. In other words, one third of these rural teachers had completed normal-school training or more. In the cities of over 10,000 population nine tenths of all elementary-school teachers possessed six years

28 *Op. cit.*, pp. 12-13.   29 *Op. cit.*, pp. 14-15.

beyond elementary school, or better, and nearly one fifth were college graduates.[30]

There is some correlation between the training and salary of rural teachers, although, for example, Delaware, New Jersey, and New Hampshire do not stand as high above neighboring states in the training as in the salaries of their rural elementary-school teachers. The correlation of training and salary is closer in American villages, which have better trained teachers than the country schools.

Standards improving. The data on the teachers in the 140 communities, together with the testimony of many school administrators, show that the standards of professional preparation for teachers was improving up to 1940. Since then, and especially since Pearl Harbor, there has been deterioration. Even in the village centers one fifth of the teachers in 1924 had received less than the traditional two-year normal-school training. Just over three fifths were college graduates. By 1936 almost two thirds were college graduates, and outside the South only one in twenty had less than normal-school graduation. The same trend was noticeable in the open-country schools, though to a less degree. In 1924 only 4.5 per cent of the white teachers in such schools held college degrees. In 1936 the figure was 21.7 per cent, practically a fivefold increase. Even among the Negro open-country teachers, 6.4 were college graduates in 1936 as against almost none in 1924.[31]

Reasons for better training. There are four reasons, among others, for this measurable improvement in the professional preparation of village teachers. First: the post-War I shortage, which attracted thousands to the profession, had given way to an oversupply in some states. This situation was sharply accentuated by the depression. Second: state boards of education have been using all their influence to raise the requirements for entry into the teaching profession. This, among other things, is the spur that sends thousands of teachers to summer school in order to get more degrees or certificates. Third: local opinion and boards of education responsive to it have demanded that local children have the best obtainable in teaching skill. Not only civic pride and economic advantage enter into this sentiment, but also the natural desire of parents to give their children the maximum educational advantages.

[30] Urban data supplied by Professor E. S. Evenden, Teachers College, Columbia University, director of the National Study of the Education of Teachers conducted from 1930 to 1933.

[31] It is believed that these data are quite representative of the national situation as those for the 1930 study agreed within two points with the rural findings of the National Study of the Education of Teachers alluded to above.

Finally: there has been a decided tendency to change two- and three-year normal schools into four-year teachers colleges.

It is interesting to note that this improvement in the training of teachers coincides with improved attendance in and greater holding power of the schools, as well as with stronger extracurricular and community programs. This is not necessarily a matter of cause and effect, but the phenomena are undoubtedly related.

Turnover of teachers. The turnover of teachers has already been mentioned with the data on salaries. It must be recognized that this was not merely a wartime problem. As long ago as 1931, the United States Office of Education estimated that each year it was necessary to replace two out of every five teachers employed in one- and two-room schools, and three out of every eleven in village schools. In towns of from 2500 to 10,000 the ratio, however, is only one in six, and in cities of from 10,000 to 100,000, one in ten. That this is probably a conservative estimate is shown by another study from the same source [32] which showed that 62.1 per cent of teachers in one-teacher schools were in their first year and another 17.5 per cent had been in that school less than two years. Large cities replace only one in twenty, or 5 per cent of their faculties each year.

If we judge by the 140 villages, there was little improvement in this situation between 1924 and 1930, although in the nineteen-thirties, during the depression, turnover declined. It is evident that although the training of the teachers of our rural schools is inadequate, as are their salaries, by peacetime standards, the situation is improving. Naturally this improvement was noticeable first in the villages. It probably will spread to the open-country schools.

The discussion now turns to what is the common concern of both teachers and pupils — the curriculum. This will be considered in a wide sense — as a social force molding the children of rural America into the citizens of the nation.

Before doing this, however, it may be well to summarize this chapter in terms of a study by the United States Chamber of Commerce, issued in 1944 through its Committee on Education and entitled, *Education an Investment in People*. The committee compared the average current expense per pupil in average daily attendance in public elementary and secondary schools for 1910, 1920, and 1930, median years of school completed by persons twenty years of age and over, per capita retail sales in 1940, number of

---

[32] Gaumitz, *Availability of Public School Education in Rural Communities.* Washington, D.C., 1931. This is based on twenty-two widely scattered representative counties.

TABLE 79. EDUCATIONAL EXPENSE COMPARED WITH SELECTED SOCIALISTIC INDICES

State	Current Expense	Median Years Completed	Per capita Sales, 1940	Telephones per 1000 Population	Circulation National Magazines	Rate of Educational Deficiencies
Ala.	$23	7.3	$154	43	120	12.9
Ariz.	85	8.8	325	115	319	5.5
Ark.	21	8.1	153	46	141	9.8
Calif.	88	10.3	462	253	431	2.8
Colo.	75	9.3	364	188	366	2.5
Conn.	67	8.8	420	200	364	1.4
Del.	58	8.8	414	159	342	3.9
Fla.	34	8.6	324	118	307	7.5
Ga.	20	7.2	200	63	133	9.2
Idaho	66	9.5	335	126	376	1.7
Ill.	67	8.8	362	212	318	1.9
Ind.	62	8.9	311	145	326	3.1
Iowa	69	9.0	324	202	370	2.0
Kans.	64	8.9	263	184	367	1.7
Ky.	27	8.3	183	71	142	7.9
La.	35	6.9	206	78	140	12.4
Maine	49	9.2	332	150	349	3.0
Md.	49	8.3	340	149	254	8.4
Mass.	73	9.4	403	197	329	2.2
Mich.	72	8.9	347	157	337	2.9
Minn.	69	8.8	364	188	341	2.5
Miss.	21	7.4	129	36	104	12.4
Mo.	47	8.7	291	154	273	2.1
Mont.	89	9.0	397	122	466	1.7
Nebr.	67	9.0	302	178	368	1.8
Nev.	102	10.1	564	175	509	1.3
N.H.	64	8.9	373	150	378	4.2
N.J.	79	8.7	380	161	303	2.2
N. Mex.	52	8.4	237	74	233	5.0
N.Y.	83	8.8	414	209	300	1.4
N.C.	24	7.4	177	51	144	9.5
N. Dak.	75	8.7	243	102	311	3.5
Ohio	66	8.9	353	170	341	1.6
Okla.	46	8.7	220	110	235	4.0
Oreg.	65	9.7	406	176	461	0.8
Pa.	57	8.7	335	144	276	1.7
R.I.	64	8.7	386	172	270	2.2
S.C.	21	6.8	175	38	125	12.6
S. Dak.	76	8.8	263	124	353	2.9
Tenn.	24	8.2	208	79	151	9.1
Texas	36	8.8	281	106	227	7.4
Utah	57	10.8	311	138	269	1.0
Vt.	61	9.0	343	150	416	2.9
Va.	29	7.6	235	88	198	10.5
Wash.	81	9.9	385	190	444	1.2
W. Va.	44	8.4	212	84	201	5.6
Wis.	62	8.7	339	181	300	2.5
Wyo.	87	9.8	398	138	426	1.5

Source: United States Chamber of Commerce Report, *Education an Investment in People*, 1945.

telephones per one thousand population in 1937, the circulation of eighteen nationally advertised magazines per one thousand population in 1940, and the rate of incidence of mental and educational deficiency per 100 Selective Service registrants examined from April, 1942, to March, 1943, all by states. The results are given in Table 79. The table shows that the volume of economic activity within various states, and the social indices that are used rise and fall with the level of educational expenditure. The table should be compared with that giving the proportion of rural population in each state.

On the basis of its study the United States Chamber of Commerce Committee concludes:

That education is an essential investment for the advance of agriculture, industry, and commerce.

That every community should ascertain its own education status and economic condition, and set to work to utilize education as a lever for its own advancement.

That the cost of adequate education is an investment which local citizens and business can well afford in increased measure.

That education programs must be made to apply more directly to the needs of the people.

That cultural education must accompany technical training if the desire for better living is to be developed.

That to maintain a representative republic, business must discover sound methods for the expansion of our dynamic economy.

DISCUSSION TOPICS

1. The exercises for this chapter will take the form of committee work. The class will be divided into five committees.

    Committee I will present a plan for organizing and administering rural elementary education on a county basis rather than a local district basis.

    Committee II will present a plan for consolidating two or more country district units.

    Committee III will present a plan for organizing and administering a high school on a town-country community basis.

    Committee IV will present a plan for organizing and administering libraries so as to be of greatest service to rural communities.

    Committee V will present a policy including editorial, reportorial, and advertising phases for a weekly newspaper, which will make it of greatest service to both its town and country constituencies.

2. Compare the per capita retail sales for selected villages and towns in a county or selected counties in a state with the per pupil costs of elementary or high schools. Can you discover any relationships?

3. Conduct a class debate on the question of federal aid to education.

REFERENCE READINGS

Brim, O. G., *Rural Education*. New York: The Macmillan Co., 1923.

Brunner, E. de S., and J. H. Kolb, *Rural Social Trends*. New York: McGraw-Hill, 1933.

Brunner, E. de S., and I. Lorge, *Rural Trends in Depression Years*. New York: Columbia University Press, 1937, chap. VII.

Clapp, Elsie R., *Community Schools in Action*. New York: Viking Press, 1939.

Cook, Lloyd Allen, *Community Backgrounds of Education*. New York: McGraw-Hill, 1938.

Cyr, F. W., *Responsibility for Rural School Administration*. New York: Teachers College Bureau of Publications, 1933.

Dawson, H. A., *Satisfactory Local School Units*. Nashville: Peabody College, 1934.

Dunn, F. W., and M. A. Everett, *Four Years in a Country School*. New York: Teachers College, 1926.

Jordan, Floyd, *The Social Composition of the Secondary Schools of the Southern States*. Nashville: Peabody College, 1933.

Langfitt, R. E., F. W. Cyr, and H. Newson, *The Small High School at Work*. New York: American Book Co., 1936.

Lewis, C. D., *The Rural Community and Its Schools*. New York: American Book Co., 1937.

Little, H. A., *Potential Economies in Reorganization of Local School Units*. New York: Teachers College Bureau of Publications, 1934.

Mort, Paul R., *State Support for Public Education*. Washington, D.C.: American Council on Education, 1933.

Mort, Paul R., and Francis G. Cornell, *American Schools in Transition*. New York: Teachers College Bureau of Publications, 1941.

Norton, John K., and Eugene S. Lawler, *Unfinished Business in American Education*. Washington, D.C.: National Education Association, 1946.

Regents of the State of New York, *Education for American Life*. New York: McGraw-Hill, 1938.

Report of the Advisory Committee on Education. Washington, D.C.: Government Printing Office, 1938.

Rural Education Number, *Teachers College Record*, January, 1940.

Rural Schools for Tomorrow. Washington, D.C.: *Yearbook,* Department of Rural Education, National Educational Association, February, 1945.

Schools in Small Communities. Washington, D.C.: American Association of School Administrators, 1939.

Sheffer, W. E., *The Co-operative School Area in Kansas.* Topeka: State Printing Plant, 1934.

Smith, M. B., *A Sociological Analysis of Rural Education in Louisiana.* Baton Rouge: Louisiana State University Press, 1938.

Stromberg, E. T., *The Influence of the Central Rural High Schools on Community Organization.* Ithaca: Agricultural Experiment Station, Bulletin 699, 1938.

Terry, Paul W., and Verner M. Sims, *They Live on the Land.* University: Bureau of Educational Research, University of Alabama, 1940, chap. VIII.

Wofford, K. V., *Modern Education in the Small Rural School.* New York: The Macmillan Co., 1938.

Works, George A., and Simon O. Lesser, *Rural America Today.* Chicago: University of Chicago Press, 1942.

19

The School Curriculum - A Social Force

THE CURRICULUM of the rural school, like that of its city counterpart, is becoming more pliant with the times; it is forsaking the rigidity of the nineteenth century and is attempting to adopt newer methods.

The curriculum today is a tool for educating the child for the world — so far as education can educate; for equipping him with the armor to battle his way through life, wrest a living from it, and to live it more completely than the common man has ever done before. For the glory of American democracy is to give each person a chance to live life fully, as far as is possible under an infinite variety of economic and social conditions, and the common free education provided by the state is one of the chief instruments in gaining this fuller life.

With all the shortcomings of our process of public education, especially in rural America, no country has ever given so much education to so many.

Next to his association with his family, the child spends more of his maturing years in school than anywhere else. Thus the school is influential in forming his attitudes, in regulating his social adjustments to his fellows, and often improving or teaching new skills. It is all this and more which gives the school its great social significance. It is this which makes the teacher so important. Instruction, which is the prime purpose of the school, is contingent upon the ability of the teachers. Administration, finance, buildings and other aspects of the institution of education are designed simply to facilitate this chief purpose.

Many people do not realize the constant changes going on within education, in order to accomplish its purposes and meet its responsibility to society. The strengthening of the state boards of education and the consolidation of school districts which were discussed in the last chapter are illustrative of this fact. Another development of significance is the employment by the state boards of education of supervisors, helping teachers, or persons with other titles, whose function it is to assist teachers and local schools to obtain the best possible results from their work. Since the younger, less experienced teachers are given the smaller salaries and go to the weaker schools, there is a considerable amount of this supervisory work in rural schools of the states which make provision for it. It should also be added that probably no profession works so constantly at improving itself as does education. Despite the handicap of low salaries, tens of thousands of teachers annually attend summer schools at colleges and universities.

The primary purpose of the school being what it is, the focal point of much of this drive for improvement is in the curriculum of the local school, in its content and in methods of teaching. Despite all the difficulties of rural education, the village and country schools of the United States share in this trend. Between 1924 and 1936 in the 140 village-centered communities surveyed more than 600 changes in the curriculum were made. In six out of seven changes a course of a department was added; in one of seven a course of a department was dropped. There were twice as many changes in the latter half of this period as in the first half. Even these changes do not tell the whole story. Courses dropped because of depression necessities, and later restored are not included in these figures. Moreover, sixteen school systems, more than one tenth of the total number, undertook complete revision of their curricula, one half of them either in co-operation with the schools of education at their state universities or in connection with state-wide programs sponsored by state boards of education.

The open-country schools, largely of the one- or two-teacher type, which enroll nearly three fourths of the open-country elementary-school children, experienced far fewer changes for reasons inherent in the structure and organization of these schools discussed in the previous chapter. Exceptions to this generalization occurred in connection with state programs of curriculum revision and in a few communities where progressive county superintendents of schools had taken the lead in reorganizing the work of the open-country schools. The curriculum of open-country schools was also being enriched in counties or groups of townships where traveling teachers in music and art were employed who visited each school at stated intervals. Better trained teachers were also introducing new elements and methods into these small schools. While there has been less change in these smaller schools than in those in villages, there has been encouraging progress in many open-country situations in this sample of thrice-studied communities. Some of this progress, moreover, was not of the sort that could be tabulated. It has better methods, better ways of organizing the work of the one-room school in which the average enrollment of twenty-one, in charge of a single teacher, often contains students in all eight grades of the elementary school. The bibliography contains references which discuss such plans in detail.

The developing curriculum. Certain patterns emerged from an analysis of the changes made in the 140 villages, which are quite illustrative of trends up to the time of the war in open-country, consolidated, and village schools. The social sciences have become far more important than formerly; that is, subjects grouped under the headings of sociology, economics, social problems, and social studies. Using the older term "civics," no junior or senior high school lacked some offering in this general field. Gains in the social studies and the cultural topics was compensated for by dropping Latin, by consolidating various courses in history — other than American — into a single course in world history, and by offering every other year such college preparatory subjects as physics, chemistry, and higher mathematics.

The next major change related to vocational education in the high schools. The offerings in home economics and agriculture increased, and these departments were found respectively in 115 and 102 of the 140 school systems. Departments of, or courses in, commercial education multiplied, with 107 schools having such offerings, twice the number in 1924. Despite the depression agitation against so-called "fads and frills," the cultural subjects which were often so classified, survived. Music was found in six schools out of seven, drama in almost half the schools, and art in two out of five schools.

The final trend of importance is in the direction of vocational guidance, now found in almost half the schools compared to none at all in 1924, and in mental adjustment, including home relations, offerings in this field being found in about one school in twelve. Much of this work was necessarily very superficial, a bare beginning in answer to a growing and deepening conviction in educational circles that something must be done in these fields.

The war brings changes. It was natural that World War II should bring many changes to the schools. The first of these manifested itself before Pearl Harbor with the inception of the defense program. The Office of Education received large sums for the expansion of vocational education, with special emphasis on skills needed in the war industries. After Pearl Harbor, more and more attention was paid to teaching subjects and skills useful in the war effort. As might be expected, this work, especially the emergency courses in vocational education, was conducted on a larger scale in the cities than in the rural areas, although even in village schools there was a wartime change of curriculum.

This experience has presented a problem to the future. There are those who claim that such activities should have a large and permanent place in the school curriculum. They point to the fact that the armed services turned illiterate men into literates in a matter of months, and imply that the school has been wasting time, should discard "boondoggling" and operate education efficiently.

There is small danger that this point of view will prevail. It is one thing to take mature adults who have been deprived of educational opportunities and make them literate for military purposes by an intensive teaching program. It is quite another thing to take immature children and introduce them to the accumulated culture of their society. The school's job of producing citizens for a free and democratic society is both supremely important and very difficult. It can be done better than it is at present, but it cannot be forced beyond the maturation process of the children. The report of the Committee on Education of the United States Chamber of Commerce, quoted at the end of the previous chapter, recognizes this in its case for including liberal or cultural subjects in the curriculum.

Forces affecting the curriculum. The reader of this book in perhaps 1950 may wonder why the above paragraphs were even introduced. They have an importance beyond the moment because they illustrate the pressures which develop from society or groups within it, upon the schools to co-operate with contemporary issues. It was fitting that all schools, rural and urban, should aid in the war effort. Not all pressures are as reasonable. Save for the frequent American phrase, "There ought to be a law," there is no more superficial solution proposed for a social problem than the phrase, "There ought to be a course." It is particularly unfortunate for rural schools when these two phrases are combined in legislative enactments regarding the school curriculum. Every state has at one time or another enacted legislation concerning the curriculum of the public schools. Schools have in this way been directed to do more than fifty different things, and have been restrained from doing as many more. One or more states require special observance of twenty-one different holidays, flag salutes, Bible reading, weekly fire drills, etc. Schools have been commanded to promote patriotism or nationalism, and with regard to the curriculum itself, certain subjects have been made mandatory: drawing in ten states, cotton grading in one, and so on. In all more than one thousand enactments have been placed on the statute books relating to the spending of time in the public schools.

Between 1913 and 1923 there was a 23 per cent increase in the number of such laws passed, and the movement has probably gained since that time. Pressure is frequently exerted upon the legislature to pass laws demanded by special interests. The Woman's Christian Temperance Union began, for example, even in the last century, to advocate laws directing instruction concerning the harmful effects of alcohol; various patriotic bodies have lobbied laws requiring the periodic reading of and instruction in the Constitution of the United States. Sometimes the manner of teaching and the amount of time to be expended are decreed, often in violation of the best pedagogic principles.

Enactments of this kind apply usually with equal force to urban and rural schools. These mandatory duties often work hardship on the rural teacher who has from four to eight grades to teach. Time is lacking for work in the non-subject-matter requirements especially. The compulsory inclusion of music and drawing in the curriculum raises problems for the country teacher, who, however excellent she may be in the fundamental subjects, may have little or no skill in such specialized subjects. Moreover, a small, weak school district may incur considerable expense in obeying such laws. School boards or teachers are faced with the alternative of ignoring the law or of handicapping the conduct of more essential work if the law is complied with. In hundreds of small communities the law therefore becomes a dead letter, this solution to the problem being admittedly the lesser of two evils.

It is, of course, not only well-meaning legislatures that are responsible for curriculum changes and difficulties. Educators themselves may be too much influenced by local pressures, or by some new theory not applicable to their local situation. Illustrative of this is the doubling of subjects in commercial education in the 140 villages already mentioned. In the nineteen-thirties, graduates of these departments were turned out far in excess of the power of their communities, or even counties, to absorb them. Failing marriage for the girls, or the finding of some other job outside their special scope of training, the only market for these skills was in the cities. Such an educational program, therefore, stimulated urban migration, but practically no cases were found where the curriculum of the village school contained any offerings designed to help these

migrants adjust to city life. The Rural Project of the American
Youth Commission found many instances where such inadequately
trained rural youth returned to their home communities because of
their inability to adjust to urban life and working conditions.

The fundamental problem. It should be remembered, however,
that far more fundamental than changes in courses and programs
are changes in teaching methods and in the contents of courses.
To appraise a course adequately, it would be necessary to answer
such questions as: How many modern problems of immediate importance are considered in, for example, the study of civics? How
many techniques of contemporary life are treated in the new commercial subjects? What opportunity do teachers have to select
content and invent procedures that will lead pupils to a better understanding of some of the pivotal issues of rural life? What conception of social and economic theory do the teachers themselves
have?

Unfortunately, the answers to such questions require intensive
surveys which have not yet been made. A number of cities and
rural districts have, however, made much progress in this direction,
and the State of Virginia has revised its whole curriculum after
taking these questions into consideration.

Virginia's curriculum revision. The Virginia Department of Education has devised courses of study dealing fundamentally with
the major functions of society as they are exemplified in the local
community. They study, for example, personal development, protection of life and resources, production, distribution and consumption of goods and services, consumption, transportation and communication, extension of individual freedom, education, recreation, and the expression of esthetic and religious impulses.
Within such a framework the rural teacher explains the local
social and economic organism, and then guides the pupils
through books to distant places and periods, from the particular and the local to the remote and abstract. The center of
interest in this curriculum is neither the child nor the community,
but the child growing up in the community. The teacher's work is
spoken of as "guiding child-learning in the social world with which
he is constantly interacting." This state course is built close to the
teacher-pupil relation, but the teacher is left free to select her
centers of study and material in terms of the community in which
she works and the children she teaches. Indeed, she is called upon
to do so. This new course of study, however, is still weak when
the problems of the one- and two-teacher school are considered.

Other tendencies. These innovations and tendencies are by no means confined to Virginia, but are spreading to an increasing number of rural schools. Other states have worked with revised curricula, though often the consideration given the special problems of the open-country schools is inadequate. Interestingly enough, two industrial states, Pennsylvania and New Jersey, are perhaps more aware of the problems of rural education at present than any others and are facing them more effectively. California also has developed much good curriculum work in small schools through its rural supervisors.

Education is promoted and disseminated by means of many activities that utilize the environment: hikes and picnics, dramatics, pageantry and sometimes the cinema. Occasionally the activities of the school are extended through the enlistment of local residents for demonstration and interpretation of activities of historical or immediate social significance. The school is at the service of the community and through parent-teacher associations and other agencies, adult education is being undertaken more and more. In many communities, at the end of the year, the director can report evidence of increasing appreciation of education, not only in the school, but also among the adult population, as well as satisfactory advancement by the pupils from grade to grade.

Broader Bases and Problems of the Curriculum

The discussion thus far has mostly concerned itself with the curriculum in what might be called the internal or more strictly educational aspects of its development. But the school does not exist in a vacuum, set apart from its community and the society of which it is a part. There are certain trends within rural society which are replete with educational implications for rural schools. Some of these are, or can well become, bases on which to construct sound curricula. Others present problems.

Returning veterans and war workers. One of the most immediate of the latter is the readjustment of war veterans and returned war workers. In terms of education, the problem here is the recent experience of these people. Warfare has become so mechanized that about two thirds of those in the armed services, and of course most war workers, have had their immediate vocational experience in what the census calls manufacturing and mechanical industries. Probably the United States at the peak of the war effort had proportionately two and one half or even three times as many persons classified under this heading as in normal times. Naturally all these persons are not continuing in this type of employment. A huge readjustment, and perhaps retraining, problem lies ahead.

Of course, mechanical training is valuable in an agriculture that is becoming increasingly machine-powered. Expansion of the rural electrification and road-building programs will absorb many who return to rural areas. But rural America is also desperately short of many services, and on the basis of trends before World War II these services will furnish employment outlets. But the skills required will be different and the time needed to acquire them will vary greatly. A clerk in a store can become efficient far more quickly than a teacher, nurse, or doctor. Rural America is proportionately shorter of these last services than of clerks or electricians.

Despite projected and actual federal programs, the greater share of the responsibility in meeting this problem lies with the local community. Assistance to veterans is a responsibility of the local draft boards under the Selective Service Act.

It is easy to say that the schools must co-operate. They will. But the extent of that co-operation will be limited by the ability of the school, which already has heavy responsibilities for the children and youth of the community, and which in rural America is handicapped as the previous chapter has told. It seems clear that additional resources, state and federal, will have to be made available if the school is to make its fundamental contribution to society.

More guidance essential. One aspect of this task will be guidance to those who are not able or willing to return to the jobs they left. This guidance must be based on tests for aptitudes and personality traits, and on a study of the individual. The whole guidance movement in education is relatively new, and there are few trained counselors as yet.

Guidance to veterans and returned war workers is an emergency job. Guidance to each new generation of rural youth will be a continuing obligation. Shall a given youth stay on the farm, seek employment in the village or city, and if so, what type of work, or go to college? Wrong decisions will mean social loss and individual frustration. We do not know yet what the war has done to the vocational aspirations of rural youth; their horizons reached farther in 1936 than in 1924.[1] In the latter year high-school boys listed

[1] The following nine paragraphs relating to vocational guidance have been summarized from an article by Brunner, Lorge, and Price, entitled "Vocational Guidance in Village High Schools." Cf. *Teachers College Record*, vol. 39, no. 3, pp. 218-29, December, 1937.

sixty different preferred occupations; girls, thirty. This was three and four times as many, respectively, as in the earlier year. This in itself is significant. It may be the result of the work in guidance. It may be influenced by the great increase in urban newspaper circulation, in the use of the radio, and in the broadening of school curricula that characterized the 140 villages between 1930 and 1936. It certainly indicates some of the problems for those at work in giving vocational guidance to rural boys and girls.

Not only was the range of choice broader than in 1924, but the relative position of some occupations in the esteem of the high-school seniors had changed. In the first place the number undecided as to their future was 40 per cent among the boys, almost double the 1924 proportion, and 29 per cent among the girls, or about one third more than previously.

Of those who had decided, for the moment at least, on a vocation the preferences in the two years, 1924 and 1936, show these significant findings: The proportion of boys electing agriculture rose from 18 per cent to 28 per cent. The number interested in the professions, of which nine were listed, doubled, rising from 8 to 17 per cent. Business was attracting 9 per cent of the class of 1936 as against 10 per cent in 1924. Engineering, as occupation and as profession, suffered the greatest loss, dropping from nearly 65 per cent in 1924 to 15 per cent in 1936. Aviation, quite naturally, took up part of this loss, with exactly one tenth of the boys hoping to become aviators. Five per cent more were headed for industry. Public service, elected by one boy in 1924, appealed in 1936 to 6 per cent.

Among the girls the most marked change was in the attitude toward teaching, a profession elected by one half in 1924 but by only one fourth in 1936. This is doubtless a reflection of the serious straits in which rural schools and their teachers found themselves during the depression. Nursing gained from 12 per cent to 17 per cent. All other professions, nine in number, attracted 9 per cent as against 6 per cent in the earlier years. Business held its own in attractiveness, securing 39 per cent of the choices in each period. Perhaps to this should be added the 10 per cent of the girls who hoped to become beauticians, an entirely new category, but one not to be wondered at, since the number of beauty parlors in these villages had increased from almost none in 1924 to an average of 1.25 per village in 1936.

It must be remembered that only broad categories have been used here. The girls classified under the general head of business, for instance, include those planning to be stenographers or secretaries, bookkeepers, cashiers, clerks in stores, hostesses, buyers, clothing saleswomen, and dry cleaners. It must also be remembered that the above compilations are based merely on stated vocational preferences of the seniors in the high schools. Many will change their choice either on the basis of wider experience or because of economic compulsion. The most significant aspect of the data is the wider range of interest and choice expressed in 1936 as compared with 1924.

It is quite evident also that these choices bear little relation to the present occupational distribution in these communities. For instance, 89 per cent of the farm male population and 12 per cent of the rural non-farm population were engaged in agriculture in 1930. Trade or business occupied slightly less than one sixth of both males and females, professional and public service 7 and 17.5 per cent respectively of men and women.

If these high-school pupils are going to engage in the occupations of their present choice, many of them must leave home. This, 53 per cent expect to do, which includes two thirds of those who hope to continue their education — a smaller proportion, however, than in 1924, when about two thirds planned to leave home. Part of the explanation for the excess of males over females in rural areas lies here. Sixteen per cent more girls than boys are continuing school. Thirteen per cent more girls than boys expect to leave the community in order to continue their education. Vocational education must assume part of the responsibility for this situation, especially as to the overloaded courses in commercial education, already referred to. The pupil undoubtedly accepts that fact and expects to migrate. Seventy-one per cent of the pupils choosing this field expect to leave the community.

One interesting finding of the study was that for boys and girls combined, vocational indecision which, as stated, had increased, was one third higher in the schools in which vocational guidance workers had had some professional training for their work than in those schools where they had had none. The proportion of students vocationally undecided in the two groups was respectively 40 and 30 per cent.

This may be due to the larger range of possible vocational opportunities opened to the ken of rural youth by means of the increasing work in vocational guidance or the other factors mentioned above. Many of the possibilities rural youth may not be well acquainted with and hence they remain undecided until they have more knowledge or experience. Again, the increase in vocational indecision may be due to the inexpertness of the vocational guidance itself, and inexpert it certainly is. It is within the range of possibility that in some schools what guidance was offered may have been worse than no guidance at all.

It is reiterated that no one knows what the war may have done to the vocational thinking of rural youth. The school program has been pointed toward the war. After 1941, boys could look forward only to military service. There is an even greater need now, therefore, for guidance than in the past.

As already stated, the larger village high schools are moving to begin an attack on this problem. In this connection a community enterprise in a Virginia village is of interest. Disturbed by the number of youth from the community unable to hold jobs after migrating to the city, a banker organized a group of about twenty professional and business people to study the problem and form a panel from which youth could seek guidance. The school and churches co-operated. The State Employment Service and the State Board of Education co-operated in offering a twelve-session course in fundamentals of guidance for this group.

Another interesting attack on this problem was made in Michigan in 1941. Several state agencies united in a weekend "careers conference" which brought together rural youth and agency leaders at the lakeside camp of one of the organizations. The conferees were its guests. Another agency planned and managed the program. Another furnished a staff member to guide the conference procedures, evaluate the enterprise, and prepare a report of findings. A number of others furnished speakers and consultants. The method of this conference successfully encouraged a large degree of giveand-take and of participation on the part of the rural youth themselves. Finally, the procedure and conference follow-up was designed to produce a maximum of influence on the decisions and activities of the young people after their return home, and to demonstrate to the agency personnel, through participation and the follow-up activities of the youth themselves, the scope of the needs to be met.[2]

Implications of migration. The influx of country youth into village high schools requires a reconsideration of the curriculum in terms of the needs of the two groups, the farm children and the village children, each of equal strength and importance. It has

---

[2] Brunner, Edmund de S., *Working with Rural Youth*, pp. 32-33. Washington, D.C.: American Council on Education, 1942.

been safe to assume in the past that the village boy and girl who did not stay in his home town would head cityward. In normal times, the exodus of village youth to the city has been greater proportionately than the better-advertised big parade from farm to city. A rural high-school training with a distinctly urban slant is, therefore, quite understandable, even though perhaps debatable. It was often contended that farm youths who received such training thirty or forty years ago were probably destined to go to the city. But whether or not such assumptions were correct in 1900 or 1910, are they safe under postwar conditions?

The rural high school, small at best, has the difficult problem of preparing its students, not only for farm or village life, but also for city jobs and college. These four disparate areas are the consumers of its product. And as pointed out elsewhere, in the nineteen-thirties, youth themselves were asking for more, better, and different education, for more guidance and for more effective help in home and family life. This is a colossal order for an institution with an average enrollment of 128 pupils the nation over. In the cities there are more or less specialized high or trade schools. In rural America a single institution must carry the whole burden, in too many cases with little aid from the state.

Vocational education important but not the solution. There are some who would say that vocational education is the best solution that can be made of these problems. Vocational education, if well done, is important, but it is far from the final solution of any of the problems raised. Life is more than vocation, important as that is. Moreover, vocational education in rural high schools is limited to agriculture, home economics, and the distributive trades. Agriculture is the most widely offered of these subjects, but despite federal aid it is found in only about 7500 of the 17,600 rural high schools, slightly more than two out of five. In them it reaches a minority of the students. In terms of the village high schools in the 140 communities an almost equal proportion of the boys chose agricultural pursuits where there was vocational agricultural education offered as where there was no such course offered. Among the girls, a higher proportion hoped to engage in work requiring domestic science: 6.9 per cent in schools where there were no offerings in domestic science and 4.2 per cent in schools where there were. Likewise, the proportion intending to go into commerce and trade was two points higher where the high school had no commercial courses than where it had.[3]

3 *Ibid.*

How shall agriculture be taught? Part of the problem resolves itself into the question, Shall agriculture be taught as a discipline or a practical subject, as a thing apart or integrated with the rest of the curriculum? Shall it be taught so that the farm-bent youth may learn that agriculture has social relations and obligations, involving processes of marketing in national and world markets? Shall he learn that the carrying-on of these processes requires an understanding of economic trends and co-operative movements, in addition to the fundamental skills of seed-testing, tree-spraying, and all those facts which enter into the productive side of agriculture?

There are few communities which have not witnessed foreclosure and tax sales, which have not received refugees fleeing from hunger in the cities during the nineteen-thirties, or which have not profited from full employment in the cities and unprecedented demands for food from abroad during the first two thirds of the nineteen-forties. The causes of these phenomena, the measures for meeting the resultant problems, the measures for their solutions, their implications for our national well-being and political organization cannot safely be omitted in the training of rural youth, about half of whom cease full-time education when they graduate from high school.

That agriculture is usually not taught in this way is chargeable to the degree of control over the curriculum exerted by the Office of Education under the Smith-Hughes law, which created the system of federal aid for vocational education in local schools.[4]

It should be added that in many places vocational teachers have overcome these handicaps and have become effective leaders in their communities, either directly as teachers or indirectly as citizens. They have been instrumental in organizing community co-operative canneries, freezing plants, potato storage or drying plants, and so on. In a number of places these were located on the school grounds or close to them. Sometimes these enterprises were part of a well-rounded continuing program of community development.[5]

In one community of over 5000 population the school vocational agricultural department employed a full-time teacher who gave his time wholly to out-of-school youth and adults. Apart from the usual classes for adults, two "Young Farmer" part-time classes were conducted, enrolling thirty-six out-of-school young men. Scores of

[4] It is possible that this control may become more rather than less vigorous. A bill before Congress in 1945, providing for greatly increased appropriations for postwar vocational education, defined the purposes for which the agricultural proportion of these funds should be spent in very narrow terms.

[5] Cf. Brunner, E. de S., *Community Organization and Adult Education.* Chapel Hill: University of North Carolina Press, 1942.

changed practices in farming resulted, and the boys gave much attention to agricultural law, learning the various ways of securing credit, contracts, and leases.

A unique feature of the program was the agricultural apprenticing of ten boys to good farmers in the community. Half of these boys divided their time equally between the farm and the regular school; the others spent all day on the farm and attended night classes. The instructor not only taught them all, but constantly visited the farms of class members, especially those co-operating in the apprenticeship program.

Valuable as have been the technical results of this program, certain unexpected results also accrued. There had been numerous cases in the county of youth being sold less desirable farm property at above its value, or being shaded on a deal for animals or equipment. The teacher soon became a one-man consultation bureau if Johnny wanted to buy a farm, Alex a calf, or if Eddie needed a loan. Soon no deal was consummated until it had been thoroughly discussed with and approved by the teacher. The banks and credit organizations co-operated. One of the best farmers in the community stated that this contribution alone was worth double the teacher's salary every year. As a result of this program, a number of young men have made their start in farming several years earlier than would have otherwise been possible.

The program described began to attract the attention of townspeople, and because of its location helped in improving relations between town and county. The plan will be continued, and those concerned believe it will be widely copied because of the very evident needs it has met, the practical results it has accomplished, and the interest it has aroused throughout the state.[6]

It should be noted, in passing, that one of the strength points of vocational education is its combination of school work with actual practice. Agriculture on the home farm becomes a project wholly conducted by the student under the supervision of the teacher. It would be highly desirable if definite work experience, integrated with the educational program, could be provided for all rural students during their high-school years.[7]

An expanded program of vocational education, integrated with the curriculum of the rural school, is to be desired. However, the

[6] Brunner, E. de S., *Working with Rural Youth,* p. 54. Washington, D.C.: American Council on Education, 1942.

[7] Cf. American Association of School Administrators, *Schools and Manpower.* Washington, 1943.

unlimited development of this field at the expense of a well-rounded curriculum would be unfortunate.[8]

School and community. It is clear that the best bases for building the school curriculum is the life of the community of which it is a part. The Virginia state course of study, noted earlier in this chapter, is evidence of this. So are a rapidly increasing number of local enterprises. The public school in rural Carroll County, Georgia, operated in co-operation with West Georgia College, is one such place. The whole curriculum is geared to the life and needs of the school and its community. This school has even produced its own textbooks, such as *Let's Plant Grass, Let's Raise Pigs, A Primer on Food, The Doctor Is Coming.* Arithmetic, agriculture, home economics, social studies, all come into these texts. The lastnamed was produced because a plan to immunize pupils against infectious diseases failed when the children became alarmed at the prospect of being "shot" and played hookey the day the doctor was to come. After the book had been studied, more children were on hand when the doctor was expected than on any other day of the session. Furthermore, fathers, mothers, and babies turned up, too, to get their "shots."

In Wisconsin, a Committee on Rural Community High Schools entered into a co-operative experiment with seven schools. After careful study, curricula were revised and made more flexible. Supervised correspondence study was substituted for courses which had very small enrollment. The teachers' time, freed in this way, was used on more important work. Social studies and English classes in one school united in a joint project with such units as "Earning a Living in W——"; "How Can I Select a Life Work"; "Recreation in W——"; "How Can I Best Spend My Leisure Time"; "Solving the Problems of Agriculture in America." These schools made community surveys, some limited, some comprehensive, to get local data needed for their classwork. Such surveys affected not only the pupils but also the community. Businessmen, churches, even local government, changed policies. Interest grew, and an

[8] Legislation pending in Congress in 1945 will, if passed, bring federal appropriations for vocational education on a per pupil basis up to the total per pupil expenditure for all education in a few of the populous but poorer rural states. In view of the data presented in the previous chapter, it may be questioned whether this is the best use of federal funds from the point of view of the national welfare.

For a careful appraisal of the whole area of vocational education, rural and urban, cf. Russell, John Dale, and Associates, *Vocational Education*, President's Advisory Committee on Education. Washington, 1938.

adult education program developed over a three-county area, especially in current affairs, international, national, and local.

From Virginia come other stories of a consolidated school in cooperation with a men's service club making and using a survey.

In such schools it should be emphasized that only the start of education is in the local community. Its part in the larger society soon becomes clear. The community emphasis is no effort to promote agrarianism. It is not content with the goal of economic and cultural subsistence, and should not be.

Programs of this sort point toward a new day in rural education. They show what can be done. They produce social change on the community level.

Two cases. Two cases among a large number that could be used, and drawn from the 140 communities, illustrate this. The first is from Cattaraugus County, New York, where for eight years ending in 1931, county-wide health demonstration was financed by the Milbank Fund. Paralleling the county health organization itself there developed three other movements:

1. A school program including full medical examinations, nutrition work, clinics, attention to the heating and ventilating equipment of the schools, and instruction of the pupils by the school nurse.
2. A program of popular health instruction through the press, speeches before clubs, churches and other organizations, posters and the like.
3. Co-operation with the social service agencies for specific work with the cases handled by such organizations.

This program achieved certain definite and measurable results. Cattaraugus County high-school students attained grades in health preferences and habits superior to those of a control group in another county. Death rates in the community had by 1929 decreased for all ages up to fifty-four when compared with 1920-22, especially for those less than a year old (41 per cent), for ages one to four (31 per cent) and fifteen to forty-four (27 to 36 per cent). "The mortality rates for diphtheria, tuberculosis, and the diseases of infancy dropped so sharply and suddenly, and to a degree involving a deviation from previous trends so pronounced as to be far beyond any reasonable influence of chance." [9]

It is interesting to note that this work proceeded on the basis not only of a health survey but as an exhaustive social investigation

[9] Quoted from Winslow, C. E., *Health on the Farm and in the Village.* New York: The Macmillan Co., 1933.

covering among other things, the history of the community, economic conditions and income, and a careful analysis of the racial, age, and sex composition of the population. Here, then, is a case in which, under outside stimulus, education of many sorts, of children as well as adults, resulted in important changes affecting the health of an entire county.

Let us take another illustration. Nestled in the southwestern foothills of the Appalachian Highlands, there existed for many decades a small village, away from the railroad, but at the nucleus of many roads leading up into the mountains. During a great part of the year these roads were impassable and the district isolated. Strangers were regarded suspiciously as recently as 1924. By 1930 the population of the village and its trade area had doubled. Roads had been improved and open-country schools were consolidated with the village school. Strangers found the inhabitants approachable and in greater contact with the outside world. Farm and domestic conditions had also definitely improved.

Behind this transformation was the school, and particularly an agricultural teacher and the principal. After some individual propaganda, they opened a few courses for adults. They instituted a county fair, and revived all-day sings and community picnics. They invited everybody to visit the school building in the evenings to listen to a radio which had been installed. They improved and modernized school methods. In time a service club was started, which helped to expand the school and community program and revitalized the church. In 1930 there was a complete school survey, far more sociological than is usual, on the basis of which a new educational program was developed.

Extracurricular activities expanded. In this discussion of the curriculum it should not be forgotten that schools are recognizing the potential educational value of leisure time and have organized an increasing number of extracurricular activities, especially in consolidated and village schools where numbers permit it, and to a certain extent, even in the smaller country schools.

The chief activity is athletics, now frequently under the control of a director of physical education. Musical affairs have tended to increase, too, particularly orchestras and glee clubs, which were found in from two thirds to three fourths of the high schools of the 140 village communities. One sixth also had bands. The development of music can be traced to the influence of state universities, some of which conduct annual high-school band, orchestra, or glee club contests.

Dramatics has now found a place in virtually all high schools, and nearly half of them give some attention to pageantry. About three fifths — that is, nearly twice as many as in 1924 — have organized debating. There is an increased interest on the part of parents in this forensic and dramatic activity, an interest carefully nursed by the school authorities. Attendance at all public school functions was reported to be rising, especially where roads had been improved and the school made accessible. There was clearly an encouraging increase in both the open-country and the village part of these communities in the contribution of the schools to the social and cultural life of their communities. Poor, discouraging, even bad situations still existed, but the trend was one of improvement and progress. This trend is important, for it shows the broadening concepts of education within the school and the enlarging place of the school as a factor in community life, another evidence of which will be discussed in connection with the social significance of adult education.

Summary. These two chapters have shown the various trends and tendencies of rural public education in our century, with emphasis on developments within the last two decades, decades during which rural education, like urban education, has made strides. Perhaps the achievements of greatest importance were the consolidation movement and the resulting centralization of educational opportunity for rural people in villages and towns. We have recorded, at least up to 1940, a steady improvement in the professional preparation of rural teachers and a consistent lowering of per pupil costs. We have noted also an increase in enrollment and attendance, especially in high schools, and a marked tendency for more rural youth, especially from the villages, to continue their education at college or at other institutions above the high-school level. We have described the movement for a more socialized curriculum, and for a closer relation of the curriculum to practical life, not omitting to notice that everywhere education was embracing more and more cultural subjects, in the interests of a fuller emotional and spiritual rural life.

. It has been indicated that the influence of the state in local school administration is steadily increasing, especially in matters of teachers' qualifications, the erection, remodeling and maintenance of buildings, and in courses of study and curricula. Finally, it has been shown that an effective curriculum is a powerful social force in the community.

Our record has, however, left out of account one highly important and advancing movement in modern education, namely, the instruction of adults. It is gradually being recognized that social and technological change is so rapid that even college education can no longer impart final technical skill in vocational subjects; much less can it impart a general knowledge sufficient for all adult life in this Gargantuan twentieth century with its revolutionary conception of science and the physical world, a conception involving volcanic changes in the social, political and economic fabrics. The issues which disturbed the statesmen of the nineteen-thirties, and on which the voters had to pass judgment, were unknown or scarcely heard of twenty years ago. At that time, for example, the gold standard was unchallenged, war debts unknown, farm bankruptcies and tax sales rare, federal relief for millions of unemployed and agricultural processing taxes and crop control inconceivable — to name only a few of the cataclysmic issues of the last tragic decades. Finally, added to all these, came the more tremendous issues of world organization and of reconversion after World War II. Another powerful force in promoting adult education is increased leisure because of unemployment and shorter working days made possible by technological advance, involving farm and factory alike. Hence adult education has assumed a remarkable importance, and to this subject the discussion will turn in the next chapter.

DISCUSSION TOPICS

1. Should rural high schools restrict their teaching of agriculture to the production and marketing phases? Defend your opinion.

2. List five or six of the most important social changes affecting American rural life and indicate the curriculum implications growing out of each of these changes in terms of either elementary school, junior high school or senior high school.

3. Block out the main outlines of a course of study in high-school civics, sociology or economics that would meet the point of view expressed in this chapter.

4. Secure from your own high school or from schools near your institution outlines of courses of study in the social studies field. What trends do these show? How adequately do they meet the current situation judged either from the point of view of the chapter or from your own point of view if it differs from that expressed?

REFERENCE READINGS

Ade, Lester, *Special Opportunities of Small Rural Schools*. Harrisburg: Pennsylvania Department of Public Instruction, 1939.

Baldwin, B. T., *Farm Children*. An investigation of rural child life in selected areas of Iowa. New York: D. Appleton & Co., 1930.

Bowen, Genevieve, *Living and Learning in a Rural School*. New York: The Macmillan Co., 1944.

Brunner, E. de S., and I. Lorge, *Rural Trends in Depression Years*, pp. 161-68. New York: Columbia University Press, 1937.

Cartwright, Morse A., and Glen Burch, *Adult Adjustment*. New York: Institute of Adult Education, Teachers College, 1945.

Clapp, Elsie R., *Community Schools in Action*. New York: Viking Press, 1939.

Committee on Rural Community High Schools, *Adventures in Rural Education*. Madison: State Board of Education, 1944.

Department of Rural Education of the National Educational Association Yearbooks: *Child Development and Tool Subjects in Rural Areas*, 1941; *Community Resources in Rural Schools*, 1939; *Conservation Education in Rural Schools*, 1943; *Guidance in Rural Schools*, 1942; *Newer Types of Instruction in Small Rural Schools*, 1938.

Dunn, F. W., "Adjustment of the Elementary Curriculum to the Schools of Extremely Isolated Areas," *Teachers College Record*, February, 1931.

Elementary Education in Two Communities of the Tennessee Valley. Lexington: Bulletin no. 3, vol. 14, Bureau of School Service, University of Kentucky.

Hulsizer, Allan, *Religion and Culture in the Curriculum of the Navaho and the Dakota*. The author. Washington, D.C.: Office of Indian Affairs, 1940.

Potter, Gladys L., *Exploring Your Community*. Washington, D.C.: Bulletin of Association for Childhood Education.

Rural Education Number, *Teachers College Record*, January, 1940.

Rural Schools for Tomorrow. Washington, D.C.: *Yearbook*, Department of Rural Education, National Education Association, February, 1945.

Schools in Small Communities. Washington, D.C.: American Association of School Administrators, 1939.

Strang, Ruth, and Latham Hatcher, *Child Development and Guidance in Rural Schools*. New York: Harper & Bros., 1943.

Tireman, Lloyd Spence, and Mary Watson, *La communidad*. Albuquerque: Report of the Nambé Community School, University of New Mexico, 1943.

West Georgia College, *With Great Awareness*. Carrollton, 1944.

Wofford, K. V., *Modern Education in the Small Rural School*. New York: The Macmillan Company, 1938.

20

Adult Education

ONE of the chief social developments of the Great Depression of the nineteen-thirties was a heightened interest in adult education. In a time of rapid spiritual and material change, it is argued, the schools and colleges cannot give youth a complete cultural and vocational equipment for life. The intellectual climate alters profoundly from the time of adolescence or young manhood to the time of middle age. Technological progress renders some trades quickly obsolete and creates others for which labor has to be trained. The progress of world events precipitates problems not envisaged in the curricula of educational institutions a few years ago; witness the New Deal and its novel sociological and economic implications and the huge issues growing out of World War II. Moreover, mankind seems to be on the threshold of greater leisure than has yet been enjoyed by the masses, and if this is actualized, there will be sufficient time for adults to continue their education.

The adult education movement is rather new. The American Association for Adult Education was founded less than twenty-five years ago. It subtends a score or more of educational fields, involving vocational, cultural and recreational activities, designed to help in the solution of personal and group problems, and carried on by public and private agencies.

THE AGRICULTURAL EXTENSION SERVICE

The largest and best financed division of adult education is entirely rural in nature: the tax-supported Agricultural Extension Service, whose administration and subsidy are a joint effort of the United States Department of Agriculture, the State Agricultural Colleges, county governments, and in some states, local farmers' organizations. It was organized in its present pattern under the Smith-Lever law in 1914, but had begun to develop a decade before, and expanded enormously during the World War.

The budget and staff. The total budget for this work reached its peak in the fiscal year ending June 30, 1944, when $36,739,968 was expended. Of this $18,996,950 was contributed by the federal government and the rest from sources within the states and territories.

On December 31, 1944, the employed professional personnel numbered 9180 persons, including 450 boys' and girls' club workers. The normal staff for adult work, therefore, numbered 8700 on this date. Of these, over 1100 are technical specialists attached to state staffs, over half of them devoted to agronomy, dairying, poultry, publicity, horticulture, animal husbandry, and marketing.[1]

Objective of the Extension Service. The aim of the Extension Service is to educate the farmers and their wives in all the facets of their occupation: it is practical to the core, such education being both technological and commercial, as a study of the preceding list of subjects will show. The Extension Service fulfills its aim by assimilating and disseminating the technical data and research discoveries of the colleges of agriculture and their experiment stations, through the state specialists who relay it by way of county agents to the ultimate consumers, the farmers and their wives.

Attention is also being given increasingly to "extending" the findings of the social sciences in areas other than marketing, and involving such things as the meaning of world trends for the farmer, community organization, and the like.

This system now functions in almost all of the counties of the nation, as the following table on the proportion of counties served shows:

	Per cent of Counties	
Year	Served by Men Agents	Served by Women Agents
1915....................	37.0	11.4
1918....................	79.3	55.8
1920....................	66.2	25.5
1925....................	69.1	30.2
1930....................	77.2	43.3
1934....................	91.1	41.8
1938....................	96.0	60.0
1945....................	96.0	69.9

[1] The remainder are allocated among the following subjects: agricultural engineering, animal diseases, child care and training, clothing, entomology, exhibits, extension schools, farm management, forestry, health and sanitation, home economics (general), home furnishings, home management, nutrition, plant pathology, poultry, publicity, rodent pests, and rural sociology.

In the early days of the Extension Service much of the teaching was done on a personal, on-the-farm, basis. Great reliance was placed upon actual demonstrations of improved methods. With the increasing use of the automobile and the acceptance by the farm people of this agency, and with the broadening of the program beyond narrowly vocational projects, more and more group work has been done. This has called for organization.

Accomplishment. The amount of work accomplished is impressive. County agents actually visit more than a million and a quarter farm homes annually, conduct about a million group meetings and arrange over a million demonstrations (by men and women) on an almost infinite number of projects. One of the most illuminating features of the work, the success of which has made it indispensable, is the voluntary recruiting of over seven hundred thousand men and women as unpaid local group or project leaders, each one of whom contributes, on the average, nearly two or three weeks each year. Training conferences for volunteer assistants are held by official leaders. So successful has the Extension Service been that a number of countries have emulated it.

Despite rapidly changing economic and social contours in rural America, and the provision of added funds for the Service, the proportion of time and money spent on the various aspects of the work changed but slightly, at least up to 1940. There was little difference in departmental arrangements even among the geographic regions. The increased service has been spread fairly evenly. Community activities have taken 6 per cent of the total time since 1925.

This fact, by the way, lends support to the criticism that the Extension Service program is highly standardized and inflexible in meeting changing needs. It must be remembered, however, that widely divergent activities may be actually conducted under each of the categories officially summarized. Adaptation to depression conditions had to be made, particularly in home demonstrations. The Agricultural Adjustment Program would probably not have succeeded if the Extension Service had not already created the machinery, the channels, and the contacts for conveying governmental plans to individual farmers, describing and explaining the action of the plan to them, though preoccupation with that program at the expense of more usual activities is a matter of concern to the Land Grant Colleges Association.

The concern over the effect of the new programs of the Department of Agriculture on Agricultural Extension is not only due to the interference of such projects with the former routine of Extension activities and teaching. It is due also to the fact that the AAA and soils program call for action, and there is some fear that the county agricultural advisers or agents will be held responsible for getting desired action. Should this happen, it would interfere with their educational function and with the objectives of the Service to bring all pertinent information to bear on subjects of vital concern to the farm population, but to allow individuals to reach their own decisions. This issue is an excellent illustration of the impact of changing conditions upon a social institution and of the demands, resistances, and tensions which are part of the process of reaching decisions. It is worth pointing out that such a clash of opinion as to the function of a tax-supported adult education agency could arise only in a democracy. Under a dictatorship the agency would do what the central government ordered or it would cease to be.

With the development of the programs of the nineteen-thirties, however, the action agencies have developed their procedures and staffs. More and more, therefore, the Extension Service has properly come to be regarded as the educational arm of the Department of Agriculture.

War shifts drastic. Then came World War II and, as in its beginning, the Extension Service planned action programs, put them into operation, and extended its educational tasks. The neighborhood leader plan, described in the chapter on neighborhoods, was one of these. At the peak of this program the number of volunteer leaders exceeded a million persons. The Extension Service also had charge of the emergency farm labor programs, making about four million placements in some years. It investigated and advised draft boards on deferments based on agricultural necessity, and was responsible in many ways for increased food production.

Results of extension work. Among the known results of the Service are the facts that between one third and one half of all farm homes are reached by it; several million persons have been assisted in solving their occupational and home-economic problems through information acquired from it; changed agricultural practices have resulted from it and the increased efficiency of American agriculture may be partly ascribed to it; co-operative action has been stimulated, local leadership developed, and community improvements furthered. Of late, the Extension Service has attempted interesting excursions into recreational or cultural fields, in music and drama, for example, and to some extent in literature and art.

Significant recent developments. One of the most interesting prewar developments has been the organization of groups all over the country for the discussion of public affairs which in a democracy must be understood by citizens if effective decisions are to be made. Opinions on such issues are too often influenced by propaganda and are formed on the basis of meager evidence. No national summary of the program has been issued as plans and procedures varied widely, but in 1936 four fifths of the counties in twenty-nine Middle and Far Western States were organized. In typical states there were ten groups per county. In one Southern state there were over five hundred local groups and almost every county was reached. In this state thirty-eight persons per county attended discussion leaders' training conferences. Discussion materials were prepared and distributed by both the federal and state agencies, in which every effort was made to present various alternative proposals impartially. One of the most significant aspects of this enterprise lies in its effort to help citizens make up their minds as to public issues. It is designed to equip them to act or vote on the basis of all the major facts in any given situation.

County planning. Another recent development has been the holding of conferences to work out programs for agriculture and rural life on a county-by-county basis. Some two thousand counties a year have participated in this project. One criterion for such planning in many but unfortunately not all states, is the use of land in such a way as to win a better material and non-material standard of living. These conferences have the advantage of bringing together all the forces of a county interested in rural welfare.

Though this work at the federal level had to be practically abandoned, many states continued it, and increasing state and federal attention was given to postwar planning.

Expanded social program. Because of the depression and a developing philosophy of adult education, much of the work in clothing, nutrition, health, home furnishings, and similar phases of home demonstration became less merely technical and more and more socialized. In several states the emphasis was placed on appreciation of beauty in the home and a utilization of materials at hand. It is impossible to do more than illustrate this trend. Thousands of families in the aggregate renovated furniture, reseated chairs, rehung pictures, and refinished floors and walls. Home Bureau clubs made tours to museums and to attractively furnished homes. Art exhibits were arranged and circulated among the groups. In one state, two thousand persons were enrolled in a project that eventuated in home flower gardens and so-called outdoor living-rooms.

Nutrition work grappled with the problem of adequate diet in the face of declining income, and this activity quickly expanded beyond the home and into the school. In Massachusetts, for instance, the Extension Service co-operated in a study of the school-lunch situation along with the State Departments of Education and Public Health, the P.T.A.'s, and the Federated Women's Clubs. As a result, a co-operative effort was made with the W.P.A. to serve a hot dish in the schools to supplement lunches brought from home.

In Missouri, 249 homemakers' clubs supplied hot dishes or whole lunches daily to more than 6500 children in 344 rural schools. In addition, 412 Home Economics Extension clubs assisted in improving the plane of nutrition in their communities from which W.P.A. nurses had reported some thousands of cases of malnutrition among children. These instances are simply illustrations of a wide variety of activities stimulated by Home Economics Extension and carried through by the local groups under their own leadership. One interesting development growing out of all this has been greatly increased attention to the knotty problem of consumption and consumer education.[2]

More concern with consumption. The word *consumption* as here used is related both to the individual and the community standard of living, and includes material goods, social utilities, and non-material spiritual and esthetic values. The criterion for production and farm management, as a number of farm groups as widely separated as South Dakota, Wisconsin, and Connecticut have recently announced, therefore, becomes the usage of land in the light of available consumer markets in such a way as to secure a desired standard of living, including both material and non-material elements. These matters are alluded to in another chapter. The announcements referred to, superficial as experts may consider them, are a long step forward; and the fact that these meetings were held under Extension Service auspices is an encouraging sign.

Child development and parent education.[3] It is a short step from such projects to the whole field of child development and parent education, and extension has taken that step. There is now a

[2] Brunner, E. de S., and I. Lorge, *Rural Trends in Depression Years*, pp. 185-86. New York: Columbia University Press, 1937.

[3] The following five paragraphs and four lines of the sixth paragraph, with the exception of some of the paragraph headings, are quoted from Brunner, E. de S., and I. Lorge, *Rural Trends in Depression Years*, pp. 187-91. New York: Columbia University Press, 1937.

specialist in this field on the national staff, and twenty-one states have also employed state specialists. The programs are varied, and reflect somewhat the interests of the state specialist in charge, the needs of the local co-operating groups, and the age of the activity.

Leisure-time activities increase. But perhaps the greatest development has taken place in the field of leisure-time activities, especially those of drama, music, art, reading, and recreation. This type of work also antedated the nineteen-thirties, but developed surprisingly, especially in the present decade.

Of the forty states responding to a questionnaire, thirty-two had well-defined programs in general recreation, and the other eight were all doing "a little." Drama was part of the program in twenty-six, music in twenty, arts and crafts in twelve, reading in eight, training in speech in two, and folk-dancing in one. In three other states nothing is being done along these lines, because such activities are cared for either by the state universities or by the state board of education.

A list of the total number of recreational activities would tax the space available for this chapter. Games of many kinds are included, both group and athletic, for home and community, as is dancing, especially folk-dancing. Home-talent chautauquas are frequent. . . . Twenty-four states hold state-wide or district institutes or schools for the local volunteer recreation leaders.

Drama. Most interesting, perhaps, of recent developments has been the great interest in drama. The training of local leaders has proceeded in the same way as with recreation. Literally thousands of rural groups have participated. Many of the colleges of agriculture maintain loan libraries of plays to assist groups in their selections. In one Middle Western state alone, 4040 plays were lent to such groups in 1935. But many of the plays are original (often the work of farmers' wives) and utilize local materials. Some of these are of very good quality. Some states are stimulating the development of the drama by holding play-writing contests; and these report that the quality of the manuscripts submitted improves with each year.

In the best organized states, the local groups put on county drama festivals, and the best companies, or those with the most significant plays, are selected from the entire state to appear at the state college during Farmers' Week.

In several states, especially in the Middle West, the number of persons actively engaged in the drama program exceeds four thousand a year. In 1939, North Dakota celebrated the twenty-fifth anniversary of the drama work of their Little Theater, originated and directed through all these years by Professor Arvold. The work in

North Dakota influenced Professor F. H. Koch, who went to the University of North Carolina and organized the Carolina Playmakers in 1920, a group which has exercised a national influence on rural drama. Their original plays have been folk plays mainly, indigenous to the soil, built of the mores, traditions, and lives of the people of the state. Now there are in the state one hundred high-school and sixty adult dramatic clubs.

Music and art. In the other cultural activities of the Extension Service, the set-up is much the same as in that for the drama. This is true in reference to organization, leadership training, and county or regional festivals or demonstrations, as well as to the appearance of local orchestras, bands, choruses, glee clubs, opera groups, and the like at state college Farm Weeks, or at state fairs, or on radio programs. These enterprises are being carried on in twenty states, and are therefore second only to drama in their popularity. The Extension Service assists, not only in training, but also in organizing, such groups when requested.[4]

An illustration of growing musical appreciation among farm people came as a result of an experiment of the Iowa State College radio station in broadcasting popular and classical music. Of 10,000 responses tabulated, 9634 persons preferred the latter.[5]

Rural community organization extension. A significant development is the addition of extension rural sociologists to the staffs of twelve colleges of agriculture, who devote themselves largely to community organization and relationships. In Iowa, for instance, the 1932 program included 12 types of recreational activities, 261 meetings and 56 local leader-training conferences dealing with community structure and planning, and assistance to churches and other types of institutions through surveys and community-planning programs. This program is still functioning.

Despite the small number of state employees in this field, county extension agents conduct some such work, the aggregate of which is very large. In 1931, according to the *Report of Extension Work in Agriculture and Home Economics in the United States,* issued by the Department of Agriculture, recreational activities were developed or assisted in 10,697 communities, and over 1000 localities established community houses or rest rooms; 6558 county-wide or community plays or pageants were presented, some of them by 4-H and not strictly adult clubs. Increasingly, however, there is a

[4] Brunner, E. de S., and I. Lorge, *Rural Trends in Depression Years,* pp. 192-93. New York: Columbia University Press, 1937.

[5] Quoted from *The American Magazine of Art,* December, 1929.

tendency for the recreational to be separated from those activities which make the findings of rural sociology available to extension workers and rural people. The latter have to do with the contributions that rural society can make to community organization and to the understanding of rural society. World-wide attention is being given to the cultural field of Extension and the interaction of the Extension program and the culture.

The general objective of rural sociological extension is to stimulate specific activities contributing to the development of human values and rural talent, and to assist rural people in developing and co-ordinating their various groups and institutions in relation to their priority and emphasis in community building.

A study of the Extension Service shows that, far from being a routine program, it is flexible and adaptable in comparison with other similar institutions of its size and scope. It has no "set" program save to serve farm, and, increasingly, rural non-farm, people in terms of their expressed needs. The close contacts which county workers maintain with the consumers of the Service keep it close to the needs of the constituents. It has developed progressive educational methods, Continually it is studying its own program and the results of its application in order to improve the service it renders. It is a highly important agency for serving rural people in their educational needs and social relationships.

As this is written, it seems probable that there will be an increase in appropriations for the Extension Service, through which the staff will be enlarged. Several states are re-examining their whole program and are making ambitious plans for expanded service and for broader and more thorough training for the professional personnel.

It is quite clear that in the future Extension work must be more with organized groups, with neighborhoods and communities. In the early days, much of the county agent's work was essentially personal service to demonstrate better methods. These personal contacts were, and will continue to be, very valuable, but the changes in technology and in rural society foretell that the amount of time spent in personal service will of necessity be less than in the beginning years of Extension history.

No one has ever determined how large a county territory or how many farm homes can be most efficiently cared for by an Extension agent. Some counties have been greatly undermanned. This has often resulted in service only to those who were the most interested or easiest to reach. In counties where co-operation came through a local farm organization, the agents seem to have made their services available to organization members only, rather than to all farmers. It is significant in this connection that up to a third of the new wartime neighborhood leaders in some states, and nationally about a fifth, had had no previous contact with the Extension Service, though of course an indeterminable number of these were villagers. With added funds the goal of reaching all farm homes should be measurably achieved.

In the discussion thus far it is plain that the program of Extension is growing in coverage and in scope. There has been progress in many of the states, and in the federal office rural youth programs are an important new aspect of Extension work. One state has decided that the county Extension office is to be the local office of the state university; another state is considering the same step. This will mean a different type of organization in the county, and more supervisory and specialized help in the state office. It will greatly broaden the potential program in the counties, and hasten the bringing of the Extension Service to all rural people, not simply to farmers, a trend which is already seen in many states.

University extension. State universities are also playing their part in rural adult education, not merely by sending lecturers into rural communities but also by inducing a constantly increasing number of people to take their correspondence courses. In one Wisconsin village one fifth of the adult population were thus enrolled in 1936. Universities send out study-guides for clubs, news letters and package libraries of pamphlets, articles and clippings on matters of current interest. A number of state universities as well as colleges of agriculture maintain radio stations or are allotted regular time by commercial stations.[6]

The Public School

Many leaders see in the public schools an instrument for widespread adult education. In the cities, it is observed, public schools have long catered to adults by holding night sessions in vocational and primary subjects, thus combating illiteracy and augmenting the technical equipment of artisans and laborers.

Extent of illiteracy. The problem of illiteracy bulks large in rural America, which in 1930 had altogether 6.9 per cent illiterates among

---

[6] Cf. Tyler, T. F., *An Appraisal of Radio Broadcasting in Land Grant Colleges and State Universities.* Washington, D.C.: National Committee on Education by Radio, 1933.

the rural farm population ten years of age and over, and 4.8 per cent in the rural non-farm population. Although in the Middle-Atlantic and Middle-Western regions less than 1 per cent of the population ten years of age and over was illiterate and the figure in the Far West was only 1.4 per cent.

As a previous chapter has shown, the 1940 Census gave a better measure than ever before of the educational status of the rural population, farm and non-farm. It indicates that the median years of schooling completed by the farm population 25 years of age and over was 8.2. For the rural non-farm the figure was 8.7 years. Almost 1,200,000 rural persons of this age, 58 per cent of them on farms, had had no schooling. Three and eighth-tenths millions more, 60.5 per cent on farms, had had less than five years of completed schooling and thus fell in the category of functional illiterates as defined by the army and navy. So we find that 5,000,000 rural persons are wholly or partly illiterate. Nearly one third of these 5,000,000 persons are Negroes, of course, most of them in the South. This is evidence of the serious problems of rural education in this region.

Expressed another way, 13.6 per cent of the rural farm and 9 per cent of the rural non-farm population over twenty-four years of age are functionally or entirely illiterate, as contrasted with 4.5 per cent of the comparable urban group. Among rural Negroes, 59.1 per cent of the farm and 48.2 per cent of the rural non-farm, compared to 30.3 per cent of the urban population fall in this category. From these facts there are clear indications of need for an agency like the Extension Service and for public schools.

The Southern states are quite conscious of their problems and have been trying to meet them. Many of them have divisions of adult education in their state departments of education, and in some states much progress was made from 1934 to 1940, when relief funds were used for literacy classes in and outside of the schools.

But while this is a specific need, the reasons for the present interest in adult education are as operative in rural as in urban America. The public school, an omnipresent institution, is meeting such needs, and is, moreover, not confined to specific educational activities as is the Extension Service.

Perhaps the best example of large-scale adult education is to be found in California, although Delaware has had a comparable program for many years. Classes in adult education are offered by the public schools and by the extension division of the state university. The public-school adult education classes receive state aid just as the regular school program does. At one time in the middle thirties, about one fifth of the adult citizens of California were enrolled. In one Delaware county with about 30,000 adult population, over a thousand persons were enrolled in school classes in a rural county for a number of years. The programs of the adult education classes are as wide in scope as the interests of the people. In 1944, Michigan began a state-wide adult education program with a special appropriation from the legislature.

Increasing adult education interest in village schools. In 1924, only nine schools in the 140 village-centered rural communities were offering courses for adults. In 1936 there were offerings in forty-four with an average of 2.5 courses per school and a total of twenty topics. The adult enrollment in each averaged 81.4 and more than four fifths completed the work. The longer a school had had adult education work, the more courses it was likely to offer.

The program was heavily weighted on the vocational side, four fifths of the courses falling in this category. This is undoubtedly due to the presence of Smith-Hughes law vocational teachers in the village schools. Their professional organization and the Office of Education at Washington promote such adult activities. As a result in only a few schools was a balanced program found. The offerings, while supported as indicated, bore little relation to the normal distribution of adult education offerings in other types of communities, to the expressed interests of adults where secured, or to the balance of the day-school curriculum. If the schools are to contribute as they might to adult education, the number of general and cultural courses should be increased without reducing the vocational offerings. The inclusive adult enrollment in vocational agriculture in 1943-44 was under 200,000.[7]

That such a development would be welcomed by the rural adults seems to be indicated by the experience of the emergency adult education program of the W.P.A. There were many problems with this program in the very nature of the case. The teachers were poorly trained for adult work. The turnover was high. The relief rather than the educational features were emphasized by administrators and the choice of offerings was dependent on the interests and skills of the relief teachers. Nonetheless, non-vocational subjects made up from one third to one half the offerings and these

[7] For a full discussion of the regular adult education program in village schools, with descriptions of some of the better programs, see Brunner and Lorge, *Rural Trends in Depression Years*, pp. 218-28. New York: Columbia University Press, 1937.

were distinctly popular. In the communities where local educators judged the work "fair" to "good," and in which the programs continued more than one year, the enrollment had increased to 138 per village, or over 46 per cent above the first year, and the proportion completing courses was higher than in the regular adult courses supported by the schools.

It should be added that the vocational teachers of agriculture and home economics have a real opportunity in adult education if they could broaden their offerings. The technical phases of these subjects are fraught with social implications. According to the President's Advisory Committee on Education, the home economics teachers have made more progress than the agricultural teachers have, in these directions. Both groups in their adult work have a real opportunity with out-of-school youth, which will soon include hundreds of thousands of returned veterans.

Another evidence of this is that throughout the country increasing interest in adult education is manifesting itself in forums, discussion groups, lyceums using university extension lecturers, all of which center about the public school. A few schools and some community organizations are reporting the use of surveys and so-called "interest-finders" to discover the educational and leisure-time needs and wants of adults in their localities.[8] Parent-teacher's associations, or other educational groups existed in about two thirds of the village and perhaps one fifth of the open-country schools in 1936, and affiliated with state federations, are entering into adult education work with leadership and program materials supplied by the latter. Apparently there is a large potential future for adult education in village-centered rural communities. There has been no nation-wide study of rural public school adult education since 1936, but increasing interest is obvious.[9]

Nor is the open country, well served as it is by Agricultural and Home Economics Extension, standing still with respect to adult education. Typical of many adult education enterprises is the following instance from an Ohio hamlet of some two hundred people. The local leader of the annual farmers' institute enlisted the cooperation of the school and arranged for a program covering public affairs, taxation, psychology, and several technical courses in agriculture and home economics. Instructors in a near-by college were

[8] Cf. Hudson, Robert, *Radburn: A Plan for Living*. New York: American Association for Adult Education, 1934.

[9] See closing pages of chapter for a discussion of the emergency program of adult education initiated by the federal government in 1933.

very willing to co-operate, and extension service experts were also drawn upon. The cost was $1.25 per *family* plus the cost of lighting and heating the school. The enterprise was highly successful and is being continued.

Rural Libraries

Although proof is increasing that in urban communities the public library is a vastly important agency of adult education, it has long been known that rural America was largely without library service. An American Library Association study in 1926 revealed that 86 per cent of the rural population had no access to public libraries, as against 5 per cent in the cities. Since that time some real progress has been made in the country, but the proportion of persons without library service is still over 65 per cent. Rural library needs are being satisfied in a number of ways.

Community libraries. Many localities have libraries of one sort or another, especially in New England, where about 1400 libraries are to be found outside of cities, often, however, pathetically inadequate. The unit of service is "the town," or township, as it is called elsewhere. In Massachusetts and Rhode Island no town lacks at least one library. A Massachusetts town somewhat above the average, of about 7000 people, with an area of about fifty square miles, possesses a main library, three branches, over 14,000 books, and has an annual circulation of more than 35,000. The budget is about $6500 or $1 per capita. An article in the weekly newspaper introduces the new books to the community, and best-selling fiction and non-fiction books are now topics of conversation. New England, as a matter of fact, has four fifths of all American township libraries. The remainder, about 500 in number, have largely followed the migrant New Englander into New York and some Mid-Western states, notably Indiana.

Elsewhere the problem of rural library service is more difficult; in some states, particularly in the South, it has been helped by opening school libraries to the general public. Such libraries, however, have been built up with specific educational objectives in view and seldom meet the needs of the general reader unless special attention is paid to him.

The village situation. The study of 140 villages showed that about three fifths of them had a local library, although the proportion in the South was only one fourth and in the Far West, four fifths. The higher the retail sales in a community, the more likely it was to have a library. Larger communities were better supplied than smaller ones. Twenty-four communities had school libraries open to the public and twenty-one at periodic intervals received traveling libraries from the State Library Commission or a comparable agency. Some of these makeshift efforts at library service were quite successful. One school in a community of 2300 population with 2800 volumes reported a public circulation of 40,000 volumes in 1936. The circulation seems also to be increasing slowly among the total population and certainly among those who are borrowers.

TABLE 80. CIRCULATION OF BOOKS PER INHABITANT, BY REGION — 140 VILLAGES

	Circulation per Inhabitant *		
	1924	1930	1935
Middle Atlantic.................	2.9	2.7	3.7
South........................	1.1	0.5	0.9
Middle West...................	3.0	4.8	4.9
Far West.....................	3.6	4.5	4.3

* Circulation per borrower increased from 9.6 per year to 14.6 in 1930 and 16.3 in 1935.

The income of these libraries was small, averaging thirty-one cents per inhabitant in the total community, with the South showing ony five cents. Most of the available money came from tax sources, though one sixth of the libraries were entirely financed by memberships and contributions and another one eighth had to supplement tax funds by other means. The average library in these communities had 4835 books in 1936, a gain of 18 per cent over 1930, or just half the rate of gain between 1924 and 1930.

These libraries, like many other of rural America's social institutions, are located in the village or town center of the community, but they have not made nearly as effective an appeal to the open-country population as have other agencies. Outside the Middle West the ratio of open-country borrowers to population was less than 5 per cent. In the region named it was almost 25 per cent. Among villages, outside the South, more than one half the population were borrowers. Circulation per borrower was steadily increasing. It went from 9.6 books a year in 1924, to 14.6 in 1930 and 16.3 in 1936. Circulation per inhabitant was 4.3, about half the

American Library Association's standard for places of less than 10,000 population.

Local library leadership. These local libraries, spreading over three fifths of our villages, a majority of them not connected with county systems and a minority unaided by tax funds, are significant vanes in the progress of national culture. Judged by professional standards, they are usually woefully inadequate. But behind each is likely to be the devotion and perseverance of a Woman's Club, a Ladies' Aid Society, or a similar organization whose members keep the library going by their volunteer, unpaid continuous service, year in and year out. The survival of these libraries is testimony to the magic of books, to the communal need for the culture, the rich mental stimulation, the broadening agency of the printed page. It is obvious from the facts presented, however, that community libraries will not make progress sufficient to fill up the great vacuum in library service in rural America. Other means must be sought, perhaps state aid and certainly county library systems.

The county library. The county library is tax-supported, maintains a headquarters, branches in towns and villages, and stations to which small book collections are sent periodically, perhaps to rural schools and stores or homes in more remote areas. Sometimes there is direct service by "bookmobile." The central library is open to everybody, it usually serves individuals by mail or telephone, and secures for serious students any needed book in the county or state libraries.

The first modern county libraries were established in Van Wert County, Ohio, and Washington County, Maryland, in 1898. From this start, the number grew to 99 counties in 1920, 176 in 1925, 228 in 1936 and 651 in 1944. This increase seems to have come as a result of state aid, interest aroused through W.P.A. rural book projects and long-time campaigns in individual counties. It is interesting to note that only about three fifths of these county libraries subsist as independent units. The others contract with urban libraries for rural service, a heartening illustration of rural-urban co-operation.

Properly speaking, a number of these 651 county libraries cover more than one county as a result of co-operative arrangements between county governments and previously existing libraries. The American Library Association calls them regional libraries. Close to a thousand counties, about one third of those in the nation, are now reached by either county or regional libraries.

The trend toward districts or regions larger than a county is also more marked. Most of the states have now set up some sort of state plan for library development and practically all of these include emphasis on regions. Some actual results are seen in Vermont, Louisiana, and in connection with the T.V.A. Apparently, the small local library and even the small governmental unit will co-operate with the state more readily than with adjoining governmental units.

As with education, it becomes clear that state aid is necessary if library service is to be expanded. About ten states now extend it. While efforts to secure such aid have failed so far in some states, no state that has made an appropriation has ever ceased to renew it by vote and a number have increased the original grants.

The American Library Association has been active in promoting this movement and in improving rural library service in general. Their recommended minimum appropriation is one dollar per capita. An unpublished study by Miss Elsa Burner, made in 1934 under the direction of the Department of Adult Education of Teachers College, Columbia University, showed that under existing conditions and in view of the average population density, a service far better than what is possible on a haphazard community basis could be secured for perhaps twenty-five to thirty cents. Because of the increase in costs of the last few years both these figures should be increased.

Many reports and records of county librarians read like romance. Books are sent to remote ranches and received by people who reach their rural mail boxes on snowshoes, horseback or in canoes. Even the statistics are meaningful. The second year after reorganization a Louisiana parish (county) library operating on a budget of $16,000 in a community having a large percentage of Negroes circulated six books per capita among less than 30,000, a high average. This system put deposits into all Negro schools. California's forty-three county libraries circulate over 11,000,000 books a year.[10] There can be no question about the response of rural people to library service when it is offered.

Advantages of the county library. The advantages of county libraries, which are now permitted by law in all but four states, excepting New England, lie chiefly in the fact that the unit of operation is large enough to obtain support for an adequate book stock and a trained librarian. It must be remembered, however, as another chapter shows, that the county is not necessarily the best unit

[10] Cf. Fair, Ethel M., *County-Wide Library Service* (American Library Association, Chicago, 1934), for an interesting compilation of various methods and expediencies by which libraries are serving rural people.

of operation for certain social services; steps have already been taken in various regions for the amalgamation of groups of counties as operating library units. This augurs well for the progress of rural reading facilities, and is another indication that county lines must eventually yield to social exigencies.

Interesting, too, are the beginnings in several states of additional library services such as the circulation of pictures, periodicals, music and phonograph records, and of co-operation among various rural adult education agencies. Typical of such innovations is the five-year reading project sponsored by the South Dakota Agricultural Extension Service and the South Dakota Library Commission. For the first year's study the state library worker prepared a general outline on "Reading in the Home," mimeographed and distributed by the Extension Service. For the second year a course on the novel was prepared (also printed and distributed by the Extension Service), and training schools were conducted in thirteen counties to introduce the project to leaders of farm women's clubs organized by the Extension Service. Books were supplied by state traveling libraries and by county and local branches.

State colleges help. The state colleges of agriculture are making other contributions to the problem of furnishing reading materials for rural people. Extension bulletins and circulars are issued to an annual average of twenty-seven per state. In few states does the distribution fall below one hundred thousand; in some it exceeds a million.

> The average Texas farm and village home requests a pamphlet every three weeks. In New York, a request comes from every rural home about six times a month. It should be recalled that in more than two thirds of the states, publications are sent out only on request, so that the recipient has spent at least one cent for a postal card and the time involved in writing.[11]

A number of states conduct book hours over the radio and several promote the organization of libraries. Written requests as to what to read on specific subjects have grown so heavy that six states offer what librarians call readers' advisory service.

Next steps in library service. Despite these various enterprises the rural library situation falls far below the urban level. In the

---

[11] Brunner, E. de S., and I. Lorge, *Rural Trends in Depression Years*, p. 215. New York: Columbia University Press, 1937. These comparisons include all circulation of state bulletins with no deduction for out-of-state and urban circulation, which is probably relatively small. The circulation of federal bulletins is not included.

main it has been strengthened during the years 1930-45. Rural people are standing loyally by such libraries as they have, the county movement has again shown a gain, and the new plan for district or regional service, the latter already approved by a majority of the states, should under normal conditions result in a further forward step in the huge task of bringing library service to rural America closer to the plane it occupies in the city. The movement for state aid to libraries also holds hope in achieving this objective.

The President's Advisory Committee on Education has drawn attention to the deficiencies and has urged some federal aid to rural libraries in order to begin to remove the obvious inequalities. Coupled with the move for more state aid, this step, if it comes, will make for significant progress in rural library service in the decade ahead.

OTHER ACTIVITIES IN ADULT EDUCATION

Other rural adult education agencies. There are many other agencies of rural adult education, some of them of long standing, some comparatively new. The Grange has for more than fifty years in all its eight thousand locals stressed its "lecture hour," which is often an open forum of considerable educational value. Materials are specially created for it and leaders trained. The Farm and Home Bureaus, closely associated in some states with the Agricultural Extension Service, have played a large rôle in rural adult education. The women's clubs and certain other agencies, described in another chapter, have their educational features. The churches are beginning to be attracted to adult education. More than one fourth of the village and about one tenth of the open-country churches in 1930 arranged for lectures or lecture courses. About one tenth of the village churches, in addition to their Bible classes connected with the Sunday School, organized adult classes of one sort or another. Though these church figures were lower in 1935 the loss was probably a temporary depression influence. There has been some recovery since, at least on the basis of a few surveys.

Radio. Somewhat similar reactions to broadcasting were found in questionnaires and surveys conducted by such magazines as *The Woman's World* and by some of the farm press. Regardless of the musical preferences of rural people, however, there is no doubt that the radio has been an enormous cultural influence amongst them, an influence which has thus far largely escaped precise analysis by social scientists. It is clear that the radio has broadened rural lives, affected daily rural conversation, and possibly buying habits. It has pierced the isolation of rural life and made the voice of the nation's chief executive, informally discussing national problems, more familiar than that of the county sheriff.

The scattered data available during the war seem to show that rural groups were as avid as urban to listen to newscasts and comments. Radios were found in more than one fifth of the farm and about one half of the rural non-farm homes in 1930. In 1938 seven tenths of all rural families had radios, according to an estimate of two of the big broadcasting companies. This figure was substantially confirmed by the 1940 Census, which found radios in 79 per cent of the rural non-farm homes and 60 per cent of the farm homes. Of course, there were the usual regional variations. For both rural population groups, the whites and the property-owners had proportionately more radios than tenants or non-whites in all categories. The single exception was among non-white tenants in the West, owing to the fact that perforce Japanese farmers were tenants.

TABLE 81. PROPORTION OF RURAL HOMES WITH RADIOS BY TENURE AND COLOR FOR THE UNITED STATES AND MAJOR REGIONS

	Owners		Tenants	
	White	Non-White	White	Non-White
United States rural non-farm . . .	87.3	37.8	78.0	28.1
United States rural farm	74.1	21.6	59.0	10.8
North rural non-farm	90.4	65.1	85.7	61.0
North rural farm . . . . . , ...	81.7	51.2	76.2	37.4
South rural non-farm	79.9	32.9	66.1	23.8
South rural farm	62.0	19.7	42.3	9.5
West rural non-farm . . . . , ...	88.2	39.9	81.0	57.6
West rural farm	83.9	23.8	72.7	59.0

Source: *Sixteenth Census of the United States, Housing*, vol. II, Part I, pp. 389.

The survey showed that rural people with radios listened on an average of slightly over five hours a day.[12]

The federal government, in its Farm and Home Hour and in its more technical broadcasts, and the considerable number of the state universities and colleges of agriculture are bringing information,

[12] *The Joint Committee Study of Rural Radio Ownership and Use in the United States.* New York, 1939.

news, wholesome entertainment to rural people. Such national features as the Town Meeting of the Air are popular in rural America and numerous local discussion groups make this program the basis for their own meetings. This is not to say that rural people have different tastes from urban. Commercial surveys [13] show that a number of national hook-up features have great attractive power. Four fifths of all rural homes listened to Major Bowes and nine tenths listen to one of the best-known humorists. More than one fourth tune in regularly on the New York Philharmonic concerts. In this case there is a sharp difference by income groups. Of the top third in income, 35 per cent listen to this feature. Only half as many of the low third get it, but even this group represents half a million rural homes.

> A most obvious and possibly most important contribution of the radio is the opportunity it affords the homemaker to gain some enjoyment or profit during the time spent in such routine household chores as dishwashing, mending, or dusting. In an extensive inquiry, one of the rural women's magazines found that over half the women reporting utilized the radio in this way.[14]

There are numerous evidences that rural people have been as eager as any other group to listen to news commentators during the war and to educative discussions of public policy. The big radio chains appear to be conscious of their public responsibility and, with all their limitations and faults, several have educational directors and are putting on improved programs. The impending developments in FM broadcasting open large possibilities for the further use of the radio by schools and other educational institutions in adult education.

The moving picture. Like the radio, the moving picture is, apart from strictly educational films, both recreational and educational. Concerning the cultural value of the movies, conflict is always raging. It is accused of inciting crime and undermining morals. It is censured, and yet it is lauded as a great educational force. It has, on the whole, from a sociological standpoint, been too little studied.[15]

[13] Cf. *Columbia's R.F.D. Audience.* New York: Columbia Broadcasting System, 1939.

[14] Brunner, E. de S., and I. Lorge, *Rural Trends in Depression Years,* p. 200. New York: Columbia University Press, 1937.

[15] The best attempt to date is the ambitious series of studies made at New York University, Department of Sociology.

Movies in villages. Even in 1929-30 the local village movie was losing ground. Attendance had been declining slowly and steadily since 1920. Not even the change to sound pictures checked this movement in some of the places studied. All told, 112 of the 140 villages had moving-picture houses, six less than in 1924. The difficulties of the local theaters were explained by radio and urban competition, but even in many neighboring cities of 10,000 to 50,000 rural attendance was reported to have fallen off, particularly since 1930.

The influence of the movies on dress, customs, morals, standards and speech of rural people is probably exaggerated. This influence needs to be studied, however, if proper techniques can be devised. At the same time, it must be remembered that country people have other means of learning about the world at large. Their cars take them to town and city very frequently, where they can observe life and people in urban surroundings. The Home Demonstration agents have taught rural women more about style and dress than Greta Garbo or Lana Turner.

It is evident that more skillful use is being made of educational movies and so-called documentaries. As these have been improved technically, they have been occasionally used in commercial theaters. The United States Department of Agriculture, the state colleges of agriculture, and a few commercial or semi-commercial agencies are making increasing use of the moving picture for educational purposes. This may be greatly accelerated when television becomes available.

The newspaper. The newspaper is an important factor in rural adult education. It has a real function to fill in relaying important local news and in interpreting the local meaning of other events. A number of agricultural colleges and state universities are co-operating with rural editors in developing better papers, and the urban daily is finding its way more and more into farm and village homes. Associations of editors are also building up morale. It is probable that urban competition and the depression have forced the weaker, less useful sheets to the wall in these last years. Indeed, in city and country alike the number of newspapers has been declining for more than a decade. The quality of the surviving ones appears to be improved. This is not to say that many of them do not have the faults reported in a study of Connecticut weeklies made nearly a decade ago,[16] such as inadequate coverage of local,

[16] Willey, M. M., *The Country Newspaper.* Chapel Hill: The University of North Carolina Press, 1926. This study was based on Connecticut weeklies.

political, and socially significant news and either no editorials or meaningless ones. On the other hand, if the study alluded to were made today or its basis broadened to include papers in a larger number of rural areas, some papers would be found that were distinctive, and whose editorials contained vigorous and progressive comment on local, county and state issues and exerted real leadership. County and local news in such papers is often well reported, and in some of the weeklies of the villages studied even book reviews, contributed by the local librarian or a library committee, were found in most issues. No one knows the proportion of local newspapers so edited but those that are were not only socially significant; they were also firmly established.

In this connection the influence of the farm press is not to be ignored. Some of these papers have circulations running into hundreds of thousands and in not a few cases, even millions. The annual analysis of the editorial opinion of these papers published each September in the Information Service of the Federal Council of Churches shows that many of them are presenting important material dealing with the social and economic issues and events of rural America, as well as with national issues affecting the well being of agriculture.

Special problems of youth adult education. There is one aspect of rural adult education which deserves special attention. It pervades all those which have been mentioned. It relates to rural youth. During the depression of the nineteen-thirties, the nation suddenly became worried about its youth. Studies were made. A well-financed national commission was organized. Education was obviously one answer to the problem. A number of colleges of agriculture added youth specialists to their staffs. Conferences and workshops were held. The work has continued, even though hundreds of thousands of youth went into the armed services during the war and others into war industry, handicapping many projected programs. As this is written, men and women, rural as well as urban, are returning from the war. The United States Department of Agriculture has appointed a special Committee on Rural Youth and is stimulating efforts throughout the states to continue the interrupted program.

In all this work, and especially in its educational aspects, much information was acquired during the latter half of the nineteen-thirties and until war broke out. Of the four demands of rural youth which recurred oftenest in almost all of over one hundred studies, two were definitely within the scope of this discussion. They wanted, next to jobs, more education. As one young man put it,

"More, but none of the same." All over the nation youth seemed to feel that the schooling they had had was weak, or too narrow on the vocational side; that it had failed to help them fit into or to understand their personal problems of adjustment. These criticisms are interesting in relation to the curriculum trends described in the previous chapter.

They also wanted opportunity for marriage, and asked for information as to how, under the existing conditions, homes could be established.

The American Youth Commission's Rural Committee organized what could be called a demonstration program in five states and fifteen counties. State co-ordinators worked with state and county agencies, and above all with youth on programs in which youth had a major share in formulating and carrying on. Education was a prominent feature of the programs in most of the counties, though usually "standardized classes" were avoided. Among the leading activities were classes in metal- and wood-working, discussion of personal, local, and national problems and policies, handicrafts and public speaking.[17]

Adapting the folk-school idea. For rural youth preparing to live their lives on farms, much of traditional education falls short of meeting their needs. In times of rapid social and economic adjustment, a new type of rural citizenship and leadership is required. The informal and dynamic emphasis found chiefly in the folk-school plan of adult education has possibilities which should be explored. The genius of the Danes was shown when they created a new educational spirit and technique to meet a disastrous economic and cultural depression. Their approach was essentially democratic. In the classroom the emphasis was upon the "living word" or the inspired lecture, while friendly conversation characterized the life about the school and in the homes of teachers. There were no entrance requirements, examinations, or diplomas. The value of vocational subjects was recognized, especially when taught in their social setting, but the folk-school leaders concentrated on the so-called humanics: social science, liberal arts, literature, and above all, history.

While the outward form of the folk school has not seemed to thrive in the American and Anglo-Saxon environment, and while any attempt to transplant its mechanics of books, buildings, or curriculum would be foolish indeed, yet there is an increased in-

[17] For a full discussion of this project see Brunner, E. de S., *Working with Rural Youth.* Washington, D.C.: American Youth Commission, 1942.

terest on the part of educators and thoughtful people in the substance and spirit of this kind of education. When so many problems face modern society, social as well as technical in nature, here
may be an idea worth adapting in order to help develop a new
educational interest and enthusiasm on the part of older rural
youth or, for that matter, urban youth, as well as to create a new
sense of citizenship, commensurate with the problems with which
they are faced.

One effort, among others, at this kind of adapting and exploring
is now in progress at the University of Wisconsin, and has been for
ten years or more. Adaptations have now been made in other
institutions, but the Wisconsin plan is described because of its
long and successful history. An agricultural short course of long
standing, with a typical emphasis on technical and vocational subjects, was reorganized in 1932 to include the social and economic
fields of agriculture, as well as the cultural phases of rural living.
The four-month winter course is for young men in their early
twenties, living on farms. There are no academic requirements,
although a majority have completed high school. The plan of
courses is built around the social and cultural needs, as well as the
vocational and technical needs of these young men. In fact, the
very essence of this venture is the attempt at synchronizing these
two educational objectives. Therefore, in addition to practical training in the many features of scientific farming, time and place are
found for history, economics, marketing, co-operation, sociology,
public speaking and discussion, music, art, and literature. An important feature is the common life in dormitories and dining room,
a feature which goes far in the personal, social, and cultural development of these rural youth. Another innovation with promise is
the "evening forums." Two or three times each week throughout
the period, stimulating personalities from on and off the campus,
leaders not only in the field of agriculture, but also in industry,
business, labor, education, government, art, literature, and music,
are brought to the auditorium in the dormitory building to talk, but
mostly to discuss, in forum fashion, important subjects of the day.

The response on the part of young farmers to this new type of
educational opportunity has been very gratifying. During the past
three winters the dormitory facilities have been taxed to capacity
with about three hundred and fifty young men, coming from every
county in the state and from several neighboring states.

This experiment may be summed up in the words of its leader,
the dean of the College of Agriculture: "We are trying to give the

young men on Wisconsin farms a training which will fit them for active participation in the whole life of a democratic, highly interdependent community. We are trying to educate rural youth not to leave the country for the city, but to give their best to improving rural civilization, including now, as it does, (1) an awakened and enlightened farm population, and (2) a rural leadership capable of manning the affairs of distribution as well as production."[18]

THE FUTURE OF RURAL ADULT EDUCATION

The future of rural adult education is, in many respects, uncertain. The Agricultural and Home Economics Extension Services at least are likely to remain through any predictable future, and there are some indications that their programs are becoming wider and more socially significant. That these services have a potential function of paramount significance in the field of rural adult education is beyond doubt. How this potentiality can be realized has already been indicated in part. Whether it will be fulfilled depends on many factors and may involve a change in the basic law or a liberalization of administrative interpretations and regulations under the law.

That the schools are becoming increasingly interested in adult education is clear. There are indications that the intentions to expand in this realm, discovered in the study, *Rural Trends in Depression Years,* were carried out, at least up to Pearl Harbor. Many emergency vocational classes were organized after our entry into World War II. Retraining for some types of veterans will be necessary and to some extent this will be a local responsibility. Federal aid to education, if decided upon, will result in some increase in adult education in the schools, in some states particularly. Other agencies seem to be moving forward, though at different speeds, and there is as yet no indication that the demand of the rural public for such services is lessening, despite local failures. For the immediate future the upward curve of interest and participation in adult education in rural America seems likely to continue its course.

[18] Christensen, Deal C. L., "Significance of the Folk-School Type of Adult Education," *American Co-operation,* 1938. Collection of papers comprising the Fourteenth Annual Session of the American Institute of Co-operation.

DISCUSSION TOPICS

1. Describe the activities of the Agricultural Extension Service in your county and indicate what changes you would make in its program and why.

2. Draw up a practical plan for library service for your county or community.

3. List and describe the adult education activities, formal and informal, in your community. Do these activities meet all recognizable needs? What changes would you make in the adult education set up? Why?

4. Write either an affirmative or a negative brief on the question: Resolved, that adult education should be included in the public school program at public expense.

5. Should the Extension Service expand its program to include all rural people? Defend your opinion.

REFERENCE READINGS

General

American Country Life Association, *Adult Education and Rural Life*. Chicago: University of Chicago Press, 1933.

Brunner, E. de S., and Irving Lorge, *Rural Trends in Depression Years*, chap. XIII. New York: Columbia University Press, 1937.

Bryson, Lyman, *A State Plan for Adult Education*. New York: American Association for Adult Education, 1934.

Cartwright, Morse H., *Ten Years of Adult Education*. New York: McGraw-Hill, 1935.

Hudson, Robert, *Radburn: A Plan for Living*. New York: American Association for Adult Education, 1934.

Landis, B. Y., and John Willard, *Rural Adult Education*. New York: The Macmillan Co., 1933.

Stacy, William, *The Integration of Adult Education*. New York: Teachers College, Columbia University, Bureau of Publication, 1935.

Studebaker, John W., *The American Way*. New York: McGraw-Hill, 1935.

Thorndike, E. L., *Adult Interests*. New York: McGraw-Hill, 1935.

Agricultural extension

Baker, Gladys, *The County Agent*. Chicago: University of Chicago Press, 1932.

Brunner, E. de S., and Irving Lorge, *Rural Trends in Depression Years*, chap. IX. New York: Columbia University Press, 1937.

McKimmon, Jane S., *When We're Green We Grow.* Chapel Hill: The University of North Carolina Press, 1945.

Patten, M., *Arts Workshop of Rural America.* New York: Columbia University Press, 1937.

Smith, C. B., and M. C. Wilson, *The Agricultural Extension System of the United States.* New York: Wiley, 1930.

True, A. C., *History of Agricultural Extension Work in the United States.* Washington, D.C.: United States Department of Agriculture, November, 1928.

Warburton, C. W., *Leaders of the Land.* Report of the Co-operative Extension Work in Agriculture and Home Economics. Washington, D.C.: Government Printing Office, 1940.

Yang, Hsin-Pao, *A Study of the Co-operative Agricultural Extension Service of the United States.* A doctoral project at Teachers College, New York, 1945. (Forthcoming.)

Rural libraries

Barker, T. D., *Libraries of the South.* Chicago: American Library Association, 1936.

Fair, E. M., *County-Wide Library Service,* chaps. I, IV, V, VII, VIII. Chicago: American Library Association, 1934.

Felton, R., and M. Beal, *The Library of the Open Road.* Ithaca: Cornell College of Agriculture, 1929.

Humble, M., *Rural America Reads.* New York: American Association for Adult Education, 1938.

Joekel, C. B., *Library Service.* Study no. 11, The President's Advisory Committee on Education. Washington, D.C.: Government Printing Office, 1938.

Lathrop, Edith A., *A Study of Rural School Library Practices and Services.* Chicago: American Library Association, 1934.

Long, H. C., *County Library Service.* Chicago: American Library Association, 1925.

Nason, W. C., *Rural Libraries.* Washington, D.C.: Department of Agriculture, Farmers' Bulletin 1559, 1928.

Ridington, John, Chairman, *Libraries in Canada.* Toronto: Ryerson Press, 1933. Especially chapters II, III, VI, VII, VIII, IX, XI, XIII, XIV.

Wilson, L. R., and E. A. Wight, *County Library Service in the South.* Chicago: University of Chicago Press, 1935.

Newspapers

Gee, Wilson, *The Social Economics of Agriculture,* pp. 656-60. New York: The Macmillan Co., 1932.

Willey, M. M., *The Country Newspaper*. Chapel Hill: University of North Carolina Press, 1926.

Recreation

Frayser, Mary E., *The Uses of Leisure in Selected Rural Areas of South Carolina*. Clemson College, South Carolina, 1930.

Murchie, R. W., *State-Wide Recreation Program*. Minneapolis: University of Minnesota, 1934.

Steiner, J. F., *Americans at Play*. New York: McGraw-Hill, 1933.

Radio

Benson, John, Chairman of Joint Committee, *Study of Rural Radio Ownership and Use in the United States*. New York: The Columbia Broadcasting System and the National Broadcasting Company, 1939.

Tyler, T. F., *An Appraisal of Radio Broadcasting in Land Grant Colleges and State Universities*. Washington, D.C.: National Committee on Education by Radio, 1933.

Youth

Brunner, E. de S., *Working with Rural Youth*. Washington, D.C.: American Youth Commission, 1942.

Kirkpatrick, E. L., *Guideposts for Rural Youth*, chap. III. Washington, D.C.: American Youth Commission, 1940.

21

Religion and the Rural Church

IN TERMS of the number of units, of the total amount of current income and capital invested, of the number of people employed, population enlisted and attendance secured, the rural church outranks all other types of rural social organizations combined, with the single exception of the public school. In some communities the church is an even greater institution than the school.

This chapter considers the rural church as a social institution. It deals first, therefore, with the number of rural churches, their constituencies, organization, leadership, financing and denominational interrelationships; elements which, although common to all social institutions, are in the church, especially, influenced and even conditioned by the intellectual and religious climate and by the basic policies of national organization to which local units adhere.

How Many Rural Churches Are There?

In 1926 there were, according to the United States Census of Religious Bodies, approximately 175,000 rural churches, including those in villages and those in the open country. They were distributed over the nation more or less in proportion to the population, but not entirely so, for the lower the density of population, the smaller the number of churches for every 1000 persons. Conversely, the greater the population density, the larger the number of churches for every 1000 people. The problem of overchurching, characteristic of rural America, is mainly a problem peculiar to the older and more thickly settled areas of the East, South, and Middle West. In terms of regions, the range is from one church for every 317 persons in the South to one for every 1219 in the Rocky Mountain states. In terms of a survey of 179 counties, the density factor for Protestants operates as follows:

Counties with a density of   1 to 10 persons per square mile have 1 church per
701 persons
11 to 20 persons per square mile have 1 church per
460 persons
21 to 30 persons per square mile have 1 church per
422 persons
31 to 40 persons per square mile have 1 church per
414 persons
over 40 persons per square mile have 1 church per
405 persons

The data in the above paragraph are twenty years old. A serious underenumeration in the 1936 religious census, especially in the South, because of non-co-operation on the part of the clergy, has prevented any later nation-wide compilation. In broad outlines the picture is, however, unchanged, although, as will be shown, the number of rural churches has declined, perhaps to 150,000.

Factors affecting church distribution. Neither population density nor economic prosperity is the final explanation for the great number of rural churches. Other factors are:

(1) The number and strength of non-Protestant churches.

(2) The degree of intensity of the rivalry among Protestant sects. The stronger this is the more churches there are.

(3) The frequency and size of community units. The restriction of the community unit and the development of neighborhood life tend to multiply churches.

(4) Where the density of population approaches the extreme in either direction, it operates more invariably to affect the number of churches. For example, a very sparse population has difficulty in assembling enough people to establish and maintain a church; the possibilities of duplication of churches are, therefore, reduced, and the areas which have no churches at all are more extended. On the other hand, the concentration of a large number of people within a small area makes division along the lines of denominational preference easier and reduces the areas which are unsupplied with churches.

(5) In those sections where the church is more securely established and where it is most deeply rooted in the affections of the people, as in the South, and perhaps more especially in the Middle-Atlantic and Middle-Western areas, there tend to be more churches proportionately.

(6) Racial groups, like the Southern Negroes, and large numbers of foreign-born farmers also tend to increase the number of churches.

General statements such as these give little or no true indication of the importance of the church in local communities. The average village-centered locality had, in 1930, 5.6 churches in the village itself, and 3.9 churches in the open-country hinterland, a total of 9.5 churches for every community, or half a church less than in 1924, a loss occurring exclusively in the open country. In 1936 the number of churches per community was 9.2.

This is not to say that there have been no changes in the distribution of village churches. Between 1924 and 1930 a new church was founded in two out of every five villages, but during the same period, as many died. Even in the open country, from which it is popularly supposed churches are slowly vanishing, one out of two communities saw a church born, while in each such community one church died. In other words, in the villages, the birth and death rate of churches exactly balanced at 6.6 per 100. In the open country the death rate of 22 per hundred almost doubled the birth rate of 11.6.

Much the same trend carried on through the depression years 1930-36. Among the villages there was a net loss of 2 per cent in the number of churches though the gross death rate was 9.2 per one hundred churches. In the open country within this period almost 21 per cent of the churches died but the net decline was but 3.4 per cent, or at a considerably lower rate than in the period from 1920 or 1924 to 1930. It is possible social forces have eliminated the great majority of the weakest churches. Such a conclusion must await further study because many of the new churches were opened by unemployed ministers or former ministers who had lost their positions and were returning to the church as a haven, perhaps only temporarily. These ministers were prepared to preach for little more than subsistence and sought churches formerly abandoned.

Another view of the decline in the total number of rural churches is to be had from a state-wide study in Indiana.[1] Of the twelve leading denominations, all but one showed a net decline in the number of churches from 1926, ranging from 7 per cent for the Roman Catholics to 33 per cent for one of the Protestant bodies. The median decline was 17 per cent.

No nation-wide survey of rural churches, even on a sampling basis, has been undertaken since 1936. Hence, there is no definitive data as to the effect of World War II on the rural church. There has been a heavy drain on ministerial manpower during the con-

[1] *Hoosier Churches.* Muncie: Indiana Congregational Christian Conference, 1943.

flict because of the need for chaplains. On the other hand, restrictions on travel have tended to keep neighborhood churches functioning, though with decreased service. Certain denominational surveys indicate that the circuits have been enlarged, and manpower is spread more thinly than ever before. Taking into account the trends discussed in this chapter and the data on migration given in an earlier section, it seems safe to conclude that the number of rural churches, especially in the open country, will continue to decline.

In the years 1924-36, in which the 140 village-centered communities have been subjected to review, nearly 400 of the original 1400 churches have been closed, less than one tenth of them by any planned or co-operative arrangement. There are surely great social losses in this situation, and tragedy for many individuals. True, this gross loss is relatively smaller than among social organizations in the same communities but the churches presumably have the advantage of overhead leadership and in some cases of financial assistance. Moreover, most of the churches that have been born had little if any sociological or economic justification in terms of the population to be served or the resources available to support a program and pay for an adequate amount of ministerial service.

Birth and death rates have various explanations. What are the causes of this instability of rural churches which obviously entails certain hardships and losses to their constituencies?

Population shifts troublesome. The demise of a church is not difficult to understand. It is usually due to population change. More two fifths of the gross loss in the number of churches occurred in localities which had lost population in preceding years, losses which were traceable, for example, to the departure of Negroes for the North, or of farmers to town or city.

High tenancy ratios serious. Farm tenancy played its part in the mobility of churches. Where it was decreasing, the church at least held its own; where it increased, the number of people reached by the church declined. Studies by the Institute of Social and Religious Research have repeatedly demonstrated that when the tenancy ratio exceeds one fifth, the church and other social organizations begin to decline. In counties where tenants operated half or more of the farms, the church enrolled two to four times more owners than tenants. The causes of this phenomenon were discussed in another chapter.

Emotional sects unstable. Another large factor in the death of rural churches is the ephemeral character of some denominations, particularly the highly emotional sects so numerous in America. They rise and vanish with the arrival or departure of some extraordinary leader who claims divine eloquence. Such, for example, were the churches inspired by Aimee McPherson and her evangelical radio broadcasting. These bizarre sects seem to attract the economically oppressed, the highly emotional seeking release through religious media, in short, the psychologically unstable. For these reasons their organizations lack the stability and discipline of denominational supervision, which is one of the important assets of the old and traditional sects. Mortality among new sects is high. Indeed, they were less important in 1930 than in 1924, although scattered reports indicate some gains in the nineteen-thirties.

Administrative errors. Again, churches die because their administrative arrangements can no longer keep them functioning, because they have become outmoded, like the one-room school. In early days, some of the larger denominations attempted to plant their churches in every village and in every open-country neighborhood. With modern high-speed transportation these isolated congregations are needless. Just as the automobile has, as shown elsewhere, enlarged community boundaries, and as noted in another chapter, made possible school consolidation, so it has accelerated the marked inclination of rural religious organizations to become centralized in village and town.

The villageward trend. In 1920, 22.6 per cent of the membership of village and 6.0 per cent of town churches came from the open country. In 1930 the respective figures were 39.3 and 23.9. The bulk of this increase occurred prior to 1925, but continued thereafter at a steady pace. By 1936, 40 per cent of the members of village churches came from the open country and similarly the proportion of open-country members in town churches again increased sharply, reaching 35.9 per cent. The reasons for this trend are many. It is largely a response to the growing tendency to group rural organizational activities in the village. From the point of view of the people, it illustrates the desire to enjoy the better-trained ministers and richer programs of village and town churches, to worship in large congregations and thereby benefit from increased social opportunities, and to follow into the church the village people with whom they participate in other activities. Of course, it is usually the more prosperous families who transfer their memberships from the "little brown church in the vale" to village and town congregations. In this manner the open-country church is undermined and eventually dies, but the farther it is from village or town, the more healthy its roots, and the greater its chance of survival, as has been mathematically demonstrated.[2] Moreover, village churches rarely, if ever, absorb all the constituents of abandoned country congregations, many of whom cease going to church altogether, especially if they do not own automobiles.

The village trend is likely to continue. More than once in the survey of the 140 villages, field workers were told of country congregations in which a majority of the members desired to amalgamate with a church of their own faith in the village, but refrained out of deference to a few older members. A number of cases of this have indeed occurred in the half dozen of the 140 communities surveyed since 1936. In the Middle-West field, workers were frequently told that the number of open-country members in village churches could easily be increased if the village pastors would cultivate the rural hinterland. The complaint was made that village ministers seemed quite unaware of the closing of open-country churches, though this was not always the case. Three village churches were found which brought country members in by buses; a service which had greatly increased their farm constituency.

Rural Church Membership

According to the United States Census of Religious Bodies of 1926, the average rural church had 98 members. This figure includes both village and open-country data. Separated, the average village membership in 1936 was 171, an increase of 23 over 1924, and the average country church had 93 parishioners, as against 80 in 1924. This small increase occurred in every region, although there were regional deviations, which were, to be sure, slight everywhere except in the Far West. The Negro churches in the South have declined slightly since 1924. Roman Catholic congregations had about twice as many parishioners as the national average, but declined in number. They comprise ten per cent of all open-country churches.

The elimination of the weakest churches, already described, partly accounted for the increase in average church memberships. Thus, in 1924, 44.8 per cent of all open-country churches had less than fifty members. In 1936 the proportion was 30.8 per cent. Such a diminution obviously tended to lift the average membership in churches. Again, between 1924 and 1930 half the village and

[2] Cf. Morse and Brunner, The Town and Country Church in the United States. New York: Harper & Bros., 1923.

nearly two fifths of the open-country churches registered a net membership gain.

Inactive members. These average figures, 171 in the village and 93 in the country, must be qualified, since one fifth of the members are classed as inactive. That is, they have ceased to contribute to or attend regularly the churches which still retain their names on the rolls. In the South, three tenths of all church members were inactive. In addition, one eighth of all members (one sixth in the South) are no longer resident in the community, although they retain their connection with and contribute to their churches. This phenomenon is one of the results of the rural-urban migration, but shows the power of sentiment in causing people to cling to home ties after they migrate to new places.

The hold of the rural church on its constituency. The adherence of members to their church can be measured by the proportion of the population enrolled in church and by the attendance of members and adherents at church services. The ratio of church membership to community population for the 140 communities, dropped from 35.3 to 32.8 per cent between 1924 and 1936. It has declined further in the six of these places studied between 1936 and 1945. In the Far West at both periods the proportion was about one quarter, in the others, over one third. Counting children not listed as full members, these proportions would, of course, be in the neighborhood of one half. There has been a slight but perceptible loosening of church ties among the village and farm population. This is shown also by the Indiana study mentioned above.

During the period from 1926 on, ten of the twelve bodies experienced a loss in rural church membership ranging from 3 per cent to 32 per cent, with a median decline of 25 per cent for the Protestant group against 20 per cent for the Catholic Church.

The situation as of 1945 is problematical. Some millions of rural youth are in the armed services and even more rural people have migrated to war industrial centers. Various surveys by the United States Department of Agriculture on the effect of the war on rural communities, which were made in 1943 and 1944, indicate that the church has lost ground in many respects, but usually less than other social organizations. A state-wide study of Congregational Christian churches in South Dakota states: "During the war years, the Conference has lost strength in every way, excepting in financial contributions."[3]

[3] Tripp, T. A., *Congregationalism in South Dakota.* New York: Board of Home Missions, 1945.

Regional strength varies. Regional variations are partially explained by population mobility. The ratio of adults in the church varies directly with the proportion of the population born in the state of their residence and inversely with the rate of population increase. Thus the seven states reporting the largest proportion of adult population affiliated with the church had increased their populations but 39.27 per cent between 1900 and 1920, and only 12.5 per cent of their inhabitants in 1920 were born in other states. The seven states with the smallest proportion of the population in the church had grown three times as fast and received proportionately four times as many people from other states. These tendencies are revealed graphically in Figure 35 which, however, is national, not rural, in scope.

This analysis tends to take the mystery out of the fact that some states and regions of the nation are distinctly more religious than others. Their inequality proves to be partly a phenomenon of unequal population growth and stability. The church as an institution has not yet caught up with the more rapidly changing parts of the nation. It has never found a means of ministering adequately to those who lived in sparsely settled areas and who soon learned to exist without such ministry. Such persons, too, as their very migration showed, were of the restless brood of American pioneers upon whom tradition made but slight impression.[4]

On the other hand, with the more stable populations of the eastern seaboard, loyalty to the church, like the other social traditions, has long been ingrained. Church membership is a token of respectability, and for that reason its customs and mores are more binding upon the social group.[5]

Population changes in local communities. The principles here elucidated are true even for local communities, and a consideration of them adds to our knowledge of the influence of population change on church memberships. When the church records of villages which gained population more rapidly than the nation as a whole (16.1 per cent) were examined, it was found that the net membership increase was 4 per cent, or less than one fourth the rate of population gain. The proportion of all people belonging to a church thus declined from 33 to 29 per cent of the population. On the other hand, in the villages which lost more than 10 per

---

[4] Cf. Hooker, *Hinterlands of the Church.* New York: Harper & Bros., 1930.
[5] Cf. Douglass and Brunner, *The Protestant Church as a Social Institution.* New York: Harper & Bros., 1935. See chapter IX, from which several sentences in the above paragraph are taken with minor changes.

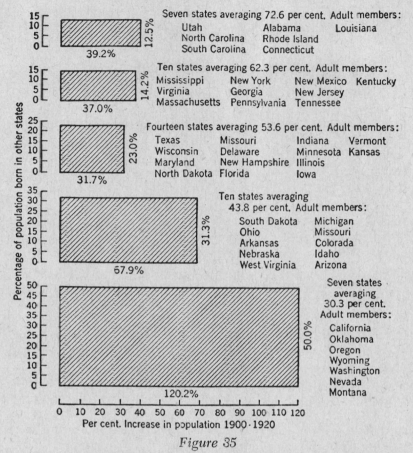

Percentage of population born in other states

Seven states averaging 72.6 per cent. Adult members:

Utah	Alabama	Louisiana
North Carolina	Rhode Island	
South Carolina	Connecticut	

39.2% — 12.5%

Ten states averaging 62.3 per cent. Adult members:

Mississippi	New York	New Mexico	Kentucky
Virginia	Georgia	New Jersey	
Massachusetts	Pennsylvania	Tennessee	

37.0% — 14.2%

Fourteen states averaging 53.6 per cent. Adult members:

Texas	Missouri	Indiana	Vermont
Wisconsin	Delaware	Minnesota	Kansas
Maryland	New Hampshire	Illinois	
North Dakota	Florida	Iowa	

31.7% — 23.0%

Ten states averaging 43.8 per cent. Adult members:

South Dakota	Michigan
Ohio	Missouri
Arkansas	Colorada
Nebraska	Idaho
West Virginia	Arizona

67.9% — 31.3%

Seven states averaging 30.3 per cent. Adult members:

California
Oklahoma
Oregon
Wyoming
Washington
Nevada
Montana

120.2% — 50.0%

Per cent. Increase in population 1900-1920

Figure 35

INFLUENCE OF MOBILITY OF POPULATION OF
CHURCH MEMBERSHIP IN THE STATES
Courtesy of Harper and Brothers.

cent of the population between 1920 and 1930 (the average loss, where loss occurred, was 17.4 per cent) church membership declined only 6.2 per cent, while the number of non-residents simultaneously increased. This tendency for church membership to decline more slowly than population and to increase less rapidly than population may be considered a well-established phenomenon. It has been met in many studies in both city and country.[6]

[6] See especially, Fry, *Diagnosing the Rural Church* (New York: Institute of Social and Religious Research, 1924); and Sanderson, *The Strategy of City Church Planning* (New York: Institute of Social and Religious Research, 1932).

Some might explain the lessening hold of the church on the ground that it was losing the confidence, and was failing to supply the needs of particular groups, but this is not borne out by an analysis of church rolls. There has been, for example, no disproportionate decline in the number of men or young people in the rural church. Whatever the cause, the fact remains that the decline in the ratio of church membership to community population has been accompanied by a falling off in attendance as well. In these 140 communities the average person went to church nine times in 1930 and eight in 1936 for every ten attendances in 1924.

Changing attitudes as explanations. Any further explanation for this data will have to be drawn from changes in the religious climate for which, obviously, no barometer has yet been devised. The great increase in informal recreation — the lure of the open road on the Sabbath to those possessing automobiles — might have affected rural church attendance. There has also been increasing criticism of the limitations of the rural clergy, who must now bear comparison with the nation's best preachers broadcasting their powerful sermons on the radio.

Radio competition. Broadcast sermons, with the prestige of a great speaker behind them, also bring doctrinal views which perhaps express or rationalize the experience of some rural people more adequately than the views of the local preacher. In other words, there are lacunae in provincial religious tradition, just as there are gaps in the whole rural cultural *milieu,* and they are perhaps more apparent today than they were two decades ago, and therefore more unsettling.

Weariness with competition. Again, some people have grown weary of competition among churches. Wherever proposed church co-operation has for any reason been prevented, local leaders have lapsed into inactivity. Finally, the very ease with which Sunday movies have been legalized in some Middle-Atlantic States villages, where fifteen years before attempts to legalize them would have met with strong protests by church people, indicates some changes of attitude or shifts in voting power. Whether this means a softening of the moral and religious fiber of rural people, or a purposeful increase in tolerance and broadening conception of the rôle of religion in rural life, many debate but none can decide.

It is important to recognize that churches are social groups, voluntary in nature and bound together theoretically, and often actually by allegiance to a stated set of principles. But there is overwhelming testimony that the differences in these principles are less important to most members than they were in the past. The Massachusetts Puritans, who about three centuries ago expelled the Baptists from the colony, now pride themselves on their religious tolerance. Intermarriage and migration have played their parts in the declining emphasis upon those things which, theologically, divide churches. Yet, despite the amalgamation of some denominations and active discussions of proposed unions by several more, the different churches continue to exist in local communities. One explanation for this fact lies in the group nature of these local church institutions. While in some areas and among some denominations, theological differences are real and sincerely believed, it is also often true that churches reflect social differences as well. The emotionally centered church tends to serve the poorer people "on the other side of the track." The large landowners and professional people and their families tend to predominate in one church, the tenant farmers in another. The problem of how the church can become "all things to all men" in rural America has not been solved.

The Organization and Program of the Rural Church

We have seen that by virtue of the number of its units and an enormous constituency, the church is a very important part of the rural social structure, but that because of regional differences, fluctuations in population and changes in religious attitudes, it is enrolling a slightly smaller proportion of the population than formerly. Here then is a great social institution facing changes that seem to indicate need for adaptation to altering conditions. What has the rural church done in this exigency? To answer that question, it is necessary to turn first to its program and organization.

Supervision. Each church is part of a denominational body, and each of these bodies in its own way makes suggestions regarding specific activities and goals and provides supervision. But the supervisory unit can render only small assistance to the local congregation. Denominational concern is almost wholly with administrative matters. Supervision is far less adequate than for the public school. Some denominations, to be sure, have special rural church departments, but their number is few.

The keystone of the organization is obviously the local minister. The ideal situation and declared objective would be a full-time resident minister for every church. But since 1920, and particularly since 1924, there has been regress rather than progress in this matter. About seven tenths of the open-country churches have non-resident service, and the same is true of about one fifth of the village churches. Less than one tenth of the open-country and only a few more than two fifths of the village churches have full-time resident clergy. The rest have pastors who give part-time attention to churches elsewhere. The obvious reason for this situation is the large number of churches and the resulting small memberships, which are unable, at the present or at any predictable salary level, to support a full-time minister. As already indicated, the war made this situation worse, though perhaps only temporarily.

Preaching. The largest part of the church program is preaching. Every effort is made to have at least one service a Sunday, an ideal realized by seven eighths of the village and nearly two fifths of the country churches, which is a gain over past performance attributable in part to the automobile, and attained in the face of decreasing attendance and at the expense of other possible features of the program.

Religious education. Ninety-two per cent of the village and 86 per cent of the open-country churches maintain Sunday Schools enrolling an average of 125 and 75 students respectively, and securing about two thirds of the enrollment on any given Sunday. These schools, which are now enlisting adults, a fact which accounts for their slow but steady growth in enrollment from 1920 to 1930, teach the Bible and Christian doctrine. About one eighth of those enrolled are teachers or officers, so that this program, more than any other activity, involves the continuous service of the laity. The educational procedure is quite simple. The handicaps of small buildings, of churches which in a majority of cases have no classrooms, and of teachers largely untrained, are not conducive to good pedagogy, even of the traditional type. There has been some improvement in village Sunday School facilities, as will be noted; but for some years back only one eighth even of the village churches conduct teacher-training classes. Indicative of the difficulties in conducting effective religious education is Doctor Tripp's finding in the South Dakota study, mentioned earlier, that since 1920 Congregational Christian churches in that state have lost half their Sunday School enrollment, and 28.4 per cent of the churches had no Sunday Schools.

The best advance in educational procedures has been in the development of daily Vacation Bible Schools, now conducted for from two to six weeks by one fourth of the rural congregations.

In these, for at least three hours daily, some worth-while educational practice is being developed.

The presence of subsidiary organizations, which largely carry an expansion of the church program beyond preaching, is influenced by the amount of pastoral service. The Indiana survey alluded to reports that churches with resident pastors had 5.3 of the eight most common program activities, including full-time preaching. Those with non-resident ministers averaged 2.7.

Other organizations. About 70 per cent of all rural churches possess an average of two and a half subsidiary organizations each, comprising chiefly women's and young people's groups, but also some men's organizations. Boys' and girls' organizations are declining with the rapid spread of 4-H clubs. During the nineteen-twenties about three tenths of the village and one tenth of the open country churches broadened their programs to include such things as lectures, concerts, and dramatics. There was some evidence in 1936 that such activities had suffered during the depression years. Whether because of budget difficulties or because of the competition of more interesting activities by various social organizations or by emergency federal agencies such as the W.P.A. recreational program, it is not easy to determine. In one village,[7] a social-minded pastor, concerned over the obvious revolt of youth against moral conventions and mores, initiated a program of activities and discussion for the young people of the community. To compete with roadhouses, weekly dances were included. The response of the youth was almost unanimous. Immediately, quite unanimous opposition arose from the other churches. Proselyting was charged. The program was, therefore, discontinued; and the youth problem rapidly assumed more serious proportions. In another village, a young people's program in a well-equipped community building was offered to the W.P.A. recreation officials; but the building was closed and the program discontinued when it was discovered that W.P.A. leadership meant that persons of any church could be admitted.

There are many evidences, however, that youth are interested in the church. This was very apparent in the rural project of the American Youth Commission conducted in fifteen counties. Here rural youth, planning their own programs, often included various activities in churches and with church youth groups.

[7] From here to the end of the paragraph and the following four paragraphs are quoted from Brunner, E. de S., and Irving Lorge, *Rural Trends in Depression Years*, pp. 314-16. New York: Columbia University Press, 1937.

One Negro church is conducting a full program of recreation, including athletics and education on Sunday afternoons, which has proved very popular. Despite criticisms from the ministers of other churches of both races, this program is locally credited with measurably improving conditions among Negro youth.

Clashing philosophies also are apparent in the attitudes of clergy and laity. Contrasting with the forums and classes noted above is the church in which the men's organization insisted on discussing the religious implications of modern social and economic problems, but was opposed by the pastor on the ground that such activities were not "spiritual." The contrasting incident is that of a young, social-minded pastor who lost his church after a discussion of the Soil Conservation program of the Department of Agriculture under the title "Our Stewardship of God's Land." The leading laymen of this church explained the action thus: "When we really need rain, God will send it. And, brother, we won't attend a church where a minister uses notes; for the Lord has said he would fill their mouths."

There was great concern among the clergy over the return of legalized liquor, and much denunciation of youth and women for drinking; yet, with few exceptions, the testimony of the schoolmen, physicians, and other leaders among the laity was to the effect that moral conditions were better than in the latter half of the nineteen-twenties and were improving. This was true even where the churches were clearly declining in influence. In fact, some of the worst situations apparently existed in the half-dozen and more villages where the churches had been strong enough to prevent chaperoned dances or other activities deemed too liberal in the local community, thereby forcing those interested in such activities into seeking them under commercial auspices.

It is quite clear that the issues involved in an individualistic, as against a social, interpretation of religion are by no means settled; and that in fact there is also an issue between the generations as to church policy. Rural youth is not interested in an interpretation of religion solely in terms of doctrine or ritual. This was found even in a number of Roman Catholic churches. It is not interested in denominational divisions. It is resentful in the extreme when such divisions balk "going" programs. Three times as many pastors reported that youth were losing interest in the church and its program as felt that the interest of youth was quickening. Where the latter report was made to field workers, the churches concerned were catering to youth in terms of youth's needs. These issues appeared more serious than at any time since this series of studies began.

Leadership. Since it is clear that the church has not yet made any considerable adaptation to its emerging problems, the question arises, how competent is its professional leadership to meet the new situations as they arise? The handicap under which that leadership works through the necessity of dividing individual attention among a number of churches, has already been pointed out. Even resident pastors serve on the average nearly two churches, and nonresidents serve three. Their training, however, may have a bearing on the problem.

Little professional training. The data indicate a rather low level of professional training among the Protestant rural clergy, who constitute the great majority of rural ministers. The standard accepted training includes a college education and graduation from a theological seminary. According to the federal religious census of 1926, more than half the Protestant rural clergy, excluding the Negro denominations, lacked both of these desiderata. Twenty-two and six tenths per cent had both, the rest, about 25 per cent, either one or the other. The majority of the better-trained rural clergy are, of course, in the villages. More than two thirds of the village ministers possessed either a college or seminary degree or both. The better-trained were also more likely to be resident rather than non-resident pastors, so that the task of serving the difficult and backward open-country parishes was entrusted to the poorly trained. On the other hand, all but a few of the older Roman Catholic clergy have had both college and seminary training.

Conditions of work. A partial explanation of this situation may possibly be found in the conditions under which rural clergy work. The average length of tenure is less than three years, a short time in which to gain the spiritual confidence and respect of a community. The compensation, too, is not large, averaging, in 1936, slightly over $1200 a year for Protestant resident village ministers and $858 for all nonresidents. In the half-dozen of the 140 communities surveyed in the early nineteen-forties, ministers' salaries showed a 14 per cent gain over 1936. The Census of 1940 covering the labor force of the nation procured data on the salaries of 82 per cent of the 136,669 clergymen, rural and urban. Of these, 51 per cent received $1199 a year or less. The great majority of this group were doubtless rural. This compensation is less than the lowest category of federal employees. Slightly over 90 per cent of all clergy received less than $2500. These data, of course, give no effect to the rental value of parsonages, nor to income from other occupations. Most of the rural clergymen and many of the urban also enjoyed the free use of a house. The Roman Catholic priests averaged $1200 and a rectory; Negro pastors, $480. These salaries represent a 26 per cent decline since 1930, but they compare favorably with those of school teachers, who are somewhat better trained, but a far larger proportion of whom are unmarried. Viewed in terms of support for a family, ministerial salaries appear inadequate and have forced nearly one fourth of the Protestant clergy to supplement their income by working part-time at another occupation. This further weakens their efficiency as ecclesiastical leaders.

The minister, of course, does not expect to make money. His is a profession which requires sacrifice. According to tradition, his chief concern is with the things of the spirit and he is more or less oblivious in his personal attitude and work to external conditions. A minister must, nevertheless, contrive to keep out of debt. The profession requires therefore a certain strong psychological equipment. The local church recognizes this and seeks a leader who has a very "human personality." The material emphasis crowds in upon the spiritual and the minister is torn between material security and spiritual forces.

Enough has been said to show that the rural clergy are not in a very happy situation. Frequent changes of location and the fact that one fourth of a professional group is attempting to earn outside funds do not bespeak a high morale. Is it affecting the future? Douglass shows that "on the side of formal education, the trend of a minority is regrettably downward." [8] The 1930 Census returns for the agricultural villages indicated that nearly three fifths of the village clergy are over 45 years of age, one tenth over 65. Ministers are on the average younger than village doctors, but as is the case with the doctors, rural communities are not attracting enough recruits to the ministry to maintain indefinitely the present religious set-up. This average has probably not changed greatly. In 1940 the median age of all clergy was 45.8 years, with 2 per cent under 25 years and 10 per cent 65 or over.

CHURCH FINANCES

The plight of the clergy raises the question of support for the rural church. Each of the 140 village centered communities spent

[8] *Op. cit.*

$16,000 annually for its churches on the average in 1930 and $10,300 in 1936. The average budget fell from $2400 to $1910 in the village Protestant churches and from $709 to $560 in the open country between these years, declines of more than 20 per cent. The Roman Catholic churches spent about $800 and $400 more, respectively, than the Protestant. By 1944, total budgets had come back practically to the 1930 level but some idea of the havoc of the long agricultural depression is gained from the South Dakota survey. This showed a drop of 49.5 per cent in contributions to local expenses and benevolences between 1920 and 1943. South Dakota was, of course, more severely affected than many other states by the depression.

The average rural church is obviously not a strong financial institution. Without church consolidation it cannot be, and ministers, especially in the open country, must serve more than one church in order to earn enough to live. However, the proportion of the average dollar going to the ministers is steadily increasing. In the village churches the minister received 43.6 cents of each dollar contributed in 1924, but practically 50 cents in 1936. In the open-country churches the change in these years was from 48 to 56 cents. There is an obvious generalization here, confirmed by every study of the rural church: namely, the smaller the church the larger the proportion of its receipts which goes for ministerial services. It is also true that the smaller the church the less service it receives. Here lies one of the serious dilemmas of the Protestant rural church.

Benevolences declining. It follows that the share of each church dollar going to the benevolent causes of the denominations has declined as other expenses took larger portions. In the village church such purposes received 31.8 cents in 1924; in the open country the figure was 32 cents. By 1936, this had dropped to 17.1 and 20 cents respectively. On a per member basis these changing proportions represent a decline of from $5.64 per year in 1924 to $3.54 in 1936 in the villages, and from $3.28 to $2.15 in the open country. These trends obtained in all regions.

Total per member gifts also declined in the period under survey, as Table 82 indicates. Regional differences, by size of village, on both total church expenses and per capita contributions indicate that Middle Atlantic churches and those in large villages had the largest budgets, that the Middle-Western, open-country churches had the largest per member expenses for this group, while in the South, per capita expenses were less than one half those in the other regions.

TABLE 82. PER MEMBER EXPENDITURES IN VILLAGE AND
COUNTRY PROTESTANT CHURCHES BY REGION

Region	Village			Country		
	1924	1930	1936	1924	1930	1936
All regions	$16.89	$16.38	$10.45	$ 8.13	$ 8.57	$5.67
Middle Atlantic	17.09	18.61	12.70	12.40	12.34	8.30
South	16.33	15.22	8.51	5.38	5.40	3.02
Middle West	17.81	16.25	9.93	12.39	12.57	8.81
Far West	19.35	19.54	12.79	12.33	16.13	6.68

Source: Brunner, E. de S., and I. Lorge, *Rural Trends in Depression Years.* New York: Columbia University Press, 1937.

The Negro churches reported an average current expense of $289, or $2.56 per member per year, a decline on both items of about 50 per cent between 1924 and 1936. The Roman Catholic Church budgets dropped slightly more than one fifth, to $2490 per church; but the per member offerings declined to $6.20 from $12.03, or almost half.

A case illustration. An indication of what has happened to the financial support of the church is the case of a substantial and relatively prosperous community in the Middle Atlantic region, restudied in 1945. The total budgets of the five Protestant churches amounted to $26,426 in 1923, reached a peak of $27,205 in 1929, dropped to $22,022 in 1935, and recovered to $26,137 in 1944-45. During this period the membership gained almost 30 per cent. In the same period the Roman Catholic Church doubled its membership to 1600 souls and its budget went from $17,776 to $24,022.

Giving reflects attitudes. These fluctuations in giving reflect, among other things, the attitudes of the givers. Enthusiasm for missions and other benevolences reached a high point in the great church "drives" of 1919-20, which carried gifts in rural churches to 10 to 20 per cent above the 1929-30 levels. As the agricultural depression deepened, it was these same causes which proved the most vulnerable in the church budgets. The survival of the church as an institution depended upon the retention of a minister and the upkeep of the building in which the activities were carried on. Such expenses became the primary obligation. It is also true that giving specific amounts to the church is, perhaps, determined in part by habit. In part it is also an evidence of the transcendent interest which inevitably, if immeasurably, protrudes itself into the background of every study of institutionalized religion. In other words, when the heap of economic statistics is sifted, when ratios are worked out and conclusions reached, there is always the great human factor, oblivious to trends, to economic decline or progress. Man cares for his soul as well as his body, and his benevolence to the church is constant, because he feels that apart from the hard reality of earning a livelihood and supporting a family there is the imponderable reality of religion, demanding his financial as well as his spiritual support. As Douglass says:

> The most revealing factor in human economics is the spending of material resources upon ideals and passions rather than upon necessities. It is as the fulfillment of a dream rather than the maintenance of a particularly efficient instrument that the believing masses, from generation to generation, continue to pour out their substance upon the church. Consequently, the masses are not greatly impressed either by the magnitude of the social institution or by the vast sums which the church costs. Compared to the glory of God which the church reflects, these things are the small dust of the balance.[9]

Influence of economic conditions on church. This is not to say that economic conditions do not influence contributions to the church. Studies by the Institute of Social and Religious Research have repeatedly demonstrated that there is a relation between economic adversity or prosperity and church support. From the mass of available data the following is selected as the simplest and most recent on this point.

Where the per capita retail sales in the village community, as determined by the 1930 United States Census of Distribution, amounted to less than $200 a year, the average per member contributions to the churches were only $9.84. The remaining figures follow in tabular form:

Sales	Contributions
$200 to $300	$13.05
$300 to $400	14.48
$400 to $500	18.38
Over $500	16.92

The decline when sales passed $500 per persons checks with many other similar results obtained by using different measuring rods. It is probably an index of the highly stereotyped program of the rural church, an institution which does not know how to exist without at least the part-time service of a minister and a place to meet.

[9] *Op. cit.,* chap. XIV.

When, however, it has achieved a dignified and well-equipped edifice, a full-time minister with perhaps an assistant, and a better than average program, measured in terms of what churches are known usually to do, it has no items that call for money, save benevolence. Churches are larger in wealthier communities. The per capita cost of the highly standardized program consequently declines. It is in such areas that the surplus available for benevolences goes into county-wide social and socio-religious agencies with paid executives. Unless they are subsidized from the outside, it is only in such wealthier areas that such agencies are found.[10]

Church buildings. Part of the problem of church finance in rural America and especially in the villages is complicated by the large capital investment of recent years. In the 140 village communities practically $2,500,000 was added to this investment between 1924 and 1930, bringing the total value of church plants to over $15,000,-000 or about $110,000 per community, although the average village and open-country church was valued at $16,000 and $4000 respectively.

Church buildings are to some degree representative of the ideas of their builders about the function of the church. The majority of country edifices are of one or two rooms, and the main objective is to secure an auditorium for preaching, the primary activity of the church. If resources are limited, perhaps only an auditorium can be provided, other activities being dispensed with or conducted under difficulty. How fundamental is the idea of the church as primarily a tabernacle for preaching, is shown in the disproportionate space — judged by modern standards — allotted to the auditorium in the older and larger churches. The second most important part of the church is "the basement" for kitchen use and for the use of the primary department of the church school; in larger edifices, separate rooms for the church school are provided. In a few of the more spacious recent buildings, rooms are equipped for community-house activities of a more or less elaborate kind, but these are the exception rather than the rule.

This analysis has shown that the rural church, especially in the open country, and in the village as well, is a small, poorly financed organization, existing under the leadership of a minister who perhaps fails to rise to a desired standard of professional training, and who, more often than not, must divide his services among several

---

[10] Douglass and Brunner, *op. cit.* Consult also Brunner and Kolb, *Rural Social Trends*, Appendix G; Brunner, Hughes, and Patten, *American Agricultural Villages*, chap. X; Fry, *Diagnosing the Rural Church.*

congregations. Its program is usually highly stereotyped, and there is some evidence that its hold upon its constituency is slowly diminishing. It is too small to afford better service, and it is difficult to improve the situation without better leadership. Its smallness arises in part from a multiplicity of units, a situation arising out of an administrative policy created before the advent of modern transportation facilities, and out of historic doctrinal differences which have perpetuated themselves in about two score major and more than one hundred and fifty minor denominations. These are the things, which, sociologically speaking, hold the ministry and the churches on the horns of a very difficult dilemma.

The operation of traditional, sentimental loyalty to a particular church counteracts somewhat the changing material and physical conditions tending to bring about the abandonment of churches, particularly in the open country. The church is by nature conservative, the great repository of tradition, slow to change or recognize what is called modernity, so that individual churches are less ready to adapt themselves to change or die more slowly than other social institutions. But fundamentally the church is closely intertwined with the community; it is therefore important to analyze the relations of rural churches with their communities and with one another.

EFFECT OF COMPETITION

It has already been shown that competition among rural churches is inevitable under present conditions. If every man, woman and child in rural America were connected with some church, the average community would recruit only about three hundred persons per church or about three churches for 1000 population. The national rural church executives of the various Protestant denominational boards have declared one church for each thousand persons of like nationality or tradition to be the desirable norm or ideal toward which to strive. The implication of this is a confession that these same denominations are parties to competitive overchurching.

Measuring effects of competition. Some evidence bearing on the proposed norm is obtainable by various indices of church progress for 1924 and 1930 in the 140 village communities. The data, given in Table 83, show that during the earlier period, while churches which enjoyed comparative freedom from competition in terms of fewer units per 1000 people were larger, better-manned, better-

TABLE 83. SPECIFIED DATA ACCORDING TO NUMBER OF CHURCHES
PER 1000 POPULATION — 140 VILLAGES

	Number of Churches per 1000 Population							
	Under 2		2 to 3		3 to 4		4 and over	
	1924	1930	1924	1930	1924	1930	1924	1930
Number of communities.....	21	28	49	48	40	32	28	32
Number of churches........	122	172	475	457	413	329	366	378
Average membership.......	172	192	146	139	103	111	82	91
Per cent with resident minister...............	55.7	76.8	46.3	58.5	38.7	54.8	30.1	40.2
Per cent of churches gaining last year...............	65.3	64.3	58.7	65.6	52.0	62.8	50.0	55.7
Average attendance principal service..........	151	107	121	91	108	83	125	69
Average Sunday-School enrollment..............	114	120	104	106	89	96	83	86
Average expenditure........	$2,193	$2,937	$2,097	$1,899	$1,544	$1,648	$935	$1,081
Per capita expenditure......	$13.02	$16.00	$14.12	$13.57	$14.44	$14.60	$11.23	$11.71
Average benevolence........	$5.65	$5.71	$6.59	$4.30	$4.61	$3.48	$3.19	$2.26
Per cent of churches with home mission aid........	13.9	10.4	7.2	15.0	10.0	17.3	12.1	16.9
Per cent of population in church membership......	27.4	26.3	36.0	31.3	34.8	35.4	43.4	44.0
Number of resident ministers per 1000 inhabitants......	0.9	1.0	1.2	1.2	1.3	1.7	1.6	1.8
Per cent of population enrolled in Sunday school.........	15.8	16.0	22.3	22.1	25.2	27.6	37.4	36.4
Local expenditures of church per inhabitant..........	$2.50	$3.62	$3.39	$4.12	$3.37	$5.14	$3.20	$5.00
Home mission aid per inhabitant...............	$0.12	$0.06	$0.05	$0.08	$0.10	$0.16	$0.12	$0.14

attended, and richer, it was found that these churches enlisted a smaller proportion of the population in church membership, if no correction was made for inactive members.

In the main these statements still hold; but careful examination of the table shows, among other things, that the proportion of communities with fewer than two churches for each 1000 inhabitants has increased by one fourth; that churches in these communities showed a greater gain in average membership, in total budget, in per capita contributions to all causes and to benevolent enterprises, than in communities in which the number of churches was greater. In fact, in some particulars the churches in this group were the only ones to show gains, while those in the more competitive regions registered losses. These gains were scored despite the fact that denominational policy increased the number of resident ministers in competitive situations.[11]

One interesting thing in this connection is that the slow-working

[11] If the sample of communities were large enough to warrant analysis on a regional basis, the results would show even greater relative progress in the

social forces already discussed, which account for the death of rural churches, resulted between 1924 and 1930 in a decline of one half church per 1000 persons, a decline occurring in all regions, although at slightly varying rates.

The place of home mission aid. The situation is somewhat complicated by the historic practice of most denominations of extending aid to local units unable to support themselves. Originally this practice developed in the effort to assist the small but growing denominational groups along the Western frontier to remain within the sect of their first allegiance. It is also used to bring a minister to small communities with limited resources. But as the country developed and stabilized, millions of dollars were given annually by the denominations to churches which appeared to be in competitive situations. Moreover, the grants-in-aid were larger in competitive situations than elsewhere. Thus in the 140 village-centered communities where two or more churches were aided, the average grant in 1930 was $421 per church. Where only one church was aided the amount was $271.[12] Furthermore, there was a higher proportion, 18.6 per cent, of aided churches in small villages (which have been shown to have the most churches per 1000 population) than in the medium or large villages where 15 per cent and 13.6 per cent, respectively, were receiving aid.

National administrations less competitive than state. It was also noticeable that the great increase in grants occurred in those states in which the national board executives have practically nothing to say about the policy of the state unit, since the state raises all the money it needs within its borders and contributes to the national costs as well. On the other hand, the number of grants made directly by national boards in non-self-supporting states declined, and had measurably shifted from competitive to non-competitive projects, such as larger parishes and allocated fields.

The unavoidable conclusion is that many of these minor units of Protestant denominations are competing more and more, not to gain any particular advantage, but because they are generous with their resources in competitive situations as long as their particular congregation is considered to have a chance to survive.

less competitive situations. A somewhat larger proportion of non-competitive communities are found in the Far West than elsewhere; but the Far West, as a region, makes a poorer record than other regions in a number of measurements of church efficiency. This weights the results in favor of the more competitive centers where regional factors make for better support of organized religion.

[12] In 1936 the average grants for all aided churches were respectively $289 in the village and $126 in the country.

Effect of depression. Liberals in all Protestant bodies have been attacking competition for over three decades, and the Home Missions Council, the organization of the large majority of national Protestant home mission boards, has for the last ten years or more called conferences and conducted surveys in many states for the purpose of reducing both "overchurching" and "underchurching." This movement has been greatly stimulated by a drop in the amount of contributions since 1930, which has resulted in reductions of from 25 to 90 per cent in the total amount of aid given by the various boards. In 1934 five of the large denominations prepared master lists of all aided churches for comparison, and as this work goes to press, there seems to be a real possibility that the national denominations home mission boards will measurably reduce competitive projects. The same procedure is being urged upon state and district units. Moreover, a few national church boards have in recent years undertaken careful studies of the whole grant-in-aid situation in the light of the needs as now understood, and of the social and economic conditions, such as population trends. As a result of such studies, effective policies are in the making.

Social effects of competition. Nonetheless, it is obvious that competition still exists. Table 83 reflects some of the results upon the church itself. From the social standpoint, strong competition is much more serious, interfering mainly with community solidarity and intensifying group divisions. Competition keeps churches small and weak, thus preventing the acquisition of competent and well-trained ministers, and weakening the social and ethical aspects of religion in the community.

It must be remembered, however, that church competition is not exclusively a matter of doctrinal differences. In many places the real differentiating factors are economic and social. For example, tenants may gravitate to one church, owners to another, the élite of the community to a third, the small business and skilled labor class to a fourth, the very poor to a fifth. In areas where the economic make-up consists of farming, industry and other non-agricultural pursuits, factory people and farmers seldom join the same churches.

Influence of race on churching the community. In localities dominated by diverse nationality backgrounds, race heritage determines church affiliation. The Hollander attends the Dutch Reformed Church, the Rhine German the German Reformed; the Saxon is Lutheran; the North German may be Lutheran or he may join the

Evangelical Synod of North America, which was a transplantation of Frederick William the Third's German State Church. In such cases language and customs vary, and denominational connections are the product of ethnic and social variations. The progenitors of such a group, for example, may have come to America partly because they opposed the union of Lutheran and Reformed bodies in Europe. Transition from one denomination to another, especially where denominations represent different nationality groups, is not easily effected.[13]

It is significant to summarize the most important conclusion of the preceding section: in spite of its ideals, the church has had to submit to social and economic factors more often than it has conquered them. The public school has been freer from such bondage, although neither church nor school has by any means achieved social autonomy.

Religious Co-operation in Rural America

Real progress has been made, however, in minimizing denominational differences, and actual co-operation has been achieved in some cases. National and (to a considerable extent) state home missions councils have erected the machinery for co-operative handling of competitive situations. The work of the five mission boards already alluded to may prove significant. Localities all over the nation have taken matters into their own hands and worked out adjustments which can be classified under several heads.

The non-denominational church. Such churches are cut off from denominational supervision and leadership and have an uncertain source of ministerial supply. Nevertheless, this severance of sectarian ties has, despite the difficulties it entails, been carried out by more than one hundred existing rural churches.

Affiliated churches. A variation of the non-denominational church is the affiliated type which remains substantially independent but maintains a loose connection with some denomination to insure a source of ministerial supply and now and then some supervision and suggestion. In 1925 there were about sixty or seventy such churches.

Federated churches. Federated churches are local combinations of congregations of two or more denominations into a single functional organization without severance of the previous denomina-

13 Cf. Brunner, *Immigrant Farmers and Their Children*, especially chap. VI. New York: Institute of Social and Religious Research, 1929.

tional ties of combining units. There are perhaps about four hundred in rural America. Only 10 per cent of the federations, however, concern more than two denominations. Rural federated churches are about one half larger than the average denominational churches of the bodies generally participating in them, while urban federated churches surpass the average city church in size. Churches federate, in the main, only under great pressure of adverse circumstances.

Such churches operate as a unit in all local matters but retain their denominational ties. Benevolences are equitably divided. Frequently the ministers alternate between the bodies represented in the federation. A frequent and highly unsatisfactory aspect of the federated church is the unfederated subsidiary. Minor organizations, such as denominational women's societies, insist on perpetuating themselves, usually because of social cleavages in the community. Within a supposedly united group, this does not make for great success.

Long-continued successful federation, however, frequently, though not universally, weakens desire to maintain separate denominations. A solution for such a condition is sometimes found in a bi-denominational relationship. The church becomes legally one, but is recognized by both denominations to which its members previously belonged. This has proved an acceptable solution in the case of the more liberal bodies.

Denominational community churches. These, the most numerous of united churches, have been elsewhere defined and described as follows in a work in which one of the authors collaborated:

> A denominational community church is one formally recognized as such by other denominations. A group of co-operating denominations agree to accord an exclusive field to the church of one of their members, usually upon condition that it broadens the terms of membership and maintains a definite community outlook, with or without an equivalent exchange of fields. This method remedies past division and prevents future competition.
>
> The act by which a denominational church merely widens the terms of its membership so as to admit members of all denominations without condition, such as assent to a particular creed or rebaptism, is not accepted by the writers as a true criterion of the type. This has always been the theory of the more liberal churches of the congregational type, and has been the actual practice of multitudes of others, as proved by the interchangeable use of denominational churches by large populations.

Denominational churches which have community aspirations and ideals but which have no authorization to represent a co-operating group of denominations, and have done nothing to change their ecclesiastical status, fall entirely outside of the definition of local church unions adopted by this study. They do not affect any ecclesiastical remedy for the religious division of communities, and their efforts are often so unconvincing as not to be demonstrable to anyone outside their own numbers.

One needs to recognize the realities behind even so attenuated a version of the community church. It testifies to the softening of denominational asperities and to an atmosphere favorable to integration. Such churches should be kept distinct from those spurious cases where the label "community church" has been adopted for promotional purposes only.

With respect to all the types of churches enumerated above, a realistic viewpoint is far more important than a discussion of changes of formal ecclesiastical status. In the main only partial local union of two or at most three denominations is accomplished. Moreover, even after remedial adjustments have been made and a broader outlook and constituency secured, these churches sometimes fail to make a really positive demonstration of unity in community religion.

A very real challenge is expressed by an experienced witness, who writes: "A community church is not really an inclusive church. . . . Its invitation is inclusive, but the very prejudice and traditions of the people, ranging from true conservatives to modern liberals, so work as to make the membership of a community church a selective one." The ideal of really making a single church the religious organ of a community is, to say the least, an exciting one.[14]

Nevertheless, many denominational officials still oppose local community mergers. They point to the numerous failures of such amalgams, but surely denominational churches also fail and die in large numbers. It is significant, too, that the movement is very largely rural; more than four fifths of the churches on the lists of the Community Church Workers are rural, and of Miss Hooker's "United Churches," all of which were rural, more than two thirds were in the open country and in places of less than one thousand. There is little recent information on these so-called community churches. The national organization of the ministers of such churches ceased to function during the depression.

[14] Douglass and Brunner, *The Protestant Church as a Social Institution*, chap. XII. New York: Harper & Bros., 1935. For a full discussion of these types of federated churches see Hooker, *United Churches* (Harper & Bros., 1927), a study of nearly 1000 cases undertaken in 1924 and 1925 by the Institute of Social and Religious Research.

The future of co-operation. Will the movement continue? It is difficult to answer this question despite the fact that the trend is more approved, better entrenched than ever. Four fifths of some 4200 Methodist laymen and ministers replied affirmatively to the question, "Should rural churches be federated on community lines?"

On the other hand, since 1930 unemployed clergymen in many places have reopened closed churches, especially if a parsonage was available, and have been conducting services and reorganizing the congregation in the hope of eking out some sort of living. This has often increased competition. War conditions countered this trend and caused a number of formal and informal co-operative arrangements on the local level.

Denominations recognize problem. One of the hopeful aspects of the rural church situation is the strong interest in the larger denominations. There is a real country life movement among the churches. Six or seven of the larger Protestant bodies have country church departments. Many others are represented in a strong and inclusive interdenominational committee under the Home Missions Council, which is affiliated with the Federal Council of Churches. There is also an effective Catholic Country Life Conference.

The enduring trend seems to point, however, to greater co-operation among a majority of the Protestant bodies, evidence for which lies not merely in the co-operative arrangements already described, but also in modifications of the spiritual environment. An example of this is given above in the Methodist questionnaire; another illustration is the freedom with which individuals pass back and forth between denominations, showing that their religious needs can be satisfied in more than one sect. Ministers, too, change faiths. Almost half of those ordained in the Congregational Church, and about 40 per cent of those ordained in the Presbyterian Church, in 1929, came from other denominations.[15] Moreover, religious prejudice has declined markedly and now rests at a low level in respect to most American denominations.[16]

This highly condensed review of the rural church as a social institution reveals, then, that the church is the most conservative of all rural organizations with the exception of local government, discussed later. Five trends, however, rise into prominence regarding the church:

(1) There is an increasing proportion of village church-memberships resident in the country. On the other hand, there are a smaller number of country churches.

[15] Cf. Douglass and Brunner, *op. cit.*, chap. XII.   [16] *Ibid.*

(2) Rural churches, considering village and country together, are somewhat fewer in number, though larger in average membership; yet a smaller proportion of the total population is represented in the membership.

(3) The leadership and programs of work, while different in detail, give little evidence of changing attitudes.

(4) Buildings of the stronger churches have improved and become more functional in the last twenty-five years.

(5) Budgets, after sinking sharply during the depression, have almost recovered former levels in many places and improved nearly everywhere, but the uses to which funds are put show a significant change.

(6) Adjustments involving more co-operation are apparent; yet evidence of competition exists.

The preceding discussion has shown, too, that the church reflects economic and social determinants. Yet, in spite of its religious values, it is a type of institution which functions according to its own institutional nature, subject, of course, to the limitations of its environment. But while this makes it possible to plan for the church effectively in social terms, deep-seated convictions, theological and historical differences, and a sense of the transcendental and eternal as apart from the mundane and temporal limit the effectiveness of action along such lines. The church has to function as a religious as well as a social body, a condition which may explain some of its dilemmas and seeming contradictions.

DISCUSSION TOPICS

1. Discuss critically Sorokin and Zimmerman's comparison of rural and urban religions.

2. Outline a standard or a method by which you would be willing to advise, if asked, as to whether a particular town-country community had too many or too few churches.

3. What types of "united churches" did Miss Hooker find have increased most since 1910? Discuss some reasons.

4. Describe the rural service plan and program of some local church, country or village, with which you are acquainted.

5. Describe the rural service plan and policy of some national church body with which you are acquainted.

6. Analyze the program of some rural church you know. How would you change it? Why?

REFERENCE READINGS

Brunner, E. de S., G. S. Hughes, and M. Patten, *American Agricultural Villages*, chap. VI. New York: Harper & Bros., 1927.

Brunner, E. de S., and J. H. Kolb, *Rural Social Trends*, chap. VIII. New York: McGraw-Hill, 1933.

Brunner, E. de S., and Irving Lorge, *Rural Trends in Depression Years*, chap. XII. New York: Columbia University Press, 1937.

Butterfield, K. L., *A Christian Program for the Rural Community*. New York: Doubleday Doran, 1923.

Cain, B. H., *The Church Ministering to Rural Life*. The Church of the United Brethren, 1941.

Dawber, M. A., *Rebuilding Rural America*. New York: Missionary Education Movement, 1938.

Douglass, H. P., and Edmund de S. Brunner, *The Protestant Church as a Social Institution*. New York: Harper & Bros., 1935.

Felton, Ralph A., *The Rural Church in the Far East*. New York: Baptist Mission Press, 1938.

Fry, C. Luther, *Diagnosing the Rural Church*. New York: Harper & Bros., 1924.

Fry, C. Luther, *The United States Looks at its Churches*. New York: Harper & Bros., 1930.

Hooker, E. R., *United Churches*. New York: Harper & Bros., 1926.

Hooker, E. R., *Hinterlands of the Church*. New York: Harper & Bros., 1930.

Lindstrom, David E., *The Church in Rural Life*. Champagne, Ill.: The Garrard Press, 1939.

Morse, H. N., and E. de S. Brunner, *The Town and Country Church in the United States*. New York: Harper & Bros., 1923.

O'Hara, E. V., *The Church and the Country Community*. New York: The Macmillan Co., 1927.

Rich, Mark, and others, *Youth Work in the Rural Church*. St. Louis: The Bethany Press, 1940.

Teague, Margaret W., *Forward into Rural America*. National Council of the Protestant Episcopal Church, 1938.

Terry, Paul W., and Verna M. Sims, *They Live on the Land*, chap. VII. Bureau of Educational Research, University of Alabama, 1940.

Wilson, W. H., *The Farmer's Church*. New York: Century, 1925.

22

Recreation and Cultural Activities

RURAL PEOPLE are often reluctant to admit that they are not always busy or that they have any "leisure time," but they are usually ready to go to a picnic or party, or to stop work and visit a while. Work and play have not been sharply separated, nor has work been considered only a necessary evil to be endured and strictly divorced from play. This general attitude has influenced the emphasis placed upon recreation, the forms and activities which it has assumed, and the organizations and agencies which have been developed for its promotion.

CHANGING EMPHASIS ON RECREATION IN RURAL LIFE

Rural society has shared, although in its own way, the general movement toward a greater emphasis on recreation which has been designated as one of the significant trends of recent times.[1] This increased emphasis takes so many different forms and expresses itself in so many diverse activities that it is difficult to trace; it ramifies society at nearly every point.

Rural recreation, during an earlier period, which might be roughly compassed by the years 1890 to 1920, could be described as largely informal and home-made, carried out on a home and local neighborhood basis. Popular activities included corn husking bees, quilting bees, box socials, picnics, special day celebrations, ring games, and social parties. Play was closely associated with work. Frontier conditions necessitated neighborhood co-operation for such things as threshing or construction of buildings. "Bees" such as barn "raisings" were a combination of work and play, and the fall threshing was a social occasion for whole families to get together. But the increasing use of agricultural machinery since 1920 has reduced the need for local co-operative labor. Occasions for combining recreation and work have become less frequent. The

[1] Steiner, J. F., "Recreation and Leisure Time Activities," *Recent Social Trends*, vol. II, chap. XVIII, p. 912. New York: McGraw-Hill, 1933.

general use of the automobile and the improvement of roads have provided rural people with the means of seeking recreation beyond the home and immediate locality. On the other hand, since 1930 a noticeable trend in rural social life has been the increase of informal recreation, and of home-talent activity.[2] Just as farmers and their families are turning to home and neighborhood-grown foods, so rural organizations are turning to their own members for talent and leadership.

Puritan traditions of emphasis upon the virtue of work doubtless limited recreation in many rural communities, for as Doctor Galpin has suggested, the "jaunty air of holiday," "the dressed-up costumes of leisure," and "the trappings of indolence," associated with urban life were unwelcome in farm life where the virtue of hard work had the backing of public opinion.[3] Despite all this background many kinds of leisure activities did develop, as has been shown, and more recently a greatly increased emphasis on the importance of the intelligent use of leisure time has augmented their variety and number.

Some rural leaders say that recreation should be a supplement or adjunct to other forms of activity. "People work together better when they learn to play together," says Doctor C. B. Smith of the United States Department of Agriculture Extension Service.[4] A 4—H club leader in a western state said that the work of the National Recreation Association in his county made it easier to carry on his regular extension program and to enter new communities. It also induced better attendance at all meetings. An evaluation of recreation by such leaders has been expressed in the following terms: "Recreation is a tool in organization work," "co-operation taught through recreation," "recreation develops experience in group action," and "an insurance against discontent."

More recently recreational activities are being undertaken for their own sakes, the ends sought being enjoyment, personality development, group experience, and appreciation of cultural values. This is the spirit of the Little Country Theater in North Dakota[5] and of the North Carolina Playmakers, as described in the chapter on "Adult Education." Rural leaders urging this emphasis ex-

[2] Brunner and Kolb, *Rural Social Trends*, p. 266. New York: McGraw-Hill, 1933.
[3] Galpin, C. J., *Rural Life*, p. 261. New York: Century Co.
[4] Smith, C. B., *Relationships and Needs in Rural Sociology Extension*. American Sociology Society Papers, vol. 24, p. 216. 1929.
[5] Kolb, J. H., "Twenty-five Years of the Little Country Theater," *Rural America*, May, 1939.

press their purpose as follows: "Activities are undertaken for their own sakes and not for any reward beyond themselves; they are relatively free, spontaneous, and enjoyable," and "development of socialized personality through self-expression and of higher ideals and standards in home and community through the cultural arts." With such motives many new recreational and cultural activities are being made available to country people, and their response is ample proof of their appreciation. Lynn Rohrbough, Director of Church Recreation Service, writes: "I've personally shifted almost entirely in a new direction in the past three years and find a big response to the new materials which might be classified as (1) craft side of games and other leisure tools. (2) rhythmic fun of folk origin, singing games, folk dances, folk songs, (3) traditional games themselves, and games of skill."

Specialization by interest and by locality. Nationally there has been a steady broadening of recreational activities and a great increase in the number of people taking part in them. Rural people have shared in this general expansion and they have also experienced, although at a considerably slower rate, the tendency toward specialization. Steiner has summarized this trend for urban society in the following manner: "The supplanting of the more simple pleasures of an earlier day by games and sports and social activities of a more elaborate nature requiring expensive facilities for their enjoyment has ushered in a regime of clubs and associations that have become a characteristic feature of modern recreation. The devotee of sport or the aspirant for social diversions attains his goal most readily by affiliation with organizations that specialize in activities of his choice."[6]

The rise of special interest groups in rural society has been traced in another chapter. It was evident there that recreational and sociability interests were important in the formation of these groups. Forms of recreation which now prevail in rural society or show a tendency to increase include drama, music and art, social parties, picnics and festivals, group games and athletics.

Specialization has taken place in the direction of locality as well as of interest. Certain neighborhoods and town-country communities have found pleasure and profit in developing and perfecting distinctive activities. There are abundant illustrations including rose festivals, community fairs, county-wide play days, adult and children's massed musical productions, homecomings, family reunions, annual dramatic events, even the annual presentation of

[6] Steiner, J. F., *Americans at Play*, p. 122. New York: McGraw-Hill, 1933.

the *Passion Play* or *Wilhelm Tell,* distinctive flower and vegetable gardens, lilac drives, home and school grounds beautification, fish frys, community picnics or dinners featuring locally produced foods or those characteristic of nationality groups.

Wider contacts with larger groups. The tendency for rural people to specialize their formal and informal recreation by interests and localities does not preclude their wider contact with the outside world. First evidence of such wider recreational contacts is the increased participation of country people in village athletics, in musical, patriotic and youth-serving groups.[7] This friendly and more intimate recreational association of farmer and villager has done much toward the creation of the larger town-country community described in Chapter 14.

The automobile has made possible an increasing number of rural and urban contacts. City residents in greatly increasing numbers are using the country for hunting, fishing, camping, picnicking and summer living. Country residents are likewise seeking facilities offered by urban centers for theatricals, musicales, art exhibitions, athletic contests, motion-picture productions and public dancing and amusement places. Trips and tours of all kinds offer an opportunity for wider contacts with secondary or more impersonal groups.

Greater opportunities for recreation also bring problems. The points of the old romance triangle — the boy, the girl, the place — can now be shifted from the neighborhood with its personal and primary controls to three far-flung points. The farm boy may seek his companion in another community where he is little known and take her for an evening of entertainment to a distant, impersonal and commercialized amusement hall. This shifting emphasis requires newer forms of social control, lest the triangle become one of tragedy instead of romance.

Rise of the commercial amusements. Rural people have never been strangers to certain kinds of commercialized sports and entertainment. What country boy, at least of the generation previous to the one now in college, has not seen a horse race through the crack in the board fence at the county fair or has not had the responsibility for getting the whole family off to the circus under the big tent on the vacant town lots? In the more modern rural world, motion pictures and the radio have probably attained widest popularity. They reach directly into the rural community or the farm home with their programs and their advertising features. Thus

[7] Brunner and Kolb, *Rural Social Trends,* p. 250. New York: McGraw-Hill, 1933.

rural and urban people are exposed at the same time to the same forms of entertainment. While the proportion of radio sets in farm homes is smaller than in urban homes, and while the high cost of installing sound equipment accounts for the absence of regular motion-picture programs in many of the smaller rural villages, nevertheless these two forms of commercial entertainment are more widespread than any other in rural society. Arguments continue pro and con as to the extent to which they fulfill the definition set forth for recreation. For example, opposition to certain types of motion-picture productions on the ground of morality has been strongly voiced by such organizations as the Legion of Decency. Agitation has started in certain groups for the return of broadcasting to public control, thus eliminating, as in England and France, private exploitation of this great source of entertainment and education.

Another form of commercial amusement which is making a problem for rural people according to a farmer opinion canvass reported by the magazine, *Successful Farming*, is the tavern with its liquor and its dances. Both youth and adult, according to this canvass, were agreed upon the issue. Old forms of local government seem poorly adapted to the modernized institutions. Some counties are attempting to cope with the problem through zoning ordinances. Business districts are set aside, often in open-country areas, and all business enterprises, including taverns, dance halls, filling stations, and stores, are confined to them. Within the districts regulations are imposed such as setback lines for buildings, space for parking, and other provisions intended to insure health, safety, and morals.

In the depression years. The opinion of rural leaders everywhere seems to be that there has been a notable increase in interest during the depression period in local and non-commercial recreation activity.[8] This has come about only naturally because funds were lacking and increased numbers of young people remained in rural communities. They and the adults developed home-talent activities, rediscovered folk games and dances, and revived out-of-door recreation. The movement was encouraged and stimulated by the Agricultural Extension Service, by leaders employed through W.P.A., and by greater attention given to recreation by schools, especially consolidated schools, by churches, and by various rural organizations. As the depression lifts, there seems to be somewhat of a tendency to revert, at least in some areas, to a greater patronage of

8 Sanderson, Dwight, *Research Memorandum on Rural Life in Depression Years.* New York: Bulletin 34, Social Science Research Council, 1937.

commercial amusements, such as moving pictures. Sunday movies are said to be increasing again in villages and small towns in some states. However this may be, it is certainly true that both farm men and farm women, as well as their children, do take time for recreation and for social activity of various kinds, and the number and variety of these activities appear to be increasing.

Recreation comes of age in wartime. With the speeding-up of work and the quickening of activity everywhere has come the recognition that recreation is an essential. It is high on priority lists concerned with physical fitness, mental health, emotional stability, and building group morale. It is essential on all fronts, at home and abroad, civilian and military, public and private, rural and urban. Doctor McCloskey, speaking from the Office of Community War Service, is emphatic in his statement that war-born accelerated programs of all kinds have confirmed recreation as a legitimate public responsibility on a par with such other services as education, health, and welfare.[9] For some communities this point of view has meant the assumption of new responsibilities; for others it has involved the reorganization of outmoded facilities and programs. For many rural communities it has resulted in more varied activities and in the training of more local, voluntary leaders.

Recognition has, therefore, dawned that, like education, recreation is a year-round, cradle-to-grave experience. It need not, indeed cannot and should not, be organized or formalized all of the time, but neither can it be ignored or placed on the moratory list. Life goes on, even though the playwright may claim that "Death Takes a Holiday."

Rural Recreation Activities Present Varied Possibilities

Many reasons can be found for the very wide variety of recreational activities in rural society. Many forms of leisure or semi-leisure activity were developed in various sections of the country and then transferred to other sections as the people moved. Holidays and festivals of eastern American and European origin were carried to the new places of settlement. Recreational activities are often combined with those of an educational, cultural or even vocational character; for example, the harvest festival or the community

---

[9] McCloskey, Mark A., Introduction to *Community Recreation Comes of Age.* Federal Security Agency, Office of Community War Service, Division of Recreation, 1944.

fair has its demonstrations and exhibits, as well as its games and dances.

Rural people have likewise been more interested in those types of activities which provide opportunity for participation as well as attendance. The highly commercialized facilities for the enjoyment of passive amusements have been more characteristic of the city than the country.[10] This has made for a wide variety of activities in rural areas.

The inference should not be drawn from the enumeration which follows, that all rural communities are well cared for, although every activity listed is actually in use in one or more communities. Some of these activities were also included in the chapter on "Adult Education"; one reason for the popularity of adult education is its appeal to recreational interests.

Music — group singing, chorus, glee club, quartet, orchestra, band, and festival. In any gathering, public or private, there is nothing that will afford everyone better opportunity for expression and enjoyment than will participation in some form of music, especially singing. Music has had and continues to have a very large place in the many organizations and activities of rural life.

The emphasis placed upon group singing during the war gave its development a decided impetus. It is a valuable means of creating group morale. Community leaders say that "sings" are most successful when strictly informal, and when all members of the group join in freely. They say that the matter of leading such singing, sometimes considered a problem, is not difficult to solve.

Choruses are organized on a neighborhood or community basis for adults or for young people or even for children. A children's chorus is an especially attractive form of group singing, and with the wealth of published music now available can easily become a part of the program of most schools, churches, and community clubs.

The quartet, either single or double, although bringing fewer members of the community together, forms a more specialized kind of musical organization. It gives opportunity for doing more intensive and more finished work than the larger group. It is often named after the community from which its members are drawn, but its influence may extend far beyond its own locality.

Orchestral music may blend both string and wind instruments and bring together individuals with varying degrees of skill and

[10] Steiner, J. F., *Recent Social Trends*, vol. II, p. 95. New York: McGraw-Hill, 1933.

training. Many communities have persons qualified to direct an orchestra; others find it possible to engage the services of a trained director who can come once or twice a month, and who may serve, as well, as private tutor for beginners. Frequently an arrangement is worked out with the local high school whereby one of its teachers can help with the community orchestra.

The band probably has a more popular appeal in many communities than almost any other form of musical organization. Its success depends largely on good leadership and faithful membership. Leadership can be secured on much the same plan as that suggested for the orchestra. Many local bands are maintained at partial public expense by village or school districts. One of the factors in the improvement of town-country relations which was repeatedly noticed in the studies of local communities was the band and its weekly concerts. The whole countryside turned out for the concert. Members of the organization were drawn from both farm and village.

The music festival, whether on a large or small scale, on a community, county, or state basis, is a fitting finale to a season's program. Choral as well as orchestral groups can be brought together in a massed ensemble under skilled leadership. In fact, there is no finer way of bringing country and city people together than through their interest in music. This was done, for example, in one county recently when about 1000 rural children and 500 rural adults, comprising the chorus, joined with the city civic orchestra under its accomplished director in providing an afternoon of real enjoyment.

Drama and pageantry — plays, pageants, folk dancing, pantomime, readings, story telling, marionettes, and puppetry. Recent surveys in a number of states reveal a greatly increased activity in dramatics. In addition to its sociability, drama quickens the imagination, cultivates and gives opportunity for the expression of emotions, and provides group experience. Not only the actors but other members of the community or the organization are drawn into the enterprise. For example, in the production of that interesting folk-play, *The Merry, Merry Cuckoo,* the men of a rural community club came together at the schoolhouse and constructed the house front and the picket fence. The women made the costumes and the curtains for the stage set.

The play is probably the most common form of drama to be found in rural communities. The one-act play is especially popular and lends itself to rural groups. The choice of the play and careful attention to the casting of characters are especially important for its success. Much latent talent is available and many stories could be told of how intensive work on such a character as Jean Valjean, for example, had literally transformed a personality by releasing it from suppressions which traced back to boyhood.

The pageant has many possibilities for rural communities since it deals with historical, mythical or allegorical subjects more largely than does the play. It is a means of education as well as of entertainment. Many rural groups have presented an effective pageant based on local history and produced by the descendants of the original characters. In one community so much enthusiasm was developed in the undertaking and so many interesting historic things were discovered that a local museum was established.

Folk-dancing and interpretative dancing may be considered a form of pantomime. Accompanied by music, they are an effective way of portraying grace and beauty of movement. Folk dancing, especially, has been receiving increased attention in many sections of the country whose residents trace their forbears to foreign lands. Many first generation Americans are rather anxious to throw off foreign traditions and customs, while those of the second generation often welcome the chance to ransack attic trunks for costumes and to revive folk ways in dance, song, play, and story.

Good story-telling is an art which is greatly appreciated. The country and small town abound with story-tellers who ply their art in small, informal groups, but many communities have not learned how to incorporate them into the more formal meetings, or how to use them for constructive entertainment. Folk tales are a rich source of material. This seems to be a world-wide trait of rural people. The traveling story-teller is still an institution and a social force in parts of Asia.

The art of puppetry and marionettes has also been revived in recent years in many country districts. A wide range of activity is provided because the ancillary arts of the theater can be practiced by painting the drops, making the costumes, constructing the properties, as well as selecting or writing the stories or plays. Thus, the arts and handicrafts along with literature, folklore, religion or health can be made topics for study.

Holidays and festivals. Christmas, New Year's, Washington's and Lincoln's birthdays, April Fool's Day, the Fourth of July, Labor Day, Valentine's Day, and Thanksgiving, as well as other special days, are all occasions for rural community programs or festivals.

A beautiful and growing custom for rural villages or small towns is the community Christmas celebration. A tree is lighted in the public square, and streets, stores and homes are decorated with pines and candles. There is often the song festival, a cantata or a Christmas play, such as Douglas Hyde's *The Nativity*.

Picnics and field days. The picnic is sure to stand very high on any list of popular recreational events. Mention cannot be made of the many forms which it may take. One rural community has carried the idea of an annual picnic to a very high degree of organization by establishing and incorporating a picnic association under the laws of the state. Each year since 1905 the event has been held as a town and country enterprise attended by thousands of people. Surrounding communities would not think of holding rival picnics on that day.

Children and adults often gather for play days which are held in some school yard. One rural school may act as host for the neighboring schools or even for all the schools in a county. If the affair is large, many committees are needed and preparations are made far in advance. Games and events must be suited to all the different groups present, the picnic dinner made a success, and the afternoon ball game becomes a fitting climax.

The community fair in many localities is a kind of field day or harvest festival. It is often held before and as a sort of local preparation for the county fair. It may center about the work of the agricultural department of the local high school, or it may be the occasion for neighborhood clubs to meet in friendly rivalry at a central community headquarters.

Social parties and group games. During winter months, social parties and games are especially popular in rural communities. They may be organized around occasions such as holidays, or they may occur informally when neighbors and congenial groups gather for visiting, card playing, dancing or singing.

A wide variety of activity is included under the title of group games. There has been a revival of interest in these games, especially during the depression, when it has been difficult to buy gas for the automobile or pay admission to commercial entertainment. There are the circle games, shuttle relays, table games, checkers, chess, ping pong, croquet, stunts, mixing games, horse-shoe pitching, folk and square dances, and the social dance. Folk games are being revived in some communities and foreign games, especially the Oriental, are being studied and introduced.

Community athletics and sports. Outdoor and indoor sports and athletics have long been favorites of farm and village people. Baseball, basketball, volley ball, and horse shoes or quoits are probably the most common, and the ones which develop the largest groups and stimulate the most community interest and enthusiasm. Teams for contests may be composed of either open-country or small-town groups or both. Baseball and quoits are particularly adapted to the country, while basketball, because it is played indoors during winter months, is usually centered in town or village.

The automobile and good roads make it possible to organize inter-community leagues of many kinds, kitten-ball for women, men, girls, or boys, men's baseball leagues, quoit-pitching tournaments and tug-of-war contests. Amateur rules are drawn and schedules arranged. Plans may include eliminations until a county play-off is arranged in order to select a team to go to state finals; for example, to the State Fair. This kind of recreational program raises important questions regarding parks and playgrounds in rural areas, which will be discussed briefly in the last section of the chapter.

Arts and handicrafts. Interest in the arts and handicrafts has not been widely developed in all rural areas. Some communities, however, have made much of them and have found in them not only gratifying recreation but profitable sources of auxiliary income. Difficulty is sometimes experienced in financing such group projects and in finding competent leaders. In some communities, however, older members of the community, grandmothers perhaps, have been induced to revive their early or their old-country crafts, and to teach the younger generation knitting, crocheting, hooking, embroidery or appliqué work. Old or discarded materials are used where possible. Wood carving, block printing, building bird houses and kites are taught to boys and men. Far too little has been done with the fine arts, painting, sculpture, engraving or etching. Many simple and inexpensive ways of learning principles of line, design and color, as well as rhythm, balance and harmony can be worked out if leaders will put their best thought into it.

Regional literature and rural-life fiction. Reading should not be a lost art. It is a leisure-time activity which presents many possibilities, especially when rural people recognize more fully than they do that a new type of rural literature is developing which has the quality of the older classic novels, and the strong appeal of rural life, the soil, the plain or mountain scene, and the region which one loves best. This type of rural-life fiction pictures the life and the culture of real families and communities, and gives them an emotional flavor and content which may be completely taken for granted by those readers who live in the environments described. Through these novels, rural dwellers gain a sense of belonging in the rural scene and the importance of it in the general scheme. There are countless examples. "One cannot read Ruth Suckow's *Odyssey to a Nice Girl* without sensing the authentic portrayal of life in a small town of the Middle West. Similarly, we realize the Southern setting of *The Yearling,* the Wisconsin flavor in *Restless Is the River,* the local Maine color in *As the Earth Turns.*"

"In *Old Jules* and *Sod and Stubble* we see the life of pioneer farm people portrayed in new and fascinating biographical form by members of their families, realistic and yet faithful to the lives of the struggling pioneer. Other volumes concern themselves with conflict situations and social adjustment. There are to be found even a number of rural novels about the developing co-operative movement. It all constitutes a wide field, capable of appealing to the interests of many groups." [11]

The more recent writings have their earlier counterparts, and together they become an interpretation of the unfolding life of a pioneering people. There is Rolvaag's *Giants in the Earth,* Hamlin Garland's *Son of the Middle Border,* Willa Cather's *O Pioneers,* Zona Gale's *Friendship Village,* Martha Ostenso's *Wild Geese.*

Whether in forms of fiction, drama, verse, or biography, rural-life literature offers an enlarging field for cultural activities and for personal enjoyment. And finally, it should be pointed out that these forms of expression are not entirely in hands of professionals. Writing, as well as reading and acting, holds many possibilities, as a recent experiment with farm boys in an agricultural short course bears testimony.[12] They are means for creative self-expression.

Cultural and social implication. At the risk of seeming to try to carry "coals to Newcastle," a few implications are suggested here. First, the above brief cataloguing of the wide range and variety of recreational and cultural activities is, in itself, an earnest of the place they hold in our rural society. The great numbers and types of activities are a sort of democratic guarantee that everyone can have recreational experiences, and that every agency and organization can make some contribution to the enjoyment of rural life.

Then, there are the opportunities which such activities offer for group solidarity. "Young persons particularly, experience a driving curiosity regarding the characteristic behavior of others, much of

[11] Barton, John R., *Rural Cultural Arts.* Madison: Special Circular, June, 1940, Extension Service College of Agriculture, University of Wisconsin.

[12] *From the Fields,* a collection of poetry, sketches, and short stories written by some fifty students in the Farm Short Course, College of Agriculture, University of Wisconsin, 1939.

which is freely expressed in the arts and play." [13] "It is the function of art, literature, and the humanities to create understandings which make for moral unity and solidarity in the community." [14]

Finally, there is the implication for our own American culture. The resources of Europe have flowed freely into this, our new country. Now that many of those sources have been destroyed and the people exhausted by wars, it remains for this country to develop an authentic culture deeply rooted in a new land where the millions can look with confidence, not only to their own future, but to give back to their mother countries some of the fruits of that early culture. This is the spirit of the *Folk-Singer* in which have been gathered the choicest folk-songs of many countries whose younger generations are now in this country. In its introduction it suggests that tuneful songs are enjoyed by everyone. "They travel unarmed to all countries and are received by all classes of society. To the extent that people use them, they are a language that is universally understood." [15] If there ever was a time when people, not only of European backgrounds, but all people of the earth, needed to understand one another better and to feel a greater sense of human kinship, this seems to be the time.

It is a matter of great satisfaction that a lifelong student and connoisseur of art interest should conclude that we are already on the way toward the goal of artistic development. "Where formerly an esthetic touch would have been considered effeminate and superfluous, more and more, art is being treated as an essential and vital element in American life, not as something apart." [16]

This conclusion is amply borne out in the six annual Wisconsin rural art exhibits. Of the seventy exhibitors in 1945, more than half were showing for the first time.

SOCIAL ORGANIZATIONS AND AGENCIES

Most social agencies, organizations, and institutions concerned with the general welfare of rural society are giving increased attention to recreation. The attention is varied and covers a wide number of activities, ranging from sports to entertainment, from

[13] Boyd, Neva L., *Social Group Work*. Division of Social Work, vol. I, Bulletin I, April, 1937. Chicago: University College, Northwestern University.

[14] Park, Robert E., "Education and the Cultural Crisis," *The American Journal of Sociology*, May, 1943, p. 728.

[15] Vornholt, Dan E., editor, *Folk-Singer*. Madison: Special Circular, February, 1943. Extension Service, College of Agriculture, University of Wisconsin.

[16] Keppel, Frederick P., "The Arts," *Recent Social Changes in the United States*, June, 1932.

formal and informal group games to the cultural activities of art, drama, literature, and music. This is true of local, state, and national agencies, both private and public. This characteristic of variety offers many opportunities to many different types of organizations, and at the same time it produces a problem of co-ordination for the local rural community and of administration for the county.

The depression period restricted budgets, and most rural families reduced expenditures for recreation, especially for those requiring cash outlay — subscriptions to magazines, payments for books, tickets for concerts and motion-picture shows. There was resort to the more informal, home-talent types of activities. In those times social welfare agencies helped to promote "amateur nights" and classes for encouraging the handicrafts, and they paid leaders for summer playgrounds. The Works Progress Administration promoted art, drama, and music, as well as general recreational enterprises.[17] Sometimes this was done through the school system, sometimes with locally sponsored groups, and in some states, as in New Hampshire, with the Agricultural Extension Service. In that state, county recreation leaders were employed with the help of federal funds. Out of such and other experiences has come the idea that recreation is a responsibility to be assumed by school, community, county, or municipality.

Recreation was an integral part of the war effort on both the home and fighting fronts, as has been said earlier in the chapter. Many private as well as governmental agencies, both military and civilian, sponsored recreation as an essential part of health, physical fitness, and morale-building programs. In communities near munition factories, training fields, or military camps, there was the United Service Organization, the Red Cross, the many citizen and public committees and agencies.

Youth centers. Those young people who remained in villages, small towns, or other rural areas responded eagerly to community festivals, leadership training laboratories, and workshops of various kinds. Some had their imagination kindled by stories of urban "youth centers," and undertook themselves or pressed their elders to establish counterparts in the local rural community. Sponsorship was assumed by teachers, school or village boards, or committees in which the young people were represented. They were the first to insist that such centers should have more than the adver-

[17] W.P.A., *Community Recreation Programs: A Study of W.P.A. Recreation Projects.* Washington, D.C., February, 1940.

tised "coke-bar" and "juke-box." Those with the most imagination
and insight into local affairs saw recreation related to education,
health, and other activities. Some attempts to carry over urban
patterns to rural situations failed. There could not be a similar
high degree of specialization in physical equipment, type of program, or leadership. However, in the rural community, country and
village, youth and adult can share at least some of their enjoyment,
emotional experiences, and good times.

Home, school, church, as recreation agencies. When recreation
is thus regarded as having a part in the larger rural community
betterment plan, the local social institutions of home, school, and
church can readily find their places in the scheme of things. The
rural home has always been a recreational center for its own members and for intimate friends and neighbors as well. Visiting and
"breaking bread" together — that is, eating — are much more than
incidents in rural living; they are the personal, "face-to-face" contacts upon which Professor Cooley placed such emphasis in his explanation of personality development and cultural values.

To be sure, the range of social activities in some rural homes is
limited and restricted, forcing their young people outside for their
amusement and warping their emotional responses. According to
numerous farm family studies, members spend more time in reading and listening to the radio than to any other form of home
recreation. Under certain conditions both of these really valuable
recreations can lead to unsocial tendencies. It will be recalled that
among farm families reporting recreation expenditures in 1935-36,
radio purchases ranked first and attending movies second, and that
among non-farm rural families the order was reversed.

Schools and churches are also taking a more active leadership in
rural recreation, although it must be recorded that many of them,
through lack of facilities, trained personnel, or because of limited
vision, are lagging far behind. Local as well as other studies indicate rather clearly that consolidated schools, on the average, are
giving greater attention to recreation than small-unit schools.[18] As
was pointed out in previous chapters, progressive village high
schools in agricultural communities are leading the way in community-wide programs, and, as has been said, there are evidences
of a quickening interest in recreation on the part of rural churches.

Social organizations in town and village-country communities.
Increased emphasis upon recreation, together with evidences of
specialization, have led to a wide variety of social organizations and

[18] Steiner, J. F., *Americans at Play*, p. 155. New York: McGraw-Hill, 1933.

to activities in rural communities which are instigated by country and village or town people. Whether formal or informal in character, they have been designed to help individuals or groups secure more of the amenities and pleasures of life. On the whole, they are less formal and less institutional than many of the other organizations described in preceding chapters, and therefore can respond more readily to changing conditions. The restudy of 140 agricultural villages afforded an opportunity to examine at close range the various organizations in rural society which were devoted to recreation and sociability, and to analyze the changing trends over a period of about twelve years.[19]

Nearly one third of all organizations found in 1930 were inactive or had died entirely by 1936. Scarcely two fifths of those studied in 1924 were to be found in 1936. During the period 1930 to 1936 the number of new or reorganized groups equaled about one fourth of those which were active in 1930. Between 1924 and 1930 the new organizations slightly exceeded those that had died, while in the latter period, 1930 to 1936, the reverse was true. Table 84 gives the changes in numbers by type during the latter period.

TABLE 84. CHANGES IN NUMBER OF SOCIAL ORGANIZATIONS, BY TYPE — 140 VILLAGES

Type of Organization	Organizations in 1930		Organizations in 1936		Net Change
	Total Number	Av. per Village	Total Number	Av. per Village	
All types.....................	2925	20.9	2753	19.7	− 172
Athletic..................	94	.7	69	.5	− 25
Civic.....................	293	2.1	255	1.8	− 38
Educational..............	187	1.3	197	1.4	+ 10
Fraternal.................	906	6.4	750	5.4	− 156
Musical..................	80	.6	64	.5	− 16
Patriotic.................	256	1.8	264	1.9	+ 8
Social...................	223	1.6	214	1.5	− 9
Bridge...................	195	1.4	280	2.0	+ 85
Socio-religious...........	25	.2	24	.2	− 1
Socio-economic...........	142	1.0	146	1.0	+ 4
Farm Bureau.............	111	.8	98	.7	− 13
Grange...................	55	.4	55	.4	0
Political.................	...	...	4	.0	+ 4
Townsend and Social Justice	...	...	59	.4	+ 59
Youth-serving............	192	1.4	163	1.2	− 29
4–H.....................	166	1.2	111	.8	− 55

[19] Brunner and Kolb, "Social and Recreational Organizations," *Rural Social Trends,* chap. IX. New York: McGraw-Hill, 1933.

The actual number of organizations declined about 6 per cent in the six-year period and the average per village decreased from 20.9 to 19.7, although there was an actual gain during this time in the village population. The greatest decline in actual number was among those organizations of a fraternal nature. This was generally true in all sizes of villages and in all regions. Lodge memberships were also dropping and attendance was reported as becoming poor. Young people were not joining these organizations. Despite the decline in number and strength, fraternal organizations are still about triple in number of any single type; the next most numerous being bridge clubs, which increased at rapid rates during the past five years. Organizations given to athletics and sports continued to drop out after 1930 as they had in the previous period. The same was true of musical organizations. Both of these types are high in cost, as will be shown later, their financial outlay being two or three times that of other types. Therefore, the depression took its toll among them.

It is possible by use of such enumeration to calculate both birth and death rates for social organizations. From such a calculation it was found that the death rates exceed birth rates for all types except educational, political, socio-economic, and the bridge clubs. The most stable were those that showed some gains in membership. Social and socio-religious organizations declined very little. New types appearing for the first time in the later period were the Townsend and Social Justice Clubs. Organizers for the Townsend Clubs succeeded in establishing units in 100 of the 140 village communities. The depression gave them ready candidates for members among the unemployed, the elderly people, and those generally disgruntled with the times. Their number rose quickly, but during more recent years there was evidence of their decline. They did not prove popular among the citizens who did not wish to join, although many feared their political strength.

Variations in types and numbers of social organizations were greater by geographic regions than by size of village. The Far West was the most highly organized region in 1924, but there was a decline in number of such organizations in small and middle-sized villages by 1930. Nevertheless, this region continues to have increased numbers of organizations per village. It was the only region in which numbers increased after 1930. The South continues to have the least number of organizations per village. The Middle Atlantic region showed greatest stability between 1930 and 1936, although in the earlier period it experienced rapid increases.

The comparisons show that organizations with some overhead connections or intercommunity affiliation and with some help or supervision of salaried leaders, both of which were found in Farm and Home Bureaus, Parent-Teacher Associations, and in local Chambers of Commerce, are most likely not only to survive but also to multiply.

Changes within the organizations. Changes within organizations are usually more important for the community they serve than changes in type and number. No analysis of the inner life and programs of organizations will be attempted here, but some clue to internal conditions can be found from a brief description of changes in memberships, attendance, finances, and physical equipment.

(1) *Memberships decreased.* The tendency among all organizations to lose members, found in the period 1924 to 1930, continued to 1936. The average decline was from 60 persons to 55.6 for the later period.

If the newly organized Townsend and Social Justice Clubs, which reported large memberships, had been omitted from the table, the average would be still lower. During the same periods, as has been previously noted, the population of the local village communities increased. Therefore, it is apparent that social organizations have failed, at least numerically, to hold their own. Table 85 shows that the following types of organization increased their membership rolls: athletic clubs, 4–H clubs, youth-serving, social, musical, socio-religious, socio-economic, and farm bureau. All others had lost. Among the fraternal groups the losses were most noticeable, while the farm economic organizations made greatest gains. The A.A.A. program described in an earlier chapter may have some relation to these changes in membership among farmers.

When those social organizations which had continued throughout the two periods of study were considered separately, it was evident that size of organization is related to ability to survive. In general, groups that did survive were about double the size of those that did not. They were also larger than those organized after the depression began. Groups seemed to find it more difficult to recruit new members during this period, but once in the organization, the tendency was for the members to remain.

(2) *Attendance increased.* Attendance is probably a better index of vitality than membership. Therefore, the improvement in attendance throughout the two periods under study, in the face of

TABLE 85. MEMBERSHIP IN SOCIAL ORGANIZATIONS, BY TYPE
— 140 VILLAGES

Type of Organization	Number Reporting		Average Membership	
	1930	1936	1930	1936
All types...................	2495	2381	60.0	55.6
Athletic...................	82	51	41.0	57.3
Civic......................	264	240	51.8	50.6
Educational................	159	168	65.9	57.0
Fraternal..................	834	700	91.1	79.2
Musical....................	79	57	26.6	30.6
Patriotic..................	244	258	52.5	44.7
Social.....................	185	198	33.2	34.7
Bridge.....................	114	152	14.3	13.5
Socio-religious............	25	23	68.8	75.1
Socio-economic.............	133	139	40.5	47.9
Farm Bureau................	83	78	45.6	50.9
Grange.....................	51	50	121.4	120.3
Political..................	...	4	...	32.0
Townsend and Social Justice....	...	15	...	293.7
Youth-serving..............	172	152	29.6	30.8
4–H.......................	70	96	19.4	23.9

loss of membership, is significant. It suggests that surviving organizations are meeting social and recreational needs even more satisfactorily than when the rolls are larger but contain inactive members. Improvement was found in every region, particularly in the South and in the Far West.

The life cycle for special-interest groups outlined in an earlier chapter is clearly shown in the social organizations found in these village communities. The younger organizations had a larger proportion of their members in attendance at meetings; interest was great during the first years. However, there are other factors than attendance which must account for the demise of such organizations, since there was a tendency for attendance to keep up to the end, at least for the organizations found in the 140 agricultural village communities.

(3) *Finances decline.* The tendency to reduce expenditures, evident before 1930, continued until 1936. The decline during the period was almost 30 per cent, which is slightly smaller than the reduction made by the churches in these same communities. In 1930 the per member expenditure for all types of social organizations was $5.67 and in 1936 it was $4.03. Variation among types of organizations can be seen in the table. Athletic organizations

TABLE 86. ATTENDANCE AND PER MEMBER EXPENDITURES FOR
SOCIAL ORGANIZATIONS, BY TYPE — 140 VILLAGES

Type of Organization	Per cent of Attendance		Per Member Expenditures	
	1930	1936	1930	1936
All types....................	39.8	43.3	$5.67	$4.03
Athletic....................	93.2	45.8	18.55	8.66
Civic.......................	51.3	51.8	6.17	5.97
Educational.................	58.8	61.1	1.69	1.41
Fraternal...................	25.2	28.5	4.33	3.89
Musical.....................	79.6	85.2	14.83	10.45
Patriotic...................	34.0	40.7	6.20	3.79
Social......................	60.4	57.7	6.46	1.62
Bridge......................	94.5	99.8	1.98	1.22
Socio-religious..............	34.0	36.7	3.87	4.90
Socio-economic..............	69.2	61.1	18.79	8.42
Farm Bureau.................	41.8	57.0	5.74	4.63
Grange......................	29.9	29.5	1.91	2.55
Political...................	...	51.6	...	2.39
Townsend and Social Justice....	...	48.3	...	.35
Youth-serving...............	75.8	71.4	3.27	2.19
4–H........................	87.8	91.4	1.63	1.01

cut per capita costs by more than one half, yet they are still relatively high. Musical organizations are highest, while the Townsend
Clubs are lowest. This trend for social organizations to follow the
business cycle in financial affairs was general in every geographic
region. In the Far West the drop was most violent. A comparison
between those organizations which continued throughout the whole
period beginning with 1924 and those that fell by the way suggests
that conservative financing is associated with long life. The per
capita costs for those organizations that died averaged about 35
per cent higher than for those which survived.

(4) *Buildings and equipment increased.* Slightly more than 10
per cent of the organizations studied had their own buildings in
1930. More than half of the buildings were lodge halls, but these
types of buildings are not the ones that are increasing in number.
The increase is in the number of publicly owned community buildings, swimming pools, and playgrounds. In a canvass of agricultural extension leaders in all states, one third reported an unprecedented call for help in planning community buildings; another
one sixth reported some requests. The movement was greatly augmented by the availability of W.P.A. labor and by the apparent
desire for rural people to have a place in which to house their

recreational and social activities. One rural New England State reported plans completed for one hundred such community buildings, while fifty-five others already approved by W.P.A. administrators were in process. In addition, school buildings and equipment are being used in increasing numbers for community and social purposes.

Country and village relations in social organizations. Although few social organizations are designed for country or village people exclusively, yet in reality there is a tendency to specialize according to interests and localities. as has been observed. Such organizations as the Grange, Farm Bureau, and farmers' clubs are designed for country groups, although they do not exclude villagers; in fact, their meetings are often held in the village. In some sections of the country, notably the East and South, members from the village are frequently found in 4–H clubs and homemakers' groups. Country groups are usually organized about the more strictly social and home-talent interest; they are personal and primary in character, and include kinship, neighborhood, or congeniality groups.

Increased patronage by country people of what can be considered village social organizations was found, although the statistical increases were not as marked as the testimony of country and village people would lead one to expect. The proportion of country members in all social organizations increased only slightly from 1930 to 1936, from 34.2 to 35.3 per cent respectively. Athletic groups have a relatively high percentage of country members, although there was a decline in the last period. Civic and educational organizations in the South and Far West show an increased percentage of country members. Likewise in the Far West, open-country people participated more largely in musical organizations in 1936 than they did in 1930. There appeared to be relative exclusion of country people from social clubs in the South and from bridge clubs in all regions. Socio-religious organizations, on the other hand, were more likely to include a relatively larger proportion of country members. This was also true of the Townsend Clubs, as well as of those organizations which have definite farm backgrounds, such as 4–H clubs, Farm Bureau, and Grange. In the South and in the Far West, the Farm Bureau had a larger portion of its members from the village in 1936, but for the nation as a whole the reverse was true.

County-wide organization, a new development. The trend for local groups to federate and to form county-wide associations as described in the chapter on "Special Interest Groups," is pronounced among recreational and social organizations. Such groups as Grange, Farm Bureau, 4–H clubs, and Parent-Teacher Associations used this plan from the first. Other types of organizations have followed, but in recent years some of the newer types, for example, those for older rural youth, use the county as their local unit of organization. Good roads, more automobiles, and the tendency to specialize one's social interests all contribute to this movement. Other influences toward county plans are the experiences gained through W.P.A. county recreation programs and the demands coming from some organized groups for recreation to be on a county-wide basis. At a conference of farm women held in Washington in 1934, the idea was advanced that each county should have a recreational leader, publicly paid.[20]

There is no doubt that county agencies and county federations have come to stay and to assume greater significance in rural social affairs. Yet many a county is too poor or has too low a population density to make a complete county plan possible. The question may also be raised as to whether the county can actually become more than an administrative unit for those organizations which are local or community in type and function. This problem will be considered again in the chapter dealing with the social implications of local government.

What of rural youth and social organizations — enough or too many? In most studies of rural youth, either by its own representatives or by the social scientists, recreational activities rank high on the list of "urgent needs." The conception of recreation among young people, however, is often rather different from that of their elders. Youth thinks of many activities, and the more active the better. The urge is for personal development and for group contacts, many of which can be quite informal and unorganized, rather than for forms of relaxation, as is frequently the case with older people. What rural young people do with their leisure time depends partly on their initiative and partly on the availability of desired recreational or educational opportunities. There are wide variations in the popularity and availability of possible activities among the many groups surveyed. In the main, reading is the most frequently listed and one of the most popular. In Wisconsin, attending movies, listening to the radio, playing cards, sports, and dancing followed in order. In specific communities, however, the

[20] Sanderson, Dwight, *Research Memorandum on Rural Life in Depression Years.* New York: Bulletin 34, Social Science Research Council, 1937.

presence of a well-organized and successful project in the realms of drama or music, for instance, sharply influences both the preferences and the expenditure of time by youth.

Another form of recreation dependent upon organization is that of sports and athletic activities. In well-organized areas these interests rank high. Elsewhere outdoor leisure activities incline to be more individual in character, such as hunting and trapping.

Organizational meetings and activities are a frequent use of leisure time, and here, too, differences are great. For instance, in the New York studies, almost nine tenths of the young women and two thirds of the young men belonged to church. In the Maryland Youth Survey,[21] only about one half belonged. In New York almost half the youth belonged to one young people's group and about one fifth to the Grange. In Maryland, six sevenths of the farm youth did not belong to any organization not connected with the church.

In the main, it appears that, although in the aggregate many organizations court rural youth, rural youth does not have wide organizational contacts. Indeed, youth is not interested in many organizations because their programs are too readymade or standardized, too much dominated by older persons. Apparently this observation need not be confined to rural North America, since in the account of Littledene, New Zealand, one reads, "There is a tendency for the more enlightened youth of the place to be absorbed and robbed of their leisure by a monstrous overorganization."

Rural young people solve own leisure-time organization problems. All over the nation young people have been getting together to solve their social organization problems. Typical of the more successful of these efforts is a club in the Middle-West states, started, as many were, by young college graduates forced by the depression to remain in their home community.

In November, 1933, an article on rural recreation in the county paper brought one of the group to the county agent. As a result of the visit, a small group attended a three-day recreational institute for rural leaders, conducted by the Agricultural Extension Service. Forthwith, they started a club, Country Youth, in their home township, beginning with fourteen members. The first year's activities began with a highly successful play which built both morale and community approval. Forty-five other events or activities were embarked on in the first year, including the building of a tennis

21 Lister, J. J., and E. L. Kirkpatrick, *Rural Youth Speak*. Washington, D.C.: American Youth Commission, 1931.

court, horseshoe-pitching tourneys, soft ball, programs at the various schools, suppers, basketball, and a country-wide drama festival. Other things, insignificant as such, helped. A broken victrola was repaired by one of the members and placed in the Farm Bureau Hall. Selling of ice cream and soft drinks at summer gatherings brought enough money to purchase and install a piano in the same hall.

In the following years the program broadened with parties, excursions, summer picnics, and the giving of programs before various community organizations, about forty a year. Community service units were formed in connection with two thirds of the county schools. Dances were included and participation in a number of state youth activities. Money was spent to secure lecturers on topics in which the members were interested.

The membership of Country Youth is county-wide. In its five years it has grown from 14 to 345. All of the thirteen townships in the county are represented, but six of them have three fourths of the total.

This group is significant. It has earned its way despite an ever-broadening program. Its service program is quite effective. It has deepened interest and increased participation in drama and music all over the county. It has revived the spirit of recreation and extended the meaning of education. It has convinced the farm youth that they can achieve. Interestingly enough, twelve of the fourteen charter members are still in their home county, eleven on farms.[22]

In another county a youth group, working under the sponsorship of an adult committee, by use of a self-survey, attempted to find out what rural young people between the ages of fifteen and twenty-eight think about present conditions and what they think can and should be done. Within fifteen months after the survey was completed, a number of different moves were made to meet the needs of young people in the county as revealed by the study. A County Youth Committee was formed; a county-wide youth conference was held, focusing attention on the findings of the survey. A summer young people's camp was held; a folk-school and camp was set up and carried on for three months; some new organizations for young people were started in areas where there were none; a series of meetings was held over the county by young people themselves in an attempt to get part-time schools, classes, and recreational programs set up in local community centers. Some of the young people

[22] Todd, Kirby, *Country Youth*. Unpublished paper.

were encouraged to continue their formal education. Other counties, seeing the success of such effort, undertook similar surveys.

Another interesting development, antedating the depression, is a national rural youth conference held at the same time as the annual conference of the American Country Life Association. It has been sponsored largely by collegiate country life clubs. In some regions state conferences have been held that are proving quite influential in helping youth to help themselves and their communities.

RECREATION AS LIVELIHOOD AND LAND-USE

"All over New England a new industry is receiving recognition. The rapid and widespread growth of public, private, and commercial recreation in these states during the last decade indicates that continued expansion may be expected." [23] "The entire cut-over area of the three Lake states has recreational possibilities and recreation has been listed as one of the primary land-uses." [24] Statements of this order from two regions of the United States portend future developments which have significance, not only for these areas but for many others. The social implications are far-reaching and involve both private and public interests. It is of special importance to find in the report of the New England study that park areas are used primarily by local people. Lands unsuited to agricultural uses could, therefore, be acquired by towns and made available to their own residents.

The majority of visitors to such recreation areas were, of course, urban residents, but it was not realized what a high proportion was in the medium- or even low-income groups. To provide recreation for them requires reasonable accessibility, equipment, and facilities within their means. It would suggest recreation areas near to urban centers of population.

In the cut-over area, the recreational use of land means that a stage of development has been reached in which agriculture is nearly stable; that is, it is as near to the margin as it can profitably

[23] Niederfrank, E. J., and C. R. Draper, *Use of Recreation Sites Developed on Federal Submarginal Land-Purchase Areas in Maine.* College of Agriculture, University of Maine, Maine Bulletin 280, July, 1940.

[24] Wehrwein, George S., and Hugh A. Johnson, "A Recreation Livelihood Area," *Journal of Land and Public Utility Economics,* vol. XIX, no. 2, May, 1943; "Zoning Land for Recreation," *Journal of Land and Public Utility,* February, 1942; Wehrwein, George S., and Kenneth H. Parsons, *Recreation as a Land Use.* Madison: Bulletin 422, Agricultural Experiment Station, University of Wisconsin, April, 1932.

go. It also implies that private enterprise has failed to use the land, once the timber has been removed; therefore, much of it has become county, state, and federally owned. This represents a transition period in which many readjustments are required. For example, with much land in public ownership, the local tax base has been reduced so much that local government finds itself with new responsibilities of land management at the same time that its revenues are more restricted. With new forest-crop laws and the extension of opportunities for recreation as a livelihood, the future holds new prospects.

Consideration must be given to changes in the highway system as well as to the local school system. Problems of taxation, zoning, and land-use controls must be solved. It might be easily assumed that tourist or resort business could readily supplement a limited farming enterprise. However, closer examination reveals that the two, if combined, require very careful management. The resort season is short and comes in the very months when major farm work must be done. Then, the social habits of "summer boarders" may run counter to the mores of the local people. What commercial amusements will be patronized and how they shall be controlled is one question among many. There will be more of recreation for all after the war's recreational experience. That seems assured.

RECREATION AS RE-CREATION AND THE PUBLIC INTERESTS

In whatever way recreation in rural society is approached, it is evident that the public is becoming increasingly concerned and more directly involved. The great rise in commercialized recreation is one result and it cannot be traced or appraised within the compass of this chapter. Among the most common private enterprises in rural society are the motion-picture theaters, poolrooms, and public dance-halls. In many rural communities the tavern is closely associated with the latter two, and it, with its predecessor, the saloon, has had a long history as a local social institution. Now, with the expansion of travel, dance-halls and taverns may be located in the country, but they can scarcely be said to be socially of it. They are frequented by people far removed from local interests.

Profits are the motive of most commercial projects, and when their vested interests are challenged, the public interests must be defined and defended. Recreation must be re-creation, and its opportunities in this definition are enlarging, as the evidence has shown. Its expansion is urged by social welfare leaders as one means for preventing juvenile delinquency, and also by health authorities as one form of therapy for emotional maladjustments. For these and other reasons, social control, involving legal measures and governmental supervision, is increasingly necessary. Such measures include zoning ordinances, set-back lines for buildings and parking areas, building codes for health and safety, and other sanitation provisions, and it would mark a new day if in this postwar period there could be added to such bare minimum standards the terms suggested by the Royal Institute of British Activities and the Town and Country Planning Association, namely, that buildings, playgrounds, and the towns themselves shall be not only convenient but pleasant, attractive, and artistic.[25] It is by such means that youth may keep its romanticism and play-spirit as long as it can, and avoid where possible, its tragedies.

On the constructive side, public policies are needed to grasp the many opportunities for recreation in modern rural life — parks, playgrounds, scenic and historic spots, wild-life sanctuaries, community buildings and equipment, and, most important, trained and competent leadership. Steiner points out that the need for public recreational facilities and policies first arose in congested urban districts, but that the situation at present requires an extended view, reaching beyond either rural or urban interests to a national scope.[26] The invasions of village and open country by new types of organizations modeled on urban patterns and affiliated on a county or nation-wide basis, together with the excursions of urban people into the country, seeking recreation and respite, are not only modifying the leisure-time habits of both rural and urban residents, but are linking them together in the need for national and regional planning.

In rural communities, schools have opportunities which they have thus far not fully realized. They are the public institutions of greatest frequency in rural society; they have the most physical equipment, and the largest paid personnel, as Chapter 18 has definitely shown. Theirs is the task of stimulating greater recognition of recreational need, of directing it into wholesome channels of activity, and of providing in larger measure leadership and equipment for youth, both in school and out, and for the adult members of their communities, as the chapter on adult education has already emphasized.

Local government has opportunities before it also. One of its

[25] British Information Service, *Postwar Planning in Britain*. New York, 1943.
[26] Steiner, J. F., chapter 18 in *Recent Social Trends*, vol. II. New York: McGraw-Hill, 1933.

chief contributions can be in the sphere of planning beyond local corporate boundaries. The playground of the modern city must extend into surrounding territory. Towns, villages, and the open country are immediately involved. This train of thinking takes one into the whole question of land and policies regarding its most appropriate uses. Several states are definitely attempting land-use planning under various legal forms in which recreation is recognized as a legitimate land use. May it not be considered one of its highest uses?

The importance given to public welfare in modern life is stated very well by a State Supreme Court Justice in the following terms:

> In this day none will dispute that government in the exercise of its police power may impose restrictions upon the use of property in the interest of public health, morals, and safety. That the same restrictions may be imposed upon the use of property in promotion of the public welfare, convenience, and general prosperity is perhaps not so well understood, but nevertheless is firmly established by the decisions of this and the Federal Supreme Court.[27]

Thus, a consideration of rural recreation, its changing emphasis, its many forms and agencies, and its public interest implications has led directly to questions of welfare and policy. This in itself is a significant and encouraging modern trend, and leads on to the further discussion of health and social welfare to be considered in the chapters which follow.

DISCUSSION TOPICS

The topics suggested below may be assigned to individual students or the class may be divided into committees, each assuming responsibility for one topic. The separate committee reports with recommendations may be presented before the whole class, thus becoming the basis for further discussion.

1. A plan for organizing and carrying to completion a dramatic program for rural groups in a county or district.
2. A plan for organizing and carrying to completion a music program for rural groups in a county or district.
3. A plan for conducting a county-wide baseball tournament in which rural groups participate.
4. A plan for conducting a town-country community fair.
5. A plan whereby a high school may give leadership and direction to a town-country community, year-around recreation program.

[27] Justice Owen, in State *ex rel.* Carter *vs.* Harper, 182 Wis. 148, p. 154.

6. A plan for enlisting, encouraging and training rural young people in the arts and crafts by such devices as exhibits, contests, testing aptitudes, or bringing in artists.

7. By use of the ten-point scale of essentials for a public recreation system, rate your own community and discuss its merits and its shortcomings:

   a. *Know your community* — the character and distribution of population, the traditions, needs, problems, resources of the community.

   b. *Pool your resources.* Work together for full use of all potential assets: from public and private agencies, neighborhood groups, organizations, and individual leaders.

   c. *Check your legislation.* Determine what legislation you need and what you have, and then, if necessary, work to get laws that provide an adequate legal base. Authority to develop public recreation depends upon state and local laws.

   d. *Establish a legal managing authority* — a responsible lay board with legal authority to administer the program, assuring recreation the community status it warrants.

   e. *Get good leadership.* Insist on a trained, full-time executive, responsible to the board, on the job the year round, and subordinate leaders chosen with equal care on a basis of qualifications and training. Select and use competent volunteers within this framework of professional leadership.

   f. *Make the most of existing facilities* — municipally owned schools, buildings, parks, playfields and playgrounds, and water areas. These may be supplemented by use of privately owned property.

   g. *Secure separate budget.* Obtain a definite, adequate amount of public funds through special tax levy or other public appropriations, earmarked for the sole purpose of community recreation.

   h. *See that your program is community-wide, year-round, has broad appeal* — with interests for young and old, indoor and outdoor activities, sports, athletics, games, music, arts, crafts, drama, lectures, forums, social recreation, and community events.

   i. *Maintain public partnership.* Keep popular opinion abreast of your program. Use all media available to interpret community recreation and win public support for it.

   j. *Plan for the future.* Make a place for recreation in long-range town planning. Good planning should include not only physical facilities, but also program, leadership, and finance.

The above scale is taken from *Community Recreation Comes of Age.* Federal Security Agency, Office of Community War Service, Division of Recreation. United States Government Printing Office, 1944.

REFERENCE READINGS

Arvold, Alfred G., *The Little Country Theater*. New York: The Macmillan Co., 1912. Possibilities of the theater in rural life.

Elsom, James C., *Community Recreation*. New York: Century Co., 1929. A practical guide for community leaders.

Halbert, Blanche, *Community Buildings for Farm Families*. Washington, D.C.: United States Department of Agriculture, Farmers' Bulletin 1804, 1938.

Halsey, A. F., *The Historical Pageant in the Rural Community*. Ithaca: Cornell Extension Bulletin 54, 1922.

Mitchell, E. D., and B. S. Mason, *The Theory of Play*. New York: A. S. Barnes & Co., 1941.

Nason, W. C., *Rural Planning (The Social Aspects of Recreation Places)*. Washington, D.C.: United States Department of Agriculture, 1924. Description of recreation places and their social values.

National Recreation Association of America, *Rural and Small Community Recreation*. New York, 1929. A guide for leaders.

Neumeyer, M. H. and E. S., *Leisure and Recreation*. New York: A. S. Barnes & Co., 1936. A social view of recreation, its background and trends, and theories of play.

Pangburn, W. W., *Adventures in Recreation*. New York: A. S. Barnes & Co., 1936. An interpretation of the recreation movement addressed to students.

Patten, Marjorie, *The Arts Workshop of Rural America*. New York: Columbia University Press, 1937. A study of the rural arts program of the agricultural extension service.

Steiner, Jesse F., *Americans at Play*. New York: McGraw-Hill, 1933. A recent social trends monograph.

Terry, Paul W., and Verner M. Sims, *They Live on the Land; Life in an Open-Country Southern Community*. Tuscaloosa: Bureau of Educational Research, University of Alabama, 1940.

Van de Wall, Willem, *The Music of the People*. American Association for Adult Education, New York, 1938.

West, James, *Plainville, U.S.A.*, pp. 81-114. New York: Columbia University Press, 1945.

Wileden, Rockwell, Borchers, *Dramatics for Amateur Groups*. Madison: Circular 257. Extension Service, College of Agriculture, University of Wisconsin, 1933. Practical suggestions for putting on plays.

W.P.A., *Community Recreation Programs: A Study of W.P.A. Recreation Projects*. Washington, D.C., 1940.

23

Rural Health and Medical Services

PEOPLE are a nation's most important resource; their health and welfare are its primary concern. Wars and depressions have made this plain. Public attention has probably never been so strongly focused upon any one social problem, excepting perhaps education, as it has been recently upon health. There are the startling figures of the Selective Service System, the casualties of war with the subsequent records of miracles of modern medicine and surgery, programs of physical fitness and mental alertness, the wartime campaigns for better food and nutrition, for health and medical service schemes, and unrecorded multitudes of committee meetings on postwar health plans.

Rural people and rural problems have found themselves up in front in many of these considerations. There was a time when rural leaders boasted, with justification, of the natural advantages of rural life — fresh air, sunshine, and direct access to food. They pointed to lower disease and death rates in the country than in the city, to a longer life expectancy, and to smaller chances of contracting diseases spread by personal contacts.

Recently many of these trends have been reversed. It is not that the rates are increasing in rural areas; they are decreasing in both the rural and urban, but the health of city people has been improving rapidly, while progress in rural areas has been relatively slow. This is illustrated in the case of death rates. In 1900, the rural death rate was 50 per cent under the urban, but in 1940, it was only 10 per cent lower than the urban. Of even greater significance was the fact that death rates from preventable diseases tended to be higher in rural than in urban areas. This would suggest differences in locations, in attitudes, and in individual and social action. These are matters in which the student of rural society has special interest and concern. He may not become expert in the diagnosis of disease, in child care, in public health standards, or in hospital construction. He cannot, however, avoid giving his attention to the incidence of death, disease, and accident; to the study of the relations of rural people with medical care and health agencies; and attempting to understand the interaction of health with other aspects of rural life. These are fundamental to family life, to community welfare, and to the future of the nation itself. It is to these problems, then, and from this point of view that this chapter will be addressed.

RURAL HEALTH SITUATION — SOME MEASURES AND SOME IMPLICATIONS

The quest for good health in rural society, in the past at least, has not been a deliberate thing. Being born, growing up, keeping well, have been more or less taken for granted. When there was trouble too difficult to cope with in the family circle, there was resort to the doctor, or, in dire distress, the hospital. There has not been systematic effort over large areas and with organized agencies to protect health. Promotion of sanitation and control of disease through public measures, such as immunization and quarantine, had to justify themselves in rural society. Public health nurses have had to win their way in country communities just as professionally trained agriculturists, home economists, and social welfare workers have had to do.

The country doctor, of course, has a fine place in the tradition of rural life. He was a part of the community; he was respected and beloved; and, in fact, he was almost a social institution in himself. Yet he was usually the only doctor in the community or for miles around, and consequently was so busy saving life and responding to emergencies that he had little time or energy, nor did he have a special training, to work in organized ways for promoting better health.

Hospitals, clinics, public health nurses, sanitary engineers, and protection programs have appeared in rural areas during the more recent years, but not in sufficient quantity and quality to give rural people a health parity equal to that of urban people.

Rejection rates, Selective Service System. Probably the most startling verification of this disparity between rural and urban health and fitness is found in the tabulation of rejection rates by broad occupational groups of the eighteen- and nineteen-year-old registrants, prepared for the American Medical Association. Table 87 indicates that farmers were rejected to a greater extent than were those of any other major occupational group — 41 per cent, which is sixteen points above the general average of 25 per cent.

TABLE 87. REJECTION RATES, BY BROAD OCCUPATIONAL GROUP, OF EIGHTEEN- AND NINETEEN-YEAR-OLD REGISTRANTS

Occupation Group	Rate per Hundred Examined		
	White and Negro	White *	Negro
All occupations................................	25.4	23.8	45.4
Professional and semi-professional workers.........	20.5	20.5	†
Farmers.......................................	41.1	36.4	58.0
Proprietors, clerical, sales and kindred workers......	21.0	20.9	26.9
Craftsmen, foremen and kindred workers...........	20.4	19.9	39.6
Operatives and kindred workers...................	22.2	21.6	39.6
Service workers.................................	28.9	25.8	35.9
Laborers except farm and mine...................	28.2	25.3	46.0
Emergency workers and unemployed...............	37.7	37.2	44.9
Students......................................	23.3	23.0	31.6

* Includes all races other than Negro.
† Insufficient data for calculation of rate.
Source: *Journal of the American Medical Association*, September 25, 1943, vol. 123, pp. 181–185.

Among white youth, the highest rate was among emergency workers, the farmers standing second; among Negroes, the farmers had the highest rate. This is the opposite of the situation in World War I, and while questions may be raised regarding classifications and techniques employed, it cannot be said that all is well with rural youth.

The seven leading causes of rejection among those white registrants eighteen and nineteen years old were in the decreasing order of occurrence: eye defects, mental disease, musculo-skeletal defects, cardio-vascular defects, educational defects, underweight, and mental deficiency.

The chart (Figure 36) shows the ten leading causes of rejection for Negroes of the same age. Half the rejections of these Negro youths resulted from educational deficiency or from syphilis. These conclusions are drawn from figures based on local board and induction station examinations made during December, 1942, and January and February, 1943. Calculations based on other ages and other periods were somewhat different. For example, mental disease led the list of ten for white registrants for the period April, 1942, to March, 1943, with 14.2 per cent all rejections, also for the period April, 1943, to December, 1943, with 19.2 per cent. Musculo-

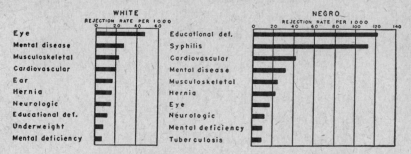

Figure 36

TEN LEADING CAUSES OF REJECTION BY RACE, 18 TO 19-YEAR-OLD REGISTRANTS, DECEMBER, 1942 — FEBRUARY, 1943

skeletal defects were second in both periods.[1] Rejections increased in direct relation to increasing age, and from the middle thirties on, reached over 50 per cent of all those examined. There were variations between and within regions. The highest rejection rates were in the South and the lowest were found in states in the Northwest. This was largely the result of the differential between white and Negro registrants.

Defects, diseases, deaths, in rural areas. A general view of the health situation in rural society, as measured by mortality or death rates and morbidity or sickness rates, can be gained from general census reports and from local studies. Comparisons of rural with urban conditions serve to call attention to special rural problems. They may also lead to wrong conclusions unless made carefully, because many different situations are bound together in the general averages for both the rural and the urban classifications.

The general death rates of rural people are still slightly less than for urban people, but, as was stated earlier, the decline has been less rapid in the country than in cities.

The first two mortality rates in the above simplified table should give real pause to those concerned with rural society. In the earlier chapter on the family, it was suggested that infant mortality is an index of the cultural level of a people; it is a sensitive sign of a people's general welfare and of their scale of values. In 1942, the death rate of babies under one year of age was over one fourth

[1] "Physical Examinations of Selective Service Registrants During Wartime," *Medical Statistics Bulletin* no. 3. Washington, D.C.: Selective Service System, November 1, 1944.

TABLE 88. UNITED STATES CENSUS BUREAU MORTALITY
SUMMARIES FOR 1940 — RATES PER 100,000

Disease	Urban	Rural
Infant mortality *	42.3	50.7
Maternal mortality *	3.4	4.0
Typhoid, paratyphoid fever	.6	1.6
Diphtheria	.6	1.5
Malaria	.3	1.8
Pellagra	.8	2.3
Pneumonia, influenza	63.4	76.6

* Rates per 1000 live births.
Source: *Fact Sheet on Rural Health and Sanitation.* Washington, D.C.: United States Department of Agriculture, Office of Information, January 3, 1945.

higher in rural than in urban society. The fact to remember is that rural areas produce the future population of the nation. This is shown in Figure 37 (page 578), giving percentages of live births to residents of rural areas. In some states the percentage of live births to rural residents is as high as 75 per cent or more of all births. In many of the most rural states both the infant and maternal death rates are highest. They are usually correlated with the use made of hospital services, per capita wealth, and the proportion of urban to rural population of the states.

Maternal mortality — that is, deaths of mothers in connection with childbirth — in 1941 was nearly one third higher in rural areas than in large cities. Table 88 also indicates the general rate to be somewhat more favorable in the urban than in the rural population. The map (Figure 38) shows the general maternal mortality rate for each state.

Diseases fatal to both children and adults which modern science and sanitation are best able to prevent are highest in many rural areas. As Table 88 shows, these include typhoid, malaria, and pellagra, the very diseases which are considered nearly conquered in many urban situations. The thirteen-point difference in pneumonia between rural and urban probably reflects, at least in part, the tardier and less frequent use of the new sulpha drugs and penicillin in country districts and in villages and towns than in the larger cities. The same general tendencies are also found by studies of local situations, counties in New York and Ohio being examples.[2] Chronic illness was found to be surprisingly high among

[2] Sanderson, Dwight, *A Survey of Sickness in Rural Areas in Cortland County, New York.* Ithaca: Memoir 112, Cornell University Agricultural Experiment Station, 1938; Lively, C. E., and P. G. Beck, *The Rural Health Facilities of Ross County, Ohio.* Columbus: Bulletin 412, Ohio Agricultural Experiment Station, 1927.

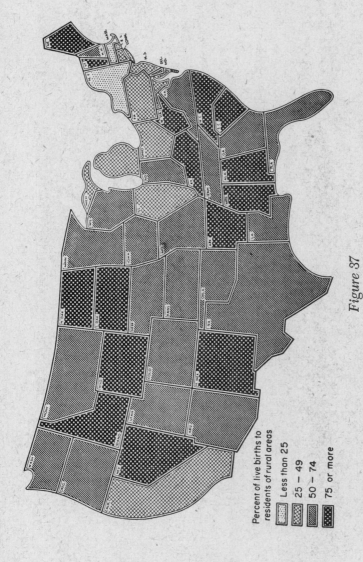

Percent of live births to
residents of rural areas

Less than 25
25 – 49
50 – 74
75 or more

Figure 37

PERCENTAGE OF LIVE BIRTHS TO RESIDENTS OF RURAL AREAS OF EACH
STATE – UNITED STATES, 1940

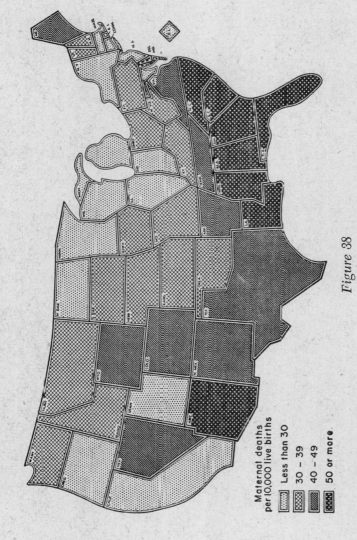

Maternal deaths
per 10,000 live births

Less than 30

30 – 39

40 – 49

50 or more

Figure 38

MATERNAL MORTALITY RATE IN EACH STATE – UNITED STATES, 1940

persons in rural Missouri.[3] During the year considered, one person in every six was ill three months or longer, and one in every nine throughout the year. The rates varied directly with age and with income. They were unequally distributed by families and by areas in the state; for example, four fifths of the total days of illness occurred in less than one third of the households. There was also a very unequal use of medical services.

Chronic illnesses are a drain on people's energies, causing loss of time and money. Many of them trace back to some unremedied defect or some untreated heart condition. It is reported that at least one sixth of the defects for which men were rejected through the Selective Service System could be readily remedied as far as medical science is concerned.[4] About 1,500,000 men with major defects were inducted and made fit for military duty, including 1,000,000 with dental defects, more than 250,000 with impaired vision, and 100,000 with syphilis, and more than 7000 with serious hernia.

Studies made by the Farm Security Administration found an average of 3.5 defects per person examined among thousands of low-income farm families. In seventeen states, for example, 14 per cent of the men and the women had varicose veins, one farm operator in twelve had a hernia, many had defective vision and infected tonsils.

Mental disorders. While it is not yet possible to draw accurate comparisons between rural and urban or between farm and nonfarm, it is well to record a health situation which has recently startled many people. It is the high rate of military rejections and of discharges for the so-called "neuropsychiatric" causes. At least some of these high rates could have been predicted, and many were, by students and authorities of mental hygiene. An example is the Interim Report of the Senate Committee on "Wartime Health and Education" in which it points out that about two thirds of the illness encountered in general medical practice is essentially neuropsychiatric in origin, and that half of the patients in hospitals at any one time are there because of serious mental disorders.[5] The report even predicts that in any group of fifteen-year-olds, one out of

[3] Kaufman, Harold F., *Extent of Illness and Use of Medical Services in Rural Missouri.* Columbia: Progress Report 5, April, 1945, University of Missouri Agricultural Experiment Station.

[4] Interim Report from the Subcommittee on *Wartime Health and Education.* 78th Congress, Subcommittee Report 3, January, 1945.

[5] *Ibid.*, and Subcommittee Report no. 4, *Health Needs of Veterans.*

twenty-two will some day be committed to a mental institution. This is sobering, indeed.

The causes for both rejections and discharges include various degrees of nervousness, emotional instability, personality disorders, and inadequacies. Many — how many no one knows — of the men with these difficulties can adjust themselves satisfactorily to civilian life back in their home communities or in other occupational situations. In rural communities many "queer" people or children "not very bright" are hidden away in homes or are seen on occasion in the country or in villages. They have not been included in the statistical summaries of hospital beds occupied or on mental hygiene clinic registers. It is safe to suggest that many cases, whether or not so enumerated, would, upon analysis, trace back to some unremedied physical defect or to some unattended functional disorder. In the local community or in the country or village school they might have been regarded as the "bad" boy or the "neglected" girl in the broken family. More adequate counsel in the schools and a greater availability of psychiatric services could greatly reduce the incidence of such mental and emotional disorders.

Accidents. Finally, accidents to American farmers, according to the director of the Farm Division of the National Safety Council, cause enough loss of time to produce the average annual wheat crop and the economic loss is nearly a billion dollars annually.[6] More than seventeen thousand farm people died in 1944 as the result of accidents and another million were injured, many of whom were permanently crippled. While not the highest among all occupations, a rate of fifty-four deaths by accidents per one hundred thousand agricultural workers in 1943 is more than double the rate of twenty deaths for the same number of workers in manufacturing industries. Farm machinery was involved with most of the fatal accidents; therefore, with the advance of technology on the farm must come changes in habits and attitudes.

Many factors involved in rural health situations. First of all, it must be borne in mind that unless otherwise specified, the census vital statistics include as rural the open country and all incorporated places up to 10,000 population. This means not only open country and villages, but towns as herein defined. Special tabulations indicate that, in 1940, death rates at every age level — in fact, preschool, youth, middle and old age — were highest in towns; that is, incor-

6 Coe, M., "Farm Safety Work," *Better Farming Methods,* p. 24, May-June, 1945.

porated places between 2500 and 10,000.[7] Places of this size are often more disadvantaged in matters of health protection than is the open country or the small village.

A second qualification is that in some states, when mortality and morbidity rates are reclassified according to residence of the deceased instead of place of death, the rural and urban differences are reversed. For example, the general mortality rate for Wisconsin in 1933 was higher for urban than for rural areas, but when the deaths were allocated according to residence the rural rates were higher than the urban.[8] This accounting by residence increased the urban rate for tuberculosis, however, since many sanatoria are located in country areas.

Similarly, in New York and Ohio Dorn found that, when deaths were allocated to usual places of residence and were standardized for differences in age, the rural mortality rates were lower than the urban.[9] By the same method it was determined that certain sickness rates were higher for villages and towns of less than five thousand population than for the open country. Infant mortality rates were decreasing less rapidly in the rural than in urban areas, while life expectancy increased more for the urban than the rural populations. All of these comparisons seem to indicate clearly enough that the relative advantage lies with the cities by virtue of their better organization of health facilities and services, a greater relative proportion of professional servants, and greater attention to protective and sanitary measures.

This general reversal of health trends to the advantage of urban areas can be accounted for, at least in part, by three major factors, namely, geographic factors and population density, ability to pay, and differences in attitudes and traditions.

Some geographic handicaps in rural society. Living in rural areas is not in itself, good health insurance. With the improvements in transportation and the freer movements of people have also come certain risks to health. Even oceans are not effective barriers today against infectious diseases, such as diphtheria and malaria. Scattered country populations or clustered small village groups are confronted with problems involving adequate sanitation and public

[7] *Medical Care and Health Services for Rural People.* Farm Foundation, 600 South Michigan Avenue, Chicago 5, April, 1944.

[8] Hutchcroft, L. W., "The Truth About Rural and Urban Death Rates." Madison: *Wisconsin State Board of Health Bulletin,* vol. 5, no. 19, 1934.

[9] Dorn, Harold F., "The Relative Amount of Ill-Health in Rural and Urban Communities." Washington, D.C.: *United States Public Health Service, Public Health Reports,* vol. 53, 1938.

health services. They must overcome the distance factor by paying more for medical services; this they are frequently not able to do. It means, as the next section of the chapter will show, that, relative to population, rural areas are low in number of doctors, dentists, nurses, hospitals, and clinics. Even a warm climate and soil type may constitute handicaps to good health. In Southern rural sections is found an environment favorable to the spread of malaria and a kind of sandy soil which makes it easy to transmit hookworm diseases.

Ability to pay. It is a paradox, a vicious circle, or whatever metaphor is preferred, that receipt of medical care should be correlated with income rather than with need. Whatever comparative methods are used, it is always evident that, as the income groups go up, the percentage of families goes down. The opposite is true for the amount spent for medical care; it rises directly as income advances. Obviously, the differences do not turn upon the relative degree of illness, but when people have more money they spend more for medical care. This was evident in the budgets of the Farm Security Administration clients reviewed in the chapter on rural standards of living. It is clear in the accompanying chart (Figure 39) and it holds for farm families, village families, and city families.

Table 89, giving the comparisons of incomes and expenditures for medical care for 33,500,000 families in the United States, indicates that, even in the relatively prosperous year of 1942, at least 70 per cent of the families had incomes of $3000 or less. The average

TABLE 89. INCOME AND MEDICAL EXPENDITURES OF 33,500,000
FAMILY UNITS, 1942 *

Aggregate Money Income During 1942	Families in Each Group		Average Spent for Medical Care †	
	Number	Per cent	Per Family	Per cent
Total...........................	33,400,000	100	$100	3.6
Less than $1,000.................	6,900,000	21	42	6.8
$1,000 to $2,000.................	9,800,000	29	68	4.5
$2,000 to $3,000.................	6,800,000	20	96	3.9
$3,000 to $5,000.................	6,700,000	20	143	3.7
More than $5,000.................	3,200,000	10	241	2.4

* Based on data from *Civilian Spending and Saving 1941 and 1942*. Washington, D.C.: Division of Research Consumer Income and Demand Branch, Office of Price Administration, March, 1943.
† Includes medical, hospital, surgical, dental, and nursing service.

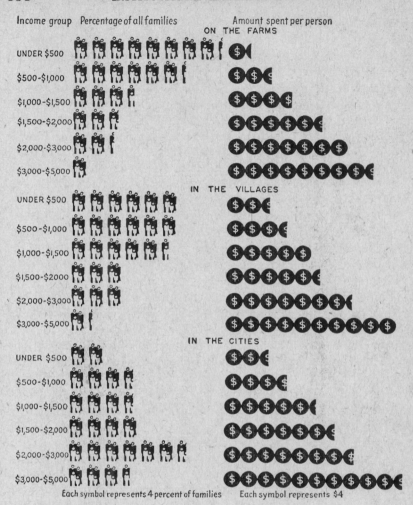

Figure 39

WHAT FAMILIES SPEND FOR MEDICAL CARE

Source: *Farm Foundation Conference on Rural Health*, April, 1944.

family expenditure for medical care was estimated at $100, but families with incomes under $3000 spent considerably less; the low-income families spent a larger proportion of their income for medical care than did the higher-income families. For farm families the average expenditure was probably nearer to $60 a year.

The joker in the health card-pack is, of course, that medical expenses are relatively unpredictable. In any one year there are comparatively few families that have large doctor or hospital bills. In an average year about 68 per cent of all rural families, for example, pay only about 23 per cent of the total medical care expenditures of all rural people. But the difficulty arises from the fact that the lower-income groups have to spend a high percentage of their meager incomes in order to pay such bills, and even then they have to be satisfied with less than adequate care. This is probably true, not simply because their incomes are so low, but because they actually have a greater amount of illness than those families in the higher-income brackets. It is likewise in these families where the relatively larger number of children is to be found. Both of these relationships have been indicated earlier.

To be sure, modern medical care costs money, but there are many health authorities who can show that, if the amount of money already being spent was spent more wisely, the whole situation could be greatly improved. Likewise, if the costs could be spread over more years and among more people, the burden upon any one family would not be too great. This idea will be expanded in the next section, but it is a principle which rural people have long since applied to another unforetellable menace — fires.

Some psychological handicaps among rural people. Finally, it is evident to those acquainted with the health situation among rural people that the factors of attitudes and understanding are involved. Some of the health deficiencies and some of the lack of good medical care arise from a lack of understanding, failure to recognize early symptoms of trouble, to realize the serious consequences of some kinds of illnesses, and to respond to modern facilities available. The facilities may lie a little beyond the accustomed route of travel, as the hospital or clinic in the not-too-far-away urban center. Or it may be public opinion is too little developed to give the county board courage to hire the second nurse, or the full-time, specially trained public health officer, or a sanitary engineer.

Attitudes and traditions must also come in for their share of scrutiny. They are a part of the culture pattern and the system of values which traditionally belong to a people. But it is a mistaken idea to think that they are static or unchangeable. There are some farm people, and village and city people as well, who simply "do not like" doctors, dentists, or hospitals. In some rural communities it is tantamount to a confession of weakness to be seen coming from a doctor's office. Hospitals are places where people "go to die." You can imagine the reply of the frontiersman to the suggestion that he go to a hospital — "Not me. I'll take mine at home and die with my boots on." Modification in reactions comes with experience, actual and vicarious, as via education, and frequently the changes come quickly. It is a game of choice, as suggested in the chapter on standards of living. People set about getting what they want, what they value highly, and what they have seen others have. The attitude may soon prevail in rural quarters that you "cannot afford" to be without good medical care.

It should scarcely be necessary to call attention again to the interaction between health and income. The circle can be vicious and closed, or it can be spiral and leading up and out. Doctor Will Alexander, the first administrator of the F.S.A., remarked in its early days that "it was just plain good business to get rid of the hookworm"; therefore, there was a regular item for health in family budgets; families that did not have to feed the hookworm could and did pay their principal and interest, and on time.

The situation respecting rural health was summarized by a group called together recently to disuss medical care and health services for rural people, in terms of three lacks: (1) lack of adequate health education, facilities, and doctors; (2) lack of financial resources and interest to establish or maintain the necessary medical centers properly equipped and adequately staffed; and (3) lack of sufficient income to afford even the necessary medical services when they are available.[10]

PLANKS IN A RURAL HEALTH PLATFORM

The principle upon which those who are in the van of the rural health movement agree is that health is not only an individual and family concern, but also a social responsibility, and that medical care in the broad sense must be made available to all of the people regardless of economic status, race, or geography. This they maintain is the only way by which people can be efficient and happy. Three general measures or planks are essential for such a program or platform: first, protection and prevention; second, facilities and services; third, spreading costs. Such an outline is oversimplified, and there are many details and other considerations which cannot be included here, but it will serve the purpose of the present discussion.

Improved preventive services needed. The health situation as described is far from hopeless. Great advances have been made in

[10] *Medical Care and Health Services for Rural People,* Farm Foundation, 600 South Michigan Avenue, Chicago 5, April, 1944.

forty years of this century. The general death rate per one thousand population has been cut from 17.2 to 10.8, a reduction of nearly 60 per cent. Infant death rates have been reduced 65 per cent since 1922. Greatest improvements have come in those diseases which respond to better sanitation and immunization procedures. The examples are the reduction in death rates from typhoid and paratyphoid fever by 97 per cent, from diarrhea and enteritis by 92 per cent, and from diphtheria by 97 per cent. These are great gains, and much credit goes to the many agencies concerned with medical care and public health. However, the total of 4,500,000 young men in the 4F classification is a mighty challenge as to what still remains to be done, especially since officials of the Selective Service System report that at least one sixth of the defects for which the men were rejected could be remedied with relative ease.

Preventive measures are developed and distributed very unevenly with respect to classes and location of families. In rural areas the United States Public Health Service points out that 5000 communities need new water systems, 6500 need new water extensions or improvements. New sewage systems are needed in 7700 communities with a population of over 25,000,000 people who do not have any form of sewage treatment. It is only more evidence of the situation in villages and small towns, in many ways the "forgotten people," too small for urban measures and too different for the various organized agricultural services to consider them.

Rural homes are in great need of improvement. About 5,250,000 need new or improved water supplies, 5,000,000 need sanitary toilet facilities. The United States Health Service reports that pasteurization plants for milk are needed in more than 400 small communities, and they serve an aggregate population of more than 1,500,000 people. Here, then, is a great field for postwar activities, projects which should give real impetus to industry and opportunities for employment, chances to "plow back" into better standards of living those public and private resources which have accumulated during the war years.

Expansion of public health services required. Early diagnosis of trouble and prompt remedy are primary factors in protection of health and in prevention of illness. It is now generally recognized that effective services of this nature must be organized on a public plan. While public health agencies of federal, state, and local governments have expanded greatly in recent years, yet, as recently as 1935, only 615 of the more than three thousand counties had full-time public health agencies. Under the encouragement and assistance of the Social Security Act, the number of counties served by such agencies had nearly tripled by 1942. Nevertheless, 40 per cent of the counties were still without a full-time local public health officer.

The map (Figure 40) shows the counties with a full-time health officer in June, 1942. It is gratifying, indeed, to note the rather complete coverage in those areas of the South where many disease and death rates, noted earlier, were relatively high. Although there is no standardized organization, the average county unit has a health officer, a sanitary inspector, one or more nurses, and a bacteriologist — all under the direction of a trained physician. Organization, of course, is not the only consideration; administration and trained personnel are fully as important. To improve sanitary conditions, it is necessary to have inspections; to detect diseases and their effects at their incipient stages, frequent health examinations are needed; and to secure co-operation from people themselves, continuous health education is essential.

According to representatives of the American Public Health Association, a good health department should have one public health nurse for each 5000 people, a sanitary officer for each 25,000 people, a trained public health engineer for a unit of 50,000, a veterinarian for every 100,000 population. The smallest operating unit which health authorities advocate is made up of a full-time health officer, a nurse, sanitarian, and office clerk. The Association advocates that counties too small to meet such requirements combine with other counties and with the towns in them to compose a district of at least 50,000 people.

Delegates of the farm organizations to the Conference on Medical Care and Health Service, to which reference has been made, pointed out that a program in rural areas should include both the prevention and the care of disease, rather than one limited either to preventive work only or to treatment of illness only.

Many state boards of health, working with a committee of the National Public Health and Medical Associations, are urging legislation whereby their states can be redistricted into smaller units, and given more trained personnel. They contend that this is necessary in order to secure more effective discovery of disease, better reporting, and improved sanitation. Federal funds are available to help, but the states must participate. In order for rural people in local communities to gain benefits from such "overhead" organization, they must work out their own plans, programs, and staff, as will be pointed out in the last section of the chapter.

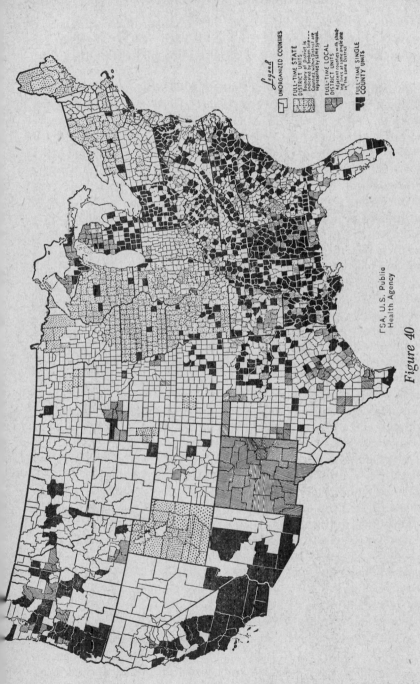

FSA, U.S. Public
Health Agency

Figure 40

COUNTIES WITH THE SERVICE OF A FULL-TIME HEALTH OFFICER, JUNE 30, 1942

Health education and more education, in school and out of school. It is recognized that rural people must become aware of the medical facilities and health services that are now available. This should lead to a greater and better utilization of them. Rural people need to be stimulated to recognize the values of good health and the importance of preventive measures and adequate medical services. Finally, they must be more willing to budget in advance and then to pay more for health purposes. This simply means a continuous course of education. There are many practical means which can be employed. A primary responsibility lies with the public health service and with the school system. Health authorities say that a local expenditure of one dollar per person is the minimum to spend on education directed toward the protection of health and the prevention of illness. When a local community is willing to spend its own money, it is in a position to ask for help from state and federal sources.

An Agricultural Health Association, in its report on Newton County, Mississippi, urges that more money be spent for educational work, and that Negro leaders should be commissioned to carry information especially regarding the preventive aspects of rural health programs to the Negro population of the county, and that when a second nurse is employed, she should be a colored person.[11]

Health programs in the schools need to include, not only medical examinations and immunization, but in many situations hot lunches and actual medical and dental services. The directly educational phases need to be related to nutrition, the biological and social sciences, and to a constructive recreational activity program in the school and in the community.

Private and voluntary agencies have a wide scope for activity in the field of health. There are notable private agencies working in rural areas — Visiting Nurses' Associations, National Tuberculosis Associations, American Social Hygiene Associations, the American Red Cross. Farm organizations have health programs, and some sponsor sickness-indemnity plans covering both sickness and accidents. Then there are the many local organizations and clubs which could do much more than they now do. They could extend their health discussion programs, their demonstrations, courses in first aid, campaigns for fire and accident prevention.

[11] Montgomery, James E., *Newton County, Mississippi, Agricultural Health Association*. Washington, D.C.: United States Department of Agriculture, August, 1944.

More medical people — doctors, dentists, nurses. In the second plank of the rural health platform, the medical services of doctors, dentists, and nurses hold central position. Everyone is conscious of the fact that there are not enough of them in rural areas. The wartime shortages, however, were only exaggerated symptoms of a long-standing maldistribution. Strictly rural counties in 1938 had only one third as many physicians in proportion to population as did urban counties. Recent reports by the Procurement and Assignment Service show that the 81 counties reporting no active physician, and the 141 counties with more than 5000 people per active physician, were practically all rural counties. This disparity in distribution is associated with a number of related circumstances. One of these is the changing in age of doctors in rural areas and the relation it bears to their mobility toward urban centers.

Not only were there fewer doctors in rural areas in 1930 than in 1920, but those who remained were older than city physicians and older, on the average, than rural doctors in 1920. In the four states, the average age was progressively lower as the population of the center increased. In New York, for example, doctors in the country and in small villages averaged ten years older, and those in medium and large villages more than eight years older, than the physicians in cities of over 100,000. In Iowa the differences were from four to ten years, and in Washington state, from two to six years. In other states, for most types of communities the average age of physicians increased, but the rural increase was always greater than the urban.

From 1930 to the outbreak of World War II, there were evidences in some regions of a reversal of previous trends. The dean of the College of Medicine at Syracuse, New York, who has been studying the location of graduates of the medical colleges for the past twenty years, reports a movement of young graduates to rural areas. He found about 25 per cent of the 1930 graduates located in communities of less than 5000, as compared with 18 per cent of the 1925 graduates so located in 1931. It may be reasonable to suppose that recent graduates, finding less practice among the unemployed in the cities, tried to establish themselves among a rural clientèle. In Michigan the 1910 to 1920 trend of physicians moving into the city of Detroit was reversed some time between 1920 and 1930, but seemed to reach a high point in the period 1929 to 1931. In this study a higher ratio of physicians was found for places under 2500 than for the larger communities.[12]

[12] Sinai, Nathan, *Report of the Committee on Medical Services and Health Agencies.* Lansing: Michigan State Medical Society, 1933.

In the restudy of agricultural village communities, an increase of 7 per cent was found in the number of physicians between 1930 and 1936. The distribution of the doctors varied somewhat according to the size of the villages, but even in the smaller ones the number held at least to the 1930 levels.

The changing situation is shown graphically for the nation as a whole, in the chart (Figure 41). The comparisons in the chart are between the years 1923 and 1938 and the general aging of physicians is evident in both years. Although in 1923 the majority even in rural areas were within the age group thirty to thirty-five, by 1938 there were only two major groups: one, the young physicians twenty-five to thirty-five years, and the other, the older men, fifty-five to seventy or over. The older men are not able to perform the additional work needed and, furthermore, they are dying more rapidly than they are being replaced by younger doctors. The United States Public Health Service estimates that following January, 1944, there will be a net annual loss of about 2100 physicians.

A second factor is the purchasing power of communities. Again, in 1938, counties with a per capita income of more than six hundred dollars had eight times as great a proportion of doctors to population as did counties with per capita income of less than one hundred dollars. Another associated factor certainly is the lack of hospital, diagnostic, and laboratory facilities in rural areas. Hospitals, independent of wealth or size of community, seem to attract doctors. This is suggested by the results of a study by the United States Public Health Service which indicates that among counties with per capita incomes of less than three hundred dollars, those with no hospital beds had 60 per cent fewer doctors in proportion to population than did those counties with two hundred and fifty or more general hospital beds. The hospital, it has been pointed out, is a sort of symbol of health in the community just as the school is the symbol of education.[13]

Numerous local and state studies bear out the general trends just reviewed. In North Carolina, for example, the number of doctors in the strictly rural area fell from 1125 in 1914, to 719 in 1940. In the latter year, 73 per cent of the population lived in rural territory, although only 31 per cent of the state's physicians were found there.[14]

[13] *Medical Care and Health Services for Rural People*, Farm Foundation, 600 South Michigan Avenue, Chicago, April, 1944. (Elin Anderson, p. 213.)

[14] *Medical Care and Hospital Facilities for Rural People in North Carolina*, summary report and recommendations of the Committee on Hospitals and Medical Care for Rural People, submitted to the Governor's Commission on Hospitals and Medical Care, October 11, 1944.

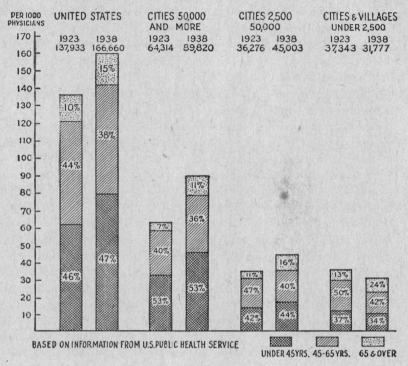

Figure 41

AGE DISTRIBUTION OF PHYSICIANS IN THE U.S. AND
OF THOSE IN LARGE CITIES, SMALL CITIES,
AND RURAL AREAS, 1923 AND 1938

A sharp increase in percentage of aging rural physicians can be
noted.

Source: *Medical Care and Health Service for Rural People,* Farm
Foundation, April, 1944.

The American Medical Association estimates that a critical level
is reached when there is one physician for every 1500 people. Below
that, health and productivity are endangered. To meet this standard
in rural communities, much hard work will be required. The odds
are already against them, since opinion polls taken among young
army and navy doctors show that the vast majority want specialists'
training and practice, and preferably with a group. Only 12.5 per
cent indicated a desire for rural practice.[15]

[15] Interim Report from the Subcommittee on *Wartime Health and Education.* 78th Congress, Subcommittee Report 3, January, 1945.

The answers to the question, "Is there a doctor in town?" will then depend upon hospital facilities, opportunity to be associated with other physicians, a chance to earn a good living and have a comfortable home.[16]

Farmers and villagers will have to revise their family expenditure budgets a good deal to bring about this condition, because it will be recalled that payments for specialists' services were nearly an absent item among both the rural farm and non-farm families.

More dentists in rural areas. Dentists have not followed the same trends as doctors. The number in villages for which special census tabulations were secured remained practically constant between 1920 and 1930. To be sure, about one seventh of the villages had no dentists, but most of such places had less than a thousand population. Between 1930 and 1936 the number of dentists in the 140 agricultural villages increased about 10 per cent, although the gain was unevenly distributed among the four geographical regions. They were also younger than the physicians by nearly a decade, averaging about forty-four years at both census periods.

There are several possible explanations for the different proportions of dentists and physicians in agricultural villages. The general public has been taught in the last decades to take better care of teeth than formerly, thus bringing increased patronage to the village dentist. On the other hand, the physician has suffered because rural people have used urban medical facilities more and more. Moreover, the average dentist needs neither the years of training nor the elaborate laboratory equipment that have become necessary for the best medical work.

The general rural situation is far below standard, however; that is, if there should be one dentist for not more than 1500 people. Most rural areas have less than a third of this ratio. Before the war there was one dentist for every 1400 persons in the cities, compared to one for every 4200 in rural areas.

Network of hospitals and medical centers. It doesn't seem to matter where you start in your thinking about better medical care, you soon find yourself at a hospital or a medical or health center. Formerly hospitals, at least in most rural areas, were considered a place of last resort for cases of very severe illness or serious accident, and all too often, as has been suggested earlier, as places in which to die. The modern conception is quite different. It calls

[16] *Is There a Doctor in Town?* Washington, D.C.: Community Health Series no. 5. Federal Security Agency, United States Health Service.

for the combining into one institution, or at least in one building or center, the three major functions of medical care — preventive, diagnostic, and therapeutic services. It means bringing together doctors and their offices, needed laboratory equipment, hospital beds for patients, and even the preventive work. It encourages group practice by physicians, surgeons, and dentists. It makes possible research and experimentation, and it stimulates the desire to exchange and to disseminate medical knowledge and better health information.

Doctors, under these circumstances, will not need to become defensive regarding the private ownership of some house which they have transformed into a hospital at their own expense and so consider it the bailiwick for only their own patients. With some of these worries removed, they can raise their sights to some of the preventive health problems of their communities. Such a change in perspective and in motive is likely to have an important effect upon the thinking of the people themselves in regard to health matters. In most cities it has been recognized for a long time that it is in the people's interests to have hospitals and health centers run by the entire community through the municipal government, or by non-profit associations, such as co-operatives, churches, fraternal or other social groups.

Hospital problems in rural areas tend to pyramid — there are not enough hospital beds, there is low occupancy, there is poor quality in hospital service. There is not complete agreement among hospital and medical authorities as to what should be considered adequate hospital service in rural areas. In recent discussions a standard of 3.5 or four general beds per 1000 population has been considered; fifty or more beds per that population unit may be required in cities. Most rural areas do not have even two beds for each 1000 people, and there are hundreds of rural communities with no hospitals at all. There are 450 counties in which there are only proprietary hospitals — that is, operated for profit — and in these same counties there were only 1.5 beds per 1000 population. Another disturbing factor is that many hospitals in rural communities are not fully occupied. This brings up the costs per unit or reduces the amount and quality of services. It is estimated that beds should have at least an 80 to 85 per cent occupancy. Reasons for these conditions are not simple; attitudes to which references have been made are involved, also costs, distances, and incomes.

Then there is the quality of hospital service. In 1944 it was reported that the American Medical Association had registered 6655 hospitals. Of the 3300 hospitals not registered, the vast majority were in small towns or rural areas. The American College of Surgeons also has an approval program. Its representatives will not even consider a hospital of fewer than twenty-five beds; experience has shown that it is not worth while to do so. In Ohio only one in six small hospitals of less than fifty beds was able to meet the minimum requirements of this agency.[17]

General agreement as to minimum size for a hospital seems to be changing from thirty to fifty beds. If the upper standard of four beds per 1000 rural people is assumed, then a population of 12,500 would be required for a fifty-bed hospital, obviously beyond the range of possibility for many rural communities, especially when it is considered that at least $250,000 would be needed to build and properly equip it.

This line of argument is not only oversimplified, but it assumes an unsound premise. Not every community can expect to be self-sufficient and supply all the social institutions and services needed by its citizens. The trends traced in other chapters are in the other direction, the direction of some specialization and of greater inter-dependence of communities, rural with rural and rural with urban as well. Then, as with education, health is not the sole responsibility of local communities and local units of government. The principle of equalization has come to be recognized; its application to health programs for rural society offers an opportunity to postwar planners.

Doctors, dollars, beds, and patients. To this point we have drawn together at least four elements in the second plank of facilities and services in a rural health program — doctors, dollars, beds, and patients. Each must be considered in its special relationship. Patients, for example, are still people, and people are persons in families, and citizens, not only of local communities, but of county, state, and nation. All of which should give point to the proposals by the Surgeon General of the United States Public Health Service, to plans being considered by rural health committees in a number of states, and to the recent recommendations of the subcommittee on Wartime Health and Education to the Committees on Education and Labor, United States Senate.

The network of facilities which the Surgeon General advocates includes four basic types of medical centers: a community health center, a local rural hospital, a district hospital, and a base hospital.

[17] Mangus, A. R., *Hospitals for Rural People in Ohio*. Columbus: Ohio State University and •Ohio Agricultural Experiment Station, Mimeograph Bulletin 184, February, 1945.

The plan does not assume all new construction, since many of the types already exist in many areas. It does mean a better organization and a closer co-ordination of all available facilities, and the building of new units as required. In some instances it could be done with alterations, additions, or adjustments to the larger plan.

The community health center might include offices for local physicians and dentists, facilities for emergency medical and surgical work, a few beds for obstetrical care, some laboratory facilities for X-ray, blood and bacteria tests, offices for the health department, and quarters for clinics as needed.

The rural hospital might be so located as to be accessible to several local health centers, and in places large enough to warrant larger construction so as to provide additional medical, surgical, obstetrical, and laboratory services. The district hospitals, in turn, might be related to a number of the smaller hospitals so that increased specialization in both medical facilities and personnel could be available. Specialists might visit the small hospitals on occasion or be ready when patients were brought in. Instruction for internes and facilities for group work of various kinds could be provided in the district center.

The base hospital would be the central unit or hub of the whole system. Its service area might include a whole state, two states, or a section of one large state. The base hospital would be the teaching hospital, staffed with medical and surgical specialists, equipped for complete diagnostic services and designed to carry on extensive post-graduate work and important research. Studies would include tuberculosis, nervous and mental diseases, contagious diseases, and orthopedic and chronic diseases. Supplementary facilities of various kinds could be devised. For sparsely settled areas of low income capacity, there must be mobile clinics staffed by a physician and nurse or a dentist and technician. They could undertake services and instruction in maternal and child care, in mental hygiene or immunization programs. Salaries and equipment could come from public funds or by a group prepayment plan or a combination of both. Ambulance service could also be arranged from out-district clinics to local or regional hospitals. Experiences of the battlefields, with motor equipment, including planes, should prove valuable here.

Such a network of medical centers would constitute a great ideal toward which to work in the postwar days. It would help communities to deal with the problems of their own returning veterans. It would create employment opportunities for very many of the

50,000 medical and dental men who will be returning from duties with the armed forces. It can be the master plan for such new construction as will be required, and for the replacement of those units now obsolete. Estimates by the United States Public Health Service claim that 100,000 new general hospital beds, 94,000 new beds for nervous and mental cases, and 44,000 new beds for tuberculosis patients are needed. In addition to replacements, 2400 modern structures are needed as headquarters for local health departments. Such a plan can include both private and public enterprises and become the basis for state and federal grants-in-aid, wherever such are necessary. Careful administration will have to be devised. The focus must be in the local community upon the needs of its people.

The Interim Health Report, to which reference has been made, recommends federal grants and loans as well as principles for organization so that such plans can be carried into effect. It urges that state and local governments establish full-time local public health units. It suggests that the army consider the possibility of expanding its rehabilitation program to those men rejected for military service because of physical and mental defects. It calls for increased medical personnel trained in psychology and psychiatry with the view to providing child guidance and mental hygiene clinics on a far wider scale.

Spreading costs is the third plank. Evidence has been accumulating which points to the conclusion that something will have to be done to bring about better health conditions in both rural and urban areas. Low incomes are highly correlated with the greatest needs for medical care, as has been shown repeatedly. Variations in health conditions and medical facilities are very great. A child's chances for living and being healthy depend very much upon where he chooses to be born. Traditional systems of trying to "pay as you go" and with the fee-for-service principle are simply not fitted for the present situation. Ways and means must be devised to meet the needs of most people, and to equalize the distribution of costs of high-quality medical care. Such plans should encourage rather than deter people in seeking help early. They should be so arranged that the unexpected illness or accident does not wipe out a family's entire savings or mortgage its future; yet doctor bills and hospital bills must not be allowed to pile up. They must be paid currently so that both doctor and hospital can carry on.

Distributing the burden over long periods of time. One application of the principle of spreading the costs of medical care is to distribute them over long periods of time, starting to pay before the bill appears. Health insurance and group prepayment plans for hospital, medical, and dental care have developed rapidly as one way of accomplishing this objective. Farmers and villagers are beginning to try in matters of health the insurance principle they long ago accepted in regard to fire risks. Groups are organized on a voluntary basis with primary control in the hands of the people as members. Prepayment plans for hospital services have become popular in the United States and memberships have greatly increased.

Equalizing responsibility among a large number of people. A second application of the spread-the-cost idea is to involve more people; whether all the people by compulsory contributions is still a matter for wide difference of opinion. The pro argument runs that, since good health is not only an individual and family responsibility, but also a general social responsibility, the burden of costs should be in keeping with this joint responsibility. The con argument holds that the voluntary element is sacrificed, the freedom of choice of physician is impaired, and government systems are clumsy and too expensive to operate.

However the arguments finally terminate, it is quite clear, from the evidence presented in this chapter, that the "public," which simply means people working together in community, county, state, or nation, must expect in the future to assume a larger proportion of the costs of rearing children and keeping them healthy. The question naturally arises, how much the different levels of government should contribute and how the plans shall be administered. The wide differences observed in the economic and social situations of families and the high mobility of some families can be offset only by some manner of sharing responsibilities. Only in this way will it be possible for every child to be "well born" and guaranteed an equal chance to health. The principle is accepted in many other nations, as will be shown directly.

Voluntary versus compulsory plans. The crux of the argument is largely the voluntary versus the compulsory features of the various systems. In the end it will probably not be an either-or proposition, but some combination of several procedures. Advocates of voluntary health insurance, such as the Blue Cross hospitalization plans and medical society prepayment plans, contend that such systems will be adequate if given time in which to extend them, and if supplemented by tax grants for medical care to those who receive public assistance. Others believe that only a small percentage of the people, and perhaps those needing it least, will ever obtain complete medical care through voluntary prepayment plans. They point out that, particularly in rural situations, to include only the low-income families will never bring about better medical care for whole communities. They urge compulsory health insurance along some such lines as are proposed in the Wagner-Murray-Dingell Bill. The latest version of this bill (S. 1606, 79th Congress) provides for state grants, over a ten-year period, for hospital construction; for public health services, for maternal and child health services, and for unemployment compensation and temporary disability insurance. Senator Wagner says the bill provides for using existing group health organizations, and that such groups would be as free as they are today to select their own staffs and to follow their own methods of paying physicians.

Still others maintain that the health situation of the whole country can be met most satisfactorily and economically through a universal system of tax-supported medicine. Some other countries have certain forms of such a plan in force.

Examples of group financing schemes. There are already many different kinds of schemes in use for financing medical care; some are voluntary, some are compulsory.

(1) *Farm Security Administration medical care program.* The plan is the outgrowth of the general rehabilitation efforts of the agency. It is based on the voluntary prepayment principle. The rates paid have been based on the average ability of its borrowers in any area to pay, with very little use of subsidy. Plans, with few exceptions, have been worked out in co-operation with local medical societies on the basis of agreements with state medical associations. There is a wide variety of such plans, especially as to detail of operation.[18]

(2) *Sandhills Region Health Association, Thedford, Nebraska.* The Association has a voluntary medical care prepayment plan. It allows members to have the services of the physician in their own home at a mileage rate, which is lower to members than to non-members, and the fee is less. The organization is also interested in preventive practices. Since it is in a sparsely settled region, the nearest hospital is sixty miles away; therefore, interest is growing in plans for a hospital. The physician is employed by the Association and receives a base salary and money for travel plus a percentage of the fees for surgery and fracture work.

(3) *Co-operative Health Association, Taos County, New Mexico.* Taos is one of the oldest settlements in New Mexico and therefore

[18] *Group Medical Care for Farmers.* Washington, D.C.: Farm Security Administration Publication 75, 1941.

of the United States. Spanish settlers came as early as 1615, and a rather large segment of the population is still what is referred to as Spanish-American. The health association was organized with the help of the University, the Farm Security Administration, and the local doctors. The plan provides for three health centers, each to have a resident graduate nurse, and one ambulance. It also provides for a medical staff on a salary basis, of one full-time medical director, two full-time physicians, two part-time surgeons, and a dentist. The hospitals and the druggists of the area participate by contract, and there is provision for co-ordination with public health and public welfare departments.[19]

(4) *Farmers' Union Hospital Association, Elk City, Oklahoma.* One of the pioneer and better-known co-operative hospitals in rural areas is operated by the above named association. The doctors are on salary, and practice as a group. Families pay a flat rate, with extras for each member beyond four, and there are extra charges for home calls, surgery, and maternity services. The high construction cost of the hospital building prevents this plan from becoming a general one for rural families. It requires a larger population base.

(5) *Michigan Medical Service plan.* This organization has an enrollment of 600,000 in Michigan, the largest in the United States. There is also a hospital service which is the second largest Blue Cross plan in the nation, with about 1,200,000 people. These plans started out to offer comprehensive hospital and medical services. Numerous modifications and adaptations have been made, the comprehensive medical-care portion was finally abandoned, and at present it includes all expenses connected with hospitalized illness.

(6) *Blue Cross plans.* These are non-profit hospital service organizations for the prepayment of hospital bills. There are seventy-seven of them in the United States, and in 1945 the eighteen millionth man signed his membership card. Most of the subscribers are in urban centers. A chief problem in providing this kind of insurance to farm, village, and small-town people is the development of some system for the periodic collection of premiums. In some states the Farm Bureaus and the co-operatives have taken over responsibilities for promotion and collection.[20]

[19] Longmore, T. Wilson, and Theo. L. Vaughan, *Taos County Co-operative Health Association,* 1942-43, United States Department of Agriculture, Washington, D.C.; and Bureau of Agricultural Economics, Little Rock, Arkansas, November, 1944; Loomis, Charles P., *Putting Over a Co-operative Health Association to Spanish-Speaking Villagers, or the Organization of the Taos County Co-operative Health Association.* Washington, D.C.: Extension Service and Office of Foreign Agricultural Relations, Co-operating, September, 1944.

[20] Pink, Louis H., *The Story of Blue Cross,* Public Affairs Pamphlet 101, 1945. 30 Rockefeller Plaza, New York 20.

(7) *American Dental Association plans.* A council on dental health has recently been appointed by the national association to study various plans and to establish prepayment dental plans.

(8) *American Medical Association.* This association has consistently opposed any form of compulsory insurance, or, in fact, any plan which is not controlled by the medical profession. Many local medical societies have helped to organize a variety of schemes for the payment of medical bills.

(9) *Ten-point measuring-stick.* At the conference concerned with medical care for rural people, sponsored by the Farm Foundation to which reference has been made, Doctor Michael Davis, of the Committee on Research in Medical Economics, suggested a ten-point test by which to measure the effectiveness of any scheme.

1. *Coverage:* how large a proportion of the people needing the service offered does the plan include?

2. *Freedom:* does the plan retain freedom on the part of people to go to the physician or hospital they choose, and does it give the physicians freedom to exercise professional responsibilities?

3. *Unity:* does the plan unify people within the area served or is it divisive?

4. *Area:* does the plan provide for an area large enough in population and finances to support the needed services?

5. *Responsibility:* does it provide substantial local responsibility for the people in the area served?

6. *Physicians:* will it bring physicians, particularly young doctors, into rural areas?

7. *Prevention:* does it contain or help with the prevention services?

8. *Costs:* does it pay for services in ways to ease burdens of sickness costs?

9. *Pay:* how does the plan pay doctors?

10. *Quality:* does it maintain and advance the quality of medical care?

LOCAL COMMUNITY AND COUNTY RESPONSIBILITY

All the plans made in committees or in capitols must finally meet the test of functioning in local community situations and of being freely participated in by living people. This may be self-evident, but many otherwise worthy plans fail at this very point. Unless there is a local plan and responsibility assumed, full advantage cannot be taken by the people of those services and institutions organized on county, state, or national levels. This seems particularly true of public health services and agencies. The nurse, who personifies these services to many rural people, needs to have a familiar and working relationship with school, club, and church in the local community. The director of a large state "base" hospital is continually saying that the chief limitation to rural people in utilizing the services offered by this institution are their own local facilities for correct diagnosis, preliminary care, and prompt delivery of needy cases. Many unnecessary cases arrive. They could have been cared for somewhere along the way had there been the network of agencies available which the Surgeon General has outlined.

Small community hospital, symbol of good health. By way of summary, it can very well be that the small hospital can form the base for the needed health emphasis in modern rural society. It can be the social institution, even the building where plans and personnel are drawn together and given meaning. It offers an excellent setting in which lay leaders and professional leaders of the community may meet. This can come about because a division of labor is easily recognized. A lay board made up of representatives of the public should be concerned with the coverage and quality of the service, and be responsible for building up confidence and understanding in the community. On the professional side there is the organization of the doctors in a hospital staff. Every physician in the community should be eligible for staff membership if he is willing to accept the stated procedures of what the staff considers good medical practice. This affords the group opportunity which will be needed to attract young trained men.

With good organization and local initiative and responsibility many services can be brought together and co-ordinated into a community plan of work. These may well include special efforts in preventive work, health education, child care, and mental hygiene. As suggested earlier, not every small rural community can have a hospital of about fifty beds serving an area ranging from twenty to thirty miles. But small centers can have health clinics such as have been described. Several small centers together with their constituents can form the larger community unit.

Consider also the whole man. Finally, with a total local health program centered in the community hospital, it should be possible to minister to the needs of the total person. It has been all too easy to divide with the advance of specialization, but this does not need to be its consequence. Life can be recognized as whole and treated as such. There is an increasing recognition of the interaction of such phases of life as the physical, the psychological, the nutritional, and the social. The social is represented by a sense of security and of personal importance. Even these divisions may be misnomers which can easily lead away from, rather than toward a unitary point of view. It is commonplace that physicians are paying more and more attention to personality diagnosis and treatment, as well as to the physical phases. This is sometimes called psychosomatic (mind and body) medicine. Other expressions finding their way into popular health literature are psychotherapy, group therapy, psychodrama, socio-drama, rôle-taking, personality-culture balance, and many others. These explorations should mean much to the future of rural health, especially for wholesome childhood.

As further evidence of this changing emphasis in the health world, one needs only to enumerate titles of books as set forth in a recent folder by the Commonwealth Fund, an organization long interested in the experimental approaches to health and hospital services, and to medical care. They are: *Patients Have Families, The Patient as a Person, Juvenile Delinquents Grow Up, Mental Health in College, The War and Mental Health in England, Foundations for a Science of Personality, Psychiatric Social Work, Mental Illness, A Guide for the Family, An Introduction to Group Therapy, The Doctor and the Difficult Child.*

Doctor Plant, in his *Personality and the Cultural Pattern,* is leading the way in this reinterpretation of life. He suggests that the moment we begin to ask "Who and what is this person who learns, this one who asks charity, this other one who is delinquent or sick?" we are started on a quest which stretches far.[21]

May not this point of view be the one about which Walt Whitman was thinking when he wrote of the child:

There was a child went forth every day,
And the first object he looked up and received with wonder, pity,
    love, or dread, that object he became,
And that object became part of him for the day, or a certain part
    of the day, or for many years, or stretching cycles of years. . . .[22]

[21] Plant, James S., M.D. (Director, Essex County Juvenile Clinic), *Personality and the Cultural Pattern.* New York: The Commonwealth Fund, 1937.
[22] Whitman, Walt, "There Was a Child Went Forth," *Leaves of Grass.* Boston: Thayer & Eldridge, 1860-1861. (Doubleday Doran, copyright, 1926.)

HEALTH ON THE MARCH IN OTHER COUNTRIES

Twenty-four countries had systems of compulsory health insurance for all or some of their workers by 1937. Such systems were established in Germany, Austria, and Hungary before 1900, in Norway by 1909, and in Great Britain by 1911. Most of the plans provide for sickness benefits, maternity care, funerals, and medical care.[23]

Brief references will be made to certain plans which may be pertinent for present purposes.

(1) *The Municipal Doctor Plan, Canada.* In 1921, the Province of Saskatchewan passed legislation permitting a municipality to engage a doctor to take care of the medical needs of a community. Similar measures were enacted within five years in Manitoba, Alberta, and, in 1944, in Ontario. The doctor is hired on a salary basis and his duties are those common to a physician in a community — maternal and child care, minor surgery, and fractures. While the municipality hires the doctor, some control over the general plan is given to the health departments in each province. Before the war there were ninety-one municipalities in Saskatchewan out of a total of three hundred which had by-laws passed to supply municipal doctors. In 1944, there were one hundred and two municipalities, but only eighty-two doctors. The war had taken the medical men. In Manitoba there were twenty-one municipalities with fifteen doctors.

(2) *Canadian Federation of Agriculture presents principles.* In the period of discussion of a Draft Bill for Health Insurance, labor groups and the Farm Radio Forum groups considered the measure, and as a result made suggestions as to how the bill should be altered. The Federation proposed six principles: that the Dominion plan should be under the direction of an independent commission; that this commission should function through a similarly independent commission in each province; that the cost should be derived from the federal consolidated revenue fund; that it should include all citizens; that it should cover all services necessary to positive health, and the prevention and curing of disease — prevention being the primary purpose — and, finally, that community effort must have a place in the plan.

(3) *The Soviet Union.* The system of social insurance is comprehensive and has complete population and health coverage. The

[23] Reed, Louis S., *The Next Step in Social Security.* New York: Harper & Bros., 1937.

medical service is free and therefore available to everyone. Prevention of disease is in the foreground of the activities. It is reported that as early as 1920 more than 60 per cent of the appropriations of the Commissariat of Health was spent for the prevention of disease. All health activities are directed by central bodies, known as the People's Commissariats of Health, and the planning is done on a large scale.

> The general idea is to supervise the human being medically, in a discreet and unobtrusive way, from the moment of conception to the moment of death. Medical workers and medical institutions are placed wherever anyone, in the course of his life, is exposed to dangers. Medical supervision begins with the pregnant woman and the woman in childbirth, proceeds to the infant, the pre-school and school child, the adolescent, and finally the man and woman at work.[24]

(4) *In Great Britain.* An act was passed in 1912 for compulsory health insurance. It provides for what is generally known as "the panel system." It covers manual workers sixteen years of age and over under contract and non-manual workers earning less than two hundred and fifty dollars per year. Before the war about 18,000,000 workers were included in the plan. More comprehensive proposals are included in the Report on Social Insurance and Allied Services, drawn by Sir William H. Beveridge.

(5) *In New Zealand.* Health insurance is a part of the Social Security Act of 1939. It provides for a system of medical and hospital benefits, as well as for old age, widows', and other pensions. The benefits include services of a general practitioner, medicines, drugs, and approved appliances, hospitalization, full maternity care, and sickness benefits when a worker is unemployed because of illness.

Costs are included in a special Social Security Tax of 5 per cent on all salaries, wages, and all income, including that of companies. The general plan is fundamental to the whole social legislation history of the Dominion. It has been a pioneer in many of these social matters. For example, the public health system has been in effect since 1872, and old-age pensions have been in force since 1898, this being the first country to introduce them. It is also famous for its child welfare programs, including not only public measures, but a unique and highly successful private nursing or-

[24] Sigerist, Henry E., M.D., Professor of the History of Medicine, Johns Hopkins University, *Socialized Medicine in the Soviet Union.*

ganization, known as the Plunket Society, founded by Sir Truby King in 1907. Its aim is "to help the mothers save the babies." Its scope can be appreciated when it is realized that well over 70 per cent of the babies born come under the supervision of the Plunket nurses.

Due to these services and other constructive measures, New Zealand has long enjoyed the distinction of having the lowest infant mortality rate in the world. A new minimum rate of 29 per 1000 live births was established in 1942. In 1907 the rate was 70 per 1000 births. It will be recalled, from the table given earlier in the chapter, that the urban rate for the United States in 1940 was 42.3, and the rural rate, 50.7.

Thus we end the chapter as we began it — with the child.

DISCUSSION TOPICS

1. What do you consider the most serious health problem in your community (either rural or urban)? Present evidence from whatever health records are available to indicate the seriousness and the prevalence of this problem.
2. Select one public and one private agency, local, county, state, or national, which is working with rural health problems, and find out all you can about it. Visit local headquarters, interview officials where possible, or, if necessary, secure information by mail.
3. Organize this information in brief outline form and be prepared to present it to the class. Give particular attention to the following points:
   a. The real purpose of agency
   b. Its local forms of organization
   c. How it serves rural communities
   d. How you think such service could be improved
4. Consider one of the "group prepayment" plans described in the chapter. Discuss its workability in some rural situation with which you are well acquainted.

REFERENCE READINGS

Bureau of Human Nutrition and Home Economics, *What Farm Families Spend for Medical Care*. Washington, D.C.: United States Department of Agriculture, Miscellaneous Publication 561.

Committee on Local Health, *Local Health Units for the Nation*. The American Public Health Association, 1790 Broadway, New York 19.

Canadian Federation of Agriculture, *Health on the March*. 304 Booth Building, Ottawa, Ontario, Canada.

Davis, Graham L., "Content and Administration of a Medical Care Program," *American Journal of Public Health*, vol. 34, no. 12, December, 1944.

Department of Rural Sociology, *Medical Care Services in North Carolina*. Raleigh: North Carolina Agricultural Experiment Station, Progress Report RS-4, December, 1944, State College Station.

Duncan, O. D., "Rural Health Research," *Rural Sociology*, vol. 9, no. 1, March, 1944.

Farm Foundation, *Medical Care and Health Services for Rural People*. Farm Foundation, 600 South Michigan Avenue, Chicago.

Farm Security Administration, *Group Medical Care for Farmers*. Washington, D.C.: United States Department of Agriculture.

Guild, C. St. C., *Surveys of the Medical Facilities in Three Representative Southern Counties*. Publication of the Committee on the Costs of Medical Care, no. 23. Chicago: University of Chicago Press, 1932.

Halbert, Blanche, *Rural Community Hospitals*. Washington, D.C.: United States Department of Agriculture, 1937.

Interbureau Committee on Post-War Programs, *Better Health for Rural America*, United States Department of Agriculture, Washington, D.C., October, 1945.

Jackson, Allen J., *An Approach to a Rural Mental Health Problem*. Washington, D.C.: United States Public Health Service, 1937.

Kemp, Louise, and T. Lynn Smith, *Health and Mortality in Louisiana*. Baton Rouge: Louisiana Bulletin 390, May, 1945, Agricultural Experiment Station, Louisiana State University.

Kleinschmidt, L. S., "Better Rural Health," *Rural Sociology*, vol. 9, no. 1, March, 1944.

Levy, Hermann, *National Health Insurance*. New York: The Macmillan Co.

McNamara, Robert L., "Physicians in Rural Ohio," *Rural Sociology*, vol. 9, no. 1, March, 1944.

Mackintosh, James M., M.D., *The War and Mental Health in England*. The Commonwealth Fund, 41 East 57th Street, New York 22.

Mott, F. D., "Rural Health Parity: Federal-State Cooperation," *Land Policy Review*, Spring, 1945.

Mountin, Joseph W., Elliott H. Pennell, and Virginia Nicolay, *Location and Movement of Physicians, 1923 and 1938 General Observations*. Reprint 2403 from *Public Health Reports*, vol. 57, no. 37, September 11, 1942, pages 1363-1375.

National Farm Radio Forum, *Health Can be Planned*. Health Study Bureau, 30 Bloor Street West, Toronto 5, Ontario, Canada.

National Farm Radio Forum, *Planning for Health*. Planning for Plenty Series, no. 2. National Farm Radio Forum, 71 King Street West, Toronto, Canada, 1943.

Plant, James S., M.D., *Personality and the Cultural Pattern*. New York: The Commonwealth Fund, 1937.

Proceedings of the Second Psychotherapy Council, Chicago, January, 1944, *Psychotherapy for Children — Group Psychotherapy*. Institute for Psychoanalysis, 43 East Ohio Street, Chicago 11.

Reuss, Carl F., *Farmer Views on the Medical Situation*. V Circular 20, September, 1944. Pullman: State College of Washington, Agricultural Experiment Station.

Richardson, Henry B., M.D., *Patients Have Families*. The Commonwealth Fund, 41 East 57th Street, New York 22.

Stott, Leland H., *Personality Development in Farm, Small-Town, and City Children*. Lincoln: University of Nebraska, Agricultural Experiment Station, Research Bulletin 114, August, 1939.

Sydenstricker, Edgar, *Health and Environment*. New York: McGraw-Hill, 1933. A social trends monograph.

Treadway, Walter L., *The Place of Mental Hygiene in a Federal Health Program*. Washington, D.C.: United States Public Health Service, 1936.

Washington Committee on Post-War Program for Agriculture, *Prepaid Health Insurance for Farm Families*. Pullman: Extension Bulletin 316, October, 1944. Agricultural Extension Service, State College of Washington.

White House Conference, *White House Conference on Child Health and Protection, 1930*. New York: Century Co., 1931.

Winslow, C. E., *Health on the Farm and in the Village*. New York: The Macmillan Co., 1931.

24

Rural Welfare and Social Security

THE TRADITION is deeply graven in the social heritage of rural America that no one shall suffer distress unaided, but at the same time that no one shall be allowed to depend solely upon others without rendering some service for help received.

Mutual aid among relatives, friends, or neighbors has been the traditional way of meeting personal and family health and social hazards in rural society. It continues to be the accepted way in some areas, although modified in manner to suit changing circumstances. Established agencies, such as school, church, and social club, have also done their share, as previous chapters have shown. While such services continued during the distress which accompanied the onset of the Great Depression, there emerged a broader concept known as "social security." From the standpoint of public attention and legislation, it traces back to a report to the President made by the Committee on Economic Security and to the Social Security Act which became law in August, 1935.

The social security idea, as well as the legislation, comprehends a wide field of activity including employment assurance, unemployment insurance, old-age pensions and annuities, child welfare, public health, social insurance, and public assistance. It strikes at problems of insecurity, some of which have old and deep roots and some of which stem from more recent difficulties. It is raising issues and causing much discussion because no great scrutiny is necessary to discover that many theories about social security and public welfare are hazy, unrelated to sources of trouble, and even inconsistent with each other.

Here, then, is a relatively new phase in large-scale social organization of rural society. Many queries are involved, the answers to which are not readily apparent. To what extent should society rather than family, for example, assume responsibility for distressed and harassed individuals? Can public welfare services be devised, financed, and administered without disrupting the integrity and self-dependence of individuals and groups, and in fact, of the estab-

610

lished order? What is the basis for social legislation and group action which will reflect the will of the majority over sufficiently long periods to make them effective?

The purpose of this chapter is to explore some of the backgrounds from which social difficulties in rural society come, to trace more recent trends, and to examine briefly the social institutions and agencies, public and private, which are attempting to bring about greater social security and welfare. These are appropriate inquiries, since it has been shown elsewhere that there is an increasing interdependence of the various units in a modern society. Uncontrolled sickness, unabated indigence, and far-flung ignorance are public menaces endangering everyone. Many studies make it very evident that there is a close interrelationship among such social maladies as poverty, ill health, unemployment, lack of education, and family disorganization. These represent the seamy side of life, but they are none the less social realities which the student of rural society must face.

The crises in the decade 1930 to 1940 were so severe in both rural society and general society that actual social revolution was produced. This is the point at which our discussion may well begin. However, it must not obscure the fact that agriculture's depression actually began in the nineteen-twenties when her foreign market collapsed while her productive capacity was still greatly expanded in response to wartime demands. Neither should the erroneous conclusion be reached that a social crisis develops quickly and in a vacuum; it has deep roots, long-time causes, and arises out of complicated social situations, as the next paragraph will show. To combat the onslaught of the depression, numerous action programs were organized including farm relief, farm blocs, and the alphabetical agencies which are now household terms even in urban society, but which continue to be subjects for lively debate and political controversy.

Then Came the Great Depression

About three or three and a half million rural families turned to one or more of the relief agencies for help during the Great Depression of the early nineteen-thirties. This wholesale breakdown of self-dependency was something new in American rural life. It does not follow, however, that only those on relief were in dire straits. The mores of rural life, as suggested earlier, made rural people reluctant to seek public assistance even when their scale of living fell far below the standards regarded by them and their neighbors as "socially desirable." Many disadvantaged families struggled on, hoping against hope that the depression would lift, allowing them to get back to "normalcy." Other depressions they had heard about or had experienced themselves had done so.

A blind faith, however, on the part of rural people in the restorative powers of "natural laws" is open to question, as is also the idea that rural citizens will not accommodate themselves to receiving public help. The effects of federal relief, of social security aids, and of the A.A.A. benefit payments do not seem to point in that direction. After all, subsidy payments are not new in this country. From certain standpoints the A.A.A. might be considered an extension to farmers of the tariff arrangements favoring much of urban industry or as being comparable to shipping subsidies. This is not suggested as justification, but by way of possible explanation.

Some classes of rural people were especially distressed, such as the poor tenants and croppers of the South, the migratory and seasonal agricultural workers of the West, the many marginal families on marginal land, or the unskilled and part-time laborers in villages and small towns. Such a brief array does not explore all the disadvantaged groups, but it does give some conception of those whose severe insecurities threatened the security of rural society itself. Some distressed groups were hidden from public view; they were thinly scattered over the whole countryside; they did not form in breadlines as needy urban people often did, nor did they appear at the county agricultural agent's office for a benefit payment or at the county welfare office for a relief grant. Their difficulties, however, were very real and to overlook them even now when the cloud has lifted is to miss some of the inherent social and economic problems of our times.

Rural insecurities not new. Lest the impression be gained that insecurity is something recent, it is well to glance back for a moment to the history of rural society. From the days of the Pilgrim founders, there have been rural hazards to threaten the well-being of all. Plagues were not unknown, starvation in some communities followed such crises as the Revolutionary War and the Civil War. There have been periods of depression many times before. The records of public dependency in rural Massachusetts, for example, extending over three centuries, show that there was no year in which local communities were without relief cases. There were the widows, the orphans, and those families which were "on the town."

While previous distress periods witnessed poverty and dependency, the more recent widespread depression resulted in an un-precedented loss of self-support to families, both rural and urban. Other areas had their insecurities, described in other terms, but in those days we were confronted with more intense maladjustments than heretofore. The shock reached to practically every major social institution and to every type of human activity. The question may well be asked why this was so. In part, it was because two "ways out" which had been employed in the past by rural people, especially farm people, could no longer be used with success by some, or to a sufficient extent by others. First, as was stated earlier, the frontier was gone. The social significance of this fact is not always perceived. It meant that older farmers could not make a new start in the West when their farms in the East, Middle West, or South failed. It meant that young farmers could not find good farms easily available, or, if they did, the price was beyond their limited resources. Farmers from the drought areas who were wont to seek another chance "in the West" found the struggle too severe as the novel, *Grapes of Wrath*, so effectively reveals.

Second, the city did not offer its usual avenue of escape. Many ambitious farm and village youth had sought their fortunes in the cities in earlier years. Many, not all, had reported that they had found them there. But in the depression days, every city had its own hordes of unemployed. What opportunities were there for rural youth? There were no jobs in villages, farms were not being turned over to farm youth at the same rate as they were attaining maturity; adults were holding on. Even city youth, especially those with young families and those whose early homes had been in rural areas, sought at least shelter and food there. There was the tendency for certain age groups to accumulate from both city and country, and to pile up in villages and small towns. There was also the push of certain types of families toward the marginal farming areas.

Preparation for and the prosecution of World War II changed all this. Former recent trends have been reversed, but the question can be fairly raised whether the long-time causes of the difficulties have been removed.

Six rural problem areas. When the rural counties with highest relief loads were plotted on a map of the United States, they formed patterns which have come to be known as "problem areas." They are regions of chronic trouble where poverty has become relatively deep-rooted.[1]

[1] Beck, P. G., and M. C. Forster, *Six Rural Problem Areas: Relief, Resources, Rehabilitation.* Washington, D.C.: Research Monograph 1, Works Progress Administration, 1935.

The Appalachian-Ozark area has been cultivated for generations. It was a problem area years before the depression began. Forests had been cut, mines abandoned, and hillsides gullied by erosion. The land cannot possibly supply adequate living for the present farm population which is increasing rapidly because of high birth rates. This population is nearly all native-white. Since fertility of the land is gone and cultural isolation is great because of poor roads, the level of family and community living is very low when measured by accepted standards of medical care, housing, diet, or mortality.

The eastern and western cotton areas are regions where the fertility of the soil has likewise been depleted by persistent cultivation of a single crop. Expensive commercial fertilizers must be applied in ever-increasing amounts if life is to go on. Traditionally and geographically, the eastern and western areas are different. In the former, relief rolls were crowded with both whites and Negroes, while Mexicans add to the burden of the latter.

The Lake States cut-over area, like the Appalachian-Ozark area, lost its lumbering and mining resources. A stranded population was left, but later other families moved in to join the stranded ones. Neither group of families, however, was able to get far beyond a subsistence basis because of small farms, poor land, and a short growing season. When income from industry went out, relief came in.

The northern and southern Great Plains areas were the last two to be added to the "problem" area map. They were forced on by the droughts of 1934 and 1936. Droughts have been a constant danger here since the pioneers pushed beyond the irregular twenty-inch annual rainfall line extending from Texas to the Dakotas.[2] The two areas taken together include nearly one tenth of the land area of the nation. Large government subsidies to farmers went into these areas during the seven years of severe depression, 1931 through 1937, and some assistance continues. A recent report of a study of the twenty counties in that southern area known as the "Dust Bowl" recommends that 52 per cent of the area be turned back to Nature. Just how Mother Nature is to succor such a prodigal is not suggested.

The first three areas included 40 per cent of the rural relief cases of the whole country in October, 1933. It was found, however, that

[2] Kifer, R. S., and H. L. Stewart, *Farming Hazards in the Drought Areas.* Washington, D.C.: Research Monograph 16, Works Progress Administration, 1938.

only 46 per cent of the families on relief were usually farm operators and only 55 per cent, including the tenants, were usually engaged in agriculture. It was significant that one fifth of the heads of all households receiving relief in these problem areas were judged incapable of permanent self-dependence. A major reason was age — 14 per cent, on the average, being over sixty-five years. In the Old South, where 29 per cent were considered incapable of self-support, the proportion over sixty-five years of age rose to 20 per cent. This predominance was due to aged Negroes. With the breaking-down of the "furnishing" system, old-age relief for Negroes became a major problem.

Long-time rehabilitation plans for these areas must depend, at least to some extent, upon self-help and self-direction; therefore, education assumes a major rôle. In the Old South, for example, one half of the Negro and one fourth of the white heads of households on relief reported no schooling. In the western cotton area, 25 per cent of the Negro and 10 per cent of the white heads of families had no schooling, while 60 per cent of the Negro and 35 per cent of the white had not gone beyond the fifth grade.

Other areas had distress as intense, as was found in the six rural problem areas, but it was not so widespread.

Permanently disadvantaged classes. The catastrophe of the depression could not have descended with such violence, even in the seven years which are to be described, without some antecedents. Many of the securities, such as they were, before 1930 proved fragile indeed when the crisis came. The facts were there in the records of the United States Department of Agriculture, but the increasing human risks seem to have passed all but unnoticed. Finally attention was sharply called to the fact that even in 1929, considered a prosperous year, 1,700,000 farm families, 7,700,000 persons, lived on farms which yielded a gross farm income of less than $600 annually; nearly 1,000,000 farms, 15 per cent of the total, yielded less than $400; and nearly 3,000,000, almost 50 per cent, had gross incomes of less than $1000.[3] When there were added to these families those farm laborers and tenants with low incomes, migratory families who move each year, and another 500,000 families on land so poor that the starvation wolf could hardly be kept from the door of the shack in which they lived — then you have a total which agricultural leaders estimated as one third of all farm families — *Disadvantaged Classes in American Agriculture* — trying

[3] Bean, Louis H., and Arthur P. Chew, *Economic Trends Affecting Agriculture.* United States Department of Agriculture, 1933.

to live at levels so low as to make security for the nation and self-dependence for the families a fiction.[4]

Unprecedented droughts. "Acts of God," as they are called in the legal parlance of some insurance policies, contributed more than their due share to the depression as far as agriculture was concerned. The 1928 Report of the Secretary of Agriculture gave evidence of improvement over the earlier nineteen-twenties, but then came the great industrial collapse of 1929-30. During the depths of that depression, between 1933 and 1937, there was a series of severe droughts.[5] This added to the distress of rural people, especially in the Great Plains areas. There were dust storms and the resulting dust bowls.

The seven lean years. The worst depression years, 1931 through 1937, which Doctor Woofter has called "the seven lean years," found 3,500,000 rural families — one in four — dependent on relief at some time. There were 4,000,000 urban families in similar plight. At the depth of the depression in 1935, about 2,500,000 rural families — more than 10,000,000 persons — were dependent on some form of relief.[6]

Cost of rural relief reached $3,500,000,000. The total national relief bill over the seven-year period, paid by both public and private agencies, was estimated as $13,000,000,000. The rural costs were proportionately less, because of the smaller number of cases and the smaller grants to rural than to urban families. However, rural amounts did not include many of the special loans and benefits for agriculture intended to keep farm families off relief or to reduce the needs of those compelled to apply for public aid. These figures of the numbers of families are bewildering, and the costs in terms of dollars were staggering, yet they cannot be considered a measure of the human waste, suffering, and discouragement involved. Millions of rural people were caught in the sweep of the

[4] Taylor, Carl C., Helen W. Wheeler, and E. L. Kirkpatrick, *Disadvantaged Classes in American Agriculture*. Washington, D.C.: Social Research Report 7, United States Department of Agriculture, 1938.

[5] Cronin, Francis, and Howard W. Beers, *Areas of Intense Drought Distress, 1930-36*. Washington, D.C.: Works Progress Administration, January, 1937.

[6] The analysis for the first part of the chapter follows closely two summary sources: Woofter, T. J., and Ellen Winston, *Seven Lean Years* (Chapel Hill: University of North Carolina Press, 1937), and Vance, Rupert B., *Rural Relief and Recovery* (Washington, D.C.: Social Problems Pamphlet 3, Works Progress Administration, 1939). Sources for these summaries include research monographs by the Works Progress Administration, other federal agencies, such as the Social Security Board, the Department of Agriculture, and agricultural experiment stations. Reference will be made to some in footnotes and at the close of the chapter.

depression through no fault of their own. They could not possibly free themselves without help. Furthermore, some of the misery in rural society did not originate in the recent depression, but, as suggested earlier, traces far back to destructive forces at work in rural life for many years. Finally, distressing rural conditions were closely interrelated with the whole nation-wide situation.

First, not all rural poverty was linked with agriculture. By census definition, rural population includes those in the open country and in villages with less than 2500 people. More than half of the rural relief cases lived in villages or were non-farm families living in the open country. Some villages are built around mining, lumbering, or fishing; therefore, their difficulties were linked with industrial causes. Others are service centers for farming regions, and their problems were the results of agricultural distress. Second, there are wide differences in the various regions of the country, and some areas have come to be known as "problem areas" or as chronic "sore spots." Third, there are groups of families or individuals scattered throughout rural society who have fallen victim to circumstances and who had to seek public assistance — youth, the aged, blind, disabled, the ill, or those otherwise disadvantaged.

Farmers on relief. It seems almost a contradiction of terms to write of farmers on relief; they are the ones who supply others with food. But as the depression spread wider and cut deeper, farmers sought relief offices for help in feeding their own families.[7] They were farm owners, part-time farmers, share-croppers, and other tenants and laborers.

Farm owners were best able to maintain their self-dependence. Even when the largest number of rural people were on relief, only one farm owner out of every seventeen was on a relief roll. The numbers receiving aid were lowest in the corn belt and in the hay and dairy area, and highest — one in five — in the Lake States cutover area. When the farm families on relief were compared with neighbors not on relief, some sources of their difficulties became evident. They were larger families, with three or four children and sometimes another relative; they had smaller farms, sometimes less than a third of the average acreage; and they had less livestock and equipment. Some were part-time farmers who had lost their supplementary employment, and some, as a result of heavy indebtedness, had lost all.

[7] Asch, Berta, and A. R. Mangus, *Farmers on Relief.* Washington, D.C.: Research Monograph 8, Works Progress Administration, 1937; McCormick, T. C., *Comparative Study of Rural Relief and Non-Relief Households,* Research Monograph 2, Works Progress Administration, 1935.

Farmers without land fared less well than the owners. One out of seven tenants was on relief in 1935, and it is considered probable that one fourth have been given public assistance at some time. They were like the owners who experienced trouble, except they were involved to a greater extent. Their land was poor, holdings small, livestock limited, and debts many. Compared with tenants who did keep their self-dependence, they were distinguished by their lack of education. Those with less than a grade-school education found it very difficult, if not impossible, to live unaided through those lean years.

One share tenant in twelve was on relief during the worst of the troublesome times. There would have been a larger proportion except for the attention given them through rehabilitation loans. The insecurity of this group of families was greatest in the areas where share tenancy itself was greatest, but also where many families were living at very low levels before the depression began. Nearly half the share-croppers on relief were without work of any kind. The relief stipends which they received were very low indeed, usually about nine dollars per month. Attempts to live at that level gave little hope for security or for self-dependence. A major problem of long standing lodges here.

Farm labor families were easy prey to the depression. It is difficult to determine how many were on relief, but the numbers were high — at least 150,000 in June, 1935, and probably 275,000 the winter before. The heads of these families, and of share-cropping families, were the youngest of the group being considered, and like the share-croppers they moved about a great deal. They had no experience in other kinds of work; they had little, if any, savings. In three months after losing their jobs they were on relief. The tenants could hold out for seven months, the farm-owners for thirteen, after losing their farms.

Villagers on relief. The second one half — or nearly half — of the heads of rural families reported on general relief in February, 1935, had non-agricultural occupations or lived without an occupation in villages. This group of families underwent their own kinds of vicissitudes. Those centers dependent upon the fortunes of agriculture felt the collapse of agriculture's prosperity first. Retail trade fell away, credit limits were broken, workers were unemployed, and business places closed. When 133 of the 140 agricultural villages restudied in 1936 were grouped into four classes on the basis of their relief loads, it was found that high relief loads were associated with decrease in per capita retail sales in three groups, but not in the highest relief group. This highest fourth had the lowest per capita sales even in 1929; the following three or four years seemed merely to intensify their previous problems. Leaders in many of these small communities, although definitely critical of relief as such, admitted that relief grants had actually supported the village.[8]

Those families relying on incomes derived from mining, textiles, or lumbering were among those which were hit especially hard. Some centers became the "stranded" industrial towns as the result of closing the factory or depleting commercial resources. A study of industrial workers in Massachusetts showed that this group was forced to seek relief in greater proportions than any other occupational group, even including the farmers. It was likewise found that industries replacing those closed were all too often exploitive schemes which brought no lasting jobs or permanent income to the towns. Part-time farmers found their income insufficient to carry them through the period when the mills were closed.[9]

Thus, by the winter of 1934-35 a million rural non-farm families were on relief. In June, 1935, one out of every eight village families, exclusive of the non-agricultural families living in the open country, was receiving public assistance. Not all villages, however, suffered alike. In the last month studied, relief in some villages was eighty-seven times as great as in others.

Analysis of the reasons given by villagers for seeking relief shows, from another angle, the picture of the village as that in-between group described in the chapter on villages. They became involved in problems of both industry and agriculture. Loss of employment and loss of assets were the prevailing reasons given for distress in villages in every section of the country. Over one half the village workers with any work history, who were on relief from July through October, 1935, had lost their jobs in private industry. This was a period when there was supposed to have been business recovery. Two fifths of the villagers on relief were unskilled workers, one fourth reported some agricultural experience, one fifth were skilled or semi-skilled workers. There were few "white-collar" workers on village relief rolls.

A situation peculiar to villages was revealed by the large proportion — 17 per cent — of relief households with women as economic

[8] Brunner, Edmund de S., and Irving Lorge, *Rural Trends in Depression Years*. New York: Columbia University Press, 1937.

[9] Useem, John, *A Study of Social Security in the Rural Communities of Massachusetts*. Ph.D. thesis, University of Wisconsin, 1939.

heads or living alone. About 8 per cent of the relief cases were men living alone. Aged people were also numerous, and many families had no person who was employable or considered capable of holding a job.

Plans for rather fundamental readjustments are needed for the many small industrial and agricultural centers if any measure of security is to be found for American villagers. Readjustments will involve not only internal rearrangements but questions of occupational outlook and volume of business necessary to render worthwhile services to agricultural communities.

Special rural groups in trouble. Cutting across the various classes of families and types of areas, and scattered throughout rural society, were special groups of people who have turned to the government for help. Mention can be made of only a few of them.[10]

First were two groups at either end of the age pyramid — children and youth on the one end, and the aged on the other. Rural youth had their own particular difficulties, as has been considered in another chapter.[11] In rural relief families whose only dependents were *children* under sixteen years of age, the proportion of families which had three children or more increased from 43.8 per cent in New England to 52.2 per cent in the Appalachian-Ozark area and to 55.9 per cent in the spring wheat area. White families on relief had fewer dependent children than Negro families in both the eastern and western cotton areas. In these areas over one half of the Negro families and about 46 per cent of the white families had three dependent children or more. This suggests that the separation of many Negro households resulted in placing a disproportionately large number of families with children on relief, but likewise that numbers of children were not the only reason for relief among the white families.

Of the rural families on relief which had only *aged* dependents, three out of four had one person, and one out of four had two persons, while practically none had three or more such persons. In the eastern cotton area, 29.9 per cent of the families in the open country had two aged dependents as contrasted with 19.9 per cent of the village families. In the western cotton area, 32.5 per cent of the open-country families had two aged dependents as compared with

[10] Zimmerman, Carle C., and Nathan L. Whetten, *Rural Families on Relief.* Washington, D.C.: Research Monograph 17, Works Progress Administration, 1938.

[11] Melvin, Bruce L., *Rural Youth on Relief.* Washington, D.C.: Research Monograph 11, Works Progress Administration, 1937.

21.7 per cent in the villages. The proportion of families with one aged dependent varied from four out of five in the Lake States cut-over and ranching areas to three out of five in the western wheat area.

In general, it may be said that the number of dependents in a family indicates either high birth rate, resulting in large families, or a high degree of family solidarity. For example, a family may cling together and when finally it is forced upon relief a large number of persons are found within a single unit, or, as is shown by the families in the cotton areas, there may be a splitting-up of families with a tendency to place the aged persons on public assistance and to leave the younger employables to work for themselves without responsibility for the others.

One-person households presented special problems to relief administrators. Such households may originate as the result of the breaking up of a family leaving aged persons alone, or because of economic and social conditions. Such families constituted less than 10 per cent of all rural families on relief in June, 1935, except in the eastern cotton, hay and dairy, New England, ranching, and the Lake States cut-over areas. Three times as many one-person families were found among Negroes as among whites in the two cotton areas.

The serious condition of many rural relief families is likewise evidenced by the fact that 12.9 per cent had no worker, and an additional 7.5 per cent had female workers only. The cotton areas had the highest proportion of families with only female workers. The proportion of all rural relief families having only male workers was 4.5 per cent higher in the open country than in villages, while the proportion of unemployable and potentially *unemployable families* was 6.7 per cent higher in the villages. This is evidence from another source that open-country families are likely to be normal families composed of an employable man, his wife, and their children. Disorganized families tend to concentrate in villages.

It must be evident that the insecurities which trouble rural families are complicated and intertwined. There is no single factor to explain them all. There are good farmers on relatively poor land or with no claim to land. Some farms yield relatively high incomes, but the level of existence of those families who live on them is comparatively low. Ambitious youth and industrious old age have restricted opportunities. To help all those distressed and insecure families and persons who have been described in this section has called forth a multitude of public and private welfare agencies and programs.

The Quest for Social Security

The period of the depression left its stamp upon American life, and upon its rural life especially. Deep fears were aroused; much effort and legislation was directed, not only toward immediate relief, but so "it would never happen again." It brought farmers into government programs as never before. It stimulated farmer organizations, farm blocs, and pressure groups beginning in the nineteen-twenties, with the MacNary-Haugen agitation. Probably not since the Granger days of the eighteen-seventies or the Alliance and Populist movements of the eighteen-eighties and nineties have farmers been more involved in political and government activities.

It was a transition period in the rural economy and in the rural social relationships of the nation, just as it was in industry and labor. Before 1933, for example, trade-union agreements gave limited attention to regulating lay-offs. Now every agreement contains such a clause. The focus of demand is for a guaranteed annual wage — the basis for some sense of security.[12] With the greater use of machinery and the wider advance of science and technology on the farms have come problems of social and economic stratification suggested earlier. With them has also come the demand for more of security, less of the risks associated with pioneering days. This demand expresses itself in "parity" price demands described in an earlier chapter, and in a variety of other social legislation. The wartime rise in curves of prices, incomes, and profits has for the time being diverted public attention, but it is doubtful that many of the fundamental conditions of such fears have been alleviated.

Relief agencies. The federal government in the latter part of 1932 began to lend funds to state and local government units for the relief of the unemployed. By May, 1933, a Federal Emergency Relief Administration was set up and authorized to allocate funds to the states for emergency unemployment relief purposes. This was discontinued in December, 1935, when the works program provided for in the Federal Emergency Relief Appropriation Act was inaugurated to furnish employment to those needy and employable. From its beginning in 1931, unemployment relief tended to overshadow poor relief in this general field of public assistance, while the need for a longer-time program was recognized in 1935.

Prior to 1933, the responsibility for the administration and financ-

[12] Chernich, Jack, and George Hellikson, *Guaranteed Annual Wages.* Minneapolis: University of Minnesota Press.

ing of relief or other forms of public assistance was most frequently placed upon local units of government. Since 1935, however, the prevailing practice has changed until at present the majority of states have laws which provide for state responsibility and direct administration or supervision by a single state agency. By January, 1939, very few states did not have legislation which provided for all types of relief and public assistance.[13]

Emergency agencies. Perhaps some conception of the wide variety and complexity of emergency programs can be gained from the assistance chart (Figure 42) which shows the trend of public assistance and the earnings of persons employed under federal works programs in the United States from January, 1933, to May, 1939. In the latter month, as an example, earnings of persons employed on works projects operated by the Works Progress Administration amounted to $140,700,000 and payments to general relief cases $39,100,000. Together these two types of aid account for nearly 60 per cent of all public assistance in that month. Payments to recipi-

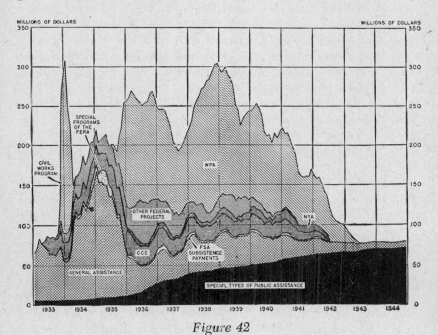

Figure 42

SPECIAL TYPES OF PUBLIC ASSISTANCE

[13] Lowe, Robert C., *State Public Welfare Legislation.* Washington, D.C.: Research Monograph 20, Works Progress Administration, 1939.

ents of old-age assistance, aid to dependent children, and aid to the blind totaled $46,200,000, comprising 15 per cent of the total. Earnings of persons employed on other federal work were $45,700,000, nearly 15 per cent of the total. Earnings of persons enrolled in the Civilian Conservation Corps were $20,400,000, or about 7 per cent of the total. The National Youth Administration's account was $6,700,000, slightly more than 2 per cent of the whole. Emergency subsistence payments certified by the Farm Security Administration were $1,700,000, which was only six tenths per cent of the total payment for the month.[14]

Since 1939, the curves of public relief expenditures have fallen rapidly as the larger chart shows. Nevertheless, the smaller chart (Figure 43) presents the trends for public assistance from 1941 to 1945; it suggests a tendency for the categorical aids to level off and for the old-age assistance to assume a somewhat larger proportion of the total.

Comments concerning all the emergency programs cannot be given. Two, however, are singled out for brief statement.

Social security. The Social Security Act passed in 1935 and amended in 1939 is not one particular kind of public assistance; it is rather a measure designed to cope with many types of insecurity. The rural areas of the country were not equally provided for within the program. In the provisions for old-age annuities and unemployment insurance, agricultural workers are not included although rural industrial workers are. The two insurance plans can-

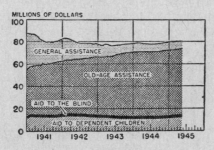

Figure 43

PUBLIC ASSISTANCE IN THE UNITED STATES,
JANUARY, 1941 — MAY, 1945

Source: *Social Security Bulletin,* vol. 8, no. 7, July, 1945, Social Security Board, Washington, D.C.

[14] Howard, Donald S., *The W.P.A. and Federal Relief Policy.* New York: Russell Sage Foundation, 1943.

not be regarded as relief measures since benefits are received, as in private insurance, on the basis of years in the program and contributions made. There is no test of need. The two plans are administered by different units of government, old-age annuities by a federal agency, and unemployment insurance by a state agency.

Of direct benefit to rural people are those forms of assistance known as the "categorical aids": old-age assistance, aid to dependent children, and aid to the blind. Unlike the insurance plans which call for flat payments, these grants are based on needs of the persons concerned. Many hard-pressed rural communities lacking local funds have been greatly aided by these provisions. Under its clauses, the federal, state, and local governments pool their resources to provide the needed funds. In all three types of assistance the federal government matches the money given by the states. In the case of old-age and blind assistance, the federal share is 50 per cent, and beginning in 1940, the aid to dependent children has been 50 per cent up to eighteen dollars for the first child and twelve dollars for each additional child.

Also of special significance to rural society are the federal grants and aids to states for the strengthening and expansion of their public service programs in the fields of maternal and child health, for crippled children, for dependent and neglected children, and for public health as a whole.

For the establishment and promotion of public health, the federal government agrees to contribute annually a total of $8,000,000. For vocational rehabilitation of the physically disabled, to aid in their return to productive employment, during the year 1939-40, the federal government appropriated $3,530,000 to the states, the District of Columbia, and Hawaii.

These sums seem very large but they are considered investments in people, and it is likely that future years will witness not smaller but larger appropriations in such public welfare activities. Changes in the program will be required; present agencies will modify practices as the result of experience, and more effective ways of preventing difficulties before they arrive will need to be discovered.

More social security for farm people. One change under consideration is the extension of old-age and survivor insurance features of the Social Security Act to include more farm people. As farmers begin to think more seriously of their postwar problems, the old fears come nearer the surface, and they are more inclined to consider security measures. The reasons they are not generally included in the insurance provisions are chiefly that they have not demanded it, and because the machinery for administering the program among the self-employed was not completed when the law was passed. Only those relatively few farmers are eligible for the insurance benefits who work at least part time in covered employment; that is, in non-farm occupations whose employees are included in the programs.

The reasons farmers are considering it now are because the farm population has an increasing number of old people, a much larger proportion of the nation's children, and because of the high incidence of unpredictable hazards which were mentioned in the previous chapter. In the Wagner Bill before Congress there are provisions for the voluntary inclusion of farmers and other self-employed persons in the social insurance system. Their contribution is set at 7 per cent of incomes up to $3000. A wage-earner, on the other hand, contributes 6 per cent of his income with an additional 6 per cent of his income being furnished by his employer. The federal program for medical care set up in the bill includes the agricultural population, as was pointed out in a previous chapter.[15]

Unlike the farmer, laborer, and industrialist, the villager and the small-town self-employed do not have their "representatives" in Washington or their "blocs" in Congress. They do, however, have a very large stake in the social security of the future, as the previous paragraphs make very evident. They are easily caught between the two pressures of the farm and the city "hard times," yet social security provisions are thus far inadequate to protect them in this intermediate position.

Farm security. Specialized relief measures for farmers began rather early. Rehabilitation loans were granted instead of direct relief or unemployment relief. This accounts for the low percentage in the May, 1939, budget described above. Three factors were depended upon to enable this form of rehabilitation program to expand: first, the spreading of risk over many borrowers; second, careful selection of borrowers or clients; and, third, close supervision, not only of the farm operation, but of the family and its household management.

In 1937, after several hundred thousand persons had been removed from the relief rolls by such rehabilitation loans, the proportion of farm families receiving different kinds of public assistance,

---

[15] Witte, Edwin E., "What to Expect of Social Security," *American Economic Review*, Supplement, vol. XXXIV, no. 1, March, 1944; Altmeyer, A. J., "Social Security for Farm People." Washington, D.C.: *Social Security Bulletin*, Social Security Board, vol. 7, no. 4, April, 1944.

exclusive of the Farm Security loans, were as follows: Works Progress Administration, 40 per cent; Farm Security direct grants — not loans — 6 per cent; aid to the aged, to the blind, and to dependent children, 39 per cent; and state and local direct relief, 15 per cent.

It was in 1937 that the Farm Security Administration was reorganized from the Rural Rehabilitation Division of the F.E.R.A., made a part of the United States Department of Agriculture, and its services enlarged to include a tenant-purchase program, homestead projects, and migratory labor camps. The significant function of the agency, as Mr. Wallace — then Secretary of Agriculture — explained, was to lend to low-income farm families unable to get adequate credit elsewhere, and to provide guidance to the borrower by a sound system of farm and home management.[16] The families were also to form co-operatives including group medical care, and in many cases to change over from a one-crop farming system to a diversified subsistence program. The farm and home plans included the home production of most of the family's food supply and feed for the livestock, the development of two or more enterprises which could yield products to sell in the market, and the use of farm practices which would build up the fertility of the soil. Much credit for the success of the plan goes to that group of farm and home advisers who were drawn into the work hurriedly, and who had to cope with the problems of a newly constituted government agency. Few of them had been trained in the techniques of family case work; they came largely from agricultural and home economics experiences and education, but they did apply the principles involved in the interrelations of the family and its farm — the man and his land. So-called "specialists" are likely to consider the crops, the livestock, or the children's clothing problems separately. The needs of the Farm Security clients involved the whole family-farm relationships.

The results of the rehabilitation loans and the family-farm planning showed that the average net increase in wealth of the families was $253 per year up to and including the crop year 1937-38. Since that time the war influences have made the increases greater. During the year 1939-40, rehabilitation loans of $93,000,000 were made to 286,000 families, 73,000 of which were new clients; the others had been on the program previously. In total about 700,000 families have been in the program.

The total cost to the United States government, up to the open-

16 Wallace, H. A., *Report of the Secretary of Agriculture.* Washington, D.C.: United States Department of Agriculture, 1940.

ing of World War II, involving not only the Washington and state regional offices, but the total cost of the county field workers and the supervisors and the total losses on the loans as well as all other expenses, amounted to less than $72 per family per year. Work relief in cities averaged about $800 per family per year and rural work relief costs were $350 per family per year and up, depending upon the states.[17] In addition, these farm families nearly doubled their consumption of owner-produced meat, milk, and eggs, and stored an average of fifty-three quarts of fruit and vegetables per person per year to tide them over the winter.

It also resulted in improved health and considerably improved school attendance on the part of the children. Up to 1938, $45,-000,000 more than was required by the terms of the loans had been paid back by the rehabilitation clients, Wisconsin leading with a repayment of 152 per cent of the sums due. Debate in the recent Congress showed that up to July 1, 1944, 87.1 per cent of all loans had already been paid. Despite this record, an amendment was introduced to remove the entire rural rehabilitation appropriation. This was defeated, although the final amount granted was only a little more than half the amount requested.

Other results did not find their way into the public hearings, but from the standpoint of the future of rural society are probably most significant of all. The report of an intensive study of six hundred and six F.S.A. families living in ten carefully selected counties during the four-year period, 1938 to 1942, concludes with these two important paragraphs:

> Emotionally these families needed security; they needed to experience the feeling of being wanted; they needed a chance to be contributing members of society. Supervisors in all counties agree that group activities have done more to fulfill these needs — to stimulate production, create unity, and effect social adjustments among the families — than anything else.
>
> To dispel the feeling of inferiority, distrust in humanity, fear of meeting new situations, and so-called relief psychology, to strengthen family solidarity and to break down resistance to change — these difficult tasks had to be done before economic progress could be made. At first, evidences of changing attitudes were seen only in isolated acts — old habits and reactions predominated. Gradually new attitudes appeared with greater frequency and certain old ones were less observable. To contribute to the welfare of their community and the war gave them new confidence. Better health,

[17] Baldwin, C. B., *Report of the Administration of the Farm Security Administration*, Washington, D.C., 1940.

clothes, housing, a more cheerful environment and new associations
have contributed greatly to a different kind of interplay among personalities in family groups. Explosive or sullen reactions have been
replaced by more pleasurable, satisfying and constructive relationships — life has taken on a new meaning, stimulating new hope and
greater efforts. [18]

PUBLIC WELFARE IN RURAL SOCIETY

Before World War I there was little organized social work in
rural counties. Poor relief was carried on for the most part as temporary assistance to keep families out of dire need. During the
war the American Red Cross carried on home service work for the
families of men who were away. The Red Cross was able to introduce and build up standards of social work in many rural communities which had lacked them entirely before. As the depression
came on, it was necessary to organize county or town relief administrations throughout the whole country. It was likewise necessary
to devise methods of contacting families. Many counties at first
employed local workers with no professional training. Later came
an increasing recognition of the importance of good practice by
trained social workers to give families adequate care. Scholarships
in schools of social work have been obtained and inexperienced
workers given an opportunity to carry out and adapt those urban
practices of proven worth to rural society.

It is possible that one of the important outcomes of the depression period may be a new conception on the part of rural people
and their local welfare officials about the objectives of welfare work
through good family case work. They may come to understand the
importance of helping those families who sought aid during the
depression to become independent and self-reliant again. This emphasis upon the rehabilitation of the family rather than on passing
out groceries and fuel for temporary subsistence is basic to public
welfare in rural life.

A sketch of public welfare in United States. The Elizabethan
laws of England formed the basis for most colonial poor-relief policy. In the New England colonies, responsibility for poor relief
was assumed by the towns. The Southern colonies used the county
as their administrative unit, while the Middle colonies combined
the two systems with some responsibility placed upon counties and

[18] Swiger, Rachel Rowe, and Olaf F. Larson, *Climbing Toward Security.*
Washington, D.C.: Bureau of Agricultural Economics, United States Department of Agriculture, November, 1944.

some upon towns or other local units. The colonial systems were carried on almost unchanged by the state governments after the revolution.

Specialized care of dependents, defectives, and delinquents developed very slowly during the eighteenth century and the early part of the nineteenth. Classification of dependent persons did not come about to any extent until after 1900. Since that time there has been much improvement in provisions for all groups requiring care, including institutional care. Until relatively recently, however, the only legislation for the public care of needy individuals other than children and war veterans was contained in the state poor laws, and they had undergone very little change since the colonial days. "Outdoor" or non-institutional care under the poor laws was not provided to any extent before the last third of the nineteenth century. Those who did receive poor relief were usually designated "paupers," and in some states were deprived even of privileges of citizenship. Eventually, of course, there was an increased acceptance of social responsibility, and state legislatures provided for certain classes of needy persons such as dependent and neglected children or orphans, mothers with dependent children, the blind, or the aged. Aid to dependent children in their own homes was still a later development. The first statute providing for this was not enacted until 1911, but by 1920 the majority of the states had passed some kind of mothers' aid or widows' pension. The enactment of the Federal Social Security Act in 1935 required considerable revision in these state statutes.

More recent trends in emphasis. One who has long been a student and a teacher of social work, gives the following conclusions briefly summarized, after a careful analysis of recent trends: [19]

(1) Relative maturity of performance and attitude achieved in the last five to ten years.

(2) Acceptance of social work by the man in the street, although he still protests many of its methods. (But not the man in the fields.)

(3) Tremendous expansion of public social services including the social insurances and public assistance.

(4) Alliance of labor and social work. (As much cannot be said of the farmer or the villager and their organizations. The social worker is still in the process of winning her way, the family case worker probably more than the children's workers.)

[19] Clarke, Helen I., "Social Work Today," *Social Forces*, vol. 23, no. 2, December, 1944.

(5) Extension of social work skills into new areas of performance.

(6) Expansion of recreation and group work resources for the armed forces and for civilians, particularly for youth.

(7) Development of international relief structures.

(8) Renewed emphasis upon social planning and social action.

Community organization and county administration. As with health programs, so with welfare and security, the final test of their effectiveness is in the local community. Community organization is now being recognized as a subject for professional consideration in rural as well as in urban circles. One example in the urban field is the rapid expansion in the number of community funds and war chests. Social workers have long been active in community work, but only recently have there been recognized techniques for community analysis of problems and for relating the family to the constructive forces within the community.

At the county level the trend seems to be in the direction of what is called "an Integrated Public Welfare Department." Within such an organization are drawn together the administration of old-age assistance, aid to needy blind, aid to dependent children, direct relief and medical care, certification to other assistance programs, special aids and services to veterans of military and naval service in co-operation with other designated agencies, family welfare and child welfare activities, as well as maintenance of administration and reporting contacts with state departments involved in any of the programs. This kind of organization involves a legal and working arrangement with the county board of supervisors or other legal authority within the respective counties. Problems of local government to be considered in the next chapter arise at this point, as do those of county-state-federal relationships.

Working with the voluntary and other social agencies. Private or voluntary social services supported by free-will contributions and controlled by citizen boards of various descriptions, like the public services, have increased greatly in recent years. Some have grown up more or less spontaneously, some have been promoted by local lay persons, others by state or national professional workers. They are less uniform from area to area than are the publicly supported and administered agencies. And again, in rural districts including small towns, they are less frequent and less well organized and established than in urban centers.

Mention has been made of the Home Service of the Red Cross. Another nearly universal private "charity" agency in rural communities is the church. The services are often personal and informal and confined to certain groups or classes within the community. In modern public welfare programs the local church may have to modify its traditional lines of relief effort, but it may contribute a great deal to the social and emotional readjustments required to re-establish self-respect and self-dependence.

Likewise, the school has an important mission to perform in the social welfare and security realm. This can be discharged, not only through class work in the social sciences and in adult education programs, but in the whole attitude and administration of the school as one of the constructive community agencies working along with home, church, club, and government.

POLICIES AND PRACTICES OF THE FUTURE?

Public welfare as a fundamental attack on basic problems of rural destitution has just begun. Social security as a practice in rural society has scarcely started on any long-time scale. The problems reviewed rapidly in this chapter were characterized by a tone of emergency and a tempo of urgency. The difficulties seemed great and the time short. Many of both problems and difficulties were born of the two great world wars or in the depression which came between. Others were only the older ones in aggravated forms.

Policies for social security are designed to give a broader base and a longer time perspective to public as well as to private welfare practices. They are aimed to strike at the social and emotional roots as well as the relief of economic pressures. As the analysis has indicated, the situations from which these problems and difficulties arise involve many besides the economic and the physical factors. Traditional economic theories of the "input-output" shuttlecock have not in their practices brought about a welfare economy.

It must be recognized that insecurities and social problems will always be present, even in the so-called "good" or "normal" times. There are sure to be those who through misfortune or mismanagement will need help and guidance, and such help may not, and perhaps should not, be in money or in kind. But the character of a society must be judged by its reaction to such human situations. Herein lies one of the most fundamental issues facing the democratic countries of the world.

One writer, seasoned in European backgrounds and experiences, says what he sees and hears in the democracies today bears an alarming resemblance to those early stages of the movements toward totalitarianism which he had heard and seen in his own country before. He decries what he terms excessive planning in order to assure security. In the process freedom is limited, he claims.[20] Other students of modern society of American origins, sharply contest his conclusions. And it does make a difference from what assumptions and within what cultural reference one begins an analysis of current social problems.[21]

The call now is to design a wholesome social order where welfare and freedom, security and adventure, responsibility and liberty, can dwell together in one household, one community, one nation — yea, may we say, in one world? These are problems, in our time, of human relations rather than of technical proficiency. Their solution will turn upon our capacity to produce and distribute not only more and better goods and services, but finer human-social beings.

Returning more circumspectly to our rural theme, there does come the opinion from certain quarters that at least some rural people are losing or have lost their determination for self-dependence and family responsibility, that some are increasingly looking to "the government" for help or as a scapegoat to criticize for their own failures — a government which they seem to feel lies somewhere beyond them or outside their direct experience and control.

With such possibilities in mind, a few simple principles are suggested for consideration in future policies and practices of rural welfare and social security. Goals to be sought are the achievement or the re-establishment of healthy development and self-dependency for the person in his social relations. But, if the individual suffers a handicap beyond his power to overcome, then the community should assist him. An emphasis upon greater social responsibility appears at this point. Following this thought, it becomes evident that the center of activity for the state or society, whether it be the caring for the disabled, or the aiding of the dependent, or even the handling of the delinquent, hinges upon this matter of the handicap. The handicap may be physical or it may be mental; it may be social or it may be economic, but if it actually exists, society has no choice but to help to correct it. If this view is accepted as

[20] Hayek, Frederick, *The Road to Serfdom*. Chicago: University of Chicago Press, 1944.
[21] Frank, Lawrence K., "The Rising Stock of Dr. Hayek," *The Saturday Review of Literature*, May 12, 1945.

a guide to thinking and acting, it will be quickly realized that real strategy for health or for welfare programs is in the direction of prevention, striking at causes before difficulties arise, rather than merely attempting to remedy a problem already existing. This is an emphasis upon conserving and building human resources.

Several corollaries may follow from such an emphasis: [22]

(1) Early discovery and diagnosis of remedial defects or social handicaps of an individual, especially of a child, followed by prompt and adequate treatment or training, may save him as a valuable member of society.

(2) Difficulties can best be prevented and combated at their source in the local community.

(3) Prevention and treatment require that every agency and resource, public or private, be utilized and co-ordinated.

(4) Only skilled and informed personnel can deal with the myriad and perplexing problems of health and welfare.

(5) Well-organized team work between professionally trained and citizen leaders is necessary — citizen boards to determine policies, professional staffs to execute and administer them.

(6) The family should be considered the basic unit for social treatment, and if it becomes necessary to remove a member for special care, a course of treatment should be designed to permit an early return to the home. The family itself may have to be rehabilitated.

(7) The county, group of counties, or similar unit should be considered the area for local administration. It should be of such population and wealth as to make possible good administration and equitable distribution of costs.

(8) State and federal departments should assume such responsibilities as are consistent with local laws and traditions, to insure minimum standards and to equalize the vast inequalities for persons living in different areas.

(9) Brick and mortar institutions should be places of last resort, and, even there, treatment should be adapted to individual needs and toward restoring the individual to a useful place in society.

Progress in attaining such goals must be measured in the postwar days ahead.

[22] Adapted from Recommendations of Citizens' Committee on Public Welfare, Madison, 1937.

DISCUSSION TOPICS

1. What problems in the fields of public welfare and social security do you think are most important in your community? What evidence do you have for your answer?

2. Select one public and one private agency (local, county, state or national) working with welfare and security problems in rural society, and find out all you can about them. Visit local headquarters, interview members of the staff where possible, or if necessary, secure information by mail.

3. Organize this information in brief outline form and be prepared to present it to the class. Give particular attention to the following points:

   a. The real purpose of agency
   b. Its local forms of organization
   c. How it serves rural communities
   d. How do you think such service could be improved.

REFERENCE READINGS

Altmeyer, Arthur J., "Social Security for Farmers," *Land Policy Review*, vol. VIII, no. 1, Spring, 1945.

Brown, Josephine C., *The Rural Community and Social Case Work*. New York: Family Welfare Association of America, 1933. Concrete suggestions for immediate steps and for long-time programs in the development of social work in rural communities.

Browning, Grace, *Rural Public Welfare*. Chicago: University of Chicago Press, 1941. Selected records with notes and comments.

Bureau of Public Assistance, *Social Data on Recipients of Public Assistance, 1939-40*. Washington, D.C.: Memorandum 1, Federal Security Agency, April, 1941.

Colcord, Joanna C., *Your Community*. New York: Russell Sage Foundation, 1939. Provisions for health, education, safety, and welfare.

Gillin, J. L., *Poverty and Dependency*, revised edition. New York: Century Co., 1937. Contains historical and current materials for this and other countries.

Hill, Geo. W., Walter Slocum, Ruth Hill, *Man-Land Adjustment*. Madison: Research Bulletin 134, Agricultural Experiment Station, University of Wisconsin, 1938. A study of family and inter-family aspects of land retirement in the Central Wisconsin Land Purchase Area.

Howard, Donald S., *The WPA and Federal Relief Policy*. New York: Russell Sage Foundation, 1943.

Lerrigo, Ruth, and Bradley Buell, *Social Work and the Joneses*, Public Affairs Pamphlet 97. Public Affairs Committee, 30 Rockefeller Plaza, New York.

Mott, F. D., "Rural Health Parity," *Land Policy Review*, vol. VIII, no. 1, Spring, 1945.

Sanderson, Dwight, "Trends and Problems in Rural Social Work," *Rural America*, January, 1930.

Smith, Marjorie J., *Rural Casework Services*. Family Public Welfare Association, 122 East 22d Street, New York 10.

Social Security Board, *A Brief Explanation of the Social Security Act*. Washington, D.C.: Information Survey Circular 1, 1938. One of a number of popularly written pamphlets which can be readily secured.

Strode, Josephine, *Introduction to Social Case Work*. New York: Harper & Bros., 1940.

Tyler and Sunley, *The Iowa Plan for County Organization of Social Work*. Iowa City: University of Iowa, January, 1931.

Witte, Edwin E., "What to Expect of Social Security," *American Economic Review*, Supplement, vol. XXXIV, no. 1, March, 1944.

25

Local Government — Social Institution

GOVERNMENT, and particularly local government, comes well within the purview of social institution as defined earlier. It is the more or less regular and recognized way of doing things. In this case it is the more rather than the less regular, since local government has probably changed less in form and organization than any other of the local social institutions with which our study of rural society has been concerned. Yet there have been many changes in the methods by which local units perform their services, and in the relation which such local units bear to state and nation and to rural people themselves. There have also been many new agencies and authorities established in rural areas.

A significant trend is the increased assumption of various social responsibilities by different units of government, as in matters of education, health, welfare, recreation, and services to needy groups. Sometimes this is done by having local units and officials assume larger responsibilities; at other times it is accomplished by the creation of separate administrations for special tasks such as fire protection, library service, health, welfare, irrigation, sewage disposal, or public utilities. In the past decade especially, services have been extended locally by state and federal agencies. The actual number of local units of government did not change significantly as a following section will show, although there was a tendency for the number of small school districts and townships to decrease.

Questions about the future are being pressed in numerous quarters. When much of living was within the country neighborhood, many local government units, such as towns, townships, parishes, villages, and even counties, were necessarily small and locally controlled. Now, with the demand for government to take on an increasing number and amount of functions, there is need for reorganization and realignment. Population is more mobile; group relationships are changing; attitudes are shifting; costs need to be equalized over wider areas and larger numbers of people. These are all concerns for the student of rural society. But, first, it is important, especially in times of uncertainty and when some traditions are being shaken from their moorings, that we should re-examine the basis for our conception of government here in the United States of America.

AMERICAN — A B C OF ITS LAW AND GOVERNMENT

Assumptions, fundamental to all government in this country, are and always have been — not only in phrase but in fact — of, for, and by the people. A fuller comprehension of this conception should have a steadying effect just now.

Backgrounds of our law and government are found in the development of the English common law upon the soil of America. It is important to remember that it was derived from and adapted to a society which was predominantly rural and agricultural in character. The common law developed slowly and has been influenced along the way by many social, economic, civic, and even ecclesiastical forces. "But running through it all, as warp runs through cloth, were the customs, habits, and traditions of the English race. The enjoyment of political freedom which meant equality before the law was the dominant desire of that race." [1] It is recognized, of course, that other peoples and other traditions have made significant contributions; they have contributed to, not substituted for, the basic principles. Moreover, these very principles and backgrounds became a selective force to determine who came out from the Old World into the New. While this theory of government was developing, society was undergoing many changes and the story of the inter-influence of the two is most interesting.

The rural order of things has been greatly altered with the oncoming industrial movement, therefore, making necessary many readjustments, some of which were tardy in their legal reference. Chief Justice Rosenberry points out that equality before the law does not produce economic equality, and that political freedom does not insure the weaker against oppression by the stronger. In the long run, he suggests, "substantive law is mainly the crystallization of social experiences." This he illustrates in several fields. The common law of master and servant is not adequate in a highly

[1] Rosenberry, Marvin B., Chief Justice of the Supreme Court of Wisconsin. "The Development of Substantive Law on Social as Distinguished from Purely Governmental Lines," *Annals of the American Academy of Political and Social Science,* Philadelphia, March, 1928.

industrial situation. Laws have been made to authorize collective bargaining, agencies have beeen set up to curb irresponsible activities. The Interstate Commerce Commission is the illustration. Regulations have been made for bringing about a fairer distribution of the proceeds of industry. The common law dealt with nuisances, but now standards must be maintained by both legal and agency means whereby good health can be not only protected but encouraged. The Pure Food and Drug Act is an example. The free school along with free church and free government came to us from this heritage. In a technical and interdependent society, education is not only desirable, it is necessary: therefore, it was made compulsory and at public expense. The list could be expanded, but the point is that the functions of government are social control and social services, and that the functions of government change and expand as society changes and develops.

In England, the history of social legislation is similar, although in certain fields, as has been pointed out recently, it has often preceded by two or more decades similar enactments in the United States.[2]

Controls of government in the United States were guaranteed to the people in the Constitution by an elaborate system of checks and balances as they are called, and the three separate branches of government: the legislative, the judicial, and the executive. England gave up this system after brief trial. Likewise, the long and intricate provisions by which local, "home rule" government and state's rights shall be protected from the federal authority constitute further basis for popular control. This is quite a different tradition and setting from that of those peoples whose countries have long been committed to state control — statism, it is termed. Some Americans, particularly in times of distress or depression, may not realize that they are still in control. But those are the very periods when they need to be encouraged to exercise more vigorously the responsibilities of citizenship.

Trends in Local Forms and Functions

With such assumptions, backgrounds, and controls in mind, the more recent trends in the local forms and functions of government can be examined with better discrimination than with only the review of relatively recent years.

2 Lynd, Helen Merrell, *England in the Eighteen-Eighties.* New York: Oxford University Press, 1945.

The major fields of local legal and governmental services are general political, including election machinery, assessment and collection of taxes, administration of justice, protection of persons and property, and the recording and custody of legal documents; education, agriculture, health and welfare — "charities and corrections" were the early terms; public services, including highways, bridges, parks, conservation and control of natural resources. One of the more recent means of control is zoning, under the "police powers." All of these functions cannot be considered here; only those which have particular reference to the social as contrasted with the political relations in rural society.

Changes in the number of units. Professor William Anderson's condensed definition of a local unit of government is very useful, and gives ample proof of its social institutional character:

> A unit of government may be defined as a resident population occupying a defined area that has a legally authorized organization and a governing body, a separate legal identity, the power to provide certain public or governmental services, and a substantial degree of autonomy, including legal and actual power to raise at least a part of its own revenue.[3]

Governmental units in the United States as of 1942, according to the census counts, totaled 155,116. This is a large number and their various relationships present a puzzling picture to the uninitiated, and often to the professional as well.

The distribution of the number of all types of units follows no definite rule either as to size of population served or to extent of areas covered. Different regions have different combinations. They are not the results of demography or of geography, but of the traditions and the movements of the settlers, surveyors' systems, and social and political patterns.

The town is the distinguishing local unit of New England, and its democratic procedures are an American tradition.[4] The township system characteristic of New York, spread to the Northwest with westward settlement; it took on its regular geographic pattern with the rectangular survey. In Southern states the township and common school districts were unknown. It is a bit of interesting history and fortuity that in territorial days Wisconsin, being a part

---

[3] Anderson, William, *The Units of Government in the United States.* Chicago: Publication 83, Public Administration Service, 1942.

[4] Webster, Clarence M., *Town Meeting Country.* New York: Duell, Sloan & Pearce, 1945. (American Folkways Series.)

TABLE 90. SUMMARY OF GOVERNMENTAL UNITS, BY REGION, 1942

Region	All Governmental Units*	Counties	Townships and Towns	Municipalities			School Districts	Special Districts
				Total	Urban †	Rural		
United States total..........	155,116	3,050	18,919	16,220	3,332	12,888	108,579	8,299
Northeast..........	17,085	205	4,184	2,144	834	1,310	9,369	1,174
North Central..........	96,595	1,051	14,667	7,721	1,099	6,022	70,207	2,847
South..........	25,130	1,386	....	4,756	999	3,757	17,001	1,911
West..........	16,305	408	68	1,599	400	1,199	11,852	2,367

* Includes the federal government and the 48 state governments.

† Incorporated places having more than 2500 inhabitants.

Source: *Governmental Units in the United States, 1942.* Washington, D.C.: Bureau of the Census, United States Department of Commerce.

TABLE 91. GOVERNMENTAL UNITS DISTRIBUTED BY POPULATION
AND AREAS SERVED, 1942

Region	Number of Units per 1,000 Square Miles	Number of Units per 100,000 Inhabitants	Average Number of Inhabitants per Unit
United States total..............	52.1	117.8	848.8
Northeast......................	104.4	47.5	2,105.8
North Central..................	109.8	231.8	431.3
South..........................	33.3	62.6	1,597.6
West...........................	13.8	117.5	851.4

Source: *Governmental Units in the United States*, 1942. Washington, D.C.: Bureau of the Census, United States Department of Commerce.

of Virginia, had the Southern forms of government. Through an election in 1841, the New York system was adopted.[5]

According to recent studies, principal changes during the past decade have been a reduction of about 7 per cent in the number of school districts and 6 per cent in the number of towns and townships.[6] The largest decrease of school districts by states was in New York, North Carolina, Texas, California, Michigan, Montana, Missouri, Mississippi, and Ohio, and in that order. The elimination of all townships in Oklahoma accounted for more than three fourths of the total reduction in townships. Other states, in order, were Minnesota, North Dakota, South Dakota, Illinois, Nebraska, and Maine. Counties remained practically unchanged in number but, of course, not in function, as will be shown presently. It is the trend in social relationships which shall engage our attention. There can be changes in the social functions of a certain type of government unit without necessarily altering its form.

With increased social duties come demands for reorganization. It is becoming generally recognized that systems of local government need reorganization for their increasing load of duties and because of the many social and economic changes which have taken place: shifts in population characteristics and distribution, increased interdependence of country, village, and city, and a greater emphasis placed upon public education, health, and welfare. Therefore, local units of government no longer conform to the social

[5] Wehrwein, George W., *Local Government.* Manitowoc, Wisconsin, 1911.
[6] Anderson, William, *The Units of Government in the United States.* Chicago: Publication 83, Public Administration Service, 1942.

and economic groups in rural society, if indeed they ever did in some of the Middle-Western States. The civil boundaries of the town, for example, were laid out on quite artificial and arbitrary township lines. The New England town idea may have been in the minds of the pioneering planners, but their engineers set up their transits and laid off the township lines uniformly six miles square. The lines often cut across physical barriers and they were no respecters of the natural groupings of people. A citizen might cast his ballot at a town hall with one group of people and be associated in his educational, religious, and recreational activities with quite another. Certainly this is one reason for the impotency of local government in many rural areas.

During the past few years discussions and studies have turned toward improvement and reorganization of local government. The belief is apparently growing, and with a good deal of strength, that the tens of thousands of local units are a factor in the mounting tax burdens described in an earlier chapter and in the increasing difficulties and problems of local government. Evidence of this rising tide of dissatisfaction is to be found in discussions at meetings of such organizations as the American Country Life Association, Institute of Public Affairs, University of Virginia, and taxpayers' leagues.

The Governor's Commission of New York for the study of New York and the bill passed in that state for recodification of the century-old town law are examples of reorganization movements. There have been many investigations, some private, others official or quasi-official, of government in rural areas and in such states as New Jersey, Mississippi, Michigan, Wisconsin, Minnesota, and North Carolina. The National Municipal League, the American Public Health Association, and other national organizations have become increasingly interested in local government reform.

Discussion has passed on into action in a number of states. Reorganization seems to be taking two general forms. First is the tendency toward consolidation of existing units or the formation of larger units adjusted to expanded needs. This inevitably involves the abolition of certain local units, especially townships and local districts. Second is the tendency for certain functions and services to pass from local units to county, state, or even to federal control. This involves questions of administration, finance, personnel, and even of constitutional changes. Social considerations need their due share of attention, for it must be emphasized that principles for the reorganization of local government will have to be anchored to heavier arguments than the immediate interests of administrative efficiency and financial economy, important as these are.

Tendencies toward centralization and consolidation. The question of centralized control versus local control, or "home rule" as it is often called, has been debated with much fervor. It has gone even to the highest courts of the land. Originally the state legislature had complete power over counties, but the question of local control was raised again and again until the Supreme Court of the United States, only a few decades ago, ruled that "the state made it [the county] and could, in its discretion, unmake it." [7]

In spite of all this, people continually insist upon their right to circumscribe state and federal rule in their own localities. They fear betrayal of local interests by central authority. Rural people fear domination by urban interests. Constitutions, therefore, are filled with clauses and amendments preventing most states from modifying local functions and units of government unless constitutional limitations are first removed. Centralized tendencies on the part of states have been checked at many points by city home rule legislation. Villages have incorporated and set themselves off from the town government so that they may do as they choose within their boundaries, and in some states they have done so for the specific purpose of securing direct representation on county boards.

States, however, are steadily assuming more and more control over local functions and agencies. For the most part this is accomplished within the framework of existing governmental organizations in one of two ways: through the direct assumption of local functions and by means of various grants-in-aid or subventures which carry certain supervisory or controlling powers. Local units including counties under the heavy pressure of property taxes, have given way to arguments of economy and efficiency.

Grants-in-aid, already reviewed for the educational functions in another chapter, have been a favorite form of increasing state influence. The granting of subsidies by a central government to local units has long been practiced in the Old World, but in the United States it is only within the past thirty or forty years that there has been a notable expansion in the amounts, purposes, and contingent provision of such grants. The tendency is of much importance for community organization policies. Consider the schools. Between 1913 and 1929 the amount of grants increased more than four times, but the total amount of state revenues and expenditures

---

[7] Jones, Howard P., "Constitutional Barriers to the Improvement in County Government," *National Municipal Review*, August, 1932, Supplement.

during the same period increased at about the same rate. Consequently, subsidies for education remained in about the same proportion to total state expenditures.[8] To be sure, since 1930 there has been a great increase in state aids. Nevertheless, many questions regarding equality of educational opportunity for rural youth, raised in the early part of the book, remain unanswered. Local communities in many states struggle on as best they can in the face of uncertain state and national policies or in their absence.

Grants for highways come not only from state but from federal sources. Not so for education. While Professor Fairlie estimates only a twofold increase in state expenditures for local highway purposes between 1913 and 1929, in addition to local grants many states have taken over complete responsibility for the construction and maintenance of the whole state system of roads.

Grants from states to localities for public health, social welfare, hospitals, and charitable institutions have been relatively small compared with those for education and highways. Increases in such amounts as well as in control have been greatest since 1890. Professor Fairlie estimates that, from 1913 to 1929, state expenditures for charities doubled, although the proportion of total expenditures for this purpose was smaller in the latter than in the former year. Since that time, of course, all records for state and federal expenditures for relief have been broken, as the previous chapter indicated. State services, such as laboratories, clinics, and the extension of state hospitals for the insane, for charity cases and for specialized attention in order to relieve local institutions, have also increased.

The centralizing tendency with its attendant grants and controls is much less pronounced in such things as fire prevention, recreation, parks and playgrounds, and adult education.

Special districts organized for special purposes. The tendency toward special interests and the forming of special blocs has been noted. The results of such trends from the standpoint of local government can be found wherever special *ad hoc* districts have been created for the administration of such purposes, other than education, as health and sanitation, mosquito abatement, drainage, public relief, and what not. A locality was found in the East which had eleven different elections each year, some on the township basis,

---

[8] Fairlie, John A., "Subsidies to Local Governments," from the *Proceedings* of the Chicago Exploratory Research Conference on the Reorganization of the Areas and Foundation of Local Government, May, 1932. New York: Social Science Research Council, 1932. See the chapter on Education and the Schools for other figures regarding proportions of state aid.

some on the county basis, but the majority on the special district basis. Apparently under many local conditions it is easier to organize a special district for a special purpose than it is to reorganize existing units to perform new duties.

Another example is reported in a recent study of local government in the State of Washington. There the taxpayers face a total of nearly three thousand governmental units empowered to levy taxes and incur debts, and all but about 260 of them are special purpose districts.[9] Nationally, special districts for control of rural roads, bridges, and water are the largest in number. They present many problems. State and county authorities are often unaware of their existence. Records of their actions, their proposed tax levies, and even their metes and bounds are difficult to make. Their boundaries and often their functions overlap with other units. This crossing of lines is shown in Table 92, taken from the Census.

TABLE 92. NUMBER OF GOVERNMENTAL UNITS WHICH CROSS STATE OR COUNTY LINES, BY REGION, 1942

(Number of school districts located in two or more counties not compiled.)

Region	All Units	Municipalities			Special Districts
		All	Urban	Rural	
United States total:					
Interstate	15				15
Intercounty	876	278	54	224	598
Northeast:					
Interstate	7	....	....	....	7
Intercounty	24	15	8	7	9
North Central:					
Interstate	6	....	....	....	6
Intercounty	430	153	23	130	277
South:					
Interstate	0	....	....	....	0
Intercounty	301	107	22	85	194
West:					
Interstate	2	....	....	....	2
Intercounty	121	3	1	2	118

Source: *Governmental Units in the United States,* 1942. Washington, D.C.: Bureau of the Census, United States Department of Commerce.

[9] Reuss, Carl F., *County Government in Washington.* Pullman: Bulletin 400, Agricultural Experiment Station, State College of Washington, May, 1941.

Nearly six hundred special districts cross county boundaries and fifteen cut state lines.

Urban and rural municipalities also have a tendency to disregard county lines as the table indicates. Local government is, therefore, not a simple arrangement, but rather an intermesh of functions and forms. County and community, as following paragraphs will suggest, must struggle to give it some sense of system and meaning for the local citizen.

Some newer forms and working relationships. First, there are the new types of authorities for setting up local units of government, encouraged and backed by substantial appropriations from the national government. The examples are the United States Housing Authority and the Soil Conservation Service in the United States Department of Agriculture. The latter is the federal government's first venture into the arena of local government and as Professor Anderson points out, has resulted in increasing the number of local units and also in further complicating the structure of local government.

Another interesting development in federal-local government relations are the so-called "action" agencies described in an earlier chapter. Under the Agricultural Adjustment Act, for example, an acreage allotment of soil-depleting crops was set for every farmer in the country. Compliance with the allotment was the basis for benefit payments. The point of interest here is the direct line of contractual agreement from the federal government right to the individual farmer. The general administration was given to a national department and locally to county and community committees whose activities have been detailed in a previous chapter. A similar direct contract relationship was set up through the Farm Security Administration in the tenant-purchase program. The Pope-Jones Water Facilities Act provides for direct aid to individual farmers and ranchers in the development of facilities for water on private lands. This is definitely something new under the governmental sun.

Some new forms have also been devised looking toward conservation and co-ordination rather than expansion and specialization. The soil-conservation district cited above is one, but another is the principle of zoning applied to land-use. This is in the sphere of what may be called state-local relations. The state, by passing an enabling act, encourages counties to set up a zoning ordinance which becomes operative when the local units, townships, or other municipalities vote it. This is in conformity with the idea of social uses for land, also explained in an earlier chapter. Certain sections of land are "zoned" against agriculture because it is considered that there are better social uses; that is, better from the standpoint of public policy. Such uses might be forestry, recreation, wild-life refuge, or water conservation.

Developments such as those briefly reviewed can become, as two political scientists have pointed out, opportunities for partisan prize-fights or for collaboration by various levels of local governments in order to strengthen and improve their position.[10] New techniques are needed to bring about such improvement.

One experiment has been the land-use planning committees both at the community and the county level, to which reference has been made. It is not a new technique for farmers to meet together and plan, but since 1933, when the action programs came into use, the opportunity has been greatly expanded. There is no general agreement on how well some of the experiments have succeeded. In some states the areas for activity were extended from land-use to general over-all planning for agriculture, including social activities.[11] At least one of the motives, according to M. L. Wilson, director of the Federal Agricultural Extension Service, was to intensify and extend the democratic process in rural America. He said, "We must battle for a renaissance of democracy and for new democratic patterns in farm life and in the rural community." [12]

•Consideration of the agricultural extension services brings to attention an important federal-state-county government relationship often overlooked or perhaps taken for granted. It is the system including enabling legislation, appropriation, and personnel selection whereby the three levels of government — national, state, and county — work as one in the hiring and the services of agricultural representatives; "county agents" they are called locally in many states. The agents may be employed to do agricultural, home economics, junior, or even specialized, types of work within the county. It means "the agricultural agent, himself a combination of

10 Gaus, John M., address at Association of Land Grant Colleges and Universities, Chicago, November 14, 1938; and Leon Wolcott, "National Land-Use Program and the Local Governments," National Municipal Review, vol. XXVII, no. 2, February, 1939.

11 Gross, Neal C., "Post Mortem on County Planning," Journal of Farm Economics, vol. XXV, no. 3, August, 1943; Williams, Robin M., and Howard W. Beers, Farmers on Local Planning Committees in Three Kentucky Counties, 1939-1940. Lexington: Bulletin 443, Kentucky Agricultural Experiment Station, 1943.

12 Wilson, M. L., Land Policy Review, January-February, 1939.

federal, state, and local official," carries on in the county, in the community, and on the farms.[13]

The agricultural and home economics teachers in the rural community high schools are another example of national-state-community relationships in local government. They have the unique opportunity, to which frequent reference has been made, to give leadership through the high school to local community development. The hope is registered here that in the future the two lines of relationship can be more closely co-ordinated, both officially and practically; namely, the Smith-Lever provision for county agents and the Smith-Hughes and the George Dean provisions for agricultural and home economics teachers.

The T.V.A. is itself an experiment in federal-local governmental relations, as the above-cited reference suggests. Mr. Lilienthal explains that there is a sound distrust of bigness and of remote control among the rank and file of local citizens. Therefore, he believes the decentralized administration of federal functions which lend themselves to such techniques and the co-ordination in the field of such decentralized activities is one answer. Such activities in the T.V.A. have included use of farm equipment, community refrigeration, operation of power systems, wild-life conservation, and population transfers.[14]

Finally, local units of government may discharge powers and duties by co-operative methods. This may be done by joint employment of trained personnel and the construction, or at least the use by contract or other arrangement, of social institutions, such as sanitaria, fire-fighting equipment, or library services. There may be construction and maintenance on a contract basis of such public services as highways, sewers, or breakwaters. There can be co-operative purchasing of supplies or equipment or the inspection of plumbing or of weights and measures.[15] It is pointed out that savings can accrue from such joint arrangements as well as real improvement in services and facilities.

Where there is a will, a way can frequently be found, and, as has been suggested elsewhere, social practice may need to precede

[13] Lilienthal, David E., "The T.V.A.: An Experiment in the 'Grass Roots' Administration of Federal Functions." Address, Southern Political Science Association, Knoxville, Tennessee, November 10, 1939.

[14] Lilienthal, op. cit., and Democracy on the March. New York: Harper & Bros., 1944; Herman Finer, The T.V.A.: Lessons for International Application. Montreal: International Labor Office, 1945.

[15] "Joint Municipal Services," The Municipality, published by the League of Wisconsin Municipalities, Madison, August, 1944.

legal sanction. Added opportunities are, therefore, given to local government authorities, and they increase the importance of good county and community organization and administration.

GOVERNMENT IN LOCAL ACTION

The discussion thus far should lead to the conclusion that it is not local government versus state or federal government, but that the real task is to bring into local action all government in all its phases and services. The theory of conflict is giving way, even in the courts, and in its place the realization is slowly growing that the function of government is the welfare and happiness of its citizens; that there are common interests, and that these can best be served by giving attention to local situations where problems arise.[16] Poverty, delinquency, ignorance, unemployment, are problems of local origin and import, but they are no respecters of government units or boundary lines. Protection is prevention at source has proved the best motto. To conclude the chapter, therefore, brief discussion will be given to three phases of government services which may help to reach such local objectives.

State, the equalizing and servicing unit. The state, and in similar reference the nation, may be regarded, from this one standpoint of local government, as units for bringing about a better equalization throughout rural society. This function would include not only equalizing of tax burdens, but of standards in services and contracts, the qualifications of personnel through training and certification in some civil service system, in the central custody of records, and in the "orders in council" of state departments.

More vigorous service can be rendered in terms of grants-in-aid and furnishing specialized services, materials, laboratories, and personnel which cannot possibly be available in the smaller units. Of course, many complications can easily develop if the principles suggested above are not followed meticulously by all parties involved. For example, it was suggested in the Washington State Report, referred to earlier, that a generous Santa Claus could later assume the proportions of a Trojan Horse. In changed metaphor, but with the same meaning, the *Municipal Bulletin* of that state describes the situation in which some cities, and it could as well be counties, find themselves. "Through the back door of unemploy-

---

[16] Mashek, John R., "The Changing Nature of Federalism," *Iowa Farm Economist*, September, 1944.

ment relief, the federal government entered the cities and now occupies a seat in the parlor." [17] Well, perhaps the local government house needs both a back door and a parlor, but, more important, it requires some kind of management and also integration with other units in the community and nation. It cannot be a dwelling apart from the rest of society and have even its own household members adequately served. It is an excellent example of how easy it is to get into the conflict attitude of "either-or" this or that authority, rather than the co-operative position of "both-and" the local and the nation-state responsibility for common problems.

County, the administering unit. A case has been deliberately built for suggesting that the county should serve as the administrative, and the community as the working, unit for certain types of services needed in modern rural society. Whether this shall be made the prevailing pattern rests ultimately upon rural leaders and upon rural people themselves. Services and functions are concentrated at the county level. The growth of county health units, the work of county agricultural and home demonstration agents, under both state and federal grants, the movement toward county administration of education, the urge for county library services, the increase of county parks and recreation places, and the accumulation of social welfare functions on a county basis all point in this direction.

The number and variety of these agencies have been expanding until one finds two counties, one in New York State and one in California, which have thirteen and fourteen agencies, respectively, organized on a county basis.

A New York County

** Health Unit
** Farm Bureau and Agricultural Agent
** Home Bureau and Home Agent
** Junior work with 4–H Clubs
 * Council of Religious Education
   Red Cross
 * Boy Scouts
 * Girl Scouts
   Chamber of Commerce
   W.C.T.U.
** Library
   Grange
 * Dairymen's League
   Co-operative Marketing Associations

A California County

** Health Unit
** Farm Bureau and Agricultural Agent
** Home Bureau and Home Agent
** Junior work with 4–H Clubs
   Sunday-School Association
 * Welfare League
 * Y.M.C.A.
 * Boy Scouts
 * Chamber of Commerce
   Federation of Women's Clubs
   Parent-Teacher Association
 * Co-operative Marketing Associations
** Library

---

 * With paid personnel.
** Tax supported and paid personnel.

[17] Chatters, Carl H., "Local Government Finance and Democracy," *Washington Municipal Bulletin,* Report 25, May 12, 1938.

Recent experience in the administration of such service as public relief and social welfare is likewise giving the county greater prominence. For example, a federal government publication on social welfare states quite flatly that "the country has been generally accepted as a more practical local administrative unit than the individual town or township." To be sure, this is the conviction or ideal of a professional worker, not shared by all leaders, nor yet by most rural people, but it is evidence of a trend in administration. The report adds that by the beginning of 1932 only about one third of the states had developed county welfare programs but the number has increased.

National agencies, such as the Social Security Board, have made uniform county, town, or district plans prerequisite to their financial participation. These and other pressures toward county administration of social functions are definitely being felt.

Counties themselves, however, are often laid out along arbitrary lines with little or no regard for the services to be performed or for the groups to be served. Since some are small in area, wealth, and population, a movement for county consolidation has developed. Agency consolidations have taken place in about twenty states, while plans and proposals of a state-wide character are under way in seventeen others according to reports of the National Municipal League. Inability of poor counties to support needed institutions and services makes some kind of reorganization necessary. It is difficult to redraw or to wipe out county lines because of political and traditional loyalties, but it appears that more can be done to combine functions, consolidate institutions, and eventually to bring together the counties themselves. However, there is little cause for great optimism since the enumerations show, in 1942, only three fewer counties than ten years earlier.

It must be recognized that a heavy responsibility rests upon the counties. There are those who feel that county government must be something more than administrative; that it should be empowered to perform services similar to a city municipality; and that it should have an executive head. The county-manager plan, an adaptation of the city-manager plan, has been advocated for this purpose, but it has had little acceptance apart from a few largely urban counties.

Another effort to bring about better co-ordination of effort and to give some sense of direction is the county council. The idea harks back nearly thirty years to the Councils of National Defense. Likewise, during World War II, county agencies assumed larger responsibilities and co-ordinating policies were put into practice. An interesting five-year experiment with a county council was carried on in Greenville County, South Carolina, from 1936 to 1941.[18] Among its notable achievements three have point here. It aroused public interest and concern regarding local social problems; it demonstrated the need for professional and trained personnel and the importance of working closely with voluntary and lay leaders; and it indicated that success is achieved in proportion to democratic planning and the assumption of responsibility at the community level.

From whatever angle we approach, the participation of local people as citizens becomes the crux of social organizational and institutional plans. As in other relationships, voting, as one index of participation in government, reflects variations, not only in economic status, but also the family, educational, and religious influences in the community.[19]

Details of county-wide administration for rural services cannot be given here, but a summary under six general functions is suggested. They appear to be more and more dependent for promotion and administration upon the county or similar local unit.

(1) Education: youth and adult, vocational and cultural, including schools and libraries.

(2) Agriculture: services to farm, family, and youth.

(3) Health: physical and mental, remedial and preventive.

(4) Welfare: social security, child welfare, corrections.

(5) Public services: roads, bridges, parks, conservation, zoning for land-uses.

(6) Political: elections, tax levy and collection, protection and justice.

Counties unable to perform at least a majority of such functions may be in the position of being considered not worthy and not capable of permanent county status.

Community, the working unit. The community idea is posited on the theory that rural people can and wish to join together locally, to determine their common weal. Field workers in rural communities reported that local people insist that some form of local organization is necessary. They argue that the county is too

[18] Brunner, Edmund de S., *Community Organization and Adult Education.* Chapel Hill: University of North Carolina Press, 1942.

[19] McMillan, Robert T., "Voting Differentials of Rural Farm and Non-Farm Populations," *The Southwestern Journal,* vol. I, no. 2, 1944.

large and the county seat too far away. They want local officials whom they "can know and trust." Many town chairmen and clerks as well as many village officials are familiar to their constituencies and go far beyond narrow legal or semi-legal duties. They are truly "representatives of the people." Unfortunately, not all the declarations of local politicians are sincere. Just as city people turn to their ward leaders for help in untangling difficulties arising out of conflicts in governmental jurisdiction, so rural people turn to their own local officials. This is simply to say what Professor Munro has expressed more emphatically thus: "They [people of educated and propertied classes] have been obsessed with a faith in political mechanics and have been enslaved to the conviction that government is an affair of laws, not of men." [20]

. The administrative unit for many functions may be the county; but there is need for more localized working units. For example, in some states, like California and Ohio, where the county library plan has wide usage, a local branch is often maintained in the high school, not only for the pupils, but for the residents of the larger community. There may be a branch in the village also, but the whole system, both of finance and of personnel, is integrated. Needless duplications, often found among country district schools, or between country schools and village schools, or again between school and village libraries, are avoided.

County health units were also visited in which community groups of interested adults formed the real working unit of the organization. Prevention and therapeutic work was all correlated with plans carried out through the schools. Agencies for recreation, child welfare, social service, credit, and fire prevention were found working according to similar arrangements.

Church leaders are talking of the "larger parish," the central idea of which they say is "a group ministry over areas as well as churches." They point out that this is really a return to the original English practice where churches are responsible for definite and assigned "parishes." Promotion of the plan in this country is proceeding definitely upon the theory of a town-country community.

The school has been repeatedly emphasized for the part it may play in community leadership for both youth and adult. The conclusion of the South Carolina Report, to which reference has already been made, is pertinent. "A developing concept of the community school holds greatest hope for the future of a creative rural life."

[20] Munro, William B., of the California Institute of Technology, quoted from *Information Service*, New York, October 31, 1931.

A complete governmental unit on the community basis has even been proposed. Its advocates suggest that it could be flexible enough to accommodate different local situations in all of their essential functions.[21]

The problem of co-ordination and the importance of local action can perhaps be illustrated with a simple diagram. The trends toward specialization and segregation of groups and functions which have been traced herein can very easily lead to a perpendicular type of social organization. The familiar dilemma of either-or is weak; there is need for some means of deliberate integration and cross-reference. It makes very little difference where one begins or what set of agencies one chooses. The tendency can be illustrated by the accompanying chart (Figure 44), in which Doctor Small's six elementary interests are used.[22] Institutions and agencies are bearing down upon rural society with a great deal of independence of action and with much pressure from the top down, "the top" being state, regional, or national headquarters. This trend toward centralized control for many agencies has already been pointed out in earlier chapters.

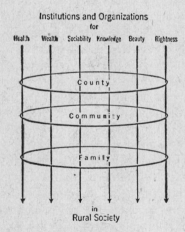

Institutions and Organizations
for

Health Wealth Sociability Knowledge Beauty Rightness

County

Community

Family

in
Rural Society

Figure 44

CHART SUGGESTING PERPENDICULAR TYPE OF
ORGANIZATION FOR SOCIAL INSTITUTIONS
IN RURAL SOCIETY

[21] Manny, Theodore B., *The Rural Municipalities*. New York: Century Co., 1930

[22] Small, A. W., *General Sociology*, p. 198. Chicago: University of Chicago Press, 1905.

The loops drawn crosswise in the diagram suggest the necessity for some linkage or integration at various levels. The three cross-loops suggested are at the family, the community, and the county level. If the picture were to be completed, it would probably be necessary to introduce a personality and a state loop. However, the concern here is more largely with local organization policies. In discussions of the increasing importance attached to group relationships in a modern and changing society, individual and state interests receive much attention. To be sure, the reconciliation of the demands and impulses of personality with the requirements of a complex society is important; yet it is to be remembered that much of life is lived in an area which is the domain neither of the individual nor the state. As a matter of fact, some of the most important and socializing experiences occur between these two spheres.

The importance of the rural family and the problems centering around its children have been detailed elsewhere. The point at issue here is, Can the rural community with courage and foresight forge a link which will bind into a unity of action those agency arrows which are bearing down upon it? Traditionally, the rural community had elements of individualism and of competitive independence. Under modern conditions it has an opportunity to work out another way of living. It might even be argued that collective action is necessary as a means of self-defense, lest independent institutions disrupt local life. From a more constructive standpoint, however, the opportunity is present for a greater awareness of local needs and for co-ordinated efforts to meet them. To accomplish this, as Sanderson says, a desire for unified action is imperative.[23] The promotion of the common welfare can be made the goal of the community only as it becomes more self-conscious and gradually assumes self-direction.

The county link binding the arrows into a sheaf brings us back to the trends and policies already discussed and to the place which the county can legitimately hope to maintain in public and in voluntary forms of social control and social action. It must be urged once more that local governmental and social organization is not for the purposes of limiting or hemming in, but rather of introducing and relating rural society to the larger society, the theme of the next and final chapter.

This chapter began with the statement that there had been little

[23] Sanderson, Dwight, *The Rural Community*, p. 559. Boston: Ginn & Co., 1932.

recent change in the forms of local government, but there have been recorded here many changes in governmental activities and devices. The interesting thing is that the form and structure of local government have not changed significantly under the impact of all this changing activity. State and federal agencies have simply caught on where and how they could. Sometimes, when finding nothing to tie to locally, they have dealt directly with individuals. However, the very contact of local people with representatives of larger units must have modified their conceptions of the purposes of social action under the aegis of this institution which we call government.

Questions, of course, arise which cannot be answered now, as to the long-time effects of this movement upon small local units. It may influence the attitudes of rural people as to the uses of government. It is certainly sharpening the division between those who welcome and those who resent the increased power of state and nation. But whatever their reactions, most rural citizens now find themselves in an intermesh of governmental relationships that have been set up because of some need. They may not be logical and they may not follow existing jurisdictions, but there they are. Soil-conservation districts, for example, were made to follow geological and geographical, not political, lines, although in some instances they have been pressed into present county patterns.

The way to get things done is to get things done. That is the way our American society works, and has worked for some time, or at least did work during the nineteen-thirties and the early nineteen-forties. Apparently the critic, with the background of recent Central European experiences, Mr. Hayek, forgot or overlooked this trait, a characteristic, however, which the Frenchman, de Tocqueville, did observe and took into account in his analysis of *Democracy in America*, nearly seventy years ago.[24]

DISCUSSION TOPICS

1. Describe the general plan of local government which is operative in your state. Indicate the relation of local units to each other.
2. Enumerate the functions which are performed by the local units of government in your state and the officials or boards which are responsible for each.
3. In establishing or maintaining a rural high-school program, what unit

[24] de Tocqueville, Alexis, *Democracy in America*, edited by Phillip Bradley. New York: Alfred A. Knopf, 1945.

requirements, such as number of people, size of district, and wealth of area, need to be considered? How do these units compare with similar units required for libraries, hospitals, townships and counties?

4. To the support of what local rural institutions must county, state or nation contribute? On what principles can you justify such support?

5. Describe evidences which you have observed of the break-down of local units of government, or of efforts (successful or otherwise) to reorganize local functions and units on larger scales.

6. Plans may be worked out for organizing all or part of the class as a county board to consider the needed programs and finances for the year. Committees presenting different phases of work such as health, agriculture, education, recreation, public welfare, and so on, would present their claims. The final adoption of a complete program and budget would rest with the class as a whole or, if organized on the small commission plan, with those members who are appointed to act as commissioners.

REFERENCE READINGS

American Country Life Association, *Rural Government, Proceedings* of the Fourteenth American Country Life Conference, Ithaca, New York. Chicago: University of Chicago Press, 1932.

Brannen, C. O., *Characteristics and Costs of County Government in Arkansas.* Fayetteville: Bulletin 338, Agricultural Experiment Station, University of Arkansas, January, 1937.

Brownlow, Louis, and Charles S. Ascher, *Less Government or More?* Chicago: American Library Association, 1933.

Catherwood, M. P., *Rural Government in New York.* Ithaca: Bulletin 331, Cornell Extension Bulletin, State College of Agriculture, Revised, January, 1936.

Davis, Joseph S., *On Agricultural Policy, 1926-1938.* Stanford University, 1939.

Fairlie and Kneier, *County Government and Administration.* New York: Century Co., 1930. A statement of all aspects of the local governmental functions.

Frank, Lawrence K., "The Rising Stock of Doctor Hayek," *The Saturday Review of Literature,* May 12, 1945.

Hammar, Conrad H., and Glen T. Barton, *The Farmer and the Cost of Local Rural Government in Missouri.* Columbia: Bulletin 385, Agricultural Experiment Station, University of Missouri, June, 1937.

Hayek, Friedrich A., *The Road to Serfdom.* Chicago: University of Chicago Press, 1944.

Jones, Howard P., "Reorganization of County Government in New York State," Institute of Public Affairs, University of Virginia, 1934.

Kumlien, W. F., *Basic Trends of Social Change in South Dakota,* VII, "Local Government." Brookings: Bulletin 347, Agricultural Experiment Station, South Dakota State College, February, 1941.

Lancaster, Lane W., *Government in Rural America.* New York: D. Van Nostrand Co., 1937. Analysis of town and county governments in the several states.

Manny, Theodore B., *Rural Municipalities.* New York: Century Co., 1930. A discussion of local rural government from the standpoint of the town-country community.

Nason, W. C., *Rural Planning, the Village.* Washington, D.C.: United States Department of Agriculture, 1925. Brief statement of what villages have done and might do.

Parsons, K. H., "Local Government Adjustments to Land Programs." Washington, D.C.: *Supplementary Report of Land Planning Committee,* Section IV, National Resources Board, titled "Certain Aspects of Land Problems and Government Land Policies.

Stromberg, Eugene C., *The Influence of the Central Rural School on Community Organization.* Ithaca: Bulletin 699, Cornell University Agricultural Experiment Station, 1938.

Taft, Charles P., "County Government Reform in Ohio," Institute of Public Affairs, University of Virginia, 1934.

Terry, Paul W., and Verner M. Sims, *They Live on the Land; Life in an Open-Country Southern Community.* Bureau of Educational Research, University of Alabama, 1940.

Wasson, C. R., and Dwight Sanderson, *Relation of Community Areas to Town Government in the State of New York.* Ithaca: Cornell University Agricultural Experiment Station, May, 1932.

Wehrwein, George S., "Town Government in Wisconsin." *Wisconsin Blue Book,* 1935.

Wehrwein, George S., "County Government in Wisconsin." *Wisconsin Blue Book,* 1933.

Wehrwein, George S., "Village Government in Wisconsin." *Wisconsin Blue Book,* 1940.

Yang, Martin C., *A Chinese Village: Taitou, Shantung Province.* New York: Columbia University Press, 1945.

26

Rural Society and the Great Society

IT HAS BECOME A TRUISM to declare that more than half the problems of the American farmer lie outside the line fences of his farms. It is, however, a truth that is not fully recognized, either on the farms or in the cities of the nation. Ours has become an interdependent society. If agriculture is depressed, business sales and profits suffer, and labor has less work. If labor is unemployed or works for low wages in comparison with the cost of food, agriculture suffers.

The complicated mechanisms of the price system, of credit, of tariffs, and foreign exchange are but social inventions devised by man to match the potentialities of his expanding technology in order the better to exchange goods and services among groups. But all these, and even money itself, only facilitate the bartering of wheat for shoes, eggs for coffee, cotton for schooling. This is likewise a truism, but one not adequately grasped by mankind, as our social behavior shows.

At the moment the world looks forward to only one certainty, that of change — fundamental change compelled by a war which has shattered half the world, destroyed untold wealth, and released secrets of atomic energy. United Nations have drawn a new plan designed to promote peace and allow men to rebuild their nations and the world of which the nations are a part. Politically, it is recognized that war anywhere is a threat to peace everywhere. The Charter of the United Nations recognizes also that political arrangements alone will be inadequate if social and economic conditions are, or become, insupportable. Hence the Social and Economic Council provided for within the framework of the new world organization.

Enormous amounts of fact-gathering, research, and planning have entered into this whole process. Comparably, nations are hard at work producing plans for meeting the problems and shocks of converting their societies from the single purpose of winning a war to the manifold purposes of achieving a better life for their citizens.[1] Nor is the United States an exception, despite the unfortunate action of Congress in refusing funds to continue the National Resources Planning Board. Government departments are concerned with this task, each in its own area of responsibility. The United States Department of Agriculture has an Inter-Bureau Committee on Post-War Planning which is concerned with all aspects of rural life — production, economic, social. Private national agencies, such as the great farm organizations, the labor unions, the United States Chamber of Commerce, educational and religious bodies, and many others, are engaged in this task of determining what their objectives should be and how they can be successfully achieved. This activity is reaching to the local level. In many states, farmers and their wives and their village neighbors, with the help of the college of agriculture, are examining their present situations and trying to plan for the future. Under the auspices of the business-financed Committee on Economic Development, about two thousand towns and cities are engrossed in a process of fact-gathering, planning, and putting into action various projects designed for this postwar period. This is as it should be. Our nation is a democracy, and its essence is that not only the civil servants of our society in government, but also the citizens themselves, where they live and work, should share in this process, and that it should be a continuous process.

There are those who fear that social planning, so-called, will lead to dictatorship. They point to the defeated Axis countries as a terrible warning. They forget that in them there was no democratic tradition built up over centuries of experience. They overlook such recent examples in rural society as the formulation of agricultural policies with the co-operation of the farmers concerned, under the Agricultural Adjustment Act, and the country planning conferences in which the best of government plans met the correction of the freely expressed opinions of local people, based on their own knowledge of their community.

Through all the ages of scarcity, when man produced feverishly to have enough to consume in order that life could be sustained, the myth grew that man was helpless to alter the unchanging social laws said to be inherent in the structure of the universe. But ever-advancing technology, in the factory and on the farm, has proved that concept to be wrong. So long as raw material lasts, an econ-

[1] Lorwin, Lewis L., *Postwar Plans of the United Nations.* New York: Second Century Fund, 1943.

omy of relative abundance is possible. All that is necessary in terms of the United States is to achieve in peace what we have already achieved in war, when, despite many handicaps, food production increased to almost 40 per cent over 1935-39 averages, and industrial production considerably more than doubled.

The so-called "economic laws" are man's creation. The alternative is not between "submission to impersonal and seemingly irrational forces of the market" and "submission to the arbitrary power of men," as Hayek maintains. The alternative is between social chaos and social control by intelligent, democratic planning. Only if Americans forget that in a democratic government there is the spirit of "we, the people"; only if they fail to recognize and to exercise their responsibilities as citizens, will there be danger.

Moreover, the die has been cast. The United Nations Charter, the Bretton Woods Agreement, the United Nations Food and Agriculture Organization, and other developments growing out of World War II, give evidence that the old defeatist attitude of mankind toward its collective fate is passing. Rather, men are coming to believe that by taking thought for the morrow they can become masters of their fate. Science, including the social sciences and technology, have made this change possible.

While the social sciences, being newer, have lagged behind the physical, they, too, are fortifying this changed attitude. Anthropologists have discovered and described successful societies that are co-operative rather than competitive.[2] Economists have found under what conditions capital is most rapidly formed and have shed new light on the behavior of the mechanism of price-making.[3] Psychologists are asking if competition is beneficial or whether it arises from feelings of inferiority. Sociologists are developing knowledge as to how society behaves in its groups, institutions, and in other manifestations. The social psychologists and the social psychiatrists are finding the person and are helping him better to relate himself to a changing physical and social environment. Such knowledge makes planning possible.

The late President Franklin D. Roosevelt, in his undelivered speech, put the challenge in this way: "Today we are faced with the pre-eminent fact that if civilization is to survive we must culti-

---

[2] Cf., for instance, Mead, Margaret, *Competition and Co-operation Among Primitive People.*

[3] *The Formation of Capital.* Washington, D.C.: Brookings Institution, 1934; and Nourse, Edwin, *Price-Making in a Democracy.* Washington, D.C.: Brookings Institution, 1944.

vate the science of human relations — the ability of all peoples, of all kinds, to live together and work together in the same world, at peace."

This is not to say that society has proceeded unplanned up to this time. That would be ridiculous. Rural America has had many plans written into law.

A great national land policy was planned in the post-Civil War days and executed with considerable success under the Homestead Law. Amid all the confusion and alarms of civil strife, we planned to bring the benefits of science to agriculture on a national scale, and therefore founded our Land Grant colleges of agriculture. Under the necessities of a greater conflict, World War I, and under the spell of a century and a half, in which each day saw more mouths to feed and backs to clothe than the day before, we re-doubled our efforts to produce ever more by planning. We estab-lished and expanded our agricultural extension service, and assisted all rural high schools that desired it to have a teacher of agriculture. The extension-service plan has been copied by other nations. Con-fronted by the problem of providing adequate credit for agricul-ture, we planned and created the Federal Land Bank System, which measurably improved the credit conditions of agriculture. What is true in agriculture is true in other branches of our national economy. But we have had scattered and sporadic plans and have not seen that often such plans when combined produced a new dilemma. We have not understood, and perhaps still do not under-stand, the difference between plans and a planning program con-stantly taking all the changing factors into account. Nor have we understood the difference between a "planned economy" in the German sense and a society that embarks democratically on a con-tinuing process of social planning, by all and for all.

Social science is not wholly prepared to accept the challenge to guide society more rigorously in the paths of social wisdom. But that attempt must be made inevitably; indeed, it is even now being made in the United States. This chapter, then, is concerned with summarizing some of the more important trends in the rural soci-ety of the United States which have been previously discussed, and will also outline a few projected policies. The summary will not, however, so much rehearse facts as raise questions and indicate possible further policies. It will ask if population growth and move-ment can be socially controlled, and if so, how? It will appraise social relationships and attitudes, especially those concerning city and country as interdependent parts of the nation. It will raise the issue of the social uses of land, of restricted production, and seek answers for rural social problems in the light of expanding horizons of knowledge.

The assumption of the chapter is that a greater measure of social planning is essential, and that only through planning and experimentation can a larger measure of social well-being be achieved. It is quite clear, however, that what can be done in rural America in the postwar years, however good the theoretical plans, will be conditioned by the general level of well-being and productivity in the nation as a whole, and even upon the tempo and type of world recovery. This is but another indication of the interdependent nature of modern social life.

POPULATION PROBLEMS AND POLICIES

Consider first the complicated problem of population. Two thirds of the world's population live on and till the land. A vast majority are close to bare subsistence, ill-fed, clothed, and housed. This is especially true in the Far East, and in the countries between the Baltic and the Aegean Seas, where almost three fourths of the hundred million population are on farms, yet the standard of living is low, farmers are underemployed, discontent is endemic, poverty is widespread.[4] Yields per acre are one fourth what they are in northwestern Europe.

Even in the United States such conditions exist. The cotton croppers of the South, the hill-dwellers of the Ozarks and Appalachians, are far removed from the vaunted American standard of living.

It is in precisely these areas that there is the largest number of children in comparison with the adult population. There have been large migrations during the history of the United States, as has been shown. If world conditions should grow worse and a depression should set in, the rural-urban migration might again fall off and the rural emigrées to urban industries return to the farm. If this happens, will farms increase in number, but decrease in size, causing the standard of living to decline? Or will rural America thus regain political dominance, become even more self-conscious, and move in unexpected ways seeking a more generous distribution of the wealth and income of the nation that will favor rural rather than urban dwellers, thus perhaps causing sectional conflict?

[4] Cf. Royal Institute of International Affairs, *Agrarian Problems from the Baltic to the Aegean*. London, 1944.

If, on the other hand, the earnest efforts toward world recovery succeed, and if prosperity is maintained at home, will hundreds of thousands, perhaps millions, again leave rural for urban America in an unguided rush?

Can social policy affect the birth rate? But perhaps a question more fundamental than location of population is that which concerns its rate of growth. New trends indicate that the nation which has grown by millions with every decade, seems likely to cease to grow in 1970 or 1980. The proportion of old people in the total population is already mounting. An increase in the death rate will inevitably follow. A declining population, which is a probability if present trends continue, would mean painful readjustments for industry, real estate, and agriculture. The cities have always been consumers rather than producers of population. They are not reproducing themselves today, and their population deficit is so large that many whole states are not propagating enough children to keep the city population stable without immigration from outside. Rural America, while still having and producing a surplus of children, is now sharing in the declining birth rate.

It is true that in the early nineteen-forties the birth rate rose sharply, as did the marriage rate, due first to the threat and then to the fact of war. This will once more raise school enrollments and produce a new peak in the number of youth in the late nineteen-fifties and early nineteen-sixties. But the trend in the birth rate was downward, from 1924 for a decade and more, and, as was shown, the ratio of children under five to women sixteen to forty-four years of age has declined for over a century.

Like our migrations, the declining birth rate is a conscious social phenomenon made up of the individual responses of millions of families to the economic and social conditions that they face. Can planning affect such a problem? It is impossible to answer because such planning has never been tried on any large scale. But it seems logical to believe that greater security might influence the birth rate. It rose in the United States as the depression lightened in the middle thirties. Greater security had a similar result in prolific Russia. Old-age pensions, maternity benefits, or family allowances, as given in a number of countries and most recently in Canada, unemployment insurance, cheaper, better housing, increased income, tax exemptions for children, are all social policies designed to improve the birth rate and to cut down mortality rates.

Population and land. Some may object that in many rural areas there is no need for increasing the birth rate. It is already too high in some places, putting too much pressure on land, forcing migration of rural youth, none too well prepared for adjustment, to urban life. If ever a population policy is adopted, it must be linked with a land policy. This is another illustration of the way in which social considerations intermesh.

During the nineteen-thirties, some embryonic attempts were made to link population and land policies by moving people from sub-marginal to better land. With the development of the great dams along the Columbia, Colorado, and other rivers, with the resultant irrigation of fertile soil, such a policy could be worked out, and marginal, or at least sub-marginal, lands zoned against agriculture, as they have been in a few states.

There is, of course, not enough reclaimed land to care for all the farm population now on poor soil, even assuming the people would wish to move. Nor is a policy of forced migration advocated. Americans have always been free to move where and when they would across the face of the continent. It would be quite possible, however, for society to produce conditions that would stimulate such migration under guided conditions.

The arguments in favor of such projects are not merely those often dismissed as "idealistic." During the nineteen-thirties there was an appreciable number of counties in which the total value of federal and state payments for rural relief and rehabilitation, agricultural adjustment, aid to rural schools, and the like, exceeded the value of products produced.

LAND-USE AND HUMAN WELFARE

This consideration raises squarely the whole issue of the relationship between land-use and human welfare. Under all is the land, but on the land are people, and without this human factor the best land in the world is unproductive. It is also true that the best land in the world can be ruined by overcropping, overgrazing, and other bad farm management practices. Our basic capital resource, the soil, can be wasted and destroyed: what is worse, it has been. The dramatic evidences of wind erosion were the dust storms of the Great Plains states during the droughts of 1934 and 1936, which even darkened the streets of Eastern seaboard cities on some days. Less dramatic, but just as alarming, are the evidences of water erosion, in the muddy waters of a thousand rivers and creeks after heavy rains, in the silt shoals fanning out for many a square mile at the mouth of the Mississippi River, made up of the precious top soils of the huge territory it drains. The evidences are in such stories as Arthur Moore tells of his McLean County, Illinois, concerning land cleared of its first-growth timber and planted to corn for the first time in 1941, which produced one hundred and twenty bushels to the acre against a county average of fifty-five bushels, the difference being a measure of the land's decline.[5] Annual farm records showed profits, but society was taking a loss. All told, we in the United States have destroyed 50,000,000 acres in our three centuries of occupancy and severely damaged as much more. Half the original top soil is gone on another 100,000,000 acres — all this out of our less than 400,000,000 acres of crop land. The land we settled was so rich, we assumed it was inexhaustible. We are slowly learning that it is not. The problem is not the soil; it is the man.

In this country, we have at last moved to attack this problem through the Soil-Conservation Act of about a decade ago. This provides for federal, state, and local co-operation, thus far through some 1100 soil-conservation districts in forty-five states, involving about one half the farmers of the nation. By June 30, 1944, under this plan 65,000,000 acres were in process of being completely protected. Nearly all of over 9000 farmers interviewed, in a sample survey by the Department of Agriculture, reported these practices had been effective in controlling erosion, and 96.6 per cent reported increased yields on protected acres.

Increase in soil fertility has been reported in some areas, but the demands for top production during the war have caused further deterioration on unprotected acres. According to the Soil-Conservation Service inventory of the nation's farm land, the total acreage to which one or another of the nine major conservation practices should be applied is almost 900,000,000 acres.[6] Obviously, therefore, many of our acres need more than one sort of treatment.

A proposed planning program. In 1934, Doctor H. R. Tolley, Chief of the Bureau of Agricultural Economics, indicated some of the basic needs of rural planning as he saw them. Some of the data called for have been gathered, and much in the program is as pertinent for the present postwar period as when it was announced. Included in this program is an analysis of the needs of the nation for the goods which land produces — food, fiber, wood, areas for recreation, for water supply and wild-life refuges. This analysis involves appraisal of population trends, of probable levels

[5] Moore, Arthur, *The Farmer and the Rest of Us,* chap. V. Boston: Little, Brown & Co., 1945.
[6] *Report of the Secretary of Agriculture,* 1944, p. 65. Washington, D.C.: Government Printing Office.

of living, and markets here and abroad. There must next be an inventory of our resources for meeting the discovered needs, and finally a practical program to bring the resources and the basic problems together.

Early proposals of the National Resources Planning Board along these lines called for the location of industries in disadvantaged rural areas; integrating agricultural and industrial employment and also agriculture with employment on public lands; prevention of settlement of public lands unsuitable for agriculture, use of state grants-in-aid for education and other social utilities, and also federal relief funds to discourage settlement in unsuitable areas.

In addition to the National Resources Planning Board, unfortunately ended by Congress in 1944, there are about forty states that have organized state planning commissions of varying degrees of efficiency. Some are proceeding within the states on much the same basis as the National Committee was dealing with the country as a whole. Their experience has brought out that regional planning is also a necessity. The Shenandoah Valley, the Tennessee Valley, and other areas transcend state lines.

There is, of course, in all this no hint as yet of the problems that may arise from rapid changes in agricultural production through advanced technology nor of the results of the possible development of artificial substitutes, especially for textile products.

The human side. There cannot be too much emphasis in all this program-building upon the human aspects, as stated in the discussion of the social-economics of agriculture. People live in families, neighborhoods, communities. They require social institutions. They must maintain adequate standards of living. No land policy can succeed unless the land of our nation provides this for rural people.

Unlimited Production?

The means and methods for achieving such a goal are not yet wholly agreed upon. In the nineteen-thirties, as an emergency measure, the production of some crops was restricted. With the world's desperate need for food and with rationing of food necessary even in the United States during World War II, there are those who today call for unlimited postwar production. Others, with an eye on the greatly expanded production of the last years, and with the certainty of the eventual recovery of European agriculture, insist that the machinery of the Agricultural Adjustment

Administration must be kept in good running order for use in the postwar period. Both groups are certain that, when machinery and fertilizer are again freely available to farmers, potential production, barring severe droughts, can exceed all prewar, and perhaps war, records, especially when full use is made of the advances in farm technology. Hybrid corn, for instance, has already increased corn yield per acre about 20 per cent.

In an ideal world, the advocates of full production would be wholly correct. In the quarter-century between the beginning of World War I and World War II, the per capita production of food in the United States dropped 8 per cent. The decline in beef cattle per capita was twice as much. In other words, the increase in food production did not keep pace with the increase in population. From 1924 to 1939, our imports of food products exceeded our exports in value.

The war years have shown that we do not have unlimited reserves of food and fiber. The statement of the Department of Agriculture in 1929 that, except in cereals, we were not producing enough food to supply our own population if per family income reached three thousand dollars a year was abundantly proved when that point was reached and passed in the early nineteen-forties, as discussed in a previous chapter.

Why, then, should anyone consider restrictions? One reason is clear, and it is an important limitation. We may have more of some crops than the nation needs, and less of others. It would be a social and economic tragedy if the South suddenly boosted its cotton acreage to 1930 levels, which would almost double that of the last years. We do not need unlimited production of cereals. Rather, human wants and needs and nutritional requirements should govern our postwar farm-management programs. One might also add that "market prospects" should influence the situation, were it not for the fact that society has subsidized the growing of cotton and cereals more often and more heavily than any other crops in the recent past. This would seem to give society the right to a voice in the discussion of how much of such crops should be raised.

But far more fundamental in the argument for restricted production is the farmer's memory of the long agricultural depression. Above everything else he fears a return of the days when there were bread lines in cities and rotting, unsold food and foreclosed mortgages on farms in rural America. He wants the machinery ready to combat a depression at its inception. He remembers that it took more than a decade of agitation and effort to get the first Agricultural Adjustment Act.

What price food? This explains the farmer's interest in the parity formula, discussed earlier, and in some protection for the prices of his products.[7] The farmer points out that business can have "administered prices" independent of government action, and indeed has had such prices, but that, since agriculture is made up of millions of separate units, government itself must administer farm prices. In a democracy, government is not an entity apart from the people. It is the organized expression of the will of the people, the tool which society uses to get certain things done.

If, then, government becomes an agency for the support or administration of farm prices, it is a recognition of the basic interest which society has in farm incomes. But it has an equal interest in determining that no group receives a disproportionate share of the national income. It must, therefore, take cognizance of the interdependencies of our major occupational groups. The interest society has in adequate farm income is that such income be used, as Schultz says, "to maximize social benefits. The governing criteria are found in social welfare." [8]

These criteria are not met when payments to agriculture are tied to income parity and payments are made according to previous production records. This results in the more prosperous farmers getting the larger sums and the poorer farmers, who most need help in raising their standard of living, getting the smaller payments. Improvement in their income would result in larger purchases of goods and services of other segments of society. Medical care is a conspicuous example. Schultz would have any payments by the government to the farmer available on equal terms, as is elementary education and rural free delivery of mail. "This would preserve certain democratic values." [9]

It is quite clear from this discussion that economics and sociology meet at this point. It is also clear that, if such a program gains adherents, the policies finally adopted must be determined in part by population trends and policies. As shown in the chapter on population, it is the more economically disadvantaged states and the families with low incomes that bear a disproportionate share of feeding, clothing, educating — in short, rearing the nation's chil-

[7] During the war, some farm leaders have put themselves in the illogical position of demanding that prices of farm products be allowed to go to their "natural level," but at the same time insisting on government guarantees of prices not less than 10 per cent below parity after the war.

[8] Schultz, T. W., *Redirecting Farm Policy*. New York: The Macmillan Co., 1944, p. 64.

[9] *Ibid.*, p. 67.

dren — and their children are as likely to spend their productive years in the city as on the farm. The fact that rural America is the nation's "seed-bed" is in itself ample justification for federal policies in aid of agriculture.

Family and farm. This suggests again the central place of the family in rural life. It is a social group; the farm is its economic base. Farming is a way of life and a way of making a living for the family on the land. This interrelation of family and farm in rural society is not built around a single motif or idea. It is a complex of a number of motivations and attitudes. Land gives security to many; it offers not only an economic base, but profit and success as well, especially to the skilled. It presents an opportunity to children for the health that contact with the sun, air, and the good earth can give. It lures those who love growing things and have a "feel" for the land. It offers social relations in neighborhood and community which are far more personal and elemental than in the cities. These factors, of course, influence different families in different degrees. They change in strength and compulsion as the family moves through its life cycle. This is aptly illustrated by the story of the past-middle-age farmer who was interviewed by a farm-management specialist while cultivating a large flower garden. When suggestions were made for changing his farming practices in order to make more profits, the farmer replied: "Yes, I know, but you don't understand. I have no son, and ma, she likes flowers."

Lessons of the war. In all this discussion, the experiences of the agricultural depression of the nineteen-twenties and thirties are evident. But the war has lifted farm incomes to unprecedented levels. Rationing in the war years was not caused by Lend-Lease shipments to our allies or by the fact that Americans in uniform ate more than they did as civilians, though these were factors. Rather, it was due to the fact that for the first time in the modern era millions of Americans had enough money to buy an adequate diet. Dramatic is a weak word for that changed situation.

The implication is clear. Full employment in the cities means full pocketbooks on the farm. The prewar years proved that the city had a larger stake in rural prosperity than was suspected. The war years proved that rural America has a high stake in urban prosperity. The interdependencies in our society are, therefore, clearer than they ever were before. Policies which urban and rural groups alike advocate must take this fact into account. Selfish promotion of group interest by agriculture, labor, or business will bring difficulty, if not ruin to all.

Confessional. It must not be forgotten that we so mismanaged our economy in the first half of the last decade that scarcity, hunger, and nakedness were our intimate companions. Labor and agriculture will not readily permit a recurrence of such conditions which deprived us as a society of goods and services to an amount equal to our share of the cost of World War II.[10] The need is obvious for the formulation of a social theory and policy regarding the use of wealth based on consumption rather than on production, and on considerations of public welfare rather than on those of maximum profit for corporate bodies or individuals. The cake must be eaten to be kept. The issues here are especially important to rural people who are, at this writing, far closer to achieving maximum production than is industry and who have seen their proportionate share of the national income dwindle despite an increase in their population.

World influences. This and some of the other questions raised have their international as well as their national roots, as is made clear by a careful study of *World Agriculture and the Depression,* by Vladimir Timoshenko.[11] He shows in detail that the prices of agricultural commodities important in foreign trade began to decline, slowly but steadily, early in the nineteen-twenties; that production of these commodities increased much more rapidly than the demand; that the consequent accumulation of surpluses was accelerated by increasing tariffs in industrial nations; that the imports of the agricultural countries were at the same time growing rapidly so that their normal favorable trade balance declined more and more until it reached the point where it could no longer take care of the interest charges on and the repayments of debts to the industrial nations; that as a result loans to these agricultural countries were drastically curtailed, and the nations were forced off the gold standard. This accelerated price declines.

Here then in briefest review is a picture on a world scale comparable to our own. Actions motivated by immediate self-interest in the protection of invested wealth, in their sum contributed to the intensification of the depression which finally engulfed the industrial as well as the agricultural nations.[12]

[10] Loeb, Harold, *et al., The Chart of Plenty: A Study of America's Product Capacity Based on the Findings of the National Survey of Potential Product Capacity.* New York: Viking Press, 1935.

[11] University of Michigan, Ann Arbor, 1933.

[12] Timoshenko does not deny that monetary factors may have contributed to the difficulties, but argues that they were not exclusively or even largely responsible. His data, which are very full and carefully gathered, support beyond reasonable doubt the conclusions summarized above.

Writing as the European phase of World War II drew to its close, Karl Brandt carried the argument further in terms of the postwar era.[13] To him the reconstruction of a healthy world agriculture hinges on the reconstruction of world trade in general, on an expanding industrial economy, and on an economic system which will relieve the pressure of underemployed rural populations on the land, especially in such areas as India, China, Japan, and the Balkans, by expanding other employment.

The main agency of agriculture in this new era of international co-operation will be the Food and Agricultural Organization. Its purposes, broadly stated, are to raise the level of nutrition and the standard of living of all peoples; to secure improvements in the efficiency of production and distribution of the world's food and fiber; and to better the condition of all rural people. In achieving these ends, it will rely on fact-finding and education. It is not an action agency and will have no authority over a member nation. It has been compared to our own Agricultural Extension Service on an international scale. It will help nations to help themselves, and should become a force in shaping world public opinion. It will send "missions" of experts to member nations asking for assistance. The proposed budget is five million dollars. One of the important tasks will be to uncover the roots of international difficulty in matters pertaining to nutrition and food and to try to find solutions. The Food and Agricultural Organization is a step in economic and social co-operation, without which political agreements have little meaning. If, as it hopes, it can help to increase agricultural production to the right amounts of the needed products, in the right places, it will improve industrial activity and business, and help to remove the causes of agrarian and industrial unrest. It may not work perfectly, but it can become a practical and effective agency.

Clearly, there is a theoretical knowledge as to how to reconstruct an adequate national economy. Clearly, the world is determined to rebuild a better structure on the ruins of the old. Whether success is attained depends upon whether nations and groups within them can rid themselves of fears, fostered through centuries of struggle, for resources inadequate to their needs because not yet touched by the magic of technology or the power of atomic energy. Should these efforts end in failure, the sheer weight of human need will force planning and policies beyond anything yet experienced in

13 Brandt, Karl, *The Reconstruction of World Agriculture*. New York: W. W. Norton & Co., 1945.

this nation. But the chance of failure is so great that the Post-War Policy Committee of the Land-Grant College Association has proposed a policy for American agriculture, both in terms of full employment and of a possible depression.

SOCIAL POLICIES FOR TODAY AND TOMORROW

Regardless of the economic fate in store for us, this Policy Committee called for enlightened social policies toward many of the areas of rural life discussed in this text. So have many of the pronouncements of farm organizations, church bodies, and other groups. Apart from the issues already discussed in this chapter, there is certain to be a large measure of agreement among these agencies and rural leaders on such policies as follow.

Improving rural education. Rural education needs a strengthening everywhere. If there is in this land the equality of opportunity which was a cardinal principle of the founding fathers, rural children should have as good an education as non-rural children. This includes not only the basic curriculum, but also guidance, broadened vocational training, special training for those handicapped physically, mentally, or emotionally, an enriched curriculum for those unable to continue their education beyond high school, and college preparatory work for others. To accomplish this, the salaries of rural teachers must be raised, buildings must be improved in a long-time program, administrative units must be enlarged, attendance units made to conform to the social boundaries of communities. Adult education in vocational, family life, social and cultural areas must be improved, and this should include the development of adequate community library service through county or district organization plans.

A program of this character cannot be financed by rural America unaided, nor should it be, since half the rural youth migrate to cities and, therefore, are the cities' equal responsibility. State and federal aid are necessary. The latter should be extended without surrendering state and local control in a way comparable to the federal grants to the colleges of agriculture for their research and extension programs, which have operated for decades.

Expanding health facilities. The problem of adequate medical care for rural people has been a serious one for half a century, and has been aggravated by wartime drains on medical personnel. Improvement is necessary, whether by some form of national legislation as proposed by the Wagner-Murray-Dingle Bill, by medical co-operatives, by the municipal doctor system of Canada, or by some other means. Curative medicine, too, must be fortified by the expansion of county health units to the one third of the counties not yet so served, as provided for under the Social Security Act.

Closely allied to this whole project is the need of improvement of the nutrition of rural people. This is proved by the proportion of draft rejections because of physical inadequacies caused by faulty diet. Educational programs in schools and among adults are needed in this sphere, and the balanced school lunch can do much, both as a corrective and as a demonstration of how to use a balanced diet.

Better housing is called for. The housing census of 1940 indicated that a large number of rural homes are in need of major repairs, while over four fifths lack running water or bathrooms. Too many are not fit for habitation. The Land-Grant College Report says, "It would seem a reasonable goal to seek farmhouses which are substantial in construction, attractive in appearance, suited to the climate, large enough to meet the needs of the family, and equipped with such facilities for light, heat, water, sewage disposal, and care of food as are adequate for the protection of health." The Report also suggests that the farm woodlot may serve as an inexpensive, ready-at-hand source of lumber.

The United States Department of Agriculture has done a considerable amount of work on farm housing, both in terms of plans for efficient homes suited to regional climate conditions, and in planning costs. The financing of such construction could well be cared for by the Farm Credit Administration, with plans comparable to those available in cities and towns under the Federal Housing Agency.

A program of farm home construction or renovation would also offer an opportunity for an expansion of the rural electrification program. This, of course, goes beyond the farm home to the barn and dairy, as well as to the school, the church, and the playground. It makes possible power, not only for light in home and barn, but for operating farm machinery, household equipment, and home freezing units.

Social Security program should include farm population. The exemption of the farm population, especially farm labor, from many of the provisions of the Social Security Act needs to be removed. The hazards of life do not cease to operate at the borders of our municipalities. Farm people are showing increasing interest in this matter. There has been sufficient experience with the operation of the act to plan for its extension to all the people.

Recreation and better social organization needed. There has been a considerable expansion of social organizations in rural communities as contrasted with the beginning of the century. But many surveys have shown that large proportions of rural people are untouched by this development. Rural youth especially are critical of recreational provisions in rural America, especially for the post-high-school group. Adequate recreational facilities are important factors in creating satisfaction with rural life. The response to the recreational programs of the Extension Service in some states is justification for more attention to this area of social life.

The problem, however, goes beyond recreation. It includes the total organizational structure of rural society. The recent decades have seen a multiplication of special interest groups. These range all the way from the national farm organizations to their local community branches, to breeders' associations, to service or purely social clubs. Yet the fundamental interests common to all who live in the same locality, be it neighborhood or community, remain; interests such as schools, roads, health, and the other social utilities.

The question arises whether this tendency to form special groups will divide rural society into as many parts as there are interests. There is much need for statesmanlike leadership and better group planning to create a better integrated community life in which legitimate specialized interests and total community development will be usefully co-ordinated.

Spiritual leadership essential. Among many other desirable forward steps in rural life, perhaps the most important is an improvement in the program and leadership of rural churches. Protestantism is the dominant persuasion of rural America, and its weakness was made clear in the chapter on the rural church. What the rural church can do as a whole is shown by hundreds of individually successful rural churches. The problem of expanding this work needs far more realistic attention than it is receiving. It goes beyond training clergy for rural parishes. It involves administrative arrangements to retrain them for such specialized responsibilities, the payment of adequate salaries, and the reduction of competition and the partial and fragmented service which results from such scattered effort. There are signs of changing attitudes and policies in the rural life movements among most of the national church bodies — Catholic, Protestant, and Jewish.

The compulsion of institutional change. In essence, these last paragraphs have been indicating that social and economic institutions must change and adapt themselves to changing times. The text has given many illustrations of this process. Social institutions are devices whereby men co-operate to accomplish certain agreed-upon purposes. These purposes grow out of recognized needs. As needs change, so do the purposes and objectives of society, and the institutions of society must change comparably. The most dramatic recent illustration of this principle, of course, is the reconversion of America and her allies in World War II from the purposes of war to those of peace. The rôle of any institution in a dynamic society is to influence, and to be influenced by and adjust to, the changing social trends and forces that operate in any society, whether the social group concerned be the neighborhood, the community, or the nation. Institutions are anchored in the past, but to survive they must be oriented to the future. The social policies suggested for the improvement of rural education, health, and social organization can be made effective only by institutional or agency action. Such action in our democratic society can come only as those concerned are convinced of the necessity of the new policies. These principles apply to voluntary associations, whether they be a village women's club or a national farm organization, and also to government from the local level up.

Social Policies Interrelated

A public opinion poll among informed persons would certainly produce a large measure of agreement on a program such as the one outlined in the previous section of this chapter. The implementing of such a program is another matter. For one thing, it would involve a considerable increase in the number of well-trained professional workers in education, health, religion, and in other fields, as well as an increase in the number of skilled artisans in construction, electrification, and other occupations. This in itself would offer expanded employment opportunities.

Again, such a program must be financed. There must be an adequate economic base in rural America to sustain the necessary institutions, or else that base must be strengthened by grants from society as a whole. But that is by no means the whole story. The implementation of such a program will make its own contribution to its cost — a fact that is little realized or understood.

The strongest practical case to be made for an adequate rural health program is the economic. A well man pays his way in this world by what he produces and by the services he renders. The measurable decline in death rates in counties that have had health units over a period of years shows that the tax support for such units has netted society a handsome profit.

Economists by the score have testified to the economic gains for society, to say nothing of the individual, from an adequate educational system.[14] Nor does the case rest on testimony. Data have already been presented on this point in the discussion on education. Compare the low standard of living in the southern Appalachian mountain region with the high standard in mountainous Switzerland. The former has twice the natural resources of the latter, but education in Switzerland is far superior to that in our southern mountains. Its system has produced some of the most skilled workers in the world and a high per capita income. Yugoslavia has average resources. Norway has poor soil, a harsh climate, a short growing season, and few natural resources. Despite its poorer soil, its yields outstrip those of Yugoslavia, indeed, outstrip all but one of the Balkan countries. Until the German invasion, it had a high per capita income. It also had an unusually high level of education. Switzerland and Norway have invested in their people. They have educated them to make the most intelligent use of the limited resources they possess.[15]

There lies in this and much other data another great social truth which Americans have not sufficiently learned, to judge by their national behavior. It is this: capital invested in human beings earns economic returns just as surely as capital invested in an acre of land, a filling station, or a steel mill. True, the return may not show on next year's balance sheet. This is why society, rather than the individual or a corporation, must share in or make the entire investment. Quarterly and annual statements of profits are not the only ways of measuring economic gain. The production of goods and services over the years is a surer index.

This principle applies even in the things of the spirit, and not merely in the sense that Henry Wallace had in mind when he remarked that a strong country church near-by was the best asset a co-operative could have. Liberty Hyde Bailey, one of the greatest deans of agriculture, once remarked that "the morals of land management are more important than the economics of land." He meant that the right use of the soil is the criterion of whether a

[14] Cf. Educational Policies Commission, *Education and Economic Well-Being in American Democracy*, Washington, 1940.

[15] Cf. Clark, Harold, *Teachers College Record*, March, 1945, pp. 360-65.

nation is civilized. The psalmist who wrote, "The earth is the Lord's and the fullness thereof," said essentially the same thing. Here again economics and sociology join hands. The essential unity of the social sciences is the fact that they are social. Social objectives can be buttressed by economic findings just as sound economic policy can be furthered by a wise use of pertinent sociological data.

WHO SHALL PLAN FOR RURAL AMERICA?

It has been reiterated in this text that implicit in democracy is the need for citizens to assume their responsibilities in determining policies of the society of which they are a part. In the county planning programs of a few years ago, still continuing in some states despite the war, in the programs of the Agricultural Adjustment Administration, in farmer participation in formulating Extension Service programs, rural people have acquired some experience in this art of planning. It needs to be built upon and expanded. Probably it should head up, as the Land-Grant College Post-War Policy Committee suggests, in a permanent national agricultural policy committee, co-operating with the Department of Agriculture. Comparably, co-operating bodies could be set up in the states and counties. Labor, business, and consumers should be represented, for the problems of agriculture and rural life are national in scope and implications. Farmers, too, should have their say on policies relating to other large areas of the economy. Ours is an interdependent society!

National interest above class. The emphasis upon national considerations, recurring as it does several times in this chapter, is extremely important. The authors reject the idea that the good life for rural America can be achieved only by making rural America class-conscious. Such a procedure is always dangerous for a minority group. Social safety and wisdom will come when we convince the nation that a square deal for agriculture and for rural people, in social and economic terms, is best for the nation as a whole. The authors suggest that it may be possible to effect a reconciliation of opposing rural and urban interests by formulating and carrying out a national policy for rural society: the old conflicts between urban and rural areas are historically explicable, and differences in objectives, more or less superficial, are still clearly discernible. The present international crisis is in part the result of lack of balance between the industrial and the agricultural countries.

Essentially what the farmer wants is to feed the hungry, to help answer the prayer for daily bread, on the basis of social and economic equality with other groups in the United States or any other society. This has been called parity, but the parity must be more than economic; it must be social as well. Indeed, it cannot be one without the other, nor can the health of society as a whole be considered sound if any important group suffers from social and economic ills.

Planning in the postwar world for the future is but planning to rebuild a world destroyed by its greatest catastrophe.

Anthropologists declare that periods of stress and social change occur when the mores that control and motivate the behavior of the local, face-to-face primary groups for some reason or reasons lose their efficacy. Social stability does not return until new mores are accepted as adequate social controls. It is also true that social change is accelerated when major conflicts between important groups develop. The final resolution of these conflicts produces a new equilibrium, a changed social pattern.

Such a period was the Renaissance. Such a period was that of the political and social revolutions in England and France when the machine worker and artisan or handicraftsman joined issue; when the slogan "Liberty, Equality, and Fraternity" challenged monarchy; when the doctrine of *laissez faire* freed the use of capital from ancient restrictions. The present, too, is such a period; two world wars have swept away the savings of generations; science has all but annihilated space and time, made the world interdependent, and given us through mass production undreamed-of potential wealth in goods, displacing entire occupations and speeding up even agricultural processes; and, finally, the ferment of democracy and its hope for the common man has spread to far-off India and China and produced in lands like Italy and Germany violent counter-movements which have ruined these lands, their satellites, and their victims for years to come. The task of the social scientist today is to plan, work for, and achieve the reconciliation of such conflicting social groups and tendencies and the acceptance of new mores befitting our resources, and thus help provide a new equilibrium between nation and nation, capital and labor, city and country.

DISCUSSION TOPICS

1. What values important to the life of the nation do you think are created or fostered in rural society?

2. What, if any, is the justification for equalization plans of financing rural social institutions, such as schools, hospitals or libraries, by moneys collected in taxes or otherwise from citizens who do not reside in rural territory?

3. What is the main agricultural policy or platform of the National Democratic, Republican, and Socialist parties, as shown by their last statements or conventions?

4. Discuss the pros and cons of pertinent sections of the Post-War Policy Report of the Land-Grant College Association in terms either of the nation or your state.

5. What are chief issues on which rural and urban interests are most likely to clash? Can these interests be reconciled in some kind of a national policy? If yes, how? If not, why?

6. Name some tests or criteria by which you are willing to judge as to whether changes in rural society are in the direction of progress.

7. Outline an adequate land utilization policy for your state; for the nation.

REFERENCE READINGS

American Country Life Association, *National Policies Affecting Rural Life*. Chicago: University of Chicago Press, 1934.

Beard, Charles and Mary, *America in Mid-Passage*. New York: The Macmillan Co., 1939.

Belshaw, Horace, *Foundations of Rural Welfare*. Montreal: International Labor Office, 1945; also in *International Labour Review*, vol. LI, no. 3.

Brandt, Karl, *The Reconstruction of World Agriculture*. New York: W. W. Norton & Co., 1945.

Country Planning: A Study of Rural Problems. Staff of the Agricultural Economic Research Institute of Oxford University. London: Oxford University Press, 1944.

Duddy, E. R., Editor, *Economic Policies for American Agriculture*. Chicago: University of Chicago Press, 1931.

Ezekiel, Mordecai, *Jobs for All*. New York: Knopf, 1939.

Land-Grant College Association, *Post-War Policy Report*, 1944.

Moore, Arthur, *The Farmer and the Rest of Us*. Boston: Little, Brown & Co., 1945.

National Resources Board, *A Report on National Planning and Public*

Works in Relation to Natural Resources, and Including Land Use and Water Resources, with Findings and Recommendations, Parts I and II. Washington, D.C.: Government Printing Office, 1934.

Agricultural Exports in Relation to Land Policy. 1935.

Soil Erosion. 1935.

Regional Factors in National Planning. December, 1935.

State Planning. June, 1935; December, 1936.

General Conditions and Tendencies Influencing the Nation's Land Requirements. 1936.

Nourse, E. G., and others, *America's Capacity to Produce.* Washington, D.C.: Brookings Institution, 1934.

Schultz, T. W., *Agriculture in an Unstable Economy.* New York: Mc-Graw-Hill Book Co., 1945.

Schultz, T. W., *Redirecting Farm Policy.* New York: The Macmillan Co., 1943.

Taylor, C. C., *Human Relations in Land Use Planning.* Washington, D.C.: United States Department of Agriculture, Bureau of Agricultural Economics, 1938 (mimeographed).

Timoshenko, V., *World Agriculture and the Depression.* Ann Arbor: University of Michigan, 1933.

Tolley, H. R., *Farmer Citizen at War.* New York: The Macmillan Co., 1943.

Wallace, Henry, *America Must Choose.* New York: Foreign Policy Association, 1934.

Wallace, Henry, *New Frontiers.* New York: Reynal and Hitchcock, 1934.

Wickard, Claude, *Report of the Secretary of Agriculture; 1944.* Washington, D.C., 1944.

APPENDIX

APPENDIX

Bibliography of Rural Life in Foreign Lands

AN INCREASING AMOUNT of work in rural sociology and research is being carried on in foreign lands, especially in Asia and Latin America. Much of it is of value, especially to graduate students in American institutions. Moreover, an increasing number of foreign students interested in rural sociology are attending American colleges and universities. The current need for and interest in the rehabilitation of war-torn countries also has added to the interest in the rural social life of overseas countries and territories, so largely rural. A brief bibliography is, therefore, appended on Rural Life in Foreign Lands.

Only a few of the references are to articles. But those interested will find a considerable source of valuable material in the issues of *Rural Sociology, Journal of Farm Economics,* and *Foreign Agriculture.* This last is a publication of the Office of Foreign Agricultural Relations of the United States Department of Agriculture. Two other regular publications sometimes carry articles of rural interest or general articles with rural references and implications, namely, the *Far Eastern Survey* of the Institute of Pacific Relations and the semi-monthly *Bulletin* of the Foreign Policy Association, both of New York City.

No pretense is made that the bibliography which follows is complete, but considerable effort has been expended to select significant books. The sections on South and Central America list a larger number of general books than the others because studies in English are few. All the books selected give considerable attention to rural life.

There are no references to rural life in Europe except Russia, for several reasons. So many countries were involved in World War II that such a section would have exceeded the space available. The destruction and other changes wrought by the war and the paucity of books after 1939 made any bibliography outdated. A few general references compensate for this lack, in part. Finally, it seemed likely that, after the immediate needs of rehabilitation, the United States would be more concerned with South America and Asia than with other parts of the world, both directly and in terms of foreign students in American colleges and universities.

It will be noted that many of these books have foreign publishers, but a number of them are obtainable from American sources. The publications of the Royal Institute of International Affairs can be obtained for the most part from the Institute of Pacific Relations in New York City.

GENERAL

Brandt, Karl, *The Reconstruction of World Agriculture.* New York: W. W. Norton, 1945.

Brunner, E. de S., I. T. Sanders, and D. Ensminger, *Farmers of The World, The Development of Agricultural Extension.* New York: Columbia University Press, 1945.

Butterfield, K. L., *The Rural Mission of the Church in Eastern Asia.* International Missionary Council, 419 Fourth Avenue, New York, or 2 Eaton Gate, London, S.W. 1. 1931.

Butterfield, Brunner, McKee, and Jones, *Christian Missions in Relation to Rural Problems.* International Missionary Council, 419 Fourth Avenue, New York. 1929.

Contribution of Extension Methods and Techniques Toward the Rehabilitation of War-Torn Countries. Washington, D.C.: United States Department of Agriculture, 1946.

Cressey, George B., *Asia's Lands and Peoples.* New York: McGraw-Hill, 1945.

Doreen, Paul and Warriner, *Food and Farming in Post-War Europe.* London: Oxford University Press, 1943.

Howard, L. E., *Labour in Agriculture.* Royal Institute of International Affairs, New York and London, 1935.

Lasker, Bruno, *Asia on the Move.* New York: Henry Holt & Co., 1945.

Mair, L. P., *Welfare in the British Colonies.* The Royal Institute of International Affairs, New York and London, 1944.

Pelzer, Karl J., *Agriculture and Land Settlement in South-East Asia.* New York: International Secretariat, Institute of Pacific Relations in co-operation with American Geographical Society, 1943.

Pelzer, Karl J., *Pioneer Settlement in the Asiatic Tropics.* New York: American Geographical Society, 1945.

Pim, Sir Alan, *Colonial Agricultural Production: The Contribution Made by Native Peasants and Foreign Enterprise.* Royal Institute of International Affairs, New York and London, forthcoming.

United Nations Conference on Food and Agriculture, *Final Act and Section Reports.* Washington, D.C.: United States Government Printing Office, 1943.

Watt, *What the Country Women of the World are Doing.* Available from Grace E. Frysinger, Office of Co-operative Extension Work, United States Department of Agriculture, Washington, D.C.

Wickizer, V. D., and M. K. Bennett, *The Rice Economy of Monsoon Asia.* Stanford University Press, 1945.

Wilcox, W. W., "Human Resources in Farming," *Land Policy Review,* vol. 4, no. 4, April, 1941.

The *Annual Yearbooks* of the British Commonwealths and of many of the British colonies are very valuable. They usually contain excellent chapters on population, agriculture, standards of living, social services and the like. They may be secured through the British Library of Public Information, Radio City, New York, New York.

The Oxford University Press of New York City carries quite a number of the publications relating to the British Commonwealth. G. E. Stechert and Company, 31 East 10th Street, New York, also carries social science works published abroad, including a number listed in this bibliography.

RUSSIA

Fisher, Louis, *Soviet Journey.* New York: Harrison Smith and Robert Haas, 1935.

Ossinsky, and others, *Social Economic Planning in the Union of Soviet Republics.* New York: International Industrial Relations Association, 1931.

Strong, Anna Louise, *The Soviets Conquer Wheat.* New York: Henry Holt & Co.

Volin, Lazar, "Recent Developments in Soviet Agriculture," *Foreign Agriculture,* January, 1937.

Webb, Beatrice and Sidney, *Soviet Communism: A New Civilization.* New York: Charles Scribner's Sons, 1937. Devotes a section to rural sociology.

Williams, Albert Rhys, *The Soviets.* New York: Harcourt, Brace & Co., 1937.

Yakovlev, Y. A., *Red Villages.* New York: International Publishers. A description of the collectivization of Russian farms. 1931.

AFRICA

Agriculture in Uganda, Staff, Department of Agriculture, Uganda. London: Oxford University Press, 1940.

Albertyn, J. R., *Sociological Report: The Poor White and Society.* Part V of *The Poor White Problem in South Africa.* Report of the Carnegie Commission, 1932.

Buell, Raymond L., *The Native Problem in Africa.* New York: The Macmillan Co., 1928. In two volumes.

Clough, O., *Report on African Affairs for 1930.* Guildford: Billings & Son.

Cook, Peter A. W., *The Education of a South African Tribe*. Cape Town: Juta & Co., 1934.

Coulten, Charles W., "Problems Arising from Industrialization of Native Life in Central Africa," *American Journal of Sociology*, vol. XL, no. 5, March, 1935.

Frankel, Herbert, *Capital Investment in Africa*. New York and London: Royal Institute of International Affairs, 1938.

Grosskopf, J. R. S., *Economic Report: Rural Impoverishment and Rural Exodus*. Part I of *The Poor White Problem in South Africa*. Report of the Carnegie Commission, 1932.

Hailey, Lord, *African Survey: A Study of Problems Arising in Africa South of the Sahara*. New York and London: Royal Institute of International Affairs, 1938.

Issawi, Charles, *Egypt: An Economic and Social Analysis*. New York and London: Royal Institute of International Affairs, forthcoming.

Kuczynski, R. R., *Cameroons and Togoland: A Demographic Study*. New York and London: Royal Institute of International Affairs, 1939.

Leubuscher, C., *Tanganyika Territory: A Study of Economic Policy Under Mandate*. New York and London: Royal Institute of International Affairs, 1944.

Light, Richard U., *Focus on Africa*. New York: American Geographic Society, 1941.

Malherbe, E. G., *Educational Report: Education and the Poor White*. Part III of *The Poor White Problem in South Africa*. Report of the Carnegie Commission, 1932.

Murray, W. A., *Health Report: Health Factors in the Poor White Problem*. Part IV of *The Poor White Problem in South Africa*. Report of the Carnegie Commission, 1932.

Neek, Macmillan, and Hussey, *Europe and West Africa: Some Problems and Adjustments.* London: Oxford University Press, 1940.

Wilcocks, R. W., *Psychological Report: The Poor White*. Part II of *The Poor White Problem in South Africa*. Report of the Carnegie Commission, 1932.

Woolbert, W. G. and M. S., *Look at Africa*. New York: Foreign Policy Association, no. 43, 1943.

AUSTRALIA AND NEW ZEALAND

Alexander, Fred, *Australia and the United States*. Boston: World Peace Foundation, 1941.

Alley, G. T., and D. O. Hall, *The Farmer in New Zealand*. Wellington: Department of Internal Affairs, 1941.

Belshaw, H., and others, *Agricultural Organization in New Zealand.* Published for the New Zealand Council of the Institute of Pacific Relations by the Melbourne University Press, 1936.

Belshaw, Horace, *Reconstruction in New Zealand with Special Reference to International Aspects.* Wellington: New Zealand Institute of International Affairs, 1945.

Belshaw, Horace, *Recovery Measures in New Zealand.* Wellington: New Zealand Council of the Institute of Pacific Relations, 1936.

Brunner, E. de S., *Rural Australia and New Zealand.* New York: Institute of Pacific Relations, 1938.

Bush, Alice, *et al.*, *A National Health Service.* Wellington: Progressive Publishing Society, 1943.

Campbell, A. E., *Educating New Zealand.* Wellington: Department of Internal Affairs, 1941.

Campbell, A. E., *The Feilding Community Centre.* New Zealand Council for Educational Research, 1945.

Cole, P. R., editor, *The Rural School in Australia.* Melbourne University Press, 1937.

Copland, D. B., and C. V. Janes, *Australia Marketing Problems.* Sydney: Angus and Robertson, 1938.

Cowan, James, *Settlers and Pioneers.* Wellington: Department of Internal Affairs, 1940.

Doig, W. T., *A Survey of Standards of Life of New Zealand Dairy-Farmers.* Wellington: Department of Scientific and Industrial Research, Bulletin 75, 1940.

Duff, Oliver, *New Zealand Now.* Wellington: Department of Internal Affairs, 1941.

Duncan, W. G. K., and C. V. Janes, editors, *The Future of Immigration with Australia and New Zealand.* Sydney: Angus and Robertson, 1938.

Eggleston, F. W., *Australian Standards of Living.* Australian Institute of Internal Affairs. Melbourne University Press, 1939.

Harris, H. L., editor, *Australia's National Interests and National Policies.* Melbourne University Press, 1938.

Hill, Ernestine, *Water into Gold.* Melbourne: Robertson and Mullins, 1937.

Mason, Hon. H. G. R., *Education Today and Tomorrow.* Wellington, 1945.

McIntyre, A. J. and J. J., *Country Towns of Victoria; A Social Survey.* Melbourne University Press, Carlton, N. 3, Victoria, 1944. New York distributors: G. E. Stechert and Company.

New Zealand Department of Internal Affairs, *Making New Zealand.* Wellington: Department of Internal Affairs, 1940.

New Zealand Institute of International Affairs, *Contemporary New Zealand.* Wellington: Whitcombe and Tombs, Ltd., 1938.

"New Zealand Security Program," *Fortune,* July, 1944.

The Peopling of Australia. First and Second Series. The Institute of Pacific Relations. Melbourne University Press, 1928 and 1933.

Publications of the Bank of New South Wales, especially the following issue of *The Circular:*

Vol. 6, no. 1, February, 1936: *Australian Population Growth or Decline.*

Vol. 6, no. 3, August, 1936: *Australia's Vast Empty Spaces.*

Radford, W. C., *The Educational Needs of a Rural Community.* Melbourne University Press, 1939.

The Rural Reconstruction Commission:
1. *A General Rural Survey.*
2. *Settlement and Employment of Returned Men on the Land.*
3. *Land Utilization and Farm Settlement.*
4. *Financial and Economic Reconstruction of Farms.*

L. F. Johnston, Commonwealth Government Printer, Canberra, 1943.

Somerset, H. C. D., *Littledene: A New Zealand Rural Community.* Wellington: New Zealand Council for Educational Research, 1938.

PACIFIC ISLANDS

Buss, Claude, "Philippines," *Fortune,* December, 1944.

Coulter, John W., *Land Utilization in American Samoa.* Honolulu: Bernice P. Bishop Museum, 1941.

Coulter, John W., *Fiji, Little India of the Pacific.* Chicago: University of Chicago Press, 1942.

Firth, Raymond, *We, The Tikopia.* New York: American Book Co., 1944.

Hart, G. H. C., *Towards Economic Democracy in the Netherlands Indies.* New York: The Netherlands and Netherlands Indies Council of the Institute of Pacific Relations, 1942.

Keesing, Felix M., *Education in Pacific Countries.* Shanghai: Kelly and Walsh, Ltd., 1937.

Keesing, Felix M., *The South Seas in the Modern World.* New York: Institute of Pacific Relations, 1941.

Lind, Andrew W., *An Island Community* (Hawaii). Chicago: University of Chicago Press, 1938.

Malinowski, Bronislaw, *Coral Gardens and Their Magic.* New York: American Book Co., 1944.

Thompson, Laura, *Guam and Its People.* New York: American Council, Institute of Pacific Relations, 1942.

Vander Plas, Charles O., *Recent Developments in the Netherlands East Indies*. New York: The Netherlands and Netherlands East Indies Council, Institute of Pacific Relations, 1942.

Wenworth, Edna Clark, *Filipino Plantation Workers in Hawaii*. New York: Institute of Pacific Affairs, 1941.

CHINA

Alley, Rewi, "China's Industrial Future," *Free World*, August, 1944.

Barnett, R. W., *China — America's Ally*. New York: American Council, Institute of Pacific Relations, 1942.

Buck, J. L., *An Agricultural Survey of Szechuan*. Chungking: The Farmers Bank of China, 1943.

Buck, J. L., *Farm Economy in China*. Chicago: University of Chicago Press, 1930.

Buck, J. L., *Land Utilization in China*. Chicago: University of Chicago Press, 1938. 3 vols.

Buck, J. Lossing, *Agricultural Survey of Szechwan Province*. New York: International Secretariat, Institute of Pacific Relations, 1943 (Mimeographed).

Buck, Pearl (Mrs. J. L.), *The Good Earth*. A novel of rural life in China. New York, The John Day Co.

Buck, Pearl S., *Tell the People — Mass Education in China*. New York: American Council, Institute of Pacific Relations, 1945.

Chang, Hsiao-mei, editor, *Economic Survey of Yunnan*. Chungking: China Economic Research Institute, 1942.

Chen, Hang-Seng, *Agrarian Problems in Southmost China*. Shanghai: Kelly and Walsh, 1936.

Chen, Ta, *Emigrant Communities in South China*. New York: Institute of Pacific Relations, 1940.

Chiang, Kai-Shek, "China's Destiny," *Contemporary China*, vol. II, no. 22, March 22, 1943. New York: Chinese News Service, 1943.

Chiang, Tung-po, *New Szechwan*. Chungking, 1940.

China Handbook, 1937-1943. Chungking: China Ministry of Information, 1943.

"China Post-war Plans," *Fortune*, October, 1943.

"China's Post-war Economic Reconstruction," *Contemporary China*, vol. II, no. 18, January 25, 1942. New York: Chinese News Service, 1942.

Cressey, George B., *China's Geographic Foundations*. New York: McGraw-Hill, 1945.

Fei, Hsiao-Tung, *Peasant Life in China*. New York: E. P. Dutton Co., 1939.

Fei, Hsaio-Tung, and Chih-I. Chang, *Earthbound — China*. Chicago: University of Chicago Press, 1945.

Hsu, Y. Y., "The Pao-Chia System in China," *Far Eastern Survey*, vol. XXII, no. 24, December 8, 1943.

Kulp, D. H., *Country Life in South China; The Sociology of Familism*. New York: Bureau of Publications, Teachers College, Columbia University, 1925.

Lee, F. C. H., and T. Chin, *Village Families in the Vicinity of Peiping*. Peiping: Bulletin 2, April, 1929, Social Research Department, China Foundation.

Leong, Y. K., and L. K. Tao, *Village and Town Life in China*. London: Allen and Unwin, Ltd., 1915.

Lou, Yu-wên, *China, Kwangsi*. Luchow: Agricultural Experiment Station, 1939.

Norins, Martin R., *Gateway to Asia, Sinkiang*. New York: International Secretariat, Institute of Pacific Relations, 1945.

Soong, T. V., "China's Achievements and Aims," *Contemporary China*, vol. III, no. 8, September 6, 1943. New York: Chinese News Service, 1943.

Stewart, John R., "Manchurian Agriculture," *Far Eastern Survey*, vol. X, no. 7, April 21, 1941.

Tang, C. Y., *Economic Study of Chinese Agriculture*. Nanking, 1936.

Tawney, R. H., *Land and Labor in China*. New York: Harcourt, Brace & Co., 1932.

Wu, Ching-Chao, "Reflections on Industrialization in Post-War China," *Contemporary China*, vol. III, no. 8, September 6, 1943. New York: Chinese News Service, 1943.

Yang, Martin C., *A Chinese Village: Taitou, Shantung Province*. New York: Columbia University Press, 1945.

Publications on China by Chinese agencies are summarized in the *Quarterly Bulletin of Chinese Bibliography*.

INDIA

Andrus, R., *Rural Reconstruction in Burma*. London: Oxford University Press, 1936.

Blunt, Sir Edward, *Social Service in India*. London: His Majesty's Stationery Office, 1938.

Brayne, F. L., *Better Villages*. London: Oxford University Press, 1937.

Darling, Malcolm Lyall, *Wisdom and Waste in a Punjab Village*. London: Oxford University Press, 1934.

Dutt, R. P., *A Guide to the Problem of Rural India: A Survey of Agrarian Structure, Poverty, and Overpopulation*. London: Gollancz, 1942.

Farley, Miriam, *Speaking of India*. New York: American Council, Institute of Pacific Relations, 1943.

Ghurye, G. S., *Indian Population Problems*. Bombay: Karnatak Publishing House, 1938.

Hatch, S., *Further Upward in Rural India*. London: Oxford University Press, 1938.

Hatch, S., *Up From Poverty in Rural India*. London: Oxford University Press, 1936.

Jathar, Ganesh B., and Beri, Shridhar G., *Indian Economics: A Comprehensive and Critical Survey*. London: H. Milford, Oxford University Press, 1942.

Karve, D. S., *Poverty and Population in India*. London: Oxford University Press, 1936.

Lal, P. C., *Reconstruction and Education in Rural India*. London: Allen and Unwin, Ltd., 1932.

Lucas, E. D., and Das F. Thakur, *The Rural Church in the Punjab*. Lahore, 1938.

Nanavati, Manilal B., and J. J. Anjaria, *The Indian Rural Problem*. Bombay: Indian Society of Agricultural Economics, 1944.

Olcott, M., *Better Village Schools*. Calcutta: Y.M.C.A., Press, 1936.

Rao, Vijendra K. R. V., *The National Income of British India, 1931-1932*. London: Macmillan, 1940.

Slater, Gilbert, *Some South India Villages*. London: Oxford University Press, 1918.

Sovani, N. V., *The Population Problem in India: A Regional Approach*. Poona: Gokhale Institute of Politics and Economics, 1942.

Strickland, C. F., *Rural Welfare in India*. London: Oxford University Press, 1936.

The Board of Economic Inquiry, Punjab, *India Punjab Village Studies*. Thirteen volumes covering as many areas.

Williams, L. F. R., *India*. Toronto: Oxford University Press, 1940.

Wiser, C. V. and W. H., *Behind Mud Walls*. New York: R. R. Smith, Inc., 1930.

Wiser, W. H., *Building the Social and Economic Foundations for an Indigenous Church in the United Provinces*. Lucknow Publishing House, 1940.

Wiser, W. H., *The Hindu Jajmani System*. Lucknow Publishing House, 1936.

Japan and Formosa

Bisson, T. A., *Shadow Over Asia; The Rise of Militant Japan*. New York: The Foreign Policy Association, 1941.

Embree, John F., *Suye Mura: A Japanese Village*. Chicago: University of Chicago Press, 1939.

Embree, John F., *The Japanese Nation: A Social Survey*. New York: Farrar & Rinehart, 1945.

Grajdanzev, Andrew J., *Formosa Today*. New York: Institute of Pacific Relations, 1942.

"Japan," *Fortune*, September, 1936, and April, 1944.

"Japanese Empire, The," *Fortune*. New York, September, 1936.

Japanese Population Policy. Population Index, vol. 7, no. 4, 1941.

Jones, Thomas E., *Mountain Folk of Japan*. New York, 1926.

Ladejinsky, W., "Japan's Agriculture Crisis," *Journal of Farm Economics*, vol. XXI, no. 3, Part 1, August, 1939.

Nasu, S., *Aspects of Japanese Agriculture: A Preliminary Survey*. New York: Institute of Pacific Relations, 1941.

Nasu, S., *Land Utilization in Japan*. Tokyo: Institute of Pacific Relations, 1929.

Orchard, *Japan's Economic Position*. New York: McGraw-Hill, 1930. See especially chapters I, II, III, XIII, XV, XVII, XXV.

Smith, Guy-Harold; Dorothy Good, *Japan: A Geographical View*. New York: American Geographical Society, 1943.

Steiner, J. F., "Population Trends in Japan," *American Sociological Review*, vol. 9, no. 1, February, 1944.

Trewartha, Glenn T., *Japan: A Physical, Cultural and Regional Geography*. Madison: University of Wisconsin Press, 1945. Especially chapters IV, V, VII, IX.

Yoder, Fred R., "The Japanese Rural Community," *Rural Sociology*, vol. 1, no. 4, December, 1936.

KOREA

Brunner, Edmund de S., *Rural Korea*. New York and London: International Missionary Council, 1928. Also reprinted in vol. VI, *Proceedings of the International Missionary Council*, 1929, and translated into Japanese by the Governor-General of Chosen.

Grajdanzev, Andrew J., *Modern Korea*. New York: Institute of Pacific Relations, 1944.

Kim, Helen K., *Rural Education for the Regeneration of Korea*. Methodist Board of Foreign Missions, 150 Fifth Avenue, New York.

Lee, Hoon K., *Land Utilization and Rural Economy in Korea*. Chicago: University of Chicago Press, 1936.

Siam (Thailand)

Anderson, J. M., *Siam, Second Rural Economic Survey*. Bangkok: Times Press, 1936.

Deignan, H. G., *Siam — Land of Free Men*. Washington, D.C.: Smithsonian Institution, 1943.

Thompson, V. M., *Thailand: The New Siam*. New York: Institute of Pacific Relations, 1941.

Zimmerman, Carle C., *Siam, A Rural Economic Survey*. Bangkok: Times Press, 1931.

Near and Middle East

Badeau, John S., *East and West of Suez*. New York: The Foreign Policy Association, 1943.

Haas, William S., *Iran*. New York: Columbia University Press, 1945.

Hourani, A. H., *Syria and Lebanon*. New York and London: Royal Institute of International Affairs (forthcoming).

Infield, H. F., *Co-operative Living in Palestine*. New York: The Dryden Press, 1944.

Jamali, M. F., *The New Iraq*. New York: Teachers College, Columbia University, 1934.

Monroe, Paul, *The Educational Commission of Inquiry*. Baghdad: Government Press, 1932.

Tannous, A. I., "Social Change in an Arab Village," *American Sociological Review*, vol. VI, no. 5, October, 1941.

Tannous, A. I., "Rural Problems and Village Welfare in the Middle East," *Rural Sociology*, vol. VIII, no. 3, September, 1943.

South and Central America

For those especially interested in the Southern Hemisphere there are three sources of special value: *The Bulletin of the Pan American Union*, Washington 6, D.C., a monthly; *Agriculture in the Americas*, Office of Foreign Agricultural Relations, United States Department of Agriculture, Washington 25, D.C., a monthly; and Bernstein, Sylvia P., *Bibliography on Labor and Social Welfare in Latin America*, Pan-American Union, Washington, D.C., 1944.

The bibliography below is divided into three main sections: General, South America, and Central America. Those using it are reminded that there is great interest in this area of the world. Important studies are under way. A few are in press. A number of the books listed below may be superseded, and more specifically rural life studies are likely to appear. These should be watched for.

SOUTH AMERICA

General

Dunne, Peter Masten: *A Padre Views South America.* Milwaukee: Bruce Publishing Co., 1945.

Hanson, Earl Parker, *The Amazon: A New Frontier.* New York: Headline Series, Foreign Policy Association, no. 45, March, 1944.

Herring, H., *Good Neighbors.* New Haven: Yale University Press, 1941.

"Human Geography of Latin America," Population Index, vol. 7, no. 4, October, 1941, p. 261.

Inman, Samuel G., *Latin America — Its Place in World Life.* New York: Harcourt, Brace & Co., 1942.

James, Prestone, *Latin America.* New York: The Odyssey Press, 1942.

Latin America and Freedom from Want. Washington, D.C.: National Planning Association, 1942. (328 pages, mimeographed.)

Loomis, Charles P., "Extension Work for Latin America," *Applied Anthropology,* vol. 3, no. 4.

Moore, R. E., *What Shall the Americas Grow?* May, 1943.

Platt, R. R., *Opportunities for Agricultural Colonization in the Eastern Border Valleys of the Andes.* New York, 1932.

Quintanilla, Luiz, *A Latin American Speaks.* New York: The Macmillan Co., 1943.

Raushenbush, Joan, *Look at Latin America.* New York: The Foreign Policy Association, 1940.

Ribra, A. F., *The Co-operation Movement in Latin America: Its Significance in Hemisphere Solidarity.* Albuquerque: University of New Mexico Press, 1943.

Second Inter-American Congress of Agriculture, *Final Act.* Washington, D.C.: Pan-American Union, 1942.

Soule, George, David Efron, and Norman T. Ness, *Latin America in the Future World.* New York: Farrar & Rinehart, 1945.

Wythe, George, *Industry and Nationalism in Latin America.* New York, 1945.

Argentine Republic

Herring, Hubert, *Good Neighbors, Argentina, Brazil, Chile, and Seventeen Other Countries.* New Haven: Yale University Press, 1941.

Herron, Francis, *Letters From the Argentine*. New York: G. P. Putnam's Sons, 1943.

Jefferson, Mark, *Peopling the Argentine Pampa*. New York: American Geographical Society, 1936.

Macdonald, Austin F., *Government of the Argentine Republic*. New York: Thomas Y. Crowell Co., 1942.

Schmieder, O., "The Pampa; A Natural or Culturally Induced Grassland?" Berkeley: *University of California Publications in Geography*, vol. 2, 1927.

Taylor, Carl C., "Argentina Loves Her Cattle," *Agriculture in the Americas*, vol. III, no. 3, March, 1943.

Taylor, Carl C., *Argentine Rural Life*. Baton Rouge: Louisiana State University Press, 1946.

Taylor, Carl C., "Farming and Farm Life in the Major Production Areas of Argentina," *Foreign Agriculture*, vol. 7, no. 7, July, 1943.

Taylor, Carl C., "Land Ownership and Status in Argentina," *Land Policy Review*, Summer, 1943.

Taylor, Carl C., *Programs of Colonization and Resettlement in Argentina*. Washington, D.C.: Library of Congress, 1944.

Taylor, Carl C., "Rural Locality Groups in Argentina," *American Sociological Review*, vol. IX, no. 2, April, 1944.

Weil, Felix J., *Argentine Riddle*. New York: John Day Co., 1944.

Brazil

Cooke, Morris L., *Brazil on the March*. New York: Whittlesey House, 1945.

Deffontaines, P., "Mountain Settlement in the Central Brazilian Plateau," *Geographical Review*, vol. 27, 1937.

Deffontaines, P., "The Origin and Growth of the Brazilian Network of Towns," *Geographical Review*, vol. 27, 1938.

Gauld, C. A., "Brazil Takes a Census," *Journal of Geography*, 40 (4), April, 1941.

Harding, Jack, *I Like Brazil*. New York: Bobbs-Merrill Co., 1941.

"Immigration and Settlement in Brazil, Argentina and Uruguay," *International Labour Reviews*, vol. 35, 1937.

James, P. E., "The Changing Patterns of Population in Sao Paulo State, Brazil," *Geographical Review*, vol. 27, 1938.

James, P. E., "The Coffee Lands of Southeastern Brazil," *Geographical Review*, vol. 22, 1932.

James, P. E., "The Expanding Settlements of Southern Brazil," *Geographical Review*, vol. 30, 1940.

Maurette, F., *Some Social Aspects of Present and Economic Development in Brazil*. Geneva: International Labour Office, 1937.

Normano, J. F., *Brazil, A Study in Economic Types*. Chapel Hill: University of North Carolina Press.

Pierson, Donald, *Negroes in Brazil*. Chicago: University of Chicago Press, 1941.

Schmieder, O., "The Brazilian Culture Heart." Berkeley: *University of California Publications on Geography*, vol. 3, 1929.

Smith, T. Lynn, *Brazil, People and Institutions*. Baton Rouge: Louisiana State University Press (forthcoming).

Smith, T. Lynn, "The Locality Group Structure of Brazil," *American Sociological Review*, vol. 9, no. 1, February, 1944.

Will, L. W., "Changes in the Agriculture of South Central Brazil," *Journal of Farm Economics*, vol. XXV, no. 3, August, 1943.

Willems, E., "Cultural Conflict in Rural Brazil," *Rural Sociology*, vol. 7, no. 4, December, 1942.

Zweig, Stefan, *Brazil, Land of the Future*. New York: Viking Press, 1941.

Chile

Ellsworth, P. T., *Chile: An Economy in Transition*. New York: The Macmillan Co., 1945.

Hanson, Earl P., *Chile, Land of Progress*. New York: Reynal & Hitchcock, 1941.

Venezuela

"Venezuela," *Fortune*, March, 1939.

Wylie, Kathryn H., *Venezuela's Agricultural Problem*. 1942.

CENTRAL AMERICA

General

Biesanz, John and Mavis, *Costa Rican Life*. New York: Columbia University Press, 1944.

Hooper, O., "The Plight of Education in Rural Panama," *Rural Sociology*, vol. 9, no. 1, March, 1933, p. 50.

Hooper, O., "Rural Panama: Its Needs and Prospects," *Rural Sociology*, vol. 8, no. 3, September, 1943, p. 247.

Jones, C. L., "Costa Rica and Civilization in the Caribbean." Madison: *University of Wisconsin Studies*, no. 23, 1935.

Jones, C. L., *Guatemala, Past and Present*. Minneapolis: University of Minnesota Press, 1940.

Kepner, Charles D., *The Banana Empire*. New York: Vanguard Press, 1935.

Munro, D. G., *Five Republics of Central America, Their Political and Economic Development and Their Relations with the United States*. New York: Oxford University Press, 1918.

Price, A. G., "White Settlement in the Panama Canal Zone," *Geographical Review*, vol. 25, 1935.

Wisdom, Charles, *The Chorti Indians of Guatemala*. Chicago: University of Chicago Press, 1936.

Mexico

Chase, Stuart, *Mexico*. New York: The Macmillan Co., 1931.

Cook, Katherine M., *Rural Education in Mexico*. Washington, D.C.: Bulletin from the United States Department of Education.

Fernandez, R., "Land Tenure in Mexico," *Journal of Farm Economics*, vol. XXV, no. 1, February, 1943.

Gaona, A., "So Much Land, So Many People," *Land Policy Review*, vol. IV, no. 2, February, 1941.

Herring, Hubert, *Mexico — The Making of a Nation*. New York: The Foreign Policy Association, 1942.

Humphrey, N. D., "The Generic Folk Culture of Mexico," *Rural Sociology*, vol. 8, no. 4, December, 1943.

Kluckhohn, Frank L., *The Mexican Challenge*. New York: Doubleday, Doran, 1939.

Mexico Today. Annals of the American Academy of Political and Social Science, March, 1940.

Munguía, Enriques, "The Agrarian Problem in Mexico," *International Labour Review*, July, 1937, pp. 49-85, and August, 1937, pp. 200-238.

Niggli, Josephina, *Mexican Village*. Chapel Hill: University of North Carolina Press, 1945.

Parsons, Elsie C., *Milta: Town of the Souls*. Chicago: University of Chicago Press, 1936.

Powell, Jane S., *Agriculture in Mexico*. Pan-American Union, Washington, 1942 (mimeographed).

Redfield, Robert, *The Folk Culture of Yucatan*. Chicago: University of Chicago Press, 1941.

Redfield, Robert, *Tepaztlan, A Mexican Village*. Chicago: University of Chicago Publications, 1930.

Saenz, Moises, and H. L. Priestly, *Some Mexican Problems*, chap. III. Chicago: University of Chicago Press.

Sánchez, George I., *Mexico, A Revolution by Education*. New York: Viking Press, 1936.

Simpson, E. N., *The Ejido: Mexico's Way Out*. Chapel Hill: University of North Carolina Press, 1937.

Tannenbaum, Frank, *The Mexican Agrarian Revolution*. New York: The Macmillan Co., 1933.

Watson, Goodwin, *Education and Social Welfare in Mexico*. New York: Council for Pan-American Democracy, 1940.

LIST OF FIGURES_____

LIST OF TABLES

INDEX

Index

Adams, James T., 32
Advertising, influence on standards of living, 427. *See also* Radio, Newspaper
Agricultural Adjustment Act, result of in South, 121-122; program for land use, 156; regain of parity, 181; effect and results, 187-193; acreage allotment, 647
Agricultural Education, 476-477
Agricultural investment in industry, 103-105
Agricultural occupation, 275
Agricultural Adjustment Administration, problem of surplus control, 110; Program Planning Division, 156; postwar period, 668-669
Agricultural Extension Service, land-use program, 242-243; and farm families, 418; in rural adult education, 484-493; and school-lunch program, 489; Home Economics, 496; and recreational activities, 547
Aid. *See* Relief, Government Aid, Extension Service
Alexander, Dr. Will, 586
Alta, Iowa, case study of, 290-300
Altmeyer, A. J., 626
American Association for Adult Education, 484
American Country Life Association, 2, 567
American Library Association, 498-499
American Public Health Association, 588
American Red Cross, recreation in the war, 556; in field of health, 590; rural social work, 629
American Social Hygiene Associations, 590
American Youth Commission, educational program, 507; church activities, 525
Anderson, W. A., 218, 640, 642
Architecture, rural, 419
Argentine, locality groupings, 308

Arts and handicrafts, as recreation, 553
Asch, Berta, 617
Ashby, A. W., 393-394
Australia, country towns, 304; community effort, 321; organizations in Victoria, 338
Automobiles, effect on social groups, 238-239; and rural-urban contacts, 546

Bailey, E. Z., 77
Bailey, L. H., 77, 678-679
Baker, O. E., 39, 43, 60
Baldwin, B. T., 72
Baldwin, C. B., 628
Ballinger, R. A., 405
Barry, M. W., 217
Barton, J. R., 554
Bean, L. H., 110, 615
Beard, Charles, 5
Beck, P. G., 97, 577, 613
Bee, L. S., 316
Beers, Howard, 315, 616, 648
Belleville, New York, a community study of, 293-294
Bennett, E. H., 44
Bennett, H. H., 107
Bennett, J. W., 323, 411
Birth rate, in rural districts, 371-372
Black, J. D., 395
Blue Cross, 599, 601
Bodie, Alice, 409
Boss, 217
Bossard, J. H. S., 215
Boyd, Neva L., 555
Boy Scouts, 234
Brandt, Karl, 673
Brazil, locality groups, 310-311
Brennan, C. O., 226
Brigham, Reuben, 243
Brunner, E. de S., on Co-operation in Coopersburg, 18; on immigrant population, 19, 61-62; on regional classification, 27; on pioneer migration, 33; on intelligence, 72; on rural male population, 114; on

709